Preparing for the Praxis
Your Guide to Licensure

Learning about the Praxis Series Statewide Testing Licensure

Many states require prospective teachers to take standardized tests for licensure. The following questions and answers will help you learn more about this important step to becoming a teacher.

What kinds of tests do states require for certification?

Some tests assess students' competency in basic skills of reading, writing, and mathematics, often prior to admission to a professional teacher education program. Many states also require standardized tests at the end of a teacher education program; these tests assess prospective teachers' competency and knowledge in their subject area and about teaching and learning.

Do all states use the same test for certification?

No. The most commonly used test is the *Praxis Series*™, published by the Educational Testing Service (ETS); as of January 2003, thirty-five states required some form of the *Praxis Series*™ for certification. You can also see a list of states requiring the Praxis tests on the ETS home page (*http://www.ets.org/praxis*). You can learn about each state's testing requirements by checking its department of education website or contacting the state department of education by mail or telephone. The University of Kentucky has developed a website with the web addresses for all fifty states' certification requirements (*http://www.uky.edu/Education/TEP/usacert.html*).

What is the *Praxis Series*™, and what is the difference between Praxis I, Praxis II, and Praxis III?

The *Praxis Series*™ is a set of three levels of standardized tests developed by the Educational Testing Service.

Praxis I assesses reading, writing, and mathematics skills. Many states require minimum passing scores on the three Praxis I subtests (also sometimes called the **Preprofessional Skills Test**, or **PPST**) prior to admission to a teacher education program.

Praxis II measures prospective teachers' knowledge of the teaching and learning process and the subjects they will teach. Praxis II includes tests on Principles of Learning and Teaching, specific subject assessments, and multiple subject assessments. Many states require that prospective teachers pass both a subtest on principles of teaching and learning appropriate to the grade level to be taught and either a single-subject or multiple-subject test appropriate to the area of certification. It is important to check with an advisor, testing center, or state certification office about the appropriate Praxis II tests to take for certification.

Praxis III focuses on classroom performance assessment and is usually taken by teachers in their first year of teaching. Prospective teachers who are applying for initial certification are not required to take Praxis III.

If my state uses the *Praxis Series*™, how do I know which tests to take?

Contact your advisor or student services center if you are currently a student in a teacher education program. If you are applying for certification through an alternative certification program, contact the state department of education's certification office.

What is the format of the Principles of Learning and Teaching (PLT) test?

The Principles of Learning and Teaching Tests are two hours in length, and consist of forty-five multiple-choice questions and six constructed-response (short-answer) questions. Each test includes three case histories followed by seven multiple-choice and two short-answer questions and twenty-four additional multiple choice questions.

What does the PLT test cover?

The PLT covers four broad content categories:

- Organizing Content Knowledge for Student Learning
- Creating an Environment for Student Learning
- Teaching for Student Learning
- Teacher Professionalism

ETS provides descriptions of topics covered in each category on their website (*http://www.ets.org/praxis*) and in their free *Test at a Glance* booklet.

What courses in my teacher preparation program might apply to the PLT?

Almost all of your teacher preparation courses relate to the PLT in some way. This book, *Foundations of Education: The Challenge of Professional Practice*, addresses many concepts that are assessed in the PLT tests, particularly in the areas of Creating an Environment for Student Learning and Teacher Professionalism. You have probably studied or will study concepts and knowledge related to the four content categories in courses such as educational foundations, educational psychology or human growth and development, classroom management, curriculum and methods, and evaluation and assessment. You may have had or will have field experiences and seminars that provide knowledge about these concepts.

How should I prepare for the PLT?
Test-taking tips are provided in the next section.

Test-Taking Tips

Test-Taking Tip 1: Know the Test
- **Review the topics covered in the exam.** For the *Praxis Series™*, the ETS booklet *Test at a Glance* (available online at *http://www.ets.org/praxis* or free by mail) includes detailed descriptions of topics covered in each of the four content categories.
- **Take the sample tests.** The ETS provides sample tests for the *Praxis Series™* on their website and in their print materials. Analyze the kinds of questions asked, the correct answers, and the knowledge necessary to answer the questions correctly.
- **Analyze the sample questions and the standards used for scoring the responses to open-ended (constructed response) questions.** Read the scoring guides carefully; the test readers will use these criteria to score your written response. Write your own responses to the sample questions and analyze them using the test-scoring guide. If your responses do not meet all the criteria for a score of 3 on Praxis (or the highest score for your test), revise them.

Test-Taking Tip 2: Know the Content
- **Plan ahead.** You can begin preparing for Praxis and other standardized teacher certification tests early in your program. Think about how each of your courses relates to the concepts and content of the exam.
- **Review what you learned in each course in relation to the topics covered in the test.** Review course textbooks and class notes for relevant concepts and information. At the end of each course, record reminders of how the course's content and knowledge relate to concepts on the test.

- **Think across courses.** The Praxis case studies draw on knowledge from several courses. As you prepare for the exam, think about how knowledge, skills, and concepts from the courses that you took relate to each other. For example, you might have learned about aspects of working with parents in a foundations course, an educational psychology course, and a methods course. Be prepared to integrate that knowledge.
- **Review the content with others.** Meet with a study group and review the test and your coursework together. Brainstorm about relevant content using the ETS descriptions or other descriptions of each test's categories and representative topics as a guideline.

Test-Taking Tip 3: Apply Good Test-Taking Strategies
- **Read the test directions carefully.** Even though you have previewed the test format and directions as part of learning about the test, make sure you understand the directions for this test.

For multiple-choice questions:
- **Read each question carefully.** Pay attention to key words such as *not*, *all*, *except*, *always*, or *never*.
- **Try to anticipate the answer to the question before looking at the possible responses.** If your answer is among the choices, it is likely to be correct. Before automatically choosing it, however, carefully read the alternative answers.
- **Answer questions you are certain of first.** Return to questions you are uncertain about later.
- **If you are unsure of the answer, eliminate obviously incorrect responses first.**

For short open-ended response questions:
- **Read the directions carefully.** Look for key words and respond directly to exactly what is asked.
- **Repeat key words from the question to focus your response.** For example, if you are asked to list two advantages of a method, state "Two advantages are (1) . . . and (2) . . ."
- **Be explicit and concrete.** Short-answer responses should be direct and to the point.

For essay questions:
- **Read the question carefully and pay close attention to key words, especially verbs.** Make sure you understand all parts of the question. For example, if the question asks you to list advantages and disadvantages, be sure to answer both parts.
- **Before you write your response, list key points or make an outline.** The few minutes you take to organize your thoughts will pay off in a better organized essay.

■ **Use the question's words in your response**. For example, if the question asks for three advantages, list each in a sentence, "The first advantage is . . .", "The second advantage is . . .", and "The third advantage is . . . ." Make it easy for the reader to score your response.

■ **Stay on topic**. Answer the question fully and in detail, but do not go beyond what the question asks or add irrelevant material.

Sample State Licensure Test Questions

The following sample questions illustrate the kinds of questions in the *Praxis Series™* Principles of Learning and Teaching tests and other state licensure tests. The case study focuses on elementary education, which is the focus of Principles of Learning and Teaching: Grades K-6 (0522). Praxis tests for Principles of Learning and Teaching: Grades 5-9 (0523) and Principles of Learning and Teaching: Grades 7-12 (0524) would include case histories appropriate to those grade levels.

The Principles of Learning and Teaching tests focus on four broad content categories:

■ Organizing Content Knowledge for Student Learning
■ Creating an Environment for Student Learning
■ Teaching for Student Learning
■ Teacher Professionalism

The sample questions that follow include one case study followed by three related multiple-choice questions, two constructed-response questions, and three additional discrete multiple-choice questions. An actual Praxis Principles of Learning and Teaching test would include three case histories, each with seven related multiple-choice questions; two constructed-response questions; and twenty-four additional discrete multiple-choice questions. It would draw from many courses and field experiences in your teacher education program.

These sample questions focus only on content and issues in *Foundations of Education: The Challenge of Professional Practice* 4/e; they are not representative of the actual test in scope, content, or difficulty. Learn more about Praxis and try more sample questions on the Educational Testing Service website at *http://www.ets.org/praxis*.

Following the sample questions are answers with explanations and references to Praxis topics and appropriate parts of this book.

Sample Case Study and Related Questions
Case History: K-6

Columbus, New Mexico, is an agricultural community near the international boundaries separating Mexico and the United States. It's a quiet town where traditional views of community and territory are being challenged. Just three miles from the border is Columbus Elementary School, a bilingual school for kindergarten through fifth grade students. Of the some 340 students enrolled at Columbus Elementary, approximately 97% are on free or reduced price lunches. The school is unique because about 49% of the students live in Mexico and attend Columbus Elementary at U.S. taxpayer expense. Columbus Elementary is a fully bilingual school. In the early grades, basic skills are taught in Spanish, but by the third grade level, students have begun to make the transition to English. Most of the teachers at Columbus Elementary School are English speakers; some have limited Spanish skills. The school also employs teaching assistants who are fluent in Spanish and can assist the teachers in these bilingual classrooms.

Dennis Armijo, the principal of Columbus Elementary School, describes the unique relationship between Columbus and its neighboring community, Palomas, Mexico.

Most of the people who live in Columbus, New Mexico, have relatives in Palomas, Mexico. At one point or another, many Columbus residents were Mexican residents and they came over and established a life here. And so they still have ties to Mexico and a lot of uncles and aunts and grandparents still live in Palomas. They have a kind of family togetherness, where they just go back and forth all the time. The kids that are coming over from Mexico, most of those are

American citizens who have been born in the United States. Now the parents may not be able to cross because of illegal status, but the kids are U.S. citizens; they have been born in U.S. hospitals.

Columbus Elementary School's international enrollment poses special challenges for family and parental involvement. Mr. Armijo notes that parental contact is often not as frequent as he would like it to be. The school occasionally runs into problems reaching parents because many don't have telephones and must be reached through an emergency number in Mexico that might be as far as three blocks away or through a relative on the United States side of the border. In many cases, school personnel go into Mexico and talk to the parents or write them a letter so they can cross the border legally to come to the school. Despite these barriers, however, Mr. Armijo says that cooperation from the parents is great. "They'll do anything to help out this school."

The parents who send their children across the border to Columbus Elementary are willing to face the logistical difficulties of getting their children to Columbus each day because they want their children to have the benefits of a bilingual education. Mr. Armijo notes that the only reason that many parents from across the border send their kids to Columbus is to learn English. He describes a potential conflict that sometimes arises from this expectation:

> There's—I wouldn't call it a controversy, but there's some misunderstanding, mainly because parents don't understand what a bilingual program is. Some of them don't want their children to speak Spanish at all; they say they are sending the children to our school just to learn English. A true bilingual program will take kids that are monolingual speakers of any language and combine them together. At Columbus Elementary, for example, if you have a monolingual English speaker and a monolingual Spanish speaker, if they are in a true bilingual program you hope that the Spanish speaker will learn English and the English speaker will learn Spanish. And if they live here for the rest of their lives, they will be able to communicate with anybody. So when the students from Mexico come over, they need, as far as I know, they need to learn the skills or the way of life, the American way of life, the American dream, if you will, of an education. Because at some point or another, they might want to come over. Remember, these students are United States citizens, even though they live with their parents in Mexico. I'm almost sure that most of those kids are going to come over across to the United States and live here and so they need to have this education.

Perspective of Linda Lebya, Third Grade Teacher

Linda Lebya is her third year of teaching third grade at Columbus Elementary School. She lives nearby on a ranch with her husband, who is a deputy sheriff. She speaks conversational Spanish, although she is not a native Spanish speaker. About 95 percent of her third-grade students are Spanish-speaking.

Linda's classroom is small but inviting. Colorful posters and pictures on the wall reflect the students' culture and many words and phrases are posted in Spanish and English. Desks are grouped in clusters of four so students can sit together facing one another. A list of vocabulary words, written in English and Spanish, is on the blackboard.

Linda describes her teaching approaches and some of the challenges she faces. First, she describes a typical spelling lesson:

> On Monday as an introduction for spelling vocabulary we have ten vocabulary words written in English and Spanish. The intent is for them to learn it in English; I also put up the Spanish words with the intent of helping them to learn what the English word means. We discuss the words in English and Spanish, then use them in sentences in each language.

Columbus Elementary is a poor school, and Linda reports that resources are limited: "Lack of books is a problem because we're supposed to be teaching in Spanish for part of the day but the only thing we have in Spanish are the readers. All the other materials are in English so that is a problem."

One resource that Ms. Lebya does have is a Spanish-speaking instructional assistant. She describes the assistant's role in her classroom:

> *All of the teachers here at Columbus K–3 have an instructional assistant to help out with different things. My assistant this year is really wonderful; she helps out a great deal. She teaches the Spanish reading to the students because I'm not as fluent to teach it. I can speak it and I can understand, but to actually teach it, I wouldn't know how; my Spanish is not strong enough.*

Linda describes her understanding of multicultural education:

> *Multicultural education here means that most of the students are from a different culture. We have a few Anglos but most of the students are Mexicans or Hispanics, and when you are teaching multicultural education, you want to make sure that the students understand that their culture is just as important as the dominant culture. For example, one of our vocabulary words was "fiesta" or "party." Some of our students were not in school that day because they were making their First Holy Communion and their families were having a big celebration. We talked about official fiestas like Cinco de mayo and family or traditional fiestas like today and the students made English and Spanish sentences about fiestas and parties. It all helps them to value their culture while they learn about the culture of the United States.*

> *And as far as the Spanish sentences, that's just giving them an opportunity to do something well because they already know it in Spanish. They have the vocabulary in Spanish, so they're able to do a good job in making the sentences, and that's something they can feel good about and help their self-esteem. (Kent, Larsen, & Becker 1998)*

DIRECTIONS: Each of the multiple-choice questions below is followed by four choices. Select the one that is best in each case.

1. Which approach best describes the philosophy of the bilingual program at Columbus Elementary School?

    (A) Children should receive instruction in both English and their native language and culture throughout their school years, making a gradual transition to English.

    (B) Students should make the transition to English through ongoing, intensive instruction in English as a Second Language.

    (C) Students should be removed from their regular classes to receive special help in English or in reading in their native language.

    (D) Students should be immersed in English, then placed in English-speaking classes.

2. Sleeter and Grant describe five approaches to multicultural education. Which approach best characterizes the Columbus Elementary School program, based on the comments of Ms. Lebya?

    (A) Human Relations approaches

    (B) Single-Group Studies

    (C) Teaching the Exceptionally and Culturally Different

    (D) Education that Is Multicultural and Social Reconstructionist

3. Ms. Lebya's instructional approach to teaching vocabulary could best be described as

    (A) individualized instruction

    (B) cooperative learning

    (C) inquiry learning

    (D) direct instruction

Sample Short-Answer Questions

The Principles of Learning and Teaching tests include two open-ended short-answer questions related to the case study. A well-constructed short-answer response demonstrates an understanding of the aspects of the case that are relevant to the question, responds to all parts of the question, supports explanations with relevant evidence, and demonstrates a strong knowledge of appropriate concepts, theories, or methodologies relevant to the question. Two readers who are practicing teachers will score the responses according to an ETS scoring guide. (To view the scoring guide, go to the ETS webpage: (*http://www.ets.org/praxis*).

The following sample open-ended questions draw from knowledge and concepts covered in this book only. In an actual Praxis Principles of Learning and Teaching test, respondents should use knowledge and concepts derived from all parts of their teacher education program.

4. Ms. Lebya says that she relies on her instructional assistant to teach reading in Spanish because "I'm not fluent enough to teach it. I can speak it and understand it, but to actually teach it, I wouldn't know how." List at least one positive and one negative possible consequence of this teaching arrangement.

5. Is it possible to teach well without textbooks? If so, in what situations? If not, why not?

Sample Discrete Multiple-Choice Questions

The Principles of Teaching and Learning tests include twenty-four discrete multiple-choice questions that cover an array of teaching and learning topics. In an actual Praxis Principles of Learning and Teaching test, respondents would draw from knowledge and concepts learned in all aspects of an undergraduate teacher preparation program.

6. On the first day of school, Mr. Jones told his eighth grade class that all students must arrive at class on time and with all their materials. He posted the same rule on the bulletin board by the door.

On Tuesday of the second week of school, a classroom visitor observed the following: two students arrived about five minutes late for class and took their seats without any comment from Mr. Jones; one student received permission to go his locker to get an assignment the class was reviewing; another student borrowed a pen from Mr. Jones so she could complete an in-class activity.

The student actions and teacher response suggest which of the following:

(A) Mr. Jones did not establish a set of expectations at the beginning of the year.

(B) Mr. Jones did not make consequences clear and apply them consistently.

(C) Mr. Jones taught and retaught desired behaviors.

(D) Mr. Jones demonstrated "with-it-ness" when working with the students.

7. Mr. Williams placed a pitcher of water and several containers of different sizes and shapes on a table. He asked a small group of students, "Which container holds the most water? Which holds the least? How can you figure it out?"

Mr. Williams' philosophical orientation probably is:

(A) behaviorism

(B) perennialism

(C) constructivism

(D) essentialism

8. Ms. Jackson was planning a unit of study for her eleventh grade American history class. She wanted to determine what students already know and want to know about the topic prior to beginning the unit. Which forms of pre-assessment would be most useful?

(A) a norm-referenced test

(B) a teacher-made assessment

(C) a criterion-referenced test

(D) a summative assessment

Answers

1. The best answer is A. In the Columbus School's bilingual program, children learn primarily in Spanish during their first few grades, then begin the transition to English in the third grade. They are not experiencing an intensive English instruction or pullout program, nor are they immersed in English.

Related Praxis Topics: I. Organizing Content Knowledge for Student Learning/Needs and characteristics of students from diverse populations; II. Creating an Environment for Student Learning/Appropriate teacher responses to individual and cultural diversity; III. Teaching for Student Learning/Needs and characteristics of students from diverse populations

Related material in this book: Chapter 3: The Richness of Classroom Cultures

2. The best answer is C. Both Mr. Armijo and Ms. Lebya emphasize that the purpose of their bilingual program is to help the students assimilate into American culture and acquire language and skills that well help them be successful if they choose to live in the United States.

Related Praxis Topics: I. Organizing Content Knowledge for Student Learning/Needs and characteristics of students from diverse populations; II. Creating an Environment for Student Learning/Appropriate teacher responses to individual and cultural diversity

Related material in this book: Chapter 3: The Richness of Classroom Cultures

3. The best answer is D. Ms. Lebya uses a teacher-directed approach, in which she asks specific questions of the students and provides praise or corrective feedback.

   Related Praxis Topics: I. Organizing Content for Student Learning/Creating or selecting teaching methods, learning activities, and instructional materials or other resources that are appropriate for the students and are aligned with the goals of the lesson; III. Teaching for Student Learning/Repertoire of flexible teaching and learning strategies

   Related material in this book: Chapter 10: Curriculum and Instruction

4. A strong response to this open-ended question will explicitly state at least one potential positive consequence and one potential negative consequence of the teaching arrangement. The respondent will use or paraphrase the question and answer explicitly in complete sentences.

   Sample Response: One potential positive consequence of having the Spanish-speaking teaching assistant teach reading in Spanish is that the students will acquire better reading skills in Spanish. If they become good readers in Spanish, they may find it easier to become good readers in English later. One potential negative consequence of having the Spanish-speaking teaching assistant teach reading in Spanish is that she may not have the knowledge or skills to teach reading. (Many teaching assistants have not had the educational preparation that licensed teachers have.) Ms. Lebya's Spanish may not be strong enough to pick up on those problems or correct them. Thus, the children may not become strong readers in Spanish.

   Related Praxis Topic: III. Teaching for Student Learning/Making content comprehensible to students; IV Teacher Professionalism/Reflecting on the extent to which learning goals were met

   Related material in this book: Chapter 3: The Richness of Classroom Cultures

5. A strong response to this open-ended question will explicitly take a position on the necessity of textbooks and will defend that position. The respondent will use or paraphrase the question and answer explicitly in complete sentences.

   Sample Response: It is entirely possible to teach well without textbooks. Although textbooks can be an invaluable resource for teachers, they are only one kind of resource that can be used for instruction. Instead of textbooks, teachers could use a collection of printed materials, such as articles or primary resources, or websites from the Internet. The teacher could also use multimedia resources, such as films, videotapes, or audiotapes. To teach well without textbooks, however, the teacher must have clear goals and must spend time looking for good alternative materials.

   Related Praxis Topic: I. Organizing Content Knowledge for Student Learning/ Creating or selecting teaching methods, learning activities, and instructional materials or other resources that are appropriate for the students and are aligned with the goals of the lesson

   Related material in this book: Chapter 10: Curriculum and Instruction

6. The best answer is B. Although Mr. Jones established and posted classroom procedures at the beginning of the school year, he did not make consequences clear. When students did not follow the procedures, he did not correct the students or remind them of the established classroom expectations.

   Related Praxis Topic: II. Creating an Environment for Student Learning/Establishing and maintaining consistent standards of classroom behavior

   Related material in this book: Chapter 10: Curriculum and Instruction

7. The best answer is C. Mr. Williams encouraged the students to construct meaning or make sense of information for themselves, one of the characteristics of constructivism.

   Related Praxis Topic: I. Organizing Content Knowledge for Student Learning/ Major theories of human development and learning; III. Teaching for Student Learning/Stages and patterns of cognitive and cultural development

   Related material in this book: Chapter 6: Why Teachers Behave As They Do

8. The best answer is B. Ms. Jackson can best find out what students know and want to know by designing her own instrument.

   Related Praxis Topic: I. Organizing Content Knowledge for Student Learning/Structuring lessons based on the knowledge, experiences, skills, strategies, and interests of the students in relation to the curriculum

   Related material in this book: Chapter 10: Curriculum and Instruction

References

Educational Testing Service (2002). *Tests at a Glance: Praxis II Subject Assessments/Principles of Learning and Teaching*. Available online: http://www.ets.org/praxis/prxtest:html

Kent, T.W., Larsen, V.A., & Becker, F.J. (1998). *Educational Border Culture in New Mexico*. Boston: Allyn & Bacon.

Foundations of Education

Fourth Edition

*F*oundations of Education
The Challenge of Professional Practice

Robert F. McNergney
University of Virginia

Joanne M. McNergney
University of Virginia

PEARSON

Boston ■ New York ■ San Francisco
Mexico City ■ Montreal ■ Toronto ■ London ■ Madrid ■ Munich ■ Paris
Hong Kong ■ Singapore ■ Tokyo ■ Cape Town ■ Sydney

Vice President, Editor in Chief: Paul Smith
Executive Editor: Stephen D. Dragin
Developmental Editor: Sonny Regelman
Associate Editor: Tom Jefferies
Senior Editorial Assistant: Barbara Strickland
Senior Editorial-Production Administrator: Beth Houston
Composition Buyer: Linda Cox
Editorial-Production Service: WordCrafters Editorial Services, Inc.
Manufacturing Buyer: Andrew Turso
Cover Coordinator: Linda Knowles
Text Designer: Glenna Collett
Photo Researcher: Katharine S. Cook
Text Composition: Publishers' Design and Production Services, Inc.

Between the time website information is gathered and then published it is not unusual for some sites to have closed. Also, the transcription of URLs can result in typographical errors. The publishers would appreciate notification of errors so that they may be corrected in subsequent editions.

Library of Congress Cataloging-in-Publication Data
McNergney, Robert F.
    Foundations of education : the challenge of professional practice / Robert F. McNergney, Joanne M. McNergney.—4th ed.
        p.   cm.
    Includes bibliographical references and index.
    ISBN 0-205-38928-7
    1. Teaching—Vocational guidance—United States. 2. Education—United States. I. McNergney, Joanne M. II. Title.
LB1775.2.M32 2004
370'.973—dc21   2003040380

Photo credits appear on pages 443–444, which constitute an extension of the copyright page.

Printed in the United States of America
10 9 8 7 6 5 4 3 2 1   06 05 04 03

To our parents,
Quentin and Thelma McNergney,
and
Elmore and Arvilla May,
and to our children,
Erin, Jonathan, Carrie, Andrew, and Mimi,
with love.

Brief Contents

PART ONE	Teaching from the Inside Out	1
Chapter 1	A Teacher's Role	2
Chapter 2	Challenges Teachers and Schools Face	29
Chapter 3	The Richness of Classroom Cultures	56

PART TWO	Our Educational Heritage	85
Chapter 4	Education in America: The Early Years	86
Chapter 5	Education in America: Then and Now	114
Chapter 6	Why Teachers Behave As They Do	143

PART THREE	Education from the Outside In	170
Chapter 7	Where Teachers Work: Schools	171
Chapter 8	Leading, Governing, and Funding Schools	200
Chapter 9	The Influence of the Law	233

PART FOUR	Helping Students Succeed	269
Chapter 10	Curriculum and Instruction	270
Chapter 11	Recognizing Educational Success: Standards and Assessment	303

PART FIVE	A Connected Future	329
Chapter 12	A Global Educational Context	330
Chapter 13	What Lies Ahead	362

Contents

Part One	Teaching from the Inside Out	1

1   A Teacher's Role   2

Is Teaching a Profession?   3
   Teaching Is a Profession   3
   Teaching Is a Semiprofession   5
How Are Views of Teaching Changing?   6
   A View of Teaching as Basic Professional
     Competence: INTASC   7
   A View of Teaching as Expert Behavior: NBPTS   8
What Career Issues Do Beginning Teachers Face?   10
   Teacher Licensure   10
   Availability of Jobs   12
   Teacher Salaries   14
   Successfully Performing Responsibilities   16
How Are Teachers Evaluated?   16
   Competency Testing   16
   Performance Evaluations of Teachers   18
   Portfolios   18
   National Teacher Examinations: *The Praxis Series*™   18
   ■ Your Teaching Life in Practice: The Voice of
     Experience   19
How Are Teachers Supported and Rewarded?   19
   ■ Technology in Practice: Digital Teaching
     Portfolios   20
   Mentoring Programs   20
   Career Ladders and Merit Pay   21
   ■ Voices: Helping Others Understand the
     Importance of Teachers   22
   National Certification   22
How Do Teachers Demonstrate Professional
Leadership?   23
   Advanced College Degrees   23
   Working with Professional Organizations   23
   ■ Cultural Awareness: An African American's
     View of the Profession   24
   Meeting the Challenges of Professional Practice   25

Summary   26
Terms and Concepts   26
Reflective Practice: Choosing a Teaching Path   26
Additional Readings   27
Web Resources   27
Video Workshop Extra!   28

2   Challenges Teachers and Schools Face   29

What Are Society's Expectations for Schools?   30
How Does Poverty Place Students at Risk of
School Failure?   32
How Can Schools Intervene to Help Students
at Risk?   33
   ■ Your Teaching Life in Practice: Mentoring
     Programs for Teachers   35
   Providing Early Intervention Programs   35
   Keeping Students in School   36
   Providing Compensatory Education   37
   Providing Before- and After-School Programs   38
   Offering Incentives and Disincentives   39
   Providing Mentors and Tutors   39
How Can Schools Get Parents Involved in Their
Children's Education?   40
   Implementing Parental Involvement Programs   40
   Providing Family Services through Full-Service
     Schools   41
   ■ Voices: Learning to Work with Parents   43
How Can Schools Reduce Risks That Threaten
Children's Health and Safety?   43
   Preventing Child Abuse and Neglect   44
   ■ Technology in Practice: Protecting Children's
     Privacy   45
   Preventing and Responding to Teen Pregnancy   45
   ■ Issues in School Reform: A Mentoring
     Program for Adolescent Girls   46

Preventing the Spread of AIDS and Other
Communicable Diseases   47
Preventing Suicide and Accidental Injury or Death 48
Preventing School Violence   49
Preventing Substance Abuse   52
Summary   **53**
Terms and Concepts   **53**
Reflective Practice: The Achievement Gap **53**
Additional Readings   **54**
Web Resources   **54**
Video Workshop Extra!   **55**

3 The Richness of Classroom Cultures   56

What Is Diversity?   **57**
Culture   57
Race and Ethnicity   58
What Other Concepts Define Diversity? **59**
From the Perspective of Immigrants   59
From the Perspective of Being a Language
Minority or Bilingual Person   61
■ Your Teaching Life in Practice: Bias in the
African American Community   61
From the Perspective of Gender   62
From the Perspective of Exceptionality   64
From the Perspective of Sexual Orientation 65
What Is Multicultural Education?   **65**
Teaching the Culturally Different   66
Human Relations Approaches   67
Single-Group Studies   68

Multicultural Approaches   68
Education That Is Multicultural and Social
Reconstructionist   68
**What Types of Multicultural Education Curricula
Exist and How Are They Evaluated?**   **69**
Accountability Issues   69
**How Are Educational Services Adapted for
Students with Exceptionalities?**   **72**
Delivering Services to Students with Disabilities 72
■ Technology in Practice: Studying Online Hate 73
■ Issues in School Reform: Serving Children with
Special Needs through Inclusion   74
Delivering Services to Gifted and Talented
Students   76
**How Can Teachers Create Culturally Relevant
Classrooms?**   **77**
Cultural Mismatches   77
■ Voices: The Power of Literature   78
Responsive Instruction   78
Summary   **79**
Terms and Concepts   **79**
Reflective Practice: One Immigrant's Success Story **79**
Additional Readings   **80**
Web Resources   **80**
Video Workshop Extra!   **81**

**Benchmarks: Historical and Philosophical
Touchstones in Education**   **82**
**Developing a Professional Portfolio:
Digital Portfolios**   **83**
Online Activity: The Learning Network **84**

PART TWO   Our Educational Heritage   85

4 Education in America: The Early Years   86

Which Europeans Influenced Early Education? **87**
Comenius: Value of Structure   87
Locke and Rousseau: Enlightened Views   87
Pestalozzi and Herbart: Encouraging
Development   88
Froebel: Start Early   89
**How Did Information Education Develop before
the Civil War?**   **89**
Education in the Southern Colonies   90
■ Your Teaching Life in Practice: Competition or
Cooperation?   91
Education in the Middle Atlantic Colonies 92
Education in the New England Colonies   92
A National View of Education   92

What Were the Aims of Education?   **94**
The Role of Religion   95
Industry Affects Education   96
■ Voices: Alexis De Tocqueville   96
Education for Slaves   97
Education for Native Americans   98
Education in Spain's American Colonies   99
Education for Women   101
Education for People with Disabilities   101
**How Did Formal Education Develop in America
before the Civil War?**   **102**
Life in Colonial Schools   103
Curricula   104
■ Issues in School Reform: *McGuffey Readers* 105
Recognizing Educational Success and Failure 106
The Monitorial Method and the American
Lyceum   106

The Latin School and the English Academy:
  No Girls Allowed   107
Early Ideas of Public Education   107
Leaders in the Movement for Universal
  Education   108
■ Technology in Practice: The Organization of
  American Historians Online   109
The Development of Parochial Schools   110
The Growth of Institutions of Higher Education   110
Summary   111
Terms and Concepts   112
Reflective Practice: Eliza Pinckney   112
Additional Readings   113
Web Resources   113
Video Workshop Extra!   113

5 Education in America: Then and Now — 114

**How Did Educational Life Change after the
Civil War?**   115
Ending Slavery and Reconstructing the South   115
We Need Educational and Social Reform   116
Science and Philanthropy Combine to Educate   117
Learning from Mass Media   117
■ Voices: Lewis Terman and Walter Lippman   118
Federal Influence on Education   119
Who Are "We the People"?   120
Native Americans   121
European Americans   123
African Americans   123
■ Technology in Practice: United States
  Holocaust Memorial Museum   124
■ Cultural Awareness: Charles Hamilton
  Houston   126
Hispanic Americans   128
Asian Americans   128
■ Your Teaching Life in Practice: Illegal
  Immigrants   129
Exceptional Learners in America   131
American Women   131
How Did Teaching Change after the Civil War?   132
Status of Women in Teaching Changes   132
The Progressive Movement Begins   133
We Attempt to Educate the Nation   133
How Did Schools Change during the Modern Era? 134
Consolidation and Bureaucratization   134
New Links between Schools and Communities   134
Rise of Preschools   135
The Middle School Movement   135
Comprehensive High Schools   135
Homeschooling   136
Adult Education   136
Opportunities for Higher Education   136

Why Was Curriculum So Important?   137
Standardized Curriculum   137
Diversified Curriculum   138
Censorship and Core Curricula   138
Innovative Curriculum   139
**How Do We Typically Judge Educational Success
and Failure?**   139
Summary   140
Terms and Concepts   141
**Reflective Practice: Cycles of Educational
Pluralism**   141
Additional Readings   142
Web Resources   142
Video Workshop Extra!   142

6 Why Teachers Behave As They Do — 143

**What Does Philosophy Have to Do with You
As a Teacher?**   144
Philosophy Influences Education   144
■ Your Teaching Life in Practice: The Core
  Philosophies of Public Schools   145
**What Are the Roots of American Educational
Philosophies?**   146
Idealism   147
Realism   148
Humanism   149
**What Modern Philosophies Influence Western
Education?**   150
Existentialism   150
Marxism   152
Behaviorism and Cognitivism   153
Pragmatism   154
■ Technology in Practice: ThinkQuest   155
Perennialism and Essentialism   156
Social Reconstructionism   158
**What Non-Western Philosophies Influence American
Education?**   158
Hinduism   159
Buddhism   159
Islam   160
African and Native American Philosophies   161
■ Cultural Awareness: Islamic Schools Step Up
  Security   161
**What Shapes Teachers' Personal Philosophies of
Education?**   162
Learning from Teaching: Reflection   162
■ Voices: A Teacher's Philosophy   163
Summary   163
Terms and Concepts   164
Reflective Practice: Philosophical Differences   164
Additional Readings   165
Web Resources   165

Video Workshop Extra!   165

Benchmarks: Professional Teaching in a
Diverse Society   167

Developing a Professional Portfolio:
Your Own Philosophy of Teaching   169
Online Activity: Exploring the Library of
Congress   169

PART THREE   Education from the Outside In   170

7 Where Teachers Work: Schools   171

What Is a School?   172
  School Districts   172
  Types of Schools   172
How Is Public Schooling Organized in the United
States?   174
  Early Childhood Education   174
  Kindergarten   175
  Elementary Schools   176
  Junior High Schools and Middle Schools   176
  High Schools   178
  Higher Education   178
  ■ Issues in School Reform: School
    Consolidation   179
What Are Some Schooling Alternatives?   179
  Magnet Schools   179
  Vocational–Technical Schools   180
  Montessori and Waldorf Schools   181
  Private and Independent Schools   182
  For-Profit Schools   183
  Charter Schools   183
  ■ Your Teaching Life in Practice: Charter
    Schools   184
  Parochial Schools   185
  Home Schools   186
How Are Schools Administered?   186
  The School Superintendent   187
  Principals and Assistant Principals   188
What Organizational and Policy Issues Do
Schools Face?   189
  Retention   189
  Class Schedule and Class Size   190
  ■ Technology in Practice: Tracking
    Attendance   191
  Tracking   192
What Makes Some Schools More Effective Than
Others?   192
  Positive School Environments   194
  Relations   194
  ■ Voices: First Day of School America   196
Summary   196
Terms and Concepts   197

Reflective Practice: A New Paradigm for School
Goals   197
Additional Readings   198
Web Resources   199
Video Workshop Extra!   199

8 Leading, Governing, and Funding Schools   200

What Are School Governance and Education
Finance?   201
  How Schools Are Run   201
  How Schools Are Funded   202
  Connections between Education and the
    Economy   202
  ■ Issues in School Reform: Urban
    Superintendents   204
  Political Influences on Public Education   205
How Does the Federal Government Influence
Education?   208
  Federal Funding for Education   209
  National Goals   211
How Is Education Financed and Controlled by
the States?   211
  State Funding   211
  State Education Oversight   216
  Cooperation among School Districts   218
How Are Schools Financed and Managed at
the Local Level?   218
  Property Taxes   218
  Local School Boards   219
  ■ Technology in Practice: How Do Schools'
    Expenditures and Revenues Compare?   220
  School District Budgets   220
How Are Governance and Funding Related to
Educational Success?   223
  The Issue of Funding Equity   225
  The Issue of School Choice   226
  ■ Voices: On Privatization   227
  ■ Your Teaching Life in Practice: Public
    Supports for Private Schools?   228
  The Issue of Site-Based Management   229
Summary   230

Terms and Concepts   230
Reflective Practice: School Board Membership   231
Additional Readings   231
Web Resources   232
Video Workshop Extra!   232

9 The Influence of the Law   233

How Does Government Influence Education?   233
What Legal Principles Affect Public Education?   235
What Are Parents' Rights and Responsibilities?   237
    A Question of Religious Principle   238
    You Can't Spank My Child!   239
    Do Some Parents Have Special Rights?   240
What Are Students' Rights and Responsibilities?   240
    In God Somebody Trusts   241
    Playing Fairly   242
    ■ Your Teaching Life in Practice: Zero
        Tolerance   243
    Show Me What's in There!   244
    Are There Limits on Student Expression?   245
    Treating Different Students Differently—Illegal
        Discrimination?   246
    Would You Check These Papers for Me?   247
    ■ Cultural Awareness: School Mascots   248
What Are Teachers' Rights and Responsibilities?   249
    To Join or Not to Join   249
    There's Got to be a Way to Keep This Job!   250

A Line between Personhood and Professionalism   251
What Do You Mean I'm Violating Copyright
    Laws?   252
Maybe She Is Just a Sickly Child   253
You Should Have Known Better   254
    ■ Voices: Teaching about Rights and
        Responsibilities Since September 11   257
What Are School Districts' Rights and
Responsibilities?   258
    Balancing Academic Freedom   258
    Equal Treatment   259
    How Could You Let This Happen to a Student?   260
    Somebody Will Pay!   260
    What Kind of Choice Is This?   261
    ■ Technology in Practice: The Oyez Project   262
Summary   263
Terms and Concepts   264
Reflective Practice: Sexual Harassment and
Schools   264
Additional Readings   265
Web Resources   265
Video Workshop Extra!   265

Benchmarks: Important Events in Educational
Governance, Finance, and Law   266
Developing a Professional Portfolio: Planning
Your Professional Development   268
Online Activity: Oyez Project   268

PART FOUR   Helping Students Succeed   269

10 Curriculum and Instruction   270

What Is Curriculum?   271
    Explicit and Implicit Curricula   271
    Null Curriculum   272
    Extracurriculum   273
    Integrated Curriculum   273
What Forces for Change Affect Curriculum
Content?   274
    ■ Your Teaching Life in Practice: To
        Standardize or Not to Standardize the
        Curriculum   275
    The National Interest   275
    State and Local Priorities   276
    Social Issues and Public Opinion   277
    Professional Groups and Individuals   278
    Educational Publishing and Mass Media   280
How Are Curriculum and Instruction Planned
and Organized?   281

Aims of Education   283
Teacher Planning for Instruction   284
    ■ Voices: On Backward Design of Curriculum   284
What Are Four General Models of Instruction?   285
    Behavioral Systems Strategies   285
    Social Strategies   287
    Information-Processing Strategies   289
    Personal Sources Strategies   290
What Is Effective Instruction?   292
    Understanding Students   292
    Communicating   292
    Creating Learning Environments   293
    ■ Cultural Awareness: Éxito Para Todos   294
    Adapting Instruction for Students with Special
        Needs   294
    Evaluating Student Learning   295
How Do Teachers Manage Students Effectively?   296
    Research Informs Teacher Management
        Behavior   296
    Relationships between Teachers and Students   297

- ■ Technology in Practice: Amplifying
  Teachers' Voices   298
  Classroom Management: An Environment of
  Self-Control   298
- **Summary**   **300**
- **Terms and Concepts**   **300**
- **Reflective Practice: Making Real-Life Connections**   **300**
- **Additional Readings**   **301**
- **Web Resources**   **301**
- **Video Workshop Extra!**   **302**

11 Recognizing Educational Success: Standards and Assessment   303

- **How Do We Know What Works in Education?**   **304**
  Personal Standards   304
  National Goals and Standards   305
  The Nation's Report Card   306
  State Standards   307
  ■ Issues in School Reform: Urban Academy—
  Where Testing Is Anything But Standard   308
  Opportunity Standards   310
- **What Types of Classroom Assessments Do Teachers Use?**   **310**
  Classroom Assessment Triad   311
  Cognition and Learning   311
  Standardized Testing   312
  ■ Your Teaching Life in Practice: Are
  Standardized Tests Useful?   314

  Minimum Competency Testing   314
  Asking Questions   315
  ■ Voices: James Popham Speaks about
  Assessment   316
  Authentic Assessment   317
  Grading and Recommendations   320
  Student's Role   320
  ■ Technology in Practice: Posting
  Students' Work   321
- **How Can Teachers Know If They Are Assessing Students Fairly?**   **322**
  Bias in Assessment   322
  Teaching to the Test   322
  Multiple Measures   323
- **Summary**   **323**
- **Terms and Concepts**   **324**
- **Reflective Practice: Arithmetic Test**   **324**
- **Additional Readings**   **325**
- **Web Resources**   **325**
- **Video Workshop Extra!**   **325**

- **Benchmarks: Milestones in Curriculum, Instruction, and Assessment**   **326**
- **Developing a Professional Portfolio: Assessing Students through Observation**   **327**
- **Online Activity: Teaching with Census Information**   **328**

PART FIVE   A Connected Future   329

12 A Global Educational Context   330

- **Why Learn about Educational Life outside the United States?**   **331**
  Preparing for the Future   331
  ■ Your Teaching Life in Practice: Are There
  Global Limits to Our Tolerance?   332
  Becoming Globally Aware   333
  ■ Voices: Teaching in Israel   336
- **Why Study Education in Other Countries?**   **337**
  Education in Canada   338
  Education in Mexico   340
  ■ Technology in Practice: The Journey North
  Project   340
  Education in Japan   342
  Education in India   345
  Education in the United Kingdom   347
  Education in Singapore   350
  Education in South Africa   352

- **How Might We Enhance Understanding of Global Interdependence?**   **354**
  Trends in International Mathematics and Science
  Study   354
  ■ Issues in School Reform: Working Locally to
  Strengthen Ourselves Globally   355
  International Comparisons: Smoke and Mirrors?   356
  Comparisons that Foster a Global View   356
- **Summary**   **359**
- **Terms and Concepts**   **359**
- **Reflective Practice: Project Cuba**   **359**
- **Additional Readings**   **360**
- **Web Resources**   **360**
- **Video Workshop Extra!**   **361**

13 What Lies Ahead   362

- **How Are Teachers' Professional Roles Changing?**   **363**
  Trends toward Common Educational
  Expectations   363

■ Cultural Awareness: Japanese School
Reform 364
Trends toward Comprehensive Curriculum and
Assessment 365
Trends toward Education for Diversity 367
Trends toward Defining Diversity in Economic
Terms 368
Trends toward Character Education 368
■ Voices: How Do Teachers Develop Students'
Character? 370
How Are Links to Technology Changing the
Foundations of Education? 371
The Internet and the World Wide Web 372
■ Your Teaching Life in Practice: Are Student
Laptops a Luxury? 374
Distance Learning 375
■ Technology in Practice: eSchools 376
Telecommunications Capabilities in the Schools 376
How Are Collaborative Networks Transforming
Teaching and Learning? 379
Targeting Students at Risk 380
Increasing Parental Involvement 383
Enhancing Relationships among Educators 383
How Can Professional Educators Prepare for
the Future? 385

Using Professional Knowledge 385
Reflecting on Professional Practice 389
Summary 390
Terms and Concepts 390
Reflective Practice: Turning Classrooms over to
Interns 391
Additional Readings 391
Web Resources 392
Video Workshop Extra! 392

Benchmarks: From the Past Comes
the Future 393
Developing a Professional Portfolio:
Preparing Your Résumé 394
Online Activity: Teaching Overseas 395

Glossary 397

References 407

Name Index 423

Subject Index 429

Preface

The Challenge of Professional Practice

Today, when the professionalism of educators is being challenged by such phenomena as teacher-competency tests, state-mandated evaluations of student performance, and the mounting social tensions that exist in schools, future teachers must be educated to be professionals.

Professionals, regardless of their field, use knowledge to solve problems and to capitalize on opportunities. Teachers and other professionals face the challenge of professional practice by acquiring and learning how to apply specialized knowledge. This text presents preservice teachers with the foundations of American education and helps them apply that information to classroom practice. This fourth edition of *Foundations of Education: The Challenge of Professional Practice* has been completely revised and enhanced to serve that purpose.

Changes to This Edition

- **Completely revised and streamlined chapters** present the foundations basics and highlight how those basics apply to everyday classroom teaching and learning.
- **New parts and chapter organization.** Chapters are organized into parts to highlight the links among chapter topics. New part opening and closing sections provide additional explanation and features.
- **New! Chapter 11** focuses on **standards and assessment,** issues that are constantly under discussion and are becoming increasingly important to all teachers.
- **New, practical features** include Your Teaching Life in Practice, Technology in Practice, INTASC Correlations, Themes of the Times, Preparing for the Praxis, and VideoWorkshop correlations.

Special Features and Pedagogy in the Fourth Edition

- **New! Your Teaching Life in Practice** This feature in every chapter presents important topics that teachers face every day in their classrooms.

Your Teaching Life in Practice
THE VOICE OF EXPERIENCE

Deborah White, a first-year teacher, loves her job but is beginning to realize that it is much more complicated and demanding than she imagined. She exchanges e-mail messages with her mother, a veteran teacher, in hopes of gaining insight into her own experiences.

Dear Mom,

I'm exhausted. I had no idea how much energy teaching requires. When I was a bank teller I had to compute like a wizard, paste a smile on my face, and do my job. I used to come home tired, but nothing like I do now.

Love, Deb

Dear Deb,

Good teachers are probably not good at compartmentalizing their lives. They are so deeply involved in their work that they give it their all, without even realizing it. They use calculators, chalkboards, computers, and other tools, but their most important tools are themselves. They use their intellect, their emotions, their physical energy—their whole being—to create conditions that inspire and support their students to learn. You don't turn those attributes on and off on command. If you love the challenge of teaching, you don't leave the old toolbox on the work site. You take it with you everywhere you go. No wonder you're tired!

Love, Mom 8-)

Dear Mom,

Remember the time you spent helping me learn how to use a spreadsheet? If you had not been so supportive, I might never have developed the skills I needed for my senior thesis! For some reason,

I do not seem to be having the same effect on my own students. They don't get it. They seem to think they just have to go through the motions and they will be stellar students. They are wonderful, bright, sweet kids, but there is some kind of communication problem here that I can't figure out. Any suggestions?

Love, Deb

Dear Deb,

The skill training I gave you as you worked on your project really wasn't intended to get at the deeper levels of understanding or motivation you want to encourage in your students. I know you want to help shape who they are—pass on the spark that you picked up somewhere along the line and nurtured over time. But I have learned through my own teaching that sometimes what I did on the surface really had no effect on my students at a deeper level. And sometimes I fell into the trap of thinking so much about myself that I forgot about my students' needs and interests. I learned that I needed to get to know my students, find out what they did for fun, what they liked to read—anything that might help me think of ways to relate what we were learning in class to their personal lives. As you go on, try to think of ways to put your students at the center of your work. Keep smiling!

Love, Mom 8-)

Critical Thinking Questions
Do you remember one or more teachers who put students at the center of their work? How did they do so?

To answer these questions online and e-mail your answer to your professor, go to Chapter 1 of the Companion Website (ablongman.com/mcnergney4e) and click on Your Teaching Life in Practice.

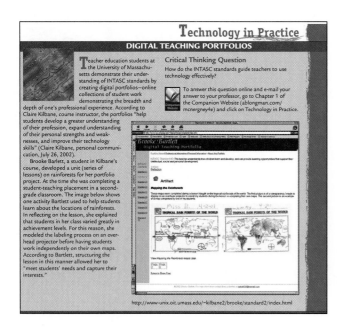

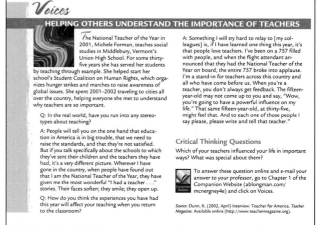

■ **New! Technology in Practice**   This feature illustrates many different classroom applications for technology available to teachers and students.

■ **Voices**   Completely updated, the Voices feature provides firsthand accounts from professionals such as teachers, teacher educators, researchers, and philosophers on teaching topics.

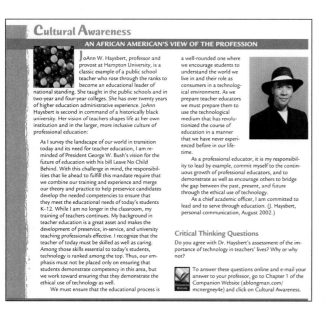

■ **Cultural Awareness**   Completely revised, Cultural Awareness highlights the influence of diversity on classroom practice.

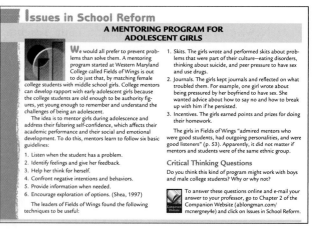

■ **Issues in School Reform**   This totally revised feature presents trends in school reform and explains how they help to improve life in U.S. schools.

■ **Reflective Practice** Completely updated, this end-of-chapter feature serves as a capstone activity for chapters and takes the form of a mini–case study that asks students to apply knowledge from the chapter.

 eflective Practice

Choosing a Teaching Path

Renae Johnson was three weeks into her first teacher education course, and she was having second thoughts about her choice of secondary English as her licensure area. "I wish I could be as certain as you are about what I want to teach," she said to her friend, Nancy Hildebrand. "It's nice that there is flexibility in the teacher education program. Unfortunately, I may need more than one semester to decide on a major. The more I learn in class about the different paths teachers can take, the more confused I get!"

"Take it easy," advised Nancy. "I agree that the classroom

teachers who have spoken to our group make every area of teaching sound appealing. But each speaker had different reasons for entering the profession and at least one of them changed directions after entering the field. Remember? She was the one who started out as an elementary teacher and then became a gifted education teacher. According to her, all teachers take professional development classes, either through the school system or a university, so it is possible to add endorsements in other areas."

"You're right. I shouldn't get so worked up about this. I know I like working with teenagers, and I love English, but ever since I tutored in the after-school program, I have been

---

thinking I might like to work with students with special needs—kids who really struggle in school. I think I'll talk to Dr. Brigham about the special education program to see if that might be the best fit for me. I should also find out how many English classes I would need to have if at some point I wanted to specialize in secondary English."

Issues, Problems, Dilemmas, Opportunities

What areas of licensure is Renae considering? Is there demand for teachers in these areas in your own community?

Perceive and Value

What factors is Renae considering when trying to determine an area of licensure to pursue?

Know and Act

What do you know about licensure requirements in the state where you are hoping to teach? How difficult is it to add one or more areas of endorsement to your license?

Evaluate

What might you gain or lose by adding another teaching endorsement at this point in your program?

INTASC Principle 1

The teacher understands the central concepts, tools of inquiry, and structures of the discipline(s) he or she teaches and can create learning experiences that make these aspects of the subject matter meaningful for students.

Disposition

The teacher has enthusiasm for the discipline(s) she teaches and sees connections to everyday life. (Interstate New Teacher Assessment and Support Consortium, 1992)

Discussion Question

What more does Renae need to know about teaching English and teaching special needs students that will help her make a decision?

■ **New! INTASC Correlations** This chapter-end feature relates the Reflective Practice features to INTASC standards, exposing students to the professional standards they will be expected to follow.

■ **New! Preparing for the Praxis** This special section at the front of the book provides students with a brief tutorial of FAQs, test-taking tips, and sample test questions intended to remove some of the intimidation of this important professional step.

Learning about the Praxis Series Statewide Testing Licensure

Many states require prospective teachers to take standardized tests for licensure. The following questions and answers will help you learn more about this important step to becoming a teacher.

What kinds of tests do states require for certification?

Some tests assess students' competency in basic skills of reading, writing, and mathematics, often prior to admission to a professional teacher education program. Many states also require standardized tests at the end of a teacher education program; these tests assess prospective teachers' competency and knowledge in their subject area and about teaching and learning.

Do all states use the same test for certification?

No. The most commonly used test is the *Praxis Series*™, published by the Educational Testing Service (ETS); as of January 2003, thirty-five states required some form of the *Praxis Series*™ for certification. You can also see a list of states requiring the Praxis tests on the ETS home page (*http://www.ets.org/praxis*). You can learn about each state's testing requirements by checking its department of education website or contacting the state department of education by mail or telephone. The University of Kentucky has developed a website with the web addresses for all fifty states' certification requirements (*http://www.uky.edu/Education/TEP/usacert.html*).

What is the *Praxis Series*™, and what is the difference between Praxis I, Praxis II, and Praxis III?

The *Praxis Series*™ is a set of three levels of standardized tests developed by the Educational Testing Service.

Praxis I assesses reading, writing, and mathematics skills. Many states require minimum passing scores on the three Praxis I subtests (also sometimes called the **Preprofessional Skills Test, or PPST**) prior to admission to a teacher education program.

Praxis II measures prospective teachers' knowledge of the teaching and learning process and the subjects they will teach. Praxis II includes tests on Principles of Learning and Teaching, specific subject assessments, and multiple subject assessments. Many states require that prospective teachers pass both a subtest on principles of teaching and learning appropriate to the grade level to be taught and either a single-subject or multiple-subject test appropriate to the area of certification. It is important to check with an advisor, testing center, or state certification office about the appropriate Praxis II tests to take for certification.

Praxis III focuses on classroom performance assessment and is usually taken by teachers in their first year of teaching. Prospective teachers who are applying for initial certification are not required to take Praxis III.

If my state uses the *Praxis Series*™, how do I know which tests to take?

Contact your advisor or student services center if you are currently a student in a teacher education program. If you are applying for certification through an alternative certification program, contact the state department of education's certification office.

What is the format of the Principles of Learning and Teaching (PLT) test?

The Principles of Learning and Teaching Tests are two hours in length, and consist of forty-five multiple-choice questions and six constructed-response (short-answer) questions. Each test includes three case histories followed by seven multiple-choice and two short-answer questions and twenty-four additional multiple choice questions.

What does the PLT test cover?

The PLT covers four broad content categories:

■ Organizing Content Knowledge for Student Learning
■ Creating an Environment for Student Learning
■ Teaching for Student Learning
■ Teacher Professionalism

ETS provides descriptions of topics covered in each category on their website (*http://www.ets.org/praxis*) and in their free *Test at a Glance* booklet.

What courses in my teacher preparation program might apply to the PLT?

Almost all of your teacher preparation courses relate to the PLT in some way. This book, *Foundations of Education: The Challenge of Professional Practice*, addresses many concepts that are assessed in the PLT tests, particularly in the areas of Creating an Environment for Student Learning and Teacher Professionalism. You have probably studied or will study concepts and knowledge related to the four content categories in courses such as educational

---

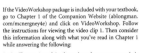

Video**Workshop** Extra!

If the VideoWorkshop package is included with your textbook, go to Chapter 1 of the Companion Website (ablongman.com/mcnergney4e) and click on VideoWorkshop. Follow the instructions for viewing the video clip for Chapter 1. Then consider this information along with what you've read in Chapter 1 while answering the following:

1. As Chapter 1 explained, teachers face numerous challenges in terms of professional practice. Compare the expectations that teachers and students have before the first

day of class, using information from the video clip to support your ideas.

2. The video clip presents suggestions that might aid a novice teacher who is preparing for a new teaching job. Imagine you are about to start the school year. Rank your top five concerns in order of importance, from least important to most important, and explain your choices in light of information presented in the video clip.

■ **New! VideoWorkshop Extra!** Questions correlated to Allyn and Bacon's VideoWorkshop for Foundations of Education program are located at the end of each chapter to encourage students to watch the video clips and think about their implications for classroom instruction.

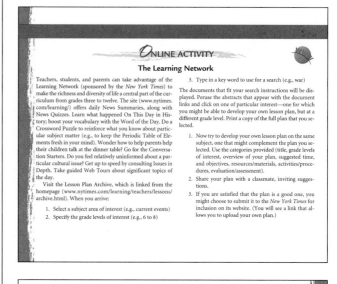

BENCHMARKS

Historical and Philosophical Touchstones in Education

1857	The National Education Association (NEA) is established as a professional organization for teachers.
1916	American Federation of Teachers (AFT) is formed as a labor union for classroom teachers.
1945	*Human Relations: Promising Practices and Intergroup and Intercultural Education in the Social Studies*, 16th yearbook of the National Council for the Social Studies, is edited by Hilda Taba and William VanTil.
1958	National Defense Education Act (NDEA, Public Law 85-864) provides federal funds to improve the teaching of science, mathematics, and modern foreign languages and to help schools provide guidance services.
1964	Economic Opportunity Act of 1964 (Public Law 88-452) authorizes grants for college work-study programs for students from low-income families; establishes a Job Corps program and authorizes support for work-training programs to provide educational and vocational training and work experience opportunities in welfare programs; authorizes support of education and training activities and of community action programs, including Head Start, Follow Through, and Upward Bound; and authorizes the establishment of Volunteers in Service to America (VISTA).
1965	Higher Education Act of 1965 (Public Law 89-329) establishes a National Teacher Corps devoted to teaching in the nation's poverty-stricken areas.
1965	Elementary and Secondary Education Act (ESEA) and subsequent amendments provide funding to aid students from low-income families through programs such as Title I (see Chapter 2).
1974	Juvenile Justice and Delinquency Prevention Act of 1974 (Public Law 93-415) provides for technical assistance, staff training, centralized research, and resources to develop and implement programs to keep students in elementary and secondary schools.
1977	*Standards for the Accreditation of Teacher Education*, issued by the National Council for the Accreditation of Teacher Education, includes a requirement for multicultural education in teacher education programs.
1986	Drug-Free Schools and Committees Act of 1986 (Part of Public Law 99-570), part of the Anti-Drug Abuse Act of 1986, authorizes funding for programs for drug abuse education and prevention, coordinated with related community efforts and resources.
1987	National Board for Professional Teaching Standards (NBPTS) established.
1989	National Goals of Education issued from the White House.
1990	Children's Television Act of 1990 (Public Law 101-437) requires the Federal Communications Commission to reinstate restrictions on advertising during children's television programs and enforces the obligation of broadcasters to meet the educational and informational needs of the child audience.
	School Dropout and Basic Skills Improvement Act of 1990 (Public Law 101–600) targets secondary school programs for basic skills improvements and dropout reduction.

82

■ **New! Part-end Features**   Useful features located at the end of each part include **Benchmark timelines, Online Activities,** and new **Developing a Professional Portfolio** activities.

ONLINE ACTIVITY

The Learning Network

Teachers, students, and parents can take advantage of the Learning Network (sponsored by the *New York Times*) to make the richness and diversity of life a central part of the curriculum from grades three to twelve. The site (www.nytimes.com/learning/) offers daily News Summaries, along with News Quizzes. Learn what happened On This Day in History; boost your vocabulary with the Word of the Day. Do a Crossword Puzzle to reinforce what you know about particular subject matter (e.g., to keep the Periodic Table of Elements fresh in your mind). Wonder how to help parents help their children talk at the dinner table? Go for the Conversation Starters. Do you feel relatively uninformed about a particular cultural issue? Get up to speed by consulting Issues in Depth. Take guided Web Tours about significant topics of the day.

Visit the Lesson Plan Archive, which is linked from the homepage (www.nytimes.com/learning/teachers/lessons/archive.html). When you arrive:

1. Select a subject area of interest (e.g., current events)
2. Specify the grade levels of interest (e.g., 6 to 8)

3. Type in a key word to use for a search (e.g., war)

The documents that fit your search instructions will be displayed. Peruse the abstracts that appear with the document links and click on one of particular interest—one for which you might be able to develop your own lesson plan, but at a different grade level. Print a copy of the full plan that you selected.

1. Now try to develop your own lesson plan on the same subject, one that might complement the plan you selected. Use the categories provided (title, grade levels of interest, overview of your plan, suggested time, and objectives, resources/materials, activities/procedures, evaluation/assessment).
2. Share your plan with a classmate, inviting suggestions.
3. If you are satisfied that the plan is a good one, you might choose to submit it to the *New York Times* for inclusion on its website. (You will see a link that allows you to upload your own plan.)

DEVELOPING A PROFESSIONAL PORTFOLIO

Digital Portfolios

A portfolio is a collection of materials teachers create to document their professional growth as educators. Many of you may choose to create a digital portfolio on the Web or on a CD-ROM because the technology is available, you know how to use it or want to learn, and you want to demonstrate that you possess special skills that make you an attractive candidate to employers and graduate programs.

There are some other benefits of making your portfolio digital. Kilbane and Milman (2003) suggest that a teacher with a digital portfolio demonstrates that she has the competency to affect students' abilities to use technology; that is, if she has the computer skills, then she can share them with her students. Digital portfolios are also more portable than hard-copy materials. They can be easily revised and copied, as well as shared inexpensively and widely.

Kilbane and Milman point their readers to several online samples of teachers' portfolios. For instance, see the work of Carter Shreves, a former preservice teacher at the University of Virginia (http://curry.edschool.virginia.edu/curry/class/edlf/589-07/Carter_Shreves). This is a simple, but not simplistic, example of what can be done on the Web. It does not require large storage capacity or special applications to make portfolio materials accessible to others.

You can also access examples of the kinds of portfolio entries required by the National Board for Professional Teaching Standards (NBPTS). See the Early Adolescence English Language Arts Certification (http://www2.ncsu.edu/unity/lockers/project/portfolios/nbcfile3.html). This example is important for two reasons. First, it is wise to keep standards in mind as you think about what kinds of materials are appropriate for inclusion in your portfolio. Second, the NBPTS standards are a look ahead at your career at the point when you might seek national certification. It is never too soon to think about using your portfolio to plan and document your own professional development.

As you explore the use of digital portfolios, ask yourself what items of professional information you might include in your own portfolio. What technologies and design features might you use to communicate your knowledge, skills, and values to others? What might you do today to begin to prepare yourself to create an electronic portfolio?

Keep in mind that the digital presentation of your portfolio is a complement to the contents of your portfolio. In the end there is no substitute for substance, so you must focus on the materials you collect for your portfolio and how they reflect your professional goals as an educator.

83

General Organization and Content of the Fourth Edition

The book's new organization reflects an updated conception of teaching as a profession. The current demanding environment in U.S. schools makes it necessary for future teachers to possess foundational knowledge of teaching and to apply it. It is also necessary to understand the links among foundational topics.

The chapters in Part One, Teaching from the Inside Out, explain the foundations of teacher professionalism and include an introduction to teaching as a profession, an overview of school and classroom challenges, and a discussion of the richness of classroom cultures.

The chapters in Part Two, Our Educational Heritage, illustrate how history and philosophy have defined education in the United States, and present the origins of ideas and values that make American education what it is today and what it will be tomorrow.

Part Three, Education from the Outside In, presents chapters that explain why it is important for teachers to understand how schools compare, how they are managed by school leaders and governed by law, and why proper financing is so critical to their success.

In Part Four, Helping Students Succeed, a brand new chapter explores the issues of standards and assessment and how they affect the teaching profession. A second chapter explains how teachers combine what they know about curriculum and instruction to increase chances that students will succeed in school.

Finally, Part Five, A Connected Future, contains chapters that stretch beyond our borders to consider international and global education; it anticipates an exciting future for educational professionals in an increasingly connected and interdependent world.

Supplements for Instructors and Students

Supplements for Instructors

- **Instructor's Resource Manual with Test Bank** includes a wealth of interesting ideas and activities designed to help instructors teach the course. Each chapter includes: a chapter overview; a chapter-at-a-glance organizer that correlates chapter outlines, learning objectives, and teaching supplements; an Annotated Lecture Outline that provides examples, discussion questions, and student activities; suggestions for additional resources; and handout masters that provide additional lecture support materials. In addition, the manual includes web-based student activities correlated to the Companion Website for the text. The test bank features hundreds of questions, including multiple choice items, essay questions, case studies, and alternative assessments, plus text page references and answer feedback (including optional VideoWorkshop test items).

- **Computerized Test Bank** The printed test bank is also available electronically through our computerized testing system: TestGen EQ. Instructors can use TestGen EQ to create exams in just minutes by selecting from the existing database of questions, editing questions, or writing original questions.

- **Allyn & Bacon Interactive Video: Issues in Education** features news reports from around the country on topics covered in the text. The VHS video contains ten modules of up-to-date news clips exploring current issues and debates in education. Some of the topics include: teacher shortages, alternative schools, community–school partnerships, standardized testing, and bilingual classrooms. An accompanying instructor's guide outlines teaching strategies and discussion questions to use with the clips.

- **Allyn & Bacon Transparencies for Foundations of Education/Introduction to Teaching, 2002,** is a set of one hundred acetate transparencies related to topics in the text.

- **Digital Media Archive for Foundations of Education/Introduction to Teaching** This CD-ROM contains a variety of media elements that instructors can use to create electronic presentations in the classroom. It includes hundreds of original images, as well as selected art from Allyn and Bacon foundations and introduction to teaching texts, providing instructors with a broad selection of graphs, charts, and tables. For classrooms with full multimedia capability, it also contains video segments and Web links.

■ **Online Course Management Systems**   Powered by Blackboard and hosted nationally, Allyn and Bacon's own course management system, **CourseCompass,** helps you manage all aspects of teaching your course. It features preloaded content to support Foundations of Education and Introduction to Teaching courses (your sales rep can provide additional information). For colleges and universities with **Blackboard**™ licenses, special course management packages are available in this format as well.

■ **VideoWorkshop for Foundations of Education** is a new way to bring video into your course for maximized learning! This total teaching and learning system includes quality video footage on an easy-to-use CD-ROM plus a Student Learning Guide and an Instructor's Teaching Guide—both with textbook-specific Correlation Grids. The result? A program that brings textbook concepts to life with ease and that helps your students understand, analyze, and apply the objectives of the course. VideoWorkshop is available for your students as a free value-pack option with this textbook.

Supplements for Students

■ Students who visit the **Companion Website** that accompanies the text (www. ablongman.com/mcnergney4e) will find many features and activities to help them in their studies: web links, learning activities linked to the features in the text, practice tests, video and audio clips, and vocabulary flash cards. The website also features an interactive **Education Timeline** that highlights the people and events that have shaped education through history, plus a direct link to specially selected *New York Times* articles through **Themes of the Times.** These articles offer students the opportunity to read differing perspectives on contemporary education topics. The website also features **Syllabus Manager,** an online syllabus creation and management tool. Instructors can easily create syllabi with direct links to the Companion Website, to other online resources, and to student assignments. Students may access the syllabus at any time to help them with research projects and to complete the assignments.

■ **VideoWorkshop for Foundations of Education CD-ROM** This exciting new supplement puts digitized video footage of children and classrooms directly into the hands of the student! The VideoWorkshop Extra! feature at the end of each chapter relates the video clips to the chapter content. The VideoWorkshop CD-ROM also comes with a Student Learning Guide.

■ **Research Navigator**™ **(with ContentSelect Research Database) (Access Code Required)** Research Navigator™ (researchnavigator.com) is the easiest way for students to start a research assignment or research paper. Complete with extensive help on the research process and three exclusive online databases of credible and reliable source material including EBSCO's ContentSelect™ Academic Journal Database, *New York Times* Search by Subject Archive, and "Best of the Web" Link Library, Research Navigator™ helps students quickly and efficiently make the most of their research time. Research Navigator™ is free when packaged with the textbook and requires an Access Code.

■ **Research Navigator**™ **Guide for Education** This free reference guide includes tips, resources, activities, and URLs to help students use the Internet for their research projects. The first part introduces students to the basics of the Internet and the World Wide Web. Part Two includes many Net activities that tie into the content of the text. Part Three lists hundreds of education Internet resources. Part Four outlines how to use the Research Navigator™ resources. The guide also includes information on how to cite research correctly, and a guide to building an online glossary. Includes Access Code for Research Navigator™.

*A*cknowledgments

We thank the people who devoted time and energy to this fourth edition. The following reviewers offered helpful suggestions on various stages of the revision:

Robert L. Brumley, Oakland City University
Lesley S. J. Farmer, California State University—Long Beach
Richard K. Gordon, California State University—Dominguez Hills
Elizabeth L. Ihle, James Madison University
Gary W. Jackson, McNeese State University
Gayla H. Lawson, University of Houston—Victoria
Anne Pierce, Hampton University
James L. Ruffa, Virginia State University
Bobbie Sferra, Scottsdale Community College
Barbara Slater Stern, James Madison University
Dale Titus, Kutztown University
Johnette J. Williams, Glendale Community College

Our colleagues at Allyn and Bacon run the best publishing house in the business. Nancy Forsyth, President, demands quality and never fails to marshal whatever support we need to do our work to the best of our abilities. Steve Dragin, our editor, is at the top of his game. He makes good things happen because he knows quality when he sees it. Sonny Regelman, our developmental editor, has been a delight to work with, with great ideas, a propensity for action, and a lovely touch with people.

We also owe a great deal of thanks to the individuals involved in the production and marketing of the text, including Tara Whorf, marketing manager, and Beth Houston, production editor. We also acknowledge Heather Mead, Mary Ducharme, and Lisa Fiore for their extensive contributions to this revision.

Our University of Virginia colleagues teach us by the examples they set. Marsha Gartland, Scott Imig, Kim Waid, and Fred Smith have piloted this material with their classes and have shared what they learned. Paula Price, David Locascio, and Eisha Jain have done hours of research and documentation. We thank them all.

Thelma McNergney, a teacher in the best sense of the word, died June 1, 2002. We are grateful for having had her in our lives.

About the Authors

Robert F. McNergney, professor in the Curry School of Education at the University of Virginia, has also been a faculty member at State University of New York, Potsdam, and University of Minnesota, Minneapolis. He has taught and coached in public schools in Iowa and Vermont. Co-author of three books and editor of four, his writing has appeared in the *Handbook of Research on Teacher Education, Educational Researcher, Journal of Teacher Education,* the *Washington Post,* and the *New York Times.* McNergney co-authored the Research Clues column for *NEA Today* for three years. He has chaired the Technology Committee for the American Association of Colleges for Teacher Education and has written the technology column for *AACTE Briefs.* He has served as secretary of Division K in the American Educational Research Association and as editor of the *Division K Newsletter.* He has chaired the Commission on Case-Method Teaching and Learning for the Association of Teacher Educators. McNergney teaches courses in foundations, evaluation, writing for publication, and research on teaching. He is cofounder and president of CaseNEX, LLC, a spin-off company from the University of Virginia that provides online professional development for teachers and school administrators.

Joanne May McNergney is an associate professor in the Department of Curriculum, Instruction, and Special Education and Assistant Dean of Admissions at the Curry School of Education, University of Virginia. She teaches courses in curriculum, instruction, assessment, and educational foundations.

A former teacher in the Charlottesville Public Schools, Charlottesville, Virginia, Joanne McNergney has fifteen years' experience working with children in grades K–4. Her writings have been published in the *Journal of Personnel Evaluation in Education, Journal of Research and Development in Education, Journal of Information Technology for Teacher Education, Journal of Curriculum and Supervision,* and *Journal of Teacher Education.*

Teaching from the Inside Out

THE NATION NEEDS YOU!

"I Love New York." This is not just a slogan to boost tourism. If you are a visitor, the hum New York City creates in your bones when you first see it never quite leaves you. If you are a native of the city, you are likely to feel like the cab driver who said, "It's a great place to live—tough, but great. And if you make it here, you know you can survive anywhere." Since September 11, 2001, New York has reflected the soul of our nation, and as diligently as any other group, the city's teachers have watched over it.

> If the opening days of school in September 2001 were different from any others, so was the school year that followed. It was a time of uncommon civility and generosity and of a collective search for meanings. At first grieving and shaken, my students were soon bursting with an unquenchable determination to understand what had happened and to be a part of the healing process. At our school, not far from what we were soon calling Ground Zero, they organized a moving candlelight ceremony, and a few weeks later, a community sing with local police officers and firefighters. Throughout the year, they wrote essays and stories, they painted bold images, they mounted theater productions, and they engaged in countless classroom discussions and debates—all in an effort to grapple with the meanings, the consequences, and the implications of September 11. An art history class installed a mural in the school's common room, weaving from the shards of individual memories a powerful, collective expression of what it was like to be there that fateful day. In the spring, I taught an urban studies seminar in which students examined the city with newfound passion. Colleagues from other schools have told me of similar outpourings of creativity and serious engagement with the entire gamut of unprecedented issues that suddenly confronted the students and educators of New York last fall. (O'Han, 2002, p. 32)

The chapters in Part 1 explain the foundations of teacher professionalism. Although the situation reflected in the excerpt above is an extreme example, the tasks that teachers confront are challenging and the students they serve are diverse, but these aspects make teaching really rewarding.

If teaching were easy, everyone would do it. Nobody says it is easy. But remember, as you consider your own place in the profession, that no career is more important than teaching.

1

THE NATION NEEDS YOU!

A Teacher's Role

CHAPTER CONTENTS

Is Teaching a Profession?

How Are Views of
Teaching Changing?

What Career Issues Do
Beginning Teachers
Face?

How Are Teachers
Evaluated?

How Are Teachers
Supported and
Rewarded?

How Do Teachers
Demonstrate
Professional
Leadership?

Teaching is a rewarding but challenging job. No one can describe the complexity of the profession better than a teacher:

Carpooling home one day a few years ago with a fellow English teacher, we heard an interview on National Public Radio with a poet who was describing her work habits. The poet, whose name I don't recall, spoke about her work as "drinking in the stillness and receiving the pulse of the land." She described sitting quietly while words and images wove themselves into slow coherence. Playfully, my colleague asked in an NPR-esque voice, "Well, Sam, what words characterize your work habits?"

In the spirit of two men who spent their day exhorting students to bang words and language together, we reeled off a list that aptly characterized our days. As English teachers, we tried to spark interest, raise questions, provoke insight, generate momentum, facilitate conversations, introduce new material, review for upcoming exams, and establish a schema for understanding and assessing the progress of our students. As teachers of adolescents, we counseled, listened, humored, disciplined, and tried to be present in their complicated lives as best we could. We also attended meetings, called parents, photocopied materials, and marked papers.

If the poet's words were languorous, gentle, and contoured, ours were charged, careening, and jagged. The poet described her work as contemplative. We described our work as a crazy quilt of roles and tasks. If the poet strolls forth taking the world in, the teacher bustles about trying to create those high-octane connections between students, subject matter, and teacher. (Intrator, 2002, pp. 1–2)

This chapter explores teaching as a profession and your place in it. As you read, think about why people teach, why they choose not to teach, how people become teachers, and what keeps them motivated.

Is Teaching a Profession?

You have spent many years as a student, but have you ever thought seriously about being a teacher, about what it means to be a *professional* in the field? Sometimes people have to "try it on for size" before they can really imagine themselves teaching. Use the short survey in Figure 1.1 to evaluate your own thoughts about being a teacher. These initial thoughts about teaching are likely to be as influential as any other information you find. **From your perspective, what does it mean to be a professional?**

Teaching Is a Profession

Teaching, like medicine and law, can be thought of as a profession for a variety of reasons:

- *Teachers possess and can use specialized knowledge.* Teachers do not simply acquire knowledge of teaching and of one or more content areas. They apply what they know in real-life settings to improve people's lives.

- *Teachers must fulfill licensure requirements in order to practice.* They must demonstrate that they are knowledgeable and competent in order to earn a license, and they must update it periodically by staying informed of current trends in their fields. Teachers need at least a bachelor's degree, special preparation in their content areas, and a supervised internship to be licensed.

- *Teachers are decision makers.* Some people might argue that the standards and curricula with which teachers must work allow them little freedom or personal choice, but this is not true. Teachers are free to make many decisions about teaching, learning, and evaluation of students.

- *Teachers get paid for their services.* Professionals get paid for what they know and what they can do. Professionals often volunteer or donate their services to worthy causes, but this is the exception, not the rule.

- *Teachers do not simply do a job; they leave a legacy.* Teachers influence people's expectations in the present, and they live on in others' memories and actions long after they have completed their work.

- *Teachers add intellectual value to an organization.* Schools staffed with accomplished professionals have greater capacity to produce desirable results—students who have been educated well—than schools short on professional talent.

- *Teachers operate according to a professional set of standards and ethics.*

- *Teachers are compelled or driven by a sense of responsibility to perform their work.*

expect the world®

The New York Times
nytimes.com

Themes of the Times!

Expand your knowledge of the concepts discussed in this chapter by reading current and historical articles from the *New York Times* by visiting the **Themes of the Times** section of the Companion Website (ablongman.com/mcnergney4e).

FIGURE 1.1   What Are Your Thoughts about Being a Teacher?

I want to have my summers off.

| STRONGLY DISAGREE | 1 | 2 | 3 | 4 | 5 | STRONGLY AGREE |

It is important that I have a predictable salary and health insurance.

| STRONGLY DISAGREE | 1 | 2 | 3 | 4 | 5 | STRONGLY AGREE |

I want to be respected.

| STRONGLY DISAGREE | 1 | 2 | 3 | 4 | 5 | STRONGLY AGREE |

I want the chance to be a leader.

| STRONGLY DISAGREE | 1 | 2 | 3 | 4 | 5 | STRONGLY AGREE |

I want to contribute to society.

| STRONGLY DISAGREE | 1 | 2 | 3 | 4 | 5 | STRONGLY AGREE |

I like the idea of having colleagues.

| STRONGLY DISAGREE | 1 | 2 | 3 | 4 | 5 | STRONGLY AGREE |

I want to help other people.

| STRONGLY DISAGREE | 1 | 2 | 3 | 4 | 5 | STRONGLY AGREE |

I can see myself getting higher college degrees.

| STRONGLY DISAGREE | 1 | 2 | 3 | 4 | 5 | STRONGLY AGREE |

I want to work with young people.

| STRONGLY DISAGREE | 1 | 2 | 3 | 4 | 5 | STRONGLY AGREE |

Teaching allows me to keep my career options open.

| STRONGLY DISAGREE | 1 | 2 | 3 | 4 | 5 | STRONGLY AGREE |

What is your average rating? What is most important or least important about the idea of being a teacher?

Both the **American Federation of Teachers (AFT)** and the **National Education Association (NEA)**—professional organizations for teachers, sometimes called **teacher unions**—acknowledge in their codes of ethics teachers' responsibility to perform their work. The NEA's 1975 preamble to its Code of Ethics (Figure 1.2) describes this responsibility as follows:

> The educator, believing in the worth and dignity of each human being, recognizes the supreme importance of the pursuit of truth, devotion to excellence, and the nurture of the democratic principles. Essential to these goals is the protection of freedom to learn and to teach and the guarantee of equal educational opportunity for all. The educator accepts the responsibility to adhere to the highest ethical standards.

Can you think of ways in which your teachers have demonstrated these standards?

𝐹IGURE 1.2   NEA Code of Ethics

PRINCIPLE I

Commitment to the Student

The educator strives to help each student realize his or her potential as a worthy and effective member of society. The educator therefore works to stimulate the spirit of inquiry, the acquisition of knowledge and understanding, and the thoughtful formulation of worthy goals.

In fulfillment of the obligation to the student, the educator—

1. Shall not unreasonably restrain the student from independent action in the pursuit of learning.

2. Shall not unreasonably deny the student's access to varying points of view.

3. Shall not deliberately suppress or distort subject matter relevant to the student's progress.

4. Shall make reasonable effort to protect the student from conditions harmful to learning or to health and safety.

5. Shall not intentionally expose the student to embarrassment or disparagement.

6. Shall not on the basis of race, color, creed, sex, national origin, marital status, political or religious beliefs, family, social, or cultural background, or sexual orientation, unfairly—

   a. Exclude any student from participation in any program

   b. Deny benefits to any student

   c. Grant any advantage to any student

7. Shall not use professional relationships with students for private advantage.

8. Shall not disclose information about students obtained in the course of professional service unless disclosure serves a compelling professional purpose or is required by law.

PRINCIPLE II

Commitment to the Profession

The education profession is vested by the public with a trust and responsibility requiring the highest ideals of professional service.

In the belief that the quality of the services of the education profession directly influences the nation and its citizens, the educator shall exert every effort to raise professional standards, to promote a climate that encourages the exercise of professional judgment, to achieve conditions that attract persons worthy of the trust to careers in education, and to assist in preventing the practice of the profession by unqualified persons.

In fulfillment of the obligation to the profession, the educator—

1. Shall not in an application for a professional position deliberately make a false statement or fail to disclose a material fact related to competency and qualifications.

2. Shall not misrepresent his/her professional qualifications.

3. Shall not assist any entry into the profession of a person known to be unqualified in respect to character, education, or other relevant attribute.

4. Shall not knowingly make a false statement concerning the qualifications of a candidate for a professional position.

5. Shall not assist a noneducator in the unauthorized practice of teaching.

6. Shall not disclose information about colleagues obtained in the course of professional service unless disclosure serves a compelling professional purpose or is required by law.

7. Shall not knowingly make false or malicious statements about a colleague.

8. Shall not accept any gratuity, gift, or favor that might impair or appear to influence professional decisions or action.

Source: "The Code of Ethics of the Education Profession," National Education Association, Washington, DC. Available at http://www.nea.org/info/code.html

Teaching Is a Semiprofession

Teaching is sometimes called a *semiprofession* because teachers do not enjoy the same privileges as some other professions. The reasons why teaching might be described as a semiprofession include:

■ *Possible lack of rigorous training.* When schools need teachers, requirements for preparation and licensure often take a back seat to filling empty slots. This can mean that inexperienced teachers are assigned to teach outside their areas of expertise with minimal or no supervision. Teacher shortages also can mean that new teachers participate in *alternative licensure* programs, which often do not expect the same length or level of professional preparation as do programs offered in colleges or universities. As a result, such programs reinforce the idea that training adds no value.

Natalia Mehlman, an investment-banking analyst who left her position to take a job as a teacher in a kindergarten through eighth grade school, quickly learned that teaching is harder than it seems. She said:

> I believed I was prepared to head a class, but a strong academic background and years in an office are not preparation for teaching. . . . As an untrained teacher, I made my share of mistakes this year. I raised my voice at misbehaving students, trying to sound menacing, only to find that yelling was almost always ineffective. (Mehlman, 2002)

The fact that children can legally be homeschooled by their parents also reinforces the belief that teaching must not require any special ability.

■ *Lack of control over entry and exit.* Unlike other professionals, teachers have little say about hiring or dismissing colleagues. School administrators and school boards—often with teacher input—make decisions about hiring. Administrators also often decide when to terminate a teacher's contract.

■ *Lack of control over schedule and workload.* Teachers neither pick the students they teach nor set their work schedules. On average, full-time public school teachers are required to be at school thirty-three hours per week, but they are actually there about forty-five hours. They spend an extra twelve to thirteen hours each week on student-related activities. Generally, they teach about twenty-four students per class.

You may want to interview one or two teachers to learn more about areas in which they believe they have the greatest amount of influence or control. **How much control do teachers have over selecting textbooks and other learning materials, determining content to be taught, selecting teaching techniques, evaluating and grading students, disciplining students, and determining how often and how much homework is assigned?**

How Are Views of Teaching Changing?

The traditional view suggests that teachers must commit themselves to lifetime careers in classrooms to exhibit professional behavior. When college and university faculty who hold this view interview candidates for admission to teacher education programs, they often look for a commitment to the profession. They wonder whether applicants are serious about being teachers, or if they are applying because they don't know what else to do. Increasingly, however, this traditional view of teacher commitment is being challenged.

Critics of this view believe prospective teachers have been forced to make these commitments too early in their college careers, indeed too early in their lives. At age nineteen, twenty, or twenty-one, even reasonable, bright, emotionally mature people are not ready to commit themselves to a lifetime career path when so many competing career options are available. Some people may want to try teaching for a while, but then move on to another career. Or they may choose teaching as a second career. Jerry, formerly a software developer, put it this way:

> I'm a career changer. I figured, why not explore a new field? . . . [I wanted to] make a difference in kids' lives and fulfill my larger mission in life, which is to

Traditional views of teaching are changing. Students studying to be teachers may decide only to teach for a few years, then change careers, while others may remain in the profession for their entire careers. What is your view?

bring more choices to people or to help people be more powerful in their own lives. And education is a pretty direct way of doing that. So I decided to take the plunge. (Peske, Liu, Johnson, Kauffman, and Kardos, 2001, p. 306)

Researchers have found that most teachers now close to retirement were committed to teaching as a lifelong career from the beginning. But the next generation of teachers includes many people like Jerry, who think of their careers and their commitment to teaching in different ways. Judging from this change, the implications for the profession seem clear:

If public education is to tap the talents and interests of this entire pool and schools are to recruit the best possible candidates into the classroom, policies must not require that all candidates conform to a single career pattern. In the end, a generic career structure is not likely to attract and retain enough good teachers. (Peske, Liu, Johnson, Kauffman, and Kardos, 2001, p. 306)

As people question the necessity of a long-term commitment, they emphasize the importance of teacher performance. That is, they are looking at what teachers do in their classrooms.

A View of Teaching as Basic Professional Competence: INTASC

Education as a profession is often criticized for its lack of agreement about what knowledge a teacher must have and be able to apply. In recent years, however, a consensus has emerged in the form of the **Interstate New Teacher Assessment and Support Consortium Standards (INTASC).** The **Council of Chief State School Officers**—state superintendents of public instruction—began the discussion about necessary knowledge, dispositions, and performances for all teachers, regardless of their subject areas (specialties). Representatives to INTASC from seventeen state education agencies then crafted the standard requirements for a beginning professional teacher, as described in Figure 1.3.

Currently, the core standards are being translated into standards for teaching individual content areas. Underlying all the standards is the belief that children benefit from current knowledge about teaching and learning only if schools and education programs are held to the highest standards. A criticism of the standards is that they may overly regulate what and how teachers teach, preventing them from being autonomous, reflective practitioners.

For you to become more familiar with the standards, the Reflective Practice feature at the end of each chapter is correlated to an appropriate INTASC standard. (See page 27 for an example.)

A View of Teaching as Expert Behavior: NBPTS

While INTASC offers a basic view of what it means to be a professional teacher, the **National Board for Professional Teaching Standards (NBPTS)** describes the characteristics of an expert teacher. Created in 1987, the NBPTS is an independent, nonprofit, nonpartisan organization governed by a sixty-three-member board of directors, most of whom are teachers. Other board members include school administrators,

*F*IGURE 1.3   **INTASC Standards for Beginning Teachers**

Standard One: Subject Matter

The teacher understands the central concepts, tools of inquiry, and structures of the discipline(s) he or she teaches and can create learning experiences that make these aspects of subject matter meaningful for students.

Standard Two: Student Learning

The teacher understands how children and youth learn and develop and can provide learning opportunities that support their intellectual, social, and personal development.

Standard Three: Diverse Learners

The teacher understands how learners differ in their approaches to learning and creates instructional opportunities that are adapted to learners from diverse cultural backgrounds and with exceptionalities.

Standard Four: Instructional Strategies

The teacher understands and uses a variety of instructional strategies to encourage the students' development of critical thinking, problem solving, and performance skills.

Standard Five: Learning Environment

The teacher uses an understanding of individual and group motivation and behavior to create a learning environment that encourages positive social interaction, active engagement in learning, and self-motivation.

Standard Six: Communication

The teacher uses knowledge of effective verbal, nonverbal, and media communication techniques to foster active inquiry, collaboration, and supportive interaction in the classroom.

Standard Seven: Planning Instruction

The teacher plans and manages instruction based upon knowledge of subject matter, students, the community, and curriculum goals.

Standard Eight: Assessment

The teacher understands and uses formal and informal assessment strategies to evaluate and ensure the continuous intellectual, social, and physical development of his/her learners.

Standard Nine: Reflection and Professional Development

The teacher is a reflective practitioner who continually evaluates the effects of his/her choices and actions on others (students, parents, and other professionals in the learning community) and who actively seeks out opportunities to grow professionally.

Standard Ten: Collaboration, Ethics, and Relationships

A teacher communicates and interacts with parents/guardians, families, school colleagues, and the community to support the students' learning and well-being.

Source: Interstate new teacher assessment and support consortium (1992). Model standards for beginning teacher licensing and development: A resource for state dialogue. Available online: http://www.ccsso.org/intascs.html#draft

school board leaders, and business and community leaders. Teachers who meet NBPTS standards must enhance student learning and demonstrate the high level of knowledge, skills, abilities, and commitments reflected in five core standards (see Figure 1.4).

The National Board considers people for **certification** if they have a baccalaureate degree from an accredited institution and have completed three years of successful teaching while holding a valid state teaching license.

FIGURE 1.4   NBPTS Standards for Accomplished Teachers

1. **Teachers are committed to students and their learning.** Accomplished teachers . . . [believe] all students can learn. They treat students equitably . . . [and] adjust their practice based on . . . students' interests, abilities, skills, knowledge, family circumstances and peer relationships.

   Accomplished teachers understand how students develop and learn . . . [and] are aware of the influence of context and culture on behavior. They develop students' cognitive capacity and their respect for learning. Equally important, they foster students' self-esteem, motivation, character, civic responsibility and their respect for individual, cultural, religious and racial differences.

2. **Teachers know the subjects they teach and how to teach those subjects to students.** Accomplished teachers have a rich understanding of the subject(s) they teach. . . . While faithfully representing the collective wisdom of our culture and upholding the value of disciplinary knowledge, they also develop the critical and analytical capacities of their students.

   Accomplished teachers . . . are aware of . . . [students'] background knowledge . . . and of strategies and instructional materials that can be of assistance. They understand where difficulties are likely to arise and modify their practice accordingly. Their instructional repertoire allows them to create multiple paths to the subjects they teach, and they are adept at teaching students how to pose and solve their own problems.

3. **Teachers are responsible for managing and monitoring student learning.** Accomplished teachers . . . capture and sustain the interest of their students and make the most effective use of time. They also are adept at engaging students and adults to assist their teaching and at enlisting their colleagues' knowledge and expertise to complement their own. Accomplished teachers command a range of generic instructional techniques, know when each is appropriate and can implement them as needed. . . . They are adept at setting norms for social interaction among students and between students and teachers. . . . [They also] employ multiple methods for measuring student growth and understanding and can clearly explain student performance to parents.

4. **Teachers think systematically about their practice and learn from experience.** Accomplished teachers . . . [model] . . . the virtues they seek to inspire in students—curiosity, tolerance, honesty, fairness, respect for diversity and appreciation of cultural differences—and the capacities that are prerequisites for intellectual growth: the ability to reason and take multiple perspectives, to be creative and take risks, and to adopt an experimental and problem-solving orientation.

   Accomplished teachers draw on their knowledge of human development, subject matter and instruction, and their understanding of their students to make principled judgments about sound practice. Their decisions are not only grounded in the literature, but also in their experience. They . . . [critically examine their own practice] . . . and engage in lifelong learning.

5. **Teachers are members of learning committees.** Accomplished teachers . . . [work] collaboratively with other professionals on instructional policy, curriculum development and staff development. They . . . [are familiar with] state and local educational objectives . . . [and] about specialized school and community resources that . . . [are available] for their students' benefit. . . . Accomplished teachers . . . [also] work collaboratively and creatively with parents, engaging them productively in the work of the school.

Source: National Board for Professional Teaching Standards (1987). Policy position (five core propositions). Available online: http://www.nbpts.org. Reprinted with permission.

In what ways can teachers earn licensure? Do you think each of these routes produces equally qualified teachers? Why or why not?

What Career Issues Do Beginning Teachers Face?

Teachers at the beginning of their careers face some issues that more experienced teachers do not encounter. These include becoming licensed to teach, getting a first job, and successfully performing their responsibilities.

Teacher Licensure

Increasingly, people use the term **licensure** to mean the process of meeting basic requirements and standards for becoming a practicing teacher. A teacher, like a physician or lawyer, needs a license to practice. For years, the terms *licensure* and *certification* were used interchangeably in education. However, recently the terms *certification, certified,* and *certificate* have acquired new meaning.

Being licensed does not suggest that a teacher is an expert or even exceptionally well qualified. In fact, processes of licensure are established and controlled by state governments to protect the public from harmful teaching practices backed by false claims of professional expertise. Prospective teachers do have several government-approved options for obtaining teaching licenses.

APPROVED PROGRAMS

Teaching licenses are typically granted in two ways: by transcript assessment and by completing an approved program. The transcript assessment process requires the candidate to submit his or her college transcript directly to the state education department. The department then compares the transcript to the state requirements and grants or denies the request for certification. The second approach requires the candidate to complete a teacher education program that has been approved or accredited by the state. (**Accreditation** is a process of review in which outside experts decide whether a program is worthy of preparing professionals.) Approved programs submit transcripts of all graduates, and the state grants licensure.

RECIPROCITY AGREEMENTS

Licensure requirements for teachers differ from state to state. When a college or university student graduates from an accredited teacher education program, he or she receives licensure to teach in the state where the program is located. But many states recognize each other's licensure; that is, states have **reciprocity agreements** by which teachers licensed in one state are eligible for licensure in another state. Because states sometimes change their licensure requirements, the list of states having reciprocity agreements changes. Where reciprocity agreements do not exist, the additional requirements often can be fulfilled by taking some additional college courses.

ALTERNATIVE AND EMERGENCY LICENSURE

Forty-five out of fifty states now offer **alternative licensure,** which is the approval to teach without having participated in a traditional, state-approved teacher education program. Alternative teacher licensure programs allow people with different educational backgrounds and from different walks of life, such as the military, liberal arts, or early retirement, to become teachers. Teachers licensed in this manner take education courses while they teach. On-the-job supervision, assistance, and formal instruction typically are provided for these new teachers (New Jersey Department of Education, 1999). From 2000 to 2002, 75,000 teachers were licensed through alternative routes, and some 175,000 people have been licensed in this manner in recent years (Feistritzer, 2002).

Some states temporarily grant **emergency licensure** until requirements are met. When school superintendents are unable to find a licensed teacher to fill a position, they petition their state departments of education to hire an unlicensed person on an emergency basis. This strategy buys time for the person to become licensed or for the school district to find another teacher who possesses valid licensure.

In recent years, a philosophical war has been waged over the value of teacher education programs. In 2002, U.S. Secretary of Education Rod Paige called the traditional system "broken" (Glickman & Babyak, 2002). The secretary's report noted state-level problems with standards for teachers, existing licensure tests, burdensome requirements, and poor hiring practices. Policy advisor Rick Hess (2002) also has argued that existing systems of licensure should be "torn down" and replaced with background checks and tests of content knowledge.

Others have argued that the nation needs to build on its already sound teacher education system. "More teacher education appears to be better than less—particularly when it includes well-constructed practical experiences interwoven with course work on curriculum, learning, and teaching" (Darling-Hammond, 1998). Jane Leibbrand, of the National Council for the Accreditation of Teacher Education, argues that "Against state and professional standards for teacher preparation, teacher candidates . . . are doing a commendable job" (personal communication, June 20, 2002).

Do we need more or less teacher education, or is it just about right?

INTERNSHIPS FOR UNCERTIFIED TEACHERS

The program Teach for America (TFA) provides college graduates who do not have teacher education backgrounds with the opportunity to become teachers. Wendy S. Kopp's senior thesis at Princeton University was the catalyst for starting this national teacher corps in 1989. The Teach for America program began with five hundred recruits from across the nation who were trained for eight weeks before assuming teaching responsibilities. By 2002, Teach for America had placed more than 8,000 of their members in sixteen urban and rural areas. Initially, funding from various foundations and corporations paid the salaries of TFA recruits. Today, their salaries are paid by the school systems where they work.

TROOPS TO TEACHERS

In January 1994 the Department of Defense established the Troops to Teachers program. The program is designed to help Department of Defense and Department of Energy civilian employees affected by military reductions develop new careers in public education. Other goals are to provide positive role models for young people in schools and to help relieve teacher shortages, especially in math and science. First Lady Laura Bush has helped make Troops to Teachers a visible priority during her husband's administration.

Availability of Jobs

Two factors influence the availability of teaching jobs: the number of properly qualified teachers available and the demand for these teachers. Demand for elementary and secondary teachers in any school year is determined by enrollment changes, class size policies, budget considerations, changes in methods for classifying and educating special education students, and job turnover due to retirement or attrition. Teacher attrition is the largest single factor influencing the demand for additional teachers in the nation's schools. Studies over the years indicate that about 20 percent of new teachers leave the profession within the first few years. Nonetheless, people teaching at the K–12 level are among the most stable of all employed graduates with respect to their occupations three years later (Henke & Zahn, 2001).

The supply of teachers is affected by salaries, educational and licensure requirements, interest in specific disciplines and geographical areas, the cost of living in some states, and other quality-of-life issues. The demand for teachers has steadily increased

The availability of teaching jobs is determined by the number of properly qualified teachers and the demand for these teachers. How many teaching jobs are available in the community where you live?

through the turn of the century and is predicted to continue rising through 2011, primarily due to increases in school enrollment (U.S. Department of Education, 2001).

TEACHER SHORTAGES

Why do the nation's large cities experience teacher shortages more acutely than other parts of the nation?   Inner-city schools present special challenges. The working conditions often are difficult, and teaching opportunities in other settings often draw teachers away from cities. The South and West also have unmet needs for teachers. In fact, population growth in these sections of the United States is expected to steadily increase the national demand for teachers through 2005 (National Center for Education Statistics, 2001).

The need to provide bilingual education and special education services can also influence the demand for teachers. This demand varies by state and locality. The number of students with disabilities entering and leaving school systems and changes to criteria used to define specific disabilities can have a marked effect on demand for special education teachers. In some locations and in some specialties, the need for teachers is so great that school districts offer cash bonuses, higher salary ranges, and other types of pay increases to attract and keep new teachers. Needs are especially high in special education, foreign languages, mathematics, and the sciences.

About 15 percent of the nation's teachers work in private schools, including parochial (sectarian) schools affiliated with religious groups and independent (nonsectarian) schools (U.S. Department of Education, 2002). Catholic schools employ more teachers than any other type of private school because the Catholic system is the largest private system.

States do not require teachers in private schools to meet the same level of licensure as public school teachers. Because private schools do not receive money from the government, they are free from many state regulations governing curriculum and teaching. At the same time, because private schools are supported by private funds, average teaching salaries are far below teaching salaries in public schools. The average base salary for a teacher with a bachelor's degree in a private school is about $22,000, almost $6,000 less than the starting salary for public schools.

PROJECTED STUDENT ENROLLMENTS AND SCHOOL BUDGETS

How do enrollment trends influence the availability of jobs? In elementary schools, student numbers have been increasing steadily since the mid-1980s as a result of the "echo effect"; in other words, this is when the children of the baby-boom generation began entering school. Projections suggest that enrollment in kindergarten through eighth grade will continue to increase until 2008. In secondary schools, student numbers began declining in 1976, reaching a low of 12.4 million in 1990. Since that time, enrollment has steadily increased as the baby boomers' children grow up. To that end, forecasters project enrollment in secondary schools to increase to 15.3 million by the year 2011 (U.S. Department of Education, 2001). Geographically, between 1990 and 2008, enrollment patterns will look different across regions, states, and communities. As previously mentioned, the greatest increases in public school enrollment will be in the South and West.

The federal government reports that by 2011 the student–teacher ratio in the nation's schools will be approximately 15 to 1 in public elementary and secondary schools. These figures are lower than actual class size, however, because the calculations include all the adults in schools, including many specialists, such as music, art, and physical education teachers, to mention three, who do not meet regularly with full classes. In 1993, for example, when the student–teacher ratio was a little over 17 to 1, the average class size was 24 (U.S. Department of Education, 2001).

School budgets determine the school's capacity for hiring personnel, and personnel costs require the most money in the budgets. Although considerations such as philosophy and mission drive budgets, when times are financially lean, boards of education and school administrators often fall back on pocketbook considerations. That is, when the budget is tight, positions are eliminated, most often through attrition.

Teacher Salaries

Why are direct comparisons between teachers' salaries and those of other professionals often misleading?   Many educators argue that until teachers earn as much money as other professionals, they will always be relegated to subprofessional status. But these comparisons rarely account for benefits packages that may include health insurance, dental coverage, sick leave, summer breaks, worker's compensation, and retirement. Sometimes benefits for teachers are better than the benefits other professionals receive.

Another consideration that may be overlooked is that teachers typically do not invest as much money in their education as do other professionals, who must possess a graduate degree to begin practice. Someone earning a law degree, for example, will spend several extra years in school, which translates into increased schooling costs and a later start to a paying career (often referred to as *opportunity costs*). It can take many years for professionals with education beyond a bachelor's degree to recover out-of-pocket losses.

Finally, many educators do not work year-round. Many public school teachers work forty weeks per year, whereas professionals in other fields typically work fifty weeks per year, with only two weeks' vacation.

Are teachers as poorly paid as many people seem to believe?   Given the importance of their work, their capacity to help society prevent problems, and the time and energy they devote to their work both during and after official business hours, the answer is clearly *yes*. In the early years of their careers, however, teachers may be better paid than some other professionals and people employed in highly skilled occupations.

The average salary in 1999–2000 for beginning elementary and secondary teachers in public schools across the United States was $27,989 (U.S. Department of Education, 2002). Remember, this salary was earned over a period of no more than forty weeks, once vacations and summer break are counted. The average beginning teacher might be able to earn another 20 percent of his or her salary working another job during the summer—an additional $5,600 or so—thus increasing total yearly earnings to more than $33,500.

When considering salaries, it is important to keep them in perspective. For example, if you started teaching in Fairfax, Virginia, in 2000 at a salary of $38,000 and tacked on another 20 percent ($7,600) in the summer, you would have made $45,600—a great beginning salary in Fairfax and virtually anywhere else in the country. In comparison, the average arts and sciences graduate in 2002 made $28,667. While the average computer scientist earned $50,354 as a starting salary in 2002, the average civil engineer made $40,848.

There is a great deal of regional variation in beginning teachers' salaries, just as there is in experienced teachers' salaries. Table 1.1 contains average salaries by state for beginners and experienced teachers. Note the range of salaries from North Dakota to Connecticut, and consider what the cost of living in Iowa might be in comparison to California.

When people graduate from college with certification to teach school, they usually think more about where to live and work and less about the salary. Teachers take jobs because of the school, the teaching assignment, and colleagues. But they also consider other factors. For example, they want to get a job near family and friends on the Great Plains, in a place where there is a social life, near a college or university, close to the

TABLE 1.1 Average and Beginning Teacher Salaries by State

2000–2001					
State	Average salary	Minimum (beginning) salary	State	Average salary	Minimum (beginning) salary
New England			**Southeast**		
Connecticut	$53,507	$32,203	Georgia	$42,141	$31,314
Rhode Island	50,400	29, 265	North Carolina	41,496	29,786
Massachusetts	47,789	31,115	Virginia	40,247	28,139
New Hampshire	38,301	25,020	Florida	38,230	25,786
Vermont	38,254	26, 152	South Carolina	37,938	26,314
Maine	36, 373	23,689	Alabama	37,606	28,649
Mideast			Tennessee	37,413	28,074
New Jersey	$51,955	$30,937	Kentucky	36,688	25,027
New York	51,020	32,772	West Virginia	35,888	24,889
Pennsylvania	49,528	31,127	Arkansas	34,729	24,469
District of Columbia	48,488	31,889	Louisiana	33,615	26,124
Delaware	47,047	32,281	Mississippi	31,954	23,292
Maryland	45,963	30,321	**Rocky Mountains**		
Great Lakes			Colorado	$39,184	$26,479
Michigan	$50,515	$29,401	Idaho	37,109	23,386
Illinois	47,865	31,222	Utah	36,441	24,553
Indiana	43,000	27,311	Wyoming	34,678	24,651
Ohio	42,892	24,894	Montana	33,249	21,728
Minnesota	42,212	27,003	**Far West**		
Wisconsin	40,939	26,232	California	$52,480	$33,121
Plains			Alaska	48,123	36,293
Iowa	$36,479	$26,058	Oregon	44,988	27,903
Kansas	35,766	26,010	Nevada	44,234	29,413
Missouri	35,091	27,173	Washington	42,143	27,284
Nebraska	34,258	24,356	Hawaii	40,536	29,204
North Dakota	30,891	20,675	**Outlying Areas**		
South Dakota	30,265	22,457	Guam	$34,947	$26,197
Southwest			Virgin Islands	34,784	22,751
Texas	$38,359	$29,823	Puerto Rico	25,430	18,700
Arizona	36,502	26,801	**U.S. Average**	**$43,250**	**$28,986**
New Mexico	33,531	25,999			
Oklahoma	32,545	27,016			

Source: American Federation of Teachers. Average and beginning teacher salaries in 2000-01. Available online. (This table was prepared June 2001.)

ocean, not far from the mountains, within driving distance of the city, and so on. People consider the salary, but, interestingly, this is less important in the beginning than it is later in one's career.

Successfully Performing Responsibilities

Teachers at the beginning of their careers work with probationary status. If they perform to standard, they may be granted **tenure** (a continuing contract). In some school systems, tenure occurs automatically at the end of the probationary period; in other school systems, the school board determines whether tenure should be granted. Tenured teachers can be released only when "just cause," or good reason, can be demonstrated. On the other hand, most states permit nontenured teachers to be released without cause. Therefore, tenure gives a teacher some freedom from the fear of being fired.   **What is your impression of tenure?**

How Are Teachers Evaluated?

In an opinion poll conducted by the Public Education Network and *Education Week,* 800 respondents were asked to rank a number of factors they consider most important when determining the quality of a school. As illustrated in Figure 1.5, quality of the teaching force is extremely or very important, followed by information literacy rates and data on students' access to books and other curricula (Jacobson, 2002). To ensure that teachers are performing to standard, principals use two types of evaluation.

The most common type of evaluation, called **formative assessment,** is done to shape, form, and improve teachers' knowledge and behavior. Formative assessment is not concerned with making judgments about salary status or tenure. Instead, it is a helping process aimed at improving teaching techniques.

Evaluators doing a formative assessment often concentrate on teachers' in-class performance by collecting data on teacher–student interactions during instruction and by helping teachers perceive what is happening during instruction. Formative assessment is based on these philosophical beliefs:

1. professional teachers constantly strive for continued individual excellence;
2. given sufficient information, professional teachers can and will evaluate themselves and modify their performance as well as or better than others; and
3. the evaluation procedures provide feedback designed to help teachers improve their teaching (Barber, 1990, p. 217).

Summative assessments, on the other hand, collect and interpret data over a specified period of time to evaluate such things as teachers' competence and teaching outcomes. The results of summative assessments inform decisions about teachers' hiring, compensation, status, tenure, and termination.

Competency Testing

Why do all states require some form of competency testing for preservice teachers?   States no longer rely strictly on schools, colleges, and departments of education to provide evidence of program quality. Competency tests are given to preservice teachers during the course of their teaching program and are now being used to provide alternative measures of the program's ability to prepare new teachers. Competency testing is useful because it provides perspectives on the outcomes of teacher education beyond those offered by teacher education programs. To simplify, if prospective teach-

$\mathcal{F}$IGURE 1.5   **Assessing the Quality of Public Schools**   When asked what types of information they would need to gauge school quality, poll respondents put teacher-qualification data at the top of the list.

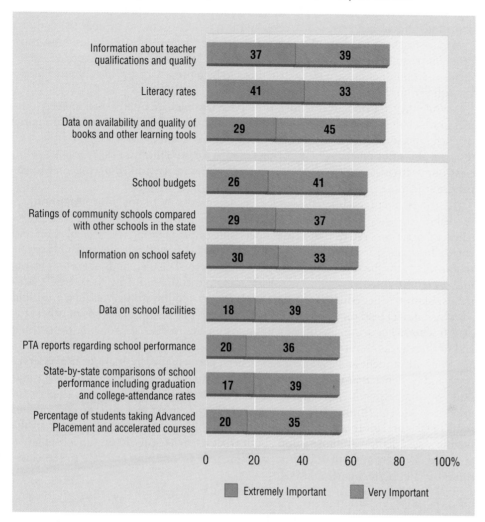

Source: "Public wants data on teacher quality." *Education Week,* vol. 21, No. 41, p. 5.
Courtesy of Public Education Network and Education Week.

ers do well on competency tests, teacher education programs can claim some of the credit for identifying and developing teaching talent. Likewise, when prospective teachers perform poorly on these tests, programs must take some of the blame.

According to their makers, competency tests simply reveal those who are minimally qualified to teach and say nothing about one's capacity to be an outstanding teacher. Nevertheless, the control of teacher education through competency tests is subtle but powerful. As preservice teachers exit their teaching programs, they must demonstrate the knowledge, skills, and dispositions that such tests claim to measure. Teacher education programs will continue to experience pressure to make sure that beginning teachers excel on these tests. In turn, teacher competency tests influence the curriculum of teacher education by focusing the program on the areas the tests measure.

Performance Evaluations of Teachers

True performance evaluations begin in field experiences, or practica, which are part of a variety of professional education courses, and they continue through **student teaching.** Student teaching involves planning, organizing, and providing instruction to students full-time over a period of weeks, and it typically occurs at or near the end of a preservice teacher's program. To prepare preservice teachers for student teaching, most programs require them to engage in a variety of field experiences. The types of assignments vary, but they are generally structured to help preservice teachers become familiar with various kinds of classrooms and schools.

While they are student teaching, preservice teachers are often asked to keep journals in which they record information about students' reading levels, mathematics proficiencies, personal interests, and classroom rules, routines, and schedules. Preservice teachers also offer one-on-one tutoring sessions for students and assist teachers with classroom activities. Classroom teachers and college instructors work together to supervise student teachers' performances.

During student teaching, preservice teachers gradually assume more classroom responsibilities. They grade papers, teach parts of lessons designed by the classroom teacher (sometimes referred to as the supervising or cooperating teacher), plan for and engage in whole-class instruction for one or two class periods, and eventually assume responsibility for the whole day's instruction. Because of the demands of student teaching, preservice teachers seldom enroll in academic courses during these field placements. Many teacher education programs, however, require student teachers to attend weekly seminars held on a college or university campus or in classrooms of other student teachers. The seminars offer them opportunities to discuss problems of teaching and to share ideas about what works.

For both student and experienced teachers, performance evaluations use observations and evidence that provide **authentic assessments** of a teacher's knowledge and skills. Such assessments are evaluations that reflect people's true abilities to perform under real-life conditions. These assessments are concerned less with recognition and recall of facts and more with people's abilities to apply what they know. To make an authentic assessment, real information about what a teacher can do on the job must be obtained. One example of authentic assessment is videotaping teachers in the classroom for later performance analysis.

Portfolios

A **teacher portfolio,** a collection of artifacts that communicates a teacher's abilities to perform his or her job, is another example of an authentic assessment. A portfolio might contain tests and homework assignments the teacher gives students, samples of students' work, lesson plans, a videotape of a lesson, and so on. Teachers' portfolios provide opportunities for teachers to have input into their evaluations. They also provide excellent ways for a teacher to demonstrate his or her abilities to understand the links between educational theory and practice.

National Teacher Examinations: *The Praxis Series*™

Before granting initial licensure, more than 30 states require candidates to take a national teacher examination as a measure of teacher competency. Most of these states use **The Praxis Series**™, a series of tests developed and sold by the Educational Testing Service (ETS), the company that also prepares the common SAT and GRE tests, as well as other exams specific to professions. Praxis assesses skills and knowledge at each stage of a beginning teacher's career, from entry into teacher education to actual classroom performance. It measures teachers' basic skills in reading, writing, and mathematics, as well as their professional education and subject matter knowledge. The teaching skills

Your Teaching Life in Practice

THE VOICE OF EXPERIENCE

Deborah White, a first-year teacher, loves her job but is beginning to realize that it is much more complicated and demanding than she imagined. She exchanges e-mail messages with her mother, a veteran teacher, in hopes of gaining insight into her own experiences.

Dear Mom,

I'm exhausted. I had no idea how much energy teaching requires. When I was a bank teller I had to compute like a wizard, paste a smile on my face, and do my job. I used to come home tired, but nothing like I do now.

Love, Deb

Dear Deb,

Good teachers are probably not good at compartmentalizing their lives. They are so deeply involved in their work that they give it their all, without even realizing it. They use calculators, chalkboards, computers, and other tools, but their most important tools are themselves. They use their intellect, their emotions, their physical energy—their whole being—to create conditions that inspire and support their students to learn. You don't turn those attributes on and off on command. If you love the challenge of teaching, you don't leave the old toolbox on the work site. You take it with you everywhere you go. No wonder you're tired!

Love, Mom 8-)

Dear Mom,

Remember the time you spent helping me learn how to use a spreadsheet? If you had not been so supportive, I might never have developed the skills I needed for my senior thesis! For some reason,

I do not seem to be having the same effect on my own students. They don't get it. They seem to think they just have to go through the motions and they will be stellar students. They are wonderful, bright, sweet kids, but there is some kind of communication problem here that I can't figure out. Any suggestions?

Love, Deb

Dear Deb,

The skill training I gave you as you worked on your project really wasn't intended to get at the deeper levels of understanding or motivation you want to encourage in your students. I know you want to help shape who they are—pass on the spark that you picked up somewhere along the line and nurtured over time. But I have learned through my own teaching that sometimes what I did on the surface really had no effect on my students at a deeper level. And sometimes I fell into the trap of thinking so much about myself that I forgot about my students' needs and interests. I learned that I needed to get to know my students, find out what they did for fun, what they liked to read—anything that might help me think of ways to relate what we were learning in class to their personal lives. As you go on, try to think of ways to put your students at the center of your work. Keep smiling!

Love, Mom 8-)

Critical Thinking Questions

Do you remember one or more teachers who put students at the center of their work? How did they do so?

To answer these questions online and e-mail your answer to your professor, go to Chapter 1 of the Companion Website (ablongman.com/ mcnergney4e) and click on Your Teaching Life in Practice.

---

measured include instructional planning, teaching, classroom management, and assessment of student learning. See the special Preparing for the Praxis section at the beginning of this book for frequently-asked questions, test-taking tips, and sample questions like those on the Praxis teaching and learning tests.

How Are Teachers Supported and Rewarded?

All professionals—physicians, lawyers, teachers, and others—must demonstrate minimum competency levels to become licensed and certified to practice. But many drive themselves far beyond minimal expectations to excel in their fields, and teachers are no different. Many teachers take advantage of every possible opportunity to

Technology in Practice

DIGITAL TEACHING PORTFOLIOS

Teacher education students at the University of Massachusetts demonstrate their understanding of INTASC standards by creating digital portfolios—online collections of student work demonstrating the breadth and depth of one's professional experience. According to Claire Kilbane, course instructor, the portfolios "help students develop a greater understanding of their profession, expand understanding of their personal strengths and weaknesses, and improve their technology skills" (Claire Kilbane, personal communication, July 26, 2002).

Brooke Barlett, a student in Kilbane's course, developed a unit (series of lessons) on rainforests for her portfolio project. At the time she was completing a student-teaching placement in a second-grade classroom. The image below shows one activity Bartlett used to help students learn about the locations of rainforests. In reflecting on the lesson, she explained that students in her class varied greatly in achievement levels. For this reason, she modeled the labeling process on an overhead projector before having students work independently on their own maps. According to Bartlett, structuring the lesson in this manner allowed her to "meet students' needs and capture their interests."

Critical Thinking Question

How do the INTASC standards guide teachers to use technology effectively?

To answer this question online and e-mail your answer to your professor, go to Chapter 1 of the Companion Website (ablongman.com/mcnergney4e) and click on Technology in Practice.

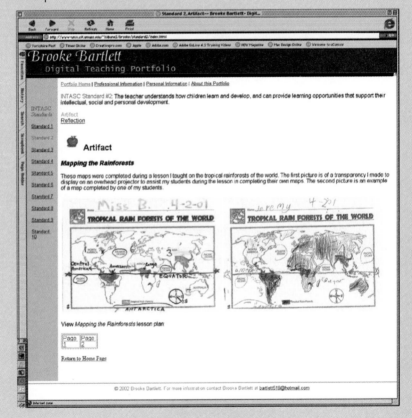

http://www.unix.oit.umass.edu/~kilbane2/brooke/standard2/index.html

acquire and demonstrate increasing levels of skill and knowledge. Mentoring programs, career ladders, merit pay, national certification, and advanced college degrees offer such opportunities.

Mentoring Programs

Does your state have a mentoring program for beginning teachers?   Most states require mentoring or **induction programs** for new teachers for their first three years on the job. These programs support experienced teachers—mentors or coaches—to help beginning teachers adjust to full-time teaching. Mentoring programs call for high levels of collaboration between beginners and experienced teachers. Participants on both sides often share a vision of what constitutes good teaching and a commitment to continuing development. Policymakers promote such programs because of the fairly high rate of attrition during the first three years of teaching; the programs are a way of relieving pressure on beginning teachers (Little, 1990).

The practice of mentoring varies considerably from place to place. Some mentors support traditional teaching practices and others foster change. Some mentoring programs avoid misunderstanding by clearly specifying how the program works. For instance, the Beginning Teacher Coaching Program of the Mt. Diablo School District in California and the Mt. Diablo Education Association spell out the responsibilities of the parties involved. They clearly state how and by whom full-time coaches are selected; how they are evaluated, rehired, and compensated; the eligibility of new teachers to participate in the program; how work schedules are developed; and the like (National Education Association, 1999).

Career Ladders and Merit Pay

Career ladder programs are examples of incentive programs for teachers. They offer status advancement, increased responsibility, and extra pay for exemplary teaching practice. Supporters of career ladder programs want teachers to examine their teaching, to think about alternative ways of teaching, and to focus on what students are learning. Career ladders typically acknowledge differences in beginners and master teachers. Dependent on school budgets, these programs come and go with the availability of funds to support them.

Like career ladders, **merit pay** tries to encourage teachers to strive for excellence by rewarding outstanding performance. Merit pay plans award either bonuses (one-time cash awards) or raises (financial increases added to teachers' base salaries). Originating in the 1920s, various plans for awarding merit pay have been tried and usually abandoned.

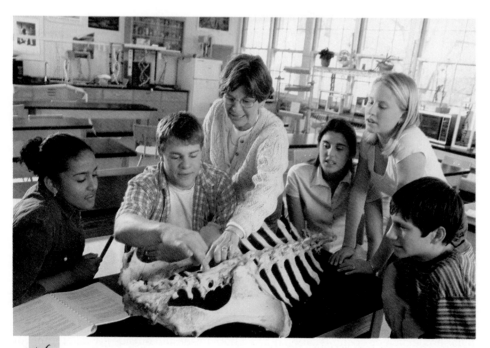

How can master teachers best be rewarded for their accomplishments? Why have some efforts, like career ladders and merit pay, been less successful than others?

HELPING OTHERS UNDERSTAND THE IMPORTANCE OF TEACHERS

The National Teacher of the Year in 2001, Michele Forman, teaches social studies in Middlebury, Vermont's Union High School. For some thirty-five years she has served her students by teaching through example. She helped start her school's Student Coalition on Human Rights, which organizes hunger strikes and marches to raise awareness of global issues. She spent 2001–2002 traveling to cities all over the country, helping everyone she met to understand why teachers are so important.

Q: In the real world, have you run into any stereotypes about teaching?

A: People will tell you on the one hand that education in America is in big trouble, that we need to raise the standards, and that they're not satisfied. But if you talk specifically about the schools to which they've sent their children and the teachers they have had, it's a very different picture. Wherever I have gone in the country, when people have found out that I am the National Teacher of the Year, they have given me the most wonderful "I had a teacher . . ." stories. Their faces soften; they smile; they open up.

Q: How do you think the experiences you have had this year will affect your teaching when you return to the classroom?

A: Something I will try hard to relay to [my colleagues] is, if I have learned one thing this year, it's that people love teachers. I've been on a 757 filled with people, and when the flight attendant announced that they had the National Teacher of the Year on board, the entire 757 broke into applause. I'm a stand-in for teachers across this country and all who have come before us. When you're a teacher, you don't always get feedback. The fifteen-year-old may not come up to you and say, "Wow, you're going to have a powerful influence on my life." That same fifteen-year-old, at thirty-five, might feel that. And to each one of those people I say please, please write and tell that teacher."

Critical Thinking Questions

Which of your teachers influenced your life in important ways? What was special about them?

To answer these question online and e-mail your answer to your professor, go to Chapter 1 of the Companion Website (ablongman.com/mcnergney4e) and click on Voices.

Source: Dunn, K. (2002, April) Interview: Teacher for America. *Teacher Magazine.* Available online (http://www.teachermagazine.org).

Merit pay plans fail most often for three reasons. First, guidelines for identifying teachers of merit are difficult to design and implement. Second, until recently, teacher unions typically have opposed merit plans, because paying some teachers more might mean paying other teachers less. Third, particularly in difficult financial times, school leaders, parents, and citizens often make other demands on funds that might go to merit pay plans. Since merit plans are frequently unsuccessful, school systems often reward excellence informally through investments in professional development. In addition, public recognition of teaching excellence is provided through state and national teacher-of-the-year programs, private organizations, grant foundations, and the mass media.

National Certification

Currently, the term *certification* denotes outstanding performance. Candidates seeking NBPTS certification, or **national certification,** are evaluated on their knowledge of subjects, understanding of students and teaching, and actual classroom practice. To demonstrate their expertise, candidates complete a portfolio and then participate in a set of exercises designed to assess their knowledge of teaching and learning. The portfolio should include documentation of work both inside and outside the classroom. For example, candidates must provide videotapes of their interactions with students during instruction and samples of student work, as well as analyses of the videos and student products. Candidates also must describe their efforts to stretch beyond the classroom and involve parents and the larger community in the education of children. Teachers who successfully complete NBPTS requirements earn national certification, which is good for ten years. Depending on state and local policy, certified teachers can receive salary increases, license renewal exemptions, and public recognition.

How Do Teachers Demonstrate Professional Leadership?

By definition, teachers are leaders. Teachers demonstrate professional leadership by working with others and by modeling desirable behavior. Teachers lead students, assistants, aides, parent volunteers, and many others who have a stake in schools. Teachers chair school and community committees organized to solve problems and take advantage of opportunities. Teachers create curricula. They lead workshops for their colleagues and other members of their communities. Teachers study for advanced degrees. They blaze new technological paths in education. They run professional associations. And they do much more. Sometimes teachers—Dennis Hastert, Speaker of the U.S. House of Representatives, for example—even lead Congress.

Advanced College Degrees

Many teachers demonstrate intellectual leadership through additional schooling and advanced degrees. When they do so, teachers enhance their salaries and may assume new responsibilities in the hierarchy of school systems. Over 40 percent of teachers have master's degrees, about 5 percent have education specialist degrees, and less than 1 percent have doctorates (U.S. Department of Education, 2002).

Working with Professional Organizations

As with other professionals, teachers' identities are shaped in part by the associations to which they belong and by the people and organizations that publicly represent them. Professional organizations and associations educate members, lobby Congress and state legislatures on education issues, and offer a range of professional services.

Teachers, counselors, administrators, and other professionals in education often belong to professional associations based on their disciplines. These associations offer journals, conferences, and action committees designed to provide opportunities for interacting with others who have similar interests. The largest, most visible, and most powerful teachers' organizations are the National Education Association (NEA) and the American Federation of Teachers (AFT). Like labor unions, teacher unions protect members' rights to **collective bargaining** (negotiation of the professional rights and responsibilities of teachers as a group) in contract disputes and other job-related matters.

The National Education Association was founded in 1857 to advance the professionalism of teaching. It now boasts 2.6 million members, including teachers, school administrators, college and university faculty and students, guidance counselors, and librarians, as well as school secretaries, bus drivers, and custodians. Negotiating teacher salaries, reporting educational research, and supporting teachers' professional development are among the many services that the NEA provides. The NEA is one of the most effective lobbying organizations in the nation, stating views of educational matters to legislators in Washington, D.C., in state capitols, and in communities across the country.

In 1916 the American Federation of Teachers was founded from a merger of twenty small teacher unions that formed after the turn of the century. More so than the NEA,

Cultural Awareness

AN AFRICAN AMERICAN'S VIEW OF THE PROFESSION

JoAnn W. Haysbert, professor and provost at Hampton University, is a classic example of a public school teacher who rose through the ranks to become an educational leader of national standing. She taught in the public schools and in two-year and four-year colleges. She has over twenty years of higher education administrative experience. JoAnn Haysbert is second in command of a historically black university. Her vision of teachers shapes life at her own institution and in the larger, more inclusive culture of professional education:

As I survey the landscape of our world in transition today and its need for teacher education, I am reminded of President George W. Bush's vision for the future of education with his bill Leave No Child Behind. With this challenge in mind, the responsibilities that lie ahead to fulfill this mandate require that we combine our training and experience and merge our theory and practice to help preservice candidates develop the needed competencies to ensure that they meet the educational needs of today's students K–12. While I am no longer in the classroom, my training of teachers continues. My background in teacher education is a great asset and makes the development of preservice, in-service, and university teaching professionals effective. I recognize that the teacher of today must be skilled as well as caring. Among those skills essential to today's students, technology is ranked among the top. Thus, our emphasis must not be placed only on ensuring that students demonstrate competency in this area, but we work toward ensuring that they demonstrate the ethical use of technology as well.

We must ensure that the educational process is a well-rounded one where we encourage students to understand the world we live in and their role as consumers in a technological environment. As we prepare teacher educators we must prepare them to use the technological medium that has revolutionized the course of education in a manner that we have never experienced before in our lifetime.

As a professional educator, it is my responsibility to lead by example, commit myself to the continuous growth of professional educators, and to demonstrate as well as encourage others to bridge the gap between the past, present, and future through the ethical use of technology.

As a chief academic officer, I am committed to lead and to serve through education. (J. Haysbert, personal communication, August 2002.)

Critical Thinking Questions

Do you agree with Dr. Haysbert's assessment of the importance of technology in teachers' lives? Why or why not?

To answer these questions online and e-mail your answer to your professor, go to Chapter 1 of the Companion Website (ablongman.com/mcnergney4e) and click on Cultural Awareness.

---

the AFT has been closely allied with industrial labor unions and affiliated with the AFL–CIO (American Federation of Labor–Congress of Industrial Organizations). Like the AFL–CIO, in contract disputes the AFT has sometimes advocated withholding professional services through job actions: work slowdowns, sick-outs, and strikes. Today the AFT has more than 800,000 members, mostly in urban areas.

Teacher unions are controversial, and they are frequently criticized by outsiders for shielding their members from scrutiny and for maintaining the status quo. They are also praised, however, for exercising considerable power for the improvement of public education. Both the NEA and the AFT have helped to shape school programs to promote child welfare. Both have fought for and won increases in teachers' salaries and improvements in working conditions, have heightened public awareness about the importance of involving teachers in decision-making processes, and have helped cultivate the concept that teachers are professionals.

*F*IGURE 1.6   **Reflective Teaching Process**   It is important for teachers to be able to reflect on their work so they can develop their professional knowledge and skills over time. Why is it also important for teachers to be able to explain their methods and the reasons underlying their behaviors?

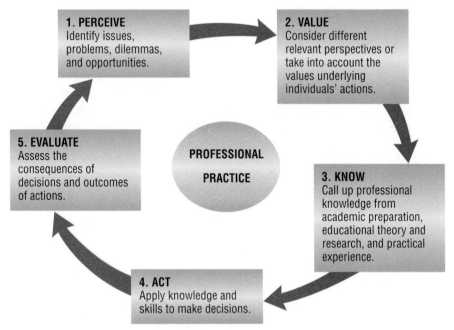

Source: "Cooperation and competition in case-based teacher education," by R. F. McNergney, J. M. Herbert, & R. E. Ford, 1994, *Journal of Teacher Education, 45*(5), pp. 339–345. Adapted by permission.

Meeting the Challenges of Professional Practice

Teachers lead most often and most effectively by example. To be a professional teacher means being able to think on one's feet and to perform in ways that support student learning. Figure 1.6 shows a model of this kind of professional practice.

A professional teacher recognizes teaching opportunities. These might be problems that need solutions, such as students' academic failure, social rejection, and emotional fragility. Or they might be opportunities to build on success, such as students' academic achievement, capacity for social inclusion, and emotional maturity. A professional perceives opportunities that increase students' chances to excel in the classroom.

Furthermore, a teacher–leader always considers the views of others who have a legitimate stake in a situation. For instance, parents and guardians hold strong values about what is right when it comes to their children. Other professionals can also provide objective perspectives. Thinking about issues from different points of view helps a teacher decide when and if a situation demands action.

To demonstrate professional practice, a teacher must possess relevant knowledge and be able to apply it to improve a situation. Such knowledge forms the basis or rationale for teaching action. INTASC, NBPTS, Praxis, and other sources of professional knowledge exist for good reason—to guide teachers' actions and to inform their performances.

Nobody knows better than a teacher in the twenty-first century that results matter. A professional is judged by the consequences of his or her actions—consequences often defined in terms of students. Did they learn? Did they enjoy it? Were they motivated to dig deeper? Did they come back for more?

As teachers confront problems and opportunities, they rise to the occasion again and again. Many of them thrive on the challenges of professional practice, getting stronger and better over time. They teach not only by sharing knowledge with their students but also by modeling what it looks like to learn (Wadsworth & Coleman, 2001).

Summary

Teaching has been described as both a profession and a semi-profession. As views of teaching change, there is less emphasis on longevity in the profession and greater emphasis on performance in the classroom. People entering the field do so through approved programs or through transcript assessment. Some of the issues they face are getting a first job, successfully performing their responsibilities, and planning for advancement in the profession. Once established, beginning teachers demonstrate leadership through their involvement in professional organizations and by modeling desirable behavior on the job—recognizing problems and opportunities, considering values of stakeholders, calling up professional knowledge, applying this knowledge through action, and assessing the consequences of such action. The challenges of professional practice are opportunities for teachers to develop and refine their expertise so they can better meet the needs of students.

Terms and Concepts

accreditation   11

alternative licensure   11

American Federation of Teachers (AFT)   4

authentic assessment   18

career ladder   21

certification   9

collective bargaining   23

Council of Chief State School Officers   7

emergency licensure   11

formative assessment   16

induction program   20

Interstate New Teacher Assessment and Support
    Consortium Standards (INTASC)   7

licensure   10

merit pay   21

National Board for Professional Teaching Standards
    (NBPTS)   8

national certification   22

National Education Association (NEA)   4

The Praxis Series™   18

reciprocity agreement   11

student teaching   18

summative assessment   16

teacher portfolio   18

teacher union   4

tenure   16

Reflective Practice

Choosing a Teaching Path

Renae Johnson was three weeks into her first teacher education course, and she was having second thoughts about her choice of secondary English as her licensure area. "I wish I could be as certain as you are about what I want to teach," she said to her friend, Nancy Hildebrand. "It's nice that there is flexibility in the teacher education program. Unfortunately, I may need more than one semester to decide on a major. The more I learn in class about the different paths teachers can take, the more confused I get!"

"Take it easy," advised Nancy. "I agree that the classroom teachers who have spoken to our group make every area of teaching sound appealing. But each speaker had different reasons for entering the profession and at least one of them changed directions after entering the field. Remember? She was the one who started out as an elementary teacher and then became a gifted education teacher. According to her, all teachers take professional development classes, either through the school system or a university, so it is possible to add endorsements in other areas."

"You're right. I shouldn't get so worked up about this. I know I like working with teenagers, and I love English, but ever since I tutored in the after-school program, I have been thinking I might like to work with students with special needs—kids who really struggle in school. I think I'll talk to Dr. Brigham about the special education program to see if that might be the best fit for me. I should also find out how many English classes I would need to have if at some point I wanted to specialize in secondary English."

Issues, Problems, Dilemmas, Opportunities

What areas of licensure is Renae considering? Is there demand for teachers in these areas in your own community?

Perceive and Value

What factors is Renae considering when trying to determine an area of licensure to pursue?

Know and Act

What do you know about licensure requirements in the state where you are hoping to teach? How difficult is it to add one or more areas of endorsement to your license?

Evaluate

What might you gain or lose by adding another teaching endorsement at this point in your program?

INTASC Principle 1

The teacher understands the central concepts, tools of inquiry, and structures of the discipline(s) he or she teaches and can create learning experiences that make these aspects of the subject matter meaningful for students.

Disposition

The teacher has enthusiasm for the discipline(s) she teaches and sees connections to everyday life. (Interstate New Teacher Assessment and Support Consortium, 1992)

Discussion Question

What more does Renae need to know about teaching English and teaching special needs students that will help her make a decision?

Additional Readings

Intrator, S. M. (2002). *Stories of the courage to teach: Honoring the teacher's heart.* New York: John Wiley & Sons, Inc.

National Center for Education Statistics (updated annually). *Condition of education.* Washington, DC: U.S. Department of Education. Available online: http://nces.ed.gov/

National Center for Education Statistics (updated annually). *Digest of education statistics.* Washington, DC: U.S. Department of Education. Available online: http://nces.ed.gov/

Rogers, D. L., & Babinski, L. M. (2002). *From isolation to conversation: Supporting new teachers' development.* Albany, NY: State University of New York Press.

Stone, E. (2002). *A boy I once knew: What a teacher learned from her student.* Chapel Hill, NC: Algonquin Books.

Thompson, J. G. (2002). *First-year teacher's survival kit: Ready-to-use strategies, tools & activities for meeting the challenges of each school day.* Paramus, NJ: Center for Applied Research in Education.

Web Resources

http://www.aft.org/

The website for the American Federation of Teachers provides information about the organization and resources for teachers.

http://www.ed.gov/pubs/survivalguide/

The Survival Guide for New Teachers is a resource for helping new teachers work effectively with veteran teachers, parents, principals, and teacher educators.

http://www.bls.gov/oco/ocos069.htm

This occupational handbook, developed by the U.S. Department of Labor, describes the conditions of teaching, job opportunities, and more.

http://www.nea.org/

The website for the National Education Association includes information about membership, services, current issues in education, and more.

http://www.ed.gov/pubs/FirstYear/

This website provides information about what to expect during your first year of teaching.

http://www.ccsso.org/index.html

The website for the Council of Chief State School Officers houses INTASC standards.

http://www.rnt.org

The website for Recruiting New Teachers, Inc. (RNT), a nonprofit organization, is an excellent resource for individuals seeking teaching positions.

Video**Workshop** Extra!

If the VideoWorkshop package is included with your textbook, go to Chapter 1 of the Companion Website (ablongman.com/mcnergney4e) and click on VideoWorkshop. Follow the instructions for viewing video clip 1. Then consider this information along with what you've read in Chapter 1 while answering the following:

1. As Chapter 1 explained, teachers face numerous challenges in terms of professional practice. Compare the expectations that teachers and students have before the first day of class, using information from the video clip to support your ideas.

2. The video clip presents suggestions that might aid a novice teacher who is preparing for a new teaching job. Imagine you are about to start the school year. Rank your top five concerns in order of importance, from least important to most important, and explain your choices in light of information presented in the video clip.

Challenges Teachers and Schools Face

Researchers interviewed inner-city middle school students in Philadelphia and other Pennsylvania cities to find out what they wanted from schools and from teachers. The students they interviewed read below grade level, performed poorly on basic mathematics tests, and wrote in an unskilled way compared to other middle-grade students around the city and in the suburbs. This performance gap mirrors a national trend in which children from economically poor backgrounds score significantly lower on various standardized tests than do children from wealthy backgrounds. Many explanations can be offered for this gap, most of which correctly suggest that this educational dilemma has deep societal roots.

> *Researcher:* Why are you getting an A in reading [now] when you did so poorly last year?
>
> *Student:* I work hard. [My teacher is] hard on us. I like that. It's helping me.
>
> *Researcher:* What does she do?
>
> *Student:* She called my house and talked to my mom. . . . She know [sic] my mom real good. She stays on my back. She says she'll call my mom. . . .
>
> *Researcher:* Why do you say you prefer a teacher who makes sure you do your work? . . . What does your teacher say to you?
>
> *Student:* You can make it. You have to work hard. You need to do more than just have a C.

CHAPTER CONTENTS

- What Are Society's Expectations for Schools?
- How Does Poverty Place Students at Risk of School Failure?
- How Can Schools Intervene to Help Students at Risk?
- How Can Schools Get Parents Involved in Their Children's Education?
- How Can Schools Reduce Risks That Threaten Children's Health and Safety?

Researcher: Why is that important?

Student: I used to be lazy. I hated school. But I realized that if I want to apply for a job, I need my education. (Wilson & Corbett, 2001, p. 72)

This chapter describes some of the challenging circumstances students experience and how teachers and schools attempt to help students overcome these obstacles. Some problems students face are shaped in part by who they are—their health, attitudes, and beliefs. Other problems depend largely on the conditions in which they live—their homes, neighborhoods, and communities. To help young people succeed, teachers and schools often stretch beyond their traditional missions in order to involve parents, social agencies, and private businesses. **What are some of the resources inside and outside school that teachers might access as they educate students?**

What Are Society's Expectations for Schools?

For many children, the years they spend in school are the best years of their lives. They interact with people who care about them and for them—people who help children to learn and to feel good about themselves and who nurture young people's hopes for the future.

In recent years, however, some critics have argued that schools have taken on too many roles. Students attending school from the beginning of kindergarten to the completion of twelfth grade will have spent only about 9 percent of their lives in the classroom (Finn, 1991). Nonetheless, expectations for schools are many, as people increasingly look to schools to solve some of society's most difficult problems (see Figure 2.1).

Although many agencies address children's problems, the public supports schools with tax dollars, so people expect educators to help students succeed, regardless of the circumstances. More and more, teachers and schools are being called on to provide services far beyond the scope of the classroom. In addition to teaching students, schools also are expected to offer counseling and support services, extracurricular activities, and programs for advancing the health and welfare of students. In short, now more than ever, society expects schools to prepare children to be functioning members of society.

At the same time, the growing number of **at-risk students**—those unlikely to complete high school and likely to have a low socioeconomic status throughout life—present unusually difficult challenges for educators. According to the U.S. Census Bureau, the following conditions suggest that students may be at varying levels of risk:

- Has at least one disability
- Retained in a grade at least once
- Speaks English less than "very well"
- Does not live with both parents
- Either parent emigrated in past five years
- Has a family income below $10,000
- Neither parent/guardian employed (Kominski, Jamieson, & Martinez, 2001)

At least 18 percent of all children (11 percent European Americans, 18 percent Asian and Pacific Islanders, 27 percent Hispanic Americans, and 34 percent African

*F*IGURE 2.1   **Some Social Issues That Affect Schools**   Think of other items that could be added to this figure. What effects might they have on teaching and learning?

Americans) experience more than one of these risk factors. Among this 18 percent, young children are as likely as older ones to have multiple risk factors. In addition, the level of risk varies by the type of risk factor or factors. For example, students who have a disability or are retained (held back) are much more likely to be at risk than are students who speak English less than "very well." The children with the highest rates of multiple risks are from families with low incomes or families in which neither parent works. Over 80 percent of the children from these families have at least one other risk factor, and 56 percent of these children have three or more risk factors (Kominski, Jamieson, & Martinez, 2001).

Schools do their best, but eventually many at-risk students drop out of school altogether. In response, communities across the country have structured schools and proposed political initiatives to meet the challenge presented by school dropouts. School choice plans try to stimulate educators to make schools places where students want to stay. Some states even redraw school attendance zones (redistricting) in an attempt to prevent certain schools from becoming way stations where students pause briefly before dropping out. Efforts to equalize funding for public schools are also undertaken to help schools in poor areas reduce their dropout and failure rates.

What is society's responsibility to students at risk?

How Does Poverty Place Students at Risk of School Failure?

Children under the age of eighteen are the people hardest hit by poverty. Some eleven million children live in families that earn less than the 2001 federal poverty level of $17,603 (U.S. Census Bureau, 2001). This figure is calculated as three times the cost of a diet that meets minimum nutritional requirements for a family of two adults and two children. The figure does not include other living expenses, such as housing, transportation, and health care.

All racial and ethnic groups are represented in every socioeconomic level. Proportionately, there are more low-income children in minority families than in majority families. But in the general U.S. population (actual numbers, not percentages), many more European American than minority group children live in poverty. Most of these children live in rural areas.

Despite what many people believe, having a job does not guarantee an escape from poverty. As Figure 2.2 indicates, poverty rates vary greatly between people living with workers and those living without workers. According to the data, families headed by single women are the ones hardest hit by poverty. While many single parents cope

FIGURE 2.2   Poverty Rates of People in Families by Family Type and Presence of Workers (in Percentages)   How does the poverty rate for married-couple families with one or more workers compare to that of female-householder families?

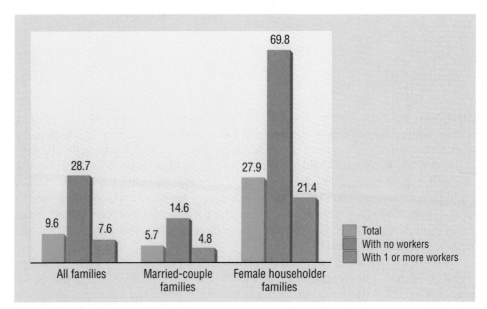

Source: U.S. Census Bureau (2001). Figure 6. Poverty rates of people in families by family type and presence of workers: 2000. Available online: http://www.census.gov/prod/2001pubs/p60-214.pdf.

admirably, the demands they must face can be formidable. Moreover, those parents most in need of child care are the ones least able to afford it.

Beyond all of these statistics, it is important to know that a basic link exists between poverty and learning. Low-income communities often mean underfunded school districts and poorer schools in virtually every way. And when child poverty and poor school funding are combined, effects on student performance can be substantial. To help understand the effects of poverty on students, imagine a child who comes to school hungry and cannot concentrate in class. Now imagine that the classroom does not have computer equipment, current textbooks, and other necessary tools. What kind of education will this student receive, especially when compared to a student from a wealthy family, attending a well-funded school?

Results of a four-state study suggest that the effects of poverty on student achievement increase in larger schools. Larger schools often mean less money is spent on each student and may mean larger classes, where students do not receive the same level of attention they would in a smaller class. The benefits of smaller schools seem to be particularly important in the middle grades, as students near the ages when they are most likely to drop out of school (The Rural School and Community Trust, 2002).

On a positive note, results of a major study of migrant children argue that socioeconomic status need not limit one's aspirations or level of achievement. The study found that when children have at least one parent who communicates high expectations for academic achievement, the children stay in school and perform well (Balli, 1996).

Although a positive family environment for learning is valuable for students, the indelible marks poverty leaves on people must not be overlooked. Some become trapped and embittered by poverty; others are resilient and motivated to defeat the circumstances in which they find themselves. In *Amazing Grace: The Lives of Children,* Jonathan Kozol (1995) describes vividly what he learned in New York City about being poor.

> The following day, I visit a soup kitchen where more than 200 people, about two thirds of whom are children, come to eat four times a week. The mothers of the children seem competitive, and almost frantic, to make sure their children get their share. A child I meet, a five-year-old boy named Emmanuel, tells me he's "in kiddie garden." His mother says he hasn't started yet, "He starts next year."
>
> "You have to remember," says one of the priests with whom I share my thoughts about these meetings, "that for this little boy whom you have met, his life is just as important to him as your life is to you. No matter how insufficient or how shabby it may seem to some, it is the only one he has"—an obvious statement that upsets me deeply nonetheless. (Kozol, 1995, p. 70)

How might children in low-income neighborhoods get better schools?

How Can Schools Intervene to Help Students at Risk?

Investing in education can foil the effects of poverty and help a large group of students at risk succeed in school and in life. For example, the U.S. Department of Education found that the availability of free or low-cost education can lead to a reduction in welfare or public assistance programs. Furthermore, it has been found that people with more education rely less on welfare and public assistance than do people with less education.

The problems facing the young involve more than economics, however, and they are often interrelated. Many people therefore advocate comprehensive, integrated

*M*ore people live in rural areas than in inner cities. Most of the poor people in the country are white, and most live in families with a wage earner.

approaches to reduce the exposure of young people to high-risk settings. Such settings are characterized by poverty, substance abuse, parental neglect, and violence in many forms.

School counselors are a primary source for helping students cope with serious social and personal problems. In general, counselors try to improve self-esteem, but many also foster career awareness and offer support groups for children affected by divorce or students who need to work on study or social skills. High school counselors, in particular, focus on college or job counseling.

In 1964, funding from the National Defense Education Act (NDEA) extended counseling services beyond high schools to include elementary schools. This action acknowledged the importance of helping children succeed early in their educational careers, with the help defined increasingly in terms of preventing problems. Counselors typically perform the following functions:

1. provide inservice training and consultation for teachers on preventing serious student problems;
2. work with parents to promote understanding of child development;
3. identify and refer children with developmental deficiencies or disabilities to others who can offer assistance; and
4. help older children make connections between school and work. (Gladding, 2000, p. 389)

For many children, these and other school-based interventions make a profound difference in their lives. Overall, one of the most important interventions that schools provide is caring teachers. Teachers collaborate with parents and other professionals to create the conditions necessary for student success. **Can you think of a teacher who had a major influence on your life?**

Your Teaching Life in Practice

MENTORING PROGRAMS FOR TEACHERS

Many school systems provide mentoring programs for new teachers. As one online mentoring program in Illinois suggests, there are opportunities to continue learning on the job. One teacher asked a mentor:

"I have a student in mind who is just a few points away from passing a course that is required for graduation," the anonymous high school instructor wrote in a message marked "urgent." "Is there ever a time when it is appropriate to bump a student up a small amount in order for them to pass a class? And if so, how large of a raise can I make while maintaining the integrity of my grading scale?" (Borja, 2002, p.12)

This question reflects real life as one beginning teacher lives it. It also suggests indirectly what makes mentoring programs—online and in person—so important. When they work well, a mentor is a trusted guide, a tutor, and a coach who offers advice and support on matters that affect new teachers.

Discussion Questions

How might a mentor be helpful to you? Would you be comfortable expressing your concerns openly to a fellow teacher serving as your mentor if she or he were more mature and/or more experienced than you? Would you prefer to do so anonymously?

To answer these questions online and e-mail your answer to your professor, go to Chapter 2 of the Companion Website (ablongman.com/mcnergney4e) and click on Your Teaching Life in Practice.

Source: Borja, R. R. (2002, April 3). E-mentors offer online support, information for novice instructors. *Education Week on the Web, 21,* 29: 12. (http://www.edweek.org/ew/newstory.cfm?slug=29mentor.h21&keywords=tenure).

Providing Early Intervention Programs

Early intervention programs provide desperately needed opportunities for student success in preschool and elementary school. Such programs offer preschool children, particularly children who may be at risk, opportunities for later educational success by laying the groundwork for effective learning. In early intervention programs, young children learn speech, cognition, and other skills that are believed to make them better students once they enter school. Based on the theory that early experiences are critical to children's development and educational progress, many of these programs have focused on educating both parents and children.

Many testaments to the value of early intervention can be found across the nation. The Perry Preschool Program, begun in 1962 by David P. Weikart in Ypsilanti, Michigan, provided a preschool and home-visit program to three- and four-year-olds from economically disadvantaged families. The program captured public attention with results from a follow-up study of its students and a matched control group. A twenty-two-year follow-up study done on 95 percent of the participants revealed that, in comparison to the control group, Perry Preschool graduates had a smaller chance of being arrested, earned approximately $2,000 more per month, were more likely to own a home, and had a higher rate of graduation from secondary schools.

Many other programs help disadvantaged students enter school ready to learn. Head Start and Early Head Start—federally subsidized programs serving children from birth to age five, pregnant women, and their families—have the goal of increasing the school readiness of children from low-income families. Besides providing an individualized curriculum, the program delivers health, nutrition, and social services to families. Parents participate in program governance and parenting classes, and they have

What are the goals of early intervention programs? How effective is early intervention and in what ways?

opportunities to do volunteer work or to be hired as staff members in Head Start classrooms.

On a practical level, some states and localities experiment with ways to supplement federal support for nutrition and health care to reach larger numbers of children. The intent of these intervention programs is to help all children be nutritionally ready for learning and to avoid labeling anyone as being low-income.

The younger the child, the more important it is not only to support good nutrition but to encourage opportunities for human interaction—time to talk and listen. Project Story Boost is an early intervention program in a small New England city that targets at-risk kindergarten children and their parents in an effort to build links between homes and schools (Wood & Salvetti, 2001). The target schools serve low socioeconomic families from public housing along with families from more affluent neighborhoods. Most of the children in the program are from single-parent families and many are immigrants.

At the beginning of the year, kindergarten teachers identify possible participants whom they think would benefit from read-aloud sessions. The adults who participate in the program, coordinated through the local university, report that students demonstrate a range of desirable behaviors. In particular, the students become familiar with stories, voluntarily choose to read, participate in whole-class read-aloud sessions, improve their vocabulary, and build their interest in books.

Keeping Students in School

How can we prevent students from dropping out of school?   Educators cannot help young people avoid potential problems or face actual problems if they are not in school. Trying to determine who is not there and why, however, is a major challenge for school officials. Some districts count as dropouts students who have died, left school to get married, taken a job, gone to vocational school, entered the armed forces, gone to jail, or been expelled. The federal government uses three measures to calculate the national number of dropouts:

1. the proportion of students who drop out in a single academic year;
2. the number of students who drop out of a specific grade level; and
3. the percentage of people in a certain age range who are not enrolled in school.

Regardless of the confusion about who is absent and why, educators are expected to keep students in school at least through twelfth grade, ultimately turning out literate, responsible, productive citizens. **Holding power,** the ability to keep students in school until they receive a high school diploma or an equivalency certificate, has increased over the decades as youth have spent more and more years in school. Although they may not choose to stay in school strictly because they want to learn, many students now recognize that they will need at least a high school diploma in order to get a decent job after they finish school.

Besides offering the possibility for a better job if students graduate from high school, teachers and schools must try to make the classroom a place students want to be. Some ways they can do this include relating the material to students' lives, offering activities that are interesting, encouraging free thinking, including all students in classroom discussion, and making school a fun place to be. To be truly effective, these methods must be in place long before students can drop out of school. Students' interest in learning must be planted early on and cultivated over time.

Providing Compensatory Education

A number of programs provide children from low-income families with additional educational opportunities beyond those offered in a school's standard program. These

With more women working, traditional roles and responsibilities of parents have changed. What new responsibilities might fathers assume?

compensatory education programs attempt to provide important educational factors (e.g., teachers, curricula, time, and materials) that may be missing in young people's lives.

TITLE I

Title I is the largest federally funded education program for at-risk elementary and secondary students. It began in 1965 as the first bill of President Lyndon Johnson's War on Poverty program. Today, the program meets the educational needs of 12.5 million low-income, low-achieving students. Title I children most often receive their services in **pull-out programs** outside the regular classroom. Instruction usually lasts for thirty to thirty-five minutes and focuses mainly on reading, mathematics, and language arts. Some 65 percent of the teaching of Title I children is done for students in grades one through six by aides or paraprofessionals. **How might you decide if a Title I program was successful?**

UPWARD BOUND

Many older children also need all the help they can get. **Upward Bound,** another federally funded program, is structured to improve the academic performance and motivational levels of low-income high school students, particularly in math and science. Participants in the program receive tutoring, counseling, and basic skills instruction. The program encourages students to finish high school and win acceptance into college. At the end of the school year, students participate in a summer residential program focusing on the improvement of study skills and content knowledge. Established in the 1960s, Upward Bound programs continue to operate across the nation.

Providing Before- and After-School Programs

In the past forty years, women have entered the work force in increasing numbers, with the sharpest increases being among married mothers of young children. Some three out of four mothers worked outside the home in 2000, compared to one out of four in 1965 (U.S. Census Bureau 2001). With more women unable to stay at home with their children, traditional roles and responsibilities of parents have changed. In some two-parent families, fathers assume child care responsibilities. In others, parents change their work schedules so that one or the other can be home with their children during the day. Working mothers of children between the ages of five and fourteen most often hire someone to provide care in the child's home. Although most children under age four have some type of supervised care, nonrelatives typically provide this care outside the child's home. About 5.5 million children in the United States live with their grandparents (U.S. Census Bureau, 1999).

Between five and fifteen million school-age children go home each day to empty houses (U.S. Department of Education, 2000). These **latchkey children,** many of whom live in low-income communities, may be without adult supervision for the several hours each day when juvenile crime is at its peak. Children who attend quality after-school programs demonstrate better behavior in school, make better grades, and spend less time watching television than those who are not enrolled in such programs. Moreover, children who participate in extracurricular activities are less likely to use drugs and less likely to become teen parents than young people who do not participate in such activities.

Schools respond to needs for child care in many different ways. Buses transport children to school in the morning and home in the afternoon. Some children arrive early enough each day to receive a hot breakfast they would not get otherwise. In the afternoon, extracurricular activities such as sports, clubs, and tutoring programs provide supervision until parents are finished with work.

In the past, children from lower socioeconomic levels in particular have had limited access to after-school programs because of transportation needs. Supplemental service provisions in the No Child Left Behind Act assure that the lowest-achieving students, regardless of income level, can enjoy the benefits of participating in high-quality programs outside regular school hours.   **What kinds of before- and after-school programs might be most useful to students who are struggling academically?**

Offering Incentives and Disincentives

Other tactics used to encourage academic success include **incentive programs.** These programs offer outside incentives—rewards for good attendance and good grades. For example, the HOPE Scholarship Program (Helping Outstanding Pupils Educationally), which is supported entirely by a state lottery, offers a free college education to all Georgia high school students with a B average who choose to attend a public college, university, or technical institute in the state. The HOPE Scholarship includes tuition, HOPE-approved mandatory fees, and a book allowance of up to $100 per quarter. Full-time enrollment in school is not required. Since its inception in 1993, the program has awarded scholarships totaling nearly $1.5 billion (Georgia Student Finance Commission, 2002).

In some instances punitive measures or disincentive programs have been employed to reduce the dropout rate. Arkansas, for example, penalizes school dropouts and students with excessive unexcused absences by revoking their driver's licenses.

Ohio's Learning, Earning, and Parenting (LEAP) program blends penalties and rewards to encourage teenage parents to stay in school and graduate. Students can earn a $62 monthly bonus in their welfare benefits for staying in school and an additional $62 for completing a grade level. LEAP deducts $62 from students' monthly benefits for poor attendance. LEAP judges success in terms of inducing dropouts to return to high school or to enroll in General Educational Development programs and promoting better attendance among those already enrolled in school. It also tracks the rates of high school graduation, GED attainment, employment, and reduced welfare payments among its participants (Ohio Welfare Information Network, 2002).

Providing Mentors and Tutors

Some programs try to improve the academic success and self-esteem of at-risk students through the use of tutors and **mentoring programs**—efforts to model appropriate behavior in one-on-one situations. For example, Big Brothers Big Sisters of America (BBBSA) has provided one-on-one mentoring relationships between adult volunteers and children at risk since 1904. The organization currently serves more than 100,000 children and youth in over five hundred agencies throughout the United States, and it promotes appreciation for racial, cultural, and ethnic diversity among the staff, volunteers, and children served.

The Mentor/Mentee (M&M) program at Arkadelphia High School in Arkansas helps students manage their time and focus on success in learning (Anderson & Blackwood, 2000). Arkadelphia High School is a rural comprehensive high school with about 530 students in grades ten through twelve. The mentors in this program counsel and guide students, encouraging strong links between home and school. Each mentor works with fifteen students on study skills, exam preparation, course registration, social skills, and conflict resolution. In addition to many informal contacts, mentors and mentees attend regular meetings once a month.   **What kinds of adults make good mentors?**

Other schools provide peer-tutoring programs in which students help one another with schoolwork. Some school-sponsored tutoring programs pair younger students with tutors from higher grade levels. Still other school-sponsored tutoring programs involve adults from the community, who are sometimes students from a local university.

FIGURE 2.3   **Average Science Scale Scores by Amount of Time Students Reported Watching Television and Videos, Grade 4 (Public and Nonpublic Schools Combined): 2000**   What can we learn from children's self-reported television watching? Why might you doubt their self-reports?

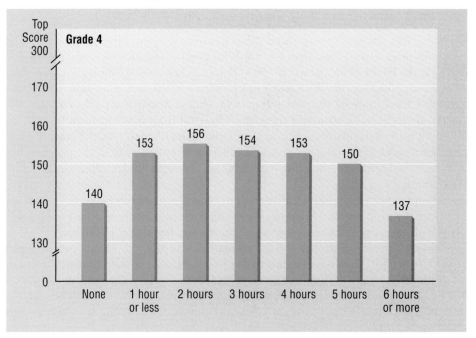

Source: National Center for Education Statistics, National assessment of educational progress (NAEP), 2000 science assessment. Available online: http://nces.ed.gov/nationsreportcard/science/results/television-g4.asp.

*H*ow Can Schools Get Parents Involved in Their Children's Education?

When schools encourage parents to get involved in their children's education, the payoffs can be high. Parental involvement in children's education from birth until they leave home has a major positive effect on children's achievement at school. But how can parents become involved?

One very important way parents influence their children's lives is through the regulation of television viewing. Watching many hours of television daily has a negative effect on students' reading performances. Studies from the National Center for Education Statistics determined that students who reported watching the most television, six hours or more a day, had the lowest average reading score (2002). Those who reported watching four to five hours a day had the next lowest score. Fourth-grade students who reported watching less television—either two or three hours or an hour or less daily—had higher scores. As Figure 2.3 demonstrates, students' science test scores also are affected negatively by heavy television viewing.

Implementing Parental Involvement Programs

For some parents, school involvement may seem like a luxury. Parents in poverty worry so much about making money to support their families that they may have little emo-

*W*hy is parents' involvement in their children's education important? How do full-service schools support family-based education?

tional energy left to devote to school activities. This is neither an indictment nor an excuse; poverty, work, and worry are facts of life for many people.

Schools have always tried to involve parents in the education of their children, but school efforts seem to have increased in recent years. Common and visible examples are parent–teacher conferences, school open houses, parent–teacher associations and organizations (PTAs and PTOs), and school advisory councils. PTAs and PTOs vary in size and level of participation in schools. Their goal is to involve parents in school activities to tackle virtually every kind of problem imaginable. In many instances, the groups' fund-raising efforts allow schools to purchase classroom materials and equipment. These funds also provide educational opportunities, such as field trips and theatrical performances.

Although opportunities such as PTOs and advisory councils exist, some parents are unable or choose not to participate. As Sandra Balli (1996) suggests, some parents may not have had positive school experiences themselves and thus are reluctant to get involved in their children's schools. Other parents may not have time to participate fully in their children's school experiences. Still other parents may not know what they can do to help their children in the classroom. The suggestions in Figure 2.4 offer a variety of ways that parents can participate as school volunteers, whether by reading stories or chaperoning field trips.

Beyond classroom volunteering, parental involvement figures heavily in efforts to reorganize schools. Concepts of parental choice, for example, are based on the idea that when parents can exercise some control over where their children attend school, schools become more responsive to their input as consumers. This ability to offer input may also encourage more parents to speak up about what they want in schools. In addition, parents are also encouraged to participate in the governing councils that plan strategies to bring about change in school systems.

Providing Family Services through Full-Service Schools

Schools today—more than ever before—are called on to offer far more than basic education for school-age students. In recognition of this fact, **full-service schools,** or

*F*IGURE 2.4   **Involving Parents as Volunteers**

Ways Volunteers Can Help at Elementary School	Ways Volunteers Can Help at Secondary School
Tell stories.	Help in the office.
Listen to children read, and read to children.	Make attendance calls.
Lead flash card drills.	Help with school events.
Help contact parents about school or classroom activities.	Reproduce materials for teachers.
Reproduce materials for teachers.	Work in the library.
Help at recess.	Help in the lunchroom.
Prepare bulletin boards.	Tutor students who need extra help.
Reinforce spelling or vocabulary words.	Work on a school-to-home newsletter.
Help in the library.	Be a resource person for teachers.
Assist with arts and crafts projects.	Act as a liaison for non-English-speaking families.
Visit with children; show that adults care.	Prepare bulletin boards.
Dramatize a story.	Participate in Saturday work parties.
Help children with handwriting.	Help with student clubs.
Help children with motor skills.	Gather resource materials.
Help non-English-speaking children.	Volunteer as a hall monitor.
Share information about occupations.	Have a monthly parent–teacher or parent–student lunch period.
Help with special programs or assemblies.	Mentor students.
Give underachievers one-on-one assistance.	Provide homework help.
Work with gifted children.	Serve on advisory committee.
Help with field trips.	
Teach a skill.	
Gather resource materials.	

Source: From *Parent involvement in education: Insights and applications from the research* by M. R. S. Stein & R. Thorkildsen, 1999, Bloomington, IN: Phi Delta Kappa International, p. 545. Reprinted with permission from Phi Delta Kappa International.

community schools, have existed around the country for about twenty years, most prominently in New York City, San Francisco, and St. Louis. The stated purpose of these programs is to offer a range of services for children and their families.

In Chicago, for example, three full-service schools work with communities to offer tutoring, arts, and sports for children, along with high-school equivalency and English classes, and job training and family therapy for adults. Services are available evenings and on Saturdays. Sophia Morales, a nine-year-old at Brentano School in Logan Square, stays after school most days for homework help as well as art and theater classes. She says, "It feels like home, except we don't have a bed" (Grossman, 2002, p.1).

Should schools provide health and social services?   The challenges of dealing with students who have a variety of health problems have added to the full-service nature of schools, prompting the establishment of school-based health centers in a number of states. These centers allow schools to coordinate health care with health curricula emphasizing preventive care. Full-care clinics provide such services as physical examinations, weight and drug counseling, treatment of illness and minor injuries, and testing for pregnancy and sexually transmitted diseases. The first of these full-care centers was established in Dallas, Texas, in 1970. Now most states have such centers.

The success of these and related full-service efforts depends on many people. Teachers, families, administrators, social service providers, health care providers, and

LEARNING TO WORK WITH PARENTS

Vivian Morris, a professor at the University of Memphis, Tennessee, believes it is critical that teachers learn to work with parents. She explains:

We really need to prepare teachers to become involved with families—it's not something that comes naturally to us. Just as we need to teach reading or social studies, we need to teach our students in education the skills they need for family involvement. There is a great deal of anxiety in talking to parents, about having to do parent conferences.

According to Morris, the key to success is infusing the curriculum with family and community involvement training. This means helping future educators question their perceptions about families and family structures and

about what involvement in schools looks like. As Morris noted, "Because many families' experiences with schools haven't been good, it's the teachers' responsibility to reach out."

Critical Thinking Questions

How might inexperienced teachers learn to reach out to parents? Can you recall instances when teachers reached out to you and your family?

 To answer these questions online and e-mail your answer to your professor, go to Chapter 2 of the Companion Website (ablongman.com/mcnergney4e) and click on Voices.

Source: Blair, L. (2002, February). The missing link: Teacher education program. *Southwest Educational Development Laboratory News, 14*(1), 9–11.

---

others must collaborate to maximize the benefit of their energies. When they do so, children's chances for living and learning in healthy environments are improved.

How Can Schools Reduce Risks That Threaten Children's Health and Safety?

If you were asked to describe the overall well-being of today's youngsters, what would you say? According to the Children's Defense Fund (CDF), a private non-profit organization dedicated to educating others about the needs of children, today's children are not doing very well (2002). Each day during a 180-day school calendar in the United States:

- 1 young person under 25 dies from HIV infection
- 5 children or youth under 20 commit suicide
- 9 children or youth under 20 are homicide victims
- 9 children or youth under 20 die from firearms
- 34 children and youth under 20 die from accidents
- 77 babies die
- 155 babies are born at very low birthweight (less than 3 lb., 4 oz.)
- 180 children are arrested for violent crimes
- 367 children are arrested for drug abuse
- 401 babies are born to mothers who had late or no prenatal care
- 825 babies are born at low birthweight (less than 5 lb., 8 oz.)
- 1,310 babies are born without health insurance
- 1,329 babies are born to teen mothers
- 2,019 babies are born to mothers who are not high school graduates

- 2,861 high school students drop out
- 3,585 babies are born to unmarried mothers
- 4,248 children are arrested
- 7,883 children are reported abused or neglected
- 17,297 public school students are suspended

At every age, among all races and income groups, and in communities throughout the nation, these and other problems threaten the well-being of young people.

Preventing Child Abuse and Neglect

Many youngsters suffer from physical, emotional, or sexual abuse, and many more may be the victims of neglect by their parents or guardians. Teachers are among those groups required by law to report suspected cases of child abuse. In 1974 Congress passed the **Child Abuse Prevention and Treatment Act** to provide financial support to states that implemented programs for identification, prevention, and treatment of child abuse and neglect. Congress passed the **Adoption and Safe Families Act of 1997** to enhance the services and extend the scope of child welfare agencies.

Problems of child abuse and neglect exist in all kinds of families and across the nation. Some 826,000 children were victims of abuse and neglect in 1999 (U.S. Department of Health and Human Services, 2001a). This figure translates to about twelve victims for every 1,000 children in the population. The government bases this estimate on data from all fifty states and, as Figure 2.5 demonstrates, abuse rates vary considerably by state.

Parenting programs are one way to increase parents' involvement in their children's lives and to break cycles of abuse and neglect. The physical and mental health of parents directly affects the health and well-being of their children. Therefore many community-based parenting programs try to provide parents with the skills and knowledge they need to cope more effectively with everyday stress and to care better for their children. For particularly young, inexperienced parents, these programs offer practical

$\mathcal{F}$IGURE 2.5   **Map of Maltreatment Rates, 1999**

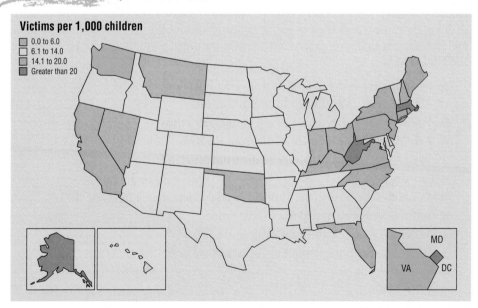

Source: U.S. Department of Health and Human Services (2001). Figure 2.1, Chapter 2: Victims. *Child Maltreatment,* 1999. Available online: http://www.acf.dhhs.gov/programs/cb/publications/cm99/cpt2.htm

Technology in Practice

PROTECTING CHILDREN'S PRIVACY

Teachers use the World Wide Web for all kinds of educational activity, from exploration to reinforcement. But these virtual worlds, like the real worlds that children inhabit, can be threatening places. A teacher has moral and legal responsibilities to protect children's privacy.

The Federal Trade Commission enforces the Children's Online Privacy Protection Act (COPPA) passed by Congress in 1999. It does so by requiring commercial website operators to get parental consent before collecting any personal information from children under age thirteen. It also allows but does not require teachers to act on behalf of parents.

Here are ways the basic provisions of COPPA affect teachers:

- Teachers are subject to their school district's policies about computer use. They may act in place of a parent in deciding to give consent to requests for information; but they do not have to assume this responsibility.
- Teachers may decide whether to approve information collection from students based on new uses for the information.
- Teachers may ask to see the information the students have submitted.
- Teachers should understand that they may revoke their consent at any time and have their students' information deleted.

Discussion Questions

What are some other ways teachers can protect children's privacy online? What are the responsibilities of website operators?

To answer these questions online and e-mail your answer to your professor, go to Chapter 2 of the Companion Website (ablongman.com/mcnergney4e) and click on Technology in Practice.

Go to the FTC website (http://www.ftc.gov/bcp/conline/pubs/online/teachers.htm) for more information about this topic.

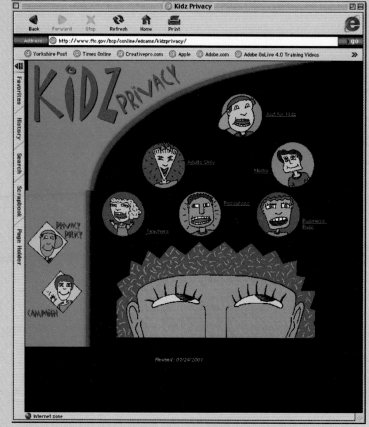

---

knowledge for taking care of themselves and their children. To reach young parents, schools often sponsor parenting programs within their own buildings. Some schools also provide day care for infants and preschool children of high school students so that parents can complete their own high school programs and avoid the life conditions that breed abuse and neglect.

Preventing and Responding to Teen Pregnancy

The more education she has, the less likely a girl is to have a baby. For teens, having a child greatly increases the chance that a young mother and her child or children will live in poverty. Furthermore, many children of teenage parents end up as teenage parents themselves, perpetuating the cycle of poverty.

The teenage birthrate declined steadily between 1991 and 1999. In 1999 the birthrate was 49.6 per 1,000 births, 20 percent lower than the 62.1 rate in 1991 (U.S. Department of Health and Human Services, 2001b). In 1999 the birthrate among Latino teenage girls ages fifteen to nineteen was 93.6 per 1,000. Among non-Latino whites, the rate was 35.2 per 1,000, and among blacks it was 85.4 per 1,000 (Center for Disease Control and Prevention, 2000a).

The overwhelming majority of states encourage some type of sex education in schools, but the content and method of courses vary widely. Instruction ranges from advocating sexual abstinence to distributing condoms within the school.

Although sex education is offered in schools, the fact remains: many teenage girls will have babies while they are students. The high dropout rate among young mothers and, in many instances, the poor health of their babies have encouraged many school systems to alter their programs to meet the needs of adolescent parents and parents-to-be. In addition to standard curriculum, some schools offer home instruction to teenage mothers during their four- to six-week postpartum period. Schools may also provide teenage parents with child care, individual and group counseling, health care, parenting education, and vocational training.

Some schools offer services to young fathers and fathers-to-be. Boston schools were among the first to establish such programs. Case managers assist young fathers by

Issues in School Reform

A MENTORING PROGRAM FOR ADOLESCENT GIRLS

We would all prefer to prevent problems than solve them. A mentoring program started at Western Maryland College called Fields of Wings is out to do just that, by matching female college students with middle school girls. College mentors can develop rapport with early adolescent girls because the college students are old enough to be authority figures, yet young enough to remember and understand the challenges of being an adolescent.

The idea is to mentor girls during adolescence and address their faltering self-confidence, which affects their academic performance and their social and emotional development. To do this, mentors learn to follow six basic guidelines:

1. Listen when the student has a problem.
2. Identify feelings and give her feedback.
3. Help her think for herself.
4. Confront negative intentions and behaviors.
5. Provide information when needed.
6. Encourage exploration of options. (Shea, 1997)

The leaders of Fields of Wings found the following techniques to be useful:

1. Skits. The girls wrote and performed skits about problems that were part of their culture—eating disorders, thinking about suicide, and peer pressure to have sex and use drugs.
2. Journals. The girls kept journals and reflected on what troubled them. For example, one girl wrote about being pressured by her boyfriend to have sex. She wanted advice about how to say no and how to break up with him if he persisted.
3. Incentives. The girls earned points and prizes for doing their homework.

The girls in Fields of Wings "admired mentors who were good students, had outgoing personalities, and were good listeners" (p. 53). Apparently, it did not matter if mentors and students were of the same ethnic group.

Critical Thinking Questions

Do you think this kind of program might work with boys and male college students? Why or why not?

To answer these questions online and e-mail your answer to your professor, go to Chapter 2 of the Companion Website (ablongman.com/mcnergney4e) and click on Issues in School Reform.

helping them find part-time jobs and steering them toward job-training programs. **Should states mandate that all middle and high schools provide sex education for all students?**

Preventing the Spread of AIDS and Other Communicable Diseases

As Figure 2.6 indicates, parents have definite ideas about what sex education programs should cover. No doubt statistics on the general well-being of young people have affected parents' attitudes. However parents choose to think about the subject, many students are having sex and should be taught about the health risks of their actions. Research indicates that students who have sex and use drugs are especially susceptible to sexually transmitted diseases, including HIV (human immunodeficiency virus), the

FIGURE 2.6   Students and Parents: What Parents Want Sex Education to Teach
Assuming students' perceptions are accurate, can you explain why there are such discrepancies between what parents want and what is covered in the curriculum?

	What Students Say Is Covered	What Parents Want Taught[a]
Core Elements		
HIV/AIDS	97	98
STDs other than HIV/AIDS, such as herpes	93	98
Basics of pregnancy and birth	90	90
Waiting to have sex	84	97
Other Topics		
Birth control	82	90
Abortion	61	79
Homosexuality and sexual orientation, that is, being gay, lesbian, or bisexual	41	76
Safer Sex and Negotiation Skills		
How to deal with pressure to have sex	79	94
How to deal with emotional issues and consequences of being sexually active	71	94
How to get tested for HIV/AIDS and other STDs	69	92
How to use condoms	68	85
How to talk with parents about sex and relationship issues	62	97
How to use and where to get other birth control	59	84
What to do if you or a friend has been raped or sexually assaulted	59	97
How to talk with a partner about birth control and STDs	58	88
n =	1099	1501

[a]"Very" and "somewhat" responses are used here.

Source: Hoff, T., & Greene, L. (2000). *Sex education in America: A series of national surveys of parents, teachers, and principals.* Menlo Park, CA: Henry J. Kaiser Family Foundation, p. 31. Reprinted with permission.

virus that causes AIDS (acquired immunodeficiency syndrome). Between 800,000 and 900,000 people in the United States are living with HIV. One-third do not know they are infected. Some 438,000 men, women, and children have lost their lives to this disease (U.S. Department of Health and Human Services, 2001c).

According to data collected by the Center for Disease Control and Prevention (2000b), 49.9 percent of high school students have had sexual intercourse; 42 percent did not use a condom.

When developing programs to prevent HIV transmission, educators should remember that many students experiment with drugs and sex at an early age. HIV prevention programs, therefore, must begin in elementary school and continue through high school. They must also be flexible enough to meet the needs of all children and take into account the possibility that some students are engaging in high-risk behavior.

One study of school-based HIV education programs revealed that the most effective interventions had the following characteristics:

- emphasize risk-taking behaviors that could lead to HIV infection;
- give students opportunities to practice refusal and communication skills through role playing and brainstorming;
- help students recognize social and media influences on sexual behavior;
- help students develop values regarding postponing sex, avoiding unprotected sex, using condoms, and avoiding high-risk partners; and
- use testimonials from respected peers to encourage a more conservative set of values (Landau, Pryor, & Haefli, 1995).

As for other communicable diseases, children who have not received preschool vaccinations before entering school are particularly vulnerable to typical childhood illnesses. Measles, mumps, pertussis (whooping cough), and rubella are threats to both health and learning. In recent years, drug-resistant strains of tuberculosis have developed and pose threats to children's health. Public health officials have expanded outreach programs to ensure the timely immunization of children. They have also increased several immunization requirements for school-age children. To enable all children to meet these requirements, many districts offer school-based medical services including immunizations.

Preventing Suicide and Accidental Injury or Death

Adolescent suicide is a serious problem in the United States. According to the American Academy of Pediatrics (2002), suicide is the fourth leading cause of death among ten- to fourteen-year-olds. Some 60 percent of children in this age group have thought about it; about 9 percent have tried it.

The academy lays the blame for the shockingly high rate of suicide on society. Boys typically use guns, while girls use pills—both are easy to get. The pressures in life are many. Competition for good grades and college admission is stiff. And violence is everywhere around them; newspapers, television, movies, and music are full of it. Moreover, parents are increasingly disconnected from their children because of divorce and the demands of work (2002).

Addressing potentially suicidal students and acquaintances of suicide victims requires special attention to young people's concepts of themselves and to signs they may be in trouble. (See Figure 2.7 for possible indicators of suicidal tendencies.) Schools also should be aware that single suicides could stimulate imitation, what some people have referred to as *cluster suicides.* Teachers and parents need to remember how acutely they felt things when they were young. Even though a problem seems small to adults, in a child's mind it can seem insurmountable. In addition, some young people have not yet developed the coping skills necessary to deal with certain life situations. School-based

*F*IGURE 2.7 **Indications of Possible Suicidal Tendencies**

Think about some young people you know and ask yourself these questions:

■ Have their personalities changed dramatically?

■ Are they having trouble with a girlfriend or boyfriend? Trouble getting along with other friends or with parents? Have they withdrawn from people they used to feel close to?

■ Is the quality of their schoolwork going down? Have they failed to live up to their own or someone else's standards (when it comes to school grades, for example)?

■ Do they always seem bored, and are they having trouble concentrating?

■ Are they acting like a rebel in an unexplained and severe way?

■ Is she pregnant and finding it hard to cope with this major life change?

■ Has he run away from home?

■ Are they abusing drugs or alcohol?

■ Are they complaining of headaches, stomachaches, etc., that may or may not be real?

■ Have their eating or sleeping habits changed?

■ Has his or her appearance changed for the worse?

■ Are they giving away some of their most prized possessions?

■ Are they writing notes or poems about death?

■ Do they talk about suicide, even jokingly? (Threatening to kill oneself precedes four out of five suicidal deaths.)

■ Have they tried to commit suicide before?

Source: American Academy of Pediatrics (2002). Some things you should know about preventing teen suicide. Available online: http://www.aap.org/advocacy/childhealthmonth/prevteensuicide.htm.

programs on suicide prevention and suicide curricula advocate careful training for teachers.

Another danger that students encounter is motor vehicle accidents, which are the leading cause of death among teenagers fifteen to nineteen years old. Many fatalities are alcohol-related, but an increasing number are attributed to low seatbelt use. According to the National Safety Council, teenagers in Montana are seven times as likely as teenagers in California to die in a crash when not wearing seatbelts (National Safety Council, 2001).

To help promote safety and driver readiness, high schools offer driver education programs that precede the granting of a license to operate a motor vehicle. In addition, insurance companies often offer incentives to students who achieve high scores in driver safety and to students who do well in academic courses. In combination with health education, driver education can potentially lower the incidence of the lethal habit of drinking and driving and motivate students to buckle their seatbelts.

Preventing School Violence

The rates of assault, homicide, vandalism, and related violent acts committed by and against young people are shockingly high in the United States. Each day ten children die from gunfire. Since 1979, more children in the United States have died from gunfire than did American soldiers during the Vietnam and Gulf Wars and in U.S. engagements in Haiti, Somalia, and Bosnia combined. African American males ages fifteen to nineteen have suffered the greatest gun toll among children and teens. They are five times as likely as European American males to be gun victims.

Although awareness of violence in schools is high, especially in the wake of a number of student attacks in the late 1990s, schools remain one of the safest places young people can be. The National Center for Education Statistics routinely states that public schools overwhelmingly report no crimes of any kind. The most prevalent type of youth crime is theft, and the most common types of violence are fist fights, bullying, and shoving matches—amazing facts given some 54 million students attend public schools (National Association of Elementary School Principals, 2002).

Violence prevention—educating young people about the senseless, cruel nature of violence—takes many forms. Foremost, violence prevention requires healthy doses of respect for others, particularly those who are different in some way. Violence prevention programs are one way to teach students that people who appear different on the outside—ethnically, racially, religiously, and the like—have the same needs and aspirations on the inside. To teach these ideas, prevention programs offer lessons in and practice using conflict resolution, anger management, and nonviolent options for handling difficult situations. Employing a different approach, character education programs address the values that underlie civil behavior. They teach that to develop character is to prepare oneself for a successful life of contribution to the greater society. In order to relate to students' lives and have a hope of preventing future violence, these programs have to address everything from drug use to gang behavior, stress management, tolerance, matters of self-esteem, and community building (Peterson & Skiba, 2001).

Have you ever participated in a violence prevention program? If so, what was your impression of the experience? If not, what type of violence prevention program might be most effective in schools?

The central issue for educators is how to ensure children's safety. A number of efforts, many school-based, aim to change the odds for children at highest risk. To deter crime and violence on buses and at school, some localities have turned to metal detectors and video cameras. Some schools employ police officers, sometimes referred to as resource officers, to help maintain order and to prevent nonstudents from going on to school grounds. In other schools, educators are trying to eliminate teasing and bullying in the early grades by encouraging positive relationships and mutual respect among students. Using such activities as story time, meeting-time discussions, drawings, art projects, journal writing, and role playing, teachers help children explore stereotypes and behaviors that get in the way of friendship.

Increasingly, educators are recognizing bullying as a critical factor in the health of school culture. Bullying, according to Peter Sheras and his colleague Sherrill Tippins (2002), occurs when a child is exposed repeatedly and over time to negative actions on the part of one or more students. These negative actions can be any physical, verbal, or socialization actions in which the bully intentionally causes injury or discomfort. Sheras believes that a chief obstacle to eliminating bullying is our inability to understand its root causes. Below are a few questions and answers from his true-or-false "Bully IQ Test" that educators can use to assess their own knowledge about the topic:

1. Most of the time what kids call bullying is simply run-of-the-mill teasing.

   FALSE. Kids are usually aware of the difference between playful teasing and deliberate bullying. Rarely will they complain to a parent if the teasing is "all in good fun." Kidding around becomes bullying when the instigator refuses to stop even after her target protests or it otherwise becomes clear that she is causing real pain.

2. It's the teacher's responsibility to make sure that bullying doesn't happen at school.

TRUE AND FALSE. Certainly, it is the teacher's responsibility to refuse to tolerate bullying and to stop it when she sees it happening. In too many instances, teachers . . . [overlook] abusive behavior in the classroom. It must be acknowledged, however, that much school-related bullying behavior takes place outside the classroom . . . where teachers may not see it. If bullying is to be curbed, parents, teachers, school administrators, and other adults must work together, as a team, to prevent abuse wherever it happens.

3. A victim is never a bully.

FALSE. Recent surveys report that roughly 40 percent of victims admit to having bullied others themselves. In some cases, a child's bullying and victim-like behaviors both stem from the same emotional difficulties or lack of social skills. In fact, victims who have found no one to help them may turn to bullying as a way of expressing their anger and attempting to escape their role as scapegoat. Bully-victims' deep feelings of rage and alienation make them the most likely children to turn to extreme forms of violence, including murder. (Sheras & Tippins, 2002, pp. 14–16)

Are you familiar with any programs or school policies that have been successful in reducing the level of bullying?

The American Psychological Association (APA) and Music Television (MTV) have collaborated to produce a warning-signs guide to recognizing and dealing with violence more broadly defined in schools and in society. The following signs suggest that violence is a serious possibility:

- Loss of temper on a daily basis.
- Frequent physical fighting.
- Significant vandalism or property damage.
- Increase in use of drugs or alcohol.
- Increase in risk-taking behavior.
- Detailed plans to commit acts of violence.
- Announcing threats or plans for hurting others.
- Enjoying hurting animals.
- Carrying a weapon.

When the following signs appear over a period of time, the potential for violence is real:

- A history of violent or aggressive behavior.
- Serious drug or alcohol use.
- Gang membership or strong desire to be in a gang.
- Access to or fascination with weapons, especially guns.
- Threatening others regularly.
- Trouble controlling feelings such as anger.
- Withdrawal from friends and usual activities.
- Feeling rejected or alone.
- Having been a victim of bullying.
- Poor school performance.
- History of discipline problems or frequent run-ins with authorities.
- Feeling constantly disrespected.
- Failing to acknowledge the feelings or rights of others. (American Psychological Association & Music Television, undated)

*F*IGURE 2.8   **Alcohol and Drug Use among High School Seniors**   Describe the
trends indicated on this graph.

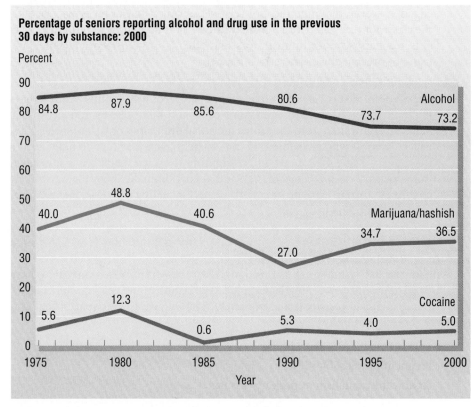

**Percentage of seniors reporting alcohol and drug use in the previous
30 days by substance: 2000**

From *Digest of education statistics,* 2001, by U.S. Department of Education, 2001. Washington, DC: U.S.
Government Printing Office. Table 149. Available online: http://nces.ed.gov/.

Preventing Substance Abuse

Surveys conducted between 1975 and 2000 reveal high school seniors' reported use of
alcohol and drugs (see Figure 2.8). Some 73 percent said they used alcohol and 36.5
percent reported use of marijuana or hashish during a thirty-day time frame (U.S.
Department of Education, 2001).

Concerns about patterns of behavior that put students at risk have prompted
parent groups in some school systems to band together to keep teenagers safe. They
sponsor all-night prom and homecoming parties in an effort to give young people
safe options for entertainment at times when alcohol and drug use typically are
elevated.

School-based programs also attempt to curb substance abuse. Project ALERT, a
curriculum developed by the RAND Corporation, and Drug Abuse Resistance Education (DARE), a program that began as a joint effort between the Los Angeles Unified
School District and the Los Angeles Police Department, are two examples of programs
designed to help elementary and junior high school students resist peer pressure to experiment with drugs and alcohol. Among program goals are helping students learn to
make their own decisions, learning drug and alcohol facts, understanding peer pressure, and developing positive self-esteem. While such programs enjoy widespread use,
they get mixed responses (Coles, 1999). Some educators prefer to develop and use their
own drug and health education programs.

Summary

Teachers work miracles, no question about it. Every year they meet a new group of students and move them farther along the academic path, regardless of where they find students on that path. If it were only so simple as "teacher meets student, teacher teaches, student learns," the case would be closed.

But many of the challenges of professional practice are far from simple and are not easily influenced by teachers. Society expects schools and teachers to succeed, if not to work miracles, on a routine basis. This means first, understanding the needs of students, particularly those at risk for academic and social failure, and second, intervening to improve students' chances for success. Interventions that work often involve parents as well as community agencies and reduce risks that threaten students' health, safety, and success.

Terms and Concepts

Adoption and Safe Families Act of 1997   44
at-risk students   30
Child Abuse Prevention and Treatment Act   44
compensatory education programs   38
early intervention   35
full-service schools   41
holding power   37

incentive programs   39
latchkey children   38
mentoring programs   39
pull-out programs   38
Title I   38
Upward Bound   38

Reflective Practice

The Achievement Gap

U.S. Secretary of Education Rod Paige made these remarks at a dinner sponsored by the Joint Center for Political and Economic Studies in Washington, D.C., on March 26, 2002.

Ladies and gentlemen, we have a problem in our great country. A problem that will hurt every part of our nation every year if we fail to solve it. A problem that must become the concern of every caring American citizen. . . .

Two-thirds of American fourth-graders cannot read at grade level. Our students rank poorly among industrialized nations on international math and science tests. Almost two-thirds of low-income eighth-graders cannot multiply or divide two-digit numbers. . . .

Tucked inside our substandard American education performance is a subproblem that contributes to the larger problem. This problem is of special interest to the African American community, but it is a problem that affects the whole country. This problem is the stubborn academic achievement gap between the races.

Consider the evidence.

On the National Assessment of Educational Progress, or NAEP, fourth-grade reading test in 1992, African American scores were 15 percent below white scores. Eight years later, neither score has improved.

On the 2000 NAEP reading assessment, 73 percent of white fourth-graders scored at or above the basic level, compared to only 37 percent of their black peers. The racial achievement gap is real, and, unfortunately, it is not shrinking.

As the National Center for Educational Statistics put it, "While white students outperform black students in reading, the gaps decreased between the early 1970s and the late 1980s. Since then, however, the gaps have remained relatively stable or increased."

The results in math are similar.

Think about that. During the whole decade of the 1990s, despite all the talk about racial progress and huge increases in spending on education, the gaps remained stable or got worse. Is that good enough? Are we even going in the right direction?

This gap is un-American and totally unacceptable. We must commit ourselves to closing it. But how?

(The full text of Secretary Paige's talk is available online at (http://www.ed.gov/Speeches/03-2002/20020326.html.)

Issues, Problems, Dilemmas, Opportunities

Secretary Paige, himself an African American, describes the problem as one of low academic achievement and, more specifically, differences in achievement between the races. What reasons, other than the fact that students vary in race and ethnicity, might explain why such achievement differences exist?

Perceive and Value

What is gained and what is lost when Secretary Paige, and indeed anyone, speaks of racial and ethnic differences in educational performance?

Know and Act

What do teachers say and do that communicate they believe all students can succeed? Role play such an exchange between a teacher and a student.

Evaluate

How do you think an individual teacher might address Secretary Paige's concern about the lagging achievement of African American students? How might teachers' beliefs about students' capabilities affect student performance?

INTASC Principle 3

The teacher understands how students differ in their approaches to learning and creates instructional opportunities that are adapted to diverse learners.

Knowledge

The teacher understands how students' learning is influenced by individual experiences, talents, and prior learning, as well as language, culture, family, and community values. (Interstate New Teacher Assessment and Support Consortium, 1992)

Discussion Question

Secretary Paige raises concerns about the achievement gap between the races. How might teachers use the kinds of knowledge suggested in this principle to try to close that gap?

Additional Readings

Barr, R. D., & Parrett, W. H. (2001). *Hope fulfilled for at-risk and violent youth: K–12 programs that work* (2nd ed.). Boston: Allyn & Bacon.

Jacobson, L. (2002, March 13). California charters are seen to benefit children in poverty. *Education Week, 26*(21), pp. 1–2.

Kozol, J. (1995). *Amazing grace.* New York: Random House.

Sheras, P., & Tippins, S. (2002). *Your child: Bully or victim. Understanding and ending school yard tyranny.* New York: Skylight Press.

Slavin, R. E., & Fashola, O. S. (1998). *Show me the evidence! Proven and promising programs for America's schools.* Thousand Oaks, CA: Corwin Press.

Web Resources

http://www.childrensdefense.org/

The website for the Children's Defense Fund, a private nonprofit organization, provides information about the status of at-risk students and efforts to meet their needs.

http://www.responsiveclassroom.org/14_2NL_1.htm

Responsive Classroom: A Newsletter for Teachers is an online magazine focusing on strategies for fostering safe, challenging, and joyful classrooms and schools, kindergarten through eighth grade.

http://www.cdc.gov/safeusa/youthviolence.htm

The Preventing Youth Violence website, developed by the

Centers for Disease Control and Prevention, offers useful information for parents, children, and school personnel.

http://curry.edschool.virginia.edu/curry/centers/youthvio/

The Virginia Youth Violence Project offers effective methods and policies for youth violence prevention, especially in school settings.

http://www.calib.com/nccanch/

The National Clearinghouse on Child Abuse and Neglect Information is a useful resource for professionals and others seeking information on child abuse and neglect and child welfare.

Video**Workshop** Extra!

If the VideoWorkshop package was included with your textbook, go to Chapter 2 of the Companion Website (www.ablongman.com/mcnergney4e) and click on VideoWorkshop. Follow the instructions for viewing video clip 2. Then consider this information along with what you've read in Chapter 2 while answering the following questions.

1. The chapter presents the issue of students at risk of school failure because of their economic status. What suggestions do you have for teachers in terms of creating a stimulating environment, when finances might make this a daunting task? Use ideas from video clip 2 to support your argument.

2. Combine the ideas of parental involvement in schools from this chapter with the notion of tapping into students' individual intelligences from video clip 2. Create a list of strategies teachers could use to bring parents and families into the classroom so that children benefit academically and socially.

The Richness of Classroom Cultures

CHAPTER CONTENTS

What Is Diversity?

What Other Concepts Define Diversity?

What Is Multicultural Education?

What Types of Multicultural Education Curricula Exist, and How Are They Evaluated?

How Are Educational Services Adapted for Students with Exceptionalities?

How Can Teachers Create Culturally Relevant Classrooms?

*S*ince the September 11 terrorist attacks against the United States, the history and culture of the Middle East and Islam—the region's dominant religion—have played a larger part in schools' curricula. The study of these topics, however, has not been without controversy. In March 2002 a student teacher in Maine was dismissed from a local high school after students and parents complained that a unit he prepared for his world history class overstepped the bounds between informing students about Islam and advocating the faith.

> [The student teacher] said he had no intention of promoting any religion. He was merely trying to engage his students in an intellectual discussion, he said, and encourage them to think critically about a complex

subject. He attributes the students' complaints to their misconceptions about Muslims, whom his students initially described as terrorists and extremists, he said. (Manzo, 2002, p. 2)

As future teachers in a culturally diverse country, you may face issues similar to this one in your own classrooms. This chapter explores the concepts of diversity and culture, and it speculates about their implications for education. People's view of society depends greatly on their perspectives, so we encourage you to begin thinking about cultural diversity from the different points of view you might find in the classroom. As you read this chapter, think about ways you might adapt your teaching to help students with diverse backgrounds succeed.

> **The New York Times**
> expect the world®
> nytimes.com
>
> ## Themes of the Times!
>
> Expand your knowledge of the concepts discussed in this chapter by reading current and historical articles from the *New York Times* by visiting the **Themes of the Times** section of the Companion Website (ablongman.com/mcnergney4e).

What Is Diversity?

What does the word "culture" mean to you?   To what characteristics does one's *ethnicity* refer, and how is ethnicity different from one's national origin, if at all? Is *race* a concept with many definitions or only those limited to physical characteristics? When educators mention *minorities*, do they mean human attributes of race and ethnicity, or do they also mean gender, sexual orientation, disabilities, giftedness, and social class? What impact, if any, does economic status have on a student's aptitude for learning?

By its very nature, the language of diversity can be confusing. People speak and write about race, culture, and ethnicity as though universal agreement exists on the meaning of the terms. In some ways and in some instances such agreement does exist, but it is usually only in general terms. Often, when the issue is pressed, the agreement breaks down. For instance, when gender is defined in a physiological way it may be easily understandable. But when the intellectual, emotional, and social characteristics of gender are thrown into the mix, not to mention, say, transgendered individuals, that easily understandable term isn't so easy. When examined, people may find that the agreement has become a stereotype that, in reality, represents no one.

In the past, public education was designed with the so-called "average" student in mind. This meant that instruction and educational materials were geared to white males from middle and upper social classes. Not surprisingly, this type of education short-changed females, people of other racial groups and cultures, and students from different economic groups. Now, instead of assuming such approaches will work for all students, researchers and curriculum developers acknowledge that differences between people can affect learning and teaching. Modern curricula must take all of these differences into account to be effective and fair to today's students.

Think back to your own experiences in school, and remember the many different kinds of students with whom you walked the halls. Try to remember how your teachers addressed (or did not address) diversity in the classroom. In what ways, if any, did you yourself feel overlooked or excluded? Chances are your feelings from back then are the same types of feelings your own students will experience.

Culture

Culture, in the larger sense of the word, refers to all of the learned characteristics of a people—language, religion, social mores, artistic expressions, beliefs, and values. In some cases a culture can be tied to a geographical region, while in other cases a culture exists largely independent of geography.

Culture also can be used in a *micro* sense to describe more narrowly defined groups of people, sometimes called subcultures or microcultures. These kinds of cultures may develop around a shared interest, circumstance, or condition. For instance, some people with hearing impairments choose to be part of the deaf culture. On the other hand, a subculture can form comprised of people who like the same music (punks) or the same television show (Trekkies).

In recent years, social scientists have begun to explore the influence of culture in classrooms. They have come to realize that culture is a much larger component of students' lives than previously understood. In fact, culture is now seen to influence practically every aspect of students' lives; it shapes their identities, beliefs, behaviors—it even shapes the *way* they learn. To ignore or misunderstand students' cultures is to risk teaching at cross-purposes with them. Therefore, educators must be informed and open to the many cultures—both macro and micro—to which their students belong.

Race and Ethnicity

One of the most obvious and often used methods of labeling a person is by identifying their racial or ethnic group. People usually think about **race** in terms of physical characteristics, especially skin color, and sometimes in terms of national origin. A person of color might refer to himself or herself as black or African American or Latino and so on. Depending on appearances, however, a Latino or a person with African ancestry might self-identify as white or Caucasian (Banks and Banks, 2001). **Ethnicity** refers to membership in a group with a common cultural tradition or common national origin. Ethnic groups function as subgroups within the larger society and may share a common language or religion, customs, or other elements of culture. While racial traits are genetically inheritable, ethnic traits are learned in social contexts such as the family.

People often find strength in their identities, and race and ethnicity are large parts of them. On a more practical level, when people complete forms for school enrollment, job applications, student loans, and the like, they are asked questions about racial and/or ethnic heritage. This information serves many purposes, such as monitoring equal opportunities in education and employment and tracking school desegregation.

One problem with defining diversity in racial and ethnic terms, as Table 3.1 indicates, is that numbers only hint at the richness of society. The arbitrariness of racial classification categories is evident, for example, in the changes in Census Bureau questions asked since 1790. In 1790, four categories were used to designate race: Free White Males, Free White Females, All Other Free Persons, and Slaves. In 1970, nine categories were used: white, Negro or black, Indian (American), Japanese, Chinese, Filipino, Hawaiian, Korean, and Other race. In the 1990 census, the designation of Mixed Race was added, reflecting demographic realities and public discontent with the standard categories used by the government.

Racial and ethnic identities can be significant parts of people's perspectives and beliefs, providing a sense of history and connection. They can also be limiting factors when applied incorrectly or when taken as the full sum of a person. What we can't escape when we talk about race and ethnicity is that diversity exists. Some people believe the current vocabulary of race, often couched in terms of black and white, is losing its meaning in a world where people are not so easily defined. Moreover, in a society like ours, where history has made race and ethnicity such charged topics, black and white carry connotations far beyond skin color or homeland. One researcher in particular believes that

> The problem is not simply that we have added new groups to the mix. The language of black-white differences is losing its meaning because Latinos and Asians

TABLE 3.1 Projected Population of the United States in 2010 Are figures lower, higher, or about the same as you would have estimated?

United States	Numbers in thousands	Percent
Total population	299,861	100
White	241,769	80.6
Black	39,982	13.3
American Indian, Eskimo, or Aleut	2,821	0.9
Asian or Pacific Islander (Chinese, Filipino, Japanese, Asian Indian, Korean, Vietnamese, Hawaiian, Samoan, Guamanian, and other Asian or Pacific Islander)	15,288	5.1
Hispanic Origin (Mexican, Puerto Rican, Cuban, and other Hispanic)[a]	43,687	14.6

[a]Spanish origin and race are distinct; thus, persons of Spanish origin may be of any race.

Percentages total more than 100% due to rounding error and interaction of race (white and black) and Hispanic origin.

Source: U.S. Census Bureau (2000). Projections of the Resident Population by Race, Hispanic Origin, and Nativity. Available online: http://www.census.gov/.

do not fit into a world in which people are permanently and definitively marked either as insiders or outsiders. (Suro, 1998, p. C2)

What is lost and what is gained by the use of racial and ethnic designations for educational purposes?

What Other Concepts Define Diversity?

We have said that effective teachers think about teaching and learning from all kinds of diverse perspectives. The viewpoints of immigrants, language minority or bilingual students, males and females, and economically disadvantaged students must be in mind when you walk into a classroom. You also need to consider the exceptionalities (special abilities or disabilities) and sexual orientations that students bring to the classroom. To be both successful and fair, teachers must be able to perceive students and situations from multiple perspectives and tailor their teaching styles and methods accordingly.

How might the experiences of immigrants differ from those of other students?

From the Perspective of Immigrants

The percentage of the U.S. population that is foreign born has increased since 1970 (see Figure 3.1). Over 2 million immigrant children enrolled in U.S. schools in the 1980s and 1990s, more than at any other time since the early twentieth century. Immigration still is largely an urban phenomenon, but it has touched suburban and rural communities as well.

How schools deal with their changing populations is linked to society's attitudes about immigration. Reflecting these societal attitudes, throughout the past century schools have encouraged both **assimilation** (making students similar) and **pluralism** (maintaining unique characteristics). Whichever approach the school is encouraging, teachers must be aware that immigrant students likely are experiencing pressures unique to their situation. Although the student's academic progress is the prime

FIGURE 3.1 Percentage of the U.S. Population That Is Foreign-Born

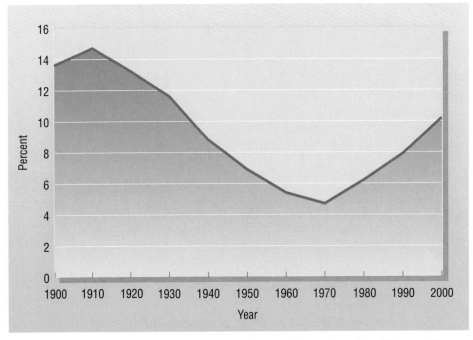

Source: From *Historical Census Statistics on the Foreign-Born Population of the United States* by J. Gibson and E. Lennon, 1999. Washington, DC: U.S. Census Bureau.

concern, teachers should think about the reasons that might be behind an immigrant student's setbacks in the classroom.

Immigrants' experiences vary widely and differ from those of other minorities. One difference that may affect students significantly is the reason behind their immigration. Some researchers have identified "castelike minorities," or involuntary immigrant minorities, as people who are Americans as a result of slavery, conquest, or colonization (Ogbu and Simons, 1998). They contend that, in addition to experiencing discrimination from others, involuntary minorities may also defeat themselves out of feelings of inferiority.

Immigrant students also face the complex issue of maintaining their traditional culture versus assimilating to their new one. This transition can be complicated by living in families and communities in which the native language and traditions are primary. Native values and belief systems may not encourage the same goals that the schools do.

This situation can be further complicated by peer pressure on immigrant and other minority students to not "act white"—speaking standard English, adopting certain clothing styles, listening to certain radio stations, or engaging in activities such as studying in the library or going camping (Hill, 1990). These researchers believe that, as members of involuntary minorities, some students view education as a process that forces them to lose their own cultural identity if they are to succeed.

Others, however, say this theory blames the victims and point out that many voluntary minorities also resist cultural assimilation. Although these minorities may value economic success, they do not view erasing or discarding all signs of their native origin and cultural identity as desirable.

So why are some immigrant children successful when others are not? Researchers attributed success in scholastic and economic terms to three factors, which they identified as "culturally based values, family life-style, and opportunity" (Caplan, Choy, & Whitmore, p. 88).

Are you personally familiar with other examples of immigrant success?

From the Perspective of Being a Language Minority or Bilingual Person

With the increasing numbers of immigrant students in U.S. classrooms, the issue of language in education gains significance. We know that language can be a formidable barrier in U.S. society. Few monolingual English speakers ever find themselves in situations where someone else does not also speak English. But many students who are categorized as **limited English proficient (LEP)** or who qualify for instruction in **English as a Second Language (ESL)** interpret life in U.S. society from behind a language barrier.

Students with limited English proficiency receive help in the form of **bilingual education,** or instruction in both English and their native languages. Bilingual programs

Your Teaching Life in Practice

BIAS IN THE AFRICAN AMERICAN COMMUNITY

The thesis of a book entitled *Losing the Race: Self-Sabotage in Black America* by John McWhorter, associate professor of linguistics at the University of California at Berkeley, is that African Americans are cheating themselves academically. Jack White analyzed the following question in an article in *Time* magazine: Is there a bias in the African American community against appearing smart?

YES [T]he lagging academic performance of African-American students isn't caused by the residual effects of prejudice or poor schools that has infected black America from ghetto to middle class. Black students, including those at elite universities . . . "are really disinclined to think hard" about subjects other than their own victimization. . . . These tendencies are legacies of segregation and the denial of equal education opportunities. . . . But today such attitudes have taken on a life of their own, and their destructive effects are worsened by racial preferences, which allow "black people [to] get the very best things doing less of a job than everybody else."

NO We've got a problem all right, but it reflects everything from the fact that white families on average have ten times more wealth than black families, to the larger proportion of uncertified teachers in mostly black schools, to the hopelessness some black kids feel because

so-called experts have told them so many times that they don't measure up. It's not going to be solved by merely exhorting blacks to pull themselves up by their bootstraps. They're already doing that. In cities like Washington where dysfunctional school systems have been cheating poor black youngsters for decades, ambitious reform vouchers would help them find alternatives to failing public schools. Such evidence puts the lie to the notion that blacks don't value education. Sure, some of us think that being bookish is uncool. But that's not so different from what George W. Bush (whose mediocre grades and SAT scores would have kept him out of Yale had he not been the son of a powerful white alumnus) thought about some of his more scholarly classmates. And look where he is today.

Critical Thinking Questions

Why do some people, regardless of their culture or ethnicity, think it is "uncool" to be smart? Why is it so important for teachers to help all students experience success in one way or another?

Companion
Website

To answer these questions online and e-mail your answer to your professor, go to Chapter 3 of the Companion Website (ablongman.com/ mcnergney4e) and click on Your Teaching Life in Practice.

Source: White, J. E. (2000, August 7). Are Blacks Biased against Braininess? *Time*, p. 81.

What are some implications of minority status for students and families? For teachers and schools? How might the experiences of immigrants differ from those of other minorities?

vary in the amount of English taught and the rapidity with which it is introduced. Definitions of bilingual programs and student success in them vary widely. Some offer instruction to students in both English and their native languages throughout their entire school career. Other programs help students move from their native languages to English by offering English as a Second Language (ESL) classes. Yet other programs remove students from regular classes to receive special help offered in their native languages. Still other programs immerse non-English-speaking students in English, sometimes providing an aide who speaks the native language, and then place students in English-speaking classes.

The reason for so many types of bilingual education is educators are divided on the best way to serve these students. Some educators believe that teaching non-English-speaking children in their native languages, the language they hear most at home, while easing them gradually into English is the only reasonable way to move these children into the mainstream. Others believe that bilingual programs teach neither language well and are bad for the country where English is the official language. **Why might some people oppose bilingual education while others advocate its use?**

How much bilingual education to offer and how long to offer it are theoretical questions open to debate. In the classroom, though, you will be dealing with actual students whose primary languages may not be English. Begin to think about what some of their unique needs might be and ways you can help these students succeed.

From the Perspective of Gender

Do you believe there is gender bias in today's schools?   When they first enter school, girls' and boys' measured academic abilities are approximately equal. Studies have shown that by the age of twelve, however, girls consistently outscore boys on tests of reading and writing. At this same age, boys outperform girls on measures of higher-level mathematics and self-esteem. These differences in academic performance may be due in part to gender bias—discriminatory treatment, often subtle or unconscious, that unfairly favors or disfavors individuals because of their gender.

Critics have long charged that girls receive less attention from teachers than boys receive and that the quality of the attention boys receive is better (Sadker & Sadker, 1993). Often subconsciously, some teachers tend to offer classroom activities that appeal more to boys' interests than to girls' and to use instructional methods that favor boys. Many teachers foster competition, for example, despite the fact that girls, and many boys, experience greater academic success when they work cooperatively (AAUW Educational Foundation & National Education Association, 1992). Some teachers also ask boys more challenging questions, encourage them to work to get a correct answer, offer them more praise and constructive criticism, and acknowledge their achievements more than they do for girls (Sadker & Sadker, 1993).

More recently, the fact that boys are also affected negatively by gender bias is becoming more evident. Studies indicate that teachers consider boys, in general, to be significantly more active, less attentive, less dexterous, and more prone to have behavioral, academic, and language problems than girls are. In addition, when schools identify children with learning disabilities, mental retardation, and reading disabilities, boys typically are identified more often than girls. And the tendency to view gender bias in the classroom as negative only for girls has perhaps helped divert policy attention from the group at most risk—African American boys. They score lowest on virtually every educational measure (Lewin, 1998).

An interesting case of perceived gender bias occurred when the principal of Seattle's Thurgood Marshall Elementary School split his enrollment into classes of all girls and all boys. Washington state officials said he was violating **Title IX**—the federal law that prohibits schools from discriminating on the basis of gender. Federal officials scrutinizing the schools disagreed, however, indicating that they planned to lessen the "rigid" interpretation of the gender-equity law. According to Assistant Secretary for Civil Rights Gerald A. Reynolds, a relaxing of the restriction would allow schools to provide more educational options for students and parents. The move toward flexibility stems from the "No Child Left Behind" Act of 2001, a law signed by President Bush that encourages innovative programs that provide more choice (Davis, 2002).

Public schools continue to experiment with the idea of single-sex education. Research continues to be done on gender bias in the classroom and its long-term effects on students. And the attention paid to making instruction less gender biased does seem to be making a difference. Recent results show gender differences are declining in some

Should these students receive instruction in Spanish? In English only? What issues are involved? What does research suggest as the best way to educate students whose first language is not English?

areas, such as mathematics (Pollina, 1995; AAUW Educational Foundation, 1998). In your own classroom, be conscious of activities and instructional methods that may exclude or be of little interest to one gender. Although culture at large is far from being free from gender bias, both female and male students deserve a classroom that promotes equality among genders.

From the Perspective of Exceptionality

Why is it important for all teachers to understand the concept of exceptionality? Nationally, about 12 percent of children have a special ability or disability that sets them apart from other children (U.S. Department of Education, 2001). In terms of education, these abilities and disabilities are called exceptionalities. Nearly 6 million **exceptional learners** across the United States possess one or more attributes that greatly affect the experiences they have at home, at school, and in the community. As knowledge of exceptionalities has grown, so too has public recognition of the importance of meeting the needs of exceptional learners in order to increase their chances for success.

Students with exceptionalities often are said to deviate from the "norm," or what is typically expected or desired by a society or culture. The definition of the norm, however, is as debatable and slippery as definitions of race. While the term "norm" indicates a single shared understanding, in a culture with so many differences, one person's norm can be another person's deviance.

In terms of education, exceptional characteristics viewed as *handicaps* only ten or twenty years ago are now characterized as *disabilities* that do not necessarily limit students' chances to advance. Also included in the category of exceptional learners are students whose skills and intellectual levels are beyond those of their peers. In practice, students with exceptionalities may possess one or more of the following characteristics.

GIFTEDNESS
Giftedness, like other types of exceptionality, has been defined in several ways. According to the 1972 Marland definition, gifted and talented students are capable of high performance and excel in one or more of the following areas: general intellectual ability, specific academic aptitude, creative or productive thinking, leadership ability, ability in the visual or performing arts, and psychomotor ability.

While a national survey indicated that 73 percent of school districts have adopted this definition of giftedness, in most schools the traditional measure of giftedness is scoring above a certain level on an IQ test. In fact, few schools use the Marland definition to identify and serve any area of giftedness other than high general intelligence, as measured by verbal IQ and achievement tests (U.S. Department of Education, Office of Educational Research and Improvement, 1993).

DISABILITIES
The majority of students who qualify for special education services have one or more of the following disabilities: speech and language disorders, learning disabilities, emotional and behavior disorders, and severe attention problems. Each of these conditions is defined by federal special education laws and regulations.

Some disabilities occur less among young people, including cognitive disabilities, hearing and visual impairments, and orthopedic or other health impairments. But teachers often must respond to these special needs as they occur in combination with other disabilities.

As more and more children are found to have exceptionalities, teachers must be prepared to have classrooms full of students representing all levels of physical and mental abilities. **Can you think of ways you could engage all students? What special needs must you be aware of?**

From the Perspective of Sexual Orientation

Education for diversity often sparks disagreement concerning which groups are identified as subcultures, and some debate on these matters seems to be about much more than student ability levels. Such is the case with students' sexual orientation and how the subject is addressed in the classroom. Sexuality is a hot-button subject, largely unaddressed in curricula. Many people believe that sexuality is not a matter for the school, but this belies the fact that, especially in high school, many students are coming to terms with their homosexuality. In addition to a lack of discussion in the classroom about homosexuality, feelings of isolation and "otherness" are increased for gay and lesbian students by the prejudice and harassment they face from other students and sometimes from teachers as well.

Beyond the classroom, homosexuality raises concern and provokes ire in the community at large. For instance, when the National Education Association passed a resolution in support of Lesbian and Gay History Month, a group called the Concerned Women for America (CWA) placed advertisements in newspapers around the country condemning the NEA's action. They billed the resolution as a "threat to morality and decency." CWA's language was so strong that two newspapers in which the ads appeared later apologized for running inappropriate statements (Ponessa, 1995).

Some people believe that gays, lesbians, and other minorities press their concerns for fair and equal treatment to the detriment of the community at large. Separate dormitories, preferential admissions, campus study centers, fiscal aid policies, and faculty hiring quotas, they argue, make people concentrate on attributes such as skin color or sexual orientation first, before they assess the content of their own or others' characters.

The work of the past decade or so has gone far toward promoting tolerance and acceptance of homosexuality in schools and in the culture at large. Dennis Carlson (1998) describes the atmosphere with regard to gays and lesbians at one university this way:

> In the fall of 1995, a new float appeared in the homecoming parade at Miami University in Oxford, Ohio—a university known for its quiet conservatism. Wedged in between floats from Greek fraternities and sororities and from several other student groups on campus was a float representing the Gay, Lesbian, and Bisexual Alliance. In bold letters, the float proclaimed: "We're here, and we're queer, and we have a float." What is perhaps most remarkable about this event is that it created hardly a stir on campus. Gays and lesbians . . . were becoming part of the new campus community, a community that (at least on the surface) was organized around the theme of respecting diversity. If multicultural education in the public schools does not yet include gay people as part of the diversity that is to be acknowledged and respected within the new American community of difference, this has not been the case in higher education. (1998, p. 107)

As future teachers, you will need to consider how you might deal with gay and lesbian students. How will you encourage other students to treat them? How will you balance this issue with all the other interests in your classroom and still provide a beneficial learning experience?

What do you think about the inclusion of gay and lesbian issues in the national conversation about diversity?

What Is Multicultural Education?

As the issues and concerns in the first part of this chapter indicate, teachers need more than ideas, enthusiasm, and love of children to be successful. Great teachers do not have "a way" of behaving toward all students or "a style" of teaching that works equally well with all people. Instead, great teachers adapt their methods to help all students succeed.

Teachers adapt their methods to help all students succeed. What strategies would you use to be sensitive to the diversity of your students' needs and abilities?

They must be able to use educational strategies that can be fit intelligently and sensitively to the diversity of their students' needs and abilities. Increasingly, educators are turning to concepts of multicultural education and inclusive education to provide such support.

Five general approaches to multicultural education are outlined below and shown in Figure 3.2 (Sleeter and Grant, 2002).

1. "Teaching the culturally different" tries to assimilate people into the cultural mainstream using transitional bridges in the regular school program.
2. "Human relations approaches" attempt to help students of differing backgrounds understand and accept each other.
3. "Single-group studies" encourage cultural pluralism by concentrating on the contributions of specific individuals and groups.
4. "Multicultural approaches" promote pluralism by reforming entire educational programs—altering curricula, integrating staffs, and affirming family languages.
5. "Education that is multicultural and social reconstructionist" actively challenges social inequalities.

Teaching the Culturally Different

Mainstreaming is an approach that attempts to assimilate students of different races, low-income students, and special education students into a single classroom, a sort of real-world approach. For years mainstreaming was the preferred approach to multicultural education. As immigrants arrived in this country, they were placed in programs designed to teach the knowledge, skills, and attitudes deemed appropriate for a successful life in the United States. Such programs often made their goals explicit. For

$\mathcal{F}$IGURE 3.2   **Five Approaches to Multicultural Education**   Think of one clear example of each of the five approaches identified in this figure.

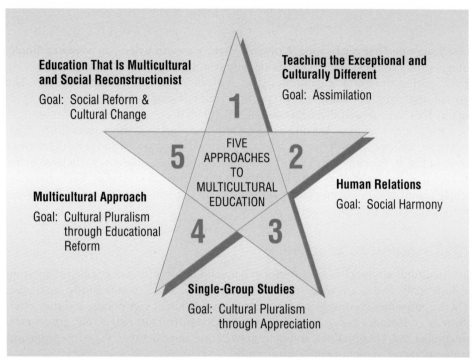

Source: *Making Choices for Multicultural Education: Five Approaches to Race, Class, and Gender* (4th ed.), by C. E. Sleeter and C. A. Grant, © 2002. New York: John Wiley & Sons, Inc. Used by permission of John Wiley & Sons, Inc.

example, students learned to read and write English, master U.S. history, and adopt prevailing social customs.

Mainstreaming programs, then and now, are also characterized by their unspoken implications. Teachers' expectations for appropriate behavior, for example, may cause students to question their backgrounds or view themselves negatively. While teachers attempt to accommodate all skill levels and backgrounds in a single classroom community, the task of meeting the needs of every student can seem next to impossible.

Human Relations Approaches

Human relations approaches to multicultural education try to help students from different backgrounds understand and accept each other on a personal level. These approaches can be as informal as teachers assigning a "friend" to a new student or forming work or play groups to improve understanding and acceptance. Human relations approaches also include formal procedures for accomplishing goals, such as **conflict mediation,** an approach that helps students resolve their differences peaceably.

One mediation program, called Teaching to Be Peacemakers, enables students to solve for themselves the daily conflicts that arise. The training helps students reject notions of winning disputes and shows them how to apply negotiation and mediation procedures. When students are trained to be their own peacemakers, discipline problems handled by teachers decrease by about 60 percent (Johnson, Johnson, Dudley, Ward, & Magnuson, 1995).

Did schools you attended use conflict resolution or other human relations approaches?

Single-Group Studies

Do you remember celebrating Women's History month when you were in school?
Single-group studies concentrate on individual and group contributions, emphasizing the importance of learning about the lives of outstanding people in various cultures. The goal of single-group studies is to help young people feel proud of their heritages and recognize that their accomplishments do not depend on their race, gender, or culture.

Single-group approaches often address affective objectives (objectives aimed at influencing feelings, attitudes, or values) and promote appreciation and respect for other ways of life. In the simplest or most traditional approaches, students participate in activities that feature the food, dress, and customs of foreign countries. Unfortunately, single-group studies can emphasize differences among groups to the extent that diversity is celebrated over unity.

Multicultural Approaches

Multicultural approaches try to reform education by revising curricula, integrating school staffs, and acknowledging the importance of families and family languages. These approaches encourage students to consider different viewpoints, and they often draw on content developed in single-group studies. Instructors also involve students by discussing real-life situations, trying to draw connections between the curriculum and students' own experiences and backgrounds.

One example of a multicultural approach is the way Robert Moses teaches algebra to sixth-grade African American students in the Mississippi delta. A firm believer that algebra is the "gatekeeper" to the college prep math sequence, Moses uses a variety of multicultural approaches to help students succeed in the course and to see themselves as thinkers. He teaches some lessons using the contrasting rhythms of African drumbeats, while other lessons are taught by having students construct their own recipes. Moses believes these and similar methods help hold student interest and make content understandable. **What are the benefits of relating academics to students' lives?**

Education That Is Multicultural and Social Reconstructionist

A multicultural, socially reconstructive approach to diversity in education challenges social inequality and seeks to restructure educational institutions in ways that will change society. Teachers who want to achieve these goals use students' life experiences as opportunities to discuss social inequalities. They encourage students to think critically about the classism, sexism, racism, and social inequities that may be present in textbooks, newspapers, and other media sources. Students are encouraged to consider alternative points of view and to think about ways they might work constructively to achieve social justice for all people.

When studying U.S. history, for example, students might investigate how the racial category of "Other" has evolved over time. They might begin by reading passages from Christopher Columbus's diary, in which he describes his encounter with the Taino Indians in the Caribbean. Through discussion, students could consider how his perceptions of the Tainos were influenced by European ideas and concepts (Banks, 2002). From there, students could discuss views of "others" in their extended families or in the larger society. Teachers might then encourage students to speculate about personal, social, and civic activities they could participate in that might change common attitudes about these "others." In this way, a history lesson becomes a way for students to build a more democratic and just society.

What Types of Multicultural Education Curricula Exist and How Are They Evaluated?

National and state initiatives related to multicultural education are numerous and varied. Overall, they relate to the larger, continuing dialogue about the meaning of *e pluribus unum*—one out of many. These initiatives are often concerned with protecting the rights of cultural and ethnic minorities. Primarily, the purpose of the legislation is to ensure **equal educational opportunity.** At the federal level, this has meant focusing on providing equal educational opportunities for female students, students of different races, LEP students, students from low-income families, and students with disabilities. This legislation, however, usually does not discuss the preparation necessary for all students to function effectively in a culturally diverse society.

National educational associations, on the other hand, promote attention to multicultural education, equity, and opportunity by advocating direct intervention at all levels of the public education system. National accreditation standards for programs and national certification programs for teachers also acknowledge the importance of multicultural education. Prominent among such standards are those promoted by the National Council for the Accreditation of Teacher Education (NCATE).

With all of the multicultural approaches available to teachers, along with national and state initiatives, it can be hard to know how to judge their effectiveness and appropriateness. James Banks offers a specific model for integrating ethnic content into elementary and high school curricula (2002). As part of the model, he provides a practical guide that teachers might use to judge various multicultural approaches (see Figure 3.3). The guide envisions a four-tiered approach to multicultural curricular reform, in which the lowest tier is "The Contributions Approach" and the highest tier is "The Action Approach." Overall, how programs are accountable for results and by what criteria a program is deemed a success are issues of primary importance when deciding what multicultural approach to use.

Accountability Issues

How would you decide whether multicultural education really works?   When deciding what form of multicultural education to adopt, a school has to consider several questions: What does multicultural education cost? How are educational activities affected? What are the outcomes of these efforts? The answers to these questions are judged acceptable or unacceptable by comparing them to the claims the program makes, to competing programs, or to the expected standards of any educational effort.

One common method of judging the success of educational programs is standardized test scores. Standardized tests often are accused of being unfair to certain groups of students and inaccurate reflections of students' progress. In general, minority-group students have not scored as well on such tests as have majority-group students. But in recent years some evidence suggests the test scores of minority group students have been increasing. As Table 3.2 indicates, members of minority groups appear to be gaining advantages from educational opportunities in ways that many had not in the past.

Many other types of outcomes can be examined to judge the effectiveness of multicultural programs. These outcomes can be acquired conveniently and inexpensively, and they can be extremely useful. For example, students' written assessments of their satisfaction with programs and with school in general can be obtained and tracked over time. These can be supplemented with student, parent, and staff interviews to determine what they do and do not like about school. One also could examine records for school attendance, dropout rates, and participation in extracurricular activities to determine a program's merits. In practice, these types of outcomes can

FIGURE 3.3   **Banks's Approaches to Multicultural Curricular Reform**   How is Banks's model similar to and different from the five approaches to multicultural education identified by Sleeter and Grant? (see Figure 3.2)

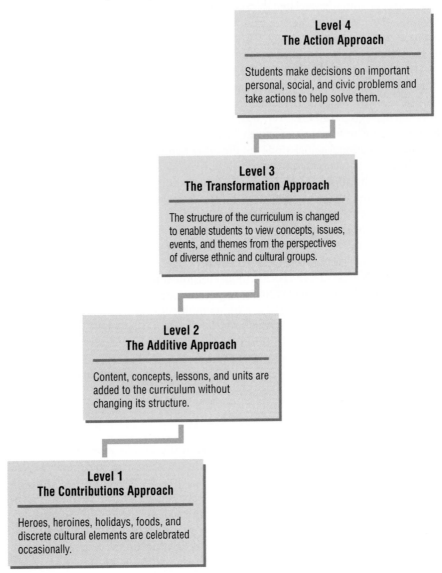

Level 4
The Action Approach

Students make decisions on important personal, social, and civic problems and take actions to help solve them.

Level 3
The Transformation Approach

The structure of the curriculum is changed to enable students to view concepts, issues, events, and themes from the perspectives of diverse ethnic and cultural groups.

Level 2
The Additive Approach

Content, concepts, lessons, and units are added to the curriculum without changing its structure.

Level 1
The Contributions Approach

Heroes, heroines, holidays, foods, and discrete cultural elements are celebrated occasionally.

Source: Approaches to Multicultural Curriculum Reform by J. A. Banks, 2002. In J. A. Banks, *An Introduction to Education,* 3rd Edition. Boston: Allyn & Bacon, 2002, p. 30. Reprinted with permission from James A. Banks.

provide more truthful and relevant insight about a program's success than can a standardized test.

INSTRUCTION

Sensitivity training and cultural awareness programs for both teachers and students promote understanding of cultures. For example, the Chicago Children's Museum features an exhibit called "Face to Face: Dealing with Prejudice and Discrimination," which aims to help students deal with discriminatory behavior. One portion of the exhibit is a full-size board game called "Race for Ubuntu" that allows children to explore

*T*ABLE 3.2 SAT[a] Scores by Racial/Ethnic Group

Racial–ethnic background	1987	2001	Score change 1987 to 2001
1	2	4	5
SAT—Verbal			
All students	**507**	506	–1
White	524	529	5
Black	428	433	5
Hispanic or Latino	464	460	–4
Mexican American	457	451	–6
Puerto Rican	436	457	21
Asian American	479	501	22
American Indian	471	481	10
Other	480	503	23
SAT—Mathematical			
All students	**501**	514	13
White	514	531	17
Black	411	426	15
Hispanic or Latino	462	465	3
Mexican American	455	458	3
Puerto Rican	432	451	19
Asian American	541	566	25
American Indian	463	479	16
Other	482	512	30

[a]Formerly known as the Scholastic Aptitude Test.

Possible scores on each part of the SAT range from 200 to 800.

Source: Scholastic Assessment Test (SAT) Score Averages, by Race/Ethnicity: 1986-87 to 2000-2001. *Digest of Education Statistics, 2001.* Available online: http://www.ncess.ed/gov/pubs2002/digest2001/tables/dt134.asp.

such issues as stereotyping, name-calling, and exclusion. The game uses photographs and information to show ways that students around the world can respond to prejudice and discrimination and move toward unity.

CURRICULA

Diversity issues in education have led to the creation of new curricula. Blues in the Schools (BITS), for example, is a curriculum shaped over the past twenty-five years by a variety of individual and cooperative efforts. The goals of the program are to affirm the cultural heritage and contributions of African Americans and to promote understanding across racial and socioeconomic lines. Participating schools find that the program offers lessons in history, music, literature, and even geography (Millard, 1999).

Some people believe that efforts to promote multicultural approaches of openness and acceptance in education have themselves become closed, producing what is known as *political correctness.* Multiculturalists have been criticized for going too far in the other direction, making the differences between students more important than the similarities. They have also been accused of focusing on moral and social issues, thereby distracting people from practical problems, such as adequately funding programs and

How ow has diversity education shaped the Blues in the *Schools curriculum? What are the advantages of a curriculum like BITS? What are the possible disadvantages?*

finding the time to use the new curricula. The challenge has been and continues to be one of finding ways to help all young people succeed—not just separately, but together—and to appreciate one another in the process.

THE FUTURE OF MULTICULTURAL EDUCATION

As with any other part of the curriculum, both the content and processes of multicultural education are subject to scrutiny. Does multicultural education promote student interest in intellectually and socially relevant activities? Does it promote academic achievement? Does it encourage understanding and acceptance among students? Can it help forge ties between schools and homes? Answers to these and similar questions will determine the fate of multicultural education.

How ow Are Educational Services Adapted for Students with Exceptionalities?

Public schools in the United States are morally and legally obligated to create environments that enhance children's learning. As a result, both curricula and instructional methods are adapted to meet the needs of all students. The ultimate goal is to create an educational opportunity that best serves the particular needs of each student.   **When you hear the term "special education," what do you think of?**

Delivering Services to Students with Disabilities

The law guarantees individuals with disabilities the right to free and appropriate education set in the least restrictive environment. This means that students with disabilities must be educated in regular classrooms wherever possible. During the 1997–1998 school year, 46 percent of students with disabilities spent 80 percent of their days in regular classrooms, alongside students without disabilities (U.S. Department of Education, 2001).

Several laws, including the 1975 **Education for All Handicapped Children Act** and the 1990 **Individuals with Disabilities Education Act (IDEA),** have established equal educational opportunities for students with disabilities. IDEA, the current Act, changed the term *handicapped* to *with disabilities* and extended the opportunity for free

Technology in Practice

STUDYING ONLINE HATE

Students in Jeffrey Morgan's high school English class investigate some representative samples of hate-group rhetoric on the Internet as part of a persuasive writing study. Besides helping students understand how to construct an argument, Morgan uses the exercise to challenge students' assumptions about the power of political language, bigotry, and free speech. Why make such assignments?

> Because hate can be as real a force in [students'] lives as love or compassion. Furthermore, hate usually doesn't come walking through the door with an automatic rifle and a pipe bomb. Hate often moves more softly; it is a subtle menace, and this is especially characteristic of the rhetoric used by many of the well-established racist hate groups. (2001, pp. 23–24)

While selecting websites, Morgan looks for those with substantive essays about a particular group's purpose or lengthy statements that urge readers to join a particular cause or group. He tries to avoid sites with vulgar language and offensive images. And before allowing the students to access the sites, he prepares them for what they might see or hear and reminds them of the purpose of the exercise. As they critique passages, the class addresses several questions:

1. What characterizes the rhetoric of hate?
2. Are there identifiable purposes behind the rhetoric of hate?

3. What assumptions about the intended audience are apparent in the rhetoric?
4. If we can dismantle hate rhetoric and explain why it is in fact *illogical,* is the language no longer dangerous?
5. Would you defend a hate group's right to free speech on the Internet if it were ever challenged? Why or why not? (p. 27)

Visit the Southern Poverty Law Center's website "Fight Hate and Promote Tolerance" at http://www.tolerance.org to learn more about propaganda online. As you do so, think about the opportunities and challenges of integrating such material into the curriculum.

Critical Thinking Questions

Would you need to seek permission from your school system to do a study like this? Would parents need to be informed in advance of the intended study? How might you prepare students for Internet-based exercises? Why might having guiding questions, such as those developed by Jeffrey Morgan, be important?

 To answer these questions online and e-mail your answer to your professor, go to Chapter 3 of the Companion Website (ablongman.com/mcnergney4e) and click on Technology in Practice.

Source: Morgan, J. H. (2001, fall). The Rhetoric of Hate: An AP English Class Unmasks Propaganda on the Internet. *Teaching Tolerance Magazine 20*, 22–27.

and appropriate public education to every individual between the ages of two and twenty-one, regardless of the nature or severity of the disability.

LAWS THAT SUPPORT INCLUSION

Today, many students with special needs receive **inclusive education,** which is education designed for and offered to all people, regardless of their physical, social, emotional, and intellectual characteristics. Most often, however, people use the term to refer to education provided in mainstream classrooms to students with disabilities. By design, inclusive education stands in contrast to special education offerings that occur in separate classrooms or segregated facilities.

The legal and moral grounds behind the concept of inclusive education can be seen in the principles laid out in the 1954 Supreme Court case *Brown* v. *Board of Education* (Mithaug, 1998). This landmark ruling said that separating children by race in order to educate them was not only illegal but morally wrong as well. The beliefs behind that case have grown since 1954, and they are now applied to the education of students with disabilities.

Issues in School Reform

SERVING CHILDREN WITH SPECIAL NEEDS THROUGH INCLUSION

Everybody wants to help children who need special attention because of their disabilities. The difficulty is knowing how to do so effectively and efficiently. As the following excerpt from special education professor Bruce Marlowe (Johnson State College, Vermont) suggests, the demands are outstripping the human and material resources.

Unfortunately, in the last ten years, inclusion has become an increasingly difficult ideology to sell to my students, and to myself. My home state of Vermont has been committed to "full inclusion" since long before it became a national issue. As a teacher educator in a state where virtually all students with disabilities are placed in regular education classrooms, I have a mandate to prepare prospective teachers for classes in which there will be a wide range of student abilities. And while mainstreaming is often a hot topic of debate with my students, the primary emphasis in my classes has always been on how to plan, manage, deliver, and evaluate instruction effectively in diverse classroom settings—as this is what new teachers must do when they graduate, regardless of their politics. . . .

Perhaps the greatest threat to inclusion is the reluctance of competent special educators to work as special educators. While there are numerous openings for special educators, few want these jobs

because of the enormous disincentives. These include: a staggering amount of paperwork, overwhelming caseloads, endless meetings, escalating discipline problems (with little support from agencies outside the school), and increasingly adversarial, uncivil, and litigious parents. In addition, many feel that the job requires almost daily compromising of one's integrity, as special educators often must choose between protecting the fiduciary interests of the school (on which their jobs depend), and the educational needs and civil rights of the students on the caseloads.

Critical Thinking Questions

How might more financial support for special education be used most effectively? Will more licensed special education teachers fix the problems? Does the system need more **paraprofessionals** (unlicensed teachers' aides)? Are there other ways to invest in children's development that might be desirable?

 To answer these questions online and e-mail your answer to your professor, go to Chapter 3 of the Companion Website (ablongman.com/mcnergney4e) and click on Issues in School Reform.

Source: Marlowe, B. (2001, April 18). The Special Education Conundrum. *Education Week, 20,* 31: 43.

PROVIDING FOR SPECIAL EDUCATION

Much like multilingual programs, schools provide special education services for students with disabilities in a variety of ways. These options range from those that fully integrate students into general education classrooms to those that seldom integrate them.

In more integrated environments, the general education teacher meets all the needs of the student. Sometimes a special educator acts as a consultant to the teacher, or a special education teacher may be within the regular classroom to offer some instruction to a student. At other times, a student goes to a resource teacher for part of the day and receives specific help. In less integrated programs, a student may spend the majority of the day in a self-contained special education class and leave only occasionally to participate in school activities. Sometimes special education students attend separate schools, or they may be in a residential setting (Hallahan & Kauffman, 2003).

Research suggests that effective elementary teachers think and behave in particular ways with children who have disabilities. After observing a large number of these teachers, researchers interviewed five individual teachers to determine why they behaved as they did toward students with special needs (McNergney & Keller, 1999). Table 3.3 shows what researchers learned about effective teachers' actions. Overall, the most effective methods to help students with disabilities in the classroom are paying attention

*T*ABLE 3.3   **Some Effective Teachers' Actions with Children with Disabilities**

1. Teachers watch students as they work on tasks:
   (a) to see if students need help.
   (b) to keep students involved.
   (c) to determine when to move on to the next activity.
2. Teachers give step-by-step directions:
   (a) to help students work independently.
   (b) to avoid interruptions during instructional time.
3. Teachers help learners by giving hints and clarifying misunderstandings:
   (a) to make the content of a lesson more meaningful.
   (b) to help students make connections between old and new material.
   (c) to get students to think.
   (d) to keep students from giving up.
   (e) to give students more time to think.
   (f) to help students succeed so they feel good about themselves.
4. Teachers recognize special needs of learners:
   (a) to give students concrete examples to help them understand.
5. Teachers summarize and review throughout the lesson:
   (a) to help students synthesize information.
   (b) to keep students involved.
6. Teachers praise learners publicly and explain why:
   (a) to encourage student involvement.
   (b) to make students feel good about their achievements.
   (c) to encourage students to behave like others.
   (d) to enhance self-concepts of students.
7. Teachers make connections to students' interests, to the outside world, and to other subjects:
   (a) to increase student attention and interest in the lesson.
   (b) to make content real or meaningful to students.
   (c) to help students see that there is an overlap in content areas.
   (d) to help students form linkages between subjects.
   (e) to reinforce what the teacher and class have just discussed.
8. Teachers urge students to answer or comment:
   (a) to get and keep student involvement.
   (b) to get students to think about the material.
   (c) to give students a chance to answer correctly and feel good about themselves.
   (d) to make students feel that what they have to say is important.
9. Teachers check understanding throughout the lesson:
   (a) to see if students are "with" the teacher.
   (b) to keep students involved in the lesson.
   (c) to get students to think on their own.
10. Teachers question and respond—they praise, acknowledge, approve, redirect, reenter, make eye contact, check status, and so on:
    (a) to keep students involved in the lesson.
    (b) to check understanding.
    (c) to get students to think.
    (d) to review concepts.
11. Teachers work to build students' self-concepts:
    (a) to help students feel that what they have to say is important.
    (b) to help students develop a feeling of power or control—a "can do" attitude.
    (c) to increase student participation.

Source: McNergney, R., & Keller, C. (1999). *Images of Mainstreaming,* Appendix: Some Effective Teachers' Actions. New York: Garland Publishing, Inc. Reprinted by permission.

to their progress, actively including them in learning activities, and offering guidance and praise for what they do accomplish.

Regardless of where children with disabilities are placed in schools, general and special educators need to work with parents and other professionals to plan an **individualized education program (IEP).** IEPs are used to make sure each student receives the best and most fitting education possible. This customized program outlines a child's current performance levels (strengths and limitations), long- and short-term goals, criteria for success, methods for assessing mastery of objectives (e.g., observation, testing), amount of time to be spent in general education classrooms, and beginning and ending dates for special services.

With people advocating both sides of almost every form of special education services, as in the debate between inclusive and segregated programs, it can be hard to know how to proceed in the classroom. Often decisions about these matters are made by students and their families. In terms of your classroom, you should keep up with current practices and be aware of what services students with disabilities might require.

Delivering Services to Gifted and Talented Students

What is the best way to educate students who are gifted or talented?   Currently, every state and many school districts have gifted and talented programs. As with special education programs for students with disabilities, programs for gifted and talented students take many forms. In one type of program, students who qualify remain in general education classrooms but are assigned accelerated curricula. Alternatively, they may be pulled out of the general education classroom for special instruction in a resource room. Sometimes gifted and talented students attend self-contained classes for talented students. They may also skip a grade in school. In later years, some of these students will take Advanced Placement courses and college courses.

Studies of students selected to participate in gifted and talented programs suggest that economically disadvantaged students are significantly underrepresented. Looking at Table 3.4, it is easy to see a direct correlation between family income and students'

TABLE 3.4   Scholastic Assessment Test[a] Score Averages by Selected Student Characteristics: 2000–2001

Selected characteristics	2000–2001	
	Verbal score	Mathematics score
All students	506	514
Family income		
Less than $10,000	421	443
$10,000 to $20,000	442	456
$20,000 to $30,000	468	474
$30,000 to $40,000	487	489
$40,000 to $50,000	501	503
$50,000 to $60,000	509	512
$60,000 to $70,000	516	519
$70,000 to $80,000	522	527
$80,000 to $100,000	534	540
More than $100,000	557	569
Highest level of parental education		
Less than high school	411	438
High school diploma	472	476
Associate degree	489	491
Bachelor's degree	525	533
Graduate degree	559	567

[a]Formerly known as the Scholastic Aptitude Test.

Possible scores on each part of the SAT range from 200 to 800.

Source: College Entrance Examination Board, *National Report: 2001 College Bound Seniors.* Copyright © 2001 by the College Entrance Examination Board. All rights reserved. www.collegeboard.com.

test scores. This and many other studies have concluded that wealth and parental educational background combine to influence student achievement. This correlation also may help explain why children in poverty are not able to take advantage of gifted and talented programs.

Studies also indicate that disproportionately fewer limited English proficient (LEP) students are included in gifted and talented programs. Although schools provide instructional assistance to these students, many people argue that the programs do not teach the language or higher-order skills that students need to perform well on placement tests. Gifted LEP students may end up in lower-level classes and even be erroneously placed in special education classes because of language barriers.

Although the teaching of gifted students defies simple prescriptions, most educators agree on some general guidelines. First, definitions of giftedness must be expanded to include criteria other than standardized test scores. Second, competition is not always conducive to academic and personal growth. Gifted students often do better when they pursue projects of particular interest to them. They need specific feedback on their performances, not comparisons of their performances to other students.

The goal of educators and families is to enable students to have the best possible education, so gifted students would seem to be at an advantage. But we shouldn't overlook the social stigma attached to being labeled gifted or talented. The fact is, sometimes students do not want to be labeled high-achieving. Being a "brainiac" is not always conducive to making and keeping friends. In addition, some students in gifted and talented programs find the combined pressure of meeting high expectations and being like other students overwhelming. As always, teachers should not underestimate the social implications of any treatment perceived to draw "special" attention to a student.

How Can Teachers Create Culturally Relevant Classrooms?

Overall, three factors influence positive attitudes in schools: the quality of teachers' relationships with students, the quality of education, and the social skills teachers impart to students (Louis Harris and Associates, 1996). When these factors are present, students view the school's social problems as less serious. They also express more confidence that people from different backgrounds receive equal treatment by adults in their community. To a large extent, these factors depend on teachers' knowledge of and attitudes toward their students.

Children and teachers who grow up in diverse communities have opportunities to learn about those who differ from themselves and about themselves in relation to others. These opportunities do not always result in social harmony. Nor do they necessarily lead to tension and conflict. But both outcomes are possible in culturally diverse schools.

Cultural Mismatches

What teachers expect from the mix of students they teach and how they act on those expectations are crucial. This process can be made even more complicated in a classroom where the teacher believes she or he has nothing in common with the students. When cultural mismatches between teachers and students occur in the classroom, the effects can be hard on each. Inner-city schools with high proportions of racial and ethnic minorities, low-income students, and at-risk learners, for example, commonly have mismatches between teachers' and students' values. Such differences can be frustrating and frightening, particularly to novice teachers. Consider the experience

Voices

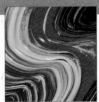

*G*loria Ladson-Billings's book *The Dreamkeepers: Successful Teachers of African American Children* (1994) describes the practices of eight teachers (three white and five African American) who create caring and democratic classroom communities with their inner-city students. One teacher, Ann Lewis, is an Italian American teacher in a largely African American community. Ladson-Billings describes why she thinks Lewis is so effective, explaining how Lewis uses a novel entitled *Charlie Pippin*. The novel is about an eleven-year-old African American girl who feels alienated from her father—a man who has buried his feelings about the Vietnam War deep inside him:

> *Charlie Pippin* became the centerpiece for a wide range of activities. One group of students began a Vietnam War research group. One group member who assumed a leadership position was a very quiet Vietnamese girl whose relatives had fought in the war. She brought in pictures, maps, letters, even a

family member to talk to the class about Vietnam. In the book, the main character—Charlie—had made origami to sell to her classmates. Lewis taught her students how to make origami. She introduced them to Eleanor Coerr's *Sadako and the Thousand Paper Cranes*. A second group of students researched nuclear proliferation. They asked Lewis to rent the video "Amazing Grace," which is about a young boy's and a professional athlete's stand against nuclear weapons. (1994, p. 110)

Critical Thinking Question

Lewis has her students "doing," not simply listening. Why is this strategy so important?

To answer this question online and e-mail your answer to your professor, go to Chapter 3 of the Companion Website (ablongman.com/mcnergney4e) and click on Voices.

---

of one teacher, Ruth Sherman, at a school in the Bushwick neighborhood of Brooklyn, New York:

> The kids in Ruth Sherman's third-grade class loved the books she read to them. . . . [T]heir favorite story was "Nappy Hair," about a black girl named Brenda with the "kinkiest, the nappiest, the fuzziest, the most screwed up, squeezed up, knotted up, tangled up, twisted up" hair. . . . Not all the parents found the story so charming. When one mother stumbled onto a few photocopied pages of the book among her child's school papers. . . , she organized a protest in the neighborhood. (Clemetson, 1998, p. 38)

When parents began to protest, Sherman was physically threatened to her face. Eventually she resigned. Although "Everyone—Sherman, administrators, and parents—now admits the situation was handled badly, " unfortunately the damage was done. **How could you prepare yourself for a classroom of students with whom you share little in terms of cultural background, experiences, and values?**

Responsive Instruction

Successful teachers create "culturally relevant" classrooms—places where curriculum and instruction are "friendly" to difference (Oakes & Lipton, 1999). But how do teachers develop such settings? Researchers suggest teachers begin by getting to know their students and their communities and then transferring that knowledge into new ways of approaching a subject. They also recommend that teachers read literature describing other teachers' experiences in diverse settings.

When teachers work with students who are bilingual or who are developing English language proficiency and literacy, making content culturally relevant can be particularly challenging. For example, the recommended strategy for increasing science literacy is to have children act as scientists, asking and answering questions to understand the world (National Research Council, 1996). But how would this approach be used with students from diverse language backgrounds who may not possess the English skills necessary to participate fully? Would they just not learn what the other students learn? On a larger scale, the question is this: Should teachers serve as *knowledge transmitters,* leading students through predetermined lessons and activities, or as *facilitators,* guiding students to ask questions and to investigate their own interests?

Teachers who share the languages and cultures of their students may choose instructional approaches that reflect students' native cultures. Researchers have worked to examine the effectiveness of different approaches not only in science, but in other content areas as well (Brown, 1994; Lehrer & Schauble, 1998; Metz, 1995; Rosebery & Warren, 1998; Valdes, 1999). Prospective teachers shouldn't think, however, that there are definite answers to these kinds of questions. Nor is there a "magic" moment when everything will be answered once and for all. Good teachers know these are ongoing issues; the answers change and sometimes even the questions change.

Summary

Differences among people take many forms and have many implications for teachers and schools. Such differences include culture, race, ethnicity, primary language group, gender, special needs and talents, and sexual orientation. How learners think about themselves matters, but how teachers think about learners matters too.

Teachers use a variety of instructional approaches adapted to their perceptions of students' needs. Teaching in a culturally responsive way means fitting instruction to learners, not fitting learners to instruction. Teachers accomplish such adaptations by selecting curricula, delivering instruction, and evaluating student progress.

Certainly people differ from one another in some important ways, but we are all similar too. To know what others think or feel—even people from cultures with which you are unfamiliar—it can be helpful to begin by looking deep within yourself. The phrase "trust your instincts" suggests that if you think or believe something others may too. But good teachers do not stop there. They observe, question, listen, read, and get out there among the people they serve.

Terms and Concepts

assimilation   59
bilingual education   61
conflict mediation   67
culture   57
Education for All Handicapped Children Act   72
English as a Second Language (ESL)   61
e pluribus unum   69
equal educational opportunity   69
ethnicity   58
exceptional learners   64

gender bias   62
giftedness   64
inclusive education   73
individualized education program (IEP)   75
Individuals with Disabilities Education Act (IDEA)   72
limited English proficient (LEP)   61
paraprofessional   74
pluralism   59
race   58
Title IX   63

Reflective Practice

One Immigrant's Success Story

Fairfax County Public Schools Superintendent Daniel Domenech is a Cuban refugee. He describes his transition from school in Cuba to school in the United States:

I started school in Cuba and went through the fifth grade. I actually started school at the age of three. I did kindergarten as a three-year-old. So when I came to the United States, I was already a fifth grader in Cuba.

I was instantly placed in a second grade class here. (Seymour, 2001, p. A1)

Nine-year-old Domenech spoke no English when he and his family arrived in the United States in 1955. He recalled, years later, the difficulty he had understanding his lessons and making himself understood while attending a Catholic boarding school in Tarrytown, New York. Domenech soon transferred to public schools in New York City and began to excel in his studies as his English improved. His path to the head of the Fairfax schools—the twelfth largest system in the nation—is a success story of personal triumph and a testament to the power of education.

Issues

What factor(s) may have given Daniel Domenech an edge in obtaining educational success in the United States?

Perspectives

Why might some people like Daniel Domenech and his family leave Cuba while others choose to stay?

Knowledge and Action

What would you want to know about the strategies Domenech's teachers, both Cuban and American, used to

help him succeed? What might you do to help immigrant children in your classroom succeed? Would you encourage non-English speakers to keep speaking their native language?

Consequences

Should non-English-speaking students' educational performance be judged differently from students who speak English fluently?

INTASC Principle 3

The teacher understands how students differ in their approaches to learning and creates instructional opportunities that are adapted to diverse learners.

Knowledge

The teacher knows about the process of second-language acquisition and about strategies to support the learning of students whose first language is not English. (Interstate New Teacher Assessment and Support Consortium, 1992)

Activity

Ask someone you know who has learned English as a second language about his or her learning experience. Did that person experience a formal program to help in learning English? What helped the person most? What was most difficult?

*A*dditional Readings

Banks, J. A. (2001). *Multicultural education: Issues and perspectives* (4th ed.). New York: John Wiley & Sons, Inc.

Banks, J. A. (2002). *An introduction to multicultural education* (3rd ed.). Boston: Allyn & Bacon.

Gollnick, D. M., & Banks, C. A. (2001). *Multicultural education in a pluralist society* (6th ed.). Columbus, OH: Merrill.

Hernandez, H. (2001). *Multicultural education: A teacher's guide to linking context, process, and content* (2nd ed.). Upper Saddle River, NJ: Prentice Hall.

Utley, C. A., & Obiakor, F. E. (eds.) (2001). *Special education, multicultural education, and school reform: Components of quality education for learners with mild disabilities.* Springfield, IL: Charles C. Thomas Publisher.

*W*eb Resources

http://inclusion.ngfl.gov.uk/

"Inclusion" is an online catalogue of resources to support individual learning needs. The catalogue is part of the British government's National Grid for Learning (NGfL) website.

http://www.tolerance.org

Visit this website for ideas on ways to alert people of all ages to problems of hate and intolerance.

http://www.census.gov

This website reveals racial statistics for the United States.

http://curry.edschool.virginia.edu/go/multicultural

The Multicultural Pavilion includes a variety of multicultural education resources for educators.

http://www.ngltf.org/

The National Gay and Lesbian Task Force works to eliminate prejudice, violence, and injustice against gay, lesbian, bisexual, and transgender people at the local, state, and national levels.

http://www.gifted.uconn.edu/nrcgt.html

The National Research Center on the Gifted and Talented provides a variety of gifted and talented education resources for educators.

Video**Workshop** Extra!

If the VideoWorkshop package is included with your textbook, go to Chapter 3 of the Companion Website (ablongman. com/mcnergney4e) and click on VideoWorkshop. Follow the instructions for viewing video clips 9, 4, and 3. Then consider this information along with what you've read in Chapter 3 while answering the following questions.

1. Teachers recognize the importance of cognitive development, which is often measured in terms of intelligence, as discussed in this chapter. How do you feel about the use of standardized tests as the most common form of assessment, as opposed to other forms discussed in video clip 9?

2. The concept of inclusion, presented in video clip 4, is complex and has powerful implications for classroom practice. How do you compare the legislative efforts to address inclusion with the practice of recognizing diversity (as presented in video clip 3) in classrooms on a daily basis?

BENCHMARKS

Historical and Philosophical Touchstones in Education

1857	The National Education Association (NEA) is established as a professional organization for teachers.
1916	American Federation of Teachers (AFT) is formed as a labor union for classroom teachers.
1945	*Human Relations: Promising Practices and Intergroup and Intercultural Education in the Social Studies,* 16th yearbook of the National Council for the Social Studies, is edited by Hilda Taba and William VanTil.
1958	National Defense Education Act (NDEA, Public Law 85-864) provides federal funds to improve the teaching of science, mathematics, and modern foreign languages and to help schools provide guidance services.
1964	Economic Opportunity Act of 1964 (Public Law 88-452) authorizes grants for college work-study programs for students from low-income families; establishes a Job Corps program and authorizes support for work-training programs to provide educational and vocational training and work experience opportunities in welfare programs; authorizes support of education and training activities and of community action programs, including Head Start, Follow Through, and Upward Bound; and authorizes the establishment of Volunteers in Service to America (VISTA).
1965	Higher Education Act of 1965 (Public Law 89-329) establishes a National Teacher Corps devoted to teaching in the nation's poverty-stricken areas.
1965	Elementary and Secondary Education Act (ESEA) and subsequent amendments provide funding to aid students from low-income families through programs such as Title I (see Chapter 2).
1974	Juvenile Justice and Delinquency Prevention Act of 1974 (Public Law 93-415) provides for technical assistance, staff training, centralized research, and resources to develop and implement programs to keep students in elementary and secondary schools.
1977	*Standards for the Accreditation of Teacher Education,* issued by the National Council for the Accreditation of Teacher Education, includes a requirement for multicultural education in teacher education programs.
1986	Drug-Free Schools and Committees Act of 1986 (Part of Public Law 99–570), part of the Anti-Drug Abuse Act of 1986, authorizes funding for programs for drug abuse education and prevention, coordinated with related community efforts and resources.
1987	National Board for Professional Teaching Standards (NBPTS) established.
1989	National Goals of Education issued from the White House.
1990	Children's Television Act of 1990 (Public Law 101–437) requires the Federal Communications Commission to reinstate restrictions on advertising during children's television programs and enforces the obligation of broadcasters to meet the educational and informational needs of the child audience. School Dropout and Basic Skills Improvement Act of 1990 (Public Law 101–600) targets secondary school programs for basic skills improvements and dropout reduction.

1994	Department of Defense establishes Troops to Teachers to help Department of Defense and Department of Energy civilian employees affected by military reductions develop new careers in public education.
1995	House Resolutions HR 1390—Children's Media Protection Act of 1995 requires television manufacturers to include a filtering device in new television sets. Requires broadcasters to provide a ratings signal for each television program to be interpreted by the filtering device.
1999	On February 16, parties in a San Francisco lawsuit reach an extraordinary settlement replacing a long-standing racial-desegregation scheme for schools with a new and creative compromise that emphasizes integration of students by economic status. Research demonstrates that American schools are becoming racially more segregated, especially in the South. A 1999 study by the Civil Rights Project, a Harvard University initiative, found that the percentage of African American students attending majority-white public schools in the South fell from its high point of 44 percent in 1988 to 35 percent in 1996.
2002	U.S. Secretary of Education Rod Paige announces ninety-five grants totaling nearly $35 million under the Transition to Teaching program to help school districts recruit skilled mid-career professionals, paraprofessionals, and recent college graduates into teaching careers.

DEVELOPING A PROFESSIONAL PORTFOLIO

Digital Portfolios

A portfolio is a collection of materials teachers create to document their professional growth as educators. Many of you may choose to create a digital portfolio on the Web or on a CD-ROM because the technology is available, you know how to use it or want to learn, and you want to demonstrate that you possess special skills that make you an attractive candidate to employers and graduate programs.

There are some other benefits of making your portfolio digital. Kilbane and Milman (2003) suggest that a teacher with a digital portfolio demonstrates that she has the competency to affect students' abilities to use technology; that is, if she has the computer skills, then she can share them with her students. Digital portfolios are also more portable than hardcopy materials. They can be easily revised and copied, as well as shared inexpensively and widely.

Kilbane and Milman point their readers to several online samples of teachers' portfolios. For instance, see the work of Carter Shreves, a former preservice teacher at the University of Virginia (http://curry.edschool.virginia.edu/curry/class/edlf/589-07/Carter_Shreves). This is a simple, but not simplistic, example of what can be done on the Web. It does not require large storage capacity or special applications to make portfolio materials accessible to others.

You can also access examples of the kinds of portfolio entries required by the National Board for Professional Teaching Standards (NBPTS). See the Early Adolescence English Language Arts Certification (http://www2.ncsu.edu/unity/lockers/project/portfolios/nbcfile3.html). This example is important for two reasons. First, it is wise to keep standards in mind as you think about what kinds of materials are appropriate for inclusion in your portfolio. Second, the NBPTS standards are a look ahead at your career at the point when you might seek national certification. It is never too soon to think about using your portfolio to plan and document your own professional development.

As you explore the use of digital portfolios, ask yourself what items of professional information you might include in your own portfolio. What technologies and design features might you use to communicate your knowledge, skills, and values to others? What might you do today to begin to prepare yourself to create an electronic portfolio?

Keep in mind that the digital presentation of your portfolio is a complement to the contents of your portfolio. In the end there is no substitute for substance, so you must focus on the materials you collect for your portfolio and how they reflect your professional goals as an educator.

The Learning Network

Teachers, students, and parents can take advantage of the Learning Network (sponsored by the *New York Times*) to make the richness and diversity of life a central part of the curriculum from grades three to twelve. The site (www.nytimes.com/learning/) offers daily News Summaries, along with News Quizzes. Learn what happened On This Day in History; boost your vocabulary with the Word of the Day. Do a Crossword Puzzle to reinforce what you know about particular subject matter (e.g., to keep the Periodic Table of Elements fresh in your mind). Wonder how to help parents help their children talk at the dinner table? Go for the Conversation Starters. Do you feel relatively uninformed about a particular cultural issue? Get up to speed by consulting Issues in Depth. Take guided Web Tours about significant topics of the day.

Visit the Lesson Plan Archive, which is linked from the homepage (www.nytimes.com/learning/teachers/lessons/archive.html). When you arrive:

1. Select a subject area of interest (e.g., current events)
2. Specify the grade levels of interest (e.g., 6 to 8)
3. Type in a key word to use for a search (e.g., war)

The documents that fit your search instructions will be displayed. Peruse the abstracts that appear with the document links and click on one of particular interest—one for which you might be able to develop your own lesson plan, but at a different grade level. Print a copy of the full plan that you selected.

1. Now try to develop your own lesson plan on the same subject, one that might complement the plan you selected. Use the categories provided (title, grade levels of interest, overview of your plan, suggested time, and objectives, resources/materials, activities/procedures, evaluation/assessment).

2. Share your plan with a classmate, inviting suggestions.

3. If you are satisfied that the plan is a good one, you might choose to submit it to the *New York Times* for inclusion on its website. (You will see a link that allows you to upload your own plan.)

*O*ur Educational Heritage

*M*any years ago when her grandmother, Nellie McGinty, died at age seventy, JoEllen felt an immense sense of loss. Nellie had always made her feel so special, even though JoEllen was just one of ten grandchildren. It seemed that her grandmother gave her undivided attention every time they were together.

At first, all JoEllen could think about was her own sorrow. But when she attended the large wake and funeral several days later, she began to understand just how important her grand-mother had been to her sprawling, far-flung family and to so many others in her little community. Nellie was a wise grand-mother, but she was also a powerful teacher. She taught school for forty-five years , touching the lives of literally thousands of people who had been in her classes or whose children had been her students.

Now, years later, JoEllen is a college history professor. She traces her own professional and personal development in part to the lessons she learned from her grandmother. Many of Mrs. McGinty's former students have also gone on to lead full, pro-ductive lives. In this sense, Nellie McGinty was an influential figure in American history. Her personal and professional philosophies, keen intellect, and unbounded energy shaped the lives of people she touched. She lives on through many people, continuing to influence the course of their collective lives through their individual actions.

We are all products of our personal and educational histo-ries—often in ways we do not even realize. The chapters in Part 2 illustrate how the forces of history and philosophy have defined education as we have come to know it in the United States. These chapters present the origins of ideas and values that make Ameri-can education what it is today and what it will be tomorrow.

4

Education in America: The Early Years

CHAPTER CONTENTS

Which Europeans
Influenced Early
Education?

How Did Informal
Education Develop
before the Civil War?

What Were the Aims of
Education?

How Did Formal
Education Develop
before the Civil War?

Ralph Waldo Emerson (1803–1882) is one of the most important figures in the history of American thought, literature, and education. He was a great spokesman for individualism and for making the most of one's life through one's own efforts. At the same time, he was a good neighbor who looked out for others and a good citizen who worked for the well-being of the community. He tackled the serious political and educational issues of his day, but he also maintained a sense of optimism. He believed in the power of people to change society for the better and in the power of teachers to make it happen. In 1834, Emerson wrote, "The whole secret of the teacher's force lies in the conviction that men are convertible." He then added cheerfully, "and they are" (Richardson, 1995, p. 169).

This Unitarian minister turned writer and lecturer may be best known for his essay entitled "Self-Reliance." He struck a chord in this essay that still rings true for many people today. He wrote, "He who knows that power is inborn, that he is weak because he has looked for good out of him and elsewhere, and so perceiving, throws himself unhesitatingly on his thought, instantly rights himself, stands in the erect position, commands his limbs, works miracles; just as a man who stands on his feet is stronger than a man who stands on his head."

This chapter examines early educational life in the United States and the forces, both within and beyond people's control, that changed life between 1600 and 1865.

Which Europeans Influenced Early Education?

Most early American colonists emigrated from England and Europe. Not surprisingly, European thinkers shaped the colonists' formal educational system. **Who were these intellectuals and what did they believe?**

Comenius: Value of Structure

Is there a danger in thinking that education is the means for improving society? John Amos Comenius (1592–1670), a Czech theologian and philosopher, thought education could improve society. Comenius believed all children should be trained methodically by teachers using quality textbooks in schools supported by governments and the clergy. He envisioned education programs divided into four distinct grades: the nursery school (birth to age six), the elementary or national school (ages six to twelve), the Latin school or gymnasium (ages thirteen to eighteen), and the Academy (gifted youths ages nineteen to twenty-four). Comenius argued that a child's mind should be "prepared" to receive instruction and that education would be "easy and pleasant" if it began early, before a child's mind was "corrupted." He also thought instruction should move from the general to the specific, with tasks arranged from easy to difficult.

Comenius thought the number of subjects studied should be manageable for children. Teachers should present lessons at a reasonable pace, use age-appropriate instruction, keep materials constantly before children's eyes, and use a single method of instruction at all times. Comenius also advocated universal textbooks and schools and a universal language (Edwards, 1972; Ulich, 1968). **Which of Comenius's ideas are relevant today in discussions about education in the United States?**

Locke and Rousseau: Enlightened Views

How did formal education encourage the idea that we, and not God, were responsible for the conduct of our lives? The English philosopher John Locke (1632–1704) believed the human mind at birth was a blank state *(tabula rasa)*, not a collection of preformed ideas placed there by God. He thought children should interact with the environment by using their five senses to gather and test ideas. In his view, teachers should tailor instruction to the individual child's talents and interests. Teachers should encourage curiosity and treat children as "rational creatures" who might unlock life's mysteries. Locke also believed that children learned through imitation; an effective teacher taught by example and suggestion, not by coercion (Gay, 1964).

Locke's ideas about education were consistent with the Age of Enlightenment, a period when reason was valued as a supreme virtue. In keeping with the beliefs of that period, Locke thought people were inherently good. It followed then that children taught by benevolent educators were bound to grow intellectually and prosper.

Swiss philosopher Jean-Jacques Rousseau (1712–1778) had ideas about education that were similar to those of Locke. Most significantly, Rousseau criticized educational

English philosopher John Locke (1632–1704)

Swiss philosopher Jean-Jacques Rousseau (1712–1778)

methods he believed were inconsistent with children's ways of thinking, seeing, and feeling. He contended that schools imposed books and abstract ideas on minds not yet ready to deal with such demands.

In his book *Emile,* Rousseau described the development of a human being from infancy to maturity, using the character of Emile. According to Rousseau's ideas about education, Emile's tutor provided experiences that matched the natural conditions of Emile's growth. From infancy through age eleven, Emile's tutor removed obstacles that might impede development. During this time, Emile explored the environment with his senses, learning through trial and error and experiencing joy and pain from naturally occurring experiences. Between ages eleven and fourteen, Emile was introduced to geography, astronomy, and his first book, Daniel Defoe's *Robinson Crusoe.* Emile also learned carpentry, a practical skill that might serve him later in life. Abstract thought processes developed during adolescence, and Emile began to compare himself to others, think about his place in the world, and explore the mysteries of the universe. Because his tutor had respected his human nature, removing obstacles that might hinder his development, Emile's educational development happened naturally (Boyd, 1962; Ulich, 1968).

Pestalozzi and Herbart: Encouraging Development

Johann Heinrich Pestalozzi (1746–1827), a Swiss educator, tested Rousseau's ideas on teachers and students at two German schools for boys. Pestalozzi (1898), like Rousseau, worried about educational conditions that stifled children's playfulness and natural curiosity. He thought young children lost their natural love of learning by being treated "like sheep" who were forced to spend their time in flocks studying boring letters and numerals.

Pestalozzi also believed that children pass through a number of stages of development. Teachers needed to be kind, and they needed to provide experiences that appealed to all the senses when teaching concepts and skills, rather than relying on verbal instruction (Gutek, 1968). In *How Gertrude Teaches Her Children,* a book written for mothers, Pestalozzi (1898) demonstrated why it was important to "always put a picture before the eye."

> It was inevitable, for instance, when [the teacher] asked, in arithmetic, How many times is seven contained in sixty-three? The child had no real background for his answer, and must, with great trouble, dig it out of his memory. Now, by the plan of putting nine times seven objects before his eyes, and letting him count them as nine sevens standing together, he has not to think any more about this question; he knows from what he has already learnt, although he is asked for the first time, that seven is contained nine times in sixty-three. (p. 97)

Pestalozzi's "object lessons" showed ways to facilitate step-by-step learning of abstract concepts. His ideas challenged educators in Germany and America to rethink instructional methods that relied on repetition and memorization. **How is Pestalozzi's approach similar to or different from math lessons taught in today's elementary schools?**

Johann Friedrich Herbart (1776–1841), a German philosopher, psychologist, and educational theorist, believed teachers should respect a child's individuality and help him develop moral strength of character. Herbart proposed several "steps of instruction" for developing a child's ability to concentrate, retain ideas, and participate in learning: (1) "clearness" (understanding of content); (2) "association" (connecting new ideas with previously learned content); (3) "system" (the analysis of new ideas and their relation to the purpose of the lesson); and (4) "method" (the ability to apply newly acquired knowledge to future problems). By the nineteenth century, many teacher education programs encouraged prospective teachers to use Herbart's methods of instruction (Ulich, 1968).

Froebel: Start Early

Friedrich Froebel (1782–1852) was a German philosopher who founded the first **kindergarten** in 1837 at Blankenburg, Germany. Froebel's kindergarten was not a school in the traditional sense, but a "general institution" where young children learned through the use of educational games and activities. He thought play was an important part of learning. In the kindergarten, much of the children's day was spent gardening, an activity aimed at helping them see the similarity between the growth of plants and their own development (Downs, 1978).

*S*wiss *educator Johann Pestalozzi (1746–1827)*

Froebel viewed mental life as the result of God's creativeness (Ulich, 1968, p. 287). To Froebel, a person's senses, emotions, and reason were the necessary attributes for learning. He valued quality early childhood experiences that focused on play, music, and art. Children were not "lumps of clay" to be molded; instead they were like plants and animals, needing time and space to develop according to natural law (Downs, 1978).

In 1855, Margaretta Schurtz, a German immigrant and one of Froebel's former students, established one of the first kindergartens in America in Watertown, Wisconsin. These early kindergartens were primarily meant to guarantee the preservation of the German heritage and language. The first kindergarten conducted in English was founded in Boston in 1860 by Elizabeth Peabody.

How do modern kindergartens seem to have changed from those in early times?

How Did Informal Education Develop before the Civil War?

European settlers who arrived on the shores of the New World in the 1600s had to adapt their European ideas to the new environment as they struggled with themselves, each other, and outside forces to survive and prosper. Education lessons and practices during this time both reflected and shaped people's values as they established their settlements along the eastern coast of America.

Students in the colonies, young men called "scholars," were educated through a tutoring system, in which the quality of education often depended on the quality of the "master." The schoolmaster typically was a member of the clergy and a prominent figure in the community. The purpose of education was to prepare young men for the ministry and for leadership. In their recollections, Meriwether Lewis, who later explored the Northwest Territories on the famous Lewis and Clark Expedition, and his younger cousin and classmate, Peachy Gilmer, complained about one of their schoolmasters and praised another. Of their schoolmaster Dr. Charles Everitt, Gilmer said he was

> afflicted with very bad health . . . peevish, capricious, and every way disagreeable. . . .
> He invented cruel punishments for the scholars. . . . His method of teaching was as
> bad as anything could be. He was imparient [sic] of interruption. We seldom
> applied for assistance, said our lessons badly, made no proficiency, and acquired
> negligent and bad habits. (Ambrose, 1996, p. 27)

In 1790, Lewis transferred to a new schoolmaster, Reverend James Waddell, who was a great contrast to the ill-tempered Everitt. Lewis called Waddell "a very polite

European settlers who arrived on the shores of the New World in the 1600s had to adapt to the new environment. What aspects of education do you think were most important at that time?

scholar," and wrote to his mother, "I expect to continue [here] for eighteen months or two years. Every civility is here paid to me and leaves me without any reason to regret the loss of a home or nearer connection. As soon as I complete my education, you shall certainly see me" (Ambrose, 1996, p. 27).

Education in the Southern Colonies

Many settlers in the southern colonies of Virginia, Maryland, Georgia, and the Carolinas lived on large plantations with rigid class distinctions. A plantation functioned as a small community where growers raised crops such as tobacco, sugar, or cotton. The owner's home often was the center of the plantation, surrounded by a kitchen, smokehouse, stable, and sometimes a school. A hired tutor usually taught the landowner's children. Education on the plantations was fairly formal, and the children were taught reading, writing, and mathematics. Learning to read was central to becoming a good Christian. If you knew how to read, you could follow the will of God as expressed in the Bible.

Slaves from Africa and indentured servants from Europe lived in cabins and barns around the property border. They were the backbone of plantation life, serving as field workers, household workers, and skilled artisans (cobblers, carpenters, tailors, blacksmiths). Slaves, servants, and their children rarely received any type of education on the plantation, and most could neither read nor write.

Small farmers in the southern colonies lived in isolated areas. Although they worked for themselves, their livelihood often was affected by plantation owners, because they had the power to purchase or sell surplus crops, rent out land, and loan money. Small farmers' decisions about where to settle were based mainly on the lay of the land, the quality of the soil, and the proximity of water. For those who struggled to make a living by working the land, there was no community of any sort, nor were there nearby schools or churches.

For the most part, education for the children of small farmers was informal. Skills that boys and girls needed to learn were taught by the family. Families also taught their

Your Teaching Life in Practice

COMPETITION OR COOPERATION?

The history of the United States and, indeed, the world is characterized by the ever-present tension between competition and cooperation. In 1857, the English philosopher Herbert Spencer, a devotee of competition, advanced the concept of Social Darwinism—a kind of philosophical, religious brand of the survival of the fittest. He believed people competed for social and class positions, with the people strongest and most skilled in social situations gaining power. The general concept, perhaps fueled by the value the nation placed on individuality, gained great popularity throughout the United States in the nineteenth century. At the time, these ideas fit well with the nation's westward expansion.

Traces of the concept of Social Darwinism still can be found in public education. Students interested in team sports, for example, usually compete for a spot on a team. Once on the team, they compete for playing time and particular positions. Some experts contend that students compete in similar ways in the classroom: for grades, class rank, access to special programs such as gifted education, and so on.

Is competition good or bad? You may hear the following positions about the purpose of testing in public schools expressed publicly and privately by people who are on both sides of the debate.

PRO Competition in schools prepares young people for real life. Sometimes people win, sometimes they lose—better to learn that lesson sooner rather than later. Grouping students on the basis of their abilities is bad only if they do not have opportunities to move in and out of programs to which they are initially assigned.

CON The focus on tests, grades, and rewards and seeing classroom learning as a competition is deeply entrenched and difficult to change. A competitive culture can be an obstacle to learning, because it can lead to labeling students as "bright" or "dull" and placing them in academic and vocational tracks based on these labels.

PRO Individuals in cooperative groups—usually made up of students of varying abilities—do not have opportunities to show what they know or can do. Typically, students earn a group grade, yet some students do more work than others.

CON Cooperation and collaboration—ideas not fostered in typical testing situations—make students better, more compassionate learners and eventually better workers. International comparative studies point out the difference between the value of competition and differentiation in the United States and the culture of belief in Japan. In Japan, for example, the common belief is the whole class can and should work together to succeed.

PRO Test results allow us to rank people from high to low in many important areas. We need information from standardized tests to make comparative judgments about who should participate in college and technical training programs. Collections of students' work, or portfolios, are unreliable estimates of student performance. They are subject to the biases of those who decide what should go in them.

CON Collections of students' work are better indications of what students know than are test scores that compare students to each other. Students' views of their own accomplishments and their potential for future success are reflected in the material; this information demonstrates a student's true potential.

Based on your experiences as a student, how should teachers think about competition?

Discussion Questions

Many educators believe that students must be able to compete and cooperate effectively if they are to succeed in school and in later life. Do you think schools have gone too far in one direction or the other? Why or why not?

 To answer these questions online and e-mail your answer to your professor, go to Chapter 4 of the Companion Website (ablongman.com/mcnergney4e) and click on Your Teaching Life in Practice.

children to read, and families conducted their own worship services until the middle of the eighteenth century, when traveling missionaries began to reach people in rural areas.

Education in the Middle Atlantic Colonies

Middle Atlantic colonists (in New York, New Jersey, Pennsylvania, and Delaware) were more diverse than were settlers in the Southern colonies. Most Middle Atlantic colonists spoke English, but there were also Dutch-, German-, French-, and Swedish-speaking families whose religious orientation varied greatly from one another. There were Catholics, Mennonites, Calvinists, Lutherans, Quakers, Presbyterians, and Jews, all eager to preserve their languages and beliefs.

Different religious groups in this area established their own **parochial schools.** English, Irish, Welsh, Dutch, and German Quakers, for instance, who settled mainly in Pennsylvania, stressed the importance of teaching religion, mathematics, reading, and writing. They also offered some vocational training to children. In accordance with their religion, teachers viewed children as inherently good and rejected the use of corporal punishment. These parochial schools were open to everyone, including Native Americans and slaves (Bullock, 1967).

Education in the New England Colonies

In the New England colonies (Massachusetts Bay, Rhode Island, New Hampshire, and Connecticut), many people shared similar values, which made it possible to establish town schools. In particular, two laws moved New Englanders in the direction of town schools. The Massachusetts Act of 1642 required that parents and master craftsmen with apprentices be monitored to ensure that children were learning to read and understand religious principles. The Massachusetts Act of 1647, sometimes referred to as the Old Deluder Satan Act, required towns to educate youth so they might thwart Satan's trickery. To produce Scripture-literate citizens, every town of fifty households had to employ a teacher of reading and writing, and every town of one hundred households had to provide a grammar school to prepare students for continuing study at Harvard University.

Many settlers in the Northern colonies were Puritans who followed the teachings of John Calvin, a Swiss religious reformer. Calvin believed God was omnipotent and good, while human beings were evil and helpless, predestined for either salvation or eternal torment. Schools were to produce literate, hardworking, frugal, and respectful men and women who could resist temptation. Calvin saw children as savage and primitive creatures who needed training and discipline to achieve a life of social conformity and religious commitment.

Colonists living in northern cities experienced a lifestyle quite different from colonists in other areas of the country. Northern cities were densely populated trading centers. Merchants, who were key people in the community, offered an array of goods and services not found elsewhere. Ships brought both goods and ideas from England and Europe that seldom made their way south. Overall, city dwellers on the eastern seaboard were among the best informed and sometimes the most influential of the colonists. In addition, many schoolteachers in the North were better educated than teachers in other parts of the country (Blum et al., 1997). **How does geography continue to influence education in our nation?**

A National View of Education

For democracy to work, people had to be literate and information had to be available. By the middle of the eighteenth century, almost every colony had a printing press churning out a daily newspaper that contained not only local and international news, but also literary and political essays. And these weekly newspapers, essays, and verse were popular reading material in the colonies. Technological advancements also made it easier for printers to produce almanacs, flyers, and books.

With all of the available information, most colonists understood how government worked, but they did not always agree on what it should do. Some argued the country should free itself from England. Others believed they should reconcile their differences with England and remain a colony. The struggle for people's loyalties, both on and off the battlefield, shaped the talk and writings of the day. Especially popular was Thomas Paine's book, *Common Sense,* published in 1776. It presented a compelling case for the country's independence and sold 100,000 copies in its first three months of publication. Paine captured the minds and hearts of the delegates to the Continental Congress and of many others outside Philadelphia, which was the nation's capital at the time (Cremin, 1970). As Figure 4.1 shows, national independence was one of several developments that significantly affected the American system of education.

As the country grew, competing forces from within continued to shape American's views of themselves and others. Plantation owners in the South protected their virtually self-sufficient communities with a permanent labor force (slaves), while abolitionists in the North battled both covertly and openly to destroy the system of slavery that supported the plantations. The Cherokee, Creek, Iroquois, and other Native American tribes fought to preserve their land and their physical and spiritual well-being, while

ᖴIGURE 4.1   Some Factors Affecting Education before the Civil War   Whose contributions might you add to this figure under the heading "Influential Early Educators and their Ideas?"

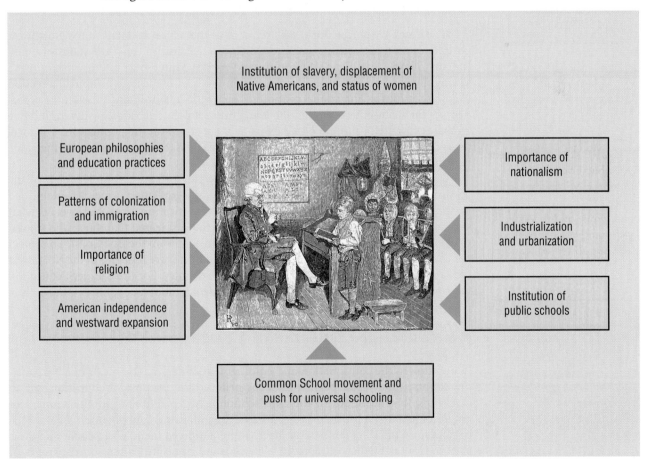

European Americans took this land by trickery and force to improve their own lives and to fulfill what they believed was their divine destiny.

Between 1800 and 1840, the value of agricultural products grew remarkably, largely due to westward expansion and continued immigration to the United States. The increased speed and volume of people heading west can be seen in the following statistic: in 1810, only about one-seventh of the total population lived west of the Appalachians, but by 1840 it was one-third of the total population. To meet the increased demand, the number of farmers increased from about five million to fifteen million during this time (Blum et al., 1997).

In the midst of all this conflict and expansion, the nation's founders believed that education was the best hope for the Republic. Freedom had to be tempered by the need to maintain social order, and education would prepare good citizens. The founders believed virtuous, disciplined, and intelligent citizens would know how to participate responsibly in a democracy. National education leaders Noah Webster (Connecticut), Benjamin Rush (Pennsylvania), and Thomas Jefferson (Virginia) argued that the ability to read, write, and compute numbers would make the people and the nation strong. Jefferson's writings (1931) indicate that he viewed education as the key to advancing civilization.   **What did Jefferson mean when he distinguished between education that is infinite and education that is indefinite?**

> Education . . . grafts a new man on the native stock, and improves what in his nature was vicious and perverse into qualities of virtue and social worth. And it cannot be but that each generation succeeding to the knowledge acquired by all those who preceded it, adding to it their own acquisitions and discoveries, and handing the mass down for successive and constant accumulation, must advance the knowledge, and well-being of mankind, not *infinitely,* as some have said, but *indefinitely,* and to a term which no one can fix and foresee. (p. 250)

The desire to educate for the betterment of the nation is stated in the Northwest Ordinance of 1785, which sliced the Northwest Territories (now the states of Ohio, Indiana, Illinois, Michigan, Wisconsin, and part of Minnesota) into townships, each having thirty-six square miles. As depicted in Figure 4.2, each township had a section of land set aside for educational purposes. The Northwest Ordinance also set the precedent for financing education through **land grant schools.** Each area was given land free of charge (granted), the size of which usually depended on the population. The local government would then use the income from this land to fund schools, thus the name land grant schools.

Most historians recognize the Ordinance as the greatest accomplishment of the government under the Articles of Confederation, the governing principles established by the Continental Congress prior to the U.S. Constitution. Fear, however, is what stimulated passage of the Ordinance. Leaders in the East feared that those who moved to the Northwest would become less civilized than people on the East Coast. To protect the Union, the framers of the Ordinance wanted to make sure residents of the Northwest did not undo democracy from their corner of the country. For these leaders, education meant socialization and the continuation of the democratic values of the young nation.

FIGURE 4.2   A Precedent for Public Education
Under the Northwest Ordinance of 1785, the sixteenth square mile of a township's land grant was reserved for town-supported education.

1 mile

6	5	4	3	2	1
7	8	9	10	11	12
18	17	16	15	14	13
19	20	21	22	23	24
30	29	28	27	26	25
31	32	33	34	35	36

What Were the Aims of Education?

In addition to the continuation and enforcement of democratic ideals in an expanding country, many European Americans believed the purpose of education was to save souls. In general, during this time schooling began at home with the family, and religion was a major aspect of education. In general, Father laid down the rules, keeping an eye on the King James Bible, and Mother enforced them. Formal schooling was patterned after English schools. In New England, legislatures reminded parents of their responsibility for their children's education, but the related laws were not well enforced.

Families and communities sometimes provided schooling for their children at inexpensive **dame schools,** or schools run by women, in the area. Dame schools taught rudimentary skills of reading, writing, and calculating. For some children, particularly girls, this was the only formal education they received. At this point, schools were private, although some received town support, and attendance was voluntary. Most wealthy Americans sent their children abroad for their education.

As the country grew both in population and land size, though, the term *educated* quickly came to mean more than learning God's law. More and more, people began to associate education with personal advancement. In addition, government leaders promoted education as a way to develop informed, wise, and honest people who would help the young democracy succeed. But education for personal advancement and civic participation was rarely extended to women and to non-European populations, such as Native Americans, Africans, and Mexicans. Later, as the nation industrialized and urbanized, education also came to mean occupational training for immigrants and low-income citizens.

The Role of Religion

Is the role of religion any more or less important in schools today than it was in colonial times, or is it merely different? Many religious groups were present in the country at this time, as religious freedom was one of the main reasons why the settlers originally came to America. In a time long before the emergence of an American popular culture, religion occupied a central place in the lives of most citizens. Religion often was a key characteristic by which people identified themselves, and it informed many other areas of their lives, including education. For example, a majority of colonists, particularly in the South, were Protestant. They believed the Scriptures were key to self-determination and to understanding God's will. Simply put, education should help save souls. As early as 1619, Virginia law made religious study on Sunday afternoons standard practice. They taught the Bible.

Except in the New England colonies, where church, state, and school were closely related, there generally was a separation of church and state. Nonetheless, church leaders greatly influenced people's thinking. Some leaders, like Cotton Mather, were among the most prolific writers in America, and some, like Michael Wigglesworth, enjoyed wide readership. Between 1662 and 1701, Wigglesworth's *The Day of Doom,* an account of the Last Judgment, went through five editions (Blum et al., 1997).

In the 1740s religious experiences were brought to thousands of people as stricter and stricter Calvinism beliefs spread among the colonies. George Whitefield, a traveling English preacher, prompted the Great Awakening with his religious revivals. Whitefield combined Calvinism and showmanship as he dramatized the pain that awaited sinners, urging his audience to confess their sins and submit to God. Jonathan Edwards, a minister from Northampton, Massachusetts, was a staunch defender of the Awakening who preached an even stricter Calvinism. His theology suggested that children were inherently evil and in need of strict discipline at home and at school (Blum et al., 1997).

By the nineteenth century the rigid beliefs of orthodox Calvinism began to soften, and Americans adopted

Religious freedom was one of the reasons why the settlers came to America. How do you think religion affected education in the 1700s?

more rational and humanistic views. As strict religious beliefs lessened, so did their in-fluence over educational methods. Many people began to challenge the traditional methods of education and demanded secular (nonreligious) curricula. Transcenden-talist philosophers Henry David Thoreau, Bronson Alcott, and Ralph Waldo Emerson were among those who advocated the radical reform of education. Transcendentalism was a school of thought that valued reason, nature, and humanity. These philosophers were concerned, in particular, with the stifling nature of education. In fact, many of their ideas about teaching methods matched those of Rousseau. According to Emerson (1884),

> Education has so cold, so hopeless a sound. A treatise on education, a convention for education, a lecture, a system, affects us with slight paralysis and a certain yawning of the jaws. . . . Education should be as broad as man. . . . The imagina-tion must be addressed. (p. 133)

Industry Affects Education

Industrialization in the Northeast shaped the character of the nation in the late eigh-teenth and early nineteenth centuries. After 1830, factories grew larger and more com-

Voices

ALEXIS DE TOCQUEVILLE

*I*n 1831, two young Frenchmen—Alexis de Tocqueville and Gustave de Beaumont—traveled to the United States to study the prison system to gain information to reform prisons in France. They were also interested in learning more about American democracy and eager to see the country. The Frenchmen traveled for nine months, as far west as Michi-gan and then south to New Orleans. They spent most of their time in Boston, New York, and Philadelphia. Rich and prominent thinkers of the early nineteenth century warmly welcomed them.

Tocqueville interviewed presidents, lawyers, bankers, and settlers. He recorded his thoughts on America's insti-tutions, its government, and the beliefs and actions of its people, including observations on their religious and educational practices. His book, *Democracy in America,* remains influential today.

> In all the States of the Union, but especially in the half-peopled country of the far West, wandering preachers may be met with who hawk about the word of God from place to place. Whole families—old men, women, and children, cross rough passes and untrodden wilds, coming from a great distance to join a camp meeting, where they totally forget for several days and nights, in listening to these dis-courses, the cares of business and even the most urgent wants of the body.

> Here and there, in the midst of American society, you meet with men, full of a fanatical and almost wild enthusiasm, which hardly exists in Europe. From time to time strange sects arise, which endeavor to strike out extraordinary paths to eternal happi-ness. Religious insanity is very common in the United States. (p. 143)
> "To be mistaken in believing that the Christian religion is true," says Pascal, "is no great loss to anyone, but how dreadful to be mistaken in believing it to be false!" (p. 134)

Alexis de Tocqueville (1805–1859)

Critical Thinking Question

Where might we be most likely to look for and find such enthusiasm for religion in today's schools?

To answer this question online and e-mail your answer to your professor, go to Chapter 4 of the Companion Website (ablongman.com/mcnergney4e) and click on Voices.

Source: Tocqueville, A. (1840). *Democracy in America.* New York: J. & H. G. Langley.

plex. As roads and shipping improved and as transportation costs decreased, people distributed their goods to mass markets.

The Northeast had all the necessary ingredients to become a center for industry: waterpower for factories and mills, iron and coal, and entrepreneurs ready to make the region the manufacturing center of the nation. Engineering marvels, such as the Erie Canal, symbolized people's technical capabilities and passion for economic prosperity. Around this time, federal law permitted people to patent their inventions, and many people took the opportunity to invent machines and products they hoped would make them rich.

While the North propelled itself toward industrialization, the South remained rural and dependent on agriculture for its economic well-being. As more colonists migrated westward into Alabama, Mississippi, and Louisiana, King Cotton continued to dominate southern agricultural life. Once Eli Whitney's cotton gin, a machine that separated seeds from cotton fibers, was invented in 1793, cotton production jumped from about 10,000 bales per year to about 500,000 bales in the 1820s (Blum et al., 1997).

Industrialization in the early nineteenth century led to an increasing emphasis on practical rather than theoretical learning. As industrial work increased, rather than study poetry and philosophy, people wanted to learn mechanics and trade skills that would lead to jobs with a paycheck. In addition, demands for cheap, reliable labor had a direct negative effect on schools' enrollment. Instead of staying in school, women and children met the increased demands for labor in the Northeast by working long hours under extremely difficult conditions. Infant schools, a concept devised by a Welsh cotton-mill owner and social reformer named Robert Owen (1771–1858), gave child factory workers a minimal education and provided an early form of day care for young children of working women. Such schools were designed to meet the mental, physical, and moral development needs of children not yet old enough to work in the factories. **Can you think of examples of industrial demands that influence the form and function of education in today's schools?**

Education for Slaves

The institution of slavery that flourished in the South made the cultures in northern, mid-Atlantic, and southern colonies vastly different from one another. Many people in the northern states, especially the Quakers, fought slavery. By the early nineteenth century, antislavery groups had produced enough pressure to achieve abolition of slavery in the northern states. But the federal Constitution recognized slavery as a local institution within the jurisdiction of individual states, so it continued in the South. For plantation owners, slavery was profitable and provided an unending supply of workers.

In the 1850s nearly half the populations of both Alabama and Louisiana and more than half the population of Mississippi were African slaves. While the number of slaves was high, actually only a few people owned most of the slaves. Three-fourths of southern European American families never owned slaves (Blum et al., 1997).

When the Civil War began in 1861, seven million slaves were living in the southern and western states. By the time the war ended in 1865, there were about four million (the rest having been freed during the war), about 5 percent of whom could read and write (Blum et al., 1997). Both before and after the war, efforts were made to provide slaves with educational opportunities. In the early 1600s, when the slave trade began, English clergy wanted to provide religious training for slaves and made some progress in achieving their goal. Presbyterians went a step further, providing formal training to African Americans to prepare them for religious leadership. In 1740 Hugh Bryan opened his school for African Americans in Charleston, South Carolina. By 1755, the Presbyterian schools had extended to Virginia, where slaves were being taught to read and write.

How was education for slaves a hidden passage to freedom for some African Americans?

During the 1800s, European American missionaries and free African Americans established African schools and black academies in the North and the South. In 1811, Christopher McPherson, a free African American, started an African school in Richmond, Virginia, to teach other free African Americans and slaves. From dusk until 9:30 each night, a European American teacher he had hired taught English, writing, arithmetic, geography, and astronomy for about $1.25 per month. Flush with success, McPherson ran an advertisement for his school in the newspaper. Southerners in positions of authority, however, were not quite as enthusiastic about his efforts. They closed his school as a public nuisance and sent McPherson to the Williamsburg Lunatic Asylum (Berlin, 1974).

Although some educational opportunities for slaves existed, not everyone supported these efforts, as evidenced by the McPherson case. In some southern colonies, laws were created that forbade teaching slaves to read and write. Teaching one or two slaves was not a serious crime, but opening schools for slaves was a different matter. Some colonists justified such laws by persuading themselves that slaves could learn only what was required to perform their menial jobs. Others believed that education would produce slaves who would lead rebellions. In fact, such leadership did evolve. In 1829, David Walker of Wilmington, North Carolina, published his widely read *Appeal*, a bold attack on slavery (Bullock, 1967).

Just before the Civil War, well-educated, vocal freed men and escaped slaves demanded equal rights and privileges. In the 1840s fearful citizens created a list of safe books that reflected the Southern viewpoint. The South Carolina Legislature made it a misdemeanor to teach a slave to write, subject to fine and imprisonment (*The Sun*, 1833, p. 2). Later safe reading lists included a Confederate edition of the New Testament. Many European immigrants in northern cities also feared and hated Africans and non-European immigrants, perceiving them as threats to their jobs and way of life.

Occasionally, slave owners themselves were sources of education for some slaves. Some slave owners placed their slaves with master craftsmen and even helped slaves establish small businesses to help them buy their freedom. Other slaves who did not receive formal education sometimes learned informally from their associations with literate European Americans. When assigned to houses, domestic workers might learn to read from their masters' personal libraries and from studying recipes, music, and the Bible. Slave children also learned from their master's children as they played school with one another, hidden from public view.

Some owners taught their slaves because it was good for business; others educated slaves out of respect and caring. Henry Bullock (1967) called these educational activities the **hidden passage** to freedom—literacy helped slaves to escape bondage and to make lives for themselves after the Civil War. **There are clear historical precedents that suggest education can be a dangerous force. Is there any evidence that such attitudes still exist today?**

Education for Native Americans

Native Americans should be "civilized," that is, taught the ways of European Americans, or so argued many settlers in Revolutionary times. On the other hand, people such as Thomas Jefferson believed that European Americans should intermingle with Native Americans and become one people. However, he also believed that African

Americans did not possess the mental capabilities to achieve equality with European Americans and should probably be resettled elsewhere. As history shows, racial and ethnic inequality and prejudice have been present in America since the first European settlers came ashore.

Assimilation of Native Americans—educating and socializing Native Americans to make them similar to the dominant culture—and their intermarriage with European Americans was rare, however. In fact, Native American tribes made every effort to protect their heritage, customs, and languages. In 1821 a Cherokee named Sequoyah devised an eighty-six character phonetic Cherokee alphabet. A printing press using Sequoyah's type churned out stories, hymns, and even a Bible in Cherokee. A newspaper, *The Cherokee Phoenix,* advanced literacy and knowledge among the tribe. Education of this sort, however, did not protect the Cherokees from the forced relocation and genocide that affected all Native American tribes during the nineteenth century.

Sequoyah (1770?–1843)

In Native American cultures, families bore the primary responsibility for education. Educators and caregivers surrounded Native American children—father and mother, grandparents, older siblings, uncles and aunts, other adults, and specialists, such as weavers, potters, warriors, and shamans (Coleman, 1993). Elders taught children by example, explanation, and imitation (Cremin, 1980). Therefore, formal schooling for Native Americans was a continuation of their education, not a beginning (Barman, Hebert, & McCaskill, 1986).

Overall, traditional Native American education emphasized observation, practice, and self-discipline:

> Close beside my mother I sat on a rug . . . with a scrap of buckskin in one hand and an awl in the other. This was the beginning of my practical observation lessons in the art of beadwork. . . . It took many trials before I learned how to knot my sinew thread on the point of my finger, as I saw her do. . . . The quietness of her oversight made me feel strongly responsible and dependent upon my own judgment. She treated me as a dignified little individual as long as I was on good behavior; and how humiliated I was when some boldness of mine drew forth a rebuke from her! . . . Always after these confining lessons I was wild with surplus spirits, and found joyous relief in running loose in the open again. (Zitkala-Sa, 1921)

During the early nineteenth century, Protestants and Catholics established **mission schools** among the Native Americans to teach English and Christianity. Brainerd Mission in Georgia, for example, tried to prepare the Cherokees for assimilation into the dominant culture. The schoolmaster even gave each child a new English name. The Mission became a self-sufficient society, producing nearly everything students needed to live. By 1830 there were eight such schools. The Brainerd Mission became the most common model for educating other eastern tribes and nations. Many believed such schools were the best answer to "the Indian problem." **Where are modern examples of education as a process of "fitting in" the dominant culture?**

Education in Spain's American Colonies

While Europeans were settling America's Eastern seaboard in the early seventeenth century, the Spanish were establishing colonies in the Southwest. In 1607 the English settled Jamestown in Virginia, and in 1609 the Spanish settled Santa Fe (now New Mexico). In 1790, there were about 23,000 Spanish-speaking people in what is now the southwestern United States. They had migrated north from Mexico, the center of the Spanish conquest. Most of these settlers were of mixed Native American and Spanish descent, Spanish-speaking, and Catholic.

The Church and its missionaries provided what little formal education existed for Mexican Americans in those early years (Manuel, 1965). The schooling was basic and heavily religious, conducted mainly by older men for younger men. But upper-class women, such as Sor Juana Ines de la Cruz (1648–1695), also had access to education:

> I was not yet three years old when my mother sent an older sister of mine to be taught to read at a school. . . . Moved by affection and a mischievous spirit, I followed her; and seeing her receive instruction, such a strong desire to read burned in me that I tried to deceive the teacher, telling her that my mother wanted her to give me lessons. . . . (Hahner, 1976, pp. 22–23)

Sor Juana Ines later studied Latin and became a nun and a writer (Flynn, 1971). Her intellectual abilities made her a favorite of the Spanish viceroy (ambassador) and his wife in Mexico City, and she served as a court poet, successfully debating teachers from the university.

Spanish colonization of the Southwest fulfilled more than one purpose. Priests established mission schools to convert Native Americans to Catholicism and thus affected peaceful conquest of the native people (Fogel, 1988). Junipero Serra, for example, was a Franciscan priest who established missions in the California territory in the 1770s. His missions taught Native Americans how to farm and ranch, while keeping them faithful to the Church. A second purpose for the Spanish missions was to capture and hold territory and resources for Spain, while making it difficult for France and Britain to do the same.

From the beginning of their interaction, the Spanish- and English-speaking peoples in the Southwest fought for control of the land. English-speaking Texans achieved their independence from Mexico in 1836. The United States, in turn, annexed Texas in 1844. In 1846, the United States and Mexico began the Mexican War. It ended two years later with Mexico's defeat and the addition of California, Utah, New Mexico, and other west-

How did Roman Catholic missions and a class system based on racial origins shape the educational experiences of Native Americans and Africans in Spanish colonies?

ern territories to the United States. These struggles, like other grand events in American history, served to educate the people involved. People's attitudes and beliefs about their neighbors were passed from generation to generation and live on even today.

Education for Women

How and why has the role of women in education changed? Women played an insignificant role in the formal education of children in colonial times. In almost every colony, however, records show one or more women being employed as teachers. These women usually taught the younger, poorer children in dame schools. Typically, women taught during the summer months (April to September) and men taught during the winter.

The Quakers in Pennsylvania did not discriminate against women to the degree that other religious sects did, so they were allowed to teach. While they were not paid as well as Quaker schoolmasters, Quaker women comprised a large proportion of the teachers in Pennsylvania (Elsbree, 1939).

The opportunities women had to be educated and their opportunities to be educators appear to have been closely linked during this period. Benjamin Rush, for example, advanced education for women in his 1787 speech "Thoughts upon Female Education." He argued that men spent so much time outside the home working that they could not possibly assume responsibility for teaching the children—women had to do it. If this were so, then women needed to prepare for the task by becoming educated themselves.

Efforts to open up formal education to women continued during the early and mid-nineteenth century. Some of these efforts called for the creation of separate schools and programs for women only. Emma Willard was among several educators who developed academically focused programs for women. In her speech to the New York legislature in 1819, Willard advocated the formation of schools that would teach geography, science, domestic skills, music, and other courses to women. Willard opened such a school in 1821 in Troy, New York. Catherine Beecher, Zilpah Grant, Mary Lyons, and George B. Emerson also established institutions expressly for the purpose of educating women (Deighton, 1971). During the mid-1800s Catherine Beecher borrowed concepts from Swedish gymnastics to introduce young women to calisthenics in order to improve their health, beauty, and strength (Steinhardt, 1992).

On the other side of the argument were people who believed women should not be formally educated. Charles Bathurst, who wrote about the young British women often emulated by women in upper-class American society, believed that women's natural liveliness and feelings ought not to be encouraged. After all, "passion was passion"— one thing could lead to another.

In studies of the foundations of education, the contributions of women traditionally have been downplayed or ignored. For instance, Elizabeth Palmer Peabody, sister-in-law of Nathaniel Hawthorne and Horace Mann, was one of America's most important writers and educational reformers from the Transcendental Movement (Ronda, 1999). Major efforts to improve formal education for women did not occur, however, until the mid-to-late nineteenth century. Until then, the education that most women received, especially those who were not from wealthy families, was informal, in the home, and short-lived.

Education for People with Disabilities

Why do you think attitudes toward people with disabilities have changed so much? The object of many superstitions, people with physical or mental disabilities in the seventeenth and eighteenth centuries most often were confined and forgotten or

Emma Willard
(1787–1870)

Catherine Beecher
(1800–1878)

Elizabeth Palmer Peabody
(1804–1894)

Thomas Gallaudet (1787–1851)

exploited. Clergymen and physicians were among the leaders in providing care and training for people with disabilities. The first permanent, state-supported school in the United States built expressly for the mentally retarded was opened in Syracuse, New York, in 1854.

Many scholars credit Jean-Jacques Rousseau (Figure 4.3) for the ideas that stimulated the development of special education. Rousseau championed the idea of encouraging children to achieve the potential they possess inherently. He wrote of the importance of sensory-motor development in young children, followed by higher intellectual development in their later years. His ideas stimulated Jean-Marc Itard (1775–1838) and Edouard Seguin (1812–1880) in France, Johann Pestalozzi (1746–1827) in Switzerland, Friedrich Froebel (1782–1852) in Germany, and Maria Montessori (1870–1952) in Italy to fit education to a child's natural development.

Samuel Gridley Howe and Thomas Gallaudet both studied abroad in the early 1800s before establishing programs in the United States to educate children with disabilities. Howe taught Laura Bridgmen, a person without sight, hearing, or speech, and achieved international fame. He also taught Anne Sullivan, who later became Helen Keller's teacher. Gallaudet founded the first residential school for the deaf in Hartford, Connecticut. Named after the pioneer in education for people with hearing impairments, Gallaudet College for the Deaf in Washington, D.C., currently is the only college for the deaf in the world.

The development of education programs specially fitted to people's needs is deeply rooted in the past (Hallahan and Kauffman, 2003). Many of today's special education practices can be traced to much earlier ideas, including prescribing instruction based on the child's characteristics, carefully sequencing tasks from simple to complex, emphasizing stimulation of the child's senses, and tutoring in functional skills.

How Did Formal Education Develop in America before the Civil War?

In colonial America, neither teachers nor lawyers required formal training. Academic qualifications of teachers, most of whom were men, ranged from having the ability to read and write to being a college graduate. The more rural the school, and the younger the children, the lower the teacher's qualifications usually were. For the most part, communities were not as interested in a candidate's scholastic preparation as they were in his character and religious orthodoxy. The Scotch Irish in Pennsylvania, for example, insisted that schoolmasters be intelligent and sufficiently pious to teach the principles of Calvinism. In 1750, Pennsylvania Lutherans required the following qualifications:

> That the schoolhouse shall always be in charge of a faithful Evangelical Lutheran schoolmaster, whose competency to teach Reading, Writing, and Arithmetic, and also to play the organ (Orgelschlagen) and to use the English language, has been proved by the pastor; special regard being had at the same time, to the purity of his doctrine and his life. He shall be required to treat all his pupils with impartial fidelity, and to instruct the children of other denominations, and of the neighborhood generally. He shall not allow the children to use profane language either in or out of school; but shall carefully teach them how, both in church and in school, and in the presence of others and upon the highway, to conduct themselves in a Christian and upright manner, and not like the Indians. (Elsbree, 1939, p. 39)

Benjamin Rush expressed another popular view of the roles of schoolmasters and their pupils. He believed the teacher should be an absolute monarch:

> The government of schools . . . should be arbitrary," wrote Rush. "By this mode of education we prepare our youth for the subordination of laws, and thereby qualify

*F*IGURE 4.3   **Braille: Deciphering the Code**

Every character in the Braille code is based on an arrangement of one to six raised dots. Each dot has a numbered position in the Braille cell. These characters make up the letters of the alphabet, punctuation marks, numbers, and everything else you can do in print.

The Braille Cell

1 ○ ○ 4
2 ○ ○ 5
3 ○ ○ 6

The letter *A* is written with only 1 dot.

The letter *D* has dots 1, 4, and 5.

The letter *Y* has dots 1, 3, 4, 5, and 6.

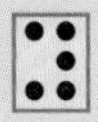

A period is written with dots 2, 5, and 6. (Do you see how it is the same shape as the letter *D*, only lower down in the cell?)

When all six dots are used, the character is called a *full cell*.

The picture below shows you how the dots are arranged in the Braille cell for each letter of the alphabet. See if you can find the letters in your name and tell the dot numbers for each.

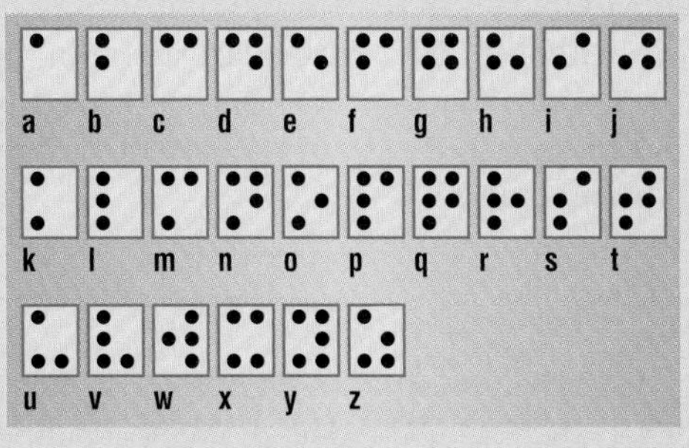

a b c d e f g h i j

k l m n o p q r s t

u v w x y z

Braille does not have a separate alphabet of capital letters as there is in print. Capital letters are indicated by placing a dot 6 in front of the letter to be capitalized. Two capital signs mean the whole word is capitalized.

One letter capitalized    Entire word capitalized

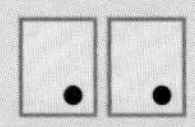

Source: American Federation for the Blind (2002). *Braille: Deciphering the code.* Available online at: http://www.afb.org/braillebug/braille_deciphering.asp

them for becoming good citizens of the republic. I am satisfied that the most useful citizens have been formed from those youth who have never known or felt their own wills till they were one and twenty years of age. . . . (Tyack, 1967, p. 88)

Life in Colonial Schools

Besides their teaching duties, schoolmasters had to perform a variety of duties outside school. In New England, some of the more common tasks included conducting religious services, leading the church choir, sweeping out the meetinghouse, ringing the bell for public worship, and digging graves (Elsbree, 1939). Schoolmasters usually juggled teaching and extra duties with one or more other jobs, ranging from surveying to innkeeping to artisanship. Teaching often was a stepping-stone for other careers, particularly the ministry; as a result, teacher turnover often was quite high (Rury, 1989).

Schoolhouses usually were one-room log or clapboard cabins attended by students from the ages of three to twenty or more. All the students were in a single class, no matter their age or education level. Most often, teaching in these large-group settings meant making students memorize facts. To do so, students had to sit quietly for long periods of time on backless benches until called on by the teachers to recite. Teachers relied on whole-group instruction and choral responses in these mixed-ability classes. The entire system depended on repetition and drill, helped along with a more than healthy dose of punishment (Boyer et al., 2000).

> Eliphalet Nott, who grew up in Connecticut in the 1780s, said, "If I was not whipped more than three times a week, I considered myself for the time peculiarly fortunate. In 1819, six-year-old James Sims was sent to a boarding school in South Carolina where new boys were always flogged, usually until the youngster vomited or wet his breeches." (Kaestle, 1983, p. 19)

During the mid-1800s, occurrences of teacher brutality toward students decreased. Historians attribute this change to the fact that graded schools came into existence. This new arrangement separated older children from younger children, so teachers who had once dealt with as many as one hundred students now dealt with smaller groups. Around this same time, women began entering the teaching profession, and they were not so cruel. In addition, educators such as Pestalozzi set out to explain to teachers the benefits of teaching students to behave in certain ways, instead of beating or coercing them into submission. Some school systems, particularly those in the cities—Syracuse, New York, for example—passed ordinances prohibiting corporal punishment (Elsbree, 1939; Kaestle, 1983). **What do you think about the fact that corporal punishment in schools is still legal in many states?**

Curricula

Curricula in the colonies were based on interpretations of God's preferences and the three Rs. The Old and New Testaments served as the main reading books in the late eighteenth and early nineteenth centuries. Arithmetic students learned from what was around them. Dealing with money, for example, reinforced the importance of math skills.

Students learned to read by first learning their ABCs. Next, they moved on to memorizing vowel sounds, such as *ab, eb, ib, ob, ub,* then one-syllable words, and then longer words and sentences. They practiced on slates with chalk and worked their way up to quill pens and copybooks. Many children studied whatever books their families sent to school with them—books that were jealously guarded. Sometimes teachers had to contend with as many different books as they had children in their schools (Kaestle, 1983).

HORNBOOKS, PRIMERS, AND ALMANACS

The **hornbook** was the first reader for many students. It was a single piece of parchment imprinted with the alphabet, vowels, syllables, and a couple of prayers. To increase its durability, the parchment was covered with a transparent sheet of cow's horn, and the two pieces were tacked to a board. The hornbook was eventually replaced with more elaborate books of several pages.

The *New England Primer* appeared in the late seventeenth century and was the prototype for the **primers**—textbooks designed to teach rudimentary reading skills—widely used in the colonies through the eighteenth century. The *Primer* was a collection of rhymes for the letters of the alphabet, adorned with woodcut drawings. Each rhyme, an admonition or prayer, reflected the religious values of the colonies (Ford, 1899).

Benjamin Franklin left his imprint on the curriculum in the eighteenth century, as he did so often on colonial life. His *Poor Richard's Almanack* extolled the virtues of thrift, hard work, and creativity. The *Almanack,* which became a mainstay in the class-

Issues in School Reform

McGUFFEY READERS

For three-quarters of a century, some 80 percent of all schoolchildren used *McGuffey Readers,* first published in 1836. About 120 million sets were sold. No other books ever had so much influence over so many children over such a long period of time.

McGuffey was intent on reforming education through his step-by-step approach to language instruction. He also taught morals through the content of the stories in his readers. For instance, charity was not expected only of the wealthy; it was a virtue to be cultivated by the young and practiced by all. Here are some of the titles of reading material in the Second, Third, and Fourth *Readers: The Greedy Girl, The Kind Girl, The Honest Boy and the Thief, The Lord's Prayer, The Effects of Rashness, On Speaking the Truth, Consequences of Bad Spelling, Happy Consequences of American Independence,* and *Decisive Integrity.*

Discussion Questions

For years, people have struggled over the teaching of morals or values in public schools. The debate often flares up over the content of instruction. Do you believe the

public schools should explicitly teach values? If so, which values? Do you have ideas about how best to offer such instruction?

To answer these questions online and e-mail your answers to your professor, go to Chapter 4 of the Companion Website (ablongman.com/ mcnergney4e) and click on Issues in School Reform.

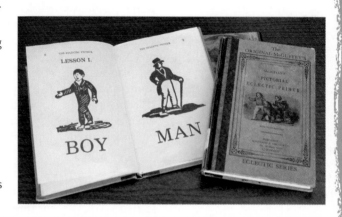

room, served as a sort of philosophical touchstone for the self-made colonist. The *Almanack* often was used in classrooms as a textbook.

GEOGRAPHIES, SPELLERS, AND DICTIONARIES

Jedidiah Morse provided an opportunity for children to think about their cultural identity as Americans when he produced his *Geography Made Easy* in 1784. The book focused on the geography of the United States, rather than on that of Europe or Britain. Much like Franklin's *Poor Richard's Almanack,* it contained patriotic and moralistic themes.

In the late 1700s and early 1800s, Noah Webster promoted a common English language. Webster's *American Spelling Book,* sometimes referred to as the **Blue-Backed Speller,** was first published in 1783; by 1837, fifteen million copies had been sold. Webster's *An American Dictionary,* first published in 1825, became the authoritative source on information about English words. Webster believed that power and prestige as a nation distinct from Britain would never come to the United States until it established its own distinctive vocabulary, spelling, and usage.

MCGUFFEY READERS

William Holmes McGuffey, a clergyman and professor of philosophy, produced his legendary reader in 1836. It was the most widely used reading book in the United States in the nineteenth century. **McGuffey Readers** taught literacy skills and sought to advance the Protestant ethic through stories and essays about thrift, honesty, and diligence. By including speeches of the nation's founders, McGuffey also used his book to promote patriotic nationalism. *McGuffey Readers* are still produced and sold.

Recognizing Educational Success and Failure

School is much more a part of life today than it was in earlier times. From the arrival of the colonists until the Civil War, few people went to school. Those who did attend public schools got a dose of reading, writing, calculating, and the Protestant ethic, and then went their own ways. Most people instead acquired the knowledge necessary to survive and prosper from their families, churches, and work. Because these communities depended on family and church to teach moral values and on work to train young people for occupations, schools were believed successful if they provided rudimentary skills at low cost. Up until about 1840, local communities viewed their schools as quite successful (Kaestle, 1983).

The narrowly defined and severely delivered education in the young nation helped those children who attended—most of whom were white, Protestant, and male—to learn the three Rs and to assimilate Protestant or Catholic values. For young people who were Native Americans, African Americans, immigrants, and living in poor, rural places, schooling, if it existed at all, was a mixed blessing. Public schools saved some of these students from illiteracy, but simultaneously reinforced the idea that one's worth was measured in terms of race and social class.

Various types of schools and educational methods were used from colonial times to just prior to the Civil War. Some schools were open to everyone, others were restricted by gender or wealth. Some were based on European concepts and institutions, others were wholly American. All of them can be seen, however, as steps taken by a new nation toward developing its own concept of successful education.

The Monitorial Method and the American Lyceum

Children started school at different ages. *Abecedarians*—beginners at school—often started as young as age three. Teachers often faced very large groups of students of varying ages who differed markedly in abilities (Kaestle, 1983). The Lancasterian or **monitorial method** of teaching provided one response to this challenge.

In the 1820s Joseph Lancaster, a Quaker, found urban classrooms to be fertile ground for the monitorial method of teaching used in Europe. In this educational pyramid scheme, the master teacher served as a "silent bystander" and "inspector." He taught the monitors, and they, in turn, taught the younger children. The older students also took attendance and kept order in the classroom. The approach made reading, writing, and arithmetic available to large numbers of children, and it was cheap.

The monitorial system was one of the most successful and widely used educational methods of the first thirty years of the nineteenth century. Efficient and easy to use, the monitorial method extended educational opportunities to increasing numbers of children from low-income families. Reformers concerned with the moral training of the poor believed the system might develop obedience, industry, and promptness in these children. At the same time, the Lancasterian system's use of monitors allowed for the training of future teachers (Kaestle, 1983).

In 1826 a wealthy Connecticut farmer, Josiah Holbrook, founded the American Lyceum, an organization devoted to the advancement of education for children and adults. Holbrook wanted to provide an economical and practical education to American youth and to encourage the application of science and education in everyday life. People belonged to a **lyceum** for $1 a year. Types of lyceums included reading circles, debating clubs, and concert bands.

The first branch of the American Lyceum formed in Millbury, Massachusetts. By 1829 the lyceum concept had spread across the country. Ralph Waldo Emerson, a frequent lecturer on the lyceum circuit, considered the American Lyceum a new form of education and a broad cultural movement. This first formal adult and community education movement thrived in the late 1820s and 1830s, but faded in the years following the Civil War.

The Latin School and the English Academy: No Girls Allowed

The **Latin grammar school,** the first formal type of secondary school in the colonies, was established in Boston in 1635. Boys entered the grammar school at age nine or ten, if they could read and write English, and attended for four to five years. Although Latin grammar schools often taught arithmetic, geography, algebra, trigonometry, or rhetoric, their main purpose was teaching Latin, Greek, and the associated literatures. The Latin grammar school was a concept borrowed from Europe, where money and social status meant power and privilege. The very few students who attended college during this time went to Latin grammar schools first. Girls were not admitted.

At the other end of the spectrum was Benjamin Franklin's English-language academy in Philadelphia, which he started in 1749. Franklin recognized the need to prepare young people for highly skilled occupations and for the world of commerce. The classics were not neglected entirely, but the **English academy** emphasized the acquisition and application of practical knowledge believed most useful to the modern man.

The academy originally taught practical subjects such as penmanship, arithmetic, and bookkeeping. Unlike in the Latin grammar school, English was the language of instruction, but students could study other languages as they needed them. Prospective merchants studied French, Spanish, or German, while prospective clergy studied Latin or Greek. Franklin's academy also taught practical skills, such as farming, carving, shipbuilding, carpentry, and printing.

Early Ideas of Public Education

Why have so many political leaders, both past and present, placed such a high premium on the value of public education?   The idea of free public education had its roots in the early Republic. Thomas Jefferson believed it was to society's benefit to educate all of its citizens so they might provide leadership and support for the country. As a member of the Virginia Assembly's Committee to Revise the Laws of the Commonwealth from 1776 to 1779, Jefferson drafted the Bill for the More General Diffusion of Knowledge, a bill he considered one of his finest pieces of work (Cremin, 1980).

The first Latin grammar school was founded in 1635 in Boston.

The bill proposed the establishment of **common schools**—tax-supported schools for reading, writing, arithmetic, and history—that children could attend free for three years and then pay thereafter. The bill also proposed the establishment of twenty grammar schools, in which Latin, Greek, English grammar, and advanced arithmetic would be taught. The brightest students from the lower schools who could not afford to pay tuition would attend these grammar schools at public expense; children whose families could afford to pay would do so. From the grammar schools, ten scholarship students would go on to the College of William and Mary for three years at public expense. Jefferson believed this system of education would allow society to safeguard liberty. Although successful in establishing a public university, Jefferson did not live to realize his dream of publicly supported schools for Virginia's children (Cremin, 1980, pp. 440–441).

The spread of common schools led to sweeping educational reform on a national scale. In the 1830s reformers in the common school movement pressed for a variety of measures: (1) taxation for public education; (2) longer school terms; (3) a focus on getting particular groups of nonattenders enrolled in schools, particularly those living in urban slums and factory tenements and the children of free blacks; (4) hierarchical school organizations (e.g., state education agencies headed by a superintendent, schools headed by a "principal teacher," graded schools); (5) consolidation of small school districts into larger-scale school units so that per-pupil expenditures would be more uniform from district to district; (6) standardization of educational methods and curriculum; and (7) teacher training (Kaestle, 1983).

Primary school enrollment rates increased over time. In the late 1700s and early 1800s, school attendance was higher in rural areas than in the cities. More girls began to go to school, particularly in the Northeast (Kaestle, 1983). Signs of literacy, such as the number of people able to sign their names and the number of newspaper subscriptions, pointed to rapid social change during this period (Cremin, 1970). From the 1600s through the early 1900s, however, no more than 10 percent of eligible school-age children ever went beyond elementary school.

In the 1820s, the public high school emerged as an alternative to the Latin grammar school and the English academy. High schools did not become important in American education, however, until the late 1800s, when courts ruled that people could raise taxes to support such schools (Krug, 1964). With this funding, high schools became public institutions that provided a classical secondary education. In other words, this early high school made available to day students the kind of education previously available only to wealthy boarding-school students (pp. 389–390).

Leaders in the Movement for Universal Education

The tax-supported system of free schools developed in the 1820s, thirty years before the Civil War. The Jeffersonian ideal of **universal schooling,** educating all citizens for the common good, came close to reality, but only for those who were not of African, Native American, and Hispanic descent. At the same time, women, through their own schooling and then by assuming roles as teachers, took advantage of new and socially acceptable opportunities for independence. More specifically, women benefited from the chance to fill jobs that men, for a number of reasons related to the expanding economy, no longer wanted. At least in this respect, progress toward universal education was made.

HORACE MANN

The name most often associated with the development of public schools in this country is Horace Mann (1796–1859). He served as secretary to the Massachusetts State Board of Education from 1837–1848. Mann revolutionized education in the United States by making it the financial responsibility of the state. He established the system of grade

Technology in Practice

THE ORGANIZATION OF AMERICAN HISTORIANS ONLINE

You can do much online to further your professional development by getting actively involved with a professional association. The Organization of American Historians is one great place to start. The online OAH Teaching History Resource Center (http://www.oah.org/teaching/index.html) provides links to and information about publications, resources, and activities for teachers of history.

■ The Organization of American Historians (http://www.oah.org), the American Historical Association (http://www.theaha.org), and the National Council for the Social Studies (http://www.ncss.org) sponsor national history conferences, which often focus on school–university collaborative innovations.

■ The Center contains information about grant programs from the U.S. Department of Education. In 2002, some $50 million was available for projects around the country to raise student achievement by improving teachers' knowledge, understanding, and appreciation of American history.

■ "Teaching the Journal of American History" (http://www.indiana.edu/~jah/teaching/) uses online tools to bridge the gap between the latest scholarly research in U.S. history and the practice of classroom teaching. JAH authors demonstrate how featured articles might be taught.

■ "Talking History," a national syndicated radio show sponsored in part by the OAH, features leading historians discussing a variety of topics. Visit the website (http://www.oah.org/activities/

talkinghistory) to access broadcasts available through the Internet.

Discussion Question

How might a teacher incorporate such materials to enrich students' understanding of history?

To answer this question online and e-mail your answers to your professor, go to Chapter 4 of the Companion Website (ablongman.com/mcnergney4e) and click on Technology in Practice.

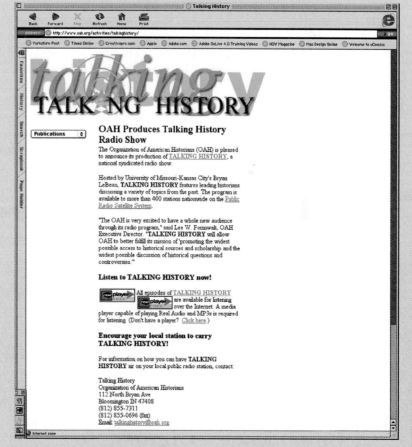

---

levels by age and performance, extended the school calendar from two or three months to ten, standardized textbooks, and made attendance mandatory (Boyer et al., 2000).

HENRY BARNARD

With Horace Mann, Henry Barnard (1811–1900) led the struggle for the common school. A journalist by training, Barnard served in various government positions related to education across the Northeast. He wrote about public education and European educational reformers such as Pestalozzi and Froebel in the *Connecticut Common School Journal* and the *American Journal of Education*. Barnard praised the teaching of civic values and basic skills, but he believed the most important subject was the English language. He wanted strong teacher preparation and enough pay to get good teachers and keep them, and he built public support for such actions.

Henry Barnard also promoted the concept of the public high school. He argued that primary schools were not up to the task of providing the intellectually rigorous education that students needed. He also believed that, by reaching out to students over a larger geographical area, the high school would serve the public better than private schools did. The high school "must make a good education common in the highest and best sense of the word common—common because it is good enough for the best, and cheap enough for the poorest family in the community" (Barnard, 1857, p. 185).

The Development of Parochial Schools

Protestants were the dominant religious group during colonial times, but there was great diversity in religious preferences. Of the 260 churches existing in 1689, 71 were Anglican, 116 Congregational, 15 Baptist, 17 Dutch Reformed, 15 Presbyterian, 12 French Reformed, 9 Roman Catholic, and 5 Lutheran. There were also loosely organized groups of Quakers, Mennonites, Huguenots, Anabaptists, and Jews (Cremin, 1970). Depending on their religious beliefs, different groups had unique ideas about the education of children, so they established parochial schools, or private schools with religious affiliations.

German Lutherans, for example, wanted to protect their language and way of life. By 1840 there were more than two hundred Lutheran parochial schools in Pennsylvania. In 1856, in return for a rent-free house, firewood, a salary of $12 per month, plus extra pay for baptisms and marriages, Lutheran minister Edmond Multanowski preached and taught members of his congregation for six hours a day, nearly eleven months a year in Carlinville, Illinois (Cremin, 1980). Groups such as the Amish and Mennonites also educated their own children and did not send them to common schools. Parents were fearful that outside influences might corrupt their sons and daughters.

In the 1840s, Catholic leaders protested the use of the King James Bible in the common schools. They also fought against the religious and ethnic slurs aimed at Irish Catholics, in particular, in the common schools. The climate was right for the establishment of their own alternative school system—one that has since grown to be the largest alternative to public education in the world. John Hughes, bishop of New York, admonished his parishioners "to build the schoolhouse first, and the church afterwards" (Lannie, 1968). By 1865, Catholic schools were teaching 16,000 students, or about one-third of the Catholic school population, in New York (Dolan, 1985).

Catholics, Lutherans, Amish, Mennonites, and others wanted to protect their children and their ways of life, as did the general public. Reformers in the common-school movement, however, viewed parochial schools as the greatest possible threat to democracy. In their minds, "the goals of a common-school system—moral training, discipline, patriotism, mutual understanding, formal equality, and cultural assimilation—could not be achieved if substantial numbers of children were in independent schools" (Kaestle, 1983, p. 116). **Why might some have viewed parochial schools as a threat to democracy?**

The Growth of Institutions of Higher Education

Oxford and Cambridge, the most prestigious universities in England, served as models of higher education for the colonists. Only six years after the Puritans landed in Massachusetts, they founded the college that was later named after its first benefactor, John Harvard (see Figure 4.4). Harvard students studied the liberal arts and sciences: Latin, Greek, Hebrew, mathematics, logic, rhetoric, astronomy, physics, metaphysics, and philosophy. The other colonial colleges that formed also promoted the idea that higher education prepared young men for lives of leadership.

As for training teachers, most prepared on the job in schools and did not attend college. Usually, new teachers first served as apprentices to teachers who had instructed them. Occasionally, they would read a textbook or attend a teachers' institute meant to transmit some new bit of scientific knowledge about teaching and learning. The first of these institutes, established by Henry Barnard at Hartford, Connecticut, in the autumn of 1839, provided six weeks of instruction focused on instructional strategies and curriculum to twenty-six young men (Cremin, 1980; Elsbree, 1939).

Private **seminaries**—academies for girls—were the primary means for advancing the skills of future teachers. In 1823 Samuel R. Hall opened a seminary with a model school at Concord, Vermont. That same year Catherine and Mary Beecher, sisters of Harriet Beecher Stowe, opened a seminary for young women in Hartford, Connecticut, that eventually became the Hartford Female Seminary. They taught grammar, geography, rhetoric, philosophy, chemistry, ancient and modern history, arithmetic, algebra, geometry, theology, and Latin (Cross, 1965). In 1827 James G. Carter, with the help of local citizens, established a teachers' seminary at Lancaster, Massachusetts. At about the same time, James Neef founded the New Harmony Community School in New Harmony, Indiana, where he introduced Pestalozzi's ideas about teaching and learning (Elsbree, 1939).

In response to the need for more teacher training programs, state-subsidized seminaries and academies began to evolve. Gradually, private and semiprivate institutions gave way to public teacher training schools called **normal schools.** Public school proponent Horace Mann opened the first normal school in Lexington, Massachusetts, in 1839 (Elsbree, 1939). Prospective teachers entered normal schools and were trained to meet high standards or "norms," hence the name. Mann borrowed the idea from the Germans, French, and English—all of whom had such schools for over one hundred years. In 1850, only a few normal schools existed in the United States, preparing young women to teach. In the years to come, however, they would flourish across the nation (Elsbree, 1939; Kaestle, 1983).

Another federal law that influenced public education was the Morrill Act (1862), which provided federal assistance for the establishment of colleges of agriculture and the mechanic or industrial arts. The act granted each state 30,000 acres of public land for each of its congressional representatives. The income from the grant went to support at least one state land grant college devoted to agricultural and mechanical instruction. The Morrill Act emphasized the importance of applied science and made higher education accessible to millions of people in the years that followed. Like the Northwest Ordinance of 1785, it foreshadowed major federal involvement in education.

*F*IGURE 4.4 **Founding of the Colonial Colleges**

How was teacher education different from college education in the 1700s?

Founding of the Colonial Colleges	
1636	Harvard
1693	William and Mary
1701	Yale
1746	Princeton
1754	Columbia
1755	Pennsylvania
1766	Brown
1766	Rutgers
1769	Dartmouth

*S*ummary

We might think about early American education as a classic psychology exercise: Is the glass half empty or half full? Our ancestors made plenty of mistakes. All sorts of negative words and phrases leap to mind in regard to education in our nation's infancy: neglectful, boring, biased, inequitable, mean-spirited, and so on. People who received even some formal education in those early days might well have thought they were the losers, even though they were among the privileged.

There are so many stories of courage and educational success, however, that the glass also appears to be overflowing. Opportunities to "get ahead," however they were defined, became increasingly dependent on what people knew and what they were able to do, not on what their name was or where they came from. Education, previously a largely informal system, began to grow visible as a reasonably well marked path to a better life. Historical forces were converging to widen the path so many people could travel it together. Despite fits and starts, our system of universal public education was to become the envy of the world.

Terms and Concepts

assimilation   99
Blue-Backed Speller   105
common schools   108
dame schools   95
English academy   107
hidden passage   98
hornbook   104
kindergarten   89
land grant schools   94
Latin grammar school   107

lyceum   106
McGuffey Readers   105
mission schools   99
monitorial method   106
normal schools   111
parochial schools   92
primers   104
seminary   111
universal schooling   108

Reflective Practice

Eliza Pinckney

Elizabeth "Eliza" Lucas Pinckney was born on the British island of Antigua in the West Indies in 1722 to a British soldier and his wife. For her mother's health, she and her family later moved to South Carolina, where her father owned three plantations. When her father was recalled to Antigua to serve as a royal governor, Eliza, at age sixteen, was placed in charge of her father's plantations.

Eliza ran a school on the plantations for the family's young slaves and was close friends with others who believed in the cause of "negro" education. She also was an avid reader, scientist, and musician,

Eliza was continually experimenting to see if a particular crop would grow well in South Carolina. She experimented with flax, hemp, and silk culture. In about 1740, she grew indigo with seeds sent by her father. Indigo had been used for thousands of years to make a beautiful blue dye. Her early efforts were failures, but by 1744 she succeeded, and she shared her methods with others. The crop eventually became the main cash crop in South Carolina.

Eliza married Charles Pinckney and had two sons who fought in the Revolutionary War with the Continental army. Both of them signed the Declaration of Independence. Eliza Pinckney died at age 71 in Philadelphia where she had gone for cancer treatment. George Washington was one of her pallbearers.

Issues, Problems, Dilemmas, Opportunities

What special challenges do you think Eliza Pinckney encountered as a female landowner during these times in this place?

Perceive and Value

Pinckney once told her son that the welfare of their whole family depended greatly on their moral virtue, religion, and learning. She told him he must fortify himself "against those Errors into which you are most easily led. . . . What I most fear for you is heat of temper. . . ." Moral weakness was a pervading theme in early America. Certainly, the times and prevailing religious beliefs accounted for this circumstance. Yet, guilt also had practical value. How might a wily landowner have wielded the force of guilt to advance her power over others?

Know and Act

Most of us do not "do science" as Pinckney did in her day. We rely on others—specialists—to do the kind of scientific investigation of which we are incapable. Eliza and others in the colonies had no choice but to be "generalists" who identified and solved their own problems in a variety of areas. What do you believe has been lost and what has been gained in the evolution of specialists in our society? How has this evolution affected the role of teachers?

Evaluate

Life in colonial times was uncomplicated in some ways, but difficult in many others. Do you think educational success and failure were easier or more difficult to identify than they are today?

INTASC Principle 8

The teacher understands and uses formal and informal assessment strategies to evaluate and ensure the continuous intellectual, social, and physical development of the learner.

Disposition

The teacher values ongoing assessment as essential to the instructional process and recognizes that many different assessment strategies, accurately and systematically used, are necessary for monitoring and promoting student learning. (Interstate New Teacher Assessment and Support Consortium, 1992)

Discussion Questions

What forms of informal assessment did Eliza use on her plantations? What similar forms of assessment might you use in a classroom?

Additional Readings

Cremin, L. A. (1970). *American education: The colonial experience, 1607–1783.* New York: Harper & Row.

Handlin, O. (1991). *Boston's immigrants, 1790–1880: A study in acculturation,* Enlarged Edition. Cambridge, MA: Harvard University Press

Hoff, D. J. (2002). History of math instruction retold through new Smithsonian exhibit. *Education Week.* Available online: http://www.edweek.org/ew

Morgan, Harry (1995). *Historical perspectives on the education of black children.* Westport, CT: Praeger.

Parkerson, D. H., & Parkerson, J. A (1998). *The emergence of the common school in the U.S. countryside.* Lewiston, NY: Mellen Press.

Ronda, B. A. (1999). *Elizabeth Palmer Peabody: A reformer in her own terms.* Cambridge, MA: Harvard University Press.

Web Resources

http://www.ilt.columbia.edu/academic/digitexts/locke/bio_JL.html

Learn more about the English philosopher John Locke.

http://www.nwhp.org

Here is a view of the world of women's history.

http://jefferson.village.virginia.edu/vshadow2/choosepart.html

The Valley of the Shadow explores two communities, one northern and one southern, through the American Civil War.

http://lcweb.loc.gov/homepage/lchp.html

The Library of Congress is a must for teachers in every discipline.

http://www.masterstech-home.com/ASLDict.html

This site contains a basic dictionary of American Sign Language terms.

http://www.afb.org

Information on Braille.

Video**Workshop** Extra!

If the VideoWorkshop package was included with your textbook, go to Chapter 4 of the Companion Website (ablongman.com/mcnergney4e) and click on VideoWorkshop. Follow the instructions for viewing video clips 3 and 4. Then consider this information along with what you've read in Chapter 4 while answering the following questions.

1. What connections can you make between the concept of service learning presented in video clip 3 and the history of the public school movement discussed in the chapter? Use examples to support your ideas.

2. Do you detect any patterns in how the aims of education (as discussed in the chapter) have changed over the years? How does a law like PL 94–142, as presented in video clip 4, fit into the pattern?

*E*ducation in America: Then and Now

CHAPTER CONTENTS

How Did Educational Life Change after the Civil War?

Who Are "We the People"?

How Did Teaching Change after the Civil War?

How Did Schools Change during the Modern Era?

Why Was Curriculum So Important?

How Do We Typically Judge Educational Success and Failure?

*I*t's almost irresistible. You see a faded old photo, and you want to slip through its surface to visit the folks peering at you across the decades. You can practically hear the clop of hooves as horses take children to a prairie schoolhouse and smell potatoes roasting in the potbellied stove at the back of the classroom. The students who put on their finery for school picture day had no idea that they would raise questions for viewers generations later. What would the girl in the frilly dress say about her teacher? What's it like for that rumpled boy in a huge Chicago high school, circa 1940? When they're not being photographed, do the kids seated at wooden desks obediently recite their lessons or slump down in adolescent petulance? (Weiner, 2002)

This chapter describes education in the United States from 1865 to the present. It provides a historical overview of slavery and the reconstruction of the South after the Civil War; of calls for educational and social reform; of the influence of science, philanthropy, and the mass media on education; and of federal involvement in schooling.

How Did Educational Life Change after the Civil War?

When the Civil War ended, people had to rebuild the nation. Slavery was abolished and with it went a set of social customs that had governed people's conduct in both the North and the South. There was no blueprint for how people would live and work together. During this time of transition, leaders and ordinary citizens redefined education both inside and outside schools. Several events and reform efforts also changed the nature of education in the United States (see Figure 5.1.).

Ending Slavery and Reconstructing the South

People's passion for intellectual freedom and civil liberties grew stronger after the Civil War. The Thirteenth, Fourteenth, and Fifteenth Amendments to the U.S. Constitution ended slavery, defined citizenship, and forbade states to deny

FIGURE 5.1   Some Factors Affecting Education in the Modern Era   Which factors do you think have had the greatest effect on your schooling?

End of Slavery
Constitutional Amendments
Landmark Supreme Court Decisions

Industrialization & Urbanization
New Immigration & Greater Cultural Diversity
Greater Federal Involvement in Education

Reconceptualizations of Schooling, e.g.:
  Preschools
  Middle Schools
  Comprehensive High Schools
  Adult Education

Progressive Social & Educational Reforms
Research on Human Behavior, Psychology, & Learning
Professionalization of Teaching

Developments in Science & Technology
Philanthropy & the Mass Media
Consolidation & Bureaucratization of Schools

National & International Events, e.g.:
  Great Depression
  World Wars
  Civil & Equal Rights Movements
  Space Race & Cold War

Curriculum Reforms, e.g.:
  Standardization
  Diversification
  Innovation
  Evaluation

nonwhite men the right to vote. The customs of segregation and discrimination, however, remained. Northerners moved to reconstruct and reeducate the South to fit their own vision. Not surprisingly, Southerners detested and resisted these actions.

The **Freedman's Bureau,** established one month before the end of the war, provided food, medicine, and seed to destitute southerners. The Bureau secured legal rights for freed slaves and created educational opportunities for them. Hundreds of northern teachers went south to teach African American children and adults. Despite opposition, the Freedman's Bureau succeeded in establishing and operating more than 4,000 primary schools, seventy-four normal schools, and sixty-one industrial schools for former slaves. The Bureau was another step toward strengthening the role of the federal government in education (Degler, 1959).

After the war, Southerners constructed **black codes** of conduct to keep "Negroes" in an inferior position. These codes, which were "halfway stations back to slavery," allowed African Americans to hold property, to sue and be sued, and to marry. On the other hand, the codes forbade them to carry firearms, to testify in court in cases involving European Americans, and to leave their jobs (Degler, 1959, p. 211).

So, while the Civil War was over, violence toward African Americans was not. Although precise numbers are impossible to determine, between 1865 and 1900, approximately 2,500 lynchings occurred, and the victims were mainly African Americans. Between 1900 and 1914, the start of World War I, more than 1,100 African Americans are known to have been lynched. Most of the lynchings happened in the South, but some took place in midwestern states (Franklin, 1967). After the start of World War I, lynchings were more rare, but they continued into the 1950s. In 1934 the **National Association for the Advancement of Colored People (NAACP)** was formed as the first nationwide special-interest group for African Americans. The NAACP lobbied for an antilynching bill, but the legislation failed to pass during the Roosevelt and Truman administrations of the 1940s and 1950s.

We Need Educational and Social Reform

Why were national development and education so closely linked in the nineteenth century? Why do they remain so closely linked today? The push for universal education that began in the 1830s gained momentum throughout the twentieth century. In 1867, Congress created a Department of Education, largely in response to pressure from the National Teachers Association. President Andrew Johnson appointed Henry Barnard to be commissioner of education and to run the department. The commissioner collected statistics and facts on education and tried to promote the cause of education throughout the country.

By the beginning of the twentieth century, critics increased pressure on public schools, particularly in the cities. Social reformers, sometimes called muckrakers, wrote about mechanical teaching and learning methods, administrative ineptitude, and parents' lack of interest in their children's welfare. Joseph Mayer Rice (1969), for instance, thought that the environment of the New York City schools was nothing short of evil: "children [are] in class-rooms the atmosphere of which is not fit for human beings to breathe, and in the charge of teachers who treat them with a degree of severity that borders on barbarism" (p. 11).

Leonard Ayres's *Laggards in Our Schools* (1909) presented what he claimed was scientific evidence that schools were filled with retarded children or children who were too old for their grade. He blamed this condition on the schools for focusing on unusually bright children and ignoring the slow or average children.

In the early twentieth century, even more problems plagued schools: an antievolution crusade, anti-immigration movements, organized campaigns against Roman Catholics, and increases in anti-Semitism, to mention but a few. In addition, people continued to exploit children as a source of cheap labor in the rapidly expanding industrial economy. To a large extent, the desire to end such abuses encouraged the development of public schools and the organization of labor. The existence of schools and mandatory attendance laws protected children by educating them and keeping them from working. In doing so, schools also protected jobs for adults.

Science and Philanthropy Combine to Educate

If science and money fueled industrialization in the nineteenth century, then the same combination of forces could fix education in the twentieth century, or so people believed. Studies on scientific management, or a system for getting greater productivity from human labor, appealed to the businessmen who ran the school boards who, in turn, hired the superintendents who ran the schools (Callahan, 1962). Encouraged by grants from private foundations, leaders in school administration encouraged educational specialization and scientific management (Tyack & Hansot, 1982).

Early scientific research in the areas of teaching and learning began to take root in schools at the turn of the century. An increase in testing for mental ability was one of the first results of the new, more scientific approach to education. Psychologist James Cattell introduced mental tests to assess people's individual differences. He then encouraged counseling agencies and schools to incorporate such tests as part of their routine procedures. The work of psychologists Alfred Binet, Lewis Terman, and, later, Edward L. Thorndike on the measurement of intelligence was hailed as a great practical advance for schools (Travers, 1983).

Other ideas about education also gained popularity. For instance, psychologist Charles Judd emphasized the importance of viewing teaching and learning as social constructs, that is, as ideas that derive meaning from their use in everyday life. In contrast, John Watson viewed behavior and learning as mechanical phenomena—elements to be manipulated continually by outside sources. His ideas prompted a revolution in the way people thought about human behavior. Although strikingly different in philosophical persuasions, these researchers all believed in the power of science to improve the human condition.

From the late nineteenth century on, society placed a premium on the value of education not only for students but for the general public as well. Several fine-art museums opened in 1870s, including New York's Metropolitan Museum of Art and Boston's Museum of Fine Arts. The Library of Congress opened its Jefferson Building in 1897, permitting wide public access to its book collection (Cole, 1979). By 1900 more than forty-five million volumes were housed in more than nine thousand public libraries across the country (Blum et al., 1997).

One reason for the increase in public works aimed at public education during this time was donations from philanthropists who profited from the industrial revolution. Andrew Carnegie and Andrew Mellon, for example, donated money for promoting public access to books and art and for establishing philanthropic foundations. Northern capitalists, such as merchant Robert Ogden, railroad man William Baldwin, and oil magnate John D. Rockefeller, also funded educational projects in the South, where industry did not have the same financial impact that it did in the North.

In 1936 the Ford Foundation, started by the Ford Motor Company, began programs intended to strengthen democratic values, reduce poverty and injustice, and advance international cooperation. Since its inception, the Ford Foundation has given some $9.3 billion in support of educational and social causes. The philanthropic spirit in education continues today, and in 2002 the William H. Gates III Foundation, which supports educational endeavors, had assets of $24.2 billion.

Learning from Mass Media

How do people learn from what they have around them? The press was a particularly powerful instrument of social education in the twentieth century. Newspapers

Voices

LEWIS TERMAN AND WALTER LIPPMAN

*W*orld War I stimulated the development of technology in many areas, including psychology and testing. Lewis Terman, a cognitive psychologist best known for his studies of intelligence, presented a model for the Army Alpha—a multiple-choice intelligence test for soldiers. Scores on the test disturbed some people when they found out that, intellectually, Americans were a nation of fourteen-year-olds. This reaction led to a debate between Terman and the journalist Walter Lippman in the 1920s about the nature and measurement of intelligence.

Lippman: Suppose you wished to judge all the pebbles in a large pile of gravel for the purpose of separating them into three piles, the first to contain the extraordinary pebbles, the second the normal pebbles, the third the insignificant pebbles. You have no scales. You first separate from the pile a much smaller pile and pick out a pebble which you guess is the average. You hold it in your left hand and pick up another pebble in your right hand. The right pebble feels heavier. You pick up another pebble. It feels lighter. You pick up a third. It feels still lighter. A fourth feels heavier than the first. By this method you can arrange all the pebbles from the smaller pile in a series running from the lightest to the heaviest. You thereupon call the middle pebble the standard pebble, and with it as a measure you determine whether any pebble in the larger pile is a subnormal, a normal or a supernormal pebble.

This is just about what the intelligence test does. It does not weigh or measure intelligence by any objective standard. It simply arranges a group of people in a series from best to worst by balancing their capacity to do certain arbitrarily selected puzzles, against the capacity of all the others. The intelligence test, in other words, is fundamentally an instrument for classifying a group of people. It may also be an instrument for measuring their intelligence, but of that we cannot be at all sure unless we believe that M. Binet and Mr. Terman and a few other psychologists have guessed correctly when they invented their tests. They may have guessed

correctly but . . . the proof is not yet at hand. (Lippman, 1922, p. 247)

Terman: Mr. Walter Lippman, alone and unaided [has challenged the value of intelligence tests].

What have intelligence tests done that they should merit such a fate? Well, what have they not done? They have [shown]:

1. That the strictly average representative of the genus homo is not a particularly intellectual animal;

2. That some members of the species are much stupider than others;

3. That school prodigies are usually brighter than school laggards;

4. That college professors are more intelligent than janitors, architects than hod-carriers, railroad presidents than switch-tenders; and (most heinous of all)

5. That the offspring of socially, economically and professionally successful parents have better mental endowment, on the average, than the offspring of said janitors, hod-carriers and switch-tenders. (Terman, 1922, p. 116)

Critical Thinking Questions

Intelligence tests gained credence in part because they seemed to be better methods for classifying people than the alternatives—birthright, wealth, social status, physical appearance, strength, political connections, and so on. Assume for a moment that there was a time when you found it desirable to classify people, for instance, to admit them to college or to assign them jobs in the military. If you had a magic intelligence test, one that was error-free, would you use it? If not, how else might you classify people? Can you explain how a teacher's beliefs about intelligence might affect her or his teaching?

 To answer these questions online and e-mail your answer to your professor, go to Chapter 5 of the Companion Website (ablongman. com/mcnergney4e) and click on Voices.

and magazines catered to the masses, often by appealing to readers' love of adventure or scandal. The sensationalism of the "yellow press" of New York City—the front pages of special editions were printed on yellow paper to catch the potential reader's eye—led by William Randolph Hearst and Joseph Pulitzer shaped American opinion on education and just about every other subject.

From 1885 to 1900, the number of periodicals published in the United States increased by 2200. By 1905 there were twenty 10¢ monthlies, with a combined circulation of 5.5 million (Blum et al., 1997). From 1920 to 1940, "newspapers and magazines continued to rival schools and churches as the chief instruments of mass education and the dissemination of ideas" (Link & Catton, 1963, p. 295).

By 1930, the United States was in an economic depression. At the same time, new communications technology was fast becoming a part of daily life. About twenty-three thousand motion picture theaters with a combined seating capacity of more than eleven million were spread across the country (Link & Catton, 1963). Especially in the midst of a national depression, movies lured people from their everyday troubles. The more subtle educational influences of the movies—their power to foster dreams of how people wanted to live—would become an enduring national issue.

Radio also captured Americans' imaginations in the 1920s, 1930s, and 1940s. The first radio broadcast was made in 1920. Just two year later, there were 220 radio stations, and by 1923 more than 2.5 million radios were scattered around the country. Approximately 80 percent of American families had radios in their homes by 1937 (Link & Catton, 1963).

Radios educated by delivering live voices of famous people into listeners' homes; television added images to these voices. Television, like radio, also increased the speed with which people heard news from home and abroad. By January 1960, nine out of ten homes in the United States had television sets, competing with, contradicting, and complementing teachers and parents. Today, American adolescents (twelve- to thirteen-year-olds) spend about 20 percent of their waking time studying in school or at home. They spend almost as much time (18 percent) being with friends, 6 percent watching television, 4 percent playing games and sports, 2 percent listening to music, and 3 percent reading magazines and books (Csikszentmihalyi, 2000).

Has time in front of the television been well spent, educationally speaking? There is no consensus on an answer. By the turn of the twenty-first century, however, evidence of the undesirable effects of TV viewing, particularly in terms of aggressive behavior in children, was substantial. Brad Bushman, a professor of psychology at Iowa State University at Ames, sees of cause for concern:

> The correlation between violent media and aggression is larger than the effect that wearing a condom has on decreasing the risk of HIV. It's larger than the correlation between exposure to lead and decreased IQ levels in kids. It's larger than the effects of exposure to asbestos. It's larger than the effect of secondhand smoke on cancer. (Vedontom, 2002, p. A01)

Federal Influence on Education

Why do people argue that the federal government must be heavily and directly involved in education, while others are so adamantly opposed to the idea?   Although it began in the 1800s, federal involvement in education became even more direct in the late 1950s, when the Supreme Court ruled that racial segregation in schools was unconstitutional. Schools became front-page news once again in the 1960s as they became battlegrounds in the war on poverty and the quest for racial equality. In the twentieth century, the federal government exerted its influence in education with money, legislation, and ideology in many arenas: desegregation, aid to schools serving children of low-income families, legislation guaranteeing racial and sexual equity, new entitlements for students with disabilities, bilingual–bicultural programs, and career education.

The most dramatic example of federal involvement was the **Elementary and Secondary Education Act (ESEA) of 1965.** The ESEA made the federal government the center of policy-making power; previously, states and localities had been the center. The act also provided funds and support for poverty programs, school libraries, textbooks and other instructional materials, counseling and health services, and remedial instruction. Research centers and laboratories to advance educational practice also were established with funds provided by the ESEA.

The New Federalism of the 1980s, under Presidents Ronald Reagan and George Bush, returned power and financial responsibility for educational programs back to individual states and localities. As federal support for education shrank in terms of actual money, talk of educational reform increased. Commissions and task forces on the national, state, and local levels called for changes in everything from how public schools are organized and schoolbooks are written to how teachers and students are taught and tested.

In the twenty-first century thus far, federal involvement in public education means maintaining existing programs and trying to improve educational practice through performance standards. The common views today are public schools are not good enough and something must be done to make them better. Setting higher academic standards is one way to raise the educational achievement of students (Jennings, 1998). But just what those standards are and how they are met are issues up for debate.

Who Are "We the People"?

The United States is one nation containing many people—*e pluribus unum*. If in no other way, we the people are similar because we are different: nearly one in four Americans in the United States is a member of an ethnic or racial minority group (Fuchs, 1990).

After the Civil War, the population of the United States grew rapidly in cities and other industrialized areas. In the 1890s about 30 percent of the population (63 million) lived in cities; by 2000, about 80 percent of the country's people lived in urban areas (U.S. Census, 2002). Although the population of the United States grew 200 percent be-

In the late nineteenth and early twentieth centuries, the children of many industrial workers often left school to work in factories.

tween 1859 and 1914, the number of workers in manufacturing jobs increased 650 percent (U.S. Census Bureau, 1975).

The late nineteenth and early twentieth centuries were particularly hard times for industrial workers. In 1910 about one-half of the men and women in the labor force lived in poverty. They worked long hours for meager wages, and their children often left school to work in factories. Only one-third of the enrolled children finished primary school; less than one-tenth finished high school.

Social reformers, nearly all of them women, worked on behalf of low-income people in various cities and industry centers. They investigated sweatshops and tenements and established settlement houses in poor neighborhoods to help immigrants adjust to life in a new country. The first of these houses was established in 1886 in New York City; by 1910, there were four-hundred such houses (Carlson, 1975). Jane Addams's Hull House in Chicago had an education program that included playgrounds, a nursery, and a library.

Life was difficult in rural areas too. The 1930 census indicated that tenant farmers and their families constituted 64 percent of the population in Alabama and 66 percent in Georgia (Dabney, 1969). *Let Us Now Praise Famous Men* was James Agee's 1960 account of the lives of three tenant farm families in Alabama. Accompanied by Walker Evans's photographs, the book created a classic documentation of the period and included the families' educational needs:

> They learn the work they will spend their lives doing, chiefly of their parents, and from their parents and from the immediate world they take their conduct, their morality, and their mental and emotional and spiritual key. One could hardly say that any further knowledge or consciousness is at all to their use or advantage, since there is nothing to read, no reason to write, and no recourse against being cheated even if one is able to do sums. (p. 268)

Poverty has been a chronic and painful condition in the United States. Even though more people go to school each year, poverty dominates the lives of millions. The rates today are the lowest they have been since the early 1970s, but more than thirty-one million people live in poverty. In 2001, the official federal poverty guideline for a family of four was an annual income of $17,650. Researchers suggest that a basic family budget for a two-parent, two-child family ranges from $27,005 a year to $52,114, depending on the community. The national median of $33,511 is roughly equal to twice the national poverty line (Catholic Campaign for Human Development, 2002).

If President Franklin Roosevelt was right when he said that a nation's compassion can be measured in how it treats its children and its elderly, what grade would you give us?

Native Americans

After the Civil War, Native Americans suffered wars with settlers and the government, the destruction of the buffalo, the expansion of railroads, confinement on reservations, and theft of their land. As Helen Hunt Jackson noted, the official abuse and neglect of Native Americans shaped *a century of dishonor*. Writing in the late nineteenth century, Jackson (1880/1977) estimated that 250,000 to 300,000 Native Americans lived in the United States, excluding those in Alaska.

The **Bureau of Indian Affairs (BIA),** established in 1824, was a government agency founded to "educate" Native Americans. Off-reservation boarding schools were meant to help Native Americans survive, but they also served to destroy their culture. Besides taking children away from their families, the schools used food, dress, regimented schedules, religion, and job and language training to impose on them the values and customs of the dominant European American culture. Students were compelled to learn English and to "breathe the atmosphere of a civilized instead of a barbarous or

Indian boarding schools were conceived as a humanitarian way to help Native American children assimilate into the culture of the United States. How did these boarding schools do more harm than good?

semi-barbarous community" (U.S. Bureau of Indian Affairs, 1974, p. 1756). One such school, the Carlisle Indian School, was established in 1879 and educated approximately four thousand children over a period of twenty-four years.

Even though it was teaching children a set of customs totally foreign and often at odds with their own history, many Native Americans of the time accepted as valid the white man's education. Some of them even helped the cause by offering the white man's education themselves. In the late nineteenth century, for example, Princess Sara Winnemucca founded a school in California for Piute children. She taught them to spell, read, write, and calculate in English. She also taught drawing and sewing (Peabody, 1886).

The Dawes Act of 1887 further undermined tribal authority by breaking up reservation land into smaller parcels and allotting these to individual Native Americans. The land allotments—most unsuitable for farming, particularly by people who had not been farmers—were initially held in trust and were supposed to be transferred to individuals at a later date. In truth, four out of five individuals were cheated out of their property (Blum et al., 1997).

The Indian Wars, a series of bloody encounters between white settlers—sometimes with the aid of U.S. troops, sometimes without—and Native Americans continued until 1890 and the massacre at Wounded Knee. At this point, Native American resistance to subjugation and displacement from their land was crushed.

Native Americans continued to live on U.S.-mandated reservations in limbo until the Citizenship Act of 1924, which made them citizens of the United States. At about the same time, the Meriam Report, a study conducted by the Brookings Institution, revealed the poor condition of education programs provided by the Education Division of the Bureau of Indian Affairs.

The 1930s and early 1940s were a period of gain for Native Americans. John Collier, commissioner of Indian affairs for Franklin Roosevelt, encouraged preservation of Native American culture by permitting reservation schools to offer instruction in Native American languages and culture. Collier also promoted the idea of local self-government, hired Native Americans in his agency, and channeled millions of dollars into improving Native American lands. Passage of the Indian Reorganization Act of 1934 returned self-government to Native Americans. It also eliminated allotment policies that had reduced tribal land holdings and prompted the improvement of the poor economic, health, and social conditions of Native Americans.

Our involvement in World War II suspended the Native American struggle for autonomy. The National Congress of American Indians, founded during World War II, was aggressive in its efforts to improve the lot of Native Americans. The American Indian Movement of 1968, composed mostly of militant urban Native Americans, resorted to violence. As Native Americans continued to press their case, Congress reversed its decision to terminate federal reservations and in 1975 passed the **Indian Self-Determination and Educational Assistance Act.**

Today, Native American cultures are tremendously diverse. Yet, collectively, Native Americans trail others statistically in terms of income, life expectancy, and level of education. Unemployment for them is much greater than that for the total population. Poverty is rampant, particularly among widowed, divorced, and aged women (Goodman, 1985). In 1990, of the approximately 235,000 Native Americans ages eighteen to twenty-four, 63 percent had graduated from high school, and 2 percent held bachelors degrees or higher (U.S. Census Bureau, 2002). These figures are well below national averages for the general population. **Why might Native Americans as a group trail in levels of educational achievement today?**

European Americans

After the Civil War, immigration made the population of the United States increasingly diverse. From 1880 to 1924, most immigrants came from southern, central, and eastern Europe. Many settled in American cities and took jobs in industry. In Chicago in 1910, for example, 75 percent of the residents were immigrants or the children of immigrants (Cremin, 1988). In the 1930s and 1940s, Europeans fled the totalitarian regimes of Italy and Germany for the freedom and safety of the United States. Survivors of the Holocaust followed in the 1950s.

Increased immigration rates meant schools had to provide basic education to more people, and they had to socialize these new arrivals to the ways of the nation. Assimilation, once again, became a major educational goal.

As the population increased, it also grew more religiously and ethnically diverse. Differences in language and culture among the new arrivals and between the immigrants and native born made assimilation slow and difficult at best.

Many immigrants retained their ethnic identities through the years, while many others shed these identities. Certainly, the push for assimilation in schools had a great effect on how immigrants responded to American culture. Based on a carefully selected sample of 524 households, in 1991 Richard Alba found that almost no ethnic people were fluent in the language of their ancestral group. About 2 percent had received help in business endeavors from other members of their group. Only 2 percent were members of ethnic social clubs, while 1 percent ate ethnic foods daily, and 11 percent lived in neighborhoods having concentrations of their own ethnic group. In some ways, then, assimilation seems to work quite well. **What factors impede assimilation into the mainstream society of some cultural and ethnic groups?**

African Americans

After the Civil War, African Americans began to participate more fully in society. In 1860, less than 2 percent of all school-age African American children were enrolled in school; by 1900 the figure had risen to 31 percent. Furthermore, illiteracy dropped from 82 percent in 1870 to 45 percent in 1900 (U.S. Census Bureau, 1990).

Technology in Practice

UNITED STATES HOLOCAUST MEMORIAL MUSEUM

The United States Holocaust Memorial Museum in Washington, D.C., is incredibly rich with possibilities for teaching and learning about the history of the Holocaust and helping people reflect on moral and ethical questions raised by that history.

The museum's online workshop for teaching about the Holocaust (http://www.ushmm.org/education/foreducators/) does not prescribe exactly how to teach the history of Germany and the Jews from 1933–1945, but it supports teachers by providing resources and intelligent guidance.

A teacher is encouraged to think carefully about what her or his students should take away from classes devoted to the material. Here are some of the questions teachers are encouraged to explore with their students:

- Where does prejudice start?
- Where can it lead?
- What steps occur along the way?
- How and why do people become bystanders to evil?
- How can a democratic government go downhill so far, so fast?

Critical Thinking Questions

If you were to teach students about the Holocaust, what other topics might you address? How might you begin the unit? Are there particular terms you would need to define before teaching? How would you place the Holocaust in historical context? Compare your ideas to those of Warren Marcus—the Museum's Director of Teacher Workshops and Conferences. His online workshop can be found at http://www.ushmm.org/education/foreducators/guidelines/.

To answer these questions online and e-mail your answer to your professor, go to Chapter 5 of the Companion Website (ablongman.com/mcnergney4e) and click on Technology in Practice.

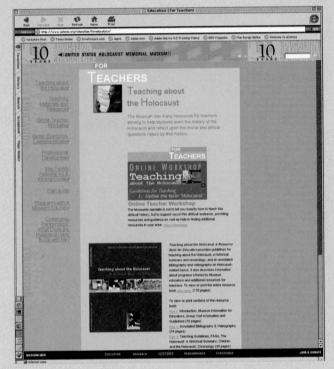

Screen capture of the United States Holocaust Memorial Museum's website courtesy of the United States Holocaust Memorial Museum, Washington, D.C.

After the Civil War, emancipated slaves and European Americans established Sunday schools and universal public education. Churches and ministers in African American communities often formed the nucleus from which educational campaigns spread. By 1868 the African Methodist Episcopal Church had already enrolled 40,000 pupils in Sabbath schools; by 1885, there were 200,000. African American teachers offered almost all the instruction. In addition, thousands of "Yankee school marms" ventured south to teach in needy schools established for African Americans (Degler, 1959).

Booker Taliaferro Washington was among the many African Americans who flocked to normal schools to become effective leaders of their people. Washington attended and later taught at Hampton Normal and Agricultural Institute in Virginia. In 1881 he went to Macon County, Alabama, to become principal of Tuskegee Institute, the newly created state normal school for African Americans. At Tuskegee, Washington built programs in academics, agriculture, industrial arts, health, religion, and music. He even created a mobile school on a horse-drawn cart that delivered basic education to ex-slaves' doorsteps. Through Washington's leadership, the Tuskegee Institute became a national model for educating African American teachers, farmers, and industrial workers.

Washington believed that vocational or industrial education was the best way for African Americans to gain financial self-sufficiency and better their lives. According to Washington (1907), "Mental development is a good thing. Gold is also a good thing, but gold is worthless without an opportunity to make itself touch the world of trade" (p. 77).

The development of Washington's ideas about the need for practical rather than academic education is evident in his autobiography, *Up from Slavery*. He discouraged African Americans from seeking education to become lawyers, doctors, or politicians. Although the war was over, African Americans were still viewed by many as inferior, and educated African Americans were a threat to white supremacy. Washington believed that achieving respectability as a trained worker contributing to the economy, and not upsetting the social order, was the key to advancement.

Booker T. Washington (1856–1915)

An opposite view was taken by Washington's severest critic, W. E. B. DuBois, an African American sociologist with a doctorate from Harvard. DuBois (1904) argued that African Americans would never achieve civil and political equality with only industrial education. Instead, DuBois advocated a more academic approach to "train the best of the Negro youth as teachers, professional men, and leaders" (p. 240). On the difficulty of being both an American and a Negro, DuBois wrote:

> The history of the American Negro is the history of this strife,—this longing to attain self-conscious manhood, to merge his double self into a better and truer self. In this merging he wishes neither of the older selves to be lost. He would not Africanize America, for America has too much to teach the world and Africa. He would not bleach his Negro soul in a flood of white Americanism, for he knows that Negro blood has a message for the world. He simply wishes to make it possible for a man to be both a Negro and an American, without being cursed and spit upon by his fellows, without having the doors of Opportunity closed roughly in his face. (1903, p. 3)

W. E. B. DuBois (1868–1963)

DuBois encouraged political activism and challenged the ideas of both African and European Americans. He helped start the Civil Rights movement that continued through the 1970s (Carr, 2000). As editor of *The Crisis,* the journal of the NAACP, DuBois helped shape the educational policy of that body: All American children and youth should have an equal opportunity to pursue an education.

Mary McLeod Bethune was also instrumental in promoting education. Bethune believed, as did other African American leaders of the time, that education was the means to better lives for all children. In 1904 she founded the Daytona Normal and Industrial School for Training Negro Girls, which later became Bethune–Cookman College. During the Depression and World War II eras, she served in the administrations of Franklin Roosevelt and Harry Truman as director of the National Youth Administration and adviser to the United Nations. As an educator concerned with practical training for upward mobility and as a political activist, Bethune represents a combination of the views of Booker T. Washington and those of W. E. B. DuBois

The efforts of leaders such as DuBois and Bethune gave rise to the Civil Rights movement that grew over the next fifty years and beyond. Yet, for years, education did little to improve economic opportunities or to create political and social equality for African Americans. Because of segregated housing and voting districts, schools for African Americans were funded from separate tax bases and were chronically underfunded.

Mary McLeod Bethune (1875–1955)

Cultural Awareness

CHARLES HAMILTON HOUSTON

The Supreme Court's decision in *Brown* v. *Board of Education* represented an important victory in the battle against segregation by overturning the decision in *Plessy* v. *Ferguson.* Despite the intent of the *Plessy* decision to establish "separate but equal" facilities for African Americans, the reality was "separate and anything but equal." Voting laws, however, restricted African Americans from exercising any political leverage on lawmakers. A small band of civil rights leaders recognized that equality would never be realized until the *Plessy* decision was overturned. The architect of this important legal effort was Charles Hamilton Houston.

Charles Houston was born in 1895, eight months before the *Plessy* decision, to a middle-class African American family in Washington, D.C. Houston's father was a lawyer and his mother was a schoolteacher turned hairdresser. After success in both all-black and predominantly white academic settings, Houston was exposed to harsh racial discrimination while serving his country in World War I. This experience, combined with his father's influence, pushed Houston toward a career in law. After entering Harvard Law School in 1919, he became the first African American elected as editor of the *Harvard Law Review.* After receiving his degree and completing an additional year of study at the University of Madrid, Houston took a faculty position at Howard University's Law School. Houston instilled in his students a sense of obligation to work for racial justice. Among his students at Howard were Oliver Hill, William Bryant, and Thurgood Marshall.

Houston concentrated on attacking the application of "separate but equal" in education. His strategy involved first arguing against the prevailing inequality of professional schools, starting with the lack of access for blacks to law schools. Houston recognized that the cost for a state to establish a separate black law school would be prohibitive and that, if they were forced by the courts to do so, some states would choose some degree of integration instead. This could establish precedent needed to chip away at *Plessy.* Houston also reasoned that white society perceived the greatest danger in desegregation to be the social intermingling of young black males with young white females. Because there were relatively few females in law schools, racial integration there might be seen as less of a threat. In cases arising in Maryland (*Murray*) and Missouri (*Gaines*), Houston successfully

presented the NAACP's case. With favorable decisions established in these law schools, he proceeded to argue for broader equal educational access in lower levels of education.

While higher-education cases were being argued before the courts, Houston's writings and actions make clear his focus on public schools and the segregation that diminished the self-esteem of young African Americans. In 1934, the year before he argued the *Murray* case, Houston began a video safari into the deep South. His goal was to document the blatant inequality of educational facilities in a manner more powerful than statistics. Hours of 16-mm film captured by Houston's camera found its way into courtroom evidence.

Charles Hamilton Houston died of a heart attack in 1950 at the age of fifty-five. Many desegregation cases were being heard by the lower courts at the time, among them the cases that would lead to the *Brown* decision. Hamilton's protégé, Thurgood Marshall, the NAACP's lead attorney in the *Brown* case, would later say in a speech at Howard University that "It all started with Charlie."

Critical Thinking Questions

Why did people in the early part of the twentieth century fight so hard to end institutionalized segregation? How did they succeed? How did they fail?

To answer these questions online and e-mail your answer to your professor, go to Chapter 5 of the Companion Website (ablongman.com/mcnergney4e) and click on Cultural Awareness.

Sources: Greenberg, J. (1994). *Crusaders in the courts.* New York, Basic-Books; Jones, N. R. (1993). Civil Rights after *Brown:* "The stormy road we trod." In *Race in America: The struggle for equality.* H. Hill, R. Jones, Jr., James E. Madison, eds.: University of Wisconsin Press; McNeil, G. R. (1999). Charles Hamilton Houston. *American national biography.* New York: Oxford University Press, 11: 273–274; Williams, J. (1987). *Eyes on the prize: America's civil rights years, 1954–1965.* New York: Viking Press.

In 1896, in ***Plessy v. Ferguson,*** the Supreme Court ruled that public facilities for European and African Americans could be separate but equal. The ruling effectively legalized school segregation. By 1917, African American schools had less than one-quarter of the financial resources that European schools had. In some rural areas, schools for European Americans received fifteen times more support. In Georgia from 1928 to 1929, for example, 99 percent of the money budgeted for teaching equipment went to European American schools, even though African Americans composed 34 percent of the population (Bond, 1934).

By 1900, African Americans outnumbered European Americans in several southern cities. African Americans had few opportunities for employment, however. Jim Crow—the colloquial name for laws and customs supporting racial segregation—sharply restricted opportunities. In 1907 in Alabama, for example, European American teachers were paid roughly five times more money than were African American teachers.

In 1900, southern states spent an average of $9.72 per pupil, compared with $20.80 per pupil in the north-central states. Between 1902 and 1910 appropriations for schools in the South doubled, enrollment of European American students increased by almost a third, and school terms increased from five to six months. Illiteracy among European Americans declined from 11.8 percent in 1900 to about 5.5 percent in 1920. During the same time period, illiteracy among African Americans ten years of age or older declined from 44.5 percent to about 22.9 percent (Link & Catton, 1963).

Poverty forced many African Americans to live in squalor. As industrialization advanced in the post–Civil War period, many African Americans migrated north, hoping to find work. After the Civil War, approximately six thousand freed slaves left Louisiana, Mississippi, and Texas for Kansas in what was called the Kansas Fever Exodus. These "exodusters" and other African Americans leaving the South prized education and sought educational opportunities as well as land in Kansas, in the West, and in northern cities (Painter, 1977).

During the 1940s and 1950s, African Americans continued to struggle for equality. In some respects and on some issues, their voices were heard. Some of the most important changes included President Harry Truman's integration of the armed forces in 1948 and 1949. In addition, many members of minority groups capitalized on their opportunities to go to college with expenses paid by the G.I. Bill.

Some of the most important changes of the period came when Thurgood Marshall of the NAACP argued constitutional cases, including the landmark ***Brown v. Board of Education of Topeka, Kansas*** in 1954. In this case, the Supreme Court ruled that segregation of students by race is unconstitutional. The Court also held that education is a right that must be available to all people on equal terms. These events marked the beginnings of the nationwide civil rights movement that Martin Luther King, Jr., and others led into the 1960s.

Although the physical separation of African American students from other students is illegal, some people argue that public schools are being resegregated by economic and demographic factors, particularly in the cities. As an example, between 1975 and 1996, African American enrollment in Detroit schools increased from 71 percent to about 94 percent, essentially making them segregated schools (Harris, 1984; Kunen, 1996). In 1979 Linda Brown-Smith, who was five years old when her father filed the historic *Brown* case on her behalf, went back to court on behalf of her own child. She charged that the Topeka, Kansas, public schools remained segregated, a condition that years of forced busing to promote integration has not cured.

Today, many African Americans remain at the lower end of the economic scale, have more health problems, have shorter life expectancy, and are statistically more prone to youth unemployment, teenage pregnancy, drug use, and violence. The percentage of African American high school graduates enrolling in college has consistently remained lower than that for European Americans.

Hispanic Americans

Hispanic Americans are the fastest growing ethnic group in America. People from Puerto Rico, Cuba, Central and South America, and Mexico have come to the United States to work and, in some cases, to escape war and political repression.

Most Cubans arrived in the United States as political refugees after Fidel Castro overthrew the Cuban dictatorship in 1959. Puerto Ricans have migrated freely between the United States and Puerto Rico since 1917. In that year, Puerto Rico became a possession of the United States with commonwealth status and its citizens became U.S. citizens. In the past, Mexican Americans came to the United States through conquest and later through annexation of their lands. For the past several decades, Mexican nationals have attempted border crossings to the United States in search of economic opportunities. Today Hispanic peoples constitute more than 70 percent of the migrant work force, which is made up mainly of farm workers (Bennett, 1999).

Like other immigrant groups, Hispanic Americans struggle to overcome prejudice and discriminatory practices directed against them. Their struggles for civil rights and political representation during the 1960s resulted in four Mexican Americans winning election to Congress. By the 1980s, Hispanic Americans were an emerging political force as they elected several members of Congress, a governor in New Mexico, and mayors in Denver, San Antonio, Miami, Tampa, and Santa Fe.

In California, Texas, and Florida, Hispanic American students are the majority in public schools. Yet educational levels of Hispanic Americans rank somewhat lower than those of other groups. High school dropout rates for fifteen- through twenty-four-year-olds who left school before October 2000 indicate that more Hispanic (7.4 percent) students fail to complete school than European Americans (4.1 percent), African Americans (6.1 percent), and Asian/Pacific Islanders (3.5 percent) (U.S. Department of Education, 2001). Income levels for Hispanic Americans averaged about the same as African Americans in 2000, but 21 percent of Hispanic American children younger than age eighteen were living in poverty (U.S. Census Bureau, 2001).

To discover why so many Hispanic American students are having academic problems, researchers studied profiles of one hundred at-risk students over a four-year period (Romo & Falbo, 1996). They followed students' grades, use of standards, gang involvement, teen motherhood, the special needs of immigrant families, and schools' administrative punitive policies. The results contend that the students' problems came from having to navigate the boundaries of three cultures in order to graduate: the culture of the home, the adult culture of the school system, and the student culture of the school. They also suggested that some schools failed to respond to the students' problems and simply placed them in low-level classes, without providing any special support.

Do you think bilingual education slows the assimilation of immigrants?

Asian Americans

Chinese immigrants entered the United States in large numbers during the 1850s. Many settled in the West, where they could get jobs. They worked in gold mines and helped build the first transcontinental railway. Most lived in Chinatowns, where they continued their traditional customs and cultural practices. Attempts by Protestant and Catholic missionaries to Americanize the Chinese failed. Other settlers used force—burning Chinatowns and cutting off the customary long braids of Chinese men—to try to destroy their "clannish" ways (Carlson, 1975).

Chinese immigrants comprised less than 1 percent of the total population in 1870. Yet Americans grew increasingly distrustful of them, particularly as union leaders began to paint the Chinese as "part of a diabolical plot to deprive white Americans of their rightful jobs and bleed the West of its wealth" (Brown & Pannell, 1985, p. 203).

Your Teaching Life in Practice

ILLEGAL IMMIGRANTS

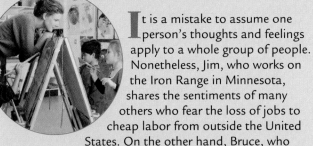

It is a mistake to assume one person's thoughts and feelings apply to a whole group of people. Nonetheless, Jim, who works on the Iron Range in Minnesota, shares the sentiments of many others who fear the loss of jobs to cheap labor from outside the United States. On the other hand, Bruce, who works for the University of Minnesota, considers himself one of the "last liberals left standing." Both men have children in the public schools.

Jim: This is the best nation on earth, and it is being overrun with illegal immigrants. Aliens come here from third-world countries and take our jobs and take advantage of educational and social services. They don't contribute—they only take.

Bruce: Illegal immigrants work here and pay taxes here. That is good for everyone.

Jim: Corporations like cheap labor. They encourage illegal immigration by hiring people who do not have proper documentation. Because of corporate greed, the average citizen ends up paying for education, medical care, and housing assistance for people who do not belong here.

Bruce: Americans refuse to do the work that illegal aliens do. They cut our grass, work in meatpacking plants, watch our children, clean our homes, and more. Sure they want a chance for a better life. Who doesn't?

Jim: Most aliens, legal or illegal, do not adopt the values of this nation. They come here and cling to their language and their customs. They keep to themselves, they do not fit in. They may not vote, but they are counted in the census, and politicians represent their interests. They exert unfair influence on our system of government.

Bruce: Illegal immigrants eventually become assimilated into American culture. They work long and hard for their families. Parents sometimes may be slow to assimilate, but their children become fully integrated into society much more quickly and easily. The children speak English. They make public education richer, more diverse, and more fully representative of the work world all students will eventually enter.

Jim: We can't afford to educate children who do not belong here. Policies of "don't ask, don't tell" with regard to determining whether children are here legally only attract students to our public schools. These kids are a drain on the system.

Bruce: It is a well-documented fact that preventing illiteracy in the young is cheaper than trying to remediate it in adults. Our own self-interest argues for educating the children of illegal immigrants. Besides, the kids aren't to blame for being here illegally. It makes no sense to punish them by withholding education, particularly when they hold the potential for making this land of immigrants even stronger than it is now.

Critical Thinking Question

What are your thoughts about the place of illegal immigrants in society?

To answer this question online and e-mail your answer to your professor, go to Chapter 5 of the Companion Website (ablongman.com/mcnergney4e) and click on Your Teaching Life in Practice.

To this end, the **Chinese Exclusion Act** was passed in 1882, aimed at stopping immigration.

By 1924 the flow of Japanese into this country was halted with the passage of the Oriental Exclusion Act. With the onset of World War II, Asian immigrants, particularly those of Japanese descent, suffered intense racism. More than 100,000 Japanese Americans were placed in temporary assembly centers, relocation centers, and internment camps, and their property was confiscated. The federal government did not officially apologize and offer Japanese Americans restitution for these actions until 1990.

In the 1950s the U.S. government began to lift restrictions on immigration according to race guidelines. In 1965 Congress abolished the quota system that based the annual number of people allowed to enter the United States on a proportion of their relatives who were already here.

Following these loosened immigration restrictions and the Korean and Vietnam wars, many immigrants from Southeast Asia made America their home. The first Korean immigrants came to Hawaii and then the United States in the early 1900s. Most Korean Americans, however, came to the United States after 1970. Like many other immigrants, Koreans typically come to the United States for greater economic opportunities. Today, more than 40 percent of Korean Americans live in the West, with the largest population living in Los Angeles. Large Korean communities also exist in New York, Philadelphia, and other large cities.

Currently, Vietnamese Americans represent only about 10 percent of the total Asian population in the United States (U.S. Census Bureau, 1995). Coming in the early 1970s, the first arrivals "were generals and peasants, schoolteachers and spies, physicians and fishermen, . . . [who] became in America a poignant symbol of the refugees' will to succeed" (Efron, 1990). These early Vietnamese immigrants have generally done well by American standards and so have their children. Vietnamese who have been immigrating since the fall of Saigon in 1975, however, have not fared so well. Most live in poverty and are poorly educated.

Cambodians, Laotians, and Thais also have begun immigrating to the United States, but not so many as the Vietnamese. These tribal peoples were deeply affected by the war in Vietnam and have had a long, hard recovery. They also have had to adjust to a society in the United States that relies on the power of science and technology to solve human and educational problems. This society is truly different from that which they left behind.

By the late 1980s and early 1990s, Asian American students were being called the new "whiz kids." Asian American students as a group have the highest SAT scores in the nation. If racial and ethnic quotas had not influenced college admissions during these years, Asian American students would have become a majority at some universities. **How might your knowledge of history influence your expectations for the performance of Asian American students in your classroom?**

$\mathcal{F}$IGURE 5.2

Exceptional Learners in America

In the 1800s, physicians, clergymen, educators, and social reformers led efforts to educate children with disabilities. Between 1817 and the Civil War, they established residential schools for people who were deaf, blind, mentally retarded, or orphaned. By the end of the Civil War, many of these schools were overcrowded, impersonal, and inhumane. A new generation of reformers wanted to close these institutions because of the conditions. Around this same time, several states began to add special classes for students with disabilities in their public schools. So as not to repeat the same inhumane conditions as the previous schools, professional organizations formed to help improve the care and treatment of children with disabilities.

The early twentieth century brought many changes in the ways scientists measured and classified types of disabilities. At the same time, more and more public schools included classes and programs for exceptional learners. Professional organizations tried to help improve the situation by offering specialized training programs for teachers. In spite of all these improvements, however, the majority of people with disabilities were placed in special-care facilities where social isolation and abuse occurred.

It was not until the 1960s that civil rights reform began to affect institutionalized people. Federal involvement at that point also helped create a Bureau for the Handicapped within the U.S. Office of Education. The bureau is now known as the Office of Special Education and Rehabilitative Services in the U.S. Department of Education.

The last two decades of the twentieth century brought dramatic changes to the field of special education (Hallahan & Kauffman, 2003). Increasingly, people with disabilities are being integrated with the larger, nondisabled society. Educators encourage early intervention, and schools offer all levels of specialized and integrated classroom programs. Today, teachers prepare people with disabilities for their transition from secondary school to adulthood. **Do you know teachers who work with exceptional learners? Have they done anything special to prepare themselves?**

American Women

Women fought for and won an amendment to the U.S. Constitution in 1920 that granted them the right to vote. The suffragettes, as the women who fought for the amendment were called, included Susan B. Anthony, a teacher; Elizabeth Blackwell, the first woman in the United States to qualify as a physician; Margaret Fuller, a teacher and foreign correspondent for the *New York Tribune;* and Elizabeth Cady Stanton, one of the organizers of the 1848 Seneca Falls Women's Rights Convention. These courageous leaders and others after them also advocated women's education.

Even after they received the right to vote, women did not participate fully in society for many years. During the Depression of the 1930s, they were laid off from their jobs before men were, had greater difficulty finding jobs, and rarely received supervisory positions. When World War II created a labor shortage, women took over many jobs that had previously been male dominated. When the men returned after the war, they took back the jobs, and women were again discouraged from having careers.

Government intervention in cases of discrimination occurred often in the 1950s and 1960s, mainly in response to the increasingly powerful civil rights movement. In 1964, the Equal Employment Act helped eliminate many types of job discrimination, including discrimination on the basis of gender. Women gradually moved out of the traditionally female dominated jobs of teaching and nursing and into nearly all professional and occupational roles, including firefighting, law enforcement, and military combat. In 1970, women accounted for approximately 5 percent of law school graduates; in the late 1980s, they constituted about 40 percent (Blum et al., 1997).

In addition, **Title IX** of the Education Amendments Act, passed in 1972, guaranteed that "no person in the United States shall, on the basis of sex, be excluded from participation in, be denied the benefits of, or be subjected to discrimination under any education program or activity receiving federal financial assistance" (Title IX, Education Amendments of 1972). The greatest impact of Title IX has been on school athletic programs. Girls cannot be excluded from any sport and must be given equal access to coaching and equipment.

The women's rights movement of the 1960s and 1970s also helped bring about legislation that affected education. The **Women's Educational Equity Act (WEEA)** of 1974 attacked sex discrimination in education and affected curriculum and instruction in the nation's schools. The law expanded programs for females in mathematics, science, technology, and athletics. It mandated nonsexist curriculum materials and implemented programs for increasing the number of female administrators in education. The law also extended educational and career opportunities to minority, disabled, and rural women.   **Do you see discrimination against women in K–12 schools today?**

Women have always comprised a large portion of the population living in poverty, and the battle continues. Between 1960 and 1980 the number of female-headed households increased twofold. By 1985 approximately ten million children lived in such homes; about six million of them were with mothers whose incomes were less than $10,000. Today, some 35 to 40 percent of the women who serve as the heads of households, with related children under age eighteen, live in poverty (U.S. Census Bureau, 2002).

How Did Teaching Change after the Civil War?

People who believe teaching is an undesirable job have not kept pace with the evolution of the role. Indeed, perceptions of the job have evolved just as the job itself has changed. At the time of the Civil War, teaching was thought of as an unattractive job. But, by 1900, teaching was perceived as a skilled vocation. As expectations for teachers' and students' performances increased in the twentieth century, so too did the status of teaching increase—use of the term *profession* became commonplace. In modern schools, teachers are essentially ambassadors to multicultural communities and promoters of democracy. Teachers transmit content knowledge and build academic skills, but they do much more. American teachers educate the whole child—cognitively, physically, emotionally, and socially.

Status of Women in Teaching Changes

By 1920, 86 percent of teachers were women, but men controlled public education as they held most of the administrative positions. Leaders of the Chicago Teachers Federation (CTF), an all-female teacher organization founded in 1897, drew attention to discrepancies in salaries between administrators and teachers. They also challenged the old male guard in the NEA and tried to force the association to focus on the concerns of women teachers. The NEA responded with some symbolic gains, such as appointing a female president every other year. Ella Flagg Young, a scholar and leader in the women's movement, spoke against the psychological control that the male management had over female teachers (Tyack & Hansot, 1982, p. 181).

One way that women teachers were controlled was with regard to marital status. That is, marriage typically was a liability for women in education but an asset for men. Even by 1940, only 22 percent of female teachers were married. In 1928 the NEA found that about three-fifths of urban districts prohibited hiring married teachers. In addition, about half of the districts prohibited teachers from keeping their jobs if they got married. During the Depression, thousands of districts passed new bans against employing married women.

The Progressive Movement Begins

From 1920 until U.S. involvement in World War II, the Progressive Movement called for increased human and material resources to improve Americans' quality of life. With regard to education, **progressivism** argued that the needs and interests of students, rather than of teachers, should be the focus of schools. Progressive teachers relied on class discussions, debates, and demonstrations, not on direct instruction and rote learning from textbooks. Teachers also experimented with individualized instruction, and the curricula encouraged practical experiences and learning outside the classroom. The teacher's role was that of a helper and guide.

Helen Parkhurst
(1886–1973)

People also were beginning to experiment with the structure of schools and the school day itself. In 1921, Helen Parkhurst implemented the Dalton Laboratory Plan in Dalton, Massachusetts. The Dalton Plan relied on students' own interests to promote learning. Officials turned off the bells and disbanded traditional classrooms. The school day was organized into subject labs, and students from fifth through twelfth grades set their own daily schedules (Edwards, 1991; Parkhurst, 1922).

John Dewey ran the Laboratory School at the University of Chicago. A strong Progressive, Dewey wanted to avoid teaching subjects in isolation. Instead, he favored the idea of integrating subjects with social activities, such as cooking, sewing, or building a playhouse, so that students might learn about cooperation among human beings (Kliebard, 1986).

After 1945 and until about 1960, people criticized progressive education because it lacked a common set of principles. Some said that progressivism pandered to individual happiness at the expense of intellectual rigor. Nevertheless, the concept of child-centered education prevailed in various forms. **What does the term *child-centered education* mean to you?**

John Dewey
(1859–1952)

We Attempt to Educate the Nation

World War II caused a teacher shortage. Although the prestige of the teaching profession had increased, the increased money of the wartime economy tempted many teachers to take other jobs. In fact, by 1945 more than one-third of the teachers employed in 1941 had left for better paying jobs in business, industry, and government. Approximately 109,000 individuals employed on emergency teaching certificates assumed some of those positions.

From 1940 to 1960, many critics expressed dissatisfaction with American education by focusing on progressive education techniques that generally attempted to make education "practical" and relevant to daily life. In 1957, the Soviet Union's launch of the first satellite, *Sputnik,* was seen as evidence of our intellectual and moral flabbiness. Schools, critics charged, had not been teaching students to think. They wanted greater emphasis placed on mathematics, science, and foreign languages.

In the **National Defense Education Act (NDEA),** passed in 1958, the federal government took the lead in improving schools. The NDEA provided funds for upgrading the teaching of mathematics, science, and foreign languages, as well as for the establishment of guidance services. It also provided low-interest loans to college students. The passage of the NDEA marked the beginning of a pattern of federal leadership, rather than just involvement, in education.

The 1970s through the 1990s saw the responsibility for national education change back and forth between the federal government and state governments. In 1979 President Jimmy Carter and Congress split the Department of Health, Education, and Welfare into two federal departments: Health and Human Services and the Department of Education. But President George Bush's 1989 Education Summit, planned and carried out in cooperation with the National Governors' Association, signaled that public education was to be largely a state, not a federal, matter.

they see high schools wanting to "maximize their holding power" (keep students from dropping out) by satisfying consumers. This outlook has led to a variety of course offerings, or "specialty shops," for high achievers, students with special needs, troublemakers, students with vocational and technical interests, athletes, and others.

Homeschooling

Homeschooling is an alternative to on-site public education. Most states allow children to be taught at home, but such arrangements are regulated in various ways. Typically, parents have to show that their children receive an education equivalent to what they would receive in public schools—comparable books, tests, and time spent on studies.

Like private schools, home schools have grown in number for both pedagogical and ideological reasons. Estimates of the numbers of students being homeschooled range from 200,000 to 300,000. The majority of these students tend to be from middle-class European American families located in the western and southern parts of the United States. The curriculum services used by homeschoolers suggest that the majority of families homeschooling children do so for religious reasons. Not surprisingly, homeschooling appears to have gotten a boost from the modern telecommunications industry. A quick tour on the Web will reveal hundreds of sites related to homeschooling.

Adult Education

Adult education took many forms in industrial America. Factories taught safety, while lyceums offered reading circles. Settlement houses taught immigrants and their children English and the skills needed to survive in a foreign culture. Beyond the cities, agricultural programs helped farmers improve their methods of growing crops and raising livestock.

The **Chautauqua movement** was the best adult education movement of its time. What began as a Methodist Sunday School Institute in 1874 at Lake Chautauqua, New York, became a secular educational institution through World War I. During those years, the Chautauqua movement pioneered the establishment of music associations, correspondence courses, lecture–study groups, youth groups, and reading circles.

More important than introducing progressive philosophy, the hard times of the 1930s forced people to use every resource they had to help young and old alike work their way out of the Depression. Many programs made it appropriate for adults and children to congregate at schools. The federally funded community education project associated with the Tennessee Valley Authority (TVA) in the mid-1930s, for example, provided educational opportunities that directly related to community needs, not just its youth (Minzey & LeTarte, 1979). These projects taught adults basic literacy and job skills to help people in the tough economy.

Adult education will likely become more important as we move into the twenty-first century. More and more corporations offer incentives for job-related education and for postsecondary adult education. Volunteer efforts such as Literacy Volunteers of America, Reading Is Fundamental, and AmeriCorps also underscore the importance of adult education. Whether it be for a degree, job training, or general self-improvement, education is being seen as a lifelong process.

Opportunities for Higher Education

Industrialization, the need for postwar development in the South, and the Morrill Act of 1862 combined to stimulate higher education in America. Technical training produced graduates for occupations and trades. Colleges and universities educated people for the professions, research, business and industry, and virtually every other field. Although higher education remained largely a man's world, by 1890 about 2,500 women a year were graduating from college, many from schools established exclusively for women. Once women's colleges took root in American society, they would develop their own rich tradition of education.

The growing middle class desired upward mobility, so colleges and universities produced experts, specialists, and managers. Technological advances called for more specialized workers, so new professional schools—in dentistry, architecture, business administration, engineering, mining, forestry, education, and social work—emerged alongside the older professions of law, medicine, and theology.

The formation of the Association of American Universities in 1900 helped raise academic standards in postsecondary (after high school) education. Slightly fewer than 1,000 colleges and universities existed in 1900, with a combined enrollment of 238,000 students. By 1920 there were 1,041 institutions of higher education, but enrollment had more than doubled to nearly 600,000 students. The prosperity of the 1920s saw increases in state aid to public universities, colleges, and junior colleges (Link & Catton, 1963).

The years 1940 to 1960 yielded phenomenal growth in higher education. Enrollment increased from 1.5 million students to about 3.5 million. After World War II, with the passage of the Servicemen's Readjustment Act of 1944 (G.I. Bill of Rights), enrollment increased even further.

A comparison of the average annual earnings of college graduates and high school graduates suggests that a college education remains a good investment. The U.S. Department of Education reports regularly that the median annual income of young adults who have not completed high school is substantially lower than that of their peers who have completed high school. Young adults who have completed a bachelor's degree or higher earn substantially more than those who have received no more than a high school diploma or GED. **Some people worry about "degree creep"—the granting of more and higher degrees, for no particular purpose other than to give and receive them. Do you imagine you will seek more degrees? Why or why not?**

*W*hy Was Curriculum So Important?

After the Civil War, advocates for common schools tried to encourage citizens to send their children to public schools. But deep divisions along class, religious, and ethnic lines made the task difficult. No single philosophy seemed broad enough to permit the integration of all Americans into the same schools. Social changes in the late nineteenth century—the growth of cities, popular journalism, and railroads—forced previously isolated, self-contained communities to live in a bigger world. Whether they wanted it or not, the world was coming into their towns and neighborhoods. These conditions stimulated the struggle for control of American curricula.

Standardized Curriculum

In 1893 the **Committee of Ten on Secondary School Studies** (established by the National Education Association in 1892) tried to standardize high school curricula across the country. Chaired by Charles Eliot, president of Harvard University, the Committee of Ten prescribed four different academic courses of study for high school students: classical, modern languages, English, and Latin–scientific. The committee urged high schools to provide four years of English and three years each of history, science, mathematics, and a foreign language. Although the goal of the curriculum was to put modern academic subjects and classical ones on an equal plane, critics viewed it as a program useful only for college-bound students.

In 1895, the **Committee of Fifteen** addressed the curriculum of elementary schools. The chairman of the committee was William Torrey Harris, U.S. Commissioner of Education. Harris advocated a curriculum that focused on "the five windows of the soul"—grammar, literature and art, mathematics, geography, and history. Harris recommended that knowledge of Western cultural heritage be passed on to students through standard literature. He believed the school's role was to be an efficient transmitter of cultural heritage through a curriculum that was graded, structured, and cumulative.

Diversified Curriculum

The purpose of schools and the content of their curriculum, as we have seen, were the subject of much debate during the nineteenth and twentieth centuries. While some educators were out to safeguard tradition, others, such as G. Stanley Hall, wanted to make the curriculum fit the stages of human development and the process of learning. Social efficiency experts advocated training for specialized skills, much like industrial training. On the other hand, Lester Frank Ward and others viewed the curriculum as an instrument for producing social change.

Progressives, such as John Dewey, diversified curricula or individualized school programs. Dewey also wanted schools to address social problems of race, ethnicity, class, and gender. He believed the standard curricula did not fit the needs of increasingly diverse classrooms. Dewey and others called for pluralism in curricula, meaning that all students were to learn a common culture, but other cultural views were to be both accepted and encouraged. By the late 1880s eight states permitted bilingual instruction in German and English in public schools. In 1872 Oregon legalized monolingual German schools (Tyack & Hansot, 1982).

Americanization efforts in schools began to intensify in 1914 at the start of World War I and continued into the early 1920s. Schools treated southern and eastern European immigrants as a special group requiring a special, nonacademic education. The curriculum for these students emphasized American government, home economics, and vocational training. During World War I, German was eliminated from the curriculum. Schools began to give report card grades not just for academic achievements but also for students' behavior. Citizenship grades were thought to be a "measure of [students] dedication to the creation of a happy harmonious America" (Carlson, 1975, p. 123).

The NEA's Commission on the Reorganization of Secondary Education in 1918 set a new direction for high schools. Its Cardinal Principles of Secondary Education called for comprehensive institutions that served all social groups and trained for many occupations (Commission on the Reorganization of Secondary Education, 1918). High schools were no longer to serve only the college bound. As the curriculum diversified, students took different courses and different programs depending on their abilities and interests, and schools assumed more responsibilities for student welfare and vocational training. **Do you think high schools are likely to become more or less diverse as the twenty-first century unfolds?**

Censorship and Core Curricula

Was God or Charles Darwin to be part of the common core curriculum? The 1920s saw an ideological fight between science and religion for control of the classroom. It was also one of the most widely supported cases of censorship in education. William Jennings Bryan was concerned about the possibility of atheists posing as teachers in public schools and undermining the Christian faith of American schoolchildren by teaching evolution (Link & Catton, 1963). He led his antievolution crusade to the 1925 Scopes trial in Dayton, Tennessee. The court upheld states' rights to ban the teaching of evolution. In the years after the Scopes trial, the scientific case for presenting Darwinism in schools eventually won out. To this day, however, the teaching of evolution in the public schools remains a heated issue.

More than 1,000 people turned out last week for a biology lesson in Columbus, Ohio. . . . Advocates of intelligent design—a small proportion of the scientific community—say that scientists still debate many of the key assumptions of Darwin's theories. Too many changes happened too quickly in fossil records, they say, for natural selection to explain them. Therefore, their argument goes, teachers should be free to discuss the possibility that an intelligent designer, such as God, intervened to shape humans and other animals. (Hoff, 2002)

Whether science classes taught Darwinism or creationism, some reformers in the 1930s believed the core curriculum of high schools was geared too heavily toward traditional academic subjects. In other words, they believed schools were more focused on college-bound students, offering little to students not going on to college. So the Progressive Education Association launched the Eight-Year Study to examine just what was being taught in high schools. They also wanted to see if students who learned from a core curriculum of traditional subjects performed better than students who did not. The results, published in 1942 and 1943, suggested that students in experimental secondary schools achieved as well in college as did students from traditional high schools. The eight-year study caused educators to modify the core curriculum to include more practical subject matter.

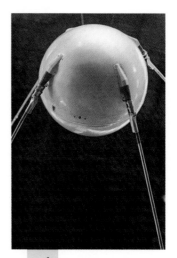

How did the Soviet Union's launch of the Sputnik I *satellite in 1957 affect education in the United States?*

Innovative Curriculum

The argument that the national curriculum is too academic or not academic enough has existed since about the 1850s. In the 1950s, critics once again harshly attacked education in America for not being academic enough. Many people believed Russian's launch of *Sputnik* was an embarrassment to the United States. At the same time, feelings of anti-intellectualism, in which practical training is preferred to high-level academics, were fairly strong. Arthur Bestor's *Educational Wastelands* (1953) described the anti-intellectualism he associated with education that emphasized "life adjustment," another term for a practical education. To counter this, he advocated intellectual training for the masses, not just for college-bound students (Kliebard, 1986).

The 1960s and 1970s brought many innovative curricula and instruction methods: School Math Study Group (SMSG), Man A Course of Study (MACOS), Physical Science Study Committee (PSSC), Harvard Project Physics, Biological Science Curriculum Study (BSCS), Chemical Education Materials Study (CHEM Study), Project English, audiolingual language laboratories, and many more. Most of these efforts tried to involve students actively in their own learning. These programs often de-emphasizing teacher-centered instruction while concentrating on methods of inquiry.

Although the curricula became innovative, some students, particularly low-income and minority students, seemed to be learning less in school every year, and the dropout rate climbed. The National Commission on Excellence in Education (1983) warned of a "rising tide of mediocrity." Many reform reports and proposals offered to fix public education. And, often, the proposed remedies come in the form of tests. President George W. Bush's No Child Left Behind legislation in 2002 called for regular testing in grades three through eight. But as opponents of these tests have pointed out, tests often report only part of the picture. Tests themselves are not a solution to educational crises. **How do you define educational excellence?**

How Do We Typically Judge Educational Success and Failure?

American education has improved dramatically during the modern era. Schools today educate and serve millions of children every year. Progress has been uneven across regions of the country and across time, but schools are dramatically better today than they were at the turn of the century.

We normally judge schools based on three levels: what goes in, what goes on, and what comes out. The inputs, processes, and products or outcomes of education are the factors people examine when making up their minds about educational success and failure.

Inputs consist of people and material resources devoted to schooling. For example, we might ask ourselves the following questions: Are our teachers well prepared? Do we have the latest textbooks and equipment? Is our per-pupil expenditure higher than our neighbor's?

The processes of education often are described in terms of the programs and curricula offered. Variety, rigor, appropriateness for students' needs and abilities, and so on, all figure into people's assessment of schooling. Educational processes also are described in terms of what teachers do in classrooms—the strategies they use and the skills they demonstrate in their interactions with students. In addition, the amount of time spent on various activities is closely and strongly related to how students learn

The products or outcomes of education can be measured in various ways. Certainly, test scores have been significant measures of outcomes through the years—the standardized achievement tests such as the Stanford Achievement Test, the Metropolitan Achievement Test, the California Achievement Test, and many more. And now the **National Assessment of Educational Progress (NAEP),** a group of achievement tests, is administered nationwide. In recent years, states have also been developing their own achievement tests, viewing them as ways to hold educators accountable for the quality of schools.

Today, test scores often are relied on as concise indications of educational quality. Many respected educational leaders, however, have warned against placing too much emphasis on test scores as either outcomes or predictors of potential to succeed in higher education. Richard Atkinson, president of the University of California, has rejected the Scholastic Aptitude (or Assessment) Test, the SAT. He does not believe it is an adequate measure of what students can do in college or of how much they learned from their K–12 education. In 2001, he proposed California scrap the test requirement for admissions to the university. Instead, he wanted the university to rely on standardized tests that assess mastery of specific subject areas. As journalist Nicholas Lemann (2000) argued, the SAT was never really "just a test." It has always been a method for sorting people and defining individuals' educational and economic opportunities. Not getting a certain number on the test can prevent a student from entering college or qualifying for financial aid, which can have a lifelong effect on the individual.

Summary

Once the Civil War ended, the nation seemed to rise up, look around, and gather itself for the headlong rush into the twentieth century. Industrialization and urbanization created the need to both care for and educate children. The end of slavery, the "re-education" of Native Americans, and the political emergence of women all put demands on education systems. The rising tide of immigration greatly intensified the pressure.

Public schools served to assimilate people into the cultural mainstream. Education was supposed to help people fit in as productive, tax-paying contributors to society—but they had to fit in the right place, in the right way. In addition, shifting demographics and cultural changes influenced education. In some ways, communities got the kinds of schools that circumstances dictated.

As people learned to read, write, speak, and calculate, they shaped their own lives. Demand for education soared. Educational leaders with strong personalities and well-defined beliefs—and millions of students and their parents—defined schooling across the nation. Despite the philosophical wars over the aims, content, and processes of teaching and learning, we have seen that U.S. public schools are remarkably resistant to change. And yet, many people ask: Why should they change? As challenged as some of these schools may be, they are part of the largest and arguably most successful universal education system in the world.

Terms and Concepts

black codes   116
Brown v. *Board of Education of Topeka, Kansas*   127
Bureau of Indian Affairs (BIA)   121
Chautauqua movement   136
Chinese Exclusion Act   129
Committee of Fifteen   137
Committee of Ten on Secondary School Studies   137
Elementary and Secondary Education Act (ESEA)
    of 1965   119
Freedman's Bureau   116
Head Start   135

Indian Self-Determination and Educational Assistance
    Act   123
National Assessment of Educational Progress (NAEP)   140
National Association for the Advancement of Colored
    People (NAACP)   116
National Defense Education Act (NDEA)   133
Plessy v. *Ferguson*   127
progressivism   133
Title IX   131
Women's Educational Equity Act (WEEA)   132

Reflective Practice

Cycles of Educational Pluralism

Change is a constant in education. Like the historical changes occurring in the larger society, educational change often occurs in cycles. Recent changes—magnet and charter schools, school voucher systems, homeschooling (parents teaching their children at home)—in the educational landscape have prompted historians to draw comparisons to the pluralism that characterized education during colonial times.

The variety of educational institutions available during the colonial period made it difficult to classify schools as either public or private. Schools that served a public purpose, such as "education for nationhood," were considered public, regardless of the percentage of public funding they received or their degree of private control. Sources of funding support, like the school structure itself, varied widely among schools. Public sources of funding, such as taxation and land grants, often were supplemented by tuition, church support, private subscriptions, donations, lotteries, and other sources of income.

Studies suggest that a similar type of pluralism has returned to education. Enrollment in Catholic schools is approximately 2.5 million, with enrollment in other religiously affiliated schools estimated at 1.8 million. In addition, the parents of more than 1 million American children have chosen home schooling. Charter schools also are experiencing tremendous growth in many parts of the country, with the current student enrollment at about 400,000.

Issues, Problems, Dilemmas, Opportunities

School reform has traditionally resulted from efforts to meet the changing needs of society. Does movement toward increased pluralism in education reflect an increasing fragmentation of society? What is the responsibility of schools to address such a trend?

Perceive and Value

In our modern return to educational pluralism, what makes a public school public?

Know and Act

Competition is a commonly named reason for increasing school options. What are some of the criticisms of attempting to apply this market metaphor to education?

Evaluate

What responsibility does our society have to support the education of all our youth, independent of the educational choices they make?

INTASC Principle 10

The teacher fosters relationships with school colleagues, parents, and agencies in the larger community to support students' learning and well-being.

Knowledge

The teacher understands schools as organizations within the larger community context and understands the operations of the relevant aspects of the system(s) within which s/he works. (Interstate New Teacher Assessment and Support Consortium, 1992)

Discussion Questions

What are all the kinds of schools that serve your community? How does each serve the larger community?

Additional Readings

Adams, D. W. (1995). *Education for extinction: American Indians and the boarding school experience, 1875–1928.* Lawrence, KS: University Press of Kansas.

Angus, D. L., & Mirel, J. E. (1999). *The failed promise of the American high school, 1890–1995.* New York: Teachers College Press, Columbia University.

Callahan, R. (1962). *Education and the cult of efficiency: A study of the social forces that have shaped the administration of the public schools.* Chicago: University of Chicago Press.

Dewey, J. (1938). *Experience and education.* New York: Macmillan.

DuBois, W. E. B. (1903). *The souls of black folk: Essays and sketches.* Chicago: A. G. McClurg.

Vinyard, J. M. (1998). *For faith and fortune: The education of Catholic immigrants in Detroit, 1805–1925.* Urbana: University of Illinois Press.

Web Resources

http://www.cedu.niu.edu/blackwell/

The Blackwell History of Education Museum at Northern Illinois University in DeKalb, Illinois, is a nonprofit organization dedicated to promoting interest in the history of American education. The website includes a variety of free materials for teachers and students.

http://www.si.edu/

The Smithsonian Institution website is a rich resource for teachers and students. Explore the section on "History

and Culture" to learn more about people and events that shaped U.S. history.

http://www.chautauqua-inst.org/

Visit the Chautauqua Institution's website to learn about educational opportunities for people of all ages.

http://www.oah.org/

The website for the Organization of American Historians promotes the study and teaching of the American past through a number of online activities.

Video**Workshop** Extra!

If the VideoWorkshop package was included with your textbook, go to Chapter 5 of the Companion Website (ablongman.com/mcnergney4e) and click on VideoWorkshop. Follow the instructions for viewing video clips 3 and 5. Then consider this information along with what you've read in Chapter 5 while answering the following questions.

1. This chapter presents examples of people and events that had an impact on modern U.S. education. Discuss the no-

tion of service learning discussed in video clip 3 in terms of the efforts made in the United States to meet individuals' needs in schools.

2. Imagine that you could control curriculum development and assessment measures for a school district. What aspects of one education movement discussed in the text resonates with your own personal philosophy, as discussed in video clip 5? Explain your reasons.

Why Teachers Behave As They Do

*H*ave you ever heard people say that some idea is "too fuzzy" or "too theoretical"? Did they want to hear "practical" ideas and listen to people with "common sense"? Did they seek advice from people who have "learned from experience" and reject things that were "too philosophical"? Famous philosopher Paolo Friere uses the metaphor of cooking to argue that educators need to be both practical and philosophical:

> Cooking presupposes certain kinds of knowledge regarding the use of the cooking stove. How to light it. How to turn the heat up and down. How to deal with possibility of fire. How to balance the ingredients in a harmonious and pleasing synthesis. With practice newcomers to the kitchen will confirm some of the things they already know. Correct others that they do not know so well, and gradually open up the way to become cooks. . . . Critical reflection on practice is a requirement of the relationship between theory and practice. Otherwise theory becomes simply "blah, blah, blah," and practice, pure activism. (Friere, 1998, pp. 29–30)

Another great educator and philosopher, Kurt Lewin, used to say nothing is so practical as good theory. What you believe, what philosophy you hold, can help you make sense out of confusion and guide you in the classroom. This chapter contains some educational philosophies that are useful to both teachers and students.

CHAPTER CONTENTS

What Does Philosophy Have To Do with You as a Teacher?

What Are the Roots of American Educational Philosophies?

What Modern Philosophies Influence Western Education?

What Non-Western Philosophies Influence American Education?

What Shapes Teachers' Personal Philosophies of Education?

What Does Philosophy Have to Do with You As a Teacher?

Philosophy can be defined as a set of ideas that answers questions about the nature of reality and about the meaning of life. What is basic human nature? What is real and true about life and the world? What is knowledge? What is worth knowing or striving for? What is just, good, right, or beautiful? Everyone asks these kinds of philosophical questions, and they are especially important questions in teachers' lives.

There are some practical reasons why philosophy is important. If we know a teacher's or a student's philosophy, then we have some clue about how that person will behave and why. John Dewey (1916) argued, "Whenever philosophy has been taken seriously, it has always been assumed that it signified achieving a wisdom which would influence the conduct of life" (p. 378). It is important for teachers and students to understand one another's philosophies if effective learning is to occur.

Philosophy Influences Education

As you begin to develop your own philosophy of teaching, can you identify examples of educational practices you believe are worthwhile?   Parents may choose or reject a school for their children because of how they believe the school's philosophy will be translated into educational experiences. Indeed, various philosophies are at work in schools, and they can be found on many different levels. For instance, principals run schools in keeping with their thoughts about managing people and administering programs. Some schools operate like businesses or factories, while others are like churches, or colleges, or football teams. Teachers plan lessons, interact with students, and judge students' performances according to their own personal views of knowledge. Sometimes their views depend heavily on their idealized conceptions of the

Teacher thinking affects teacher action.

role of teacher. In turn, prospective teachers learn a particular set of instructional methods based on their teachers' educational philosophies. Philosophy shapes the writing of curricula, the preparation and scoring of tests, and even the architecture of school buildings.

Educators disagree routinely and sometimes aggressively about philosophies. One problem with clinging to philosophies is we often forget to reexamine our views in light of changing conditions. Our actions become habitual, out of touch with the present. When this happens, philosophies limit our visions of the future more than they shape it.

It is possible, for instance, to construct educational systems with a view of the "typical" or "average" person in mind when, in reality, the system is full of "extraordinary" people. When this happens, the systems do not work, because they do not fit the people they are supposed to serve. Martin Haberman (1995) believes the education of inner-city youth and teachers in the United States illustrates this point. Colleges and universities tend to recruit, select, and educate teachers with a vision of the suburban United States in mind. Inner-city students, however, do not fit this vision. As a result,

Your Teaching Life in Practice

THE CORE PHILOSOPHIES OF PUBLIC SCHOOLS

The influence of philosophy is evident in schools. For example, we construct and maintain school buildings with a particular view of the way school is "supposed to look." Curricular programs are shaped by philosophical beliefs. Educators and parents behave according to what they believe is acceptable and unacceptable. Philosophical diversity is healthy and is part of what makes us Americans, but it also separates us. Schools should bring us together around common beliefs and expectations, not separate us.

The following two positions are expressed by many people when debating the philosophies that should underlie our American public schools. The pro position argues for a common set of values that drive what we do in schools. The con position argues for the celebration of differences and diversity in the beliefs and philosophies present in public schools.

PRO Schools need some coherent sense of what should be taught and learned. We need a common set of values that drive what we do in schools.

CON There is no consensus about what our common beliefs should be. Nobody can speak with authority about "the American way."

PRO Why don't we base schools on middle-class values—things such as hard work and good moral behavior?

CON The values of hard work and good moral behavior might be a good place to start, but what is hard work to one person may not be to another. The same might be said of good moral behavior. And even if we could agree, what about the people who want to go their own way, define life on their own terms?

PRO Schools' efforts to define common standards and expectations for student performance should reflect our shared values. People can be individuals, but they still need to conform to some expectations, for the good of the group. If we provide the necessary time and support, all children can meet or exceed our expectations.

CON The poor, minorities, and immigrants will need more time and more support. How can we bring people together to provide the resources?

Critical Thinking Question

Can you think of an activity in which parents, students, and teachers might participate that would encourage them to discuss what it means to be an American—an activity that might encourage people to look for the values they share?

Companion Website

To answer this question online and e-mail your answer to your professor, go to Chapter 6 of the Companion Website (ablongman.com/mcnergney4e) and click on Your Teaching Life in Practice.

education programs for both teachers and the students they will teach are radically out of line with life in many communities.

Philosophies different from our own can be useful because they stretch our own thinking. Someone who calls herself an "idealist," for example, cannot help but grow from a serious consideration of a "realist" view, and vice versa. There is almost always some room to change one's mind, but change is unlikely if people are unaware of the options. Big minds have room to consider more than one point of view. No one's ideas should be influenced by real or imagined pressure to be philosophically correct.

What Are the Roots of American Educational Philosophies?

Western philosophies originated with the ancient Greeks, who systematically addressed life's questions. Figure 6.1 shows how Greek thinkers divided philosophy into three branches:

1. **Metaphysics** and its two corollaries address reality. **Ontology** explores issues related to nature, existence, or being. **Cosmology** deals with the nature and origin of the universe (the cosmos).

2. **Epistemology** addresses the nature of knowledge; that is, it questions how we come to know things. We develop knowledge of truth through observation and logic—by reasoning deductively from a general principle to a particular case and by reasoning inductively from a set of particular cases to a general principle. We also develop knowledge from scientific inquiry, intuition, and our senses.

3. **Axiology** and its corollaries seek to determine what is of value. **Ethics** explores issues of morality and conduct. **Aesthetics** is concerned with beauty.

Our education system remains rooted in the Western philosophies described in the following sections. We also describe a number of non-Western philosophies that affect education in the United States as more non-Western people enter our schools and communities.

FIGURE 6.1   Summary of Branches of Philosophy   How might you have to deal with each branch of philosophy in your role as a teacher?

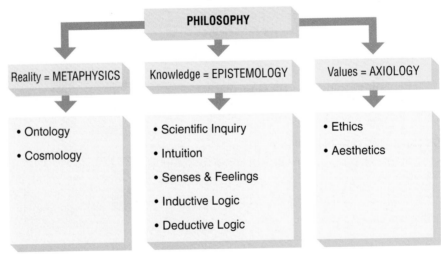

$\mathcal{F}$IGURE 6.2   **Philosophies That Undergird Western Education**   How might teachers who are idealists, realists, and humanists differ in their relationships with students and their teaching approaches?

	IDEALISM	REALISM	HUMANISM
Philosophers	**Plato**	**Aristotle**	**Erasmus**
Metaphysics	Reality is an unchanging world of perfect ideas and universal truths.	Reality is observable events, objects, and matter independent of human knowing.	Reality is also humanity's creation. People strive for personal meaning in their experience and interpretation of life on earth.
Epistemology	Knowledge is obtained when ideas are brought into consciousness through self-examination and discourse.	Knowledge is obtained when students are taught ideas that can be verified and skills that enable them to know objects they encounter.	Exploration, questioning, and critical thinking enable students to discover or construct and use knowledge.
Axiology	Wisdom of goodness; discipline, order, self-control; preservation of cultural heritage of the past.	Self-control; clear judgment and rational thought; personal excellence; balance and moderation.	Knowing and loving God; serving humanity.

Idealism

Do you believe, as Plato did, that the best and brightest people among us should lead our government?   **Idealism** says reality lies in our consciousness or our intellect (see Figure 6.2). The father of idealism is Plato (427?–347 BC), who was a student of Socrates and a citizen of Athens. Plato imagined a society driven by the pursuit of knowledge. To search for truth, justice, and beauty in the world, one needed to find meaning in one's own life and in the collective life of the community. Plato believed this search for knowledge would lead us away from the physical world of what we can see, feel, smell, hear, and taste and toward a world of ideas. The job of philosophy and philosophers was to help people think clearly about these important ideas. He further believed this search for ideas would help people govern themselves justly. According to idealism, perfect knowledge of the ideal resided outside humans as an absolute, or as God. By pursuing ideas, however, Plato believed we could move closer to living in a perfect world.

Plato explained his vision of the ideal world through imaginary conversations between Socrates and his students. These conversations, or dialogues, were written as poetry, science, and philosophy. In the dialogues, Socrates asks questions that force his students to examine their thinking about life, truth, beauty, and justice. As they interact with Socrates, students discover the errors in their thinking and form clearer, more accurate ideas about life's important questions. The **Socratic method,** then, is teaching

$\mathcal{P}$lato (427?–347 BC)

through inquiry and dialogues that help students discover and clarify knowledge. These dialogues have guided thought and action in Western civilizations since their writing, and they continue to guide people today.

Plato's most famous dialogue is *The Republic,* in which he described his ideal society. He outlined how people should think, value, behave, teach, and organize and govern society. Plato knew that this utopia was unattainable. Yet for him, and for the idealists who followed, such visions of perfection are goals we should strive to achieve in our own lifetimes. They are benchmarks against which we should judge human progress over many lifetimes.

In terms of education, Plato promoted the idea of an aristocracy based on wisdom and goodness rather than wealth and power. Although he believed all men and women should have opportunities to learn, he thought few would demonstrate the wisdom and goodness necessary to govern. In Plato's utopia people who had proved themselves worthy, remained healthy, thought clearly, and were of high moral character would govern. Rulers could come from any segment of society, but only the most talented among them would serve as philosopher kings. An intermediate class of well-trained soldiers would protect the community. And a broad base of farmers, traders, and manufacturers would support the society. Plato's curriculum for this idealized society was straightforward, rigorous, and lifelong: moral education that would make citizens realize they had responsibilities to one another.   **What is your ideal classroom?**

Realism

Aristotle advised people to seek balance in their lives. How might it be possible to find balance in a life of teaching?   Aristotle (384–322 BC) was a student of Plato, but he saw the world differently. Instead of searching for truth in the world of ideals, as Plato prescribed, Aristotle sought truth by investigating the real world around him. His work, called **realism,** forms the basis for the scientific method. At its core, realism suggests that the objects we sense or perceive exist independently of the mind. In other words, whether or not we perceive these objects, they exist in the world.

Aristotle established a vast library of manuscripts, a collection of zoological and botanical specimens, and a lyceum in Athens, where he taught many young scholars. Despite the lack of scientific equipment and basic knowledge of the laws of nature, Aristotle did much to advance science. Specifically, Aristotle acted on his belief that the study of matter would lead to a better understanding of ideas. In fact, Aristotle and his students provided much of the intellectual groundwork for Mendel's genetic theory, Darwin's theory of evolution, and the disciplines of biology and psychology.

Aristotle believed humans learn through their senses. As individuals experience the world, they develop and refine concepts about objects. Whereas idealists believe truth and knowledge can be found in the mind of the individual, realists believe knowledge exists independent of human comprehension. Therefore, realists believe the purpose of education is to teach students about the world in which they live.

Aristotle believed that happiness is the ultimate goal in humans' lives. People travel the path to true happiness by stretching their minds to the fullest of their capabilities. "Virtue, or rather excellence, will depend on clear judgment, self-control, symmetry of desire, artistry of means" (Durant, 1961, p. 60). In other words, people develop virtue by accumulating experience and not by having intent or maintaining innocence.

If excellence is desirable, excess is taboo. Aristotle counseled people to seek the middle ground, or Golden Mean, in matters of life: "between cowardice and rashness is courage; between stinginess and extravagance is liberality; between sloth and greed is ambition" (Durant, 1961, p. 60). To Aristotle, the middle ground was where training could make excellence flourish. As people practiced thinking and behaving in productive ways, they developed habits that would lead them to excellence.

Aristotle (384–322 BC)

Like Plato, Aristotle believed that an aristocracy of talented people should run the government. He envisioned a government-run education system that would emphasize balance in assigning people to the work of society. It also would teach responsibility to the state.   **What do you believe is the ultimate goal of education?**

Humanism

When, if ever, do teachers need to step aside and let students learn on their own?
Humanism advocates respect and kindness toward all people. As it relates to education, humanism says that students should receive developmentally appropriate instruction in liberal arts, social conduct, and moral principles. These beliefs are grounded in the writings of Erasmus (1466?–1536), Martin Luther (1483–1546), and Jean-Jacques Rousseau (1712–1778), some of the first humanists.

The Renaissance was a time of rebirth in Europe between the fourteenth and sixteenth centuries. After many years of war and death, the arts, literature, and classical interests experienced a revival. In some respects, humanism was the result of a renewed hopefulness for humankind after a long period of suffering. Writing during the Renaissance, Erasmus extended this rebirth to education. He said that the young should be taught with kindness and gentleness. Children were to be nurtured, not scolded and abused.

The Protestant Reformation occurred around the same time as the Renaissance, and education was an essential ingredient in both movements. The Reformation inspired the idea of public-supported education to help people take responsibility for their own lives. Specifically, the goal was to help people read and interpret the Bible for themselves. As people discovered their own ways to worship God, they also began to define how they would educate for character. For people living during the Reformation and the Renaissance, education empowered them to make their own decisions, thereby determining their destiny both on Earth and in the afterlife.

Rousseau enriched Erasmus's humanistic perspective on the needs of children and the goals of education. He suggested children not be viewed as blank slates or as miniature adults, but as individuals possessing natural goodness and needing continual support.

Humanistic psychologists in the twentieth century, including Alfred Adler, Carl Rogers, Paul Goodman, and Abraham Maslow, continued to apply humanist philosophy to schooling. They wrote and spoke often about the assumptions upon which a humanistic education should be based. Humanists believe students should not be forced to learn; they will learn what they need and want to know when they are ready. The process of learning is at least as important as the acquisition of facts and skills. Students can evaluate themselves; they do not need to be judged by teachers or other adults. Students' emotional well-being is of critical importance for learning. Schools have to be fear-free places if students are

Jean-Jacques Rousseau (1712–1778)

to take responsibility for their learning and to enjoy what they do. Most of all, humanists believe self-fulfillment is the principal aim of education.

Paulo Freire was a humanistic Brazilian educator who encouraged the teaching of illiterate, indigent workers in the developing world. With the abilities to read and write, Freire argued, people will become aware of their own essential humanness and be able to improve their social situation. **Do you believe students should be given more or less responsibility for evaluating themselves?**

What Modern Philosophies Influence Western Education?

Modern philosophies, such as existentialism, Marxism, behaviorism, and cognitivism, have influenced education in the United States. These and other modern philosophical orientations are summarized in Figure 6.3.

Existentialism

"I don't care who my teacher is. The only thing that matters is what my teacher does." Do you agree or disagree? Experts consider Sören Kierkegaard (1813–1855) to be the originator of **existentialism,** a philosophy that emphasizes the subjectivity of human experience. Here is another way to think of existentialism: every individual is the subject of his or her own reality, and no two realities are the same. Therefore, the importance of both individual creativity and personal choice in a nonrational world is key to existentialism. Friedrich Wilhelm Nietzsche (1844–1900), Martin Heidegger (1889–1976), Jean-Paul Sartre (1905–1980), Albert Camus (1913–1960), Paul Tillich (1886–1965), Martin Buber (1878–1965), and others developed existentialist thought by describing reality not as something beyond the comprehension of humans, but as the result of individual passion and life experience.

Existentialists believe the physical universe has no meaning apart from human experience. The world and forces of nature exist, but they are not ordered in some grand scheme in which humans play their appropriate part. Human life exists, but we are only what we make of ourselves. Sartre's often-quoted phrase is "Existence precedes essence" (1947, p. 28). By this statement, he means we owe our existence to nature, but we define ourselves through our actions.

Nietzsche (1924, 1961) revealed the dark side of this view (Banville, 1998). He characterized life as a grim battle requiring strength, pride, and intelligence merely to survive. Sensitivity, kindness, and consideration were signs of weakness. He did not believe in God or an eternal afterlife. Nietzsche believed we should not strive to better the majority of people, who were mostly worthless. Instead, he argued that we should promote genius and develop superior personalities through restraint and discipline.

Choice is a critical concept for existentialists. People choose who they will be. Some allow others to decide for them, but even this is a choice. Although existentialists do not reject morals or norms of behavior, they do reject unthinking adherence to them. When we make decisions based on what is right for us, we take responsibility for our actions. In other words, we should not do something simply because we are told to do it. Existentialists also believe that when we are free to choose our directions we value that freedom and want it for others.

Martin Buber, existentialist and Hasidic Jew, criticized theologians' talk of God and their pretensions about knowing God. In *I and Thou* (1970), Buber did not try to support religion or to argue that God was present in all things. Instead, he raised the possibility that life without religion lacked an important dimension. Buber proclaimed that the secular is sacred and that God is present when people engage in honest dialogue.

*F*IGURE 6.3 **Today's Philosophical Orientations** What combination of philosophical orientations best matches your own beliefs and values?

	Goal of Education	Role of Students	Role of Teachers	Teaching Methods	Subjects Studied
Existentialism	Develop authentic individuals who exercise freedom of choice and take responsibility for their actions.	Develop independence, self-discipline; set challenges and solve problems.	Encourage students to philosophize about life and to recognize and fulfill personal freedom.	Discussion and analysis, examination of choice-making in own and others' lives.	Drama Art Literature Social Sciences History
Marxism	Shape people and institutions; change material conditions of society, producing classless society.	Live and work harmoniously with others, acquire and use knowledge that will enable them to transform natural and social world.	Lead and advocate change.	Scientific methodology, practical activity (problem solving).	Emphasis on science and history.
Behaviorism	Engineer environments that efficiently maximize learning.	Respond to environmental and behavioral stimuli; become self-regulated.	Manipulate the learning environment and present stimuli, using conditioning and social learning to shape student behavior.	Programmed instruction that provides feedback on performance, behavioral contracts, reinforcement.	Learning tasks in which behavior can be directly observed, measured, and evaluated.
Cognitivism	Develop thinking skills for lifelong self-directed learning.	Construct meaningful knowledge through experience and interaction.	Stimulate cognitive development; mediate student learning and monitor thought processes.	Use of manipulatives and real-life learning opportunities relevant to students' prior experiences.	Integrated curricula; emphasis on thinking and critical thinking skills, study skills, and problem-solving skills.
Pragmatism	Develop and apply practical knowledge and skills for life in a progressive democratic society.	Active learning and participation.	Teach inductive and deductive reasoning, the scientific method, and the powers of observation and practice.	Hands-on curricula, group work, experimentation.	Emphasis on citizenship, knowledge and skills applicable to daily life, and career or job preparation.
Perennialism	Acquisition of timeless principles of reality, truth, and value; learning for the sake of learning.	Receive knowledge and academic skills.	Guide to the classics; teach basic skills.	Teacher-centered direct instruction.	Emphasis on Great Books and core curricula in the arts and sciences.
Essentialism	Acquisition of culture; cultural literacy for personal benefit.	Receive knowledge; demonstrate minimum competencies.	Deliver a standard curriculum.	Subject-centered direct instruction.	Uniform curriculum for all students that emphasizes the essence of traditional American culture.
Social Reconstructionism	Solve social problems and create a better world.	Inquire, apply critical thinking skills, and take action.	Ask questions; present social issues and problem-solving challenges; serve as organizer and information resource.	Stimulate divergent thinking and group investigation.	Emphasis on social studies, social problems, global education, and environmental issues.

Human relationships create meaning in our lives. Buber and other existentialists have influenced the development of humanistic psychology, in which relationships, free thinking, and action lead to self-actualization, or personal fulfillment.

Summerhill School in England applies existentialist–humanistic philosophy to schooling. Teachers encourage students to philosophize about life and to use their personal experiences to understand individual choice making. Students try to perceive and solve problems through dialogues with their peers and their teachers. The goal is to help students become "authentic" individuals committed to the creation of a better world. **Of the values you hold most strongly, which one will be the most important in helping you define yourself as a teacher?**

Marxism

How might education be used to promote social revolution? **Marxism** promotes the belief that forces in history prevent people from achieving economic freedom and social and political equality. Marxism is a philosophy most closely associated with communism and Russia, and they did all share some of the same ideas. Despite the collapse of the U.S.S.R. in the late 1980s and early 1990s, Marxist theory remains a powerful philosophical force.

Karl Marx (1818–1883) was a historian, philosopher, and social theorist born to Jewish parents in Germany. Marx learned from the writings of the idealist Georg Wilhelm Friedrich Hegel (1770–1831). Although Marx grew to reject Hegel's political philosophy, he was influenced greatly by Hegel's thought. He was particularly interested in Hegel's concept of the *dialectic,* or the process by which human thought and human history progress.

The dialectic is a constant intellectual movement from thesis, to antithesis, and finally to synthesis. Movement in thought occurs, for example, when one puts a thesis (idea) against its antithesis (opposite). Hegel believed this type of devil's advocacy was the reality of nature. Synthesis is the new idea that develops from the interplay between thesis and antithesis. The synthesized idea, then, generally is a more evolved or well developed idea. Hegel believed that ultimately this process would reach the Absolute Idea, similar to the idealists' conceptions of truth. He rejected the realist view that truth exists independently of our minds. People become and remain alienated, he thought, until they understand that they are thinking beings. For him, truth is a function of this self-realization.

Hegel argued that the dialectic process also works for history. Civilization progresses along a continuum toward richer, more complex syntheses. In other words, culture moves forward by building on what has come before.

Marx saw progress as a mixed blessing. He believed the dialectic of history to be a clash of economic forces in which the capitalist system exploits the worker. The ruling class seized workers' labor and offered money in return, making workers servants of the system. Capitalists, Marx contended, accumulate great wealth, but they create inequalities and dehumanize people in the process. Marx believed workers would eventually rise up and overthrow the ruling class.

Marx recognized the value of science as a way to acquire knowledge and, ultimately, power. For Marx, perception comes from experiencing the material world through one's senses, and this experience shapes one's knowledge. Therefore, human nature is malleable, meaning people and social institutions can be formed and reformed. A person's social class is a matter of education and circumstance. The aim of Marxism, then, is to change the material conditions of society so everyone shares them equally. When these conditions change, consciousness changes; when consciousness changes, ideology changes. And this is when the perfect, classless society will emerge.

In the twentieth century, Marxism has been advanced most notably by people referred to as the Frankfurt School—a school of thought based on Marxist assumptions about the social world. Some of the main voices in the school include Max Horkheimer (1895–1973), Theodor Adorno (1903–1969), Herbert Marcuse (1898–1979), and Jürgen Habermas (born 1929). Critical theorists such as Habermas try to reveal the hidden values of the upper class in schooling and society. They claim that schools alienate students and "de-skill" them by establishing the goals of education instead of encouraging students to set their own goals (Apple, 1995).   **What implicit or unspoken values influence schooling in the United States?**

Behaviorism and Cognitivism

If teachers can shape students' behaviors, how might students shape teachers' behaviors?   **Behaviorism** says that human behavior is determined by forces in the environment beyond our control and not by the exercise of free will. Behaviorism stands in stark contrast to **cognitivism,** a philosophy based on the belief that people actively construct their knowledge of the world through experience. Several names are associated with the development of behaviorism—Ivan Pavlov (1849–1936), John Watson (1878–1958), E. L. Thorndike (1874–1949), and B. F. Skinner (1904–1990).

Skinner was a psychologist who concentrated on scientific experimentation and empirical observation. Although he made his reputation with tightly controlled laboratory experimentation, he could let his mind roam freely over complex social problems. Our failure to solve social problems, he believed, was because of our failure to understand human behavior: "We have made immense strides in controlling the physical and biological worlds, but our practices in government, education, and much of economics, though adapted to very different conditions, have not greatly improved" (1971, pp. 5–6).

Skinner wanted scientists to work for a peaceful and just world by helping us understand human nature. To behaviorists, education conditions people to behave in more and less civilized ways. What is learned about human nature through scientific experiments could help develop more effective teaching and learning methods. In this way, science could be used to shape morality.

Behaviorists, like realists, rely on knowledge derived from the physical world. They examine how people develop behavior patterns in response to environmental influences. The most famous example of this type of conditioning is Pavlov and his dogs. Another example is John Watson, who conditioned and then unconditioned his young son to fear animals. For some behaviorists, including Watson, free will does not exist because it cannot be measured. In other words, all our behaviors are simply learned responses to specific stimuli.

In terms of education, behaviorists believe students are conditioned to learn. So when students are not learning, something is wrong

Skinner thought our failure to solve social problems was due to our failure to understand human behavior.

with the educational program. The way to solve the problem is to break down the program into its separate parts and fix the pieces that are broken. If too much is wrong, the program should be scrapped altogether, and a new one should be used. The challenge to educators, then, is to engineer programs that produce desired results.

The educational applications of behaviorism are many and varied. One application is the use of programmed instruction to teach mathematics, reading, and other subject matter. The subjects are organized into ordered units of study, accompanied by unit tests, opportunities for feedback on performance, and chances to practice skills. Educators also use behavioral contracts to influence student behavior. These are organized as "if. . . , then . . ." agreements between teachers and students: For example, a teacher might say, "If you do your homework correctly, then you can spend the end of the class period reading whatever you wish in the library."

The language of education is full of behavioral terminology—*reward, punishment, contingency, reinforcer, shaping, fading.* Teachers speak of "reinforcing desirable behavior." They try to "ignore inappropriate behavior." People want student motivation to become "intrinsic" rather than "extrinsic," and so forth (Cohen & Hearn, 1988). These behavioral terms reflect the scientific nature of the philosophy

Alternatives to the behaviorist outlook take a variety of forms, loosely grouped under the heading of cognitivism. The word comes from *cognition,* meaning the process of thinking and knowing. Cognitive psychologists assert that people are not passively conditioned by the environment but rather are active learners. They mentally construct their knowledge of the world and beliefs about reality through their own direct experiences and interactions. They then act upon those constructs out of free will. To summarize, cognitivists focus on thought, which cannot be observed directly, while behaviorists focus on behavior that is observable and measurable.

Cognitivism, like behaviorism, is a philosophy with implications for education. Educators who favor cognitive teaching models often use student-centered learning experiences. They assist students by teaching them study skills, thinking skills, and problem-solving skills. They try to provide conceptual foundations or **scaffolding** upon which students make sense of information for themselves. In education, the movement to modify curriculum and instruction to reflect the cognitivist outlook is called **constructivism.**   **Can you think of an experience where a teacher helped you construct your own knowledge?**

Many people are associated with cognitivism and constructivism, most notably the Swiss developmental psychologist Jean Piaget (Perkins, 1998). Piaget tested children's understanding of basic logical structures by having them perform basic tasks. These included putting a series of sticks in order from smallest to largest and estimating how the shapes of containers determined properties of liquids. Piaget encouraged teachers to become classroom experimenters to learn how students play active roles in their own development (Parziale & Fischer, 1998). By taking advantage of students' interests and abilities, teachers can provide more effective learning experiences.

Many modern constructivist teachers see themselves as action researchers seeking to understand how and why students construct knowledge as they do. They encourage students to experiment. They ask lots of open-ended questions. In a constructivist classroom, learning is student centered, not teacher centered.

Pragmatism

Pragmatism defines the truth and meaning of ideas according to their physical consequences and practical value. Charles Sanders Peirce (1839–1914), an Englishman, is acknowledged as the originator of modern pragmatism. Pragmatism is so often equated with "common sense" that many people would claim it as the unofficial American philosophy. William James (1842–1910), John Dewey (1859–1952), and, most recently,

Technology in Practice

THINKQUEST

Constructivists are alive and well on the Web, as the existence of ThinkQuest (http://www.thinkquest.org) demonstrates. ThinkQuest supports programs to advance students' direct involvement in their own education through the use of technology. This global network of students, teachers, parents, and technologists encourages young people to learn, teach, mentor, discover, research, and grow by creating their own online curricula and instruction.

Students work together in teams, using the Internet to research a topic in science, mathematics, literature, the social sciences, or the arts. They then publish their research as an educational website for peers and classrooms around the world. ThinkQuest teachers support students by being coaches, technology mentors, and subject-matter guides. They let students define projects, conduct research, and develop the Web technologies necessary for participation.

A quick glance at a ThinkQuest Library provides an idea of what this student-constructed approach can yield. For example, the Human Genome and Leukemia project exhibits the triumph and difficulties facing leukemia patients and the potential that DNA exploration offers. There are quizzes and Flash animation games designed to help others learn about these biological wonders.

Visit ThinkQuest for many examples of constructivism in action.

Critical Thinking Question

What are the pros and cons of using constructivist approaches in classrooms?

To answer this question online and e-mail your answer to your professor, go to Chapter 6 of the Companion Website (ablongman.com/mcnergney4e) and click on Technology in Practice.

Richard Rorty (born 1931) have used pragmatism to try to balance the realism of the natural sciences and the beliefs of idealists as expressed in art, religion, and politics (Rorty, 1991).

Like other philosophers, early pragmatists wrestled with the dualism of mind and matter: A subjective reality exists in our minds, an objective reality exists in the physical world around us. They agreed with the realists that a world does, in fact, exist and is not merely a figment of our imagination. However, much of the meaning we assign to objective reality comes from our subjective knowledge of the effects that objects have and the consequences that actions have. For instance, you may have been raised to believe that over time a person gets from life what he or she deserves; that is, "appropriate behavior" is rewarded, just as "inappropriate behavior" is punished. If so, you may grow to think that your present state of being, "objectively speaking," is a direct indication of what is right and just, because you have behaved in ways that make it so. The goal of pragmatists has been to seek wisdom, or truth, by thinking about the consequences of having particular beliefs and acting on them.

William James emphasized the right of individuals to create their own reality. He viewed the pragmatic method as a way to settle metaphysical disputes: "Whenever a dispute is serious, we ought to be able to show some practical difference that must follow from one side or the other's being right" (1907, p. 42).

Other pragmatists have argued that the correspondence between human beliefs and physical objects is unimportant. If we believe that something is true, and there is some gap between our beliefs and truth, we can always change our beliefs as new evidence becomes available. For pragmatists, truth is what is good for us to believe (Rorty, 1991). For all practical purposes, if something works, it is true.

William James (1842– 1910)

John Dewey linked pragmatism to educational preparation for life in a democracy, where many different viewpoints are represented. When people are educated pragmatically, Dewey argued, they are prepared for life. And when education concentrates on real-life problems, people are prepared to live fully and effectively in a democracy. Dewey believed that ordinary people possess the intelligence to govern themselves and to direct their own actions. The function of education is to enhance human potential. But he believed American public education did not meet that goal. He believed it was indoctrination—mindless and practically irrelevant. **Do you think people need to be taught how to behave democratically, or would they do so naturally if left alone?**

Pragmatists believe that children should learn how to make difficult decisions by considering the consequences their actions might have on others. Because democracy permits people to consider multiple points of view, pragmatic action and democracy complement each other. Education never ends—it is a process that continues throughout one's lifetime. People are instruments of change, capable of experiencing, experimenting, and testing their beliefs (Westbrook, 1991).

Perennialism and Essentialism

Perennialism looks backward through history and forward in time to shape understanding of the goals and processes of education. Perennialists celebrate the great ideas and accomplishments of Western civilization for their own sake and also for what these classical writings can offer to future generations. The purpose of schools, in their minds, is to develop students' intellectual capabilities.

Perennialists contend there are principles of education so important and central to the development of culture that they cannot be ignored. These include the universality of truth, the importance of rationality, and the power of aesthetics and religion to encourage ethical behavior. Like realists, perennialists believe that these enduring principles demand the attention of teachers and students. Culture is not relative to a time or a place, perennialists argue. Rationality and intellectual self-discipline are the traits most desirable in people.

Robert Maynard Hutchins (1899–1977) and Mortimer Adler (1902–2001) are noted supporters of this view. In every important way, they argue, people are basically the same, regardless of where they live and who they are. Therefore, all people need the same basic education. This education should consist of the fundamentals, including history, language, mathematics, science, literature, and humanities.

Hutchins and Adler introduced perennialism in the 1930s in response to progressive educational approaches. They argued that people are rational animals who learn to exercise self-control when their minds are disciplined by knowledge. The logic of their argument suggests that education implies teaching, teaching implies knowledge, knowledge is truth, and truth is the same everywhere. Therefore, education should be the same everywhere (Hutchins, 1936).

Perennialists believe contemporary curriculum that disregards the classics does a disservice to students and society. One must know the past to participate fully in the present and to contribute in the future; think of the old adage, "Those who don't know history are doomed to repeat it." This view led to the development of the Great Books program at the University of Chicago in the 1950s. It also led to Mortimer Adler's *Paideia Proposal* (1982), a more recent expression of perennialism that calls for a one-track system of public schooling that is the same everywhere.

The practical implications of perennialism for schooling are numerous. Perennialists prefer teacher-centered education. The teacher is the authority who must possess the knowledge and responsibility necessary to teach a core curriculum to young people. Moral education, including Bible study, is important for what it teaches about self-control and social responsibility. Concepts of academic tracking and gifted education are acceptable to perennialists, but both should emphasize the classics.

Essentialism claims the existence of a body of knowledge that all people must learn in order to function effectively in society. Like perennialists, essentialists acknowledge the timeless quality of great works. Unlike perennialists, essentialists do not base their views on realist principles. Nor do they agree on what constitutes the "essentials" that educated people should know. Essentialists simply agree that such essentials exist and that they ought to be represented in the curriculum.

One criticism shared by both perennialists and essentialists is that they define the essentials in terms of Western history and culture. But, unlike perennialists, essentialists want students to study great works not for their own sake but to become better prepared to solve contemporary problems. The sciences, too, are useful and central to the process of knowing and improving one's world.

William Bagley (1874–1946) founded the Essentialistic Education Society as a reaction against progressive, pragmatic trends in education. Bagley and his colleagues feared what they saw as an erosion of moral and intellectual standards in the young. To remedy this situation, they advocated that schools transmit a common essential core of knowledge to all students.

Robert Maynard Hutchins (1899–1977)

Essentialist curricula are rarely as specific as the recommendations of E. D. Hirsch (1987; Hirsch, Rowland, & Stanford, 1989), professor of English at the University of Virginia. Hirsch argues that society cannot function properly without communication among its members, and communication cannot occur in the absence of literacy. But true literacy, Hirsch (1996) contends, is more than the mechanical performance of reading and writing. True literacy depends on a body of information or common knowledge that everyone shares. Hirsch called this shared common knowledge **cultural literacy.**

As for specifics, Hirsch has prescribed curriculum for students in terms of what he believes children need to know by the end of sixth grade. Included in his curriculum are the subjects of literature, religion and philosophy, history, geography, mathematics, science, and technology. Based on the content of this curriculum, people criticize Hirsch's work for being **Eurocentric.** That is, some people believe his curriculum is centered on the history and cultures of Europe and represents works only by "dead white males." His supporters argue that the Core Knowledge Foundation correctly acknowledges valuable contributions from all cultures woven into the American fabric.

Defenders of essentialism, such as Allan Bloom in his book *The Closing of the American Mind* (1987), say that curricula should be exclusionary: "One should conclude from the study of non-Western cultures that not only to prefer one's own way but to believe it best, superior to all others, is primary and even natural—exactly the opposite of what is intended by requiring students to study these cultures" (p. 36). Michelle Fine (1987) and Henry Giroux (1984), on the other hand, believe the essentialist approach silences talk about instances of social, economic, and educational discrimination experienced by minority, female, and low-income students. **If we assume all students should learn the same curriculum, what is the single most important area of content for the curriculum to include?**

Social Reconstructionism

Social reconstructionism says that people are responsible for social conditions, whether good or bad. Theodore Brameld (1904–1987) and George Counts (1889–1974) advocated education as a means of preparing people to create a new society. Influenced by progressivism, Brameld, Counts, and others pushed for rapid, sweeping changes throughout society. The progressives and pragmatists of Dewey's day were politically moderate, urging gradual change, but the social reconstructionists were provocative in advocating immediate change from top to bottom.

George Counts (1889–1974)

The optimism of early social reconstructionists was based on faith in the power of science to solve human problems:

> Unless the profession can develop a superior type of social leadership, a leadership at least equal in intelligence, courage, and power to the leadership in other fields of interest with which it must contend, the profession will find itself unable to incorporate in the systems of public education the findings of educational science. (Counts, 1928, p. 361)

The same kinds of arguments made by early social reconstructionists are still used today to restructure schools and redesign professional education for teachers.

From the 1930s to the 1960s, social reconstructionists saw a world where confusion and crisis reigned. The Great Depression, World War II, the Nuclear Age, and the Cold War era raised long-running concerns about world order. Social reconstructionists wanted to build a good and just society. They believed people could not sit comfortably in their safe homes enjoying the good life while others less fortunate sat on the outside looking in. People were to bring the have-nots into a better society.

Brameld and others like him thought that the future could be bleak or promising: the choice belonged to us. They believed people had the power to take control of their lives and behave in ways that improved the human condition. But the education system itself needed to be reconstructed as a tool for transforming individuals' lives and shaping a new society.

The spirit of social reconstructionism has been nurtured in the United States by individuals and groups wanting to create change through social activism. Social reconstructionists of the late twentieth century press for schools to address ignorance, poverty, and the lack of educational and employment opportunities. Education, then, cannot be a simple response to a particular need. It must address an interdependent set of students' intellectual, emotional, personal, and social needs. Complex problems demand complex solutions. Social reconstructionists believe educators should prepare students to meet these demands.   **If you could immediately change one aspect of schools, what would it be?**

What Non-Western Philosophies Influence American Education?

Across the country, many foreign and first-, second-, and third-generation American public school students have Asian and Middle Eastern backgrounds. Buddhist Vietnamese Americans in Los Angeles, Islamic Arab Americans in Detroit, Hindu Indian Americans in New York, and others, maintain private schools and educate children and adults through cultural festivals and religious celebrations.

The influence of these many cultures and their philosophies can be found in schools across the country. Classes on world religions are commonplace in many schools. Teachers encourage students to develop secular spirituality, a personal ethical system, and inner peace. Multicultural curriculum materials provide access to past and present ideas and expressions of spirituality. And in some alternative private schools, non-Western philosophies play a significant role.

Western ways often encourage people to concentrate on personal and professional hopes for the future. In these traditions, one's sense of progress is rooted in work and one's place in society. Attendance at church or temple, the latest self-help book, or some traumatic event often prompts people to think about "meaning" in their lives. Non-Western philosophies can remind people that introspection, often undertaken with the help of a spiritual guide or teacher, is an ongoing process that leads to a fulfilling life.

Hinduism

Hinduism is more than a religion; it is a philosophy and a way of life. To use the term *Hindu* as though it represents a single philosophy is misleading. Many kinds of Hindus exist, and their beliefs and life-styles vary dramatically. Members of some Hindu sects are Stone Age worshippers of trees, snakes, and other objects and phenomena in nature. Other Hindus are sophisticated urban intellectuals who contribute to virtually all aspects of modern life.

Major Hindu writings began to appear in the form of hymns and chants, or mantras, about 1200 BC to AD 200. The three basic Hindu texts—the Vedas, the Upanishads, and the Epics—reveal a way of life that guides believers. The Vedas describe a vision of the universe consisting of Earth, the atmosphere, and heaven. Vedic believers worship many gods and assign human characteristics to nonhuman things. The god Varuna, for example, is thought to control the changes in seasons.

The Upanishads, or secret teachings, recognize a single god, Brahman. They also provide laws to govern personal conduct. These laws established the caste system, which is a social hierarchy that has since been outlawed. In the caste system, the Brahmins, or priests, teachers, and other thinkers, were at the top, while the Sudras, or untouchables, were at the bottom.

The Epics were written between 200 BC and AD 200. One of the writings included in the Epics is the Bhagavad-Gita, a poem of more than seven hundred verses that depicts a compassionate god who opens salvation to all devoted, dutiful souls. The Bhagavad-Gita also describes yoga as a means of uniting one's soul with the Absolute. Through yoga's teaching of proper posture, correct breathing, and control of the senses, one learns to free the mind and attain enlightenment.

Mohandas Gandhi, a member of the Jain sect of Hinduism, was known as the Mahatma (the Great). His influence on Western thought included his strong belief in nonviolence as a means to social reform. Martin Luther King, Jr., (1964) wrote about the use of nonviolent political action during the bus boycott in Montgomery, Alabama: "For Gandhi love was a potent instrument for social and collective transformation. It was in this Gandhian emphasis on love and nonviolence that I discovered the method for social reform that I had been seeking for many months" (p. 79).

One example of Hindu education in practice is the Shishu Bharati School of Languages and Cultures of India established in Massachusetts and New Hampshire. The school was founded by a group of parents who had immigrated to the United States from India. They wanted to teach their languages and cultural heritages to their children. The school offers language programs in Bengali, Gujarati, Hindi, Marathi, Sanskrit, Sindhi, and Tamil. In addition to language classes, education programs address Indian arts, customs, religion, history, geography, and current events. The curriculum also includes field trips to Indian cultural events, yoga, and advanced culture classes (Shishu Bharati, 2002).

Buddhism

Buddhism is not a fundamentalist religion. It is more a way of thinking about the world, part philosophy and part religion. Its basic aim is to help people gain direct insight into the truth for themselves. Buddha, or the Enlightened One, was born as Siddhartha Gautama (563–483 BC) to wealthy parents in Nepal. Tradition teaches that he led a sheltered, opulent life until the age of twenty-nine. At that point, his life was changed forever by three events. He saw an old man bent over a walking stick, a diseased man suffering with fever, and a corpse being carried to a funeral pyre. These experiences compelled him to seek a spiritual inner peace with which to face old age, sickness, and death.

In search of that peace, Gautama left his wife and son and lived an austere life of study concentrated on human suffering and its cure. The doctrine, or dharma, he taught consisted of four truths: life is full of suffering and dissatisfaction; suffering emanates from desire; suffering will cease when desire stops; and the cessation of desire can be accomplished through eight steps. These eight steps are right views, right aspirations, right speech, right conduct, right livelihood, right effort, right mindfulness, and right contemplation.

Buddhists think of life as a flowing stream. They believe in reincarnation, that is, rebirth in which people assume a new physical form and status depending on the quality of their deeds (karma). They also believe progress with Buddha's eight steps will allow them to reach *nirvana,* a state of serenity and wisdom in which they can escape the cycle of endless rebirth. Although Buddha did not believe in an Absolute or God, after his death he became revered as a god.

Zen, a sect of Buddhism, took root in Japan in the twelfth century. Shinto was the traditional religion of Japan prior to the introduction of Buddhism and Confucianism from China. Shinto focused on worshipping nature and family ancestors (Holtom, 1984). The Shinto philosophy encourages feelings of reverence toward all life, past and present, thus it mirrored, quite closely, the beliefs of Buddhists. In feudal, patriarchal Japanese society, Zen Buddhist monks stressed the dignity of physical labor, the arts, swordsmanship, and the tea ceremony. They emphasized stern discipline, selflessness, and spontaneity. Zen beliefs and rituals became integral to Japanese culture.

Islam

Islamic philosophy is based on the writings of the Koran (Quran), the holy or sacred book of Muslims. Muslims believe the word of God, or Allah, was revealed to Muhammad by the angel Gabriel. Abu-Bakr, Muhammad's father-in-law, collected Allah's words (delivered by Muhammad) in the Koran. Muhammad (570–632), then, was a prophet, like Christ, who described Allah's will. Muhammad foretold of a day when Allah would pass the Last Judgment to judge all souls by how well they lived according to Allah's will. Eternal reward is paradise and would be granted to those who succeeded. Those who failed would suffer the pain of eternal fire. The religion of Islam is rooted in both Judaism and Christianity and was strongly influenced by the Old and New Testaments (Corbin, 1993; Fakhry, 1983).

Al-Kindī (died after 870) expressed Islam's view of God as an absolute, transcendent being. God revealed truth through philosophy and religion. Al-Fārā bī (875–950) expressed the Islamic view that the goal of life is to attain immortality through education or the development of one's intellect.

In the ancient world, Muslims made important advances in science and medicine. The physician ibn-Sina (980–1037) described concepts of matter, form, and existence in a way that allowed for a Necessary Being, or God. To ibn-Sina, the prophets were teachers who used religion as philosophy for the masses. Their teachings revealed symbolic truths that helped people approach absolute truth, or God.

In the 1960s Islam gained many African American believers in the United States, particularly among urban African American males. The Koran expressly forbids discrimination on the basis of race. Submission to Allah and strict adherence to Islam guarantee automatic brotherhood and equality. In 1965 Malcolm X, an influential Black Muslim, wrote bitterly about the need for Islam at a time when many African

Americans felt disappointed that the civil rights acts of the late 1950s and early 1960s had not yet made much of a difference in people's lives:

> I am in agreement one hundred per cent with those racists who say that no government laws ever can force brotherhood. The only true world solution today is governments guided by true religion—of the spirit. Here in race-torn America, I am convinced that the Islam religion is desperately needed, particularly by the American black man. (pp. 368–369)

African and Native American Philosophies

Western thought is rational (I think, therefore I am), whereas African thought is based on feeling and sociality (I feel, and I relate to others, therefore I am) (Asante, 1987).

It is important for educators to have an understanding of African American philosophy and its bearing on educational life in America. Asante (1992) advocates a curriculum that acknowledges African history and culture:

> The African American children in your classrooms are not a black version of white people. They have different cultural and historical experiences that must be looked at and examined in a different way. To give an obvious example, African Americans did not come to America on the Mayflower. We recognize the

Cultural Awareness

ISLAMIC SCHOOLS STEP UP SECURITY

Following September 11, 2001—the day of terrorist attacks on America—students and teachers around the nation, particularly those in New York City, tried to return to their normal routines. Schools serving the children of U.S. military personnel at home and abroad closed temporarily or took other precautions to ensure the safety of their students. Many Muslim schools also took precautions, fearing their students might be harmed in reaction to reports that Muslims or Arabs were responsible for the September 11 attacks.

Some private Islamic schools closed temporarily, in response to parents' concerns for their children's safety. Other private Islamic schools and schools with many students of Middle Eastern backgrounds stayed open, often with extra surveillance from local police.

Sharifa Alkhateeb, who teaches a course on Middle Eastern culture for teachers in the Fairfax County, Virginia, schools, said Muslim leaders told their followers to keep a low profile. "I fear that average people will be so filled with fear in general," Ms. Alkhateeb said. "It will make them so depressed that as a catharsis for their general fear, they will try to find a local target."

On September 11, the Islamic Academy of Florida in Tampa stayed open to maintain a sense of normalcy. Due to parents' concerns, the school closed the following day. The school received several angry calls, in which callers used an obscenity or told Muslims to go home. But, to their surprise, someone called to say, "'I'd like you to know that we know you feel the same way we do, and I don't feel like you are different from other people.'"

Critical Thinking Questions

Do you have any firsthand evidence of acts of rejection or support for Muslims or Arabs since September 11, 2001? Assume, for example, that you had seen students taunting a Muslim girl, telling her to "go home." How should teachers deal with such acts?

To answer these questions online and e-mail your answer to your professor, go to Chapter 6 of the Companion Website (ablongman.com/ mcnergney4e) and click on Cultural Awareness.

Source: Zehr, M. (2001). Fearing potential for backlash, Islamic schools step up security. *Education Week.* Available online: http://www.edweek.org/ew/newstory.cfm?slug=03muslim.h21

Mayflower as part of the American experience, but our experience was different: We crossed the ocean packed in boats with as many as 1,000 other people, with only 18 inches of space between us and the deck above, and chained from neck to ankle. (p. 21)

Traditional Native American thought also emphasizes holistic (natural), nonrational existence and social relations. Reason and logic, for example, are not seen as superior methods of explaining events. Like African traditions, Native American traditions encourage spiritualism based on animism—belief in the presence of active supernatural forces in the natural world. Both traditions also prize humans' harmonious coexistence with nature. In these cultures, truth does not come from great books or scientific inquiry. Instead, truth is the result of personal introspection, oral traditions, and the values and knowledge handed down from ancestors.

Native American philosophies stress personal dignity, moral responsibility, and the mutual interdependence of all the people in a society or group. Group identity and well-being take precedence over individual needs and abilities. Traditional social values encourage silent reflection over verbalizing, cooperation over competition, stability over change, and continuity over progress (Banks, 1994).

African American and Native American thought, like the religious and secular philosophies of the Middle East, India, and Asia, influence the development of educational philosophies in the United States. They broaden people's minds, and they enlighten changes in curriculum and instruction that are designed to meet the needs of all students in our culturally diverse society. These curricular influences take many forms. History teachers concentrate on the contributions of different cultural groups to the building of America. Literature teachers focus students on writings of authors with different ethnic backgrounds. Art teachers encourage student expression using various media in genres endemic to certain cultures.

What Shapes Teachers' Personal Philosophies of Education?

Teachers are role models of responsible adult behavior, attitudes, and values. A teacher constructs the social system of the classroom, with its rules, norms, sanctions, and rewards. This system governs behavior for an entire school year, sometimes longer. The personality and values of the teacher reflect her or his philosophy and set the tone for how classroom life is lived. The teacher's philosophy can even find its way into students' lives outside the classroom, lasting well beyond their years in school.

Learning from Teaching: Reflection

Teachers shape their own philosophies—by what they do and by what they think about what they do. Dewey and others have given the name *reflection* to this process of thinking about what you do. Donald Schön (1987) described two types of reflection. The first, reflection-in-action, is a process that helps teachers reshape what they do as they do it. For instance, a teacher launches into a lecture and perceives that students are not listening. She stops, asks a question, takes several volunteers' responses, reinforces those who make positive contributions, and moves on with the lesson. In the thick of activity, she thinks about what is happening and learns from her own actions and those of her students. Over time, these reflections-in-action inform her more general beliefs about teaching.

The second type, reflection-on-action, is a look back at what happened previously. A teacher remembers what happened in particular circumstances and thinks about the

Voices

A TEACHER'S PHILOSOPHY

*D*onna Moffett invites a few of her first-grade students to eat lunch with her in their classroom at Public School 92 in Brooklyn, New York. These hurried meals are revered moments for the children, who yearn for private moments with their teacher.

For Ms. Moffett, a first-year teacher with only a month of training, they offer something equally valuable: glimpses of her students' lives outside school, which have remained frustratingly mysterious.

Some of the lunchtime conversations are mundane; others are heartbreaking. A cheerful girl, who is a top student, chattered about making cupcakes with her mother. Another child, who is chronically late and always asking to visit the nurse, confided that she missed her father. "I wish he'd come take me out more," she said gravely. "He's in jail now. He stole a car. It's bad when you steal people's cars."

Such confessions are eye-openers for Ms. Moffett, who abandoned her longtime job as a legal secretary in Manhattan last year to teach in Flatbush, a largely Caribbean neighborhood. Increasingly, she is haunted by the question of how far teachers should go to solve the complex problems of their students' lives—and whether it is realistic or even appropriate to try.

How much can a novice teacher do to address the impact of deeply rooted problems like poverty and transience, she wonders, when her immediate responsibilities are so consuming?

"There's a balance I have to strike between what is good for each individual student and what is good for the entire class," Ms. Moffett said recently. "My judgment is not necessarily the best judgment. But I am compelled to do the greatest good I can for the greatest number of students. . . ."

"I can see a lot of blossoming going on," Ms. Moffett said one evening, staying in her classroom long after dark to hang the children's latest artwork and writing. "I see it in their faces, in their work, in their demeanor. If I can give them reason to be motivated and somehow keep them that way, it will carry them a long way."

Critical Thinking Question

What lessons does Ms. Moffett seem to be learning from her reflections-on-action?

To answer this question online and e-mail your answer to your professor, go to Chapter 6 of the Companion Website (ablongman.com/mcnergney4e) and click on Voices.

Source: Goodnough, A. (2001, March 11). For first-year teacher, 20 minds to shape, 20 mysteries to plumb. *New York Times.* Available online (http://www.nytimes.com/2001/03/11/nyregion/11TEAC.html?pagewanted=print).

lessons he learned from the experience. The experiences he recollects might be the most vivid, but not necessarily the most successful or most satisfying. The teacher might ask himself: What did I do? Why? What might I have done differently? What might have happened if I had done something else? The people who can truly learn from what they do develop personal philosophies that help them move toward higher levels of professionalism.

Developing a personal philosophy of education and enriching that philosophy over time requires a certain amount of risk-taking behavior. A teacher who relies only on comfortable, familiar methods has nothing new to think about and very little opportunity to learn. **What did the principal mean when she said, "I want to hire a teacher with ten years of experience, not a teacher with one year of experience, ten times"?**

*S*ummary

Educational philosophies are important for teachers because they both reflect and influence what happens in schools. Our educational roots go back to the Greeks and other ancient Western thinkers. Modern philosophies with quite different views of the nature of reality and the meaning of life have had dramatic effects on curricula, teaching, and learning. Some of these philosophies are associated with mainstream Western thinking, and others have evolved from Eastern and Middle Eastern religions and from African American and Native American life.

Teachers' own philosophies about the way the educational world works develop over time. As they perform their tasks and think about what they do, teachers learn more about what professional practice means to them. The more they stretch themselves to think and behave in new ways, the richer their philosophies become.

Terms and Concepts

aesthetics   146
axiology   146
behaviorism   153
cognitivism   153
constructivism   154
cosmology   146
cultural literacy   157
epistemology   146
essentialism   157
ethics   146
Eurocentric   157
existentialism   150

humanism   149
idealism   147
Marxism   152
metaphysics   146
ontology   146
perennialism   156
philosophy   144
pragmatism   154
realism   148
scaffolding   154
social reconstructionism   157
Socratic method   147

Reflective Practice

Philosophical Differences

Stuart Hastings was reluctant to let his high school students in his team-taught class discuss their beliefs about being ethnic minorities in a predominantly white world. Even though they were studying social borders and barriers, he worried that the discussion might turn ugly. Nonetheless, he could not dissuade them. According to his colleague, Suzanne MacCormack, he even seemed to approve of the idea.

"I tell you, it was uncomfortable in there second period. How are we going to address these students' issues?" Stuart asked.

Suzanne had been shifting uneasily in her chair for several minutes. She could keep quiet no longer. "Well, what about our schedule? Your impromptu therapy session has set the whole team plan back." Suzanne could really be a pain in the neck.

"Whoa! Calm down!" Stuart blurted defensively. "What's a bigger border or barrier than the attitudes and stereotypes these kids face in the real world? We barely had time to dive in today. Now we really need more time to discuss positive ways of dealing with these problems."

Suzanne was not soothed. "Fine. Wonderful. We are all social workers. But what happened to our curriculum? These kids need to learn some basic skills and to understand that when we set deadlines they must be met. Let's talk about real-world expectations for a change. And, who do you think gets to clean up the mess after you stir these kids up? I spent the better part of my day tackling crisis after crisis. Some of these kids are just time bombs waiting to go off."

"Suzanne, I really do see your point, but it seemed like the right thing to do at the time," said Stuart.

Issues, Problems, Dilemmas, Opportunities

What issues arose in Stuart's and Suzanne's discussion about the class session?

Perceive and Value

Can you describe, in your own words, the main differences between Stuart's and Suzanne's beliefs?

Know and Act

If you were the team leader, what might you do to encourage greater cooperation between Suzanne and Stuart, and why?

Evaluate

Why might team teaching be advantageous and disadvantageous from a philosophical point of view? How would you know if more or less cooperation between the teachers made a difference in student learning?

INTASC Principle 6

The teacher uses knowledge of effective verbal, nonverbal, and media communication techniques to foster active inquiry, collaboration, and supportive interaction in the classroom.

Disposition

The teacher appreciates the cultural dimensions of communication, responds appropriately, and seeks to foster culturally sensitive communication by and among all students in the class. (Interstate New Teacher Assessment and Support Consortium, 1992)

Discussion Question

How might Stuart foster culturally sensitive communication among his students when they meet the next day?

Additional Readings

Alinsky, Saul David (1971). *Rules for radicals: A practical primer for realistic radicals.* New York: Random House.

Freire, Paulo (1993). *Pedagogy of the oppressed.* New York: Continuum.

Gutek, Gerald L. (1997). *Historical and philosophical foundations of education: A biographical introduction* (2nd ed.). Upper Saddle River, NJ: Prentice Hall/Merrill.

Illich, Ivan (1971). *Deschooling society.* New York: Harper & Row.

Kneller, George (1971). *Introduction to the philosophy of education* [by] *George Kneller.* New York: Wiley.

McGrath, Alister E. (2001). *In the beginning: The story of the King James Bible and how it changed a nation, a language, and a culture.* New York: Doubleday.

Web Resources

http://www.cie.org/

The Council on Islamic Education provides resources for teachers in the handbook *Teaching about Islam and Muslims.*

http://www.tolerance.org/

The Southern Poverty Law Center provides materials for teaching tolerance toward people of all philosophies and religions.

http://www.shishubharati.org/

The Shishu Bharati Schools in Burlington, Massachusetts, and Nashua, New Hampshire, offer programs in the languages and cultures of India for all ages.

http://www.christianhomeschoolers.com

Christian philosophy and curricula abound on the Web, and much of it is designed to school children at home.

http://www.glef.org/index.html/

The George Lucas Education Foundation promotes modern educational idealism through the use of technology.

http://cuip.uchicago.edu/jds/

The John Dewey Society advocates the use of reflection in the search for solutions to educational and cultural problems.

VideoWorkshop Extra!

If the VideoWorkshop package was included with your textbook, go to Chapter 6 of the Companion Website (ablongman.com/mcnergney4e) and click on VideoWorkshop. Follow the instructions for viewing video clip 5. Then consider this information along with what you've read in Chapter 6 while answering the following questions.

1. Explain which philosophy presented in the chapter best represents your views. How does your philosophy embrace or reject the philosophical notions discussed in video clip 5?

2. What patterns do you see within the Western philosophies presented in this chapter? Are certain emphases placed on issues from the video clip 5 that you disagree with? Why? Which non-Western philosophy is more appealing to you, and why?

BENCHMARKS

Professional Teaching in a Diverse Society

1500s–1600s	Spanish conquer Native American peoples in Mexico and the American Southwest. Dutch, English, and French settle the Atlantic seaboard and explore North America. Dutch traders bring African slaves to plantations in the southern colonies. Such actions shape the people who will educate and be educated and will influence both individual and collective educational goals across time.
1620–1630	Puritans and Pilgrims settle in New England, establishing the pattern of education for the New England and Middle Atlantic colonies.
1635–1636	Latin grammar school is established in Boston as a college preparatory school for young men. Harvard College is founded.
1642–1647	Massachusetts Act of 1642 makes citizens responsible for the education of their children and sets a precedent for the development of compulsory education.
1647	The Massachusetts Act of 1647, known as the Old Deluder Satan Act, is passed.
1801	First Roman Catholic school in New York is established.
1819	Emma Willard asks the New York legislature to extend educational opportunities to women. First public high school opens in Boston.
1825	First edition of Noah Webster's *An American Dictionary* is published.
1827	Massachusetts becomes the first state to require every town with 500 or more families to establish a public school.
1836	First of the *McGuffey Readers* is published. About 122 million copies of the series are sold after this date.
1837–1848	Horace Mann, secretary of the Board of Education in Massachusetts, calls for sweeping reforms based on the principle of universal free education for all citizens and the belief that teaching is a profession.
1839	First public normal school (teachers college) in the United States is established in Lexington, Massachusetts.
1852	Massachusetts enacts the first compulsory attendance law.
1854	Lincoln University, the nation's first college for free African Americans, is established in Pennsylvania.
1855	First kindergarten in the United States is established by Margaretta Schurtz in Watertown, Wisconsin.
1860	Elizabeth Palmer Peabody opens the first English-speaking kindergarten in Boston.
1874	A Kalamazoo, Michigan, case specifies that states may establish and support public high schools with tax funds, which contributes to the secondary school movement and eventually to compulsory high school attendance laws.

1893–1895	The Committee of Ten on Secondary School Studies and the Committee of Fifteen on Elementary School Studies attempt to standardize public high school and elementary school curricula, respectively.
1909	First junior high schools are established in Berkeley, California, and Columbus, Ohio. The NAACP is founded through the efforts of African American leaders such as W. E. B. DuBois.
1910	Ella Flagg Young, Ph.D., the first female superintendent of schools of a large city (Chicago), becomes president of the National Education Association (NEA).
1917	Congress passes the Smith–Hughes Act, which provides federal matching funds for vocational education in public high schools.
1944	GI Bill provides financial aid for veterans to attend college.
1954	The Supreme Court rules in *Brown* v. *Board of Education of Topeka, Kansas,* that separate but equal schooling is unconstitutional on the grounds that segregated schools generate feelings of racial inferiority and are inherently unequal.
1968	Bilingual Education Act enacted into law to address the special needs of students whose first language is not English.
1972	Title IX of the Education Amendments Act prohibits sex discrimination in schools receiving federal funds. Indian Education and Self-Determination Act gives Native Americans more control over their schooling.
1975	Education of the Handicapped Act (EHA) increases federal commitment to the education of children with disabilities and establishes a basis for subsequent special education legislation.
1979–1980	Department of Education is established; the U.S. secretary of education becomes a cabinet-level post.
1983	National Commission on Excellence in Education issues a report, *A Nation at Risk,* which leads to new calls for educational reform to eliminate literacy and raise SAT scores.
1989	Presidential Summit Conference on Education held in Charlottesville, Virginia, attended by President George H. Bush and the fifty governors, who agree that "Good education makes good politics, good business, and good sense."
1994	President Bill Clinton and Congress cooperate to pass the Goals 2000: Educate America Act, which adds two new education goals on teacher quality and parent involvement to the 1989 National Education Goals. Grants are also established to help states set standards and create new student assessments.

DEVELOPING A PROFESSIONAL PORTFOLIO

Your Own Philosophy of Teaching

Regardless of our levels of experience as educators, each of us has our own way of thinking about teaching and learning. Our ideas are shaped over time through human interactions and through such influences as reading and coursework. To explore your philosophy of teaching, try to respond to the questions below. Then write a two- to three-paragraph statement that summarizes your philosophy.

■ How do you define learning and how would you determine if learning has occurred?

■ What do you need to know about students to be able to teach them?

■ How do you describe good teaching?

Next, find an experienced teacher who is willing to answer the same questions. (You might want to ask her permission to audiotape her responses.) How do your responses compare to hers? Why do you think your answers are the same or different?

ONLINE ACTIVITY

Exploring the Library of Congress

No teacher should miss the opportunity to explore our nation's history via the Library of Congress online (www.loc.gov), an amazing resource for teaching and learning. Click on "America's Library: Fun for Kids and Families." You will find five links that connect to different ways to use online resources for the teaching of history and American culture. These links are described below.

First, explore the links, then rate each one for its potential motivational value for students. When you finish, compare your ratings to those of your classmates and discuss why you agree or disagree.

1. Meet Amazing Americans—discover the inventors, politicians, performers, activists, and everyday people who shaped our country's history.

    Low   Medium   High

2. Jump Back in Time—travel to an era in American history.

    Low   Medium   High

3. Explore the States—click on a state you wish to investigate.

    Low   Medium   High

4. Join America at Play—explore America's favorite pastimes, sports, and hobbies.

    Low   Medium   High

5. See, Hear and Sing—watch a movie, hear a song, or play a tune from America's past.

    Low   Medium   High

THREE *Education from the Outside In*

aribel spent her first four years of elementary school in small portable classrooms [trailers] that had no windows, no insulation, and no air conditioning. The cramped quarters were like little cells—dark and dreary spaces that were often too hot or too cold for students and teachers to work comfortably. The playground was small and the equipment was old. Many of the water fountains didn't work and those that did ran only lukewarm water that did little to quench a student's thirst on a hot Arizona afternoon.

"You'd look around and think, 'They don't even take care of this and that,'" recalls the soft-spoken fifteen-year-old. "They don't care about me."

And then, towards the end of Maribel's third-grade year, the unbelievable happened. The students, staff, and families at Capitol Elementary School received word that a new facility would be built. "It was like, Whoa! Maybe they do care about us," says Maribel. "It inspired me. It made me happy. I thought, now I really do have to study and work hard." (Furger, 2002, p.10)

Schools are not simply physical structures that serve to invite or impede learning. People and money help make them what they are. The chapters in Part 3 explain that it is important for teachers to understand how schools compare, how they are managed by school leaders and governed by law, and why proper financing is so critical to their success.

$\mathcal{W}$here Teachers Work: Schools

$\mathcal{A}$mericans have long believed that the road to a better life runs through schools. As educational researcher Gerald Bracey notes, the quality of schools is defined increasingly in terms of students' scores on standardized achievement tests.

> For almost twenty years now, some of our most prominent business leaders and politicians have sounded the same alarm about the nation's public schools. It began in earnest with that 1983 golden treasury of selected, spun and distorted education statistics, "A Nation At Risk," whose authors wrote, "If only to keep and improve on the slim competitive edge we retain in world markets, we must dedicate ourselves to the reform of our educational system." The document tightly yoked our economic position in the world to how well or poorly students bubbled in answer sheets on standardized tests.
>
> And it continued in September 2000, when a national commission on math and science teaching headed by former Ohio senator John Glenn issued a report titled "Before It's Too Late." It asked rhetorically, "In an integrated, global economy . . . will our children be able to compete?" The report's entirely predictable answer: Not if we don't improve schools *before it's too late."* (2002, p. B4)

CHAPTER CONTENTS

What Is a School?

How Is Public Schooling Organized in the United States?

What Are Some Schooling Alternatives?

How Are Schools Administered?

What Organizational and Policy Issues Do Schools Face?

What Makes Some Schools More Effective Than Others?

Today, as in the past, Americans pin their hopes for a better world on schools. As each call for change is debated, the focus of discussion is often on ways to increase learning. Opinions as to how we can accomplish that goal, however, vary greatly.

This chapter provides an overview of the different types of schools that exist in the United States, from public elementary schools and four-year universities to magnet schools and home schools. As prospective teachers you should be aware of all these schooling options so you can consider the full range of teaching options.

What Is a School?

If someone asked you what a school is, what would you say? Would you describe the physical structure of a building or talk about the activities that occur in classrooms? Or would you talk about school as a **social institution,** that is, an organization with an identifiable structure meant to preserve social order?

Although schools have unique characteristics, they share the same primary function: to move young people into the mainstream of society. The curricula, teaching, evaluation, and relationships among people in a school reinforce an ideal toward which young people are expected to work. This ideal is concerned with preserving our heritage, adapting to social change, and making change happen where needed. Therefore, school is a social institution, because it shapes the lives of students and the future of society.

Schools are places where people come together and stay together for an extended period of time. In such settings, educators work with parents, children, and outside agencies to ensure the psychological and physical well-being of students and to promote academic success. These people also work together to help students understand and accept others. In fact, many reformers focus on making changes in schools because of schools' ability to shape future generations.

School Districts

In terms of public education, the common method of organization is the **school district.** A school district is a state-defined geographical area responsible for providing public instruction to students living within that area. Grouping schools this way is efficient for administrative and financial purposes. School districts also are useful for creating uniformity in what students in different schools are learning.

Most school districts are made up of separate schools for students of different ages, such as elementary and senior high schools. During the 1999–2000 school year, there were 16,850 districts in the United States. Within those districts were 94,090 schools and 47.7 million students in prekindergarten through twelfth grade.

Because school districts are determined by geography and population, they range in size from quite small to quite large. The average U.S. school district includes 5.6 schools, but the 100 largest school districts average 155.6 schools. New York City school district—the largest in the country—has over one million students enrolled in 1,207 schools. Los Angeles Unified, the second-largest district, has 710,007 students in 655 schools (U.S. Department of Education, 2001). In contrast, Tecumseh Public Schools in Tecumseh, Nebraska, have a total enrollment of 394 students in two schools.

Types of Schools

What types of public and private schools are available to children in the United States? (See Figure 7.1.) Schools are designed for students of many different ages,

FIGURE 7.1   **Some Types of Schools in America**   It is difficult in many cases to draw solid lines between the three columns in this chart. Can you develop a hypothesis that you think might explain this difficulty?

PUBLIC SCHOOLS	PUBLIC ALTERNATIVE SCHOOLS	PRIVATE SCHOOLS
Kindergarten (K)	Head Start	Nursery Schools & Preschools
Elementary School (K/1–6 or K/1–8)	Prekindergarten Programs	"Concept School" Alternatives
• Primary (K–2)	Laboratory Schools	• Montessori Schools
• Intermediate (3–6)	Nongraded Schools	• Waldorf Schools
Middle School (5–8)	Magnet Schools	"Ethnic School" Alternatives
Secondary Schools	Charter Schools	• Afrocentric Schools (Black Academies)
• Junior High School (7–8 or 7–9)	Accelerated Schools	• Reservation Schools
• High School (7–12, 9–12, or 10–12)	Cluster Schools	Parochial/Religious Schools
Post-Secondary Schools	Vocational–Technical Schools	• Catholic Schools
• Community Colleges	Professional Development Schools	• Christian Academies
• State Colleges	Government-Run Schools	• Hebrew Schools
• State Universities	• Department of Defense Dependents Schools	• Islamic Schools
	• Native-American Schools	College Preparatory Schools
	• Career Academies	Trade Schools
	• Job Corps	Military Academies
	Home Schooling	Junior Colleges
		Colleges & Universities
		Adult Education Centers

from preschool to college. Depending on the students they serve, schools can differ in structure (organization) and function (programs and services). Although the most common type of school is the public school, many alternatives are available. Within the boundaries of most public school districts, for example, you also can find magnet schools, charter schools, alternative schools, and vocational or trade schools. These public school alternatives are discussed later in this chapter.

Other ways that schools can be categorized include elementary, middle, junior high, and senior high. In these schools, age is the determining factor. The geographical categories of rural schools, suburban schools, and urban schools each have their own set of issues and concerns, but they also share many of the same goals and purposes. Chief among these goals is providing a positive educational environment for students.

How Is Public Schooling Organized in the United States?

One of the important decisions prospective teachers must make is what level or grade of school they want to teach. In the U.S. public school system, teachers can work with students from preschool age up to the typical college age. Teachers might also work in preschool programs, or they might teach graduate school students. Each level has its own set of pros and cons, so if you choose to work in public schooling, you should be familiar with its organization.

Many children attend preschool, but enrollment rates vary according to family income and race or ethnicity, because preschool programs can be costly. By age five, when students are required by law to begin schooling, most children are enrolled in public schools. This begins their involvement with public schooling, where student organization is based primarily on students' ages. Elementary schools often classify students as primary (kindergarten through second grade) and intermediate (third through sixth grade) students. In some school districts, students in grades four through six, five through seven, or six through eight attend middle schools. In other districts students in grades seven through eight or seven through nine are enrolled in junior high schools.

High schools, or secondary schools, usually include grades nine through twelve or ten through twelve. Because parents and school leaders want high school students to continue their education, high schools try to prepare students to move up the academic ladder. When students graduate from high school, their education options include technical or vocational institutions, two-year colleges, and four-year colleges and universities. However, students' access to higher education is influenced in large part by the cost of these programs.

Early Childhood Education

Many of the first early childhood education programs in the United States were day nurseries funded by philanthropic organizations associated with settlement houses. Today, both public and private sponsors support many more kinds of preschool programs. Examples of such sponsors are Project Head Start, infant intervention and enrichment programs, nursery schools, public and private prekindergartens and kindergartens, college and university laboratory schools, church-sponsored preschools, and parent cooperatives, which all offer a variety of educational programs for young children.

Although enrollment in such programs has gradually increased over time, not all children have access to preschool. European American and African American three- and four-year-olds, for example, participate in early childhood programs at higher rates than do Latino children.

With so many agencies sponsoring preschool programs, many types of services are offered and many families are served. While some preschools offer full-day educational care, others offer only half-day programs. Certain preschools serve only children from low-income families, children of adolescent parents, or children with disabilities.

Program goals and philosophies about teaching and learning vary considerably among various preschools. The professional preparation of early childhood education staff and the quality of programs also differ greatly. Although evidence points to the benefits of early learning opportunities, some children do not participate in high-quality preschool programs. For example, children from low-income families, particularly the working poor, are least likely to have access to high-quality programs. In response to these concerns, some states now require preschool programs to earn accreditation from the **National Association for the Education of Young Children (NAEYC),** the largest professional association for early childhood educators.

Some advocates believe such accreditation efforts will improve the quality of preschool programs, but others argue that it is funding for public preschool programs that must be increased. In 2002 the national average wage for an early childhood teacher was reported to be less than $10 per hour. Such low wages make it difficult to attract and retain qualified staff—and staff ultimately make the difference in what children experience at school. **Why are preschool staff paid so poorly?**

Kindergarten

Nine states—Alaska, Colorado, Idaho, Michigan, New Hampshire, New Jersey, New York, North Dakota, and Pennsylvania—do not require school districts to offer any type of kindergarten program. In practice, however, every state pays for at least some school districts to offer half-day kindergarten programs. In addition, twenty-five states and the District of Columbia subsidize kindergarten for the full school day in districts that offer it. But only eight states and the District require schools to offer full-day kindergarten programs (Olson, 2002).

Findings from a recent study of 17,600 Philadelphia schoolchildren suggest full-time kindergarten programs may have both academic and financial benefits. By the time children in the study reached third and fourth grades, former full-day kindergartners were twice as likely as children without kindergarten experience and 26 percent more likely than children from half-day programs to have succeeded in school without repeating a grade. Researchers estimated the lower retention rates reduced the cost of full-day kindergarten education by 19 percent; that is, moving children through schools with a lower incidence of failure reduced the cost of providing full-day kindergarten. In 1999 that savings worked out to about $2 million for every one thousand kindergartners (Viadero, 2002).

In some kindergarten programs, teachers offer an academic curriculum. These classrooms offer whole-group settings, teacher-centered instruction, worksheets, and other traditional methods. Such kindergarten programs have few opportunities for small-group, individualized, or hands-on activities. Other kindergarten teachers use a more student-centered, "developmentally appropriate" curriculum. This usually means that students are expected to acquire skills and concepts at their own pace through exploration and free play. **To what extent should kindergartens focus on academics?**

How is early childhood education organized in the United States? What alternatives exist for education at the preschool and kindergarten levels?

Elementary Schools

Elementary schools exhibit many variations in curricula and instructional methods. Often, students are grouped homogeneously by ability or achievement for instructional purposes. Such grouping can occur within a single classroom or across many classrooms. In other settings, students work in **nongraded classrooms.** Such classrooms may include students of heterogeneous abilities and sometimes students of different ages. Nongraded programs, also referred to as multiage, multigrade, or family grouping programs, are most prevalent in primary schools.

Nongraded programs try to provide curriculum tailored to students' stages of intellectual, emotional, physical, or social development. They allow for individualized, continuous progress for young children. While there are standards for students' performance, the time and methods taken to reach these standards vary from student to student. Grouping for instruction is flexible and based on the abilities, interests, and needs of students. In these programs there is no formal promotion from one grade to the next. Instead, a student stays with a group of students until he or she has mastered necessary skills.

Research on elementary schools suggests that nongrading can be quite effective as a grouping method. The positive effects are greatest in situations where students are grouped across age lines in only one subject (usually reading) or in multiple subjects, with students receiving direct instruction for the majority of a class session. Experts agree that groupings should not be unchanging, however. They should be reassessed frequently and changed when student performance indicates a mismatch in instruction and achievement (Good & Brophy, 2003). **Should schools use multiage rather than graded groupings?**

Junior High Schools and Middle Schools

The first junior high school opened in 1909 as a three-year intermediate school in Columbus, Ohio. Since then, junior high schools have been an important part of the U.S. education system. Junior high school programs are meant to help students make the transition from elementary to high school by concentrating on academic subjects and by exposing students to careers and occupations. They are also helpful on a social level for students not yet ready to mix with seventeen- and eighteen-year-olds.

Most junior high schools include students who are in grades seven through nine. As in elementary schools, instruction occurs mainly in self-contained classrooms. Curriculum at the junior high school level, however, is usually more diversified; that is, more types of courses are offered. Like their colleagues at the senior high school level, junior high school teachers generally specialize in the content and teaching of a particular subject area. Junior high schools typically schedule six class periods per day, and instruction is usually teacher directed. In many respects, then, junior high schools are very similar to senior high schools.

Middle schools, which emerged in the 1960s, aim to provide an educational environment less imitative of high school and better suited to the developmental needs of ten- to fourteen-year-olds. Middle schools are particularly popular in the suburbs, where large populations of school-age children live. Between 1990 and 2001, the number of middle schools (grades four through six or six through eight) increased by 35 percent. During that same period, the number of junior high schools declined by 22 percent (U.S. Department of Education, 2002). Recently, however, middle schools have been criticized for creating programs similar to the ones they were supposed to replace. In part, this may be due to the fact that many middle school teachers have not been prepared to teach at this level (Dickenson & Butler, 2001).

The National Middle School Association (NMSA) has attempted to increase public awareness of the critical need for improved education for ten- to fifteen-year olds. In

How are middle schools different from junior high schools? Why has the middle school movement spread so successfully nationwide?

2002 the NMSA and the National Association of Elementary School Principals encouraged principals, teachers, school counselors, parents, and students at both elementary and middle school levels to work together to ease the transition to middle school. The NMSA also created an annual celebration called Month of the Young Adolescent. Held each October, this program celebrates the accomplishments of young people and creates awareness of their needs and characteristics.

Educators working to build academic programs that are developmentally appropriate for young adolescents use instructional strategies that allow for peer interaction and encourage team teaching. They also may alter the length of time that students work with teachers.

One example of this kind of program can be seen at the Indian Hills Middle School in Shawnee Mission, Kansas. There, principal Jim Wink experimented with **looping**— a grouping strategy that keeps students together for a longer period of time than in traditional schools. At Indian Hills, some teachers accompanied groups of students for two years. At the beginning of the second year of looping, teachers already knew students' strengths and weaknesses. As a result, the students were able to progress through the curriculum at a faster pace than their nonlooping peers. In addition, teachers commented that students seemed less apprehensive about starting the new year. Other outcomes of looping were greater parental involvement in school activities and a lower rate of discipline referrals. The resource teacher also noted that many of the special education students in the looping group were at grade level by the end of the second year (McCown & Sherman, 2002).

High Schools

High schools vary greatly in size. The total enrollment in alternative schools may be as low as two hundred. On the other end of the spectrum, one out of four students attends a school with an enrollment over one thousand. In fact, enrollments of two or three thousand are not uncommon. As noted in Chapter 5, comprehensive high schools—large high schools having a full range of programs—evolved over time. The comprehensive high school as it exists today emerged in the late 1950s, primarily through the efforts of former Harvard University president James B. Conant.

Large high schools can offer a wide variety of curricula fairly economically. They typically provide courses to prepare students for vocational or technical areas and for college. To graduate, students must complete a certain number of credit hours in core courses. But high schools offer many other kinds of experiences. Some schools, like Missouri's Pattonville High School, require students to spend fifty hours performing community service.

Comprehensive schools are not without their critics. The results of one study suggest conditions in small schools are more conducive to learning than the conditions in large schools. Researchers also found that teachers in smaller schools know their students better than do teachers in comprehensive schools. Additionally, teachers in smaller schools use a broader range of strategies to engage students (Walsley, Fine, Gladden, Holland, King, Mosak, & Powell, 2000).

Whether a student attends a small or a comprehensive high school, studies indicate the importance of a challenging high school curriculum. These studies show that students who took rigorous coursework in high school were more likely to receive a bachelor's degree. Specifically, researchers studied high school graduates three years after they entered a four-year degree program. They found that 87 percent of the students who took advanced coursework obtained a bachelor's degree. Only 62 percent of the students who had not exceeded the basic curriculum in high school received their bachelor's (National Center for Education Statistics, 2001). **Are high schools too big and too comprehensive?**

Higher Education

A variety of higher education opportunities are available to students once they finish high school, including two-year and four-year colleges, technical training schools, and nondegree courses. Today more than ever students are taking advantage of these opportunities. In fact, the percentage of high school graduates enrolling in college immediately after graduation has increased steadily over the past three decades. In October 2000, 63 percent of high school graduates enrolled in college, compared to 49 percent in 1972. Of the October 2000 group, the enrollment rate was higher for women (66.2 percent) than for men (59.9 percent). Among racial and ethnic groups, 64 percent of European American, 56.2 percent of African American, and 53 percent of Hispanic American students went on to college. Two-thirds of these students entered four-year institutions (U.S. Bureau of Labor Statistics, 2001).

Entering a two- or four-year college is the typical choice for many recent high school graduates. The missions of two- and four-year colleges are somewhat different. Two-year colleges typically offer basic undergraduate liberal arts and sciences courses, while providing a wide range of vocational, technical, and adult education programs. They also offer a variety of professional and preprofessional programs, including programs for nursing and education. Four-year colleges and universities generally provide a full undergraduate program, leading to a bachelor's degree. Many four-year institutions offer advanced graduate and professional degree programs as well.

Adult education programs are good for the mind, body, and budget. The increasing numbers of younger and older adults participating in such programs illustrate the

Issues in School Reform

SCHOOL CONSOLIDATION

Over the past several decades, one trend in the United States has been to consolidate small schools. In 1930, there were more than 247,000 public schools, compared to over 90,000 today.

Rural communities have tried to meet fiscal shortfalls by consolidating schools. As a response to a century-old pattern of rural decline, school consolidation has been one of American education's longest-lasting reform efforts. By combining schools, proponents argue it is possible to cut administrative and facilities expenses while still offering students a broad curriculum.

In recent years, many communities have resisted consolidation, because they like knowing and working closely with a small number of administrators and teachers. Moving their children to a larger, more distant school means parents will have less say in the day-to-day running of schools (Schwisow, 2002). Parents also contend that, while money may be saved by closing school buildings, additional transportation expenses may more than offset savings. Furthermore, the prospect of having their children spend excessive amounts of time riding buses to and from school has encouraged many parents to speak out against consolidation.

Another factor contributing to resistance to consolidation is the "small school advantage." A growing body of research suggests that small schools help students develop strong relationships with teachers and colleagues, promote greater student and parent involvement, and foster a positive school culture (Walsley et al., 2000).

Critical Thinking Question

If you were a teacher in a small school, what are some of the factors that might prompt you to support or resist school consolidation?

Companion Website

To answer this question online and e-mail your answer to your professor, go to Chapter 7 of the Companion Website (ablongman.com/ mcnergney4e) and click on Issues in School Reform.

---

possibilities for lifelong learning. Adult education classes offer opportunities for everyone to pursue interests, develop talents, and increase literacy skills, no matter how old they are. According to the second report from the National Adult Literacy Survey, adults with higher literacy skills are more likely to work full time, earn high wages, and maintain better health (U.S. Department of Education, 1998).

What Are Some Schooling Alternatives?

What do you know about alternative schools? How are they different from "regular" schools?   Many people believe alternative schools provide specialized or "nonconforming" programs for "at risk" or "bad" students. In reality, alternative schools are for all types of learners. The schools operate within the public school system, and they address the needs or interests of specific student groups.

Some **alternative schools** are self-contained programs that exist outside the general public schools. Others are organized as schools within schools. Although many models of alternative schooling can be found in the United States, they share many of the following attributes: small school size, small class size, voluntary membership, lack of ability grouping and other forms of labeling, school-based management, student involvement in governance, and extended roles for teachers that include counseling and guidance.

Magnet Schools

Magnet schools are alternative schools within a public school system that accept students from the whole district, instead of only from the local neighborhood. Magnet

What are some alternatives to the comprehensive high school model? What other schooling alternatives exist for students in preprimary grades through grade eight?

schools emerged in the 1970s, primarily as a way to desegregate schools. At that time, many people thought schools were integrated only because of mandatory busing. The goal of magnet schools was to offer an environment so appealing that a racial cross section of students would attend voluntarily. The appeal of magnet programs today is strong enough that they often have waiting lists for enrollment.

The characteristics of magnet schools are (1) an enrollment policy that opens the school to children beyond a particular geographic area, (2) a student body that is present by choice and that meets inclusion criteria, and (3) a curriculum based on a special theme or instructional method. Magnet schools are available at any level, from preschool to senior high school. They may organize their curricula around a specific area, such as mathematics and computers, the arts, or the sciences, or around general academics, such as college preparation and honors courses.

Vocational–Technical Schools

For students who do not plan to go to college, vocational–technical high schools are a helpful alternative to general high schools. Vocational–technical schools help students prepare to get a job by training them for specific trades and technical employment. These schools offer programs in areas such as the following:

- Cosmetology
- Food preparation
- Law enforcement
- Horticulture
- Automotive repair
- Tool and machine operation
- Air conditioning and refrigeration repair
- Building construction
- Masonry
- Graphic and commercial arts
- Drafting
- Electronics repair
- Data processing
- Health-related fields
- Child care

Although vocational–technical high schools prepare people to assume jobs upon graduation, students who attend these schools may go on to community colleges or four-year institutions. As you might expect, vocational–technical schools that integrate academic work with technical training are thought to provide the best opportunities for continued development.

*V*ocational–technical schools train students for specific trades and technical employment in areas such as food preparation, cosmetology, and auto repair.

One example of an innovative vocational–technical school is the Metropolitan Regional Career and Technical Center (Met) in Providence, Rhode Island. It offers a unique education program best described as "avocational" (Keough, 1999). In 2002, the Met had two small schools, each with 110 students, eight teachers (advisors), a principal, administrative staff, and specialists in college placement, internships, and special education. Advisors at the Met do not teach classes in the traditional sense. Instead, they work one-on-one with the same fourteen students over a four-year period, designing curriculum and instruction to fit individual students. Met students take at least one college course before graduating, and they may take formal courses at nearby colleges, including Brown University. Students also can choose to do a two-day-a-week internship. Other than required statewide exams, the Met does not give tests. Instead, students demonstrate learning through portfolios and projects related to their internships.

The absence of a standard curriculum and assessment process at the Met has raised more than one eyebrow. Nonetheless, staff members insist their program is effective:

> Since opening in 1996, the Met has had one-third the dropout rate, one-third the absentee rate, and one-eighteenth the suspension rate of other public high schools in Providence. Every Met graduate has been accepted to college, even though more than half are from families where no one has ever attended college. (The Met, 2002)

Do public schools put enough emphasis on vocational education?

Montessori and Waldorf Schools

Both public and private alternative schools often have broad educational philosophies. Montessori and Waldorf schools are examples of these various philosophies in action. These two alternative schools focus specifically on young students and the best ways for them to learn. Montessori preschools encourage the development of children's perceptual, motor, intellectual, and social skills. These programs are based on the ideas of Maria Montessori (1870–1952), a physician who developed preschool teaching methods in the early 1900s. She focused on students' rates of maturity and their readiness to learn particular skills at certain ages. Teachers trained in Montessori methods use materials specifically designed to help children discover the physical properties of objects. For example, as students interact with the "pink tower" (blocks of graduated size), teachers act as observers. They assist students indirectly by asking questions or providing additional materials to help students learn. Most Montessori instructional materials are graded and self-correcting, so students experience personal freedom within the structure of the classroom. Montessori schools are typically limited to early education and preschools.

At the other end of the philosophical spectrum, Waldorf education opposes the structured acquisition of specific skills. Waldorf education has its roots in the spiritual–scientific research of Rudolf Steiner (1861–1925). Steiner was an Austrian scientist and educator who believed young children learn primarily through their senses. He also believed that children's most active method of learning is imitation. In Waldorf preschools, therefore, creative play is viewed as the critical element in a child's development. With creative play, children learn at their own pace and from one another. Waldorf teachers argue that premature intellectual demands weaken the very powers of judgment and practical intelligence they are trying to build (Barnes, 1991).

There are over one hundred Waldorf schools in the United States and Canada, and most of them are private. Although the majority are elementary schools, a few secondary schools follow the Waldorf model. All Waldorf schools have a strong spiritual component, though they are not affiliated with a specific religious group. Ideally, teachers remain with the same group of students from first through eighth grades.

Private and Independent Schools

Private schools—sometimes called independent schools—are nonprofit, tax-exempt institutions governed by boards of trustees. They are financed through private funds, such as tuition, endowments, and grants. Some are religiously affiliated, while others are secular. All private schools are accredited by state departments of education, must meet state and local health and safety rules, and must observe mandatory school attendance laws.

There are 27,223 private elementary and secondary schools in the United States (National Center for Educational Statistics, 2001b). Nonreligious private schools vary in focus, structure, social organization, and size. Military schools, for example, emphasize self-discipline and encourage academic study. Elite college preparatory schools place a high premium on academic achievement. Some private schools are less easily classified and develop their own unique personalities.

Some people support private and semiprivate alternatives because they believe competition will force public schools to improve. Other people like private schools because they may offer smaller classes or more rigorous academics. In some cases, people support private schools because they serve a special interest or set of beliefs. For these reasons and more, private schools are an attractive alternative to public schools for some teachers, parents, and students.

Despite many similarities, private schools differ from public schools in several ways:

■ Public schools are tax supported, while private schools are not.

■ Private schools can set their own admissions requirements, while public schools must accept all those who come for an education.

■ Private school students are enrolled by parental or student choice, while public schools typically serve only students in their districts.

■ Private schools are free to follow philosophies that appeal to specific groups of people, while public schools must serve everyone.

Traditionally, the lines separating public from private schools have been the source of funds and the prohibition of religious activity in public schools. Those lines, however, have been continually challenged. In particular, distinctions between public and private education are obscured by (1) state loans of secular textbooks to church schools, (2) state reimbursement of funds for transportation to church schools, and (3) public funding for private and parochial schools' required standardized tests and other services. In 1999, Florida was the first state to enact legislation to permit the use of public funds for private schools. **Do you think distinctions between public and private schooling should be clarified?**

For-Profit Schools

Since the late 1980s, concepts of **for-profit schools** have gained attention as alternatives to public schools. For-profit schools do not claim tax-exempt status because they are run by private companies as businesses. Their goal is to make money. For-profit schools claim that for the same amount of money or less they can deliver better education to children than can public schools. In short, advocates of for-profit schools want to privatize education—move it out of the public realm and into the control of private enterprises.

For-profit schools must meet the same requirements as public schools. Their students must take and pass tests required by the states in which they reside. They cannot discriminate on the basis of ethnic origin, race, or gender.

One of the most visible efforts to create and sustain for-profit schools is Edison Schools, Inc., headquartered in New York City. Edison opened its first four schools in August 1995. By 2001, Edison was responsible for teaching approximately 74,000 students in 133 schools. Most of Edison's schools are in urban areas, including Dallas and San Francisco. It also runs the 1,500-student Inkster, Michigan, school district. Despite the company's visibility, Edison has lost hundreds of millions of dollars and has fallen out of favor with investors. In May 2002 Edison announced that one of its first charter schools—the Boston Renaissance Charter School, with 1,300 students in grades K through twelve—terminated a contract that was supposed to run until 2005.

At the same time, Michigan's National Heritage Academies, Inc., announced a small profit for 2001. National Heritage manages more than two dozen charter schools across the country. It is believed to be the nation's first charter school management company of significant size to make a profit (Walsh, 2002). **What are the pros and cons of running a school as a business?**

Charter Schools

Charter schools are independent public schools supported by state funds but exempt from many regulations. They are based on a contract, or charter, between school organizers (parents, teachers, or others) and a sponsor (usually a local or state board of education or, in some cases, universities). Organizers generally have the power to hire and fire staff and to budget money as they see fit. In turn, they guarantee the sponsor certain academic outcomes; that is, students will meet or exceed the levels of academic performance expected of their counterparts in public schools. Charter schools developed in the 1990s and have been described as the "upstart reform idea of the decade." To some people, charter schools offer a way to promote school accountability and excellence in educational outcomes. They also permit parents and teachers to have more say in what goes on within the school.

Like other reform initiatives, charter schools are meant to be innovative—to reach out to those students who are not being served well by the public schools. Some charter

Your Teaching Life in Practice

CHARTER SCHOOLS

The number of charter schools in the United States has grown tremendously in the past decade. Charters allow families choices; students can "shop" for an education—an idea many people find appealing. Not everyone agrees that charters are the answer for solving the nation's educational ills, however. Mary, the parent of a ninth-grader in the local high school, likes the concept of charter schools. Her neighbor, Sanchita, questions the effectiveness of charters. She also worries that each time a bright student like Mary's daughter leaves the system, the public schools are weakened.

Mary: Many students in today's schools are not succeeding academically. With the competing needs and interests of today's youth, how can we expect public schools to meet the challenge? We must have alternatives for young people who don't "fit the mold." Because many charter schools are created with a particular philosophy or special emphasis, they may be better suited to students underserved by traditional public schools.

Sanchita: The idea of choice is a reasonable one only if students everywhere are held to the same academic standard. Some district officials say charter schools have lower standards for behavior and offer an easier curriculum than public schools. Is that a good way to prepare young people for the future? How can we be sure students aren't leaving public schools because they want an easier path to a diploma?

Mary: While charters are free from the rules and regulations governing public schools, they are held accountable. Like public schools, charters usually align curriculum with state standards, because end-of-the-year tests will focus on that content. Based on test scores to date, charter schools seem to be doing a good job.

Sanchita: It may not be fair to compare test scores in public and charter schools. Charters can select their students and also ask them to leave if certain conditions are not met; public schools must serve everyone. It is also conceivable that students whose parents exercise choice are more involved in their students' education than parents of students in public schools. This may be a factor in student performance. Some public schools—already strapped financially—have experienced significant decreases in state aid when students have gone to charters. With less money in the coffers, education programs in public schools are less able to provide optimal conditions for learning.

Mary: Charter schools do compete with public schools for funding, but that may be just what our schools need. There's nothing like competition to encourage change. Some school districts have started advertising and public relations campaigns to boost their schools' images. They are thinking of strategies to involve parents, teachers, business leaders, and others in this effort. Some public schools also interview students leaving for charters to find out what prompted the move. These and other efforts suggest charters have nudged public schools out of complacency, something long overdue!

Sanchita: Let's not be too hasty to endorse charters. Most of the charter school research has focused on the characteristics of charter schools and the challenges they face. Let's take a closer look at achievement of children of similar socioeconomic levels to see if charters do make a difference in academic achievement.

Activity:

How many charter schools have been established in your state? Go to the website for the Center for Education Reform (http://www.edreform.com/charter_schools/) and click on the map of the United States to learn more about the status of charter schools across the country.

To answer this question online and e-mail your answer to your professor, go to Chapter 7 of the Companion Website (ablongman.com/mcnergney4e) and click on Your Teaching Life in Practice.

schools offer a rigorous classical education, while others integrate academics and counseling with technical and experiential training. Some charter schools serve homeless children and wards of the state. Still others are for deaf and hearing-impaired students or for dropouts and at-risk young people.

In 1991 Minnesota became the first state to approve the concept of charter schools. According to Minnesota law, only certified teachers can contract with local school boards to create charters. While the boards have a say in what outcomes charters must meet, the boards do not participate in the charters' day-to-day operations.

By 2001, thirty-seven states, the District of Columbia, and Puerto Rico had signed charter legislation into law. At that time, Arizona had the most charters (421) of any state as well as the nation's most charter-friendly laws (Sack, 2002). Other states, such as Kentucky, prohibited charter schools. But even among those states, many have altered regulations to allow schools to operate with "charterlike" autonomy.

Parochial Schools

As defined in Chapter 4, private schools operated by religious organizations are called parochial schools. Parochial schools have long been an alternative to public schools in the United States. Although they receive funding from public schools for student transportation and testing, most parochial schools charge a tuition fee. Interestingly, more than a few students attending parochial schools are not from particularly religious families. These types of schools often are believed to offer a better education than public schools for less money than private schools.

Catholic schools account for the largest number of parochial school students. The majority of these students attend schools in New York, Pennsylvania, California, Illinois, and Ohio. Other areas of the country where Catholic schools are prominent include New Orleans, Louisiana, and Detroit, Michigan.

In St. Louis, Missouri, and other cities around the country, charter schools are competing with Catholic schools. Some parents who believe inner-city public schools

Catholic schools are believed to offer a better education than public schools for less money than private schools. Why do you think this is true?

provide a low-quality education view charter schools as attractive alternatives to parochial schools. The movement of students from Catholic schools to charter schools has not gone unnoticed by Catholic educators, but it has not caused alarm. Instead, it has underscored for Catholic educators the importance of marketing (Zehr, 2002).

While Catholic schools are the most popular parochial schools, some 200,000 children attend approximately 650 Jewish day schools in North America. The majority of them are Orthodox Jewish schools. In the past twenty years, however, many schools have been founded by groups that once opposed the idea of separate schools for Jewish children. Jewish day schools are springing up not only in large Jewish population centers in the Northeast and Southern California, but also in Atlanta, for example. There, seven Jewish schools operate, representing every major movement. Each of the schools welcomes Jewish children regardless of their family's sect. In fact, about 25 percent of students attending Atlanta's Torah Day School are non-Orthodox Jews (Archer, 1998).

Fundamentalist Christian schools are growing in number more quickly than are other private schools. This growth is due primarily to the popular appeal of their philosophies and curricula. Melinda Wagner's 1990 study of nine Christian schools' philosophies in the southeastern United States suggests why this may be so. Wagner found that conservative Christians try to "create" an ideal culture to serve as a "crucible of change" for fixing the inadequacies and evils in existing culture (p. 20). Building their own schools to educate children certainly helps meet this goal.

Home Schools

Some parents choose to take on the role of teacher themselves and educate their children at home. The U.S. Department of Education (2002) estimates that more than one million primary and secondary students in the United States study in "home schools." Other estimates go as high as 1.8 million. Reliable numbers are hard to come by for several reasons. First, many states define and track homeschoolers differently. Second, some parents do not comply with state rules requiring them to register their home-schooled children. In addition, some parents do not join home school support groups, another way of counting heads.

In a survey conducted by the National Center for Education Statistics (2001c), parents were asked to list reasons for homeschooling. Among the sixteen categories parents mentioned, leading reasons included better education (48.9 percent), religious reasons (38.4 percent), and avoiding a poor public school environment (25.6 percent). (See Chapter 9 for a discussion of some legal issues involving homeschooling.)   **From your perspective, what are the pros and cons of homeschooling?**

*H*ow Are Schools Administered?

When people think about schools, they often picture a school building, teachers, and students. Missing from this picture are the people who administer the schools, who take care of the daily business of running schools so teachers and students can concentrate on learning. From the **superintendent of schools** to the general office staff, the administration of schools has changed over time. Increased demands and constraints from both inside and outside schools have greatly affected the way they operate. For one, today's school administrators have much less flexibility in making decisions than their predecessors had. As you will read in Chapter 8, they must contend with state-aid formulas, government mandates, external standards for educators' and students' performances, and a host of political interests intent on getting power. As a result, many administrators now feel caught between the need to make everyone happy and the need to make effective policy.

In the 92,000 public schools in the United States, superintendents and their associates and assistants form the **central office staff.** They, along with school principals, all tend to view their worlds in a remarkably similar way. The demands of their jobs and their training probably contribute to their common outlook. Nevertheless, it is interesting to note that administrators of schools as diverse as those we find in the United States all share some of the same issues, goals, concerns, and characteristics.

The School Superintendent

A superintendent can be thought of the chief executive officer, or CEO, of a school system, usually a school district. Superintendents are appointed by the **school board,** which is the legislative policy-making body responsible for making sure that competent individuals perform the work of schools. The school board functions like a board of directors that sets policies and then hires employees to carry them out. Because the board is made up of people with no particular expertise in school affairs, it delegates much of its power to the superintendent and his or her staff. For a better picture of the typical staff organization of public school systems, see Figure 7.2.

FIGURE 7.2   Typical Line and Staff Organization of Public School Systems
Why might the term *middle management* be used to describe principals?

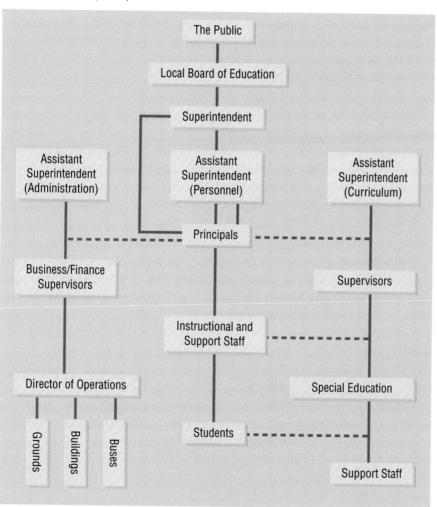

Being a superintendent can be an incredibly demanding job. Superintendents worry about financing schools, planning and goal setting, assessing educational outcomes, improving accountability and credibility, evaluating staff and administrators, developing relations with a school board, administering special education services, negotiating labor contracts, dealing with changing enrollments, and so on.

Superintendents must be able to mediate and compromise without losing the trust of people with opposing goals. They often are the go-betweens for school employees and the school board, as well as for the school and the public. With increased public and media interest in schools, the job has become especially challenging. The rapid turnover rate of superintendents reflects this trend.

The chancellor of the New York City public schools, a sort of super-superintendent, presides over thirty-two community school-district superintendents and more than 1,100 schools, 110,000 employees, and one million students. Believed to have the largest and toughest urban education challenge in the country, the chancellor is expected to be (1) an educator well versed in instruction, supervision, and administration; (2) a leader who exhibits decisiveness, shrewdness, powers of consensus building, and a commitment to children; (3) a manager having skills to run a bureaucracy with more than 100,000 employees; and (4) a strategist, good at overcoming institutional barriers.

On a smaller level, the responsibilities of the New York City school chancellor are the responsibilities of superintendents everywhere. Indeed, many more superintendents work in small communities than in large ones. One problem that faces small-town superintendents in particular is declining student enrollments, which make opportunities to offer a diverse and intellectually rich curriculum virtually impossible. Simply staffing the courses to meet minimal requirements can be a major challenge. Another challenge for rural school administrators' success is that they must be a good "fit" with their communities. In small towns, educational leaders are not nameless, faceless bureaucrats. People know where to go and who to see if they are unhappy about educational policies and practices.

Principals and Assistant Principals

Schools generally have a single administrative officer, a **principal,** responsible for the everyday operation and tone of a school. Large schools often have one or more assistant principals to help complete all the work. Although the job requires formal training, one truly becomes a principal by learning on the job.

Principals typically administer discipline and give guidance to students, deal with staff and faculty on simple to complex issues, locate substitute teachers, implement rules, conduct surveillance of halls, balance the school's budget, and maintain the building and equipment. With so many duties to perform, elementary and secondary principals are feeling the time crunch. Based on a recent survey released by the National Association of Secondary School Principals, nearly half of the 1,400 respondents reported that they work sixty hours or more a week (National Association of Secondary School Principals, 2001).

Principals in all schools perform similar everyday duties, such as observing classrooms, circulating through the building, and monitoring hallways. The ways principals interpret these activities, however, can make a big difference in their effectiveness as leaders. As indicated in Figure 7.3, effective principals share several characteristics.

One of the most important characteristics of a principal is the ability to maintain the administrative team's relationship with teachers. In the overall organization, the principal is in a position of middle management—between the superintendent and the teachers and school staff. As such, he must be able to follow and to lead. Ultimately, he must follow the policies of the school administration. But to lead the teachers and

FIGURE 7.3 **Behaviors of Effective Principals** Which of the behaviors of principals have you observed in schools? Can you think of other characteristics of effective principals?

- Lead schools in a way that emphasizes student and adult (teacher, principal, staff members) learning.
- Set high expectations and standards for the academic and social development of all students and the performance of adults.
- Demand content and instruction that ensure student achievement of agreed-upon academic standards.
- Create a culture of continuous learning for adults tied to student learning and other school goals.
- Use multiple sources of data as diagnostic tools to assess, identify, and apply instructional improvement.
- Actively engage the community to create shared responsibility for student and school success.

Source: National Association of Elementary School Principals (2001). Leading learning communities: Standards for what principals should know and be able to do (p. 2). Washington, DC: NAESP.

the support staff (guidance counselors, special education teachers, media specialists, librarians, custodians, bus drivers, and others), the principal must involve others in formulating and implementing ideas without sacrificing authority. Finding this balance between leading and following is one of the most crucial abilities principals learn on the job.

What Organizational and Policy Issues Do Schools Face?

Schools have been organized in different ways to try to meet the needs of today's students. Decisions about whether to establish separate grades, to implement multiage groupings, or to separate students by gender shape the unique character of each school. School policies about issues, from retention and tracking to class schedules and class size, also affect life in classrooms. Regardless of school setting, policies are regularly reviewed or revised. Changes can originate with teachers, administrators, parents, and students.

Retention

Flunking, the scornful term for failing a course or repeating a grade, has taken on new significance as education reformers promote high standards. In his 1999 State of the Union address, for example, President William Clinton urged educators to practice **retention,** or holding students back until they have mastered a grade level. This idea runs counter to the idea of **social promotion,** or passing children to successive grades to keep them with other children of their age.

Schools must set policies regarding retention that are fair to students. Many critics claim that students are graduating from high school without knowing how to read or how to do simple math. At the same time, other students may not have the chance to advance because other classmates need more time to learn a skill or topic.

Research suggests, however, that retention alone does not help students adjust or learn. The social stigma of being held back is painful for many students; it often seems like a punishment. At the same time, administrators need to consider the possibility that students are not learning because of a particular teaching method or because of outside influences.

Class Schedule and Class Size

One effort to restructure schools involves class schedule and class size policies. Recently, the trends have been longer class periods, fewer classes a semester, and smaller classrooms. Experimentation with class schedules and class sizes is done in hopes of providing students with better-quality learning experiences.

Block scheduling is a method of organizing classes that typically provides longer instructional periods during the school day. It is used in roughly 30 percent of the nation's secondary schools. Instead of the traditional seven- to eight-period school day, various block schedules include four periods a day, each lasting eighty-five to one hundred minutes. One model, the 4 × 4 schedule, allows students to complete four year-long courses each semester. Among the benefits of using the 4 × 4 schedule are declining failure rates, improvement in students grades, an increase in the number of students on the honor roll, and greater instructional flexibility for teachers (Rettig & Canady, 1999).

Indiana educators have divided their school year into three parts (trimesters) with five periods a day. This novel approach to block scheduling means that Westfield High School students can earn fifteen credits instead of the usual twelve during an academic year. This 3 × 5 plan is a way for Westfield to offer more joint courses with nearby universities. Students can take off up to three trimesters for travel, work, or illness and still graduate on schedule. Specific subjects, such as calculus, physics, and chemistry, can be enhanced by requiring an additional trimester. And students can take these extra courses without losing out on electives. In addition, this schedule allows students to

*R*esearch supports the value of smaller classes, but simply lowering class size does not automatically lead to increases in learning.

attend school part-time, work part-time, and still graduate with their class (Keen, 1999).

Class size has always been a controversial issue in schools. **How many children should be placed in a single room with one teacher? What happens to teaching and learning when a group becomes larger or smaller? Should the inclusion of one or more students with disabilities or students at risk affect class size?**

Research supports the value of smaller classes, those having twenty or fewer students, particularly in the early grades (U.S. Department of Education, 1999). Younger students, especially those economically disadvantaged, learn more in smaller reading and mathematics classes. Their attitudes and behavior improve too (Achilles, 1996). Critics are quick to observe, however, that simply lowering class size does not automatically lead to increases in learning. How teachers organize instruction continues to be critical to student success.

School districts report their average class size in different ways. Surprisingly, just measuring class size can cause problems. Dividing the total number of students by the total number of staff (including noninstructional staff members) yields a more

Technology in Practice

TRACKING ATTENDANCE

Attendance is an easily overlooked indicator of school success. "Big urban districts such as New York typically have 90 percent attendance rates, as opposed to 97 or 98 percent in the suburbs. Ninety percent on an exam may be an *A*, but as an attendance rate it is nothing to brag about. It means nearly a month out of class in a 183-day-a-year calendar" (Miller, 2002, A4.) For students to succeed in school, they must conform to Rule #1: Show up.

In Boston, nearly 5 percent of the 64,000 students are truant for more than five days during the school year. Eager to prevent teenagers from playing hooky, Boston Public Schools truant officers (or attendance supervisors) started the 2002 academic year with a new tool—a wireless system that displays student records instantly.

Attendance supervisors simply type a student's name into a special cellular phone to retrieve student data. The local probation or police officers who travel with supervisors have a cellphone that allows them to check court and police records, so students with outstanding arrest warrants are not returned to school.

In the past, truant officers have had to verify student information by lugging around a paper printout the size of several phone books. Technology has changed all that. According to Elliot Feldman, the Boston school system's director of alternative education, the new system will be more current because printed lists are out of date by the

time attendance supervisors receive them.

Teachers and administrators know that getting students to spend more time in school will not automatically improve achievement. They are optimistic, however, that getting students to school will be a first step in helping young people succeed.

Critical Thinking Questions

What are some other ways schools might monitor student attendance? Which do you believe might be more and less effective, and why?

To answer these questions online and e-mail your answer to your professor, go to Chapter 7 of the Companion Website (ablongman.com/ mcnergney4e) and click on Technology in Practice.

Source: Trotter, A. (2002). Boston will use new cellphones to call truants' bluff. *Education Week.* Available online: http://www.edweek.org/ew/ newstory.cfm?slug=31truant.h21&keywords=cellphones.

favorable **student–teacher ratio** than do calculations based on the number of actual classroom teachers. The obvious answer—hiring more teachers—is impossible on most schools' budgets, even if the extra teachers are available.

Tracking

Should students be grouped homogeneously or heterogeneously based on estimates of their abilities?   Assigning students believed to have similar abilities to certain instructional groups, class sections, and programs of study is a practice known as **tracking.** It has been the focus of bitter debate throughout the twentieth century.

Critics of tracking argue that students are tracked on flimsy, often biased evidence. Many assigned to "lower," or nonacademic, tracks may be there as much for behavior problems as for academic reasons. The students hurt most severely and often are disadvantaged, minority-group students (Oakes, 1995). In general, these students are the most at risk and have more needs than average students. These students often get by in lower-track classrooms because the teachers may expect little of students. Students, in turn, develop a negative self-concept, low self-esteem, poor motivation, and loss of interest in learning. Perhaps the most damning charge against tracking is the static nature of the assignments: once a student falls into the lower tracks, he or she seems caught in an academic tailspin from which few recover (Pool & Page, 1995).

On the other hand, supporters of tracking believe it is a way to group students with like abilities in the same classes. This way, more advanced students can proceed at a faster pace without leaving classmates behind. Likewise, students requiring more time and instruction can proceed through material together at an appropriate pace. Advocates think these settings provide better learning experiences for students than they receive in mixed-abilities classrooms. They contend that tracking allows teachers to focus on the whole class, rather than on a few individual students who are bored or who need more help. In this sense, as long as teachers do not write off lower-achieving students, tracking can offer a positive learning experience. Until that balance is reached, however, school policies continue to change.

*W*hat Makes Some Schools More Effective Than Others?

Effective schools—schools that can demonstrate student learning—allow substantial staff development time. In these schools, improvement goals are sharply focused, attainable, and valued by staff members. School needs guide staff, rather than standardized forms and checklists. Methods for reaching goals are often based on proven successful strategies. A blend of teacher independence and central office control characterizes improvement programs in effective schools. Effective schools also have respectful and supportive relationships among administrators, teachers, support staffs, and students. Figure 7.4 illustrates some of the elements that contribute to school effectiveness.

Effective schools are managed by effective leaders. These individuals provide the leadership necessary to create a strong curriculum and a safe environment where students can succeed. Effective leaders care about faculty needs, teacher recognition, and professional development. Good leaders also encourage parental, family, and community involvement in school activities. Many school leaders help parents and teachers assume new and powerful leadership roles.

For example, by 1999, eighty-three elementary schools had become part of the Basic School Network—another conception of effective schools. The network was created by an alliance of education foundations and groups, which based its plan on Boyer's (1995) ideas about effective schools. The alliance's goals are to help students

F̃IGURE 7.4   Elements That Contribute to School Effectiveness   What other characteristics of effective schools might you add?

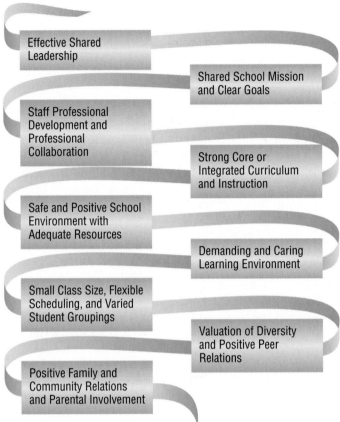

Effective Shared Leadership

Shared School Mission and Clear Goals

Staff Professional Development and Professional Collaboration

Strong Core or Integrated Curriculum and Instruction

Safe and Positive School Environment with Adequate Resources

Demanding and Caring Learning Environment

Small Class Size, Flexible Scheduling, and Varied Student Groupings

Valuation of Diversity and Positive Peer Relations

Positive Family and Community Relations and Parental Involvement

communicate effectively, acquire a core of knowledge, and become lifelong learners. Four key components distinguish these schools:

1. *The School as a Community.* Separate classrooms are connected through a clear and vital mission. Teachers serve as leaders, and the principal acts as lead teacher. Parents are viewed as partners in the learning process.

2. *A Curriculum with Coherence.* There is an emphasis on language and on core subjects, which are organized around common themes.

3. *A Climate for Learning.* Class sizes are small, teaching schedules are flexible, and student grouping arrangements are varied. Students are provided with resources ranging from building blocks to electronic tools. They also have access to basic health and counseling services and afternoon and summer enrichment programs.

4. *Character Development.* The Basic School focuses on seven core values: honesty, respect, responsibility, compassion, self-discipline, perseverance, and giving.

At Mantua Elementary School in Fairfax, Virginia, sixth graders explore a single theme for an entire year. The theme integrates multiple strands of the Basic Schools philosophy. In their classes, students learn about Native Americans in social studies, while studying weather and its impact on migration. They discover the cultural roots of mathematical patterns as they learn about the navigational methods used by early explorers. This multidisciplinary approach to learning can be particularly engaging for students, and it promotes cooperative learning and teaching.

Positive School Environments

Interviews with students from comprehensive high schools in California suggest that students see positive school environments much as the experts do. The measures students listed as indications of effective schools include:

- level of visibility and accessibility of the principal;
- amount of support students receive from teachers and staff members;
- students' perceived degree of personal safety;
- types of interactions between student groups;
- student behavior in general;
- availability of extracurricular activities;
- physical condition of the school; and
- degree to which students can speak their native language in informal settings and the availability of at least one staff member who speaks the same primary language (Phelan, Davidson, & Cao, 1992).

The students interviewed had strong opinions about schools when they attended more than one high school or when their experiences in middle school differed from those in high school. One student, a sophomore, described vividly why her high school was special:

> I don't like it; I love it! This school is something else! The teachers, they're friendlier, they're easier to work with. If you need help, they'll bend over backwards to help you, if it's after school, before school, anything—they do it. I know just about every teacher here. I'm a really friendly person. And they're wonderful. I wouldn't trade them for nothing. I loved eighth grade, but that does not compare to Lincoln [High School]. I mean you would not believe it. This school is so dedicated. That's the word, dedicated, that's what this school is to their students. They would stop what they're doing to help you. This school cares about their students. (Wasley, Hampel, & Clark, 1997, p. 10)

How would you judge the effectiveness of a school?

Relations

Good schools and good homes go together. Evidence suggests that connections between home and school help students adjust and learn. Parents boost their children's academic achievement by exposing them to intellectually stimulating experiences, teaching them directly, monitoring homework, and communicating with the school. Parents also strengthen ties by volunteering at the school, attending school conferences, requesting information, and participating in school governance.

Based on current standards, large schools are less likely than small schools to provide effective teaching and learning environments. In fact, the larger and more diverse the schools are, the less likely parents are to be involved. Students who have multiple teachers in middle and high schools and who are in classes with a lot of other students probably have weak teacher–student relationships (Dornbusch & Glasgow, 1996). Dealing with large classrooms means that teachers do not get to know their students well. Teachers also are unlikely to encourage parental involvement because they find the idea impractical. These teachers tend to focus on the strongest and weakest students because they seem to require the most attention. The parents of the students of average achievement, then, may be among those least likely to be linked closely to schools (Dornbusch & Glasgow, 1996).

Some parents who live in dangerous or resource-poor neighborhoods have less time, energy, and resources available for parenting and for getting involved with

*R*esearch shows that students do better in school when parents are involved by volunteering at the school, attending school conferences, requesting information, and participating in school governance.

schools. In these neighborhoods, "family" involvement is probably a more appropriate term than "parent" involvement, because children often are raised by people who are not their parents (Decker, Gregg, & Decker, 1995).

Furthermore, children from single-parent families and stepfamilies are more likely than are children from two-parent families to experience problems in school. Strong home–school ties are especially important for these students' success (Zill, 1996).

Research provides additional evidence that connections between home and school may be influenced by social networks and social class. Middle- and upper-class parents may think of education as a joint responsibility of school and home, whereas parents of lower socioeconomic status might view education as the teacher's job (Lareau, 1996). As poorer children grow older, their parents become less likely to be involved in school activities. The gap that exists between socioeconomic status and children's academic achievement also widens with age. This cycle makes it even more difficult for parents from low-income families to get involved in their children's schools (Alexander & Entwisle, 1996).

Some school attempts at parent involvement may actually work against home–school connections. Language barriers and differing cultural practices may halt schools' attempts to reach the parents of students needing the most help. First-year teacher Mary Ann Pacheco tried to overcome some common obstacles to communication:

> Generally, Latino parents hesitate to approach or question teachers because teaching is a highly respected position. I made myself very accessible and expressed my interest in their understanding bilingual education, student learning, and their voice in public education. I also built personal relationships, made phone calls, and made home visits. I reinforced their cultural beliefs but made them aware of certain characteristics that they might want to help their children develop. For example, during parent conferences, some parents were openly concerned with their child's tendency to talk excessively. Many times, I reminded them that in higher education, the willingness to initiate conversations, participate in group

Voices

FIRST DAY OF SCHOOL AMERICA

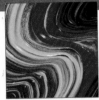

$\mathcal{T}$he First Day of School America—a grassroots movement intended to strengthen community support for schools—was initiated by Hemmings Motor News in Bennington, Vermont, in 1997. The idea was a simple one: plan a special event for the first day of school that will allow parents to establish positive relationships with teachers and administrators. Eleven schools in the Southwest Vermont Supervisory Union were the first to join the movement. Today, about four thousand schools in all fifty states, Canada, the Caribbean, and on military bases around the world have joined the campaign. Buffalo High School in Buffalo, Oklahoma, is one participant.

Although Buffalo High School is small (157 students), Principal Judith Faulkner knows the start of the school year holds plenty of unknowns for parents: "They know me, and know they can call anytime with questions," she says, "but when it comes to school–family relationships, I just don't think we can ever do too much."

When Faulkner learned about the First Day of School America campaign, she quickly pulled together a planning team

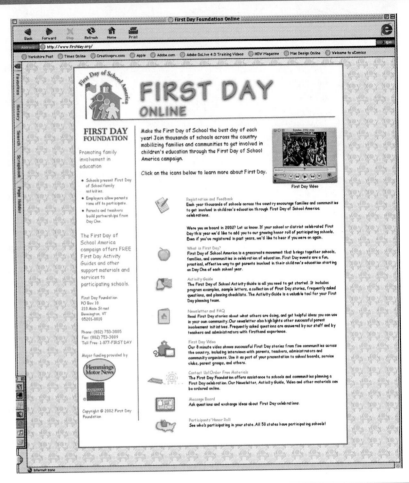

projects, and dialogue was required of students and highly valued. (Oaks & Lipton, 1999, pp. 354–355)

Teacher efforts such as those made by Ms. Pacheco to reach parents and involve them in their children's schooling have been proved to increase student success.

Summary

Schools come in all shapes and sizes and with widely varying philosophies. They address school objectives in almost every conceivable way. Administrators use a range of management strategies to deal with organizational and policy issues. Yet, troubling issues remain.

Why do schools look so much alike? Why do young people succeed in some settings and not in others? Do differences among school philosophies represent variations in only their written descriptions? What, if any, more radical approaches to schooling should we explore to help young people succeed?

When you attend your own school reunions, look around you. What was it about your school that made you and your peers want to stay in touch—to remain loyal to your conceptions of what school was all about? Why did the "no-shows" stay away?

and called area employers to solicit their participation for the 2001 school year. The school's first day began with a pep rally. "We cranked up the jock jam music as they came in," she laughs, "which got everyone in the mood to have a good time. The superintendent and I then welcomed them, after which I introduced our 'starting line-ups on the Bison teaching squad.'"

After the assembly, parents and mentors accompanied students through a shortened class schedule where teachers shared their rules and expectations for the year ahead and talked about how families could support students at home to achieve their goals. The event ended with a picnic. Faulkner was pleasantly surprised by students' and parents' reactions to the day:

> "You'd think students this age would be uncomfortable with having their parents around, but they were surprisingly cool about it," says Faulkner. "I even heard a couple of students talking in the hallway, who'd begged their parents not to come, say they'd

get them there the next year for sure. . . . Because our area employers were involved, we had parents who would never have been able to attend otherwise—parents who often don't feel as included in the life of the school as we would like," says Faulkner. "Buffalo High intends to make First Day an annual tradition."

Critical Thinking Question

What kinds of activities might you recommend for a First Day of School event? Visit the First Day Website (http://www.firstday.org/) to get additional ideas.

 To answer this question online and e-mail your answer to your professor, go to Chapter 7 of the Companion Website (ablongman.com/ mcnergney4e) and click on Voices.

Source: First Day Foundation (2002). One new first day firsthand story. Newsletter 24. Available online: http://www.firstday.org/.

Terms and Concepts

alternative school   179
block scheduling   190
central office staff   187
charter school   183
for-profit school   183
looping   177
magnet school   179
National Association for the Education of Young Children (NAEYC)   175
nongraded classroom   176

principal   188
private school   182
retention   189
school board   187
school district   172
social institution   172
social promotion   189
student–teacher ratio   192
superintendent of schools   186
tracking   192

Reflective Practice

A New Paradigm for School Goals

The current emphasis on education standards has fueled much philosophical debate about school goals. Many sectors of society question how well a standards-based educational system is meeting these goals. Among the educators who feel that standards have diverted education from its primary purposes is Peter W. Cookson, Jr., of Columbia University.

Cookson writes that society should worry less that students clear some imaginary age-graded hurdle and worry more that by high school graduation students have internalized values of personal integrity and community responsibility. Cookson proposes an innovative curricular design to foster such an internalization of values.

The early years of the child's schooling would focus on literacy and math skills within a setting emphasizing students' security. Children would develop their appreciation of the world's diversity through exposure to world languages. The cornerstones of environmental ethics would also be laid during these K to three years by opening the classroom to nature and to ecological concerns. Testing in these early grades would be limited to only diagnostic assessment that would allow teachers to create individualized learning plans that match students' unique abilities.

In grades four to six, Cookson's curriculum shifts to mastery, inquiry, and membership. The active development of analytical skills through the study of science and mathematics that will form the foundation for further learning occurs during this stage. As children proceed through the middle school years, the curriculum must support students as they undergo the transition from childhood to early adulthood. Socially relevant questions about sexuality, tolerance, and ethics would be examined. The curriculum would focus heavily on history and the humanities. By this point in the child's education, Cookson argues, the roots of democratic citizenship have been firmly set and the development of self has been nurtured.

In the high school years, Cookson's proposal veers most dramatically from the tradition of public education. Cookson wants a two-year secondary program that provides opportunities for a wider variety of students to make connections to society through internships and academic programs related to chosen professions. He criticizes the current system as unjustly reproducing social inequalities by emphasizing college preparation.

Issues, Problems, Dilemmas, Opportunities

What are some of the social forces that work against innovation in educational design such as that advocated by Cookson?

Perceive and Value

Do you agree with Cookson that public schools provide advantages to already advantaged students?

Know and Act

How does the curriculum in Cookson's model compare to the curriculum you experienced as a student? If you worked in a school using Cookson's approach, how would you organize students for instruction? How would your strategies compare to those used by your teachers?

Evaluate

Cookson argues that no student should graduate from high school without a specific plan for the next five years of his or her life. What can schools do to increase the likelihood that this occurs?

INTASC Principle 5

The teacher uses an understanding of individual and group motivation and behavior to create a learning environment that encourages positive social interaction, active engagement in learning, and self-motivation.

Knowledge

The teacher understands how participation supports commitment, and encourages the expression and use of democratic values in the classroom. (Interstate New Teacher Assessment and Support Consortium, 1992)

Discussion Question

Some might argue that Cookson's emphasis on participation in internships and academic programs related to chosen professions is at the expense of excelling in traditional academic subjects necessary for admission to college. How would you respond to that argument?

Additional Readings

Bodilly, S. (2001). *New American schools' concept of break-the-mold designs: How designs evolved and why.* Santa Monica, CA: Rand.

Education Week (April 2001–May 2001). High School: The Shifting Mission (Special Reports). Available online: http://www.edweek.org/sreports/special_reports_article.cfm?slug=highschool.htm

Gary, M., & Nelson, C. (2002). *What's public about charter schools? Lessons learned about choice and accountability.* Thousand Oaks, CA: Corwin Press.

NAESP & NMSA (2002). Supporting students in their transition to middle school: A position paper jointly adopted by the National Middle School Association and the National Association of Elementary School Principals. Ohio: National Middle School Association. Available online: http://www.nmsa.org/

Walsh, M. (2002, May 22). Businesses flock to charter frontier. *Education Week.* Available online: http://www.edweek.org/ew/newstory.cfm?slug=37chartbiz.h21

Walsley, P., Fine, M., Gladden, M., Holland, N., King, S., Mosak, E., & Powell, L. C. (2000). *Small schools: Great strides: A study of new small schools in Chicago.* New York: Bank Street College of Education.

Web Resources

http://nces.ed.gov/help/sitemap.asp

The National Center for Education Statistics fulfills a congressional mandate to collect, analyze, and report complete statistics on the condition of American education.

http://www.edweek.org/

Education Week is an online newspaper that provides daily news and special reports that help educators stay up to date on happenings in schools.

http://www.conferencepros.com/srs/

The Center for the Study of Small/Rural Schools is a cooperative effort between the University of Oklahoma's colleges of education and continuing education. The center is endorsed by the National Rural Education Association

tion as one of its five recognized rural education research centers.

http://www.acs.ohio-state.edu/urbanschools/

This website describes collaborative efforts between Ohio State University and four urban school districts in Central Ohio to promote research and programs to improve K through twelve education.

http://www.aasa.org/

The American Association of School Administrators, founded in 1865, is the professional organization for over 14,000 educational leaders across America and in many other countries. The AASA's mission is to support and develop effective school system leaders who are dedicated to the highest-quality public education for all children.

VideoWorkshop Extra!

If the VideoWorkshop package was included with your textbook, go to Chapter 7 of the Companion Website (ablongman. com/mcnergney4e) and click on the VideoWorkshop button. Follow the instructions for viewing video clip 3. Then consider this information along with what you've read in Chapter 7 while answering the following questions.

1. This chapter presents the idea that school is a social institution. Create a slogan that addresses a school's concern for students' self-worth (as discussed in the video clip). How might a school promote this idea?

2. Analyze the various alternatives covered in the chapter. Do you believe society values these alternatives as equal vehicles for developing a student's abilities? Why or why not? How does this affect students' self-concepts (as mentioned in the video clip)?

*L*eading, Governing, and Funding Schools

CHAPTER CONTENTS

What Are School Governance and Education Finance?

How Does the Federal Government Influence Education?

How Is Education Financed and Controlled by the States?

How Are Schools Financed and Managed at the Local Level?

How Are Governance and Funding Related to Educational Success?

*D*eborah Lynch, president of the Chicago Teachers Union, is a successful educational leader.

Lynch understands how essential feedback is to teachers. After all, it was just one year ago that she taught 8th graders. . . . Since then, Lynch has employed all she learned while a classroom teacher, and more, to begin pushing the 34,000-member Chicago Teachers Union in a new direction.

Not only does she advocate higher wages, better benefits, and improved working conditions, as any seasoned labor leader would, but she also insists that the labor organization instigate school improvement measures that go to the heart of teaching and learning. In her view, the CTU should work to lower class sizes, especially in the primary grades, and demand the enforcement of current school board policy on the matter. It should fight for special education students to receive appropriate schooling, rather than the one-size-fits-all education provided in many buildings. And the union should push the district to rely less on standardized testing and adopt many of the performance assessments Chicago teachers themselves have crafted. Lynch lists the achievement gap between minority and white students as the most critical one facing the CTU.

"She's a very good example of the teachers' union leader of the future," says Adam Urbanski, her counterpart in Rochester, N.Y., who has worked with Lynch for more than twenty years. . . . "She is strongly inclined toward collaboration, disinclined toward collusion, and very expert on the issues of instruction and professional issues. I think she's going to be a blessing." (Blair, 2002, p. 23)

This chapter explains how leaders shape schools and work to finance educational efforts. It presents the role of the federal government in public education and the power of state influence and localities on schools. It also illustrates the link between money and educational success, both of which influence the profession of teaching.

What Are School Governance and Education Finance?

The Tenth Amendment to the U.S. Constitution gives people the power to establish and operate public schools. Specifically, the amendment states that any powers and duties not in the domain of the federal government reside with state governments. Because the Constitution does not discuss federal responsibility for public education, the power to educate resides at the state level. That is, the states are ultimately responsible for **school governance,** or for establishing and managing public education. As the processes of public education became more complex, states delegated many educational responsibilities to local education agencies. Over time, a complex network of formal organizations at the federal, state, and local levels has made public education what it is today.

School governance controls finance, and finance shapes practice. Educators who want to have some influence on educational policy and practice must learn how the system works. They need to understand how public education is funded, where the money is allocated, and how it is eventually spent and accounted for. Some knowledge can be gained from examining the formal processes of governance and finance. But it is important to study informal processes, too.

How Schools Are Run

Schools are run through a variety of methods, but the most important factor for success is the school leader. Educational leaders—school board members, superintendents, principals, department heads, and teachers—are responsible for the governance of schools. They control and direct the conduct of schooling within a system of institutions, laws, regulations, policies, politics, and customs.

Leadership is an important quality in people who want to participate effectively in school governance. The concept of leadership can represent many different things. Even people in the same profession can have different ideas about what makes a good leader. Some characteristics of leadership that people might identify include vision and the ability to articulate it, an understanding of the group's wants or needs, a good personality, thoughtfulness and truthfulness, the ability to inspire others, knowing the right thing to say and the right time to say it, and setting a good example. These diverse characteristics suggest that there is no single model of effective leadership. Like beauty, leadership may be in the eye of the beholder. **What do you think it takes to be a good leader?** See Figure 8.1 for a questionnaire about what makes a good leader. Complete the questionnaire and discuss your results with your classmates.

$\mathcal{F}$IGURE 8.1   What Makes A Good Leader?

A Good Leader:
Takes responsibility

1	2	3	4
STRONGLY DISAGREE	DISAGREE	AGREE	STRONGLY AGREE

Develops relationships

1	2	3	4
STRONGLY DISAGREE	DISAGREE	AGREE	STRONGLY AGREE

Establishes goals

1	2	3	4
STRONGLY DISAGREE	DISAGREE	AGREE	STRONGLY AGREE

Is politically minded

1	2	3	4
STRONGLY DISAGREE	DISAGREE	AGREE	STRONGLY AGREE

Delegates authority

1	2	3	4
STRONGLY DISAGREE	DISAGREE	AGREE	STRONGLY AGREE

Encourages innovation

1	2	3	4
STRONGLY DISAGREE	DISAGREE	AGREE	STRONGLY AGREE

How Schools Are Funded

Tax money collected at the local, state, and federal levels provides most of the funding for public schools, as illustrated in Figure 8.2. More than three-quarters of the school boards in the United States have taxing authority. During the 2000–2001 school year, the total per-student expenditure in public elementary and secondary school programs was $7,079 (U.S. Department of Education, 2002). Many reformers believe more funding for public schools is necessary to increase the quality of education offered. In economically troubled times, however, few political leaders at any governmental level are willing to risk angering voters by raising taxes to support public schools.

The chances of school boards successfully raising taxes are further reduced by the fact that an increasing number of voters no longer have children in the public schools. In addition, people who are retired and on fixed incomes often are less willing and less able to support public education.

Connections between Education and the Economy

Money and education are closely linked in many ways, as policymakers will attest. For them, balancing educational funding and educational values is a way of life. The following four values continually compete for attention in many school systems and communities (Guthrie, Garms, & Pierce, 1988). Sometimes one value is at the top of a system's priorities, only to be replaced when another value becomes more urgent.

1. *Equality,* or equal educational opportunity, has been defined most often in terms of equal access to schooling. This means public school teachers, administrators, and staff try to offer education tailored to all students' strengths and

FIGURE 8.2 **Sources of Revenue for School Funding** What factors might alter the proportion of financial support that each level of government provides?

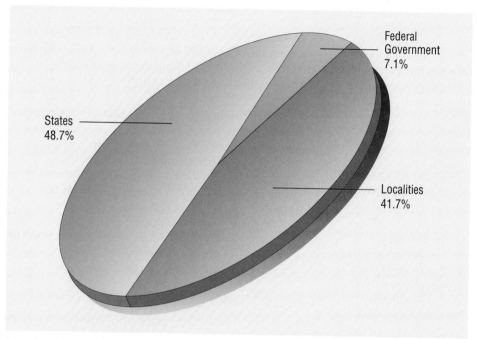

Federal
Government
7.1%

States
48.7%

Localities
41.7%

Source: From *Digest of education statistics, 2001,* by U.S. Department of Education, 2002. Washington, DC: Government Printing Office.

needs, while ensuring that all students acquire at least minimum or basic shills. Does providing equal educational opportunities mean every school has to receive the same amount of funding?

2. *Adequacy* refers to the minimum resources needed to achieve an educational outcome. Is there a minimum level beneath which funding cannot sink in order to provide basic education?

3. *Efficiency* refers to getting the maximum educational benefit for the dollar spent. How can we recognize efficient and inefficient or wasteful spending on education?

*M*oney and education are closely linked in many ways. Schools with more resources can offer better opportunities for students.

Issues in School Reform
URBAN SUPERINTENDENTS

According to a study by the Washington-based Council of the Great City Schools, urban superintendents stay in one job for only about two and a half years. A report by the National School Boards Association, however, indicates that some school chiefs, like Linda Murray—superintendent of the 34,000-student San Jose school district in California—last longer than the average. Ms. Murray, who has run the district for almost ten years, contends that listening to parents and community members, getting school board support, and building a good administrative staff are key to her longevity in the urban-superintendent hot seat. She and her staff annually survey parents, teachers, and students; track and publicize student progress; and involve local business and community leaders in district decisions. Murray also meets weekly with the president of the local teachers' union (Borea, 2002).

Superintendents contend with a variety of highly charged matters, including tight finances, high-stakes testing, taxpayer concerns, board turnover, pressure from community groups, and school reform initiatives. Currently, only one of the nation's five largest urban school districts—the Broward County, Florida, public schools—is being run by a leader with more than two years on the job. High turnover rates raise important issues that both educational leaders and their constituents need to think about:

■ Who is in charge? School boards are elected by the people to oversee and help shape schooling in their districts. Board members are often among the most vocal, visible, and involved people in their communities. Many are energetic and eager to "change" the system. Their views and values may be quite different from one another. They hire or inherit the superinten-

dent hired by a previous board and charge him or her to run the system. It is not surprising that disagreements about priorities occur among board members and between the board and the superintendent—a person who has spent his or her professional life connected to schools.

■ How much parent involvement is enough? The admonition to "get parents involved in their children's education" has become a familiar phrase. But "being involved" has many meanings. In our democratically structured and run public school system, there are many ways to be involved. Most experts agree that school reform, if it is going to stick, requires consensus building. Yet superintendents and principals can be so distracted by the perceived need to get parents involved and help them "get with the program" that they have too little time to devote to the education of children.

Critical Thinking Questions

It is true that "you can't do everything" if you are a superintendent or principal. And "getting people involved" is right up there on the list of tasks to be accomplished. To find time to do so, successful educational leaders learn how to delegate tasks to others. There is something to be gained from delegating and something to be lost, if you aren't careful. What kinds of tasks might administrators wisely delegate to others, assuming there is someone to do them? How might this be done to ensure that the delegation works?

 To answer these questions online and e-mail your answers to your professor, go to Chapter 8 of the Companion Website (ablongman.com/mcnergney4e) and click on Issues in School Reform.

4. *Liberty,* or choice, is about control over where, how, and for what purposes students are educated. Should parents be allowed to choose where and how they spend tax dollars to educate their children?

When thinking about spending money on education, it is important to remember that the connections between education and financial success in life are strong. In general, the more schooling a person has, the greater his or her potential earning power. Education, then, is seen as a way of developing "human capital" (Becker, 1964; Schultz, 1981). Students have reason to expect that the time, effort, and money they invest in their education will yield some personal benefit. Society, too, benefits because education develops productive, tax-paying citizens. Society also benefits from an educated citizenry in terms of reduced crime rates and the spread of moral values—both of which accompany education.

Political Influences on Public Education

Various individuals and organizations shape public education. Formal sources of power are found in the school governance leaders themselves. For instance, these elected and appointed officials hire, reassign, fire, and reward their staffs. But informal sources of power outside the school system are important as well. This is where politics can become a factor in public education governance. Elected lawmakers have to answer to their constituents, who often have loud opinions when it comes to public schools. In addition, citizens work on their own or in groups to create change in schools based on their political beliefs. Sometimes these informal political powers working outside the system achieve sweeping changes within the system. Figure 8.3 shows some of the

FIGURE 8.3 **Influences on Public Education** How might this figure change if you ranked the levels in terms of their power? Explain your reasoning.

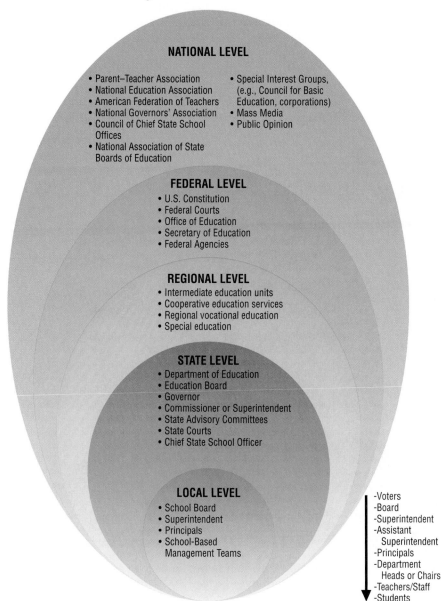

NATIONAL LEVEL

- Parent–Teacher Association
- National Education Association
- American Federation of Teachers
- National Governors' Association
- Council of Chief State School Offices
- National Association of State Boards of Education
- Special Interest Groups, (e.g., Council for Basic Education, corporations)
- Mass Media
- Public Opinion

FEDERAL LEVEL
- U.S. Constitution
- Federal Courts
- Office of Education
- Secretary of Education
- Federal Agencies

REGIONAL LEVEL
- Intermediate education units
- Cooperative education services
- Regional vocational education
- Special education

STATE LEVEL
- Department of Education
- Education Board
- Governor
- Commissioner or Superintendent
- State Advisory Committees
- State Courts
- Chief State School Officer

LOCAL LEVEL
- School Board
- Superintendent
- Principals
- School-Based Management Teams

-Voters
-Board
-Superintendent
-Assistant Superintendent
-Principals
-Department Heads or Chairs
-Teachers/Staff
-Students

influences on education at the national, federal, regional, state, and local levels, which are discussed throughout this chapter.

EDUCATION LOBBIES AND SPECIAL-INTEREST GROUPS

How do special-interest groups have a positive effect on education?   Public education is everyone's business, but some people are more powerful in influencing its direction than are others. People often gather around specific interests and try to change policy to advance their cause, hence the terms **special-interest group** and *pressure group.* These terms can have a negative meaning by suggesting that group members promote their own narrow points of view. But special-interest groups also educate the public about important issues and offer alternative solutions to problems.

Although authorities at the state level have initiated many education reforms in recent years, special interests have contributed informally to the reforms. Their members have worked publicly and behind the scenes to shape policy at the local, state, and national levels. For example, the largest volunteer education organization in the United States, the **National Parent–Teacher Association (PTA),** has long supported legislation at all levels designed to benefit children. Professional organizations such as the National School Boards Association, the National Association of State Boards of Education, and the American Association of Colleges for Teacher Education also support many education policy initiatives with work and funds.

Special-interest groups often try to influence schools on ideological issues. Such groups are sustained by their beliefs about school curricula and issues of social justice. The Council for Basic Education, for example, advocates curriculum in the liberal arts. Since the 1960s, African Americans and Native Americans have been increasingly active

In the famous 1925 Scopes trial, the ACLU arranged for Clarence Darrow to defend teacher John T. Scopes against William Jennings Bryan. Here, Darrow (l.) and Bryan (r.) are pictured in the courtroom.

in demanding that schools respond to their needs. Hispanic Americans, too, have tried to establish *unidos,* or unity, among Spanish-speaking peoples for the purpose of changing public schools.

Interest groups concerned with education want to influence curricula, instruction, and governance in public schools. For example, the Americans with Disabilities Association, Inc., provides a political voice for the community of individuals with disabilities. The ADA educates the public and works to influence political elections and legislative initiatives. This political action committee, or PAC, seeks to block threats from other groups working against the interests of people with disabilities. The ADA conducts voter registration drives, promotes get-out-the-vote programs, and raises money for candidates who support policies favorable to people with disabilities. In terms of education, their work includes fostering the development of new and useful resources for people with disabilities.

The American Civil Liberties Union (ACLU) is another PAC that has taken public positions on educational issues. Specifically, the ACLU is a legal organization that defends people against what it believes are attacks on their civil liberties. One of its most notable actions was in the Scopes trial of 1925. Tennessee law at the time forbade public school teachers from teaching any theory that denied the theory of creation described in the Bible. The ACLU offered legal representation to any Tennessee teacher who would test this law. John T. Scopes took them up on the offer and was defended by Clarence Darrow against famous orator and politician William Jennings Bryan. Their trial was the beginning of the end for antievolution forces.

Other actions of the ACLU include filing briefs on legal issues as a "friend of the court" for the purpose of educating judges and lawyers. They have endorsed exempting students from the flag salute when it is against their religion. They have also opposed the use of public funds for private education.

The Anti-Defamation League (ADL) wants to end discrimination against and ridicule of any religion or group of citizens. It has four hundred staff members in thirty U.S. field offices. In terms of education, the ADL offers a comprehensive educational program for elementary and secondary teachers and students. The program encourages tolerance through teacher awareness training, youth training, classroom discussion guides, student after-school programs, and weekend awareness retreats. According to ADL figures, it has trained more than 100,000 teachers and ten million public, private, and parochial school students.

The Legal Defense and Education Fund (LDEF), part of the National Organization for Women (NOW), works to advance women's rights in education systems across the country. In St. Louis, Missouri, for example, the board of education's policy was to transfer pregnant elementary and junior high school girls to a less desirable school when their pregnancies became obvious. The LDEF stepped in and took up the fight. As a result, the board changed its policy, allowing girls to choose to remain in regular classes or to transfer.

Since its founding in 1909, the National Association for the Advancement of Colored People (NAACP) has worked to achieve racial justice for all people and to improve the living conditions of low-income people. The association is the largest and most influential civil rights organization in the country. Over the years, the NAACP has been a major force behind open housing, job opportunities, prison reform, school desegregation, and education programs for youth and adults.

PUBLIC MEDIA

How do the mass media affect education? Public opinion on processes of governing and managing public education is a powerful influence on policy making. When it comes to public opinion, the press has two roles. First, they report what the public opinion is on various matters. Second, the press suggests what people ought to think. Both roles are important, but sometimes the line between the two gets blurred.

One view, expressed by Juan Williams, is that the job of the press is to watch governmental and educational leaders so they do not cheat the public. This time-honored role of journalism is important. Williams (1992) describes the job of the journalist on the education beat:

> The truth is, reporters and editors and, most important, readers are interested in education only as a function of political power. A major proportion of any jurisdiction's tax dollars goes into schools. Politicians have to make up those school budgets and defend them. The school or university budget has to be both sufficient to the task of educating young people and simultaneously able to withstand charges that it is really a pork-barrel project, wasting the taxpayers' money. Education budgets pay not only for teachers and books but also for construction workers, maintenance people, teachers' aides, administrators, union chiefs, and cooks. In other words, the tax dollars assigned to educate children are a major source of patronage and power in our society. Newspaper editors, as the public's watchdogs, want to know if the taxpayers are being cheated out of their money. (p. 179)

But too often, critics argue, the press goes out of its way to criticize schools. Nowadays, negative events seem more newsworthy than positive ones, and most of the stories about schools focus on something bad—school violence, low test scores, and so on. Critics say, "We think that too frequently a story is found interesting to reporters only if it is critical of the schools, if it has some scent of blood about it. Using the news lingo, if it bleeds, it leads" (Berliner and Biddle, 1995).

The media perform not only an informational function in society but an educational function as well. Television, newspapers, radio, and magazines touch more people today than at any time in our history. And they will reach more tomorrow than they do today. Some might raise this question: Are children learning more from the media than they are from their parents and schools?

How Does the Federal Government Influence Education?

Although the wording of the Tenth Amendment to the Constitution leaves control of school governance to the states, the federal government has always had a hand in shaping education. Various court cases have defined education as a property right or a civil right under the Constitution. This interpretation makes education subject to the Fourteenth Amendment, which allows the federal government to intervene in state government matters when necessary. (Section 1: "No State shall make or enforce any law which shall abridge the privileges or immunities of citizens of the United States; nor shall any State deprive any person of life, liberty, or property, without due process of law; nor deny to any person within its jurisdiction the equal protection of the laws.") The Fourteenth Amendment therefore allows the federal government to influence the education of children at the local level.

Some experts suggest that the federal agenda for education is set by the "Iron Triangle"—the combination of education interests in the executive branch, congressional committees, and interest groups outside government (Guthrie, Garms, & Pierce 1988).

The executive branch combines beliefs and programs to influence public education. Presidential staffs and cabinets speak publicly about education issues, encourage states' attention to education reform, and designate federal funds for education initiatives. In addition, the president is responsible for many departments, agencies, and programs devoted to education.

Congress' role in public education involves passing laws and appropriating funds. Although not part of the Iron Triangle, federal courts also influence public education through their decisions. For instance, the courts set policy when they rule on civil rights cases and other controversial issues, such as prayer in public schools and the use of public funds for private schools.

Federal Funding for Education

Figure 8.4 illustrates trends in total federal funding for education between 1965 and 2000. For elementary and secondary schools, for example, support increased by 144 percent between 1965 and 1975, but rose only 2 percent between 1975 and 1980. Between 1980 and 1985, funding declined 22 percent, and then rose again 47 percent between 1985 and 2000 (U.S. Department of Education, 2001).

Many of these statistics on education in the United States are collected and analyzed by the **National Center for Education Statistics (NCES),** an agency in the executive branch. The Center reported that the total federal support for education in fiscal year (FY) 2001 was $92.8 billion. As illustrated in Figure 8.5, a substantial portion of that money went to elementary and secondary education programs: 52 percent went to elementary and secondary education, 17 percent to postsecondary expenses, and 25 percent to university research. The final 6 percent funded "other" education programs, including libraries, museums, cultural activities, and miscellaneous research. Funds were distributed through the Departments of Education, Health and Human Services, Agriculture, Defense, Energy, and Labor and the National Science Foundation.

Within these federal departments and foundations, funding for education is distributed in many ways. One way is major grant programs that are established through

FIGURE 8.4 **Federal On-Budget Funds for Education by Level or Other Educational Purpose, 1965 to 2000** Why might support for elementary, secondary, and postsecondary education have declined in the 1980s?

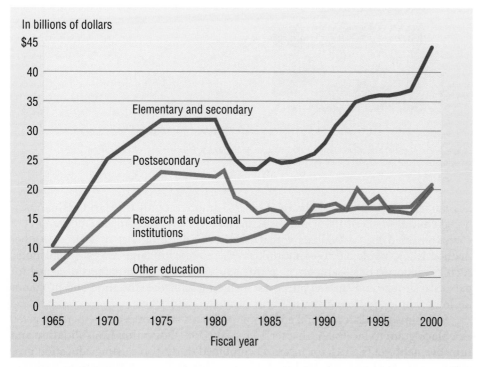

Source: From *Digest of education statistics, 2000,* by U.S. Department of Education, 2001. Washington, DC: U.S. Government Printing Office.

*F*IGURE 8.5   **Estimated Federal Education Dollar, 2001**   What proportion of the federal budget goes to elementary and secondary education?

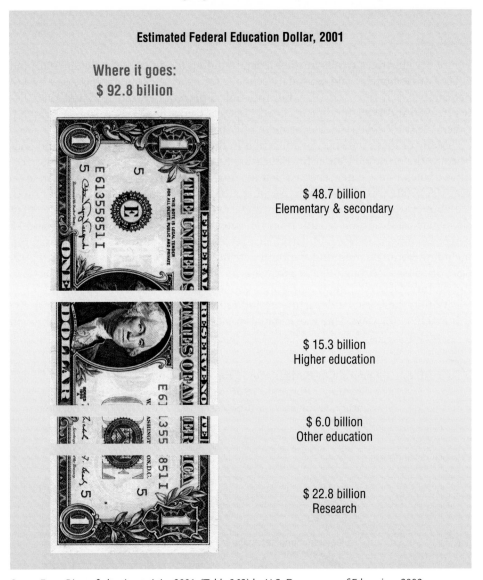

Estimated Federal Education Dollar, 2001

Where it goes:
$ 92.8 billion

$ 48.7 billion
Elementary & secondary

$ 15.3 billion
Higher education

$ 6.0 billion
Other education

$ 22.8 billion
Research

Source: From *Digest of education statistics, 2001,* (Table 362) by U.S. Department of Education, 2002. Washington, DC: U.S. Government Printing Office.

legislation, such as the Vocational Act of 1963 (more recently the Carl Perkins Vocational Education Act of 1984) and the Education for All Handicapped Children Act of 1975 (renamed the Individuals with Disabilities Education Act of 1997). Another method is to provide aid to communities where there are large federal installations, such as military bases. **Categorical grants** support education programs designed for particular groups and specific purposes, including bilingual education and programs for low-income children, such as Project Head Start and Title I.

Sometimes funds for several education programs are grouped together and given as a **block grant** to localities. Chapter Two of the 1981 **Education Consolidation and Improvement Act (ECIA),** for instance, combined thirty-two existing education programs under one block grant. This block grant was then made available to state and local education agencies for general education purposes. The amount of money states receive in this block grant is based on a student population formula. States then prepare a plan for using federal funds based on district enrollment or on measures of student need. Finally, once states receive the federal funding, they give money to local school districts for use in whichever programs need additional services.

Regardless of what type of federal funding a school district receives, the district must comply with federal guidelines when spending grant money. If a school district either does not spend the federal money or misspends it, one of several things can happen: the school system can be forced to return the money, it can be fined, and/or it can be prevented from receiving any federal funds in the future. States and school districts with educational programs or practices that are found to be in violation of federal laws also lose funding.

National Goals

How will we know if we have met our National Goals? In the 1980s and 1990s, the federal government influenced education at state and local levels by setting up what are known as National Goals. The goals are a series of educational measures that monitor states' progress in areas such as standardized test scores, graduation rates, and teachers' salaries. The purpose of National Goals is to set standards for all states and to ensure equitable educational opportunities and high levels of educational achievement for all students. A national reporting system makes public each state's progress toward meeting the goals.

Table 8.1 shows how one state in the middle of America, Nebraska, performed on Goal 1 (Ready to Learn), Goal 2 (School Completion), and Goal 3 (Student Achievement and Citizenship) from 1990 to 2000. With two exceptions, Nebraska registered either an improvement or no change on all indicators at the time of the last measurement. On Goal 3, notice that the measurement of progress has occurred infrequently. In 2002, President George W. Bush and Congress announced a plan to test academic progress every year in grades three to eight. They believe more frequent testing will better indicate if the National Goals are being met.

How Is Education Financed and Controlled by the States?

We have said that, according to the Constitution, states are responsible for public education. State governments therefore exercise more influence on public education than does the federal government—and they do so in a variety of ways. Figure 8.6 shows a typical organization of public education at the state level.

The methods of influence state governments use include taxation and distribution of revenues. States also set standards for building schools, educating teachers and school administrators, and licensing school personnel. States establish the curriculum, the minimum length of the school term, attendance requirements, and requirements for school accreditation. In addition, states provide many of the other special services school districts use. While the structure of state bureaucracies and the influence of key state officers vary, the role of state government in public education has grown through the years.

State Funding

Most of the funding for public education comes from either state or local taxes. The percentage of support the state provides to school districts, however, can vary from year to year. Of federal, state, and local support, states typically provide the most funding.

TABLE 8.1   **Nebraska and the National Goals.** Why is it important to view a state's progress over a fairly long period of time?

Indicator	1990	1991	1992	1993	1994	1995	1996	1997	1998	1999	2000	Change[a]
Goal 1: Ready to Learn												
Children's health index (%)	38	38	37	37	37	36	35	36	36	—	—	Improvement
Immunizations (%)	—	—	—	—	72	78	82	77	78	84	—	Improvement
Low birthweight (%)	5	6	6	6	6	6	6	7	7	7	—	Decline
Early prenatal care (%)	83	82	82	83	83	84	85	84	84	84	—	Improvement
Preschool programs for children with disabilities (per 1000)	—	34	38	41	41	46	46	48	52	53	—	Improvement
Goal 2: School Completion												
High school completion (%)	91	93	93	96	94	93	91	91	92	—	—	No change
High school dropouts (%)	—	—	3.6	3.8	4.6	4.5	4.5	4.3	4.4	—	—	Decline
Goal 3: Student Achievement and Citizenship												
Reading achievement, 4th grade (%)	—	—	31	—	34	—	—	—	—	—	—	No change
Reading achievement, 8th grade (%)	—	—	—	—	—	—	—	—	—	—	—	
Writing achievement, 8th grade (%)	—	—	—	—	—	—	—	—	—	—	—	
Mathematics achievement, 4th grade (%)	—	—	22	—	—	—	24	—	—	—	24	No change
Mathematics achievement, 8th grade (%)	24	—	26	—	—	—	31	—	—	—	31	Improvement
Science achievement, 8th grade (%)	—	—	—	—	—	—	35	—	—	—	—	
Advanced placement examinations (per 1000)	—	38	—	—	—	—	—	47	—	—	43	Improvement
Advanced placement performance (per 1000)	—	25	28	29	29	29	26	30	30	30	28	Improvement

[a]Improvement: statistically significant improvement; Decline: statistically significant decline; No change: no statistically significant change. —Data not collected or not available.

Source: The National Educational Goals Panel: Building a nation of learners. Available online (http:///www.negp.gov/).

FIGURE 8.6 **Typical Organization of Public Education at the State Level** Why are "The People" shown at the top of this figure? In what sense are the top and the bottom of this figure the same?

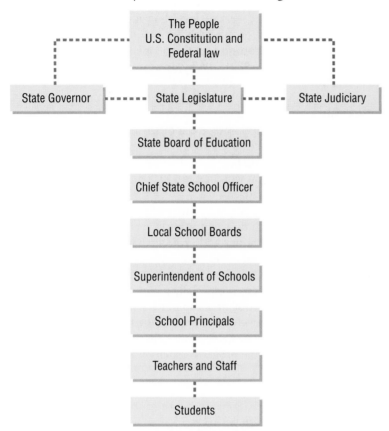

Localities usually provide an amount close to the state level of support, while federal funding supplies well under 10 percent of a school budget.

STATE SALES TAXES

Most states, excluding Alaska, Delaware, Montana, New Hampshire, and Oregon, have state sales taxes. The money collected from these sales taxes provides a large portion of the funding for public schools. The five exception states receive most of their educational funds from income or property taxes. In addition to the state sales tax, some states allow localities to add their own sales taxes to items. New York City, for example, charges 4.25 percent in addition to the New York state sales tax of 4 percent, for a total rate of 8.25 percent.

Sales taxes have great appeal because they are relatively easy and inexpensive to administer—retailers collect sales taxes at the point of sale. The state then deals directly with retailers instead of collecting money from individuals, as in the case of personal income taxes. Sales taxes are also attractive because they raise large sums of money. The more money people earn, the more they spend, and the more tax revenue collected for the state. To ease the burden on the poor and the elderly, some items, such as food and drugs, can be exempt from sales taxes. On the other hand, sales taxes on luxury items and so-called sin taxes—taxes on cigarettes and alcohol—are relatively easy to raise because most people do not object.

Sales taxes also have drawbacks, the main one being their dependence on the economy. When the economy is healthy, people buy more things and therefore pay more sales taxes. State programs that depend on sales tax revenue are well funded during these economic uptimes. When retail sales decline during an economic downtime, however, there is less money for all public services, including education. In addition, as more items become subject to taxation, people with limited incomes spend a greater percentage of their income on taxes than do wealthy people. This is referred to as **regressive taxation** (Burrup & Brimley, 1982).   **Why do states need different ways to raise money for education?**

STATE INCOME TAXES

State income taxes, both personal and corporate, are another source of revenue for education. Unlike sales taxes, income taxes are a form of **progressive taxation.** That means people pay more as they earn more. For example, a person who makes $100,000 pays more income tax than does a person who makes $30,000. Likewise, corporations pay much higher taxes than do private citizens.

For most states, income taxes are a necessary source of revenue for providing the services people demand from states, including education. Every state tries to balance a budget consisting of projects that cost money and projects that make money. Money coming in rarely if ever matches money going out. The only options are raising taxes or cutting programs, and neither option satisfies everyone.

In the 1990s, the battle over raising taxes, especially income taxes, and cutting services was common to most states. The problem of too much money going out and too little coming in forced state leaders everywhere to make difficult choices about where to spend their limited revenues. As a result, many school districts receive less financial support and have less access to state-run programs such as Head Start and special education.

STATE LOTTERIES AND OTHER SOURCES

Other sources of state aid for education include estate and inheritance taxes, miscellaneous user fees, licenses, severance taxes—fees for the privilege of extracting natural resources from land or water—and lotteries.

Early attempts to establish state lotteries were complicated and largely unsuccessful. New Hampshire, a state that had neither a sales tax nor an income tax, established a state lottery in 1964 to support public education and to hold down property taxes. New York followed in 1967. Neither state raised as much money as it had expected, because the lotteries cost too much to operate. Tickets cost several dollars each, buyers had to register, and drawings were held only twice a year.

In the 1970s other states created lotteries having streamlined procedures and more frequent payoffs. Now thirty-seven states and the District of Columbia have lotteries that, combined, put billions of dollars into state pockets. Only a small percentage of this money, however, goes for state aid to education.

STATE AID PLANS

Flat grants are a type of financial aid provided by states to local communities; these grants are classified as either uniform or variable. Uniform flat grants give school districts equal amounts of money on a per student basis, regardless of district needs or financial standing. Variable flat grants try to compensate for differing classroom needs, typically giving more money to schools having more expensive services. For example, high schools with vocational programs can require more money than can elementary schools. Districts having high demands for bilingual or special education classes may also receive more aid.

In **foundation programs,** the state guarantees a certain amount of money for educational expenditures (by pupil or by classroom). In other words, the state says that a certain dollar amount will be spent on public education in a school district. It then determines what proportion of that cost should be paid for by localities. The proportion is based on the total property value of the particular locality, and it is usually expressed in terms of *mills*. (A mill is one-tenth of a cent.) If the locality cannot raise the level of funds required, the state supplies the rest of the money. In poorer communities, for example, where property taxes are low, the state contributes more money than it does in affluent communities, where taxes are high.

Per pupil expenditures are the funds allocated for education services divided by the number of pupils to be served. Think of a $1 million dollar budget that serves 1,000 students. In this case, the per pupil expenditure would be $1,000. In practice, the dollar amount of per pupil expenditures can vary from state to state, as shown in Figure 8.7. Variations in the way states distribute funds to localities depend mainly on money available, demand for services, and cost of living.

Results from the 33rd Annual Phi Delta Kappa/Gallup Poll indicate that lack of proper financial support for schools is the greatest problem facing schools today. Responses also suggest that 68 percent of those polled believe the quality of schooling depends on the amount of money spent on students (Rose & Gallup, 2001).

One plan for putting money to better use in schools is the **district power equalization** plan. Under this plan, localities set the tax rate to collect money for educational

FIGURE 8.7 **Expenditure per Pupil in Average Daily Attendance in Public Elementary and Secondary Schools, by State: 1998–1999** What regional trends do you identify in per pupil expenditures? What factors might account for differences?

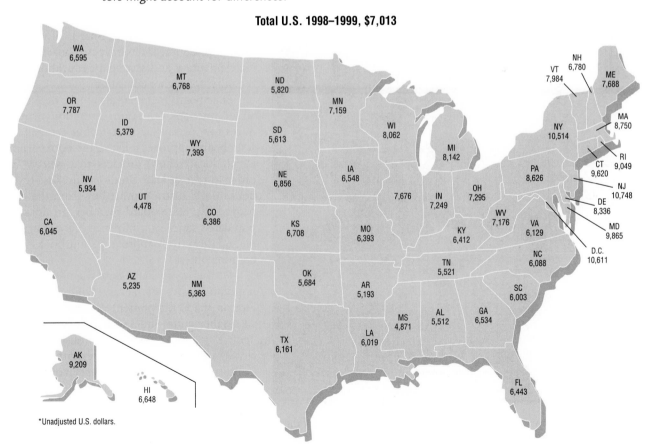

Total U.S. 1998–1999, $7,013

*Unadjusted U.S. dollars.

Source: From *Digest of education statistics, 2001,* by U.S. Department of Education, 2002. Washington, DC: U.S. Government Printing Office. Available online (http://nces.ed.gov/pubsearch).

spending. The state guarantees an amount of money proportional to the money collected from that local tax. As in the foundation program, the state supplies the rest of the funding if the local tax revenue comes up short of the amount needed. This program does not equalize education expenditures among school districts; it merely equalizes access to funds for expenditures.

Hawaii operates as a one-school-district state and provides **full state funding** for its schools. This type of funding means the state pays all educational expenses through a statewide tax. In this plan, then, all funding is equal and all taxation is equal. In other states the desire for independence causes many districts to reject the idea of full state funding. **Why might states allocate funds in different ways?**

State Education Oversight

State government has the responsibility to ensure that public education truly serves its citizens. The quantity and quality of educational services vary across communities within a state, sometimes significantly. State government, therefore, oversees educational operations so that all communities receive at least the minimal level of services required to educate state residents. State government fulfills this mission by designing and implementing educational programs, monitoring resources for public education, and evaluating the results of programs.

STATE BOARDS OF EDUCATION

The **state board of education** regulates educational practices and advises governors and state legislators about educational business. All states except Wisconsin have state boards of education. The majority of states—thirty-five to be exact—allow governors to appoint some or all board members (National Association of State Boards of Education, 1996). Some states have two boards, one for elementary and secondary education and the other for higher education.

State board members also make decisions about textbook adoption. Adoption procedures vary from state to state, but generally a state board approves a list of textbooks from which local school districts may select. In order to receive state funds to purchase textbooks, local districts must buy from the approved list. State board members in densely populated states can influence school curricula significantly by approving some books and banning others.

Furthermore, state board members in the populous states of Texas, California, and Florida shape the content of textbooks sold across the nation. States with many school students buy a lot of books, so publishers listen closely to their requests. For example, when California state board members voice concerns about the lack of multiculturalism in textbooks, textbooks soon focus more attention on multicultural life. As a result, children in less populous states, such as Montana, Kansas, or Vermont, for better or worse, use textbooks designed for other states.

How do the powers and responsibilities of state governments and the national government differ with regard to the governance and finance of education? How are the responsibilities of local boards of education or local education agencies different from those of state boards of education?

STATE EDUCATION DEPARTMENTS

A **state education department (SED)** is an organization that carries out a state's education business. An SED may administer programs directly, for instance, schools for the deaf or blind. SEDs are directed by a state superintendent, a commissioner, or a **chief state school officer.** SEDs oversee a variety of matters, such as how well elementary and secondary schools meet curriculum guidelines and how colleges conduct teacher preparation programs.

An SED also advises the executive and legislative branches of state government on a variety of issues, including school finance. It conducts staff development programs and public relations work for itself and for other governmental and nongovernmental agencies with a stake in education. Over the years, SEDs have taken on more and more tasks. As more laws are passed and regulations established, SEDs are expected to monitor schools' compliance.

Some states are trying to alter the way their state education departments are organized and the way they do their work. Michigan and Iowa, for instance, have reduced the level of services provided at the state level and the number of employees in their state education departments.

STATE STANDARDS BOARDS

Should teachers control the state standards board?   All states now have **state standards boards,** which are commissions that regulate professional practices in education. In thirteen states these boards have the final authority. In the rest of the states, they serve only in an advisory capacity to policy makers. In Alabama, for example, the State Advisory Committee on Teacher Education and Certification has about thirty members appointed by the state superintendent. As its name suggests, this committee advises state policymakers on such topics as teacher certification requirements. In contrast, standards boards in Minnesota, Nevada, Kentucky, West Virginia, and North Dakota have final authority concerning certification, entry, and exit standards for teachers. In these states teachers themselves make up a majority of the standards board members.

The National Education Association and other teachers groups have encouraged the creation of state standards boards. They believe standards boards help create and promote a concept of professionalism for teachers. Advocates also believe teachers should be the ones who serve on standards boards. Not until teachers control the state policymaking system, it is argued, will they be able to control their own professional destiny.

THE GOVERNOR'S INFLUENCE

Historically, governors have relied on their appointees to formulate and implement educational policy. Only in the past fifteen to twenty years have governors themselves become personally involved in state education issues.

The **Council of Chief State School Officers** is an informal organization for the leaders of state departments of elementary and secondary education across the United States and its jurisdictions. The Council provides a forum for education leaders to discuss their mutual ideas and concerns. The Council also sponsors a series of special programs (international education, technology, national teacher of the year, etc.), a resource center on educational equity, and a state education assessment center. These programs and activities, plus an electronic network, provide opportunities for communication among leaders of state systems of public education.

In recent years governors themselves have become major participants in education reform through the **National Governors' Association (NGA).** Founded in 1908, the NGA is a coalition of state chief executives. Many governors have come to believe that good education makes good politics. The problems in education are so challenging and so related to other areas of society that real reform demands strong, visible leadership from the very top of state government. The NGA has given governors the opportunity to influence education not only in their respective states but nationwide. The association also has a strong voice in education funding and reform at the federal level.

Cooperation among School Districts

Some educational services are so expensive, and both human and material resources so limited, that districts must band together to provide them. These cooperative efforts are run by facilities most often called **intermediate educational units (IEUs),** educational service agencies (ESAs), or boards of cooperative educational services (BOCESs). For example, every high school in a state cannot provide the kind of vocational training that students need to be competitive in the job market. To meet their students' needs, several districts may join together to construct and maintain a technical training center.

About three-fourths of all states mandate and provide support for special cooperative facilities, or units, between the state and local levels. These units further concentrate resources and support to provide high-level care that many schools could not supply on their own. Special education services, particularly for children with severe and multiple disabilities, represent opportunities for such interdistrict cooperation or even for statewide cooperation.

Sometimes school districts cooperate with organizational units besides other school districts. They do so to increase their power, to reduce uncertainty, to increase performance by ensuring a steady flow of resources, and to protect themselves (Stearns, Hoffman, & Heide, 1987). On a day-to-day level, they share information, people, funds, and equipment. For example, some schools contract with state and federal governments, universities, and private corporations to conduct research and to operate innovative educational projects. Head Start and Follow Through projects are examples of such cooperative arrangements.   **Why might vocational programs and advanced placement courses be located in IEUs?**

How Are Schools Financed and Managed at the Local Level?

Schools' personalities reflect the characters of the communities they serve. Some are dull and complacent; others are full of energy and hopefulness. Citizen participation in educational matters is apparent at a variety of events—school board meetings, gatherings of parent–teacher organizations, and high school sporting events. People affect the schools, and the schools, in turn, influence citizens both inside and outside their walls.

The local level is often the best place to observe how money and personalities interact to produce a unique mix of educational practices. In some communities the balance of power rests with a small number of people. At other times in other places, several groups compete to influence the focus and flow of educational policy. Power struggles on the local level can be particularly intense, because the people involved are concerned with the very schools where they teach and send their children. It is public education on the most personal level.

Property Taxes

In most states **local property taxes** on property almost exclusively provide the portion of school funding that localities must supply. There are two kinds of property, real and personal. **Real property** is not readily movable; it includes land, buildings, and improvements. **Personal property** is movable; it consists of machinery, livestock, crops, and automobiles, as well as money, stocks, and bonds. A community's ability to pay for education depends on the assessed value of its property. The local tax rate is a calculation of a community's total property value and the amount of money needed to fund the community budget. The citizens who own property within the community are then responsible for paying local taxes.

Using property taxes as a source of support for public schools is a widely criticized procedure (Burrup, Brimley, & Garfield, 1999). One criticism is homeowners pay an unfairly large amount of the cost for funding education. A homeowner not only pays tax on the land he owns, but on the house as well. Residents living in apartments, on the other hand, pay no taxes of this kind. Another criticism is property assessment procedures are not uniform among communities, thereby creating taxpayer inequities. These and other problems create differences in property tax revenue that ultimately lead to educational inequalities among schools.

Although property taxes often are referred to as "school taxes," in truth the money is used to meet needs other than educational ones. Property taxes also pay for things like community road maintenance, ambulance and police services, and libraries. This fact may be more problematic in some areas than in others. It can be especially problematic in cities where tax-exempt property (e.g., public buildings, churches, government property, and parks) is a large portion of the total city property. Cities, particularly those in high-crime areas, face many expenses that suburbs either do not face or face on a more modest scale. The result is less money is available to fund city schools.

In addition, cities often provide services paid for with property taxes to people who work in the city but live in the suburbs. When it snows, for example, the city must plow the streets so people can get to work. Workers who live in the suburbs benefit from the plowing of city streets, even though they do not support this activity with their own property taxes. While snow removal benefits many people, it uses up money that could be earmarked for inner-city schools.

Rural districts, too, may face considerable financial hardship by depending on property taxes to fund schools as well as other services. The main cause of rural hardship is higher per pupil costs. When a rural district builds a new school, for instance, relatively few taxpayers share the cost of the building. To ease such inequities and the burden on property taxes, the trend in recent years has been to replace declining local revenues with state aid. **Should property taxes be abandoned as a way to fund education?**

Local School Boards

Would you ever consider running for a seat on a local school board? The **local school board** is one of the most common, visible examples of democracy in action. School boards are bodies of elected or appointed public servants responsible for providing advice and consent on the operation of public schools. Because overseeing education is a power reserved to the states, local school boards are agents of the states.

The local school board is generally recognized as the policy-making body for public schools. In action, this means school board members have the right to establish schools, select the board's executive officer (the local superintendent of schools), set rules to ensure the smooth running of schools, and spend tax dollars as they see fit.

Like all public representatives, school board members try to interpret the public will, as well as exercise their own personal judgment, in governing the public education system. On some issues, board members and the people they represent are out of tune with one another. A poll conducted for the National School Boards Foundation revealed some points of tension between school boards and their constituents:

> While more than two-thirds of school board members gave their local schools an A
> or B for overall performance, less than half the general public did so. Three-quarters
> of school board members said their teachers and principals were doing a good or

Technology in Practice

HOW DO SCHOOLS' EXPENDITURES AND REVENUES COMPARE?

To understand if schools have too much money, not enough, or just about what they need to educate students, school administrators often try to "balance" their budgets with expenditures of other similar districts. In other words, many believe that it is politically wise to propose budgets that are similar to their peers' budgets.

The availability of online databases makes the task of comparing one's own educational spending to the spending of one's neighbors a simple process. Go to the Education Finance Statistics Center online at the National Center for Education Statistics (http://nces.ed.gov/edfin/index.asp). There you will find a link called "Public School District Finance Peer Search." When you click on the link, you will be asked to supply a district name. The site supplies a peer group for this district according to the total number of students, student–teacher ratio, median household income, and other factors. You might supply the name of the district where you went to high school. (No need to enter the state name; the program gives you a choice if there are multiple districts with the same name.)

When you choose to do a "standard" search, you will see your district compared to its peers by per pupil expenditures. You will also find comparisons of student–teacher ratio, administrative expenditures, sources of revenue, and other information. The screen capture on page 221 is an example of what you can expect to see.

This exercise is especially useful if you are thinking as school leaders must think. But if you are thinking like a teacher looking for a job, you might also use this website to sharpen your search techniques. For instance, once you identify your target district and its peers, it is possible to find the starting salaries of these educational systems.

Critical Thinking Questions

Imagine for a moment that you value a certain type of community as a good place to teach, but the starting salaries are quite different among many communities. How will you decide which place is best for you? What other factors will you consider? Will the diversity of the community be an issue? Will the geographical location of the job matter? Will your access to further higher education be important?

excellent job. Among the public at large, just 43 percent rated principals that highly, while 54 percent gave teachers similar votes of confidence. More than eight in ten board members said their districts were doing a good or excellent job in combating violence and drugs, but only a third of the public agreed. (Hendrie, 1999, p. 9)

When there is tension between school board members and their constituents, dissatisfaction can result in the limitation of the board's power. In some instances, the concept of local school boards has been abandoned altogether. In Chicago, advocacy groups lobbied successfully for the establishment of popularly elected councils of citizens, parents, and teachers for each school. These councils were given the right to select principals and to decide how discretionary funds should be spent. In New Jersey, community dissatisfaction with the quality of public school education took a different route. In this case, the state took over control of the Jersey City and Paterson school districts.

School District Budgets

The best way to understand local finance of public schools is to study a school district budget. Most school boards control both the staffing of local schools and the types of programs offered to students. In this sense, the budget represents a concrete statement of local values.

School districts develop long-term financial plans that represent predictions about

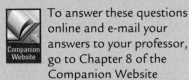

To answer these questions online and e-mail your answers to your professor, go to Chapter 8 of the Companion Website (ablongman.com/mcnergney4e) and click on Technology in Practice.

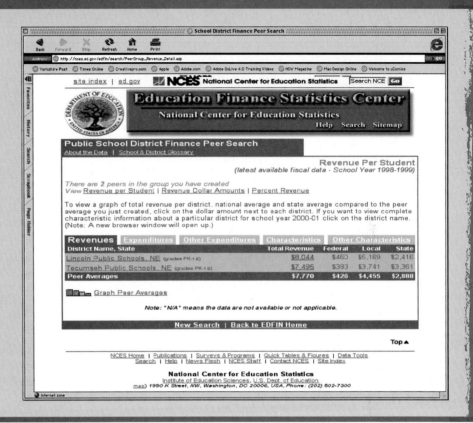

the future. They predict such things as the cost of new textbooks, money needed for building maintenance, transportation costs, and so on. District employees craft a new budget for each **fiscal year**—a twelve-month period covered by the annual budget, often corresponding with the state's fiscal year (e.g., July 1 to June 30). Once an annual budget is adopted by local officials or approved by the voters, it guides school administrators' actions. Budgets also help administrators know how much money they will need and receive from various sources, including state money and local taxes. These factors, of course, are key to determining how the school will operate in the coming year. In short, the school budget outlines where funding is coming from, what it will be used for, and what services will be provided.

So who creates school budgets, and how are they set in place? In most localities the budget-adoption process involves a number of steps (U.S. Department of Education, 1989):

1. District administrators led by the superintendent analyze needs and costs, set policies for the coming year, and plan an initial draft of the budget.
2. District administrators discuss this draft with the school board in one or more meetings.
3. District administrators make the proposed budget available for public study.
4. The school board holds one or more public hearings, at which they receive comments from citizens about the proposed budget.

5. The school board adopts an official budget based on the proposed budget, but with any amendments it believes necessary.

6. In some districts the school board vote is the final decision. In other districts the budget must then be approved by elected officials or by voter referendum.

7. A budget that has received final approval takes effect in the district.

In areas where site-based management (discussed later in this chapter) is the norm, people are experimenting with **school-based budgeting** or **site-based budgeting.** This concept puts the responsibility for budgeting resources at the level of the individual building, rather than at the level of central administration. In other words, each school's teachers, parents, and principals make decisions about how money is spent on hiring staff, professional development, and goods and services. To be effective, school-based budgeting requires that the principal and other staff members know students well enough to match available resources to students' needs (Burrup et al., 1999).

As with most types of budgets, negotiation is key to crafting and adopting school budgets that are acceptable to everyone. Many people (taxpayers, teachers, administrators, and special-interest groups) have a stake in where the money to run schools comes from and where it goes. A school budget, then, is a political document formed from compromise. At its core it should provide adequately for the educational needs of the school district's constituents. **Whose values and needs should a school budget represent?**

When presenting their next year's budgets, school officials sometimes justify only the increase over the previous year's request. In these cases, the amount the school district is spending is usually accepted as necessary. Some schools, however, must make a case for their entire financial request each year. This is referred to as **zero-base budgeting** because each year program budgets start at zero, rather than at the amount they received the previous year (Pyhrr, 1973).

Whether they are starting from scratch or building on the previous year's budget, most school districts use line-item budgets to explain their financial plans. These budgets include a beginning balance for the year, estimates of revenue by source, planned expenditures, and a projected balance at the end of the year. Sources of revenue may include moneys from federal, state, county or parish, and city government levels; income from local taxes or from the sale of bonds; payments of fees for meals and for use of sports facilities; and private donations expected during the year. Income often is set aside for use with specific groups of students (e.g., students with disabilities) or special programs (e.g., library support or school nurse).

Planned expenditures represent the most detailed portion of a school budget. As illustrated in Table 8.2, a school system can have a number of educational expenditures. Generally, districts categorize expenses in one of two ways. *Functions* are broad categories of purposes, such as instruction and support; *objects* are specific things to be paid for, such as personnel salaries and benefits.

Salaries and benefits for both instructional and noninstructional staff claim the largest portion of any school budget. For this reason, and because they are visible in the budget, salaries often become sources of irritation in communities across the country.

Even with all the work and careful planning administrators put into building a budget, the fact that one has been approved does not mean the numbers are firmly established. In reality, spending can change for a number of reasons: enrollment figures may be higher or lower than projected, unexpected weather may affect utility bills, and unforeseen events (e.g., flooding of a school gymnasium during a heavy rain) can require emergency maintenance. School administrators sometimes have the authority to transfer dollars from one line item to another to take care of unforeseen needs. In other districts, administrators must consult with the school board before making changes. When budget changes are made, however, federal regulations prohibit the removal of money from federal grants designed to benefit specific groups of students or programs.

TABLE 8.2 Hypothetical Actual and Proposed School Budget Items

	Fiscal Year 2004, Proposed Budget	Fiscal Year 2003, Actual Budget
Instruction		
Salaries	3,466,867.8	3,194,956.6
Benefits	271,911.2	271,911.2
Purchased services	67,977.8	67,977.8
Supplies	135,955.6	203,933.4
Property	407,866.8	407,866.8
Total Instruction	4,350,579.2	4,146,645.8
Support		
Salaries	1,495,511.6	1,223,600.4
Benefits	135,955.6	135,955.6
Purchased services	203,993.4	67,977.8
Supplies	135,955.6	203,993.4
Property	203,993.4	135,955.6
Total support	2,175,289.6	1,767,422.8
Noninstructional services		
Salaries	67,977.8	135,955.6
Benefits	6,797.78	13,595.56
Supplies	20,393.34	40,786.68
Property	54,382.24	67,977.8
Total noninstructional	149,551.16	258,315.64
Facilities		
Salaries	203,933.4	163,146.72
Benefits	20,393.34	16,314.46
Supplies	271,911.2	163,146.72
Property	183,540.06	65,258.9
Total facilities	679,778	407,866.8
Total expenditures	7,355,197.9	658,025.1

Source: Adapted from *Making sense of school budgets* (p. 15) by U.S. Department of Education, 2001, Washington, DC: Office of Educational Research and Improvement.

How Are Governance and Funding Related to Educational Success?

Public education uses public funds to provide educational opportunities for all children, regardless of their home circumstances. Funds relate directly to educational opportunities; that is, money can buy equipment, materials, and experiences. But the relationship between funds and learning that is measured by standardized achievement tests resists simple explanation.

Two separate researchers set out to prove just what the relationship is between how much money a school has and test scores. Eric Hanushek (1989) reviewed thirty-eight research studies and concluded there is no systematic relationship or direct connection between school expenditures and student performance. In contrast, Larry Hedges and his colleagues (Hedges, Laine, & Greenvals, 1994) reviewed the same studies using a different method and found that higher expenditures do improve school outcomes. Who is right? According to Michael Sadowski (1995), given the methods they used, both Hanusheck and Hodges are right.

So perhaps the more important question is: What do schools do with the money they have? When schools use money to reduce class size so educators can change how they offer instruction, there are remarkable gains in student learning. In contrast, when decision makers simply reduce class size but fail to adopt new curricula and methods, more money has little effect on student performance.

Unfortunately, more money is not always available. Debt and economic recession during the 1990s and beyond has halted much of the educational reform begun in the 1980s. Many states have experimented with a wide range of programs and organizational setups in hopes of getting the most out of the money they spent on public education. These programs include site-based management, high-tech classrooms, career ladders for teachers, professional development schools, better and longer educational programs for teachers, innovative curricula, restructured school calendars, and new testing of both students and teachers.

But innovations can be expensive too. Sometimes the political courage to stick with these new ideas long enough to determine their worth is difficult to come by. Many policymakers got nervous in the 1990s, as states faced budget problems and the public demanded results. They wanted "hard evidence"—test scores—that demonstrated the money spent on education was not being wasted. If teachers and students did not produce, why spend more money on people and systems that were failing?

Some critics, however, take issue with the belief that schools are failing and that funding for education is not connected to success. They argue that people interpret test results incorrectly to suggest that student performance and educational quality are declining. Moreover, they argue that test results fail to represent the real accomplishments of schools (Berliner & Biddle, 1995; Bracey, 1991; Carson, Huelskamp, & Woodall, 1991; Verstegn & McGuire, 1991).

Furthermore, statistics show that states spending the most on education consistently have many more students seeking college admission than states spending less money. Given the mission of public education in America—to accept and educate any and all students who desire an education—schools do a remarkable job.

How might this community support its schools? Why might this community have less money for education than other nearby communities or municipalities? Would funding relate to how well the students do? What measures might work to reduce disparities in funding from one school district to the next?

The Issue of Funding Equity

People make trade-offs when education dollars are limited. Sometimes the trade-offs exist as choices between educational fairness, or equity, and educational excellence. Some people believe that efforts to promote educational excellence will leave behind poor and minority-group students. Others argue that money spent on equalizing programs and opportunities for all students would be put to better use capitalizing on the strengths of outstanding students. Allan Odden (1984) contends that such choices are ill-conceived, however, because there are more connections between excellence and equity than many realize:

> On economic grounds, the simultaneous pursuit of excellence and equity is mandatory. If our national strategy for maintaining a competitive edge in the international market is to increase the per capita productivity of the U.S. work force, then all U.S. workers must have better-developed skills than their counterparts in other countries. (p. 316)

Although the various state funding formulas are intended to provide some standardization of educational quality among communities, they are unable to do so completely. For example, more affluent school districts can support high levels of education without much assistance from the state. Quite often, these districts are reluctant to support increased state taxes that would benefit other districts. Nor do such communities want to give up control of their ability to collect local taxes. Doing so would potentially reduce their ability to maintain a position of privilege (Ward, 1992).

In some parts of the country, inequalities in available funds are so great that districts poor in property have had to tax themselves three or four times as heavily as rich districts to raise revenue for their schools. On the average, however, high-poverty districts receive much more of their revenue from state and federal sources than do low-poverty districts.

Adding to the general expenses of running schools, expensive items—school buildings and their repair—can be incredible financial burdens. This is especially true in urban and rural districts where the properties and buildings (infrastructure) suffer from years of neglect. Incidentally, these are the same schools that may have less money available for such expenses. Table 8.3 provides some sense of the magnitude of the infrastructure problems across the United States.

Educational revenue inequities are not a new development; the issue goes back many years. In the 1960s people thought that inequities in school finance might be corrected by taking the issue to the courts. The landmark 1971 case of *Serrano* v. *Priest* was the first case filed in state court (California) to declare unconstitutional a state public school finance system based on taxable wealth. By focusing on the link between educational expenditures and district property wealth, this case challenged school district spending inequities across the nation. William Thro (1990) refers to these cases as the "first wave" of public school finance reform litigation.

In *San Antonio Independent School District* v. *Rodriguez* (1973), a federal district court ruled that the school finance system of San Antonio, Texas, violated the equal protection clause of the Fourteenth Amendment. The amendment applied because large disparities in school district expenditures existed across the state. The U.S. Supreme Court, however, ruled that education was not a fundamental right under the Constitution and was therefore not protected by the Fourteenth Amendment. This decision was a major setback for those who sought to reform school finance.

In 1989, three landmark school finance reform cases—in Montana, Kentucky, and Texas—invalidated school finance systems because funding disparities had grown dramatically. In part, these cases say that the right to education is fundamental or of extreme importance under state constitutions. This assertion could mean that states have

TABLE 8.3   Percent of Public Schools with Building Deficiencies and Renovation Plans   Were any schools you attended in need of repair?

Type of School Condition	All Public Schools
Estimated number of schools	78,313
Estimated enrollment, in thousands	45,000
Percent of schools with temporary buildings	39
Percent of buildings in less than adequate condition	
Original buildings	19
Permanent additions	16
Temporary buildings	19
Percent of schools with building features rated as less than adequate	
At least one feature less than adequate	50
Roofs	22
Framing, floors, and foundations	14
Exterior walls, finishes, windows, doors	24
Interior finishes, trim	17
Plumbing	25
Heating, ventilation, air conditioning	29
Electric power	22
Electrical lighting	17
Life safety features	20
Percent of schools needing to spend money to bring schools into good overall condition	76
Cost per student for all schools	$2,900
Cost per student for schools needing to spend money	$3,800

Source: U.S. Department of Education, National Center for Education Statistics, *Digest of education statistics, 2001.* http://nces.ed.gov/pubsearch.

a responsibility to ensure some measure of financial equality for public schools within their borders. These cases may eventually serve as the basis for a revolution in school finance reform.   **How might funding equity be achieved?**

The Issue of School Choice

Will school choice weaken or strengthen public schools?   School choice is the right of parents to choose the schools their children attend. Instead of being limited to the local public school, some parents prefer to send their children to parochial, vocational, or other types of alternative schools, as discussed in Chapter 7. Some people believe school choice should be common practice and argue that competition among schools would improve the overall public school system. Opponents say school choice would destroy the concept of a public education system in which children of diverse backgrounds live and learn together.

Parents who choose the schools their children attend do so for several reasons, the primary one being academics. The second most important reason that parents list is convenience. Among those who select a private school, the second most important reason is religious preferences.

People who oppose concepts of school "choice" cite many reasons for their position. They believe that, if citizens can choose where to send their children to school, schools will become racially segregated. At the very least, gains made by students who attend private schools will exacerbate class distinctions. A central purpose of public education is to prepare people to participate in our democracy, they argue, and school choice will prevent this from happening. Also, children who most need their parents' involvement in order to make wise choices will be least likely to get it. Others point out that the money available for most "choice" schools is far below what they actually cost. Therefore, the only people who will benefit are children of wealthy individuals who can pay the extra costs.

Historically, paying for private schooling has been a private matter. If parents wanted their children to be educated in a certain manner, to be taught particular values,

Voices

ON PRIVATIZATION

Milton Friedman, a senior research fellow at the Hoover Institution, won the Nobel Prize for Economics in 1976. Excerpts from a paper he wrote on vouchers appear below.

Our elementary and secondary educational system needs to be radically reconstructed. That need arises in the first instance from the defects of our current system. But it has been greatly reinforced by some of the consequences of the technological and political revolutions of the past few decades. Those revolutions promise a major increase in world output, but they also threaten advanced countries with serious social conflict arising from a widening gap between the incomes of the highly skilled (cognitive elite) and the unskilled.

A radical reconstruction of the educational system has the potential of staving off social conflict while at the same time strengthening the growth in living standards made possible by the new technology and the increasingly global market. In my view, such a radical reconstruction can be achieved only by privatizing a major segment of the educational system—i.e., by enabling a private, for-profit industry to develop that will provide a wide variety of learning opportunities and offer effective competition to public schools. Such a reconstruction cannot come about overnight. It inevitably must be gradual.

The most feasible way to bring about a gradual yet substantial transfer from government to private enterprise is to enact in each state a voucher system that enables parents to choose freely the schools their children attend. I first proposed such a voucher system 40 years ago.

Many attempts have been made in the years since to adopt educational vouchers. With minor exceptions, no one has succeeded in getting a voucher system adopted, thanks primarily to the political power of the school es-

tablishment, more recently reinforced by the National Education Association and the American Federation of Teachers, together the strongest political lobbying body in the United States. . . .

Finally, as in every other area in which there has been extensive privatization, the privatization of schooling would produce a new, highly active and profitable private industry that would provide a real opportunity for many talented people who are currently deterred from entering the teaching profession by the dreadful state of so many of our schools.

This is not a federal issue. Schooling is and should remain primarily a local responsibility. Support for free choice of schools has been growing rapidly and cannot be held back indefinitely by the vested interests of the unions and educational bureaucracy. I sense that we are on the verge of a breakthrough in one state or another, which will then sweep like a wildfire through the rest of the country as it demonstrates its effectiveness. . . .

Critical Thinking Question

How might you evaluate the success or failure of a voucher program designed to allow parents to send their children to any school of their choice, public or private? Try to synthesize what you have heard and read about vouchers into two crisp paragraphs, one for and one against.

To answer this question online and e-mail your answer to your professor, go to Chapter 8 of the Companion Website (ablongman.com/mcnergney4e) and click on Voices.

Source: From *Public schools: Make them private,* by M. Friedman, 1995. Washington, DC: CATO Institute. You can get Friedman's complete manuscript online at http://www.cato.org/.

Your Teaching Life in Practice

PUBLIC SUPPORTS FOR PRIVATE SCHOOLS?

Nothing starts a spirited debate in education these days quite as quickly as the topic of vouchers—publicly funded tuition that parents can use to send their children to private schools. If you attended a public meeting about the merits of a voucher system, here are some of the comments you might hear:

PRO Vouchers make it possible for children from lower-income families to escape weak public schools. Vouchers make educational life more equitable because they give these children the same opportunities that children from more affluent families enjoy.

CON Children need their parents' help to take advantage of vouchers, and many children from lower-income families simply will not get it.

PRO Vouchers foster competition among schools. If parents can send their children to private schools, then the public schools will improve as they compete to attract students.

CON Vouchers threaten the ideal that every child in the nation will have equal access to high-quality public schooling. Competition doesn't always serve people well. Schools must be accountable for what they do. Vouchers do not ensure proper oversight and may well be abused by corrupt managers of private schools. A few children may flee to private schools where they will be well educated, but far more will be left behind in public schools that have even fewer resources.

PRO Individual parents have the opportunity to spend their vouchers at the school of their choice. They may even decide that a religiously affiliated school will best meet their child's needs.

CON Vouchers will breach the constitutional separation of church and state by allowing parents to use public funds to send their children to religious schools.

Discussion Question

Where do you stand on the use of vouchers? Why?

To answer these questions online and e-mail your answer to your professor, go to Chapter 8 of the Companion Website (ablongman.com/mcnergney4e) and click on Your Teaching Life in Practice.

---

and to associate with certain other children, they paid for these privileges out of their own pockets. Those who could afford to send their children to private schools continued to pay their taxes, which in turn supported public schools.

While some private schools have developed and maintained their reputations by appealing to wealthy families, others have attracted people from across the socioeconomic spectrum. The largest alternative school system in the United States, the Catholic schools, teaches high- and low-income students. Catholic schools may offer scholarships and tuition breaks to encourage students from low-income families to attend. Other types of private schools, both religious and secular, may offer similar enticements. Many parents, even those who could least afford to do so, have been willing to sacrifice economically to send their children to private schools.

At the turn of the twenty-first century, the debate about public support for private elementary and secondary schools has reenergized. Now part of the debate focuses on possible methods of enacting school choice plans. One of the most widely explored methods is the school **voucher,** an idea first offered by economist Milton Friedman in 1955. He argued that local governments ought to create vouchers, or certificates, that provided parents with a sum of money to pay for each of their children's education. Parents would be free to spend this money at any school they chose, as long as it met minimum governmental standards.

Another way to set up and pay for school choice programs involves a **tuition tax credit.** This method allows taxpayers to subtract educational costs from the amount of taxes they owe. Similarly, a **tuition tax deduction** allows taxpayers to subtract educational costs from their incomes before taxes are calculated. Tax credits and tax deductions resemble vouchers in that they all are designed to give parents at least part of the money they will spend on private schooling for their children. Opponents contend that tax credits and deductions may encourage people to abandon public schools. They fear the public school system will serve only low-income families, who cannot afford to pay up front for the cost of education and wait to receive a deduction later. In addition, public schools would receive less taxpayer support, and the quality of education would decrease considerably.

The use of tuition tax credits, deductions, and vouchers must meet with state approval. When states adopt new funding mechanisms, they cannot conflict with federal law. For example, if a proposed plan denied certain people their civil rights, federal courts would rule the plan unconstitutional. Issues of the separation of church and state have been particularly confusing when it comes to school choice. In short, there is debate about whether allowing public funds to be spent on private schools violates the separation of church and state. For example, if a family decides to use its vouchers to send its children to Catholic school, is that line of separation crossed? This issue will continue to make private schools a focus of public interest and court scrutiny.

In June 2002, the U.S. Supreme Court ruled that the state-enacted school voucher program in Cleveland, Ohio, does not violate the U.S. Constitution. The program provides benefits to people defined only by financial need and residence in a particular school district. It allows individuals to exercise choice among public and private schools that are either secular or religious. The ruling ensures that some 3,700 students can continue attending private, mostly religiously affiliated schools at taxpayer expense (Walsh, 2002). It remains to be seen whether this is a one-time decision or an indication of how courts will rule on this topic in the years to come.

The Issue of Site-Based Management

Increasingly, principals lead site-based or school-based management teams composed of teachers and parents—and sometimes students. The belief is that people closest to a school best understand the school culture and have the biggest stake in its outcomes. Therefore, these are the people who should share responsibility for student learning and school decision making (Darling-Hammond & McLaughlin, 1995).

Who could argue with the idea of involving in the formation of educational policies those affected by such policies? The nation's historical commitment to the common school has meant that public education should serve all the people by involving all the people. Site-based management, then, has historical precedent and seems to make sense. But what appears reasonable in theory does not necessarily translate smoothly into practice. Moreover, certain reform efforts, such as those aimed at professionalizing education, tend to conflict with group or team decision making. Some educators believe that people working outside the public education system do not have enough training to make decisions that will affect children's educational experiences. **Why might teachers not want to participate in site-based management?**

Like other educational innovations, site-based management must overcome a number of obstacles to succeed. One of the biggest obstacles is inertia. When people are used to behaving in certain ways, it is difficult to change these patterns. For instance, teachers often resist decisions that require them to make drastic changes in the way they teach. Moreover, teachers must be convinced that reform is permanent and real, and not simply this year's trend. They need to be convinced that they can exert power over events and decisions if they are to participate enthusiastically.

At least five states—Colorado, Florida, Kentucky, North Carolina, and Texas—have mandated some form of participatory decision making in all their schools. Standards and protocols for how participatory decision making works, however, do not exist. As a result, literally hundreds of districts across the country are using different forms of local control. Large urban school systems, including Chicago, Miami, Los Angeles, San Diego, and Rochester, New York, have moved toward site-based management (*Education Week,* 2002). How other schools will implement participatory decision-making policies—and how well they will work—remains to be seen.

Regardless of where site-based management occurs, lack of resources can be a serious impediment to effective public education. With too little money, no matter how it is shared, even schools managed on site can be uninspiring and ineffective. The schools most in need of a new lease on educational life may be least able to afford it. Although the ultimate intent of restructuring schools for site-based management is to create environments that motivate teachers and help students be successful, this goal may not be met. What Jonathan Kozol observed more than a decade ago may still be true: "In many cities, what is termed 'restructuring' struck me as very little more than moving around the same old furniture within the house of poverty" (Kozol, 1991, p. 4).

Summary

A layer of control and oversight exists in public education that is not readily apparent to the untrained eye. Government at the federal, state, and local levels shapes the activities of schooling, the behaviors of leaders, and ultimately the lives of teachers and their students.

Federal funding to elementary and secondary schools, small in relation to state and local funding, comes with requirements. Increasingly, these have been translated into a national agenda for public schooling. Both incentives and sanctions exist that can be used to enhance educational performance.

States and localities, too, have increased expectations for teacher and student performance. They also have multiple ways to raise money in support of public education. What individual schools and school districts cannot do alone, they often try to accomplish by sharing resources and collaborating on services.

School leaders must contend with these disparate forces and conflicting demands. Who are the pressure groups that want to influence education policy and practice? Who will decide what is best for all the people in a community, and how will those decisions be made? Teachers, by the nature of their jobs, have an important say in these matters. The more they know about governance, finance, and leadership, the more likely they are to maximize their abilities to work successfully within the system they inhabit.

Terms and Concepts

block grant   210
categorical grant   210
chief state school officer   217
Council of Chief State School Officers   217
district power equalization   215
Education Consolidation and Improvement Act
    (ECIA)   210
fiscal year   221
flat grant   214
foundation program   214
full state funding   216
intermediate educational unit (IEU)   218
local property taxes   218
local school board   219

National Center for Education Statistics (NCES)   209
National Governors Association (NGA)   217
National Parent–Teacher Association (PTA)   206
per pupil expenditure   215
personal property   218
progressive taxation   214
real property   218
regressive taxation   214
school-based budgeting   222
school choice   226
school governance   201
site-based budgeting   222
special-interest group   206
state board of education   216

state education department (SED)   217
state standards board   217
tuition tax credit   229

tuition tax deduction   229
voucher   228
zero-base budgeting   222

Reflective Practice

School Board Membership

There is nothing quite like a school-board election to focus public attention, especially when the most pressing issue is money. That is just what Eileen Bracey learned when she ran and won a seat on her local board. Eileen's children were grown and out of school—a school system she, her husband, and her children loved dearly. She felt just as passionately about the schools as she did when her daughter and son were there. Now that she had more time devote to public service, she looked forward to helping the community protect educational quality.

However, Eileen also believed the schools wasted money, and she ran for office on that premise. School enrollment had declined while the staff had increased. The administration poured incredible resources into remodeling old buildings that really were not needed. She realized that her neighbors had grown older and were worried about educational costs. They watched young parents speak convincingly about the need to "invest in youth," while they witnessed a steady decline in the stock market that depressed the value of their savings.

Would Eileen have to resist all efforts to raise funds for education—increasing property taxes, lobbying for a sales tax hike, fighting for a larger share of the lottery proceeds, reassessing property values (which would automatically raise taxes), and any other plan that came down the pike—or could she possibly find some way to balance the need for material support with the need to hold the line on spending? Eileen's reelection and the political fate of her colleagues on the board depended on charting a course of reason and sticking to it.

Issues, Problems, Dilemmas, Opportunities

What problems and opportunities do Eileen Bracey and her fellow board members face?

Perceive and Value

If you were a young parent in this district, why might you be willing to support any attempt to raise additional funds for the schools? If you were a retired person, why might you oppose any such attempt? If you were a beginning teacher in this school system and Eileen Bracey asked you what to do, what kind of advice might you give her?

Know and Act

What kinds of ideas might the board explore for saving money? What are the pros and cons of these strategies? How might they build public support for "smarter education," that is, education that protected or enhanced the quality of teaching and learning while holding down costs?

Evaluate

How might Eileen know if she were successful in her attempt to be a good board member?

INTASC Principle 10

The teacher fosters relationships with school colleagues, parents, and agencies in the larger community to support students' learning and well-being.

Knowledge

The teacher understands schools as organizations within the larger community context and understands the operations of the relevant aspects of the system(s) within which she or he works. (Interstate New Teacher Assessment and Support Consortium, 1992)

Discussion Question

What more would you like to know about the school and the community to better understand the district's issues related to quality and funding?

Additional Readings

Hanushek, E., & D. W. Jorgenson (Eds.) (1996). *Improving America's schools: The role of incentives.* Washington, DC: National Academy Press.

Hess, F. (2002). *Revolution at the margins: The impact of competition on urban school systems.* Washington, DC: Brookings Institution.

Hoy, W. K., & Miskel, C. G. (2001). *Educational administration: Theory, research, and practice* (6th ed.). New York: McGraw-Hill.

King, R. A., Swanson, A. D., & Sweetland, S. R. (2003). *School finance: Achieving high standards* (3rd ed.). Boston: Allyn and Bacon.

Kowalski, T. J. (1999). *The school superintendent: Theory, practice, and cases.* Upper Saddle River, NJ: Prentice Hall.

LeLoup, L., & Schull, S. A. (2003). *The President and Congress: Collaboration and combat in national policymaking* (2nd ed.). Boston: Allyn and Bacon.

*W*eb Resources

http://www.aclu.org/

Visit the website for the American Civil Liberties Union to learn more about the educational issues they believe are important.

http://www.naacp.org/

The website for the National Association for the Advancement of Colored People provides information about efforts to ensure quality education for all people.

http://www.aasa.org/

See the website of the American Association of School Administrators to learn more about educational issues through the eyes of school leaders.

http://www.pta.org/index.asp

Learn about what the 6.5 million members of the National Parent–Teacher Association are doing to support children and teachers.

http://www.adl.org/main_education.asp

See the education page of the Anti-Defamation League for ideas about ways to unlearn prejudice and combat hate.

Video**Workshop** Extra!

If the VideoWorkshop package was included with your textbook, go to Chapter 8 of the Companion Website (ablongman.com/mcnergney4e) and click on the VideoWorkshop button. Follow the instructions for viewing video clip 12. Then consider this information along with what you've read in Chapter 8 while answering the following questions.

1. The idea of a "digital divide" is addressed in the video clip. Select one aspect of federal funding presented in this chapter and its effects on education. Discuss its importance in contributing to this divide.

2. Which entity should have the most influence on schools—federal, state, or local government? How can you develop an alternative source of power that would reconcile the necessity of standards presented in the video clip with the existence of government structures presented in this chapter?

The Influence of the Law

*C*harneice M. Broughton picked up her ringing telephone on the last Thursday in June to hear news that made her burst into tears of joy: The highest court in the land [the Supreme Court] had just given its blessing to the voucher program that enables her to send her 8-year-old daughter to a private school. "When I heard it, I just said, 'Oh, my God! Thank you, Jesus, God is good!' " said Ms. Broughton, a single mother in southeast Cleveland who works part time as a nursing assistant while studying for her nursing degree. "I need all the help I can get just to get through the school year." (Gewertz, 2002, p. 19)

Schools work, in part, because we agree collectively there must be rules that govern educational life—or laws that help Charneice Broughton and others find answers to educational problems. This chapter explores such problems and suggests how court cases have evolved into our present legal system in which people share rights and responsibilities for schooling.

*H*ow Does Government Influence Education?

How does government influence education? Choose your answer to this question from one of the following responses: (1) slowly, (2) with haste, (3) minimally if at all, (4) profoundly, or (5) all the above. The astute observer will probably argue that the correct answer depends on the definitions of government, influence, and maybe education, too. To best answer this question, then, one must consider exactly what these terms mean.

CHAPTER CONTENTS

How Does Government Influence Education?

What Legal Principles Affect Public Education?

What Are Parents' Rights and Responsibilities?

What Are Students' Rights and Responsibilities?

What Are Teachers' Rights and Responsibilities?

What Are School Districts' Rights and Responsibilities?

Government is organized into federal, state, and local units. As discussed in Chapter 8, the constitutional authority for making educational decisions belongs to the states. They, in turn, encourage localities to assume much responsibility for operating schools. The federal government, however, can and does exert powerful influence on schooling. The U.S. Congress and state legislatures pass laws meant to stop inappropriate behavior in schools and to encourage all that is good about teaching and learning. The chief executives (the president and the governors) must enforce these laws. And both federal and state courts interpret the laws when disagreements arise.

In one of its many functions, government decides who should go to school, how a school building is constructed, how children travel to and from school, what subjects they take, what they eat for lunch and when they eat it, who teaches the children, how, if, and when they progress, and so forth. *Government,* then, can be defined by its organizational structure and by the functions it performs.

The term *influence* is probably best measured on a scale from little or none to strong or profound. Legislation that concerns funding for educational programs may be the easiest way to think about governmental influence. Here, influence can be defined in terms of dollars and power. That is, the more dollars, the more likely the influence will be strong. Furthermore, those who supply the money have the power. In truth, however, more money buys more *potential* influence, but not necessarily actual educational power. Real influence depends on how the money is spent.

Governmental influence on education can also be defined in other ways. For instance, the president of the United States and the governors of the fifty states support a set of national standards for education. They encourage local schools to adopt these standards, because they believe these standards for world-class education will benefit the economy. The cycle continues with Congress and state legislatures. They regulate the development and use of tests meant to assess teachers' and students' success in meeting these standards. City and town councils and local school boards then look to school employees to deliver satisfactory test results. In this example, influence might be defined in terms of the resources that go into the activities of these governmental officials, the activities in which they engage, and the results of their work. All are difficult and costly to measure with any precision.

The term *education* seems simple enough. When used in relation to public policy and governmental control, education often refers to public schooling. It is education supported by public money and governmental institutions. Public schools currently serve slightly less than 90 percent of the K through twelve population, and they have been institutions in our society for many years. Public money usually is thought of in terms of tax dollars, and the source of funding for most public education is in fact tax dollars. But the issue is not that simple. While it is true that the majority of funding schools receive comes from various government levels, public schools may also receive support from private sources. Individuals buy jerseys for the football team, and local businesses and service organizations raise money for computers; large corporations give discounts and grants for facilities, programs, equipment, training, and scholarships.

Private schools may also receive public funds for their programs. In some communities children who attend private religious schools ride public school buses paid for by public funds. The renewed

Funding for private schools is just one area where law affects education.

interest in a voucher system, as we discussed in Chapter 8, would allow children to attend private schools of their choice at taxpayer expense.

So the lines between public and private education are not as black and white as some might believe they are. If the definition of education is further stretched to include educational activities that occur outside school walls, such as online access to public educational services, the definition of what constitutes education becomes even murkier.

So far in this chapter we have discussed the roles of the legislative and executive branches of the government at various levels. But what is the influence of the third branch of government, the judiciary? How and to what degree do the courts influence education?

The courts remain the one governmental authority through which individuals or groups of people, often from outside the political mainstream, can have real influence on educational policy. The courts exercise their influence by settling disputes between parties—interpreting the law in the process. As you will see, court decisions have been the basis for some of the most relevant and far-reaching policies and practices in education.

What Legal Principles Affect Public Education?

The U.S. Constitution does not specifically mention education. States' legal control over education is authorized by the Tenth Amendment's provision that gives states powers not claimed by the federal government. The Constitution is very clear, however, that such state control cannot violate the Constitution's provisions for the basic rights of individuals.

When disputes arise over educational practices or policies, the parties involved try to settle differences at the local level of governance. Depending on the type of case it is, either state courts or the federal judiciary system hear unresolved cases. As Figure 9.1 illustrates, the Supreme Court of the United States is the highest court in the land, beyond which there is no appeal.

Courts frequently consider several statutory and constitutional provisions when ruling on educational matters. One is the First Amendment to the Constitution, which contains two clauses often cited in lawsuits. The **establishment clause** prohibits favoritism toward a particular religion, and the **free exercise clause** ensures religious freedom. Here are some key legal provisions that courts rely on and reasons why they are important:

■ The First Amendment states that "Congress shall make no law respecting an establishment of religion, or prohibiting the free exercise thereof; or abridging the freedom of speech, or of the press; or the right of the people peaceably to assemble, and to petition the government for a redress of grievances."

This amendment is the basis for many lawsuits challenging aid to and regulation of nonpublic schools, public school policies that advance or inhibit religion, and actions that restrict expression by teachers and students.

■ The Fourth Amendment guarantees citizens that the right "to be secure in their persons, houses, papers, and effects, against unreasonable searches and seizures, shall not be violated, and no warrants shall issue, but upon probable cause, supported by oath or affirmation, and particularly describing the place to be searched, and the persons or things to be seized."

When a student's bookbag, locker, or person is searched for illegal or dangerous items, this amendment usually serves as the basis for judgments about the legality of such actions.

FIGURE 9.1 Levels at Which Disputes Are Heard In settling disputes, why is it important for the extra-legal grievance system to function effectively?

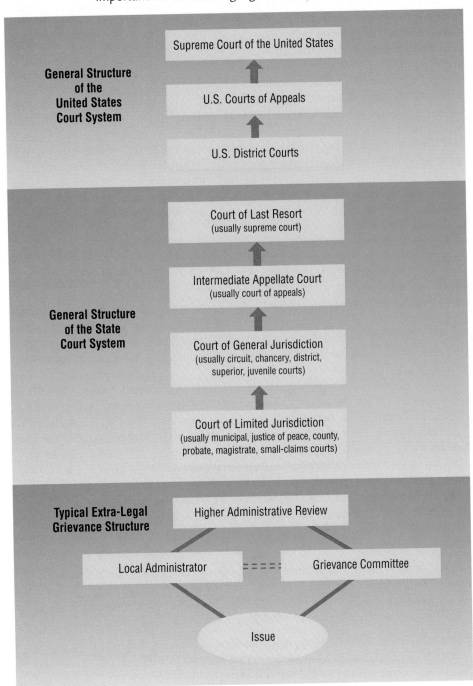

■ The Fourteenth Amendment is the most widely invoked constitutional provision in school-related cases (McCarthy, Cambron-McCabe, & Thomas, 1998). Section 1 states that "[N]o State shall make or enforce any law which shall abridge the privileges or immunities of citizens of the United States; nor shall any State deprive any person of life, liberty, or property, without due process of law; nor deny to any person within its jurisdiction the equal protection of the laws."

FIGURE 9.2 **Groups with Rights and Responsibilities under the U.S. Constitution and Federal Laws** What do overlapping areas in this diagram represent?

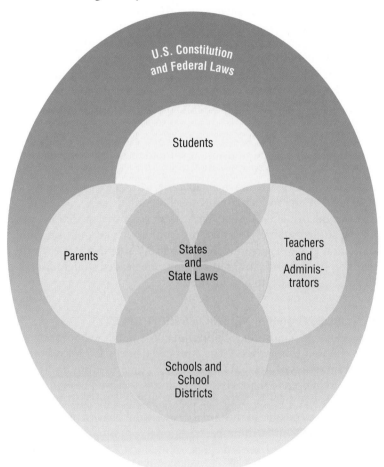

This clause, the **equal protection clause,** is significant in legal cases related to school finance, the expulsion and suspension of students, the dismissal of teachers, and discrimination on the basis of race, gender, and disability.

When disputes arise in contractual situations, Article I, Section 10 of the Constitution typically is consulted. This article states in part that "no State shall . . . pass any . . . ex post facto law, or law impairing the obligation of contracts." Courts' interpretations of this article are key to decisions about the validity of contracts and possible breaches of contracts. Figure 9.2 suggests why these disputes may arise.

In the scenarios that follow, note that the courts use constitutional provisions, state and federal legislation, rules and regulations of state and local boards, and case law (common law) to settle disputes. Note also that Supreme Court decisions have brought some uniformity to educational practices and policies across the country.

What Are Parents' Rights and Responsibilities?

A number of cases decided by the courts have dealt directly with parents' rights and responsibilities as guardians of their children. As the following scenarios suggest, knowledge of such rulings is just as important for teachers as it is for parents.

A Question of Religious Principle

At the end of the school day, Betty Anne Mason fell into stride with three of her ninth-grade students weaving their way to the locker room. The students—James, Lashanta, and Miranda—were so engrossed in conversation that they didn't notice Betty Anne until they reached the locker room. Normally friendly and outgoing in class, the students seemed suddenly fidgety and nervous when Betty Anne asked good-naturedly if they planned to attend the ninth-grade dance Friday night. Miranda muttered something about having to stay home to "do some stuff," then rushed for the front door. As Betty Anne turned toward the other two students, James blushed and whispered something to Lashanta, who bobbed her head in agreement. "Hey, what's with you guys today?" asked Betty Anne.

"Mrs. Mason," said Lashanta, "I don't know if you heard or not, but there is a meeting tonight after the Bible study session at Miranda's house. Some parents who don't like what is going on here at Walden High are getting together to talk about taking their kids out of school and teaching them at home. Miranda's parents have already told her this is her last week at Walden. Can you believe it?"

As she headed for the principal's office, Betty Anne was upset. Miranda was one of her most promising students. Surely her parents wouldn't try to pull something like this. If they did, wouldn't they be violating the compulsory attendance law? By the time she reached the office, Betty Anne's mind was racing. She headed straight for the principal, hoping to get some answers to her questions.

ANALYSIS OF "A QUESTION OF RELIGIOUS PRINCIPLE"

If parents have religious or philosophical objections to a public school program, can they exempt their children from school? The Supreme Court's 1972 decision in *Wisconsin* v. *Yoder* said members of the Old Order Amish religious community were not obligated to send their children to school beyond eighth grade, even though subsequent home instruction was not equivalent to instruction in public schools. (The Amish had argued that compulsory attendance in the upper grades would have a negative effect on the established way of life in their farm-based, traditional community.) The Court's decision was based on the religious freedom clause of the First Amendment and on evidence that the Amish way of life was an acceptable alternative to formal education (Zirkel, Richardson, & Goldberg, 1995).

What are the rights and responsibilities of parents who claim that public school curricula or the public school experience violates their religious principles?

Litigation since *Wisconsin* v. *Yoder* suggests that the "Amish exception" cannot be used by parents who wish to exempt their children from schools for philosophical or religious reasons unless evidence suggests that such schooling might destroy their own religion. For those dissatisfied with the public schools, however, compulsory attendance requirements may be fulfilled in private, alternative, or parochial schools. In all states and the District of Columbia, homeschooling is yet another option.

An examination of data collected by the Home School Legal Defense Association (1999) indicates, however, that the way states regulate homeschooling varies widely. Only thirty-seven states specifically regulate home schooling, and the vast majority (forty-one) do not require parents to have specific qualifications to teach. Only twenty-six states require students to have regular evaluations or take standardized tests (C. Klicka, personal communication, July 20, 1999). In Kentucky, for example, state law specifies that home-schooled students must spend 185 days per year focusing on five areas: reading, writing, spelling, math, and library research. There are no teacher qualifications for parents. Parents are expected to maintain an attendance register and progress reports, but no student testing is required (Home School Legal Defense Association, 1999).

In contrast, North Dakota law requires home-schooled students to study a prescribed curriculum 175 days per year, four hours per day. The elementary curriculum in North Dakota stretches beyond the Kentucky curriculum to include English grammar, geography, U.S. history, civil government, the U.S. Constitution, nature, effects of alcohol, prevention of contagious diseases, and elements of agriculture, physiology, and hygiene. Curriculum at the secondary level is equally specific. To continue studying at home, North Dakota students must meet cutoff scores on standardized tests. Parents serving as teachers must also meet standards. Those who do not possess a teaching certificate or a baccalaureate degree are required to meet or exceed the cutoff score for a national teacher exam. Alternatively, they could have a high school diploma or GED and be monitored by a certified teacher during the first two years of home instruction or until the child completes third grade, whichever is later. Monitoring must continue thereafter if the child scores below the fiftieth percentile on standardized achievement tests (Home School Legal Defense Association, 2002).

Several states, including Arizona, Colorado, Florida, Maine, Washington, and Wyoming, have passed laws requiring public schools to open sports and other extracurricular activities to home-schooled students. Other states are considering such policies, but most states leave decisions on whether to open activities to homeschoolers to local districts.

You Can't Spank My Child!

Can teachers use physical punishment on a child? Steve Donovan's face was flushed as he escorted Brian's parents to the door. As the principal, he suspected there might be some backlash from his actions the day before. But, as he had explained to Brian's parents, he had warned Brian several times that if he kept spitting on other students he was going to be spanked. When Brian repeated the offense yesterday, Steve made good on his promise. Brian's parents were furious. "We know Brian has some behavior problems," they said, "but we sent a note to Brian's teacher telling her that spanking was not to be used as a disciplinary measure. Your behavior was an infringement on our rights as parents, and we're going to see that you don't get away with something like this again!"

ANALYSIS OF "YOU CAN'T SPANK MY CHILD!"

Given that Brian's parents requested formally that their child not be spanked, would a court of law support Steve's actions? In *Ingraham* v. *Wright* (1977), the Supreme Court ruled that the Constitution does not prohibit the use of corporal punishment in schools. In so ruling, the Court concluded that cases dealing with corporal punishment should be handled at the state rather than the federal level. Whether Brian's parents have a legitimate complaint, then, depends on state and local school board policies.

In states that allow corporal punishment, parental objection to the practice does not necessarily take precedence. In *Baker* v. *Owen* (1975), a case challenging a North Carolina state law permitting reasonable corporal punishment, the federal district court recognized parents' basic right to supervise the upbringing of their children. The court also recognized the importance of maintaining order in the schools. Ultimately, the court said that parents' wishes should not interfere with methods chosen by school officials for maintaining discipline.

To head off problems down the line, some states and localities have laws requiring written permission from parents that spanking their children in school is acceptable. If there is no state or local regulation to the contrary, however, schools are not required to seek parental permission before administering corporal punishment. Educators must be aware of state laws and board policies banning or restricting the use of corporal punishment in the classroom.

Another common restriction in some states is that principals are the only ones who can use corporal punishment, doing so only in the presence of an adult witness. Educators who violate such policies may face monetary fines, dismissal, and even imprisonment (McCarthy, Cambron-McCabe, & Thomas, 1998).

Furthermore, many states restrict the methods and intensity with which corporal punishment may be used. Though often equated with paddling, corporal punishment is more broadly defined as "reasonable physical force used by school authorities to restrain unruly students, to correct unacceptable behavior, and to maintain the order necessary to conduct an educational program" (Data Research, Inc., 2002, p. 139). Sometimes teachers who have demonstrated excessive force when disciplining a student (e.g., throwing a student against a chalkboard and then pulling him upright by his hair) have been dismissed for cruelty or charged with criminal assault and battery.

Teachers working in school systems where corporal punishment is allowed must avoid excessive force and follow local guidelines when administering such punishment. Overall, corporal punishment is unacceptable in most states. Those that allow it do so only as a last resort, to be avoided if at all possible.

Do Some Parents Have Special Rights?

Kenneth and Karen Rothschild, deaf parents of nonhearing-impaired students, used American Sign Language as their primary means of communication. When the school system denied their request to hire a sign language interpreter for school-sponsored functions, the Rothschilds were forced to obtain their own interpreter at great personal expense. Subsequently, they brought action against the school district and the superintendent for violating section 504 of the Rehabilitation Act of 1973, which prohibits discrimination on the basis of a disability. School officials denied the charge, arguing that they had made good-faith efforts to accommodate the Rothschilds's needs by providing special seating arrangements at all school-sponsored functions.

ANALYSIS OF "DO SOME PARENTS HAVE SPECIAL RIGHTS?"

Must a school system provide special services, such as sign language interpreters, to parents who are disabled? In *Rothschild* v. *Grottenthaler* (1990), the U.S. Court of Appeals ruled that a public school system receiving federal financial assistance is obligated to provide a sign language interpreter, at school district expense, to deaf parents attending school-initiated events. In explaining its decision, the court said that, without an interpreter, people like the Rothschilds do not have equal opportunity to participate in activities related to their children's education. The court also noted that the Rehabilitation Act specifies that access to necessary accommodations for individuals with disabilities should not impose undue financial or administrative burdens on them. Accordingly, the school system was ordered to (1) reimburse the Rothschilds for money spent on interpreters and (2) hire an interpreter to assist the Rothschilds at school-initiated activities directly involving their children's academic or disciplinary progress.

*W*hat Are Students' Rights and Responsibilities?

In *Tinker* v. *Des Moines Independent Community School District* (1969), the Supreme Court emphasized that students do not lose their rights when they pass through the schoolhouse door. Under the Constitution they continue to be persons "possessed of fundamental rights which the state must respect." Although school authorities have broad powers for the development and implementation of an educational program, they must avoid unreasonable, vague, arbitrary actions or actions in direct conflict with students' constitutional rights and freedoms. **Can students conduct religious practices in school?**

In God Somebody Trusts

Jack Mills sat at his desk grading papers late one afternoon. He heard singing coming from the direction of the principal's office. He recognized the strains of "Onward Christian Soldiers" being sung by what sounded like a fairly large group of students. Students often sang in the building after the final bell; Omega High had many after-school activities. But they did not usually sing hymns. When Ellie Ferro, the sophomore English teacher, stormed into his room, Jack was surprised by her anger.

"Jack, the Young Crusaders for Christ are holding a prayer meeting in the gymnasium again. Apparently the principal said they could meet there whenever the basketball team was not practicing. It really ticks me off that they get to stay here when nobody else gets to use the building for church meetings. The principal has been cuddling up to those fundamentalists every chance she gets. It isn't fair. I want you to come with me to her office. I think we need to call her on this one."

ANALYSIS OF "IN GOD SOMEBODY TRUSTS"

Jack feels nervous about Ellie's anger, largely because the law on prayer clubs in schools is a mystery to him. Given the number of court cases focusing on the separation of church and state since the mid-twentieth century, Jack's confusion is understandable. In the tug of war over where the lines of separation should be drawn, some argue that the First Amendment's establishment clause prohibits religious observance of any type in public schools. Others contend that the Amendment's provisions for free speech, free exercise, and association rights prohibit schools from practicing religious discrimination.

In *Widmar* v. *Vincent* (1981), the Supreme Court ruled that refusing to give religious groups access to facilities while allowing other groups to use the same facilities was a violation of students' rights of free speech. Furthermore, the Court deemed college students less impressionable than high school students. As adults, college students could be expected to understand that the university was neutral in granting permission to a prayer club to meet on public property. With passage of the **Equal Access Act (EAA)** in 1984, Congress indicated that secondary school students were also mature enough to understand that a school does not condone religion merely by allowing prayer clubs on public property.

The EAA states that secondary public schools accepting federal aid must treat student religious groups in the same way as other extracurricular clubs. That is, if a school allows noncurriculum student groups (e.g., the computer game club or the chess club) to meet on school property during noninstructional time, other student-initiated groups, regardless of their religious, philosophical, or political views, must have equal access to school premises. In *Board of Education of the Westside Community Schools* v. *Mergens* (1990), the Supreme Court upheld the constitutionality of the EAA.

Given the Supreme Court's ruling, approving any single student club not directly tied to the curriculum prohibits schools from discriminating against other student organizations, such as the Young Crusaders for Christ. This even applies to groups having little community support, such as religious cults or white supremacists. If schools do permit noncurriculum student group meetings during noninstructional time, teachers or other school employees may be present only in a nonparticipatory capacity. Furthermore, meetings may not be coordinated or led by people other than school students (La Morte, 2002).

Below are rulings on other major cases dealing with separation of church and state that contain implications for educators:

■ *West Virginia State Board of Education* v. *Barnette* (1943)　Educators cannot require students to salute or pledge allegiance to the American flag when those students choose not to for personal or religious reasons.

- *Goetz* v. *Ansell* (1973)   Requiring students to stand quietly or to leave the room during the pledge of allegiance is unconstitutional. According to the Court, standing quietly may be seen as an act of acceptance of the pledge in spite of deeply held convictions. Leaving the room is a benign form of punishment for nonparticipation.
- *School District of Abington Township* v. *Schempp* (1963)   Prayer and Bible reading in public school classrooms are unconstitutional. However, study of the Bible as part of a secular program of education focusing on its literary and historic value is allowed.
- *Wallace* v. *Jaffree* (1985)   Educators cannot require students to pause for a moment of silence for meditation or voluntary prayer.
- *Lee* v. *Weisman* (1992)   Prayers at a high school graduation ceremony are unconstitutional. (Since *Weisman,* however, school systems in some states have skirted the ban on prayer at graduation services by allowing students to initiate, plan, and lead invocations.)

Since 1971, Supreme Court justices have often applied the three-part **Lemon test,** developed from the *Lemon* v. *Kurtzman* case (1971), when deciding whether specific practices or policies constitute an establishment of religion. Under the Lemon test, each of the following questions must be answered affirmatively to satisfy the Constitution:

1. Does the challenged practice or policy have a secular purpose?
2. Does it neither advance nor inhibit religious practices?
3. Does practice or policy avoid an excessive entanglement between government and religion?

How much longer the Lemon test will survive as the yardstick for settling establishment clause disputes is uncertain. As Justice Antonin Scalia noted, there are several problems with the Lemon test: "For my part, I agree with the long list of constitutional scholars who have criticized *Lemon* and bemoaned the strange Establishment Clause geometry of crooked lines and wavering shapes its intermittent use has produced" (Bureau of National Affairs, 1993).   **Does the Lemon test really work?**

Playing Fairly

At the end of the school day, Mary Ellen, Joe, and David went to the principal's office. Anne Jeffrey, the assistant principal, handed each of them a sealed envelope addressed to their parents. "As I understand it," she said, "each of you is suspended for three days. This notice of suspension should be given to your parents."

"Are you kidding?" said Joe. "Nobody said anything to me about this. What are the charges against us?"

"Wait a minute," interrupted Mary Ellen. "Does this have anything to do with what happened during lunch today? If it does, this is a bunch of crap. We weren't the ones who started that fight."

"Yeah," said David. "It was that bunch of rednecks. They're always mouthing off and getting in your face. How come they aren't getting suspended? They cause trouble every day! You guys just never see them!"

"Look, I don't want to hear it," said Anne. "The principal asked me to give you these forms and that's it. Now go get on the bus before you get into any more trouble."

"You mean we don't even get to tell our side of the story?" asked Joe. "Man, this is really wrong!"

If you were these students' teacher, how would you respond to their complaints about the way their suspension was handled?   Can students ever be denied the right to due process of law?

ANALYSIS OF "PLAYING FAIRLY"

In *Goss* v. *Lopez* (1975), the Supreme Court addressed the grievances of Dwight Lopez and several of his peers. They had been suspended by the principal for ten days without being given a hearing, a practice forbidden by Ohio law. Because the principal did not follow mandated legal procedures, the Court ruled the students were denied **due process of law.** Specifically, the Court noted that the principal's actions were in violation of the Fourteenth Amendment. The Court subsequently ordered school officials to remove references to the students' suspensions from school records.

The Court held that students facing temporary suspension from school must be given oral or written notice of the charges, an explanation of evidence if they disagree with the charges, and an opportunity to present their side of the story. Whenever possible, the notice and hearing are to precede suspension from school (La Morte, 2002).

Your Teaching Life in Practice

ZERO TOLERANCE

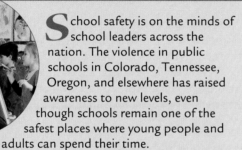

School safety is on the minds of school leaders across the nation. The violence in public schools in Colorado, Tennessee, Oregon, and elsewhere has raised awareness to new levels, even though schools remain one of the safest places where young people and adults can spend their time.

One response to the fear has been the implementation of *zero-tolerance* policies with regard to student violence—the "one-strike-and-you're-out" approach to school management means that students who threaten others or bring weapons to school are suspended or expelled. These policies raise questions about what is reasonable and legally defensible administrative behavior. They also divide people by philosophical orientation.

Zero tolerance has led to the following actions:

- A sixteen-year-old female student in Washington was met by police and expelled for using her finger to make a gun and jokingly saying, "Bang." She has since been reinstated.
- A thirteen-year-old male student in Texas was arrested and spent five days in jail awaiting a hearing for writing a spooky story about killing classmates. He is currently receiving homeschooling.
- An eighteen-year-old male student in Georgia wrote a story in his journal about a deranged student who goes on a rampage at school, which resulted in expulsion and arrest with no opportunity to graduate.
- A seven-year-old was suspended for bringing nail clippers to school in Illinois and a fifteen-year-old in Virginia was suspended for dyeing his hair blue (Essex, 2002, p. 60).

The only case to reach the courts was the one involving the account of the deranged student. The judge ruled that the student's journal did not constitute a threat. Nonetheless, the student had to change schools. Prosecutors are still considering pressing charges against him. Educators think about zero-tolerance policies in different ways.

CON Robert Frank, a special education teacher at a middle school in Boston, argues that there must be some compassion for "offbeat" behavior—some room to bend zero-tolerance policies to acknowledge the special plight of children with disabilities. To do otherwise, he contends, is to behave unfairly.

PRO Sarah Compton, an elementary school principal in Michigan, believes we should hold all children accountable, regardless of who they are, for strict and certain rules pertaining to violence. According to Compton, to do otherwise creates a sliding scale that cannot be administered fairly and which encourages disrespect for the community.

Critical Thinking Questions

With which educator do you agree? Why?

To answer these questions online and e-mail your answers to your professor, go to Chapter 9 of the Companion Website (ablongman.com/mcnergney4e) and click on Your Teaching Life in Practice.

In instances when student behavior is serious enough to warrant long-term suspension or expulsion, prudent educators provide students with a written notice stating the charges, time and place of a hearing, and procedures to be followed in the hearing. Students have the right to know what evidence will be presented and who will testify, as well as the substance of such testimony. They also have the right to cross-examine witnesses and to present witnesses to testify on their behalf. Written or taped records of proceedings and the decision of the group conducting the hearing are to be made available to students. Students are also to be informed of the right to appeal (Essex, 2002).

Show Me What's in There!

When Assistant Principal David Adams stepped outside, his attention was drawn to three students walking across the school courtyard. As he moved toward them, he noticed the boys were looking at a small black bag held by William, one of the students. The bag, a vinyl calculator case, had a suspicious bulge in its side.

When he questioned the boys about where they were going and why they were late to class, William, palming the leather case and hiding it behind his back, responded that his classes had ended and he was on his way home. Curious about what William was hiding, the assistant principal insisted, to no avail, that William show him the object in his hand. "It's nothing," said William. "Leave me alone. You have a search warrant or something?"

After sending the other two boys back to class, David took William to the office and asked an aide to witness his efforts to look at the calculator case. When William refused to let him see it, David pried it out of William's hand, unzipped it, and found marijuana and other drug paraphernalia. David called the police, and William was arrested. As he was being escorted out of the office, William turned to David and said, "You haven't seen the end of this. I know my rights. You can't be searching me or anybody else without a warrant!"

ANALYSIS OF "SHOW ME WHAT'S IN THERE!"

Does a school official have the right to search students?   The scenario of William follows closely the events that occurred in a California public school. After being convicted in juvenile court, William appealed the decision, saying the evidence against him came from an illegal search and should have been excluded from the hearing. In *In re William G.* (1985), the Supreme Court of California agreed, basing its decision on the reasonable suspicion standard set forth in *New Jersey* v. *T.L.O.* (1985).

In *New Jersey* v. *T.L.O.* (1985), the Supreme Court stated that school officials are acting not **in loco parentis** (in place of the parents) but as agents of the state when they search students under their authority. This should mean that school officials are subject to the Fourth Amendment. The Court ruled, though, that schools are special settings and thus there should be some "easing of the restrictions" normally placed on public authorities when conducting searches. Accordingly, school officials do not need to obtain a warrant or show "probable cause" when searching a stu-

State supreme courts have ruled that schools are special settings and, as such, normal restrictions placed on conducting searches do not apply. Schools can search students' backpacks if they are suspected of violating school rules or the law.

dent suspected of violating school rules or the law. Instead, when determining the legality of school searches, school officials can rely on "reason" and "common sense." Tests for determining reasonableness are whether (1) at the inception of the search there are reasonable grounds for suspecting that evidence will be found to prove a student is in violation of the law or school rules, and (2) the scope of the search is reasonably related to the objectives of the search, the age and sex of the student, and the nature of the infraction.

Such guidelines allow for much latitude among courts when interpreting Fourth Amendment rights (McCarthy, Cambron-McCabe, & Thomas, 1998). In the case of William, the court decided that the assistant principal had insufficient grounds for conducting a search. First, the assistant principal had no prior knowledge of William using or selling illegal drugs. Second, suspicion that William was late to class and William's attempt to hide the leather object provided no reasonable basis for a search. Third, William's demand for a warrant merely indicated that he wanted to preserve his constitutional rights; it was not an admission of guilt (National Organization on Legal Problems of Education, 1988).

The *New Jersey* v. *T.L.O.* case itself was a markedly different situation. In this case a student claimed that her Fourth Amendment rights were violated when a school official searched her purse. The student (T.L.O.) was one of two girls sent to the office for smoking in the girl's restroom (a violation of school rules). When questioned by the assistant vice principal, T.L.O. denied having smoked at all. However, when T.L.O. complied with the request to open her purse, the assistant vice principal found marijuana and drug paraphernalia, $40.98 in single dollar bills and change, plus a handwritten note to a friend, requesting that she sell marijuana at school. Subsequently, the school official notified T.L.O.'s mother and the police. After being advised of her rights, T.L.O. admitted to selling marijuana at the high school.

When the state brought delinquency charges against T.L.O., she claimed that the assistant vice principal had violated her Fourth Amendment rights, and thus evidence from her purse and her confession should be suppressed. The Supreme Court disagreed, saying that the search met the criteria for reasonableness. That is, a teacher had witnessed T.L.O. smoking and had a duty to investigate whether a school code had been broken (La Morte, 2002).

More recently, the Supreme Court's ruling in *Veronia School Dist. 47J* v. *Acton* (1995) gave school officials the right to screen student athletes for drug use. In explaining its decision, the Court said random urinalysis drug testing is not a violation of students' protection against unreasonable search and seizure, because schoolchildren have fewer rights than adults. The Court further held that students who participate voluntarily in sports have low expectations for privacy, because teammates undress together and shower in communal locker rooms. Furthermore, privacy rights compromised by urine samples are considered negligible, because conditions of collection are similar to public restrooms and the results are viewed only by limited authorities. Finally, the Court emphasized that governmental concern over the safety of minors under their supervision overrides the minimal, if any, intrusion in student athletes' privacy. In 1999, more than one hundred districts in at least twenty states required students to submit to urine tests if they wanted to play sports (Portner, 1999).

In 2002, the Supreme Court expanded its view of authorized drug testing. The Court ruled five to four that drug testing all students in extracurricular activities, not only those in athletics, does not violate the Fourth Amendment's prohibition against unreasonable searches.

Are There Limits on Student Expression?

Students at Kirkwood High School in suburban St. Louis, Missouri, had enjoyed much freedom in the production of the school newspaper. When the students agreed to run an ad for Planned Parenthood, Birthright (an organization concerned with reproductive issues) requested that students run an antiabortion ad to counteract Planned Parenthood's message. Several parents and local citizens considered such advertisements inappropriate and insisted that principal Franklin McCallie ban the ads from the student newspaper (Conkling, 1991). **Can school administrators censor student publications?**

ANALYSIS OF "ARE THERE LIMITS ON STUDENT EXPRESSION?"

Students had reason to cheer in 1969 when the Supreme Court ruled on *Tinker* v. *Des Moines Independent Community School District,* a case in which three public school students were suspended for wearing armbands to protest the Vietnam War. Deciding in favor of the students, the Court declared that public school authorities do not have the right to silence students' political or ideological viewpoints simply because they disagree with students' ideas. Under *Tinker,* students' verbal or symbolic expression may be restricted only in instances when student behavior could result in disorder or interfere with the rights of others.

In 1988, the Supreme Court restricted students' First Amendment rights (*Hazelwood School District* v. *Kuhlmeier*) when it ruled that principals could censor school-sponsored publications. The basis for the Court's decision was a case involving students in a high school journalism class. Those students had claimed their First Amendment rights were violated when the principal reviewed their material and removed two stories—one on divorce, the other on three students' experiences with pregnancy—from the school-sponsored newspaper. According to the Supreme Court, a student newspaper does not represent a forum for public expression when it is part of the school curriculum. Thus, school officials can censor material considered inconsistent with the educational mission of the school. This includes material that is ungrammatical, poorly researched, biased or prejudiced, vulgar, or inappropriate for an immature audience.

On the other hand, if schools have clearly established, either through practice or policy, students' rights to control editorial content, the publication is considered an open forum and restrictions under Hazelwood do not apply. At Kirkwood High School, principal Franklin McCallie firmly believed the newspaper should be an open forum for student expression. Thus he allowed student journalists to decide what to do about the controversial ads.

Treating Different Students Differently—Illegal Discrimination?

As Sam Miller's fifth-grade class lined up to leave the gymnasium, Tyrone grabbed Tony's hat and ran to the end of the line. Tony, a mainstreamed student with emotional disturbance, raced after Tyrone, knocked him to the gym floor, and punched Tyrone hard enough to bloody his nose. When Sam pulled Tony away from Tyrone, Tony swung his fist and hit another child in the stomach. Sam wrapped his arms around Tony's waist and carried him to the back of the gym before he could do any more damage. He sent one of his students to get the principal. This wasn't the first time Tony had exploded, but it was the most serious and dangerous incident.

Sam was nearing his wit's end. He had talked with the resource teacher about ways to diffuse Tony's anger, but it was sometimes impossible to intervene before Tony's quick temper caused incidents like the one in the gym. In Sam's mind, Tony threatened other students and needed to be disciplined for his misbehavior. Sam decided to ask the principal either to expel Tony or to give him a long-term suspension so Tony's

Individual Educational Plan (IEP) team could have sufficient time to rethink Tony's placement. **Can students with disabilities be expelled for dangerous conduct?**

ANALYSIS OF "TREATING DIFFERENT STUDENTS DIFFERENTLY— ILLEGAL DISCRIMINATION?"

Disciplining students with disabilities has been a controversial and confusing issue for educators and parents. Under the 1975 Education for All Handicapped Children Act (EAHCA), now called the Individuals with Disabilities Education Act (IDEA), students with disabilities are guaranteed a free and appropriate education. In 1988 the Supreme Court ruled in *Honig* v. *Doe* that expulsion of students with disabilities for behavior attributable to their disabilities would be a violation of EAHCA provisions (Data Research, Inc., 2002). The Court did agree, however, that students with disabilities who exhibit behavior dangerous to themselves or others could be temporarily suspended for up to ten days. But this suspension would be acceptable only if such punishment were the same as would be used for a nondisabled student. The 1997 IDEA amendments altered this ruling by allowing school officials to establish a forty-five-day interim educational placement. This interim placement would remove students carrying weapons, using drugs, or demonstrating behavior that might result in injury to themselves or others from the classroom while a solution was found.

IDEA regulations established in 1999 offer schools even more leeway in disciplining disruptive students with disabilities. School officials are allowed to suspend a student for up to ten days at a time for each separate act of misconduct, as long as the removals do not constitute a pattern. Special education services do not need to be provided during the first ten days of suspension. However, if a child is subsequently removed for up to ten school days for other violations of school conduct codes, services must be provided. Administrators and the special education teacher determine which services are needed. Furthermore, decisions as to whether a student's behavior is related to his or her disability are now required only for a suspension that results in a change of placement (U.S. Department of Education, 1999).

Would You Check These Papers for Me?

The terse phone call from Amy Aller's mother, a local lawyer, should have alerted Charles Armstrong to the possibility of an unpleasant parent conference. Amy was a good student, though, and, as far as Charles knew, she had been quite happy in school. Amy had left school that afternoon a little upset by the low score on her math quiz, but her grades in general were so good that he couldn't imagine one assignment prompting a parent conference. It had to be something else.

As Charles sat facing Mrs. Aller that afternoon, she explained the reason for her conference. Amy was in fact upset—not so much because of her low math score but because of the "unkind" comments about her paper made by classmates. "How did anyone else know Amy's grade on this quiz?" asked Mrs. Aller.

Charles shifted uncomfortably in his chair. "I have student helpers who grade papers for me when they finish their work," said Charles. "I guess one of them must have told the others about Amy's paper today. I'm sorry. This has never been a problem before. I'll be sure to say something to my students tomorrow so this type of thing doesn't happen again."

As she stood to leave, Mrs. Aller said, "I like you, Mr. Armstrong, but I want to tell you I don't think you should use this system

Students with disabilities cannot be expelled for behavior attributable to their disabilities, but they can be removed from class for interim placement if they endanger other students.

anymore. I believe it violates the Buckley Amendment. No student should have knowledge of another student's progress in school."

Later that night Charles pulled out his college textbook, read about the Buckley Amendment, and reflected on his conference with Mrs. Aller. If Mrs. Aller was right, did he also violate students' rights of privacy when he displayed some students' papers as examples of good work? What about when he asked students to raise their hands to indicate whether they got something right or wrong on written assignments? Was he in violation of the law when he had students work problems at the board in front of their peers? Charles made a mental note to call the legal advisor to the teachers' organization the next day to get some answers to these questions.   **Is posting grades an invasion of students' privacy?**

ANALYSIS OF "WOULD YOU CHECK THESE PAPERS FOR ME?"

Before 2002, Charles might very well have been in violation of the Buckley Amendment when he allowed students to grade each other's papers. Part of the Family Educational Rights and Privacy Act (commonly referred to as the **Buckley Amendment**) prohibits schools from releasing information about a student to third parties without parental or student permission. In 2002's *Owasso Independent School District* v. *Falvo (No. 00-1073)* case, however, the Supreme Court ruled unanimously that the classroom practice of allowing students to grade each others' papers does not violate the law.

Cultural Awareness

SCHOOL MASCOTS

Schools in cities across the country are pausing to consider the effects that mascots depicting Native Americans (such as Indians and Redskins) have on minorities in their communities. In 2002, the Seattle School Board proposed a policy banning schools from using Native Americans as mascots or symbols. West Seattle High School had been a focus of debate because of its "Indians" mascot.

The school board viewed the mascot's use as "antithetical to the Seattle School District's commitment to non-discrimination and its mission to provide an equal education to all students." Not everyone agreed. West Seattle High's Native American club collected 650 signatures of students, staff, and community members asking that the mascot be changed. They saw its use as a form of racism. But some 500 alumni voted to retain the symbol, while only seven wanted it changed. Alumni viewed the symbol as a demonstration of respect for Native Americans.

A former student body president commented that if the students were given the choice they would opt to keep the name and the mascot. "What happens if next year a group of Norwegians tells you they're offended by the Rainier Beach Vikings?" he asked.

On the other hand, Jacqueline Shopbell, a student at West Seattle High and a member of the Native American club, noted that "headdresses and traditional regalia have sacred meanings to Native Americans." She thought they should not be used as sports symbols. "It's almost as if a Catholic priest were to give Communion at a halftime show," she said.

When the Seattle School Board met to discuss the issue of mascots, they voted six to zero to prohibit the use of any American Indian or Alaskan Native as a mascot, nickname, or symbol for a school. The decision spurred the Issaquah, Washington, School Board to also require high school teams to drop their Indian identities (Jamieson, 2002).

Critical Thinking Question

Do you believe this issue should have been decided through a poll of students and alumni or by administrative action? Why?

To answer these questions online and e-mail your answer to your professor, go to Chapter 9 of the Companion Website (ablongman.com/ mcnergney4e) and click on Cultural Awareness.

Source: Denn, R. (20 June 2002). Seattle schools consider Native American mascot ban. *Seattle Post Intelligencer.* Available online: http:// seattlepi.nwsource.com/local/75354_mascot20.shtml.

What Are Teachers' Rights and Responsibilities?

Teachers enjoy a number of rights also extended to students. For example, they may be excused from saluting or pledging allegiance to the flag if such actions violate their beliefs and commitments. However, as with students, there are times when teachers' constitutional rights must be considered in light of important educational goals. Because of the nature of their jobs, teachers usually are held to higher standards of behavior than are ordinary citizens (Imber & van Geel, 1993). The scenarios that follow examine some of the issues decided by the courts in this delicate balance between teachers' rights as citizens and their rights as state employees. The scenarios also suggest some of the responsibilities inherent in teachers' jobs, particularly with regard to student safety.

To Join or Not to Join

Do teachers have to pay dues to teachers' unions if they are not members?
Megan beamed when she received a contract from the Detroit public schools in July. Although her college advisor had warned her that it might be midsummer or later before people heard about their job applications, Megan had been on pins and needles since graduation. For as long as she could remember, Megan had wanted to be a teacher. Now she also had school loans to repay, so she needed to be employed as soon as possible.

A few days after signing her contract, Megan received a letter from the Detroit Federation of Teachers (DFT) describing the benefits of belonging to the professional association and the cost of joining. Megan tossed the letter in the trash, deciding that she would wait until she had some financial stability before spending money she didn't have. During the first week of school, a representative of the DFT announced at a faculty meeting that those who had not paid dues to the DFT needed to do so or risk being dismissed from their jobs. Megan was confused. Perhaps she had misunderstood the announcement. Surely nonmembers of the DFT would not be required to pay dues.

ANALYSIS OF "TO JOIN OR NOT TO JOIN"

Federal law recognizes teachers' constitutional rights to advocate, organize, and join a teachers' union. In many states, teachers also have the right to engage in collective bargaining, a procedure for resolving disagreements between employers and employees. Teachers negotiate with their school boards, usually through their union representative, about such issues as contract hours, salaries, and fringe benefits. There are no constitutional guarantees that school boards must bargain with teachers' unions, however, so restrictions on the scope of bargaining vary greatly from state to state.

By the 1995–1996 school year about 85 percent of public school teachers belonged to either the National Education Association (NEA) or the American Federation of Teachers (AFT) (Whiting, 1997). At the same time, more than half of all states had laws requiring nonmembers to pay dues to the union as a condition of employment. Several Supreme Court rulings uphold the constitutionality of such laws. In a case (*Abood* v. *Detroit Board of Education*) heard in 1977, Christine Warczak and a number of other teachers challenged a Michigan law requiring teachers who had not become union members within sixty days to pay an amount equal to union dues or face discharge. The teachers argued that, because they did not believe in collective bargaining or agree with union activities unrelated to collective bargaining, such a law violated their right to freedom of association as guaranteed in the First and Fourteenth Amendments. The Supreme Court disagreed, noting that certain union activities benefit every employee, union member or not. Specifically, all should share the cost of the union's collective bargaining activities. The Court also decided, however, that it was a violation of First

Amendment rights to require public employees to support financially a union's political activities.

In 1984 the Supreme Court clarified this last portion of the *Abood* decision in its *Ellis* v. *Brotherhood of Railway, Airline, and S.S. Clerks* ruling. It said that a union's nonpolitical publications, conventions, and social activities are sufficiently related to the union's work in collective bargaining to justify the charging of nonunion members for such services. Litigation expenses not involving the negotiation of agreements or settlement of grievance or costs for general organizing efforts, however, cannot be charged to dissenting employees. In its 1986 ruling in *Chicago Teachers Union, Local No. 1 AFL–CIO* v. *Hudson,* the Supreme Court also stated that unions must explain the basis for the dues amount, allow dissenters a prompt opportunity to contest the fee before an impartial decision maker, and hold in escrow disputed amounts until the parties reach an agreement (Fischer, Schimmel, & Kelly, 1999).

There's Got to Be a Way to Keep This Job!

Sandra Allen, a second-year teacher, loved her teaching job. With the exception of two or three students who had difficulty controlling their actions, her class was well behaved and motivated to learn. Most students consistently completed assignments on time, and their work was accurate and neat. Sandra knew that parents had been ambivalent about their children having the "new" teacher at school, but their comments during parent conferences indicated that they, too, were pleased with their children's academic progress.

When Sandra received notice in May that she would not be rehired for the upcoming academic year, she was shocked and angry. Because her principal's midyear evaluation rated Sandra as "above average" or "outstanding" in all categories, Sandra had assumed her contract would be renewed. She needed only one more year of teaching in the system to earn tenure. Surely the school board could not force her out of the system without giving her reasons for doing so, or could it?

ANALYSIS OF "THERE'S GOT TO BE A WAY TO KEEP THIS JOB!"

Sandra's story is much like that of David Roth, an assistant professor of political science at Wisconsin State University–Oshkosh, who was hired for a fixed term of one academic year. When Roth was notified at the end of the academic term that he would not be rehired for the following year, he went to court, claiming that the decision infringed on his Fourteenth Amendment rights. In ruling on *Board of Regents of State Colleges* v. *Roth* (1972), the Supreme Court disagreed with Roth's charge, explaining that a probationary teacher does not have the same rights as a tenured teacher.

According to the Court, tenured teachers may not be removed from their positions without specific or good cause, nor may they be dismissed for arbitrary reasons (e.g., political beliefs and activities). Thus, tenured teachers have a "property interest" that merits due process protection. In most states, however, the contract of a teacher with probationary status can be terminated at the end of the year without cause (state statutes generally specify a date by which teachers must be notified of such action). This means that a probationary teacher maintains property interest only for the duration of a one-year term. In other words, the teacher is protected by due process during that term, but not afterward. However, if the probationary teacher can present evidence to suggest that nonrenewal is in retaliation for exercise of constitutional rights (e.g., freedom of speech), the employer must follow due process (Essex, 2002).

If the school board resorts to **dismissal** (removing a probationary or tenured teacher before the completion of his or her contract), the board must provide a notice, hearing, or notification of reasons for dismissal. State statutes typically list broad causes for dismissal, such as incompetency, immorality, unprofessional conduct, and neglect of duty. Lack of funding and a decline in student enrollment may also be just cause for the midyear dismissal of both tenured and nontenured teachers (La Morte, 2002). Many state laws also stipulate that nontenured teachers must be dismissed before tenured teachers, and, among tenured teachers, the least experienced must be dismissed first.

A Line between Personhood and Professionalism

Can a teacher be dismissed for private conduct? Jason O'Hara enjoyed his most-popular-teacher status at Baker Middle School. Students, parents, and colleagues respected him for his innovative ideas, sharp wit, and ability to interest students in learning. Now in his fourth year of teaching, Jason had tenure in the school system and was chair of the English department.

When Jason received a note from John Wright, the principal, requesting that he come to the office that afternoon, Jason thought nothing of it. Mr. Wright had been very supportive of Jason and his efforts to upgrade the English curriculum. As he stepped through the office door, however, Jason knew that something was wrong. Mr. Wright, a grim look on his face, handed Jason a two-page letter addressed to the superintendent. The letter, written by a teacher with whom Jason had had a brief homosexual relationship the year before, made explicit the nature of their relationship. Jason read it in stunned silence.

"Jason," said Mr. Wright, "this letter was also mailed to members of the school board. Several of them are really uptight about this. They want to dismiss you for immoral behavior. I think this is going to be an ugly battle. I'll do everything I can to help you, but I think you also need legal assistance. Do you have a good lawyer?"

ANALYSIS OF "A LINE BETWEEN PERSONHOOD AND PROFESSIONALISM"

As noted in Chapter 2, teachers in earlier times were held to rigid codes of conduct. Those who crossed the line between moral and immoral behavior resigned or were dismissed immediately from their teaching duties. In recent times, however, the line has blurred because it is often difficult to get community consensus about what constitutes immoral conduct. Actions and beliefs that were believed immoral during colonial times are not given a second thought today. Moreover, many educators believe that when the school day ends, what occurs in the privacy of their homes is their own business and should not affect negatively their status as professionals. Those who disagree argue that being a private person does not relieve educators of their duty to serve as role models for children.

Ambiguity about what constitutes moral and immoral behavior is reflected by court decisions in different states. In making employment decisions based on a teacher's sexual orientation, courts usually consider "the adverse effect on students or fellow teachers, adversity anticipated within the school system, surrounding circumstances, and possible chilling effects on discipline" (Alexander & Alexander, 2001, p. 611). Therefore, much of the decision is left to the local school board, because it is in closer touch with the beliefs of both the community and the school.

Depending on public reaction to Jason's case, then, he may or may not be dismissed from his teaching position. In 1969 the California Supreme Court heard a case (*Morrison* v. *State Board of Education*) involving a teacher, Marc Morrison, whose circumstances were much like those of Jason. When the superintendent received a letter from a male teacher who had been involved sexually with Morrison the year before, the school board voted to dismiss Morrison on grounds of immoral and unprofessional behavior. The court disagreed with the school board's actions, saying that the board's definition of immoral behavior was dangerously vague and could implicate many educators. Ruling in favor of Morrison, the court also stated that disapproval of an educator's private conduct was insufficient reason for dismissal, particularly when there was no proof that the educator's professional work was affected negatively by the conduct.

However, eight years later in *Gaylord* v. *Tacoma School District No. 10* (1977), a case heard by the state supreme court of Washington, the court upheld the dismissal of a teacher who admitted his homosexuality to the vice principal of the school. Based on the fact that at least one student and several teachers and parents had challenged the individual's fitness to teach, the court held that the teacher's continued employment would likely disrupt the educational process.

Such cases end differently in different localities because the U.S. Supreme Court has not yet recognized a constitutional privacy right to engage in homosexual behavior. Based on the 1984 ruling in *National Gay Task Force v. Board of Education of Oklahoma City*, however, teachers have the right to advocate publicly for legalization of homosexuality, as long as such activity is not disruptive to the educational process.

As indicated in the 1984 ruling in *Rowland* v. *Mad River Local School District*, advocacy does not include talking with co-workers about personal sexual preferences or those of students. In this case, an Ohio guidance counselor who had been dismissed by the school board for admitting her bisexuality to several members of the staff argued that her First and Fourteenth Amendment rights had been violated. The Court disagreed, saying that the First Amendment did not protect the guidance counselor's statements because they were not made as a citizen on matters of public concern. Rather, the counselor's statements were a matter of private concern. Furthermore, the court held that, without evidence that heterosexual employees had been or would be treated differently for discussing sexual preferences, nonrenewal of the counselor's contract did not violate the Fourteenth Amendment (Essex, 2002).

What Do You Mean I'm Violating Copyright Laws?

During summer vacation, Robert Wells, the newly appointed chair of the mathematics department at Central High, videotaped a two-part series titled "Mathematics in Today's Workplace" and added it to his growing collection of tapes. Robert's students had responded well to his occasional use of a videotape to illustrate concepts being taught in class. He believed that these newest tapes would be especially effective in the spring, when math analysis students planned projects showing real-life applications of mathematics.

As he thought about the upcoming inservice program he would conduct for department members, Robert also realized that his videotapes might be an excellent tool for helping others think about ways to vary their own instruction. Excited by the prospect, Robert contacted Dorothy James at the media center to see if she would make copies of his videotapes and place them on reserve in the school library. When Dorothy asked Robert if he had permission to videotape the copyrighted television programs, he was caught off guard. "What do you mean?" Robert said. "I'm using these tapes for teaching purposes. Lots of people do that. What's the big deal?"

"I used to think it was okay myself," said Dorothy, "but now I'm not so sure. I'll call central office and see what I can find out. Until we know, we'd better not copy any of those videotapes."   **Can teachers videotape television programs and use them for educational purposes?**

ANALYSIS OF "WHAT DO YOU MEAN I'M VIOLATING COPYRIGHT LAWS?"

What constitutes fair use?   The Supreme Court has not decided whether it is illegal for teachers to tape television broadcasts on home video recorders for later classroom use. Congressional guidelines from 1981 for off-the-air taping, however, suggest that such activities may in fact constitute copyright infringement. Guidelines specify that copyrighted television programs may be videotaped by nonprofit educational organizations. But the videotapes must be destroyed or erased after forty-five calendar days if the institution has not obtained a license for such videotaping. Teachers may use the videotapes with students at school or with students receiving homebound instruction one time during the first ten school days after recording occurs. One additional showing is allowed during the ten-day period, but only for instructional reinforcement. Additional use is limited to evaluation of the videotape's usefulness as an instructional tool (McCarthy, Cambron-McCabe, & Thomas, 1998).

In *Encyclopedia Britannica Educational Corporation* v. *Crooks* (1982), a New York federal district court found a school system guilty of violating fair use standards by engaging in extensive off-the-air taping and replaying of public television programs. The court found that such taping interfered with the marketability of producers' films. In 1984, in *Sony Corporation of America* v. *Universal City Studios,* the Supreme Court ruled that personal video recording for the purpose of "time shifting" (recording of a program for later one-time viewing), however, did not harm the television market (McCarthy, Cambron-McCabe, & Thomas, 1998).

Until the Supreme Court decides whether home taping for broader viewing by students in classrooms constitutes fair use of copyrighted materials, teachers are advised to follow congressional guidelines. Another option, of course, is to seek written permission from copyright owners to videotape their programs for classroom use.

A new question of fair use arose in the 1990s with the explosion of the World Wide Web. The Internet offers an exciting array of motion media, music, text material, graphics, illustrations, and photographs for educational purposes. When incorporating others' electronic materials in multimedia projects, however, teachers and students are obligated to act responsibly. The same level of care is expected when using print materials from textbooks, magazines, and other sources.

Laws regulate fair use of copyrighted materials such as media, music, and text material, and teachers must follow these laws.

Maybe She Is Just a Sickly Child

Theresa chose a desk near the back of the room, not near anyone in particular. She was quiet and somewhat plain in her dress, but her long brown hair was striking. Joan Mason didn't know much about eight-year-old Theresa, because Theresa had just moved to town in August. Her permanent records indicated that she was above average in ability. Although Theresa had missed a lot of school last year, her grades were about average, maybe a little low in math.

Another parent told Joan that Theresa's mother had been divorced last year and had moved here, at least in part, to get away from her former husband. The family—Theresa's mother and her younger sister; a man she called Jim, whom she described as the mother's friend; and Jim's seventeen-year-old son—lived in a small ranch house in a nice neighborhood on the outskirts of town.

As Joan worked with Theresa the first few weeks of school, Theresa seldom missed a day of school and kept up with daily assignments. By mid-October, however, things had changed. Theresa's attendance became sporadic, and Joan noticed that Theresa often was passive and uncommunicative, both with Joan and with classmates. During seatwork, Theresa chewed her fingernails, her constant gnawing sometimes drawing blood. When Joan talked with Theresa's mother during a parent–teacher conference, she did not seem overly concerned by Joan's observations. Her mom indicated that Theresa's behavior at home had not changed. She attributed Theresa's recent absences and withdrawn manner to her tendency to be a "sickly child." After the conference,

Joan still worried about Theresa, but she didn't know what to do.   **What about this situation concerns you? What, if anything, would you do if you were Theresa's teacher?**

ANALYSIS OF "MAYBE SHE IS JUST A SICKLY CHILD"

Educators, unlike physicians, social workers, and law enforcement officers, have a unique opportunity to monitor students' social behaviors, academic progress, and attitudes over time. Some patterns of behavior, especially sudden, dramatic changes, can be a warning sign of something gone awry in a child's life. Teachers need to be particularly alert to patterns of behavior that could indicate a child is the victim of abuse or neglect.

As defined by the Child Abuse Prevention and Treatment Act, child abuse and neglect include physical or mental injury, sexual abuse or exploitation, negligent treatment, or maltreatment (1) of a child younger than eighteen years of age (unless state law specifies a younger age), (2) by any person responsible for a child's welfare, (3) under circumstances that harm or threaten a child's health or welfare. Sexual abuse is defined as

> [(1)] the employment, use, persuasion, inducement, enticement or coercion of any child to engage in, or assist any other person to engage in, any sexually explicit conduct (or any simulation of such conduct) for the purpose of producing any visual depiction of such conduct, or (2) rape, molestation, prostitution, or other form of sexual exploitation of children, or incest with children. (U.S. Department of Health and Human Services, 1999)

Abuse can occur at any socioeconomic level to both males and females. In every state, educators must report cases of abuse or neglect resulting in physical injury to a child. In the majority of states, educators also must report instances of emotional, mental, or sexual abuse. Failure to report suspected abuse and neglect constitutes a misdemeanor in most states and, with a few exceptions, teachers are identified among the professionals required to make such reports. Certain behaviors or signs occurring repeatedly or in combination may cue an educator that child abuse is present in a family (see Table 9.1).

Once a teacher suspects that a student is being abused or neglected, the teacher should consult state statutes that specify procedures for reporting it. Many localities also have school board policies and procedures to encourage effective reporting of suspected child abuse. Under the Child Abuse and Neglect Act, educators are assured immunity from civil liability if reports of abuse and neglect that are made in good faith later turn out to be inaccurate.

You Should Have Known Better

Two teachers organized a trip to a museum of natural history for a group of about fifty students ranging in age from twelve to fifteen years. When they arrived at the museum, students divided into small groups to tour the museum without supervision. One student, Roberto Mancha, of his own volition joined a group and proceeded with them to the various exhibits. While out of his teacher's sight, Roberto alleged that he was accosted by a group of youths not connected with the school, was beaten by them, and as a result suffered serious injuries. In *Mancha* v. *Field Museum of Natural History* (1972), Roberto's father initiated action against the school district, the two teachers, and the museum for the injuries his son suffered while at the museum.   **When can a teacher be sued for negligence?**

ANALYSIS OF "YOU SHOULD HAVE KNOWN BETTER"

Lawsuits brought by students injured during school-related activities are the most common type of litigation in education. A teacher who demonstrates **negligence** (failure to

*T*ABLE 9.1   **Signs of Child Abuse and Neglect**

Teachers can all help end child abuse by becoming aware of the signs and reporting suspected cases of child abuse and neglect. Some signs of child maltreatment include:

Physical Abuse
Bruises, welts, or swelling
Sprains or fractures
Burns
Lacerations or abrasions

Sexual Abuse
Difficulty in walking or sitting
Torn, stained, or bloody clothing
Pain or itching in the genital area; bruises or bleeding in the external genital area
Sexually transmitted diseases
Pregnancy

Physical Neglect
Lack of adequate supervision, nutrition, or shelter
Poor hygiene
Inappropriate dress

Educational Neglect
Infrequent attendance in school

Medical Neglect
Unattended medical or dental needs

Emotional Neglect or Abuse
Speech disorders
Delayed physical development
Substance abuse

Behavioral signs of abuse or neglect
Uncomfortable with physical contact
Low self-esteem
Behavior extremes, such as appearing overly compliant and passive or very demanding and aggressive
Frequently at home with no caretaker
Lags in physical, emotional, or intellectual development

Source: New York City Administration for Children's Services. Available online: http://www.nyc.gov/html/acs/html/getinvolved/abuseprevent_signs.html.

exercise reasonable care to protect students from injury) may be held liable for damages if an injured student can prove the following:

1. the teacher had a legal duty to offer a standard of care that would have prevented the injury from occurring,
2. the teacher did not live up to the standard of care,
3. the teacher's carelessness resulted in harm to the student; and
4. the student sustained an actual injury that could be measured in monetary terms (Imber & van Geel, 1993).

*W*hat are teachers' responsibilities toward children's health and safety? If one of these children were injured by another child during recess, can the teacher supervising the playground be sued for negligence?

When accused of negligence, a teacher can try to prove that a student's injury was a mere accident, that her action or inaction was not the cause of such injury, or that some other act intervened and was the cause of the injury. Other responses to claims of negligence include contributory negligence, comparative negligence, and assumption of risk (Alexander & Alexander, 2001).

Contributory negligence occurs when the student who was injured failed to exercise the required standard of care for his or her own safety. When this condition exists, depending on such things as a child's age and mental maturity, the teacher may be absolved from liability. A high school student, for example, who has been taught how to use a power saw and observed to determine that she can operate the machine safely may be guilty of contributory negligence if injured while removing a piece of wood from the machine with her hands—a violation of safety practices the students have been taught.

In situations in which teacher and student are both held liable for an injury, there may be a charge of **comparative negligence.** Generally, this means that a teacher is held accountable for a proportion of damages in line with the degree to which he contributed to the injury. **Assumption of risk,** rarely applicable except in cases of competitive athletics, means that people who are aware of possible risks involved in an activity voluntarily participate, thus agreeing to take their chances.

In *Mancha* v. *Field Museum of Natural History* (1972), an Illinois court dismissed charges of negligence brought against the school, museum, and teachers. The lower courts did state that the teachers' action of letting students tour the museum in an unsupervised group was as an intentional act. But given the nature of the environment (a museum), it was not an act that teachers should have anticipated would result in harm to a student. In explaining their verdict, the court argued that a museum is very different from a factory, a stone quarry, or a place where there might be dangerous machinery, or a place where there might be a shooting or an assault:

> The Museum in question is itself a great educational enterprise which enables teachers, parents, and children to learn much that could be learned at school. . . . To say that the teachers had a duty to supervise and discipline the entire Museum trip would be to ignore the realities of the situation and to make such trips impossible. (*Mancha* v. *Field Museum of Natural History,* 1972, p. 902)

However, there have been several cases in which students were injured and educators were found to have breached duty of care:

- A group of students with mental retardation was left unattended for a half-hour, and a student received an eye injury when another pupil threw a wooden pointer (*Gonzalez* v. *Mackler,* 1963).
- A student who was permitted to wear mittens fell while climbing on a jungle gym (*Ward* v. *Newfield Central School District No. 1,* 1978).
- A student was burned when she and her peers were working on a project for the science fair. The accident occurred when the students tried to light a defective burner that had gone out and alcohol exploded. Although the teacher had set up the experiment and checked to see that it worked properly, the teacher was not in the room when the students lit the burner. Because the students were not advised to wait until the teacher's return to light the fire and were not personally supervised, the teacher was held liable for negligence (*Station* v. *Travelers Insurance Co.,* 1974).

Voices

TEACHING ABOUT RIGHTS AND RESPONSIBILITIES SINCE SEPTEMBER 11

*B*arbara Landau, associate professor of education at the University of Redlands in Redlands, California, has taught professional development workshops on student rights and social responsibilities for more than fifteen years. In doing so she has given quizzes to assess educators' knowledge of the law, both before and after her sessions. In a two-year period she quizzed some four hundred educators in three states. What she has learned may lead us to question our own knowledge and assumptions. Here are some responses she recounts.

> One teacher asked, with great anxiety in her voice, "Do I have to teach students their rights? Can't I just teach them their responsibilities?"
>
> One school administrator I encountered had told her faculty that students could not wear hats because the Supreme Court of the United States had ruled that hats must be banned in schools. The teachers had bought the argument simply because they did not know any better. One principal, in an effort to head off a write-in campaign being mounted for class elections, told students they would not be allowed to write names in because people could not do that in national elections. I have heard of a teacher who barred second-language learners from attending his industrial arts class because he felt that if they could not speak English, they could not handle the tools safely. I could go on.

When Landau reflects on these experiences in the context of September 11, she worries about the implications for students.

> We are now in a time when rights are being limited in order to preserve our common safety, and certainly some things will have to change in order to travel safely and protect our country's well-being. But we ought to know what is being traded away to be safe. We ought to be able to engage in social discourse and hold analytical discussions about what it is that must be preserved for the United States to maintain the democratic ideals which define the essence of who we are as a nation.
>
> A democracy is all about discourse, debate, and the open exchange of ideas. If we truly cherish the freedoms that are threatened by terrorists, there can

> be no greater patriotic act than to teach students—and to teach them well—the essence of what makes this country unique and worthy of our loyalty.

According to Landau, teachers have the perfect opportunity to teach students about constitutional rights, not just through rote memorization and tests, but through discussion of how material is relevant to their everyday lives. While it is easier to simply dictate rules, Landau contends that we will produce better citizens if students learn about rights and responsibilities and how to make appropriate decisions that balance the two.

Critical Thinking Questions

Do you have any evidence to suggest that the tragedy of September 11, 2001, is affecting the behavior of teachers and students in the United States? Are we more fearful of others who are different from us? Are we less willing to think about and discuss rights than we used to be?

To answer these questions online and e-mail your answers to your professor, go to Chapter 9 of the Companion Website (ablongman.com/mcn-ergney4e) and click on Voices.

Source: Landau, B. (2002). Educating for citizenship. *Education Week, 21*(25), 40, 44. Available online: http://www.edweek.com/ew/newstory.cfm?slug=25landau.h21&keywords=freedom%20of%20speech.

What Are School Districts' Rights and Responsibilities?

Although the courts have consistently asserted that the authority for public education resides in the state legislature, schools for the most part are administered locally. As mentioned in Chapter 8, local school boards deal with a variety of educational issues and problems. A number of court cases, in conjunction with federal and state statutes, have clarified the special responsibilities and rights of local school districts.   **Do school boards have the power to ban textbooks?**

Balancing Academic Freedom

The school board meeting raged on for several hours. Three English teachers from the high school and a number of parents voiced their opinions about the list of texts used in elective high school literature courses. When the board voted to eliminate ten texts from the diverse list of 1,285 books, the teachers were enraged. They believed all the books were necessary components of a curriculum designed to encourage debate and broaden student knowledge. Viewing the board's action as an invasion of their First Amendment right to academic freedom, the three English teachers decided to seek legal counsel. They could not believe that a local school board had ultimate authority to determine what textbooks would be used in schools.

ANALYSIS OF "BALANCING ACADEMIC FREEDOM"

Since the U.S. Supreme Court ruling in *Hazelwood School District* v. *Kuhlmeier* (1988), the Court has indicated a willingness to give local school boards the final decision regarding the curriculum and the availability of books, films, and materials in elementary and secondary classrooms. However, if school boards' actions narrow rather than expand knowledge, judicial intervention is not uncommon (Alexander & Alexander, 2001). When deciding individual cases, the courts usually consider the educational relevance of controversial material, teaching objectives, and the age and maturity of the intended audience.

In *Virgil* v. *School Board of Columbia County, Florida* (1989), the Supreme Court upheld a local school board's right to remove two readings from the curriculum because of objections to the material's vulgarity and sexual explicitness. Although the Court did not endorse the decision, stating that they seriously questioned how reading the masterpieces of Western literature could harm young people, the Court acknowledged that the school board's decision was reasonably related to "legitimate pedagogical concerns." That is, as in *Hazelwood*, school officials considered the emotional maturity of the intended audience when determining the appropriateness of readings dealing with potentially sensitive topics (Alexander & Alexander, 2001).

How much freedom does a teacher have in the selection of material for her students? In 1989 a Fifth Circuit Court of Appeals ruling held that teachers cannot assert a First Amendment right to replace an official supplementary reading list with their own list of books without first getting administrative approval. Nor may teachers delete parts of the curriculum that conflict with their personal beliefs. A kindergarten teacher, for example, who refuses to teach a unit on patriotic topics may be dismissed by the school board for not covering prescribed material (La Morte, 2002).

Teachers do have freedom in selecting teaching strategies, however. Teachers who want to assign controversial materials usually may do so, as long as the selected materials are relevant to the topic of study, appropriate to the age and maturity of the students, and unlikely to cause disruption. When a high school psychology teacher in a conservative Texas community was fired for having her students read a masculinity survey from *Psychology Today*, the court ruled that the school violated the teacher's constitutional rights. In the eyes of the court, there was no evidence that the material caused substantial disruption, and there was no clear, prior prohibition against the use of such materials (Fischer, Schimmel, & Kelly, 1999).

Equal Treatment

Fifteen African-American preschool and elementary students living in a low-income housing project in Ann Arbor, Michigan, brought suit against the board of education for practices they claimed denied them equal educational opportunities. According to the students, their language (African American English) differed from the standard English spoken by teachers and used in written materials of the school. The students claimed a violation of Title 20 of the U.S. Code, which says that no state can deny individuals educational opportunities due to their race, gender, or national origin by failing to overcome language barriers that might inhibit learning (*Martin Luther King, Jr., Elementary School Children* v. *Michigan Board of Education,* 1979).

ANALYSIS OF "EQUAL TREATMENT"

Are school boards legally obligated to make special provisions for students who speak "black English"? In its 1954 landmark decision *Brown* v. *Board of Education of Topeka, Kansas,* the Supreme Court addressed for the first time issues of educational inequality when it rejected the "separate but equal doctrine." Their decision was an attempt to put an end to racial segregation in schools. As the courts worked, and continue to work, to create united school systems, many have questioned the quality of educational opportunities for minority-group students in such settings.

One area of concern about equality has been classification of minority-group students for special services. Sometimes courts and legislatures have directed attention to discriminatory classifications of minority-group students. In other situations, such as those involving linguistic minority-group students, the courts have addressed the absence of student classifications.

In *Lau* v. *Nichols* (1974), the Supreme Court held that a school district receiving federal aid must provide special instruction for non-English-speaking students whose opportunities to learn are restricted because of language barriers. This particular case centered on the plight of about 1,800 Chinese American students in San Francisco public schools. They spoke little or no English, yet were offered no remedial English language instruction or other special compensatory program by the school system. According to the Court, such treatment of students violated Title VI of the **Civil Rights Act of 1964,** which specifies that no one, regardless of race, color, or origin, can be discriminated against or denied participation in programs receiving federal assistance.

Following *Lau,* Congress offered further protection to students when it passed the **Bilingual Act of 1974,** amended in 1988. This act calls for parental involvement in the planning of appropriate educational programs for children with limited English-speaking ability. Neither the Bilingual Act nor Title VI, however, specifies what types of programs are appropriate for addressing the needs of students with limited English-speaking abilities. Types of assistance offered to students who have difficulty understanding standard English vary greatly from state to state.

Since the *Lau* ruling, the courts have heard many cases, one of which was *Martin Luther King, Jr., Elementary School Children* v. *Michigan Board of Education* (1979). As described above, African American students who protested the use of standard English as the sole medium of instruction brought this suit before the court.

In ruling on the case, the Court acknowledged that Michigan schools had provided special assistance to these and other students through learning consultants, a speech therapist, a psychologist, a language consultant, tutors, and parent helpers. Evidence existed of good-faith efforts to meet the needs of students who spoke black English. The Court noted, however, that teachers seemed to lack knowledge about black English and thus were restricted in their ability to educate African American students. To remedy this, the Court did not order the establishment of a bilingual program, as was done in the *Lau* case. Instead, the Court required the school board to develop a plan whereby teachers would learn to recognize the home language of students. That knowledge would then be used to teach reading skills and standard English more effectively.

How Could You Let This Happen to a Student?

Are schools liable for educational malpractice?   When Peter graduated from high school, he sought $500,000 in damages from the San Francisco Unified Schools for failing to provide him with an adequate education. According to Peter, the school system was at fault for his poor skills because it had (1) failed to understand his reading disabilities, (2) assigned him to classes in which curricular materials were not geared to his reading level, (3) allowed him to pass from grade to grade without seeing that he mastered basic skills necessary for succeeding levels, (4) assigned him to teachers who did not know how to meet his learning needs, and (5) allowed him to graduate without being able to read at the eighth-grade level, as required by the Education Code. Moreover, Peter said that his mother had been told that his reading ability was not much below the school's average.

ANALYSIS OF "HOW COULD YOU LET THIS HAPPEN TO A STUDENT?"

Historically, teachers and educational institutions have been exempt from legal responsibility and accountability. Increasing numbers of educational malpractice claims, however, have forced the courts to deal frequently with issues of academic negligence. A precedent-setting case occurred in California in 1976, when Peter W., the high school graduate described above, accused the school system of negligently and intentionally depriving him of basic skills.

The state appellate court dismissed Peter W.'s suit, contending that there were no explicit "standards of care" by which schools or classroom teachers could be judged negligent in their duties. Besides conflicting ideas about the best way to educate students, the Court noted that a variety of physical, neurological, emotional, cultural, and environmental factors influence learning but were beyond a classroom teacher's control. In addition, the Court reasoned that attempts to hold school districts to a "duty of care" in academic matters would likely result in a flood of malpractice suits that would only inhibit schools' abilities to fulfill their academic functions (*Peter W.* v. *San Francisco Unified School District*, 1976).

For the most part, the California court's decision has been followed in educational malpractice litigation. However, in instances when educators have maliciously or intentionally caused injury to children, courts have allowed parents to bring action against school officials (La Morte, 2002). Such instances include cases when educators furnish false information about a child's learning problems and alter information to cover their actions (*Hunter* v. *Board of Education of Montgomery County*, 1982) or when they place a child in a program despite scores showing the placement to be inappropriate (*B.M. by Berger* v. *State of Montana*, 1982).

Somebody Will Pay!

Can students who are victims of sexual harassment sue for damages?   Christine Franklin, a tenth-grade student, felt uncomfortable around Andrew Hill, a sports coach and economics teacher at her high school in suburban Atlanta. According to Christine, Hill sexually harassed her by doing such things as asking if she would be willing to have sex with an older man, calling her at home to ask her out, and forcibly kissing her on the mouth in the school parking lot. During Christine's junior year, things got much worse; on at least three occasions, Hill allegedly pressured her into having sex. When Christine reported Hill's actions to school officials, they took no immediate steps to curtail Hill's behavior. By the time Christine had lodged a complaint with the U.S. Education Department's office for civil rights, however, Hill had resigned and the school had adopted a grievance procedure to avoid future violations.

Still angry about the abuse she had suffered at the high school, Christine decided to sue the school district for monetary damages. She argued that Hill's behavior toward her violated Title IX (a law prohibiting schools supported with federal monies from discriminating on the basis of gender). In school officials' eyes, Christine didn't stand a chance in court; they had resolved the problem and it was unlikely to occur again.

ANALYSIS OF "SOMEBODY WILL PAY!"

In 1992, when the Supreme Court heard Christine Franklin's case (*Franklin* v. *Gwinnett County Public Schools*), the Court ruled unanimously that Christine had suffered sexual harassment. Furthermore, the Court stated for the first time that schools supported by federal funds were susceptible to lawsuits and, in instances of sexual harassment and other forms of sex discrimination, liable under Title IX for monetary damages to the victims of such mistreatment.

Because *Franklin* was about a teacher's harassment of a student, some lower courts concluded that the Supreme Court's decision did not apply to student-to-student harassment. The Supreme Court's ruling in *Davis* v. *Monroe County Board of Education* (1999), however, proved this assumption about harassment erroneous. LaShonda Davis, on whose behalf the case was filed, was only ten years old when a classmate, G. W., sexually harassed her by touching her breasts and genitals, telling her he wanted to have sex with her, and rubbing up against her. Despite LaShonda's complaints to teachers, no one intervened on her behalf. One teacher even refused for more than three months to let LaShonda change seats so that she could distance herself from G. W. in the classroom. Only after LaShonda's mother filed a criminal complaint against G. W., alleging sexual battery, did the harassment stop. Concerned by her daughter's declining grades and a suicide note, LaShonda's mother next filed a lawsuit against the district, alleging that Title IX had been violated. The Supreme Court's decision in this case reversed the decision of the U.S. Court of Appeals for the 11th Circuit, which in 1998 ruled that institutions have no obligation to address complaints of student-on-student harassment. This time, the Supreme Court held that schools can in fact be held liable for monetary damages if they are deliberately indifferent to known sexual harassment (Williams, 1999).

What Kind of Choice Is This?

When the special education teacher and Anita Leopold met at the end of second grade to construct Miranda Leopold's IEP, they agreed that Miranda was at a point where she could benefit academically and socially from interactions with regular education students. Accordingly, they created a plan that would allow Miranda to be mainstreamed into a regular third-grade classroom. With the exception of daily tutorial sessions with a resource teacher, Miranda would experience the regular curriculum for third-grade students.

Anita liked her daughter's new placement. When she learned, however, that Miranda also qualified for the Milwaukee Parental Choice Program, she didn't know what to think. One of the private schools on the choice list focused on art and music, both of which Miranda loved. The idea of sending Miranda to such a school appealed to Anita. When she phoned the school for information about the program, however, Anita learned that the choice school had no resource teacher to help Miranda with her reading skills. Anita was perplexed. Didn't choice schools have to offer the same services to students with disabilities as did the public schools? How could state taxes be used for educational programs that, in a sense, discriminate against certain students? **Are choice schools held to the same standards as public schools?**

Technology in Practice

THE OYEZ PROJECT

History and government teachers seem naturally curious about the judicial branch of government, but in these days of widespread educational reform, many other teachers are becoming avid "court watchers." They are turning to the Web, in particular The Oyez Project at Northwestern University (http://oyez.nwu.edu/), for up-to-date information on the highest court in the land.

The *Zelman* v. *Simmons-Harris* case, argued before the Supreme Court on February 20, 2002, and decided on June 27, suggests why educators are so interested in the courts. The arguments and decision in this case could have dramatic implications for teachers' jobs.

Facts of the Case:

Ohio's Pilot Project Scholarship Program provides tuition aid in the form of vouchers for certain students in the Cleveland City School District to attend participating public or private schools of their parent's choosing. Both religious and nonreligious schools in the district may participate. Tuition aid is distributed to parents

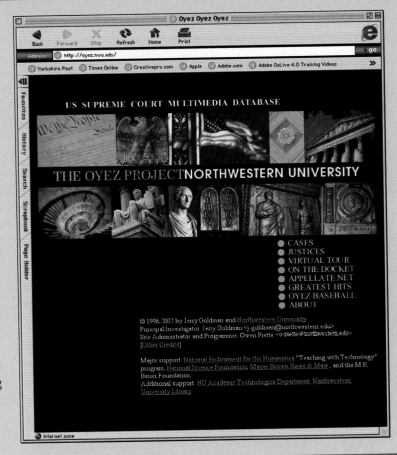

ANALYSIS OF "WHAT KIND OF CHOICE IS THIS?"

On March 3, 1992, the Wisconsin Supreme Court voted four to three to overturn a court of appeals ruling that the Milwaukee Parental Choice Plan (MPCP) was unconstitutional. Established in March 1990, the Choice Plan allowed up to one thousand low-income students in Milwaukee to receive a voucher worth $2,500 each year to attend certain private, nonsectarian schools in the city. According to Shirley S. Abrahamson, one of the dissenting justices, the majority opinion on this issue "permits the legislature to subvert the unifying, democratizing purpose of public education by using public funds to substitute private education for public education without the concomitant controls exerted over public education" (*Davis* v. *Grover*, 1992).

In 1995, the legislature approved a budget proposal initiated by Wisconsin Governor Tommy Thompson that would expand the program to include religious schools and 15 percent of the public school population, or roughly 15,000 students. The Milwaukee Teachers' Education Association and the American Civil Liberties Union immediately challenged Thompson's proposal. In 1998 the Wisconsin Supreme Court upheld the constitutionality of the revised proposal, which at the time provided vouchers of $4,400 to some 1,500 children (Walsh, 1998). Now Milwaukee enrolls some 10,000 children each year in the choice program (Gewertz, 2002).

The *Zelman* case, described in the Technology in Practice feature, may have per-

according to financial need, and where the aid is spent depends solely upon where parents choose to enroll their children. In the 1999–2000 school year, 82 percent of the participating private schools had a religious affiliation and 96 percent of the students participating in the scholarship program were enrolled in religiously affiliated schools. Sixty percent of the students were from families at or below the poverty line. A group of Ohio taxpayers sought to enjoin the program on the ground that it violated the Establishment Clause. The District Court granted them summary judgment, and the Court of Appeals affirmed.

Question Presented [to the Supreme Court]:

Does Ohio's school voucher program violate the Establishment Clause?

Conclusion:

No. In a five to four opinion delivered by Chief Justice William H. Rehnquist, the Court held that the program does not violate the Establishment Clause. The Court reasoned that, because Ohio's program is part of Ohio's general undertaking to provide educational opportunities to children, government aid reaches religious institutions only by way of the deliberate choices of numerous individual recipients, and the incidental advancement of a religious

mission, or any perceived endorsement, is reasonably attributable to the individual aid recipients, not the government. Chief Justice Rehnquist wrote that the "Ohio program is entirely neutral with respect to religion. It provides benefits directly to a wide spectrum of individuals, defined only by financial need and residence in a particular school district. It permits such individuals to exercise genuine choice among options public and private, secular and religious. The program is therefore a program of true private choice."

You can go to the Oyez site to explore other landmark education cases. It also includes the complete written decision in the *Zelman* case, described above.

Discussion Question

Discuss the practice of "court watching" with your classmates. How do websites such as this one help teachers?

 To answer this question online and e-mail your answer to your professor, go to Chapter 9 of the Companion Website (ablongman.com/ mcnergney4e) and click on Technology in Practice.

Source: The Oyez Project (2003). *Zelman* v. *Simmons-Harris:* Facts of the case. Available online: http://oyez.org/cases/cases.cgi?command= show&case_id=1496&page=abstract.

---

manently changed the legal landscape of support for the voucher system and school choice. The Supreme Court's decision to allow the use of vouchers primarily for Catholic schools will certainly strengthen the hand of those who would promote the kinds of choice programs found in Cleveland and Milwaukee.

Summary

Government at all levels influences schools by passing, enforcing, and interpreting laws and by funding educational programs. The locus of power resides at the state level, as authorized by the Tenth Amendment to the Constitution.

Public education works in the United States because we maintain a balance between our rights and our responsibilities to the communities of which we are a part. Parents have the right to expect that their children will receive an adequate basic education from school authorities. But parents must also make certain their children are cared for and that they come to school ready to learn. Students themselves must be afforded real opportunities to learn and be subjected to rules

that are fair and fairly administered. They, in turn, must behave reasonably and with respect toward others.

Teachers do not have to surrender their personhood when they go to work; they can expect to exercise their professional judgment in the performance of their duties. Teachers are responsible for teaching their students and for protecting their students' physical, intellectual, emotional, and social well-being. School systems and their leaders must provide the infrastructure to support teaching and learning and govern fairly and openly. They have the right to expect the people to provide support for public education.

Sometimes teachers must face situations that are gray or

ill-defined, legally speaking. Seeking advice is always wise. It also makes sense for teachers to ask themselves what a reasonable person would do if faced with the same situation and take their cues accordingly.

Terms and Concepts

assumption of risk   256
Bilingual Act of 1974   259
Buckley Amendment   248
Civil Rights Act of 1964   259
comparative negligence   256
contributory negligence   256
dismissal   250
due process of law   243

Equal Access Act (EAA)   241
equal protection clause   237
establishment clause   235
free exercise clause   235
in loco parentis   244
Lemon test   242
negligence   254

Reflective Practice

Lexington, North Carolina. First-grader Johnathan Prevette is accused of sexual harassment of a classmate. Johnathan kissed a female classmate on the cheek, and the girl's mother charged sexual harassment. The superintendent suspended Johnathan from school.

If Jane Ottinger, a teacher at Lincoln Middle School, had read this headline in her Sunday paper a year ago, she would have believed that it was some kind of cruel joke. Since when did a little boy kissing a little girl become sexual harassment?

But that was before she had lived through what was to become known as the Amy Christopher Incident. Amy was a bright, pretty girl in Jane's sixth-grade class. Mr. and Mrs. Christopher argued that the boys in Amy's class had treated her so badly that she had become an emotional wreck. When the Christophers complained to Jane about the behavior, Jane went immediately to the principal and recounted her conversation with them. The principal said that he would handle the matter and that Jane should be alert to signs of inappropriate behavior but not to worry too much. As nearly as Jane could remember, he said something like, "The hormones begin to rage about this time in kids' lives. Sometimes the boys, and the girls too, get carried away. This is natural. Although the school does not want and would never condone such behavior, you need to understand that some parents are fanatics who blow everything out of proportion. Flirting and teasing are part of life in the sixth grade."

Six months later the Christophers moved to another school district. Their move was accompanied by a front-page story in the local paper, in which they were quoted as saying that they had complained repeatedly to the teacher and school officials about the sexual harassment of their daughter and other children, but gotten no results.

Now, some four months later, when Jane read the story about little Johnny she felt sad. Had times changed so much since she was a child? Where would all these claims and counterclaims end?

Issues, Problems, Dilemmas, and Opportunities

How do issues such as the Amy Christopher Incident offer opportunities for teaching and learning? How do incidents of possible sexual harassment impede learning?

Perceive and Value

If you were Amy's parents, what might you say to your daughter's teacher and principal if you suspected other children of sexual harassment? If you were Amy's teacher, what would you think of the principal's response?

Know and Act

If you were a teacher faced with a situation like that presented by Amy Christopher, what more would you want to know? Assuming that you reported incidents between students and told your principal about parents' concerns, what more if anything might you do? Rank the following activities in the order in which you might undertake them. Explain your reasoning.

- Weave prevention of sexual harassment throughout the curriculum.
- Train peer leaders in awareness and prevention, and use them to teach workshops for other children.
- Provide students with safe avenues to report harassment.
- Involve parents in lessons and homework on sexual harassment (LRP Publications, 1996, p. 3).

Evaluate

Examine your own perceptions about sexual harassment. What standards guide your assessment of acceptable and unacceptable behaviors among young people? Examine a school's faculty handbook. Does it mention sexual harassment among students? If so, what does it communicate?

INTASC Principle 2

The teacher understands how children learn and develop, and can provide learning opportunities that support their intellectual, social, and personal development.

Knowledge

The teacher understands that students' physical, social, emotional, moral, and cognitive development influences learning and knows how to address these factors when making instructional decisions. (Interstate New Teacher Assessment and Support Consortium, 1992)

Discussion Questions

The Johnathan Prevette incident involves a single incident between two first-grade students. The Amy Christopher incident involves several events involving a sixth-grade girl and several sixth-grade boys. How would knowledge about development at each of these ages help you to understand these two incidents? Are these incidents examples of typical development, inappropriate behavior, or both?

Additional Readings

American Civil Liberties Union (1999). *Freedom is why we are here.* New York: author. Available online: http://www.aclu.org.

Crockett, J. B., & Kauffman, J. M. (1999). *The least restrictive environment: Its origins and interpretations in special education.* Mahwah, NJ: Erlbaum Associates.

Essex, N. L. (2002). *School law and the public schools: A practical guide for educational leaders* (2nd ed.). Boston: Allyn and Bacon.

LaMorte, M. W. (2001). *School law: Cases and concepts* (7th ed.). Boston: Allyn and Bacon.

Zirkel, P. A. (1995). *A digest of Supreme Court decisions affecting education.* Bloomington, IN: Phi Delta Kappa Educational Foundation.

Web Resources

http://www.nps.gov/brvb/

This site commemorates the landmark Supreme Court decision (*Brown* v. *Board of Education*) aimed at ending segregation in public schools.

http://www.nytimes.com/learning/index.html

Go to the *New York Times* Learning Network and search on "law" to find lesson plans on hot topics.

http://www.calib.com/nccanch/

The National Clearinghouse on Child Abuse and Neglect Information contains valuable information about these issues.

http://www.aclu.org/

The American Civil Liberties Union works to protect individual rights and liberties.

http://www.freedomforum.org/

The Freedom Forum is a nonpartisan foundation dedicated to free press, free speech, and free spirit for all people.

VideoWorkshop Extra!

If the VideoWorkshop package was included with your textbook, go to Chapter 9 of the Companion Website (ablongman.com/mcnergney4e) and click on the VideoWorkshop button. Follow the instructions for viewing video clip 6. Then consider this information along with what you've read in Chapter 9 while answering the following questions.

1. Many of students' rights revolve around what a school can or cannot do in order to keep a student safe. Which of the rights presented in the text appear to consider a student's self-esteem, as presented in the video clip? Why is this important?

2. Select one of the following issues from this chapter and explain how it relates to a student's sense of self-efficacy: ESL, civil rights, or disabilities and exceptionality. Use examples from the video clip to support your ideas.

Important Events in Educational Governance, Finance, and Law

1788	U.S. Constitution is ratified. The framers of the Constitution give the power to establish schools and license teachers to the individual states, rather than to the federal government.
1865	The American Association of School Administrators is organized in Harrisburg, Pennsylvania.
1874	Kalamazoo, Michigan, case rules that states may establish and support public high schools with tax funds, which contributes to the secondary school movement and eventually to compulsory high school attendance laws.
1916	The National Association of Secondary School Principals (NASSP) is founded in Chicago.
1917	The Smith–Hughes Act marks the first federal financial aid to public schools below college level. Funds are earmarked for vocational programs, including homemaking.
1921	National Association of Elementary School Principals (NAESP) is founded in Washington, D.C.
1943	*West Virginia State Board of Education* v. *Barnette*. Requiring students to salute or pledge to the American flag becomes unconstitutional.
1963	*School District of Abington Township* v. *Schempp*. Prayer and Bible reading in public school classrooms become unconstitutional.
1964	The Civil Rights Act of 1964 authorizes the Commissioner of Education to support educational institutions with problems caused by desegregation.
1969	*Tinker* v. *Des Moines Independent School District*. Students do not lose their constitutional rights and freedoms when they pass through the schoolhouse door.
1971	*Lemon* v. *Kurtzman*. States may not provide direct aid for secular services to parochial schools, including teacher salaries and instructional materials.
1974	*Lau* v. *Nichols*. School districts receiving federal aid must provide special instruction for non-English-speaking students whose opportunities to learn are restricted because of language barriers.
1975	The Education for All Handicapped Children Act (Public Law 94-142) provides a free and appropriate education for children with special needs.
	Goss v. *Lopez*. Students may not be suspended from school without a hearing.
1977	*Ingraham* v. *Wright*. The U.S. Constitution does not prohibit the use of corporal punishment in the schools.
	Abood v. *Detroit Board of Education*. It is constitutional for states to require nonmembers of unions to pay union dues as a condition of employment.
1979	The Department of Education Organization Act creates a cabinet-level department replacing the former U.S. Office of Education.

1981	*Widmar* v. *Vincent.* Refusing religious groups equal access to public facilities while allowing access to other groups is a violation of students' freedom of speech.
1984	*National Gay Task Force* v. *Board of Education of Oklahoma City* and *Rowland* v. *Mad River Local School District.* Teachers can advocate publicly the legalization of homosexuality unless the activity disrupts the educational process. Advocacy does not include telling co-workers about one's own or students' sexual orientation.
1985	*New Jersey* v. *T.L.O.* School officials are not required to obtain a warrant or show probable cause when searching a student suspected of violating school rules or the law.
1988	*Hazelwood School District* v. *Kuhlmeier.* School principals can censor school-sponsored publications.
1990	*Rothschild* v. *Grottenthaler.* Public school systems receiving federal funds must provide a sign language interpreter to deaf parents attending school events directly relating to their children's academic program.
1991	Minnesota enacts the first charter school legislation.
1992	*Franklin* v. *Gwinnett County Public Schools.* Schools supported by federal funds can be sued for sex discrimination and sexual harassment.
1993	*Florence County School District Four* v. *Carter.* Parents who unilaterally withdraw their child from a public school that fails to provide appropriate education under IDEA and place the child in a private school that offers such education are entitled to state reimbursement of expenses.
1995	*Missouri* v. *Jenkins.* A district court does not have the authority to fashion a desegregation program whose stipulations are broad enough to have purposes beyond the elimination of racial segregation in public schools.
	Veronia School District v. *Acton.* Random drug testing of high school athletes does not violate the reasonable search and seizure clause of the Fourth Amendment.
1999	*Cedar Rapids Community School District* v. *Garret F.* Continuous nursing services that do not involve a physician are a "related service" that a district is required to provide under IDEA.
	Davis v. *Monroe County Board of Education.* Institutions that do not address complaints of student-on-student harassment may be liable for monetary damages.
	State of Florida enacts voucher legislation to permit use of public funds for private schools.
2002	U.S. Secretary of Education Rod Paige announces the creation of the Institute of Education Sciences to support the high-quality research, evaluation, and statistical activities needed to improve education policy and practice.

DEVELOPING A PROFESSIONAL PORTFOLIO

Planning Your Professional Development

Being a professional means, in part, knowing how to strengthen your knowledge and skills. Teachers make *professional development plans* and include them in their portfolios to guide their own work and to demonstrate to others that they have clear, attainable professional goals. As you think about becoming a teacher, what is your plan for developing as a professional? Use the questions below to guide your planning, specifying the materials that you will include in your portfolio:

- What courses will you take in your program of studies?
- How will these courses enhance your knowledge of the content you plan to teach?
- Which courses have field placements?
- What types of activities will you be doing in these field placements?
- What options are there to work through school- or community-based organizations with both children and their parents? How might these options help you stretch

beyond the required program of studies to make you a better professional?

- What credentials do you need to work as a substitute teacher in the schools?
- How might substitute teaching help you think about your own eventual work as a full-time teacher in schools? At what point in your college career might you be able to serve as a substitute teacher?

Next, talk with someone in your college or university career services office about paid and volunteer work you can do to enhance your employability as an educator. Many organizations rely heavily on volunteers to support young people. They provide opportunities for you to demonstrate your abilities and your commitment to worthy causes. These include secular organizations (e.g., Big Brothers, Big Sisters, computer clubs, and after-school programs), as well as religiously affiliated organizations (e.g., Hillel, Catholic Youth Organization, Sunday school, and summer camps).

ONLINE ACTIVITY

Oyez Project

Go to Northwestern University's Oyez Project, a U.S. Supreme Court Multimedia Database (http://oyez.org). Click on the link called Cases to access a page where you can search for cases by title, citation, subject, or date. After exploring these options, click on Search by Date and enter the date on which *Santa Fe Independent School District* v. *Doe* was decided (06/19/2000).

This case addressed the question of whether a school system's policy permitting student-led, student-initiated prayer

at football games violated the Establishment Clause of the First Amendment. Click on Abstract to examine the facts of the case and the decision made by the Court. Listen to the oral argument and access the written opinion on the website. What did the Supreme Court decide? How was the Court's ruling affected by principles endorsed in *Lee* v. *Weisman* (1992)? How do you think this decision might affect your job as a teaching professional?

Helping Students Succeed

*O*ne evening as Nora Labonte, a high school algebra teacher, finished dinner, the telephone rang. "Yes, Mr. Luders, I am glad you called. You are not interrupting my dinner. This is a good time to talk," she said.

Leon Luders, a parent of one of Nora's Algebra I students, explained the reason for his call. "I'm sure you know that Gary used to worry about his algebra grades. But this past two weeks he has done his homework—I kid you not—with a smile. I ask if I can help him, and he says, 'No Dad, everything's cool. I can handle it.' I'm calling now because I want to thank you for lowering his anxiety. I don't know what you are doing with him, but it sure is working miracles with his confidence. Now, if it just shows up on his test performance, I will know we have really made progress. Thanks so much, Ms. Labonte."

If you want to know what your students and their parents think about teaching and testing, think about your own experiences as a student. What were some of the activities your teachers used that helped you learn material? How did you prepare for tests? Did you know how to study? Did you consistently do well on teacher-made tests but sometimes do poorly on standardized achievement tests? Did your test performance accurately reflect your understanding of the material?

The chapters in Part 4 present how teachers combine what they know about curriculum, instruction, and assessment to increase chances that students will succeed in school.

Curriculum and Instruction

CHAPTER CONTENTS

What Is Curriculum?

What Forces for Change
Affect Curriculum
Content?

How Are Curriculum and
Instruction Planned
and Organized?

What Are Four General
Models of Instruction?

What Is Effective
Instruction?

How Do Teachers
Manage Students
Effectively?

*P*eople typically think of *curriculum* as what is taught in school and *instruction* as the method by which curriculum is delivered. Teachers like Karen Kannapel—a Hanover County, Virginia, Beginning Teacher of the Year—suggest that such definitions are too simplistic. When developing a social studies unit on the Civil Rights movement, Karen considered the students she would be teaching—what they already knew about the subject and what more they needed to know to meet local and state standards of learning. She also thought about strategies or approaches she might use to make content meaningful:

> I think students learn best when they explore history using primary sources, learn what children their age were doing and experiencing during the time period of study, and reflect on information they discover. Technology is incorporated into this curriculum because it is one of the best tools for obtaining primary sources and providing students with engaging learning experiences. Also, by fifth grade, students in Virginia are required to meet technology standards. Therefore, this unit provides the perfect opportunity to integrate social studies and technology (personal communication, 2003).

This chapter discusses some of the more predominant ways curriculum has been defined through educational practice. It explores the forces influencing curriculum content and the goals underlying the curriculum. The ways educators design curriculum and models of instruction also are described. Finally, this chapter considers factors that determine the effectiveness of classroom instruction.

What aspects of the explicit curriculum are evident in this photograph? What aspects of the implicit curriculum might you infer?

taught implicitly, rather than explicitly, through school experiences. If a student "does his homework (though incorrectly), he raises his hand (though he usually comes up with the wrong answer), [and] he keeps his nose in the book during free study period (though he doesn't turn the page very often)," he will likely gain the teacher's approval and be labeled a "model" student (Jackson, 1990, p. 34). Students may also implicitly learn that participating in class puts them in the teacher's good favor. In these ways, students implicitly discover that mastery of content is not the only road to success in the classroom.

School routines and rituals also are part of the implicit curriculum. Teacher behavior, such as calling on students whose hands are raised while ignoring those who speak without permission, is one of the subtle ways that teachers convey values. Other implicit classroom examples teach students to cooperate with others, to have patience, and to demonstrate group skills that will serve them well later in life.

Another type of implicit curriculum relates to teachers' values and to the subject matter they teach. In other words, how a teacher presents the material can be as important as the content itself. In case studies of four high school teachers, Sigrun Gudmundsdottir (1991) found that teachers' values seeped into the curriculum through personal interpretations of subject matter and through teaching methods. For example, when English teachers were presenting *Huckleberry Finn,* one teacher viewed the book as an illustration of "an individual rebelling against conventions." The other considered it "a book about relationships [between Huck and Jim]" (p. 48). Each teacher selected passages for discussion that represented her take on the book, thereby creating different "texts" for their students.

Null Curriculum

Should schools be concerned about aspects of the curriculum that are not taught? If so, which ones?   The **null curriculum** is the curriculum that is *not* taught (Eisner, 1985, 1994). When educators develop curriculum, they select the skills and subject matter they believe students should learn. This process necessarily means that

*W*hat Is Curriculum?

The term **curriculum** in general refers to what is taught in school. In practice, curriculum can mean different things to different people, and it can cover a wide variety of ideas. A good working definition of curriculum is the knowledge and skills that schools are supposed to help students master. In this sense, books and study guides are curriculum. Movies, newspapers, computer programs, board games, animals, and songs can be curriculum as well.

For some people, the word *curriculum* can mean a set of subjects, subject content, a program of studies, a set of materials, a sequence of courses, a set of performance objectives, and a course of study. Curriculum can be regarded as everything that goes on within the school, including after-school activities, guidance, and interpersonal relationships, as well as everything taught both inside and outside school that is directed by the school or planned by school personnel. Curriculum, in short, is a series of student experiences in schools.

Because curriculum can have so many similar yet different interpretations, Americans often disagree about what children should or should not be taught in classrooms (Kliebard, 1998). Politics, economics, and religious beliefs differ among the population, and they are all elements that can change rapidly. Because states and localities control education, they are left to define curriculum. Therefore, shifts in politics, economics, and religious beliefs within the community and the state can influence schools' curricula to a large degree. In fact, if you examine battles over curriculum, you often will find political, economical, and religious beliefs at the root. In the attempt to prevent some of these battles over curriculum, states have recently made efforts to establish common educational standards and assessments. Their efforts have done much to build consensus on the practical meaning of education.

As noted, curriculum exists outside school as well as inside. Educational opportunities are not limited to only schools and universities. Business, industry, churches, prisons, and other organizations provide out-of-school training on topics as diverse as dog obedience, home sales, and natural childbirth. Curriculum is at issue when children watch *Sesame Street* and attend Scout meetings, when people study for a real estate license, and when people participate in a local library's reading program. **Who should define the curriculum in schools?**

Explicit and Implicit Curricula

Explicit curriculum is the official description of programs, courses, and objectives of study that explain specific educational expectations for both teachers and students. Explicit curriculum exists in policy statements, manuals of school procedures, instructional materials, and textbooks that stipulate what and how students should learn. Teachers are expected to teach the explicit curriculum; students are supposed to learn it. Explicit curriculum might, for example, outline what specific subject matter or skills should be taught in each grade. This is the type of curriculum for which schools are held publicly accountable.

Explicit curriculum dominates the public view, but another side of the curriculum is unvoiced, often unintended, and equally as powerful. This side reveals itself in the way teachers present subject matter and in the classroom atmosphere they establish. Philip Jackson (1990, p. 33) calls this curriculum the "hidden curriculum," and Elliot Eisner (1985, p. 89) uses the term **implicit curriculum.**

Students learn many implicit lessons while they attend school, and some of them might stay with students longer than do the facts they learn. "Trying" is one such lesson

nyt...

Them...

Expand your
concepts disc...
by reading curre...
articles from the...
visiting the **Theme...**
section of the Comp...
(ablongman.com/mc...

some skills and topics will not be taught. Sometimes the decisions about what not to include in curriculum are conscious and sometimes they are not. For instance, some critics believe many textbooks portray U.S. history and contemporary life experiences in unrealistic ways, glossing over controversial issues and avoiding discussion of discrimination and prejudice. They suggest that such texts produce citizens with a narrow sense of reality:

> For example, almost 50 percent of all marriages end in divorce, and one-third of all children will live with a single parent during part of their lives. Yet many textbooks portray the typical U.S. family as one having two adults, two children, a dog, and a house in suburbia. When controversial issues are not presented, students are denied the information they need to confront contemporary problems. (Banks & Banks, 1997, p. 133)

Time schedules for different classes and locations for instruction can also be part of the null curriculum because they communicate to students "what counts" in schools (Eisner, 1992, 1994). Time devoted to the arts, for example, is substantially less than time devoted to such courses as science and math. Moreover, the fact that art teachers are often "floaters"—moving from classroom to classroom—suggests to students that the arts are less permanent and perhaps less important than other courses.

Extracurriculum

By definition, **extracurriculum** refers to activities that do not earn credits—it is extra, or over and above the required curriculum. Yet it can be a significant part of students' lives. Students' feelings about themselves, their desire to come to school, their need to belong or be part of a group, and even their performance in academic areas can be influenced greatly by extracurricular activities. In addition, extracurriculum can help students develop skills in leadership and cooperation, as well as in the particular activity they pursue.

Sports, band, clubs, study groups, school plays, cheerleading, dance, and so on, may fall under the heading of extracurriculum. In some schools these activities may be considered *cocurricular* and weighted equally with other academic classes. Most of the time, though, these activities are viewed as being outside the typical curriculum.

Nevertheless, people frequently make conceptual and policy ties between the curriculum and the extracurriculum. If a student performs poorly on the required curriculum, someone is sure to argue the student should not be allowed to participate in the extracurriculum, at least until his or her grades improve. Others will argue the opposite—were it not for the appeal of extracurricular activities, a student with academic problems might be a dropout.

Researchers at the U.S. Department of Education's Office of Research and Improvement (OERI) found a strong connection between extracurricular activities and academic performance. Generally, extracurricular participation rates rose with students' socioeconomic levels, enrollment in an academic curriculum, and attainment of a B+ or better average.

Integrated Curriculum

Many traditional practices compartmentalize subject matter in the curriculum, with separate classes for math, English, science, and so on. Educational critics have challenged these methods of teaching and learning, however, by saying they bear little resemblance to life outside schools. Instead, these critics support an **integrated curriculum,** or a curriculum that combines concepts and skills from different subject areas (Sowell, 1996). They believe an integrated curriculum will better prepare students for life beyond school, where subject matter is not so segregated. In addition, some critics believe an integrated curriculum teaches students more, because it shows how material is connected.

In one real example of integrated curriculum, the teachers of primary grade students in a California school plan and teach science, social studies, and foreign languages to support the connections between the subjects. The teaching team helps students learn concepts, skills, and values by exploring themes that cut across subject matter. They resist separating the disciplines by class period and by the classrooms students occupy.

Another example of integrated curriculum is found with middle-school teachers in North Carolina, who take the study of science, social studies, language arts, and mathematics beyond school walls to their community—and even to Disney World. The teachers' goal is to forge connections in young minds between acquired content and applied content. Furthermore, high school teachers and administrators in Illinois have restructured blocks of time in their conventional eight-period day into four periods. They assign staff to interdisciplinary teams, change student entrance and exit requirements for courses, and incorporate an entirely new set of instructional models. By using this setup, students are able to spend longer periods of time on a topic and examine all the related subjects. All these programs, regardless of grade level and geographical location, are attempts to tear down walls that separate subject matter.

The development of integrated or interdisciplinary curriculum is made easier by emerging technologies. For example, teachers from across the United States and Canada have begun to work together on the Web to solve real-life problems by analyzing cases of interdisciplinary teaching and learning (Herbert, 1999). In addition, the Web itself has brought a world of ideas into schools, making it even easier for students to see the relationships that exist between all topics, skills, and values.

*W*hat Forces for Change Affect Curriculum Content?

Many interests shape the curriculum of public schools. Historically, some interests operate within or close to the school itself. Others' interests exercise power indirectly and from a distance, both conceptually and physically. As Figure 10.1 indicates, some of the

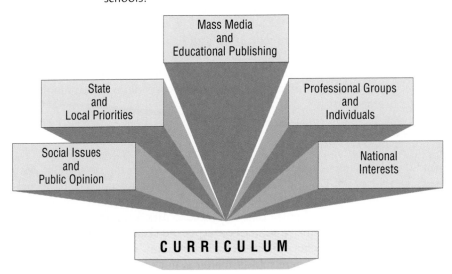

FIGURE 10.1   Forces That Shape the Curriculum   Which forces and groups are most influential in shaping the curriculum in your community's schools?

Mass Media
and
Educational Publishing

State
and
Local Priorities

Professional Groups
and
Individuals

Social Issues
and
Public Opinion

National
Interests

CURRICULUM

Your Teaching Life in Practice

TO STANDARDIZE OR NOT TO STANDARDIZE THE CURRICULUM

Some educators and community members argue for a move "back to the basics" in public education. They advocate a common or standardized curriculum to ensure that all students learn the same information and skills. They resist attempts to replace traditional subject matter with courses that are based on real-life experiences and are problem focused.

Other people support efforts to expand and diversify public school curriculum to "meet students' needs." They believe traditional curriculum and teaching–learning methods breed conformity and simply do not work for children who fall outside an imaginary band of "average" and "above-average" students. Basics, they argue, require and reinforce conformity. The diversity of our population and the rapidly changing, technologically rich society in which we live demand a responsive, flexible curriculum.

Should American public schools have a standardized curriculum, at least in elementary and middle schools? People who support standardization are typically characterized as conservative. Those who oppose it might be called progressive. However, different people from various walks of life might hold either position.

PRO A child's education should not be based on a geographical roll of the dice. You should have access to the same content regardless of the town or state in which you reside.

CON Many students do not even speak English, and many more have disabilities. They cannot be expected to learn the same content that typical students learn.

PRO If we are to stand together as a nation, we need a common conception of what it means to be a citizen of the United States of America. The only way we can get that is to have a standardized curriculum.

CON What it means to be an American is that we respect each other's right to be different. We don't need to force conformity in the curriculum to feel and act like Americans.

PRO There is too much variation in what teachers choose to teach and how they have students spend their time. Students who most need help mastering the knowledge and skills for which they will be held accountable later are cheated by differing expectations.

CON Who is to say what should constitute a standardized or common curriculum? Teachers are professionals. They know their students better than anyone else. Society should welcome their judgment about what is to be taught and learned and trust that judgment when it is offered.

Critical Thinking Questions

Do you favor one position more than the other? Why or why not?

To answer these questions online and e-mail your answers to your professor, go to Chapter 10 of the Companion Website (ablongman.com/mcnergney4e) and click on Your Teaching Life in Practice.

---

powerful forces shaping the curriculum include national interests, social issues and public opinion, and mass media.

The National Interest

What kind of curriculum is in the national interest? The influence of national government on public school curriculum has a long and rich history. Much of its work is said to be on behalf of the "national interest," which can be thought of those ideas, skills, and values that build a strong democratic nation—the things that are best for the country as a whole. Passage of the Environmental Education Act (Public Law 91-516), for example, stimulated the modern environmental education movement (DeBoer, 1991). The U.S. Congress influenced vocational education (Smith–Hughes Act of 1917) and preschool education (Economic Opportunity Act of 1964), in addition to expanding school access for students with disabilities (Education for All Handicapped Children Act of 1975 and final regulations in the Individuals with Disabilities Education Act, 1997). These laws reflect values about education that are in the national interest.

Federal influence on curriculum development also occurs through funding and advisement. In the 1990s, for example, the federal government funded states to help students meet national learning and testing standards. In 2002, President George W. Bush spoke often about his education agenda as expressed in the No Child Left Behind legislation. In almost every public address for several months, he emphasized the place of standards and the importance of testing students to provide evidence of progress. The combination of formal actions (offering a legislative agenda with funding implications) and informal efforts (urging educators to rely more heavily on testing) affected the curriculum in schools across the nation, as educators worked to align the content of instruction with the standards to be assessed.

State and Local Priorities

State laws and local policies, many promoted by special-interest groups, influence everything in public schools from textbooks to discipline. Concerns about violence in schools, for example, caused the Georgia legislature to sign into law the Improved Student Learning and Discipline Act of 1999. The law requires school districts to teach character education to students at all grade levels. The twenty-seven traits listed in Figure 10.2 are the main focus of the "character curriculum." Georgia code also specifies "such program shall . . . address, by the start of the 1999–2000 school year, methods of discouraging bullying and violent acts against fellow students."

Other ways states are forcing curriculum revisions include dictating graduation requirements, adopting state achievement tests, and, in many instances, requiring new

FIGURE 10.2 Georgia's Character-Building Traits   Which, if any, of these character traits might be controversial to special-interest groups? Why?

courage	generosity
patriotism	punctuality
citizenship	cleanliness
honesty	respect for the environment
fairness	school pride
respect for others	respect for the creator
kindness	cheerfulness
cooperation	patience
self-respect	creativity
self-control	sportsmanship
courtesy	loyalty
compassion	perseverance
tolerance	virtue
diligence	

Source: Title 20 of the Official Code of Georgia, Section 20-2-145. Available online: http://www.state.ga.us/cgi-bin/pub/ocode/ocgsearch?docname=Ocode/G/20/2/145&highlight=Section/20-2-145.

textbooks to match recommended instructional approaches. One particularly strong motivation for changing a school's curriculum is the results of student achievement tests. In response to students' poor scores on state and national reading tests, California education officials redesigned their language arts program. Officials have also revised their mathematics programs to teach basic skills. They want to move attention away from real-life application of mathematics and instead focus on students' abilities to calculate.

In addition to school curricula evolving from the input of various levels of governments, political action committees, networks of parents, professional and civic organizations, and religious groups, curricula also can be influenced by local history and geography. In the Midwest, for example, memories of the Dust Bowl days of the Great Depression still linger. So schools in Nebraska farming com-

In what ways do school curricula reflect state priorities and regional or local interests? What are the other principal sources of influence upon curriculum content?

munities teach students about the threats of soil erosion. On the Atlantic shores, students and their families do not have to own oceanfront property to be affected adversely by harsh storms. Therefore, schools on the New Jersey coast instruct students about the evils of beach erosion (Gehring, 2000).

Social Issues and Public Opinion

To what extent should the curriculum reflect local interests and values? Public schools exist to serve the community and are responsible, to some degree, for providing curricula the public supports. As noted in Chapter 8, funding from public tax dollars, as well as election and reelection concerns, causes school officials to consider public opinion and social issues when they develop curricula. Some social issues in which public opinion is heard loudly and often include teaching alternative life-styles, sex education, creationism, and multiculturalism.

Of all social issues, society's concerns about teenage pregnancy and sexually transmitted diseases (STDs) may cause the most curricular reform efforts. Perhaps the most controversial curriculum reform is *family life education,* which is now an integral part of most school programs. Family life education focuses on topics such as personal health and safety, substance abuse prevention, mental health education, human growth and development (including sex education), and STD prevention. It is probably the area of the curriculum most closely scrutinized by the public. In fact, parents often must sign a permission form for their children to participate in family life education.

Family life education programs around the country acknowledge the central role of parents in educating their children. School curricula on the topic try to help parents and fill in some of the gaps. What the curriculum covers, however, varies from place to place. In some localities, contraceptives are discussed in sex education classes; in other school systems, educators are prohibited from mentioning condoms or other contraceptives.

A provision in the 1996 federal welfare law budgeted $50 million a year for five years, beginning in fiscal year 1998, for efforts to bring some uniformity to family life education programs. States accepting federal funds for sex education were required to teach teenagers to abstain from sex until marriage. Under the law, grantees must inform young people that sex outside of a marriage can have negative psychological and physical effects. The law prohibits using funds to teach young people about contraceptives. Critics of this legislation argued that teaching only abstinence turned a blind eye to the fact that many teenagers are already having sex and need information to help them stay safe. Other critics questioned the religious and moral values that seemed to be tied to the funding.

Professional Groups and Individuals

Through professional organizations educators have influenced curriculum over time. Professional organizations offer advice on material that should be taught, methods of teaching, and forms of evaluation. They also promote teacher involvement in school policy-making activities. Some organizations, such as the National Council of Teachers of Mathematics (NCTM), have developed standards intended to guide curricular reform in schools. The NCTM's *Curriculum and Evaluation Standards for School Mathematics* (1989) comprises fifty-four value statements. Each consists of three parts that address (1) what mathematics the curriculum should include, (2) a description of student activities associated with that mathematics, and (3) instructional examples. The NCTM standards make computation serve a more important goal—the development of mathematical thinking (Association for Supervision and Curriculum Development, 1992).

The NCTM standards set out guidelines for core knowledge, or that knowledge common to all students, as well as special requirements for college-bound students. In a companion volume, entitled *Professional Standards for Teaching Mathematics* (National Council of Teachers of Mathematics, 1991), NCTM recognizes teachers as central to changing mathematics education in schools. They emphasize the need to shift instruction toward the use of logic and mathematical evidence and away from a reliance on teachers as sources of right answers. The standards also promote responsive teaching practices. Standard 6, which follows, addresses how teachers should engage in ongoing analysis of teaching and learning:

TEACHING: Standard 6—Analysis of Teaching and Learning: The teacher of mathematics should engage in ongoing analysis of teaching and learning by—

- observing, listening to, and gathering other information about students to assess what they are learning;
- examining effects of the task, discourse, and learning environment on students' mathematical knowledge, skills, and dispositions;

in order to—

- ensure that every student is learning sound and significant mathematics and is developing a positive disposition toward mathematics;
- challenge and extend students' ideas;
- adapt or change activities while teaching;
- make plans, both short- and long-range;
- describe and comment on each student's learning to parents and administrators, as well as to the students themselves. (NCTM, 1991)

Figure 10.3 illustrates two teaching activities, one of which the NCTM might consider more "worthwhile" than the other.

To what extent should teachers and professional associations determine the curriculum? As individuals leading a classroom, teachers' habits, dispositions, and areas of professional expertise influence what is taught and learned. When teachers stick to familiar tools, content, and activities, they operate as conservative—and some believe negative—forces on curriculum (Cuban, 1992). In the 1970s, criticisms of ill-

*F*IGURE 10.3 **Structuring Worthwhile Mathematics Tasks**   What skills are required to solve tasks 1 and 2? Why might the National Council for Teachers of Mathematics consider task 2 the more "worthwhile" assignment?

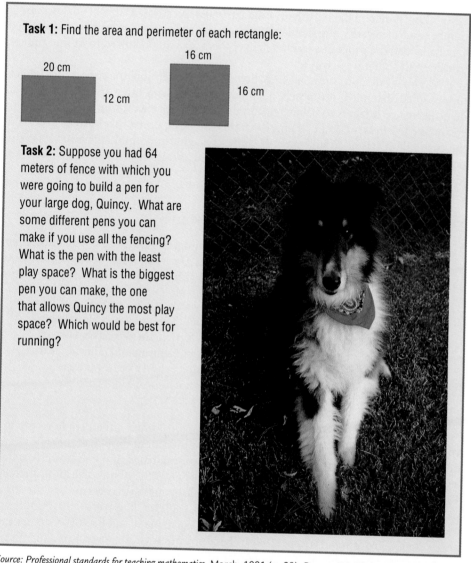

Task 1: Find the area and perimeter of each rectangle:

20 cm

12 cm

16 cm

16 cm

Task 2: Suppose you had 64 meters of fence with which you were going to build a pen for your large dog, Quincy. What are some different pens you can make if you use all the fencing? What is the pen with the least play space? What is the biggest pen you can make, the one that allows Quincy the most play space? Which would be best for running?

Source: Professional standards for teaching mathematics, March, 1991 (p. 28), Reston, VA: The National Council of Teachers of Mathematics. Reprinted with permission. All rights reserved.

prepared teachers led designers to create what are often called "teacher-proof" curricula, or curricula from which students can learn, regardless of the teacher's level of experience, interest, or skill (Grobman, 1970). Today, attitudes toward teachers as professionals are much more positive.

Creative teachers make curricula come alive. In language arts or literature-based instruction, for example, teachers with a constructivist philosophy guide students to define knowledge for themselves, using curricula as the groundwork for innovative thinking (Applebee, 1991; Langer & Applebee, 1986). Teaching in these instances is not a matter of transmitting knowledge; it is more a matter of helping students construct and interpret knowledge for themselves.

At times it seems as though everyone, from the president to the governor to the person on the street, has an idea of what schools should teach. In the midst of this, it can be easy to overlook the people all this work is for—the students. Students' needs can and must dictate the nature of some curricula. As students' problems increase in number and/or severity, the standard curriculum may have to be reduced or modified. Curricula, and the programs used to deliver them, can be organized to fit the students instead of the other way around.

When a curriculum stimulates and holds student attention, the curriculum is likely to be copied, extended, promoted, adapted, and used with other students. Also, students influence teachers to behave in certain ways in the classroom. That is, students encourage teachers, or "pull" them, to emphasize or de-emphasize various aspects of the curriculum (Hunt & Sullivan, 1974). Besides educators thinking about what students should learn and how they will best learn it, asking students to voice their own ideas on such matters can be enlightening.

Educational Publishing and Mass Media

Textbooks play an important role in student learning, and the people who select them play an important role in shaping the curriculum. Deciding which textbooks a school should buy is not always an easy process. Consider this description of one such process:

> With the Texas state school board gearing up to decide which textbooks will be used to teach history and social studies to the state's four million public school-children, the recurring battle over what students learn in the subjects has begun anew. A recent public hearing, as well as competing campaigns to influence text content and selection, reflect[s] some of the tension between conservatives and liberals. But state board members say ideology is not welcome in this debate. (Manzo, 2002, p.11)

Various conservative and liberal organizations routinely urge people to get involved in textbook selection in their states and communities. About half the states have official state-level processes by which curricula are evaluated and endorsed. A state-level endorsement in populous states that tightly control textbook selection, such as Florida, Texas, and California, can be the difference between success and failure for a particular text and for its publisher (Apple, 1998).

State-level textbook adoption policies shape curricula in public school across the entire state. According to Apple (1998), these policies exist for several reasons. First, textbooks can be purchased at a lower cost when large orders are placed (a group of school districts as opposed to a single school district). Second, the state wants to protect children from being exposed to poor-quality textbooks, so they rely on experts to make selections. Third, a minimum standard curriculum for the entire state can be more easily established if schools are using the same books. **To what extent does the textbook publishing industry determine the curriculum?**

Textbooks often are the first thing people think of when they think about curriculum. Not surprisingly, textbooks may constitute as much as 70 percent of the curriculum. Educational experts worry, however, that the drive to produce textbooks suitable for all students has instead led to textbooks that teach to the "lowest common denominator" or "dumb down" the curriculum. Furthermore, critics believe textbook publishers avoid controversial subjects in trying to appeal to schools that may be urban or rural, liberal or conservative, wealthy or poor, and so on. In addition, some textbooks teach inaccurate and erroneous information.

Educators also worry about texts in all subject areas that are structured in pedagogically poor ways.

> The next generation of math textbooks should cover fewer topics in more depth, offer teachers the tools to customize lesson plans, and try to reach students of varying ability levels. "Please give us greater depth of instruction on fewer topics," [said] Barbara Montalto, the assistant director of mathematics for the Texas Education Agency . . . "Give us longer lessons linked together." (Hoff, 2001, p. 5)

Textbook publishers, for their part, influence the curriculum through the authors they hire and the books and materials they produce. Publishers argue that they do not influence the curriculum as much as do the people who buy the books. Publishers say they simply provide what they believe people will buy. And buy they do—elementary and secondary textbooks gross nearly $4.18 billion a year (Association of American Publishers, 2003).

In addition to news coverage of school policies, school funding, and testing scores, media also provide a wealth of information through television, film, radio, publications, and the Internet. In this sense, the media are involved directly in producing their own curricula.

One example of this direct curriculum production is Channel One Network, the leading provider of television news and educational programs for students. Channel One delivers programs by satellite to some 12,000 middle schools and high schools in the United States. Participating schools receive a satellite dish and classroom television monitors in exchange for showing the programming. In turn, schools agree by contract to make Channel One available to their students on 90 percent of school days. In 2001, Channel One claimed eight million students as regular viewers. Liberals and conservatives have differing views on Channel One. Some worry about Channel One's effects on students, criticizing in particular Channel One's introduction of commercials into the classroom. Others praise this public/private partnership for bringing quality content and technology to schools free of charge (Kevin Neary, personal communication, February 6, 2003). Channel One has a 99 percent renewal rate among its installed base. In 1999, the channel charged advertisers as much as $200,000 per thirty-second commercial (Walsh, 1999). Figure 10.4 shows the Channel One homepage.

Another example of media-produced curriculum is the *New York Times* Learning Network on the Web. This website contains daily lesson plans that match each day's edition of the newspaper, an archive of previous plans, a special section on education news, education product reviews, science quizzes, special news packages on current events and historic events, and many more curricular materials. *New York Times* employees also conduct professional development sessions for teachers.

How Are Curriculum and Instruction Planned and Organized?

Ralph Waldo Emerson captured the essence of curriculum and instruction when he stated "the things taught in schools are not an education but the means for education" (Emerson, undated). In other words, teachers attempt to prepare students for life beyond school walls. They do so by considering their audience (students) and the aims of education.

As we have seen, decisions about what is taught in schools are made by many levels of government and by many organizations. Media, public opinion, and a variety of

*F*IGURE 10.4 **Channel One Network**   The Channel One homepage reflects the curriculum broadcast to some 12,000 schools in the United States.

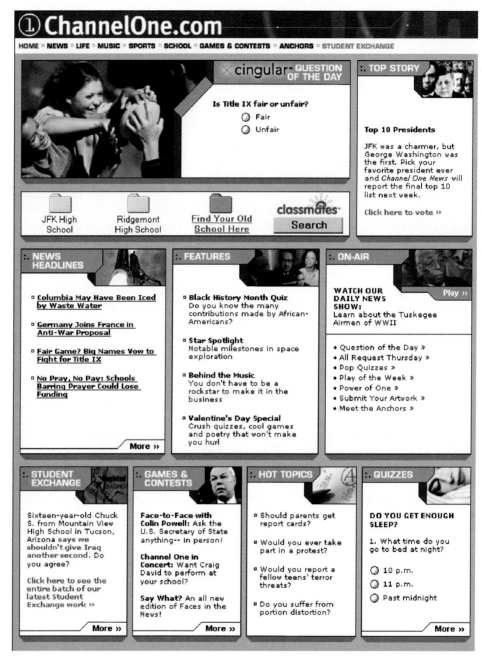

Source: http://www.channelone.com/home.html

other factors also take part in the conversation concerning school curricula. When it comes to the day-to-day business of education, however, teachers play a crucial role in developing and using curriculum to help students learn in the best ways possible. For all the decisions, ideas, and values others put into curriculum, teachers ultimately are responsible for bringing curriculum into the classroom—and making it work.

Aims of Education

Through the years, educators have had different ideas about what and how students should learn. As illustrated in Figure 10.5, some approaches put students at the center of learning, encouraging them to work with teachers to structure and evaluate their own educational experiences. Other approaches rely more on the teacher to establish goals, to present academic tasks relevant to the goals, and to determine whether students are successful. **Which of the aims of education reflected in the chart have you experienced as a student?**

FIGURE 10.5 **Five Aims of Education and Corresponding Curricular Orientations** Which aims of education and curricular orientations interest you the most at this time?

Aims of Education	Curriculum Orientation	Roles of Students and Teachers	Examples of Curriculum Content	Examples of Instructional Approaches
Teach students how to learn	Development of cognitive processes	Student centered: Students think about academic tasks and construct meaningful knowledge in relationship to prior experiences. Teachers mediate and facilitate students' learning.	Thinking skills; study skills; problem-solving skills	Scaffolding; inquiry learning
Impart culture to students	Academic rationalism	Teacher centered: Students receive instruction and demonstrate competencies.	Great ideas; great works of art; literary classics; basic skills	Direct instruction
Help students find self-fulfillment, develop effective learning styles	Personal relevance	Student centered: Students and teachers collaborate to create or match curricula to individual and group interests and needs. Teachers provide opportunities for student reflection and self-evaluation.	Opportunities for personal expression; clarification of personal values	Individualized instruction; nondirective teaching
Help students become productive citizens capable of changing the social order	Social adaptation, change, and outcomes-based views	Teacher centered: Teachers present facts, issues, problems, and learning challenges for students to act upon or apply in life.	Citizenship; communication skills; environmental, social issues, and job-related skills	Questioning; cooperative learning; project-based learning; internships
Give students the tools they need to master subjects; deliver instruction efficiently	Curriculum as technology	Subject centered: Teachers preestablish developmentally appropriate learning goals, outcomes, objectives, and criteria for assessment for a subject area. Students demonstrate minimum competencies.	Traditional subjects; basic skills	Direct instruction; mastery learning

Teacher Planning for Instruction

Teacher planning is "the thread that weaves the curriculum, or the *what* of teaching, with the instruction, or *how* of teaching" (Frieberg & Driscoll, 1996, p. 22). When planning instruction, teachers consider the curriculum, state and local goals for student learning, instructional strategies for meeting those goals, and means of assessing students' understanding. Teachers should never underestimate the importance of planning how to evaluate student learning and the effectiveness of a lesson.

When identifying goals and objectives, teachers determine what students should learn or be able to do as a result of instruction (e.g., students should be able to solve nine out of ten math problems correctly). Deciding what the intended results of learning should be helps teachers clarify their thinking about the methods and materials they

Voices

ON BACKWARD DESIGN OF CURRICULUM

*G*rant Wiggins and Jay McTighe, leading authorities on student assessment, are familiar names in research on curriculum, instruction, and evaluation. Below, they refer to the ideas of a major figure in U.S. educational history, Ralph Tyler, to explain why conventional wisdom about curricular design must be reserved:

Why do we describe the most effective curricular designed as "backward"? We do so because many teachers *begin* with textbooks, and time-honored activities rather than deriving those tools from targeted goals or standards. We are advocating the reverse: One starts with the end—the desired results (goals or standards)—and then derives the curriculum from the evidence of learning (performances) called for by the standard and the teaching needed to equip students to perform. This view is hardly radical. Ralph Tyler (1949) described the logic of backward design clearly and succinctly about fifty years ago:

Educational objectives become the criteria by which materials are selected, content is outlined, instructional procedures are developed, and tests and examinations are prepared. . . . The purpose of a statement of objectives is to indicate the kinds of changes in the student to be brought about so that instructional activities can be planned and developed in a way likely to attain these objectives. (pp. 1, 45)

Backward design may be thought of as purposeful task analysis: Given a task to be accomplished, how do we get there? Or one might call it planned coaching: What kinds of lessons and practices are needed to master key performances? The approach

to curricular design we are advocating is logically forward and commonsensical but backward in terms of conventional habits, whereby teachers typically think in terms of a series of activities . . . or how best to cover a topic. . . .

This backward approach to curricular design encourages us to think about the place of assessment in teaching. While we typically think of assessing students at the end of a lesson, we should also consider assessing students prior to teaching. The information we learn can help us shape instruction to meet students' needs. Many teachers who have adopted this design approach report that the process of "thinking like an assessor" about evidence of learning not only helps them to clarify their goals, but also results in a more sharply defined teaching and learning target so that students perform better knowing their goal. Greater coherence among desired results, key performances, and teaching and learning experiences leads to better student performance—the purpose of design.

Critical Thinking Question

Can you describe how you might use backward design to create a series of lessons to teach a particular concept, such as photosynthesis?

To answer this question online and e-mail your answer to your professor, go to Chapter 10 of the Companion Website (ablongman.com/mcnergney4e) and click on Voices.

Source: Wiggins, G., & McTighe, J. (1998). *Understanding by design.* Alexandria, VA: Association of Supervisors and Curriculum Developers. Available online: http://www.ascd.org/framebooks.html. Tyler, R. W. (1950). *Basic principles of curriculum and instruction.* Chicago: University of Chicago Press.

should use. Although educational objectives are influenced by state and local mandates, they also are shaped by teachers' perceptions of students' needs and abilities before, during, and after instruction.

To maximize students' opportunities to learn, teachers plan on their own and in teams. Sometimes team planning occurs across grade levels and even across schools. As teachers consider goals and objectives, they may create time lines indicating approximate dates when concepts and skills will be introduced. The resulting documents, sometimes referred to as **curriculum maps,** help teachers identify gaps and repetitions in the curriculum. They also are helpful for pointing out occasions when different subjects can be integrated.

When planning for instruction, teachers also think about classroom management. By establishing clear rules and routines, teachers minimize confusion and maximize instructional time. This aspect of planning is particularly important at the beginning of the year, when teachers establish patterns, limits, and expectations that set the tone for the rest of the year.

Methods for motivating students also should be part of teachers' instructional planning. According to Thomas Good and Jere Brophy (2003), teachers can motivate students by (1) establishing a supportive classroom environment in which students feel comfortable taking intellectual risks and (2) selecting activities at an appropriate level of difficulty "that teach things that are worth learning" (p. 223). Other motivational strategies include beginning the lesson by explaining how the subject matter relates to students' personal lives and to what they have already learned. Teachers should also let students know what they will need to do to demonstrate understanding of the lesson.

What Are Four General Models of Instruction?

No single best way exists to teach all things to all people. Different learners and different objectives often require different **instructional models,** or systematic approaches to teaching. Successful teachers have a variety of teaching instructional models they can use when they need them. When a teacher uses the same model of instruction over and over, only those students who learn well with that particular model will succeed. A teacher who uses different models will reach more students and will encourage them to learn in multiple ways.

As Bruce Joyce and his colleagues have found (Joyce, Weil, & Calhoun, 2000), models of teaching can be placed in four groups according to the models' purposes (see Figure 10.6). The Behavioral Systems Family models use ideas about manipulating the environment to modify students' behaviors. The Social Family capitalizes on people's social instinct to learn from and relate to one another. The Information-Processing Family focuses on increasing students' abilities to think—to seek, organize, interpret, and apply information both inductively and deductively. The Personal Family encourages self-exploration and the development of personal identity. As you read the following descriptions, see if you can determine which philosophies described in Chapter 6 influence each teaching model group. **How should decisions be made about what teaching methods to use?**

Behavioral Systems Strategies

Mastery learning is based on the idea that student learning is a function of a student's aptitude, his or her motivation, and the amount and quality of instruction received. Supporters of mastery learning define aptitude as the amount of time a student requires to master an objective and not as the student's natural ability. Students are thought to be capable of mastering almost any subject matter, given enough time, the inclination

$\mathcal{F}$**IGURE 10.6 Examples of Teaching Strategies That Contribute to a Teacher's Instructional Repertoire**   Effective teachers employ strategies and combinations of strategies from all four "families."

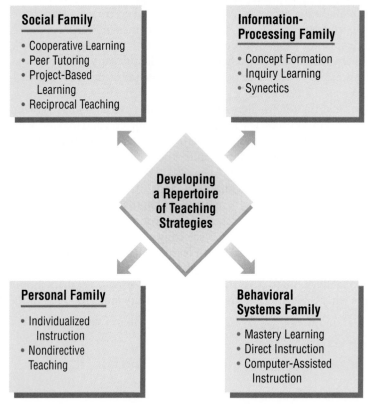

Source: Adapted from *Models of teaching* (6th ed.) by B. R. Joyce, M. Weil, & E. Calhoun, 2000. Boston: Allyn and Bacon.

to learn, and instruction fitted to their needs. The teacher's role in mastery learning is to organize instruction into manageable units, identify students' needs with respect to the material, teach in ways that meet those needs, and evaluate progress regularly. Developed by Benjamin Bloom (1971), John Carroll (1971), and their colleagues, mastery learning has proved to be a popular behavioral system model.

Teachers following the mastery learning model select learning objectives from a list of simple to complex thought processes (recall, comprehension, application, analysis, synthesis, and evaluation). Bloom's guide to learning objectives has aided the development of many curricula. Table 10.1 shows Bloom's guide and the tasks teachers must address to help students accomplish the objectives.

Like mastery learning, **direct instruction** is a highly structured, teacher-centered strategy. It relies on behavioral techniques such as modeling, feedback, and reinforcement to teach basic skills, primarily in reading and mathematics. Teachers using this model must set high but attainable goals for students. Activities and teaching environments should be structured so students succeed at a high rate. Direct instruction focuses on basic mathematics and reading objectives, not complex objectives. For this reason, and because it works, direct instruction is popular with policy makers.

BEHAVIORAL OBJECTIVES

In the 1960s and 1970s, Robert Mager (1962) encouraged educators to write instructional **behavioral objectives.** They are goal statements that specify conditions under which learning will occur and criteria for success. Since then, teaching objectives and

TABLE 10.1 **Bloom's Taxonomy of Educational Objectives**

Level	Learner Objectives	Teacher Tasks
1.00 Knowledge	To define, distinguish, acquire, identify, recall, or recognize various forms of information.	To present and/or elicit facts, conventions, categories in ways that enable learners to demonstrate knowledge.
2.00 Comprehension	To translate, transform, give in own words, illustrate, prepare, read, represent, change, rephrase, or restate various forms of information.	To present and/or elicit definitions, words, phrases, relationships, principles in ways that enable learners to demonstrate comprehension.
3.00 Application	To apply, generalize, relate, choose, develop, organize, use, transfer, restructure, or classify various forms of information.	To present and/or elicit principles, laws, conclusions in ways that enable learners to apply what they have learned.
4.00 Analysis	To distinguish, detect, identify, classify, discriminate, recognize, categorize, or deduce various forms of information.	To present and/or elicit elements, hypotheses, assumptions, statements of intent or fact in ways that encourage learners to critically analyze information.
5.00 Synthesis	To write, tell, relate, produce, originate, modify, or document various forms of information.	To present and/or elicit structures, patterns, designs, relationships in ways that encourage learners to form new structures of knowledge.
6.00 Evaluation	To judge, argue, validate, assess, appraise various forms of information.	To present and/or elicit from learners different qualitative judgments.

Source: Teacher development (p. 57) by R. F. McNergney and C. A. Carrier, 1981, New York: Macmillan.

learning objectives have become the backbone of curriculum development, particularly in subject areas that can measure learning in quantifiable terms. These statements about what students should know or be able to do after completing a unit of study form the basis of what is taught and how success is judged. As the following example illustrates, behavioral objectives should specify the intended result or product of instruction.

An Instructional Behavioral Objective in Mager's Terms

Conditions of Performance:	Given a definition and examples of a verb as a part of speech,
Behavior:	students will identify verbs in sentences
Criteria for Performance:	correctly in at least 9 of 10 instances.

Although behavioral objectives are widely used in curriculum development, when schools overemphasize them, teaching becomes simplistic and mechanized. By necessity, the objectives must be specific and structured, which can lead to staleness. Many educators resist strict adherence to behavioral approaches so they can remain open to spontaneous opportunities for learning.

Social Strategies

Instructional models in the social family help students work together to attain both academic and social goals. Teachers serve as guides, encouraging students to express their ideas and to consider others' perspectives as they deal with a variety of issues. Cooperative learning and project-based learning are two examples of strategies for classroom teaching and learning in the social family.

COOPERATIVE LEARNING

Cooperative learning is more social in nature than behavioral systems models. Cooperative learning promotes the careful, purposeful formation of mixed groups of students within classrooms to accomplish social, personal, and academic objectives. Cooperative learning is popular because it influences student self-esteem, intergroup relations, acceptance of students with academic and physical limitations, attitudes toward school, and ability to work cooperatively.

One cooperative learning technique, Students Teams–Achievement Divisions (STAD), has the teacher use direct instruction to teach students concepts or skills. Students then work in four-member, heterogeneous learning teams to help each other master the content by using study guides, worksheets, and other materials. Following group work, students take quizzes on which they may not help one another. Teams earn recognition or privileges based on the improvement made by each team member over his or her past record (Slavin & Fashola, 1998). The success of groups depends on what each individual in the group has learned, not on a single group product (Slavin, 1995).

The Education Department of the Metropolitan Opera Guild has created its own cooperative learning model. Teachers can use "Creating Original Opera" to integrate curriculum and to encourage students from all backgrounds and experiences to work together. The program, designed for students in grades three through six, emphasizes personal responsibility, constructive criticism, and the development of communication skills. Through its emphasis on the formation of an opera company, the program also demands that students work effectively in groups. One young actress explained the critical role of cooperation:

> When you act you are part of a company of people putting on the opera. Say like someone forgets their line, and you notice it. Then it is up to you not to make a face or whisper or anything. You have to think fast and make up a new line that your character might say. And that gets the same information said out loud. (Wolf, 1994, p. 30)

Teachers using "Creating Original Opera" serve as guides or coaches, helping students learn to work within a company structure. Thousands of classroom teachers and music teachers from around the world have participated in the Creating Original Opera Teacher Training Program.

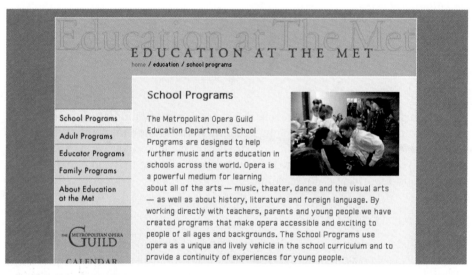

"Creating Original Opera" is one tool for cooperative learning in the classroom.

Source: The Metropolitan Opera Guild (25 August 2002). School Programs. Available online: http://www.operaed.org/index.htm#six.

OTHER FORMS OF PEER-MEDIATED INSTRUCTION

Is peer-mediated instruction as effective as teacher-mediated instruction? **Project-based learning** helps students pursue solutions to important problems raised by students, teachers, or curriculum developers. Students approach the problems by "asking and refining questions, debating ideas, making predictions, designing plans and/or experiments, collecting and analyzing data, drawing conclusions, communicating ideas and findings to others, asking new questions, and creating artifacts" (Blumenfeld, Soloway, Marx, Krajcik, Guzdial, & Palcinsar, 1991, p. 371). Artifacts are models, reports, videotapes, and computer programs representing students' problem solutions. Feedback on their artifacts helps students revise their solutions. For one project middle and high school students designed a solar house. At another school students modeled the effects of water pollution on a stream (Guzdial, 1998).

The key benefit of project-based learning is that students draw on many different curricular areas, making connections between subject matter disciplines. Also, technology allows students to work with computerized databases to conduct research and with video technology to construct products using computerized design.

Information-Processing Strategies

Models in the information-processing family stimulate the development of thinking skills such as observing, comparing, finding patterns, and generalizing. Simultaneously, students learn specific concepts or generalizations (Eggen & Kauchak, 2001). These models are built on the ideas of information-processing theorists and modern constructivists. Information-processing models take their cues for instruction from theory that explains how people think.

FORMING CONCEPTS AND GENERALIZATIONS

Teachers using the **concept formation** method of instruction want students to analyze and synthesize data to construct knowledge about a specific idea. A science teacher using concept formation during a unit on plants would likely ask students to (1) examine a variety of plant specimens, (2) place the plants into groups based on structural characteristics, and (3) create labels for each of the plant groups. The teacher might then provide additional specimens for students to classify. Although most of these plants would probably fit existing groups, students might have to create new categories for some of the plants. In a lesson of this type, students are active "creators" or "inventors" of knowledge.

THINKING AND CREATIVITY

Can creativity be taught? **Synectics** is a teaching model that seeks to increase students' problem-solving abilities, creative expression, empathy, and insight into social relations. Developed by William Gordon, a businessman from Cambridge, Massachusetts, synectics is designed to "make the familiar strange." The key teaching strategy is to force distance between the student and the object or subject matter being investigated. Through a series of exercises, students work as a team to experiment with traditional ways of thinking to discover new perspectives on topics from a wide range of fields.

Synectics activities begin with a statement of a problem or a topic. A series of *stretching exercises,* or activities, familiarizes students with using analogies in new ways. A teacher might pose a problem about water pollution, for example, and ask students to consider the effects of pollution and ways they might prevent it. For stretching exercises, students might then brainstorm responses to such questions as "Which is more dangerous to water—chemicals or construction waste? Why?" or "Which is a more powerful force for change—regulations or education? Why?" (McAuliffe & Stoskin, 1993, p. 23).

During the next phase of the synectics model, students create direct, personal, and symbolic analogies. In the lesson on pollution, for example, the teacher might help students create direct analogies by saying, "An oil slick is like what animal? Why?" or "Toxic waste is like what machine? Why?" (McAuliffe & Stoskin, 1993, p. 24). Personal analogies call for empathetic identification with a person, plant, animal, or nonliving thing or idea. The teacher might suggest, for example, that students "be" a duck: "Imagine you are a duck swimming on Lake Superior one frosty September morning. You scurry along the water's edge and, all of a sudden, find yourself paddling through an oil slick. What do you do? How do you feel?"

After students share their ideas, they develop symbolic analogies involving unusual juxtapositions of ideas. For example, students might think of word combinations, such as "awful beauty," "heavy flight," or "helpful panic" (McAuliffe & Stoskin, 1993, p. 27). By the time students return to their original problem, water pollution, they can think about solving the problem in new and creative ways.

INQUIRY LEARNING

When students engage in **inquiry learning,** they try to answer questions and solve problems based on facts and observations. They think as scientists do while analyzing data and testing theories and hypotheses. The Suchman Inquiry Model, one of several ways to structure inquiry lessons, lets students see that knowledge is tentative. That is, as new information is discovered and new theories evolve, old ideas are modified or discarded.

A biology teacher might use the Suchman model to focus instruction on fire in the balance of nature. She might provide students with the following information:

> Many small communities in the western United States are nestled in or near lush, green forests. Residents settled there for the serenity and the safety that small town life provides. Over the years, the Forest Service has thinned trees near these towns in efforts to protect them from fires. Yet, some of the towns thought to be safe are now at great risk, threatened by fire almost every summer. How might this have happened?

The teacher would then guide students through five steps:

1. define the problem;
2. formulate hypotheses;
3. gather data;
4. organize data and modify hypotheses accordingly; and
5. generalize from findings.

Personal Sources Strategies

Personal sources models of instruction try to involve students actively in deciding what and how they will learn. The goal is for students to develop lifelong character traits, rather than to focus on short-term educational goals (Joyce, Weil, & Calhoun, 2000). Specifically, teachers use personal models to help students develop effective learning styles and healthy self-concepts. The nondirective teaching model, based on the work of Carl Rogers (1971), is one approach to attaining these goals.

In the **nondirective model,** teachers facilitate students' learning based on students' own interests and concerns. In this sense, teachers are more like guides than instructors. Instead of lecturing on a topic, teachers encourage students to identify problems and feelings, to take responsibility for solving problems, and to determine how personal goals might be reached. Students' problems may relate to personal, social, or academic issues. When focusing on personal problems, students generally explore their own feel-

According to the Suchman Inquiry Model, teachers present students with a problem, such as forest fires, and then guide students through five steps of inquiry.

ings. When considering social issues, students investigate their feelings about others and how their thoughts can influence relationships. Academic concerns generally center on students' feelings about their competence and interests in certain areas (Joyce, Weil, & Calhoun, 2000).

As this lesson structure suggests, students determine classroom activities. Acting as a facilitator, the teacher follows five steps when using the nondirective model:

1. The teacher describes the learning situation, and teacher and student agree on procedures for meeting and interacting with one another. The student may also identify a problem.

2. The teacher, using strategies such as paraphrasing and asking open questions ("Can you say more about that?"), encourages the student to express positive and negative feelings and to clarify the problem.

3. The teacher uses supportive language ("Yes, it is difficult to be alone") to encourage the student to explore the problem and to develop new insight.

4. The teacher clarifies a student's plan for dealing with the problem.

5. The teacher listens as the student explains the actions she has taken. The teacher may also help the student to consider other things that might be done to solve the problem.

The five phases of the nondirective model might occur in one day or across a longer period of time. Meetings between teacher and student typically are one on one, allowing for privacy and time to explore problems and issues important to the student (Joyce, Weil, & Calhoun, 2000).

What Is Effective Instruction?

Teachers are students, too. They are always learning and applying skills in new ways to be effective in their unique situations. Even the best among them do not always know how or why they are successful. With experience, though, they grow accustomed to not having all the answers. They learn to combine the best information available about teaching and learning with their prior teaching experiences. In addition, teachers cannot rely exclusively on either creativity or technical expertise. Instead, they must build a stockpile of knowledge, methods, and practices they can call on at a moment's notice. Good teachers, like good students, push all their capabilities to the limits.

Much time is spent debating the surefire way to be an effective teacher. The literature on educating teachers is brimming with lists of skills that one expert or another claims are essential. Yet it is hard to imagine a single method that could accommodate the variety of students and material that teachers encounter during their careers. As knowledge grows and as philosophies change, programs require that teacher education students demonstrate far fewer yet more complex skills. Instead of relying on specific methods and structures, teacher education is now likely to promote some basic skills and concepts that can be adapted to a number of situations. Some of these skills and concepts are described in the sections that follow and are also listed in Figure 10.7.

Understanding Students

Good teachers learn about their students so they can challenge and support them. Teachers try to understand what students know, what they can and cannot do, how they think, what they value, and what gets in the way of their learning. Teachers learn about students formally by reading and studying student artifacts, such as tests and projects. They can also informally observe, talk with, and listen to students and their parents.

The most frequent, the most critical, and the most generous evaluators of teaching are the students themselves. Students watch what teachers do and listen to what teachers say. Good teachers understand that when they help students become critical thinkers they also encourage students to become good evaluators of teachers and teaching.

Former New York mayor Ed Koch used to ask people on the street, "How am I doing?" Whether you thought he was doing a good job or not, you had to admire the man's spunk and his willingness to listen to the people he served. Teachers might take a lesson from Koch and seek feedback from their students. Whether it's discovering their successes or their failures, teachers can learn much from their students when they take the time to do so. We remember the great students—what they did, what they said—and like to think we had something to do with their success. But too often we overlook the bored, the tired, the restless student who may be "telling" us a great deal about what does and does not work in teaching. **What might we learn about our own teaching by listening to students?**

Communicating

Good teachers are good communicators. They communicate clearly, both verbally and in writing. They transmit information about subject matter and communicate with parents, administrators, and other teachers. Good teachers also use their skills to communicate expectations for student performance, as well as empathy, positive regard, and willingness to help.

Skillful teachers know how to establish, negotiate, and help students set reasonable goals for learning. Sometimes goals are established within a curriculum, and teachers must help all students accomplish the same goals. At other times, teachers must help students set and reach their own goals.

*F*IGURE 10.7 **Teachers' Skills**   These skills underlie teachers' abilities to understand students, set goals, create learning environments, evaluate student learning, and communicate.

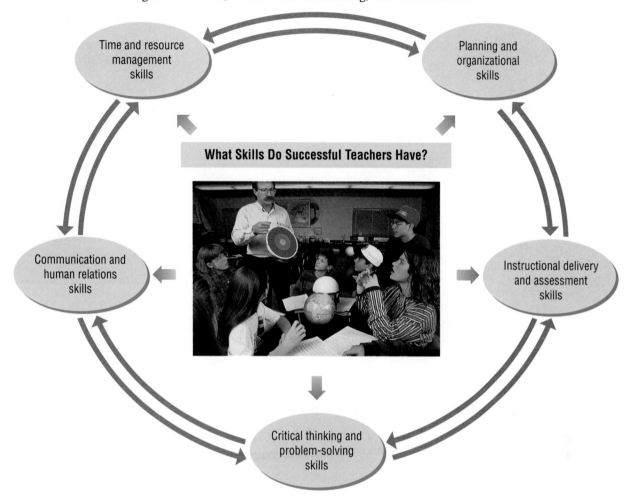

Communicating expectations for success and reinforcing success when it occurs are two of the most important skills a teacher exhibits. Teachers must state their expectations clearly so that students understand. They also must recognize students' successes and acknowledge their failures. If feedback is infrequent or unclear, students may not know if they have met or exceeded their teachers' or their own expectations. Furthermore, teachers must help students judge their own progress.

Creating Learning Environments

A great teacher is part artist, part scientist (Gage, 1978). Successful teachers adapt general principles of effective teaching to help students get involved in their work and stay that way. Successful teachers also have many ways to help students succeed and to feel good about themselves.

From her experience of teaching mathematics, Marilyn Burns offers a set of practical lessons for teachers that seem relevant to the creation of learning environments in all subject areas:

1. Whatever you do, create a clear structure at the beginning of the year. (Spend the first month helping children learn how to be effective learners.)
2. For sane planning, organize your year into units (whole-class lessons; a menu of independent activities for partners, individuals, or groups to work on).

Cultural Awareness

ÉXITO PARA TODOS

Éxito para Todos is the Spanish version of the Success for All program. The curricula are not translations from English, but consist of books and materials appropriate to the children's culture and language.

Like the Success for All mode, Éxito para Todos stresses the importance of early academic success. Éxito incorporates a number of prevention and intervention strategies designed to ensure that the Spanish-speaking children in a school develop strong foundations in reading in Spanish in the early grades. English as a Second Language instruction is closely coordinated with reading instruction in Éxito para Todos. The Éxito program is based on research findings suggesting that Spanish-dominant students perform better when they succeed in learning to read and write in Spanish in the early grades and then are supported in making a transition to English reading in the upper elementary grades.

Critical Thinking Questions

Bilingual programs are the subject of controversy all over the country. Do you think young children should learn reading and content in their native languages? Why or why not?

 To answer these questions online and e-mail your answer to your professor, go to Chapter 10 of the Companion Website (ablongman. com/mcnergney4e) and click on Cultural Awareness.

Source: Éxito para Todos (Spanish Bilingual Adaptation of Success for All). Downloaded from the World Wide Web (September 12, 1999). Available online: http://www.ed.gov/pubs/ToolsforSchools/ept.html.

3. Give students choices; this helps to motivate them.

4. Remember that children can often do more than you think they can.

5. Focus on basic facts and emphasize reasoning; these are not mutually exclusive activities.

6. Talk less in class; have children talk more.

7. Want to know what children are learning? Ask them to write about it.

8. Use homework as a vehicle to inform parents about children's learning. (1995, pp. 87–88).

Adapting Instruction for Students with Special Needs

Every child is special in some particular way. Students' needs, abilities, and interests can be helpful guides for determining how best to plan for and teach them. For example, kindergarten teachers give their students books with more pictures than words, because the children are only beginning to read and are easily overwhelmed. Chemistry teachers teach high school students about molecular bonding before they teach cell signaling, because students could not understand the latter without the former. The challenge in most teaching circumstances is to find out what students know and can do and move them forward, sometimes each in his or her own way.

Three general approaches exist for adapting instruction to differences among learners. Each has its own potential strengths and weaknesses.

The first approach is to remediate students' learning problems. If students cannot organize their thoughts to write a paper, for instance, teachers show them how to use outlining or concept-mapping techniques. In truth, teachers spend their lives, often with the assistance of parents, helping students overcome deficiencies. The appeal of remediation is obvious. It's also a matter of common sense: If students knew everything, why would they go to school? The basic idea behind teaching is to help students acquire and apply new knowledge. It can be fun to explore new intellectual territory and learn to behave in ways that are new and different.

However, this strategy has the potential to spiral downward. When everything is remediated, students may feel like they are too dumb to learn anything. Instead of being excited to learn, they may come to believe their teacher has little confidence in their abilities. In turn, students play their roles by living down to their teacher's low expectations.

The second approach is to compensate for student deficiencies that no one will ever be able to correct. Such deficiencies include poor eyesight, a small stature, or any other physical or mental setback a student may have. To compensate, teachers can say things like "If you can't see the chalkboard, take a seat closer to the front of the room," "If you can't do long division in your head, use a calculator," and "Too small for football, try wrestling." Good teachers encourage students to try new things, but they do not encourage them to pursue the impossible. And they must never make students feel bad for things beyond their control.

But what if a teacher misreads a student's capabilities and expects too little? The downside of compensating for students' weaknesses may be failing to challenge them or denying them the opportunity to learn to cope with failure. Educational history has many examples of people conquering adversity, triumphing over weakness, and doing the impossible. Knowing when and how far to push students—and when to back off—can be a hard decision.

The third approach is to capitalize on what students do well and prefer to do. Teachers know that students cannot spend all their time doing what they like to do and do well. They need to be challenged to think and behave in new ways. Yet the really great teachers learn to look for student success and build on it, so they can help students gain power over their own educational lives. "You like to read mysteries? Great, try *The Hound of the Baskervilles*." "You are an amazing piano player. You should apply for summer music camp at the university." "You are one of the few students in class who speaks two languages. Would you please write your next paper on what it is like to live in a multilingual home?" These are examples of ways teachers can use students' existing interests and abilities to further pursue learning experiences. Such occasions can also make students feel proud of what they already know, making them more willing to pursue something new.

Evaluating Student Learning

Teachers must be able to decide what works in teaching and what does not. They have access to a variety of information about students that can help them make such decisions. They can use formal measures, such as tests and quizzes, and informal measures, such as questionnaires, interviews, and observations of in-class behaviors.

Teachers make judgments daily about students' academic performance, their attitudes and interests, and their ability to work with others. Such information enables teachers to (1) determine what students already know and want to know about topics, (2) plan instruction that is appropriately challenging, (3) motivate student performance, (4) assess progress toward affective and cognitive goals, and (5) communicate progress to others.

Typically, the best indicator of students' performance is their classwork. Two types of assessment are used for classwork: formative and summative. Formative assessment is conducted while a lesson is in progress to discover information about students' errors, misunderstandings, understandings, and progress. Teachers can use this information to shape new plans that will improve student performance (Frieberg & Driscoll, 1996). Summative assessment is conducted at the end of a lesson, unit, or course to allow students to demonstrate what they have learned.

Teachers have a responsibility to use the best information available about students before making evaluative decisions. This means assessing students frequently and using procedures that allow students to demonstrate what they can do. After collecting information, teachers are obligated to protect its privacy, recognize the limits of its use in decision making, and not use it to demean or ridicule a pupil (Airasian, 2000).

*H*ow Do Teachers Manage Students Effectively?

What is the key to effective classroom management? Classrooms are often "crowded, competitive, contradictory, multidimensional, simultaneous, unpredictable, public . . . [places where] teachers work with captive groups of students on academic agendas that students have not helped to set" (Weinstein & Mignano, 2003, pp. 56). Teachers who understand the complexity of classrooms realize the importance of finding ways to gain students' cooperation. Through careful planning with many other people, these teachers can prevent problems from occurring. **Classroom management,** then, is the collective ability of teachers, students, administrators, school boards, and even police and the courts to establish a common framework for social and academic interactions (Doyle, 1986; Frieberg, Stein, & Huang, 1995; Wolfgang, Bennett, & Irvin, 1999).

Classroom management does not concern only discipline. Successful teachers create total systems of management that address various aspects of behavior. As Jere Brophy (1988, 1996) has argued, a classroom management system is designed to maximize student engagement, not merely to minimize misconduct. Teachers who create and maintain classrooms as caring communities are more successful than teachers who assert their roles as authority figures and disciplinarians.

Research Informs Teacher Management Behavior

Jacob Kounin's (1970) classic research on classroom management and discipline is timeless. He filmed hundreds of hours of teacher–student classroom interactions,

*U*sing *classroom management techniques, successful teachers create an environment that maximizes student engagement in learning.*

preschool through college levels. From his research he learned teachers often created problems for themselves. Many teachers behaved in ways that actually encouraged students to become uninvolved in classroom activities and to misbehave.

Kounin suggests that good classroom managers motivate students to get involved in learning. They prevent student boredom by varying tasks and by maintaining momentum. They avoid giving too many directions or lengthy explanations. They stop activities when students become restless and make smooth transitions from one activity to the next. The intent is to maximize student involvement and to minimize disruptions.

When disruptions occur, Kounin suggests tactics teachers can use to stop problems from escalating—tactics such as "with-it-ness" and "overlapping" behaviors. A teacher who is "with it" seems to have eyes in the back of her head. Aware of what is going on, this teacher stops students who are misbehaving and gets them back on task. Overlapping, which is a teacher's ability to handle more than one thing at a time, can occur when a teacher working with a small group of students also manages a disruption in another part of the room.

Ed Emmer and his colleagues (Emmer, Evertson, & Anderson, 1980) found that the tone teachers set in the beginning of the year affects the entire year. When teachers are organized and prepared at the start of the school year, they give students the impression that things will run smoothly. In most cases that initial impression becomes reality. In addition, when teachers teach and reteach desirable behaviors, they reinforce a classroom community where people respect each other.

Here are a few dos and don'ts from research on classroom management and discipline:

- Be motivated yourself, and communicate why—students are likely to catch the bug.
- Never demean or embarrass students.
- Help students learn to manage themselves.
- Look for ways to reduce their confusion and increase their involvement in activities.
- Make sure students understand what you expect from them.
- Build on what students already know—it helps them succeed and keeps them involved.
- Reinforce success! Reinforce success! Reinforce success!

Relationships between Teachers and Students

Personal relationships help shape how people behave and get along with one another. Educational research is full of examples of counseling and personal development approaches that are useful for defining and managing how classroom relationships should function. As any guidance counselor would tell you, a classroom management system must be based on respectful relationships between teachers and students if it has any hope of being effective (Henderson and Gysbers, 1998).

What teachers expect from students is a powerful prediction of what they will get. Robert Rosenthal and Leonore Jacobson (1968) were among the first researchers to speak of students' "self-fulfilling prophecies," or students' tendencies to behave in ways they believe teachers expect. Other researchers have further explained the influence of teacher expectations not only on teacher–student relationships and student classroom behavior, but on student achievement as well (Brophy and Good, 1971, 1974; Good and Brophy, 2003). Like Kounin before them, Good and Brophy suggest that teachers create problems for themselves and for students by communicating their expectations differently—sometimes inappropriately—to high and low achievers. In this sense, if teachers expect little from students, students will pick up on it and behave accordingly. If teachers don't expect low-achieving students to try as hard as everyone else, why would

Technology in Practice

AMPLIFYING TEACHERS' VOICES

If you ask teachers about their pet peeves, they might mention the frustration of having to talk over the hum of an air conditioning unit, the buzz from the lawnmower just outside the classroom window, or the shrieks of laughter coming from the playground. According to Evelyn Williams—director of audiology for the Rockville, Maryland-based American Speech-Language-Hearing Association—acoustics in classrooms are affected by background noises inside and outside the classroom, how much the teacher's voice bounces around the room, and how loud the teacher's voice is compared to competing sounds.

While carpeting helps with acoustics, Williams and other educators contend it is not enough. For that reason, Sparks Elementary School in Baltimore, Maryland, and a growing number of schools are equipping classrooms with wireless microphones. "It really saves your voice," said Ms. Maltese, a twenty-eight-year veteran. Ms. Maltese wears a small lapel microphone that she sometimes extends to soft-spoken students, so students can

also hear one another's responses. She wants students to learn not just from her, but from their peers as well.

When Sheila Guttman, a teacher at Sparks Elementary, had to go ten weeks without her microphone while it was being repaired, she lost her voice a couple of times and suffered several sore throats:

they try at all? Good and Brophy call the teacher behaviors listed in Table 10.2 "danger signals" if they occur often and on many levels.

Classroom Management: An Environment of Self-Control

Teachers demonstrate many techniques to encourage student self-control. For one, teachers use nonverbal signals to alert students that they recognize inappropriate behavior. Teachers use physical proximity—they move closer to students—to communicate disapproval. They show interest in students' appropriate behavior, and they ignore inappropriate student behavior. Teachers help students who need it, thus helping students help themselves, while decreasing the odds of student misbehavior. Teachers often help students by restructuring or rescheduling activities, removing distractions, or removing students from troubling situations. Teachers set routines and help students know what to expect. All these tactics teach students how to control themselves in a classroom environment by communicating what is acceptable behavior and what is not.

Trying to build a classroom community where people manage themselves in appropriate, productive, and respectful ways is a bit like looking for the secret of life. Once, when the Dalai Lama was at a gathering in New York City's Central Park, a young woman asked him, with the proper respect due the leader of Tibetan Buddhism, what he believed was the secret of life. He wrinkled his brow in thought for a moment then said with a large smile, "Be nice."

In teaching as in life, to be nice can be a sign of strength, not a sign of weakness. To smile costs nothing. To enjoy being around others is to make oneself enjoyable to be around. These simple acts may have more to do with building productive, self-regulating classrooms than we typically acknowledge.

At first, "none of us really wanted to wear these things," said Ms. Guttman. "But once you get used to it, it's hard to go back to raising your voice." And her students could tell the difference, too. Without the amplification system, "you couldn't hear her questions," said Tim Butler, a student in Ms. Guttman's third-grade class.

Student chatter also rose significantly while the system wasn't being used. . . . To illustrate the point, Ms. Guttman turned her microphone off and held a brief conversation with Mr. Ellis [the principal]. As she turned back to the students, who were all talking, she asked them to quiet down without using the microphone. Some twenty-eight students quieted down, but most kept talking. When Ms. Guttman turned on the microphone and asked the class to settle down again, the room fell silent.

According to teachers and speech and language experts, children with and without hearing impairments benefit from the new technology, because students can hear their teacher's voice from any location in the classroom. In a sense, the wireless microphones place everyone on a front-row seat—particularly important for students who do not hear well and for children with attention problems.

Critical Thinking Questions

Have you ever been a student in a school that used sound-amplification systems? If so, did you find them helpful? If not, can you think of any classes where you might have benefited from having the teachers' and students' voices amplified?

 To answer these questions online and e-mail your answer to your professor, go to Chapter 10 of the Companion Website (ablongman.com/mcnergney4e) and click on Technology in Practice.

Source: Galley, M. (2002, May 15). Classroom microphones make voice louder, clearer. *Education Week,* Available online: http://www.edweek.org/ew/newstory.cfm?slug=36headset.h21&keywords=technology.

---

*T*ABLE 10.2 **How Teachers May Treat High and Low Achievers Differently**

1. Waiting less time for lows to answer a question before giving the answer or calling on someone else
2. Giving lows answers or calling on someone else, rather than trying to improve their responses by giving clues or repeating or rephrasing questions
3. Inappropriate reinforcement: rewarding inappropriate behavior or incorrect answers by lows
4. Criticizing lows more often for failure
5. Praising lows less often for success
6. Failing to give feedback to the public responses of lows
7. Generally paying less attention to lows or interacting with them less frequently
8. Calling on lows less often to respond to questions or asking them only easier, nonanalytic questions
9. Seating lows farther away from the teacher
10. Demanding less from lows
11. Interacting with lows more privately than publicly, and monitoring and structuring their activities more closely
12. Differential administration or grading of tests or assignments, in which highs but not lows are given the benefit of the doubt in borderline cases
13. Less friendly interactions with lows, including less smiling and fewer other nonverbal indicators of support
14. Briefer and less informative feedback to questions of lows
15. Less eye contact and other nonverbal communication of attention and responsiveness
16. Less use of effective but time-consuming instructional methods with lows when time is limited
17. Less acceptance and use of lows' ideas
18. Exposing lows to an impoverished curriculum

Source: Good, T. L., & Brophy, J. E. (2000). *Looking in classrooms* (8th ed.). New York: Addison Wesley Longman, Inc., pp. 85–86.

Summary

Curriculum as we know it in schools takes many forms. You can see and touch it in books, study materials, and other physical artifacts. The expectations that teachers communicate to their students also constitute a kind of curriculum. Some curriculum is "extra" or outside normal academic requirements. And sometimes curricula are integrated around themes or particular issues.

Curriculum represents various conceptions of the knowledge, skills, and values considered critical to success in later life. Most all curriculum has been shaped by powerful forces, both inside and outside the educational world. Our elected and appointed leaders use their visibility to advance ideas that influence curriculum. Public opinion, professional education groups, and vocal individuals all work to influence the curriculum in its many forms. Influential interests in publishing and the mass media also play important roles in what is taught and learned in schools across the nation.

Teachers deliver curriculum through instruction. The forms of instruction they use depend largely on what is to be taught and on the student's needs and abilities. Clearly identifiable models of teaching are based on both theory and research. These models or strategies enable teachers to help students to develop personally, socially, cognitively, behaviorally, and academically.

Effective teaching—teaching that helps students learn—depends on teachers' abilities to understand what students know and can do. Effective teachers create environments that complement and supplement students' abilities. They assess student progress and give feedback on student performance that reinforces desirable behavior. Effective teachers are good communicators and good managers, helping students take control of their own learning.

Terms and Concepts

behavioral objectives   286
classroom management   296
concept formation   289
cooperative learning   288
curriculum   271
curriculum map   285
direct instruction   286
explicit curriculum   271
extracurriculum   273
implicit curriculum   271

inquiry learning   290
instructional model   285
integrated curriculum   273
mastery learning   285
nondirective model   290
null curriculum   272
project-based learning   289
synectics   289
teacher planning   284

Reflective Practice

Making Real-Life Connections

Bob Dunleavy approached the kick-off of his geography unit with unbridled enthusiasm. He had loved history as a kid, but geography was his favorite subject. Just as his mentor had done for him, he wanted to excite students about a subject that is too often minimized in the curriculum.

He was determined to wrap important concepts from classical geography study in a captivating story about the students' hometown, Greenville, South Carolina. He would use this story to encourage students to do their own research on a community they knew on the surface but probably did not appreciate fully. Only then, he thought, would his students engage in geography with the enthusiasm that the discipline deserved.

Bob knew that from the time of the earliest European settlers the natural advantages of Greenville County propelled the area toward prosperity. The cultural background of the settlers was one of hard work and attention to quality. From the beginning, they had exhibited the desire to capitalize on the industrial potential of the area. The people foresaw opportunities for economic development that they had dreamed of in the old country.

Rivers and waterfalls provided abundant natural power. By the 1920s, Greenville was the textile center of the world because of a nearby supply of cotton. Transportation facilities and a booming economy made Greenville one of the most successful industrial centers in the world.

The textile industry waned in modern times, to be replaced by new business and industry. Much of the new development was fueled by international investment. Open land, low taxes, reasonable cost of living, and forward-thinking government have made Greenville not only a good place to work and live, but a modern case study of the relevance of geography to everyday life.

Issues, Problems, Dilemmas, and Opportunities

What will Bob want to know about local and state educational standards before planning his unit on the importance of Greenville geography?

Perceive and Value

Why might Bob want to make certain that his students think about Greenville from the points of view of foreign investors? How might he use examples of German investment in a local BMW plant to teach curricular issues of international cooperation and competition?

Know and Act

What might Bob want his students to know about the importance of "connections" and community development? How might he introduce and reinforce concepts of "connections" using links between resources and manufacturing, suppliers and producers, marketing and consumption?

Evaluate

If you were Bob, how might you judge your students' understanding of the importance of place, or physical geography, in modern civic decision making?

INTASC Principle 7

The teacher plans instruction based upon knowledge of subject matter, students, the community, and curriculum goals.

Knowledge

The teacher knows how to take contextual considerations (instructional materials; individual student interests, needs, and aptitudes; and community resources) into account in planning instruction that creates an effective bridge between curriculum goals and students' experiences. (Interstate New Teacher Assessment and Support Consortium, 1992)

Discussion Questions

What should Bob do to learn more about the experiences, needs, and aptitudes of his students that might affect the success of this unit?

Additional Readings

Bloom, B. S. (Ed.) (1956). *Taxonomy of educational objectives; the classification of educational goals, by a committee of college and university examiners.* New York: Longman, Green.

Eisner, E. (1982). *Cognition and curriculum: A basis for deciding what to teach.* New York: Longman.

Good, T. L., & Brophy, J. E. (2000). *Looking in classrooms* (8th ed.) New York: Longman.

Joyce, B. R., Weil, M., & Calhoun, E. (2000). *Models of teaching.* Boston: Allyn and Bacon.

Tyler, R. W. (1950). *Basic principles of curriculum and instruction.* Chicago: University of Chicago Press.

Web Resources

http://www.ncte.org

The website for the National Council of Teachers of English offers a variety of resources for teaching reading, writing, and the English language arts to elementary, middle, and high school teachers.

http://www.nctm.org/

Visit the National Council of Teachers of Mathematics to learn more about mathematics standards, grant opportunities, and online resources for teachers.

http://www.aahperd.org/naspe/template.cfm

The website for the National Association for Sport and Physical Education describes quality physical education programs.

http://www.socialstudies.org

The National Council for Social Studies provides online publications, teaching resources, and curriculum information for educators.

http://nap.edu/html/nses/html/

This website describes the National Science Education Standards. You can read the teaching, content, and program standards before focusing on the professional development, assessment, and systems standards.

http://www.menc.org/

The National Association for Music Education encourages the use of music to celebrate our cultural heritages and to provide students with opportunities to develop new knowledge through expression, imagination, and creation.

Video**Workshop** Extra!

If the VideoWorkshop package was included with your textbook, go to Chapter 10 of the Companion Website (www.ablongman.com/mcnergney4e) and click on VideoWorkshop. Follow the instructions for viewing video clip 8. Then consider this information along with what you've read in Chapter 10 while answering the following questions.

1. This chapter presents several characteristics of effective instruction. Use what you know about these characteristics and determine which ones contribute most to meaningful curriculum planning (see the video clip).

2. The video clip presents the idea that curriculum enhances classroom management. Which social strategies discussed in the chapter might also encourage constructive, effective classroom environments?

Recognizing Educational Success: Standards and Assessment

"I did not cheat." That was the message from a teary-eyed but resolute Wendy Lou Waller, who . . . spoke publicly for the first time since resigning [a week earlier]. The Chesapeake teacher was accused of improperly helping her fifth-graders on a state test.

Flanked by her attorneys, she described how she reviewed Virginia Standards of Learning material with her students using a state teacher's guide at the direction of the school division. She said she quit, effective at school year's end, to stop school investigators from questioning and upsetting her students.

Chesapeake public schools spokesman Thomas A. Cupitt relayed Schools Superintendent W. Randolph Nichols' reassertion that officials can't discuss details of the case due to legal reasons.

But, Cupitt added, "If she said she did nothing wrong, we do disagree with that." (Bowers, 2001, p. 1)

This case of a teacher being accused of helping her students cheat on a standardized test is an extremely rare event in the history of American education—yet some variation

CHAPTER CONTENTS
How Do We Know What Works in Education?

What Types of Classroom Assessments Do Teachers Use?

How Can Teachers Know If They Are Assessing Students Fairly?

of this scene can loom large in teachers' nightmares. These days everyone seems to be interested in developing standards and evaluating schools, teachers, and students. With standardized tests becoming a main factor when judging the success or failure of schools across the country, pressure is on teachers and students to perform well. Indeed, evaluating students' performance, development, and knowledge is a necessary and helpful part of the educational process. But setting standards and evaluating students also can be one of the hardest and most closely watched parts of a teacher's job. The purpose of this chapter is to explore the place of standards in modern public education and to describe teachers' responsibilities for assessing students fully and fairly.

How Do We Know What Works in Education?

How can we convince others and ourselves that what teachers do makes a difference in students' lives? Deciding if an educational program or activity is valuable is always a matter of answering this question: Compared to what? **Standards** in education are the necessary or required levels of knowledge and ability a student should possess—they are the benchmarks against which we can compare programs, teaching, and learning. Standards are determined in various ways and from multiple sources. Some are defined by the school or by the teachers themselves. Other standards of educational quality are set by outside sources, such as professional education associations and state education departments.

Standards can also vary in what they measure. Some, such as **content standards,** represent the knowledge, skills, and attitudes students must attain in order to master a subject matter. For example, a fifth-grade student might be expected to use whole numbers, fractions, and decimals to solve math problems. **Performance standards,** on the other hand, indicate the level at which students should be able to use the knowledge they possess to solve problems. Thus a fifth-grader might be expected to correctly solve nine out of ten word problems requiring the use of whole numbers, fractions, and decimals.

Assessment and **measurement** are synonyms for formal attempts to determine students' knowledge, skills, and attitudes. **Evaluation** is the process of examining student performance to determine whether students have met or exceeded standards of performance set by the teacher. Although the topic of standards and assessment can be rather controversial, most people would agree they are necessary parts of the educational process. We can predict how students will respond to certain teaching methods, what they will learn from various curriculum designs, and how teacher training will influence students' acquisition of knowledge. In truth, though, these are all predictions and educated guesses. Until and unless students are evaluated according to educational standards, we do not know for certain whether our planning is effective or how well students are learning anything at all. It is important to remember that students' performance on assessment or evaluation measures is a direct indication of how well they are being taught. We cannot expect students to know what they have not been taught. In this way, assessment is as important for educators as it is for students.

Personal Standards

How do personal standards influence one's judgment of educational quality? In terms of education most of us judge quality by comparing it to what we value. The comparisons might be simple and casually made. For instance, a student might say, "I like Mr. Jackson's class. I am learning the material, and he treats me like what I have to say is important. I think it is valuable for students to learn and to feel good about themselves. Mr. Jackson cares about me. Mr. Jackson is a good teacher." From her statements, this student appears to use her conceptions of caring and learning as standards for judging a teacher's effectiveness.

Other personal assessments of educational quality can be elaborate and carefully made. For example, your own personal philosophy might suggest that good teachers do not behave the same way with all students. Instead, they take their lead from students' differing needs and abilities, and they tailor teaching to fit students' present conditions. You might think, "If students change for the better as a result of working with a teacher who behaves in this fashion, then I judge that teacher to be good."

To gather information for your judgments or standards, you would probably make several observations and ask many questions of different people. You would be seeking evidence of students' needs and abilities, of students' differences, of "tailored instruction," of changes in both students and teaching over time, and so forth. The answers to the questions in addition to your observations would help you decide whether a teacher measured up to your personal standards for effective teaching.

Likewise, if you are a supporter of equal opportunity in education, you might judge programs and curricula by how well they meet the needs of all the students in the classroom. If you value competitiveness, you might believe a cooperative classroom environment is ineffective. Traditionalists might label a school unsuccessful if it offered bilingual classes but did not offer Latin. All these judgments are based on people's personal standards for effective teaching and valuable education.

National Goals and Standards

Where is the nation headed, educationally speaking? President George Bush and the nation's governors unveiled the National Education Goals in 1989, the six goals shown in Figure 11.1. In 2000, President William Clinton and Congress added two more goals, one for teacher quality and one for parental involvement. Every major parent, education, and business group across the country endorsed these goals as soon as they were announced. Although people realized that many of the goals would remain unmet for years to come, the goals themselves raised nationwide concern for quality education. The National Goals continue to offer direction for educational change (Hoff, 1999).

How are the National Education Goals relevant to a new teacher? In essence, the National Goals form a political document or statement of values for nationwide education. They drive the development of many sets of national standards and guidelines in particular curricular areas. These standards and guidelines—specific statements about what is to be taught and learned—hold special interest for teachers who are ultimately responsible for ensuring that students succeed in school.

Other groups have created similar national standards, including the National Council of Teachers of English, the Center for Civic Education, and the National Academy of Sciences. The National Council of Teachers of Mathematics (NCTM) stands as an excellent example of how one national organization designed and explained mathematics standards. Their standards specifically outline what material should be covered and what methods should be used to teach students from prekindergarten through high school. As shown in Figure 11.2, NCTM teaching standards are complemented by general expectations for student performance. These standards and expectations are strengthened through the use of elaborate explanations and graphics meant to help teachers guide their students to perform appropriately (National Council of Teachers of Mathematics, 2000). Standards such as these help teachers prepare lesson plans for specific topics. They also help teachers stay on course with a national curriculum for a subject.

*F*IGURE 11.1 **National Education Goals**

Goal 1:   **Ready to Learn**   All children in America will start school ready to learn.

Goal 2:   **School Completion**   The high school graduation rate will increase to at least 90 percent.

Goal 3:   **Student Achievement and Citizenship**   All students will leave grades 4, 8, and 12 having demonstrated competency over challenging subject matter including English, mathematics, science, foreign languages, civics and government, economics, the arts, history, and geography, and every school in America will ensure that all students learn to use their minds well, so they may be prepared for responsible citizenship, further learning, and productive employment in our Nation's modern economy.

Goal 4:   **Teacher Education and Professional Development**   The Nation's teaching force will have access to programs for the continued improvement of their professional skills and the opportunity to acquire the knowledge and skills needed to instruct and prepare all American students for the next century.

Goal 5:   **Mathematics and Science**   United States students will be first in the world in mathematics and science achievement.

Goal 6:   **Adult Literacy and Lifelong Learning**   Every adult American will be literate and will possess the knowledge and skills necessary to compete in a global economy and exercise the rights and responsibilities of citizenship.

Goal 7:   **Safe and Disciplined Alcohol- and Drug-Free Schools**   Every school in the United States will be free of drugs, violence, and the unauthorized presence of firearms and alcohol and will offer a disciplined environment conducive to learning.

Goal 8:   **Parent Participation**   Every school will promote partnerships that will increase parental involvement and participation in promoting the social, emotional, and academic growth of children.

Source: From National Education Goals Panel (1998). *National education goals: Building a nation of learners.* Available online: http://negp.gov/webpg10.htm.

The Nation's Report Card

How are we to know if the nation is reaching its goals?   The National Assessment of Educational Progress (NAEP) is a survey designed to give policymakers and the general public information about the academic achievement of students across the United States. It serves as one kind of benchmark against which specific educational programs can be compared. The U.S. Department of Education refers to the NAEP as the Nation's Report Card—one specific set of assessment results on which we can judge progress toward some of our National Education Goals.

Since 1969, the NAEP has been administered annually to samples of students in grades four, eight, and twelve. The survey is not based on any particular curriculum. Instead, the NAEP uses broad assessment frameworks that describe the knowledge and skills being evaluated in each subject area. In other words, the NAEP is a general survey of students' knowledge in particular subject areas at various points in their educational careers, no matter what type of school they attend.

Education reformers view the NAEP as a stimulus to change teaching. Results from the survey indicate areas where U.S. students in general are strong and weak. The results are also useful because they offer a comparative view over time. For instance, the results might show that on average fourth and eighth grade students meet reading standards for

FIGURE 11.2 Geometry Standard for Prekindergarten to Grade 2   4.3 Learning Geometry and Measurement Concepts by Creating Paths and Navigating Mazes: Hiding Ladybug

Hiding Ladybug

Making Rectangles

Ladybug Mazes

The three-part ladybug example presents a rich computer environment in which young students can use their knowledge of numbers, measurement, and geometry to solve interesting problems. Planning and visualizing, estimating and measuring, and testing and revising are components of the ladybug activities. These interactive figures can help students build ideas about navigation and location, as described in the Geometry Standard, and use these ideas to solve problems, as described in the Problem Solving Standard. In the first part, Hiding Ladybug, students create a path that enables the ladybug to hide under a leaf. In the second part, Making Rectangles, students plan the steps necessary for the ladybug to draw rectangles of different sizes. In the last part, Ladybug Mazes, students plan a series of moves that will take the ladybug through a maze.

their age, but by the twelfth grade the average student is below the standard level. As a result, the NAEP can indicate subjects that need to be emphasized more than they presently are. These surveys therefore can inform teachers' decisions about lesson plans, teaching methods, and classroom management. For example, a teacher might reconsider the effectiveness of group work on science projects if NAEP results are low for science.

Although many believe the current NAEP surveys are useful, some assessment experts recommend that NAEP begin to assess broader definitions of school achievement than it currently measures (National Research Council, 2002). These new, broader concepts might include students' thinking about how problems can be represented, their use of problem-solving strategies and self-regulatory skills, and their explanations and interpretations. To measure these types of achievement, though, would require more than the fifty-minute paper-and-pencil tests on particular survey sections currently used. A broader survey might mean observing students solving problems in small groups or analyzing portfolios that students construct over a long period of time. These complex assessments could yield much more complex information and better directions for teaching.

State Standards

Why are state education standards so important for teachers to understand?

Teachers are most likely to be held accountable for state standards. State school boards and other state-level organizations determine the state standards that all schools must meet. Teachers shape instruction to match the standards, assessing student performance through both teacher-made tests and standardized tests. Because states provide much of the funding for public education, the consequences of meeting or not meeting state standards may ultimately determine the financial support for schools. At the classroom level, students who do not perform to standard may be denied entry to special programs or prevented from graduating. When tests are used in this manner, they are often referred to as **high-stakes tests.**

Although most states have their own sets of standards and tests for determining if the standards are being met, Maryland has been a leader in the development and use of state standards. They are a good example of what can be done to encourage the teaching and testing of both lower- and higher-level thinking in students. The Maryland Learner Outcomes are state standards developed by Maryland educators that were approved by the State Board of Education in 1990. They specify what students should know and be able to do as a result of their educational experiences. The Maryland State Performance Assessment Program (MSPAP) is designed to evaluate how well schools are teaching the basic and complex skills outlined in the standards. The MSPAP consists of **performance tests**—assessments that produce observable indications of how well students can apply what they have learned—in reading, mathematics, writing, language usage, science, and social studies for students in grades three, five, and eight.

The MSPAP measures a broad range of knowledge and skill competencies. Tasks require students to respond to questions or directions that lead to a solution for a prob-

Issues in School Reform

URBAN ACADEMY—WHERE TESTING IS ANYTHING BUT STANDARD

The faculty at New York City's Urban Academy is committed to individualizing teaching, learning, and assessment. Performance assessment is the primary means for determining whether student work meets state standards. Classes at Urban are unlike what you'd find at many schools throughout the country:

Here, teachers don't lecture or use textbooks as students' primary source of information on everything from algebraic formulas to the Civil Rights movement. Instead, they facilitate discussion groups, create their own curriculum, and from the first day begin to foster in students a commitment to inquiry and a respect for different opinions.

In a constitutional law class, for example, students break into teams that are charged with the task of arguing a case before the Supreme Court. Another group of students serves as the distinguished panel of judges, asking questions, poking holes in arguments, and challenging their classmates to use the law, not their own personal opinions, to defend their positions. Joining in the critique and the discussion is a group of attorneys from a Manhattan law firm. Their presence provides a real-world connection for students and sends a powerful reminder that their opinions, their analysis, and their perspectives matter. . . .

Torri Gamble's literature proficiency was based on a reading of the book *Sula* by Toni Morrison. She

discussed it with a mentor teacher, identifying themes, asking questions about interesting or difficult passages, and relating it back to other works of literature. Then, when she felt confident in her understanding of the work, she had a conversation with an outside assessor, Sehila Kosoft, who holds a degree in literature and is a Toni Morrison devotee.

The assessment system used at Urban Academy can be time consuming for students and teachers, because several faculty members may review a single student product before it is considered complete. Does the extra effort pay off? Based on the percentage of students accepted to college (91 percent compared to a citywide average of 62 percent), Urban Academy's approach seems to be working well.

Critical Thinking Questions

How do the curriculum and assessment at Urban Academy compare to your high school program? Why might teachers' use of performance assessment be demanding yet rewarding?

To answer these questions online and e-mail your answers to your professor, go to Chapter 11 of the Companion Website (ablongman.com/mcnergney4e) and click on Issues in School Reform.

Source: Roberta Furger (2002, Feb. 11) Urban Academy: Where testing is anything but standard. *Edutopia.* Available online: http://glef.org/.

lem. They also might be asked to make a recommendation or decision or to explain the reasons for their responses. Some tasks assess one content area; others assess multiple content areas. For instance, a mathematics task may be explained in the form of a long, detailed paragraph that would test both students' math and reading comprehension skills. Tasks may encompass group or individual activities; hands-on, observation, or reading activities; and activities that require extended written responses, limited written responses, lists, charts, graphs, diagrams, and/or drawings.

MSPAP tasks assess basic as well as higher-level skills and knowledge. In terms of basic knowledge, they measure reading for general understanding, writing to communicate clearly, making accurate arithmetic calculations, understanding key scientific concepts, and identifying historical and geographic information. For higher-level knowledge, the tests include tasks such as supporting an answer with information, predicting an outcome and comparing results to the prediction, and comparing and contrasting information (Maryland State Department of Education, 2000). See Figure 11.3 for an example of an MSPAP question for third graders.

*F*IGURE 11.3 **The MSPAP in Action**   Here is how a third-grade student might describe an assessment task that requires test takers to plan a zoo:

1. **Teacher gives us floor plans.**   My teacher says we're going to imagine that some people planning a new zoo in our town have asked our class to help. In our activity papers, there are pictures of three floor plans for three different animals in our zoo—a giraffe, a polar bear, and an elephant. The key says that each little square on the plan is equal to one square foot of real space. Next, we have to build a fence around each cage and figure out how much it will cost. Fencing costs $8.00 per foot, so we have to count each side of a square going around the cage. Once we find this number, it's easy to multiply it by 8 on our calculators to find out how much putting a fence around each cage will cost.

2. **More measuring and planning.**   Now we have to put some flooring in the cages to make the animals more comfortable. Each square foot of flooring costs $4.00. We have to figure out how much the flooring for each cage will cost. The easy way is just to count the squares. Then we multiply that number by 4 to find out how much it will cost to put a floor in each cage.

3. **Each animal has special needs.**   The giraffe needs a square feed box measuring four square feet, and it has to be placed in the cage so the animal can get around it on all sides. I draw a box around four squares in the cage. Since the box isn't touching any walls, the giraffe will be able to move around it on all sides. The polar bear needs a swimming pool with a perimeter of twelve feet, and the pool should be in a corner of the cage. I draw a figure against one of the corners of the cage, making sure that the perimeter equals 12. The elephant needs two trees. The elephant is easy to please. I just draw two boxes that have the same size and shape.

4. **Creating a tile pattern.**   Our zoo will have an information office, and since we want everything to look nice, we have to make up a repeating pattern for the tiles on the floor of the office. I remember the pattern of our tiles in the kitchen at home. They look like a checker board. So I color in every other box in the rows of squares until it looks like our kitchen at home. I write a sentence about how I came up with the pattern. Then we're finished. Everybody had a lot of fun planning our zoo. It doesn't seem so hard now to plan something like a zoo, or maybe something else, like a bridge or something. I bet that's not as hard as it looks either.

Source: Maryland Standards © 1995 Maryland State Department of Education. Non-exclusive permission to use granted. All other rights reserved by MSDE. Available online: http://www.mdk12.org/mspp/mspap/ 3_eyes.html.

Opportunity Standards

How might standards spread educational accountability to those in charge?
Opportunity standards (sometimes called **opportunity-to-learn standards**) are meant to hold school leaders—school board members and administrators—accountable for giving students a fair chance to succeed. The point of opportunity standards is simple: those in charge must provide students with appropriate support, in terms of books, materials, machines, highly prepared teachers, time to learn, and other tools, for students to do their work.

For a school to meet an opportunity standard, it must provide the required quantity and quality of resources, practices, and conditions necessary for student success. Supporters of these standards argue that the responsibility to meet such standards lies with the states and the districts, as well as with individual schools.

These standards are largely symbolic, however, because all schools are supposed to be meeting them already. In addition, they are not enforced by any specific organization. Any influence these standards have on actual school policy comes from persuading board members and administrators to abide by them. The intent is clear, however: leaders ought to be as accountable for their behaviors as are teachers and students.

In a unique application of opportunity standards, three education professors in Washington state have come up with an interesting twist on holding state political leaders accountable for education. They have proposed a ballot initiative that would require candidates running for local or state office to take the state's newly enacted tenth grade assessment test and post their scores on the secretary of state's website and in voters' pamphlets.

> "Part of it is the Golden Rule," explained Bob Howard, an assistant professor of education at the University of Washington in Tacoma. "In creating social policy, it seems to be a good idea to create policies that you could live with if they applied to you. If the test is truly essential," he added, "then it seems to me that we should take it seriously and apply it to people other than students." (Olson, 2002)

The professors hope to bring attention to what they view as the inappropriate, high-stakes nature of the exam. Students in the class of 2008 will have to pass the test to graduate.

*W*hat Types of Classroom Assessments Do Teachers Use?

Judging students is a controversial issue. Everybody seems to have an opinion about what it means to be a successful student, as evidenced by the multiple standards and assessments established at various levels. In addition to national and state standardized tests, classroom assessment is an important part of the overall assessment of teaching practices and students' knowledge. Because classroom assessment occurs over long periods of time and takes many different forms, some believe it is the most accurate measure of what students are learning, how well they are progressing, and how effective teaching methods and curricula are. Furthermore, classroom assessments also can say the most about teacher performance, because in measuring what students have learned, we measure what we have taught them. Student assessment should be part of an ongoing process in which teachers develop and revise their teaching plans and methods based on what does or does not work for students.

Assessing students, however, can be one of the more difficult parts of a teacher's job. The process of evaluating students—determining what they should be learning, how that will be tested, and what the results mean—can be particularly nerve wracking for new teachers. The best advice for professionals trying to meet the challenge of student assessment is to specify the goals and objectives of education, determine learners' needs and abilities, and take action to close the gap between where learners are and where they need to be (National Research Council, 2001).

Classroom Assessment Triad

What do new teachers need to know and be able to do regarding assessment to meet their job responsibilities?   Teachers have three responsibilities for classroom assessment. First, teachers need to know what is expected of students. They need a clear view of the learning goals that drive the local educational program. Teachers and students can only move forward together if they know which way to proceed. Second, teachers need to be able to determine what students presently know or can do in relation to these learning goals. This baseline information defines the starting point from which progress can be measured. Third, teachers need instructional strategies and methods to narrow the gap between where students are and where they are expected to be. This third challenge means teachers need to teach based on their readings of students' needs and abilities as identified by classroom assessments.

How do you know if a teacher has properly assessed student progress?
One simple way is to examine how well his students are learning. You could look at students' projects and grades, their classroom participation, and their ability to move on to more difficult material. If students are progressing, we may assume the teacher has properly used assessment results to guide instruction.

In addition, you may ask and try to answer the following questions: Did the teacher provide practical information to meet the needs of his primary audiences—students, parents, colleagues, and administrators? Was his evaluation realistic? Did he behave legally and diplomatically? Was his evaluation accurate—did it gather correct information about student performance? Answers to these questions can help establish whether the teacher correctly understood students' needs and abilities.

Cognition and Learning

How might assessing student thinking help teachers develop successful lessons?
The ways in which students think about their educational tasks can greatly influence their performances. A teacher who understands student thinking—who watches and assesses students' work and asks questions about how students think—can organize instruction to fit students' needs and abilities. Being in tune with students' feelings and attitudes is one sure way to know what appeals to them and what does not. From there, it becomes easier to develop lesson plans that will engage students.

Here is how this strategy can work in a math class. Given the math problem $2 + 4 = ?$, most students use the strategy of counting on from the first addend (e.g., the student thinks 2 plus 1 is 3, plus another 1 is 4, plus another 1 is 5, plus another 1 is 6). Only later do students learn to count on from the larger addend (e.g., the student thinks 4 plus 1 is 5, plus another 1 is 6). If a teacher carefully assesses a student's approach to this math problem, she might modify her instruction in several ways. She might pose a more difficult or an easier problem. She might change the size of the numbers in the set. Or she might compare and contrast different students' strategies to help them learn new ones (National Research Council, 2001).

In short, if a teacher knows more than a student's answer—if she understands how a student works toward a solution—she can use that information to improve her instruction. She can pull, push, stretch, and inspire the student to think in new ways. The teacher who assesses student thinking and not just student results in any content area is likely to increase the chances for student success.

Standardized Testing

Tests are attempts to make standards apply directly to life. If you have a standard for student learning, it is argued, you ought to have a test to see if students meet that standard. When people make this argument, they usually have in mind tests that are said to be *standardized*. In common usage, **standardized tests** are commercially prepared examinations designed to obtain samples of students' knowledge or aptitudes. They are standardized in that the same type of test is given to all students, no matter where they are, using the same directions for classroom administration and the same procedures for scoring and interpreting the results. Standardized tests are given to students at all points in their academic careers in the form of IQ tests, national standards tests, state standards tests, and so on. In addition, standardized tests often are a main factor in deciding whether a student can proceed to a higher level of education, for example, the Scholastic Aptitude Test (SAT) for entrance to college and the Law School Aptitude Test (LSAT) for entrance to law school.

How do standardized tests both help and hinder teachers' efforts to judge their students' needs and abilities?   Academic progress is assessed formally most often by standardized tests. The tests are usually, but not always, multiple-choice, paper-and-pencil assessments (Carey, 1994). The items do not necessarily reflect the knowledge that students are supposed to learn in their classes; that is, sometimes the tests and curricula are not aligned. In some cases, standardized tests measure students' potential or aptitude, rather than their actual knowledge.

Standardized tests help equalize opportunities for students to demonstrate the knowledge they have and the skills they possess. Comparing students' scores on these tests is easy, because they are standardized in terms of administration and interpretation, and they are widely applied. In other words, students are starting from the same place; they take the same type of test that is scored in the same way. Therefore, standardized tests enable nationwide comparisons of students at the same grade level or age. These comparisons can be very instructive for teachers and parents. For example,

*W*ere you required to take standardized tests in your school years? What was your experience with them? Do you think they reflected your true knowledge and abilities?

a particular student might score at the ninety-seventh percentile in reading (97% of the students in the norm group had lower scores), but only at the fifty-seventh percentile in mathematics (57% of the students in the norm group had lower scores). This information might stimulate teachers and parents to arrange for more instruction or a different kind of assistance in mathematics for this student.

Some people do not have a lot of faith in standardized tests, however, because students' scores represent estimates of their capabilities based on samples of their performance. The tests are not complete measures of students' knowledge or talents. The amount of knowledge and the number of skills that a student might be expected to command at any point in time are immense. By necessity, standardized tests must be fairly short, so the samples must be restricted in size. Thus, the items might not deliver a full representation of what a student knows and can do.

Another criticism of standardized test is that scores are derived from student performance on paper-and-pencil tasks, not from performance on real-life situations. Some students simply do not do well on tests for any number of reasons, including anxiety and pressure to do well. They might not perform well on a standardized test question that would be easy for them to solve in a classroom discussion. Furthermore, many circumstances beyond students' capabilities can affect their scores: the temperature of the room in which the test is given, lucky guesses, illness, and problems at home (Airasian, 2000).

Another set of issues arises when discussing standardized test scores, specifically their reliability, validity, and utility. To be useful, test scores must be **reliable**—a student's score today must be the same as or close to the score he would get tomorrow. A reliable test does not yield erratic results. Many standardized tests are scored by machines and therefore have black and white answers. This helps eliminate scoring disagreements—an answer is either correct or wrong. When humans score tests with variable answers, they must be able to agree on their estimates of student performance. This becomes an especially difficult and expensive requirement in the case of essay tests.

Standardized tests also must be **valid;** that is, they must measure what they are supposed to measure. For instance, if a test claims to assess students' understanding of the workings of an internal combustion engine, it should not be a test of students' reading abilities.

Also in terms of scoring, standardized tests must demonstrate a high degree of **utility.** The results need to be reported in ways that people can easily understand and apply to help students improve their performance.

When it comes to interpreting what standardized test scores mean, people usually look at them in one of two ways. On a **norm-referenced test,** students' test scores are compared to the scores of other similar students. The comparison group students are usually from the same age or grade level, with half of the scores above the average or mean score and the other half below the mean. In norm-referenced tests, then, a student's test score acquires value in relation to every other student's score. For example, if the comparison group scored particularly high on a test, a score of 340 might put a student in the fifty-fifth percentile. However, if that same score was achieved in a comparison group where the scores were particularly low, the student might be in the eighty-fifth percentile. Norm-referenced test are useful for determining where a student is in terms of other students of her age or at her level.

The other type of standardized test scores comes from a criterion-referenced test. In contrast to a norm-referenced test, a **criterion-referenced test** assesses a student's performance against a clear, external standard. Returning to the previous example, on a criterion-based test a student who scored a 340 would always be in, say, the seventy-fifth percentile. By comparing a student's score to some clearly defined benchmark, a teacher can interpret student performance in terms of instructional objectives, instead of comparing students to one another.

Your Teaching Life in Practice

ARE STANDARDIZED TESTS USEFUL?

James, a first-year teacher, meets with Mary O'Reilly, the curriculum coordinator, to discuss his students' scores on the standardized achievement tests administered in April.

James: I am not looking forward to explaining these test results to some of my students' parents. From the comments they made earlier in the year, I think many parents overvalue standardized tests.

Mary: I agree that many parents are test conscious. In part the publicity surrounding standards and student performance has probably contributed to the heightened interest in "objective measures" of student performance. Parents want to be sure their children have opportunities and learning experiences that will allow them to move up the education ladder. To some degree, standardized tests are the yardstick they use to be sure their children are challenged appropriately.

James: But just look at these scores, especially those for Billy and Sherell! They have made so much progress in English this year, but you would never know it from their scores. These multiple-choice tests measure students in a totally different way from how I taught them. I feel like such a failure!

Mary: Wait a minute, James. You know as well as I do that a standardized test offers well-developed measures of student performance, but only partial information about student achievement. Think about it . . . these tests use small collections of items to assess student learning. We also know that performance on standardized achievement tests is affected not only by what is taught in school, but by students' inherited academic aptitudes and by their experiences outside the classroom. So it is a mistake to gauge our success or failure as teachers using only test scores as a measure.

James: Are you suggesting I forget about these scores?

Mary: Quite the opposite. I think you should study the test items to determine what they are really measuring. They may offer information about student performance that we have overlooked during instruction. At the same time, I think you need to take a hard look at the kinds of evidence you are collecting on a daily basis to determine whether students have mastered significant skills. Do your assessments involve the direct evaluation of student mastery of content and effective use of skills? In other words, do you have credible evidence that students are learning? This, in combination with standardized test scores, can offer a more complete view of student achievement.

Critical Thinking Question

Why do experts recommend using multiple measures to judge both student and teacher success?

To answer this question online and e-mail your answer to your professor, go to Chapter 11 of the Companion Website (ablongman.com/mcnergney4e) and click on Your Teaching Life in Practice.

Minimum Competency Testing

Is there a common body of knowledge and minimal level of learning that all public school students should be expected to master?   People who think so support minimum competency programs, curriculum, and instruction geared toward the successful completion of **minimum competency tests.** These tests are meant to assess the lowest acceptable levels of student performance in various subject areas, including reading, writing, math, and science.

The minimum competency movement, sometimes called **outcome-centered learning** because it focuses on "results," began in the 1970s. Advocates worried about what they perceived as a declining emphasis on content and academic rigor in schools. Some wanted to end the practice of **social promotion**—promoting children through the grades to keep them with their peers even if they could not keep pace academically. Others wanted to make sure public funds were spent on **literacy,** which was defined most often as students' scores on tests of reading, writing, and calculation. The purpose of the movement was to return curricula to the basics and to make sure all students learned at least that much. The minimum competency movement defined "minimum" in terms of the knowledge and skills adults believe children need to possess in order to maintain employment in their adult lives.

Critics contend that the minimum competency movement has led to an overemphasis on high-stakes tests, which determine students' grade promotion, graduation, and access to specific fields of study. Some critics argue that high-stakes tests limit the curriculum to simplistic ideas and punish students who do not score well.

Asking Questions

Why is the ability to ask good questions one of the most important assessment skills a teacher can have? Teachers neither can nor want to test students at every possible turn of the curriculum. They do, however, ask questions while they teach. A main purpose of these questions is to assess student thinking. Students' responses can inform teachers about what students understand, as well as indicate areas where students need more time or help. Teacher questions also let students know what is important. If a teacher asks several questions about the latter portion of a history chapter, for example, students can infer that they should focus on this part of the text when studying for the upcoming test. Teachers who ask the right questions at the right time and respond appropriately to student answers are conducting effective evaluations.

What kinds of questions do teachers ask? Many schemes can be used to classify the types of questions teachers ask: closed questions (a single answer) versus open questions (many answers); divergent questions (request elaboration) versus convergent questions (narrow responses); higher-level questions (requiring respondents to analyze, apply, evaluate, or synthesize) versus lower-level questions (requiring recognition and recall). One simple but useful guide organizes teachers' questions into four categories. Students' answers to these questions can provide valuable evaluative information that will guide instruction. The four categories are:

1. Questions that elicit information from students (e.g., "Why do you think Al Gore was defeated for the presidency?").
2. Questions that establish or put information into students' minds (e.g., "If you were a newly freed slave in Alabama, what problems would you face?").
3. Questions that expand students' thinking about particular topics (e.g., "Because students are required to attend school, what subjects do you think should be required?").
4. Questions that extinguish or close down student thinking (e.g., "What kind of evidence would convince you that the statement you just made is erroneous?") (Mackey & Appleman, 1988).

How might teaching or learning conditions or settings dictate teachers' questions? Teachers ask students questions about subject matter in a variety of ways. In addition to questions on written examinations, teachers often ask questions during the common give-and-take lectures and discussions that occur in the classroom. Sometimes teachers direct these questions toward selected individuals, sometimes toward volunteers, and sometimes toward the class as a whole, in search of a

What are the different kinds of questions that teachers ask? How do students' answers guide instruction?

Voices

JAMES POPHAM SPEAKS ABOUT ASSESSMENT

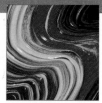

*J*ames Popham, a retired professor from the University of California, Los Angeles, was for years a regular on the annual program of the American Educational Research Association. He had written a statistics book that people used to rave about. Besides being famous for his books, Popham was always entertaining. He made people think about assessment in ways that made sense to teachers, students, and their parents. Here is what Popham said about testing:

I think that, from an instructional perspective, all teachers need to know about testing. . . . The first reason [is] instructional planning pay-offs that teachers can get from a clear understanding of what they're trying to have their students accomplish. Because a properly constructed classroom test can truly exemplify what a teacher is trying to achieve, the resulting clarity of intention helps teachers make more astute decisions when they plan their instruction.

When I recall my own early years as a high school teacher, I remember how often I simply whipped together lesson plans that seemed somewhat instructional. Yet, my planning was almost never guided by a truly clearheaded notion of what knowledge, skills, or attitudes I wanted my students to possess when the instruction was over. If I had relied on my classroom tests to clarify what I wanted my students to become, I'm certain that my lessons would have been far better focused on intended instructional outcomes.

The second reason I think all teachers should become more astute regarding assessment is also instructionally rooted—namely so that teachers can monitor students' progress. . . . With the evidence yielded by classroom formative assessments, a teacher will often fail to spot instructional inadequacies. As Black and Wilian, the British investigators, made quite clear, the instructional dividends from monitoring students' progress can be quite striking. And their views were based on solid research investigations, not wishful yearnings. My grandparents came to the United States from Great Britain, so I typically groove on anything that's asserted with a British accent. But, then, doesn't everyone? (Popham, 2002, p. 17)

Critical Thinking Question

Can you think of other reasons it is important for teachers to know about assessment for both teacher and student development?

To answer this question online and e-mail your answer to your professor, go to Chapter 11 of the Companion Website (ablongman.com/mcnergney4e) and click on Voices.

united group response (e.g., "Okay class, what is 6 × 6?"). Teachers also provide questions in written study guides or as comprehension checks to be answered after students complete assigned readings. Sometimes teachers give written questions to small groups of students and ask for either group or individual responses in oral or written form. One-on-one tutoring sessions provide opportunities for individualized questions that yield an in-depth account of a student's attitudes, beliefs, or understanding.

Questions in the classroom, however, should flow in both directions. Astute teachers know there is great value in soliciting students' questions. Students' questions can be a useful tool when teachers are trying to determine where the class is in terms of understanding the subject or skill. In fact, student questions may be a better indication of the class's level of understanding than are the teacher's questions.

Authentic Assessment

Authentic assessment is an alternative to traditional standardized tests, because it assesses student performance on real-life tasks in many forms. The idea behind authentic assessment is to encourage the application of knowledge to problems that students can expect to encounter in real life. We all know that in many real-life problems there are rarely right and wrong answers. Instead, there are more and less acceptable courses of action. Rather than ask students to perform limited tasks that are rarely seen outside standardized tests, authentic assessments ask students to synthesize ideas to find answers to real-life problems.

Many advocates support authentic assessment as a more reliable and accurate way to measure what students have learned and, perhaps more importantly, how well they can apply this knowledge. In assessment terms, however, this means that judging a student's performance becomes a complicated, time-consuming, and often expensive venture. It is also more difficult to compare the results of students' authentic assessment in terms of state and national standards.

What are some forms of authentic assessment that teachers use? Authentic assessment takes place over a period of time (weeks, semesters, etc.) during which students' work is measured in terms of the progress made and material mastered. Various means are available for observing and collecting student work for purposes of authentic assessment.

JOURNALS

Teachers can use a student's **journal** or log—written collections of students' reflections on learning—to increase their knowledge of students' needs and abilities. Journals may be hard-copy notebooks or online files that contain graphs, notes, charts, pictures, and any artifacts that students choose to include. Students can use their journals to record their feelings about a particular assignment, to describe what they learned from a project, to explain why they did or did not think a test was fair, and so on.

Journals are just one form of authentic assessment. What other forms can you think of? Which do you think are most effective?

Typically, teachers generate questions that guide students' written reflections in their journals. Teachers usually have access to the journals, but not always. Sometimes students are encouraged to designate their entries as "shared" or "private." Teachers set the ground rules for journal use up front, often cooperatively with students, and respect these rules throughout the school year.

PORTFOLIOS

A **portfolio** is a collection of a student's work, often selected by the student himself, that represents the best of his learning efforts. Portfolios might include test papers, essays, diagrams, art projects, audiotapes of musical performances, videotapes of drama productions, computer programs, and the like. Portfolios can exist as physical collections of work or as electronic files. The work that students include in a portfolio may be accompanied by their own or their peers' critiques. Sometimes students share their portfolios with would-be employers to demonstrate their accomplishments and to show their potential value as employees.

Portfolios are alternatives to traditional tests because they document student performance in outcomes not typically measured by tests that take place over an hour or two. For example, a writing portfolio may include writing assignments that a student has completed over the course of a marking period or an entire school year. As a result, portfolios may offer some of the best available evidence of student learning and progress. Teachers and parents can use portfolios to enrich their understanding of student learning and to better plan how to encourage student progress.

RUBRICS

A **rubric** is a scoring key. Teachers create and use rubrics to help assess how well students have grasped important aspects of learning activities. Rubrics are sometimes as simple as checklists that help teachers note the presence or absence of specific attributes in students' performances or products. For example, a teacher may have a checklist for a group math activity that includes such items as "mastered the computational skill," "arrived at the correct answer," "worked cooperatively with rest of group," "applied previous lessons to current work," and so on.

Rubrics can also be used to note the strength of various aspects of students' work. These sliding-scale judgments replace the all-or-nothing characteristic of a checklist. For instance, a teacher might use a 3-point scale with the following descriptors of student work: 3 = excellent, 2 = satisfactory, 1 = unsatisfactory.

TEACHER-MADE TESTS

Teachers usually build their own tests to measure students' grasp of material taught in their classrooms. One useful tool for building tests is a test **blueprint,** which is a set of specifications for the content and objectives to be assessed. Designing a blueprint is an excellent way for teachers to plan ahead—they can make sure their lesson plans cover the content that will be assessed on the test, and vice versa.

A sample test blueprint is shown in Table 11.1. It outlines ten areas of content and four types of exercises (requiring two lower-level and two higher-level types of thinking) that students will face. The higher-level exercises (application and analysis) are weighted more heavily in the teacher's test than are the lower-level exercises (knowledge and comprehension). In other words, the test will have more exercises (a total of sixty-five items) that require students to apply and analyze ideas, much as they might have to do in real-life settings. After looking at the sample blueprint in Table 11.1, do you see how the teacher might have an easier time developing a lesson plan with the blueprint in place?

CURRICULUM-BASED ASSESSMENT

Curriculum-based assessment measures students' competence in various areas using the materials (books, readings, etc.) students encounter in the classroom. This type of

TABLE 11.1 Blueprint for a Test on Bodies of Water

Course Content	Knowledge	Comprehension	Application	Analysis	Total
Salt water	2	3	2	3	10
Fresh water	2	2	3	3	10
Plants	1	2	4	3	10
Currents	1	1	3	5	10
Animals	1	2	4	3	10
Tides	2	3	3	2	10
Temperature	2	2	4	2	10
Maritime law	1	2	4	3	10
Commercial	2	2	4	2	10
Recreation	1	1	4	4	10
Total	15	20	35	30	100

assessment assumes that academic success is heavily dependent on reading and writing skills and that such skills are most fairly and accurately measured using material somewhat familiar to students (Jones, Southern, & Brigham, 1998).

One example of a curriculum-based assessment is a timed oral reading assessment. In such an assessment the teacher might identify a previously unread passage from a class text and ask the student to read aloud from it for one minute. The teacher would then count the words the student reads correctly as a percentage of the total words read. (Reading fluency is highly related to reading comprehension.) A similar strategy is for the teacher to read one sentence that is the beginning of a story. The student listens, thinks for one minute, and then writes for three minutes. Scoring is based on the student's number of correct words, correct word sequences, and so forth.

SELF-ASSESSMENT

Why not ask students to evaluate themselves?   Too often, teachers overlook the obvious source of information about what does and does not work in the classroom: students themselves. They know what they like and dislike. They often know what they can and cannot do. They also know the consequences of taking and not taking risks in their learning experiences.

Good teachers take advantage of this plentiful resource in classroom assessment and ask students to evaluate themselves. The process of **self-assessment** requires students to evaluate their own participation and their own products. In practice, this means teachers should ask students such questions as these:

- How hard did you try?
- How difficult was the assignment for you?
- If you were to do this assignment again, what might you do differently?
- What did you learn?
- How well did you like this work?

Students are most likely to respond to these kinds of questions in honest, useful ways when they believe they are in a nonthreatening environment. Therefore, their responses should never be used against them. When done properly, student self-assessment can provide a wealth of information to both teachers and students about classroom learning experiences. It can also involve students more closely with their education and help build strong relationships between teachers and students.

Grading and Recommendations

Why is grading such a difficult issue for teachers? Grades are more than letters or numerals on a report card; they are used to reward students, to give feedback to students and parents on performance, and to provide estimates of students' potential for postsecondary study. In reality, grades determine a student's future. For example, grades often are a key factor in a student being assigned to a particular course of study (college prep or remedial), winning awards and scholarships, and being admitted to various colleges and training programs. Thus, grades play an influential role in how students feel about themselves and about their academic careers because they count for so much.

Grades result from student assessments. As previously discussed, assessments can take many forms. Some school systems use collections of students' work to report students' progress instead of using traditional grades. But using such methods to replace grades is rare. Most schools continue to use traditional assessment methods—unit tests, quizzes, midterms, final exams, classroom participation, general progress, and so on—to determine grades.

Grades take various forms: the familiar letter grades (A to F), pass/fail (P/F), satisfactory/unsatisfactory (S/U) and numerical values (90 to 100 = A range, 80 to 89 = B range, etc.). Grades are frequently supplemented with teachers' comments or estimates of student effort, attitudes, work habits, and the like.

Although they sometimes appear to be determined by a scientific formula, grades usually are determined by teachers. This can be an overwhelming responsibility, especially for new teachers. Teachers at all levels of experience often feel pulled by opposing desires when grading: to use grades to build students' confidence by rewarding effort and progress and to assign value to students' performances in some "objective" fashion. These sometimes contradictory demands can force teachers to examine their own reasons for giving grades. Planning for evaluation and grading early on helps teachers resolve such dilemmas when they arise.

Recommendations are another way teachers convey information about student performance. Letters teachers write in support of their students may be some of the most important writing teachers ever do. These letters of recommendation and character references can be used by students seeking awards, honors, loans, and so on. A character reference, as the phrase suggests, is a reflection on the personal qualities and traits of a student. The strongest letters are usually those that explain general sentiments with specific examples of a student's behavior. (For instance, Jack Smith is one of the top two students I have ever taught. Jack's personal diligence and creativity were never more evident than in his senior thesis. . . .) Because teachers often know their students better than most other adults know them and because teachers write well, these letters can carry a lot of weight with readers.

Teachers also write letters of recommendation for student admission to college and training programs, scholarships, and jobs. These letters often take the form of reflections on a student's past performances, with an eye toward his or her aptitude for future success. A letter says as much about the writer as it does about the person for whom it is written. Wise writers follow principles of composition and share a draft with an editor before mailing.

Student's Role

Why is it so important for teachers to understand what students can do and want to do? Researchers have found that about 50 percent of a student's success with learning new topics can be explained by his attitudes and prior knowledge (Bloom, 1982). In other words, what students already know and their feelings toward particular

Technology in Practice

POSTING STUDENTS' WORK

Ms. May's sophomore biology class is in the computer lab completing their final projects on amphibians. Their assignment is to create a website that will teach other students about the characteristics of amphibians. As she walks by Jeremy and Orlando, who are collaborating on the project, Ms. May is impressed with the images they have downloaded from the Web. She tells the boys that they are likely to get some interesting reactions from students around the country, and perhaps overseas as well, when others view their work. Later in the day, when Ms. May discusses the project with Mr. Roberts, the librarian, he raises questions about her instructions to students and the propriety of the Internet assignment. What concerns might Mr. Roberts have? How might an *Acceptable Use Policy* help Ms. May and her students in this situation?

Electronic availability of student work is an important issue for two reasons: student safety and intellectual property. Schools protect their students in such matters by crafting an Acceptable Use Policy. The policy guides teachers' actions with regard to the use of the Internet. These policies vary from place to place, but all are meant to reduce confusion and ambiguity. For instance, most policies dictate that teachers should not post a student's last name, e-mail address, or photo without a signed release from the student's parent or guardian. The idea, of course, is to protect students' identities.

A good Acceptable Use Policy also protects students' rights of creation. For example, stories that people write or ideas they have are considered personal property, or

intellectual property. These artifacts also may have monetary value. The rule of thumb is to get parent or guardian permission before posting any student work.

An Acceptable Use Policy may also address the issue of students using other people's intellectual property. For example, Mr. Roberts may instruct Ms. May to make sure the students get permission to post the downloaded images on their website.

Activity

Search for some high schools' acceptable use policies online and compare them. What might be some of the most difficult obstacles to overcome when trying to enforce an acceptable use policy?

 To answer this question online and e-mail your answer to your professor, go to Chapter 11 of the Companion Website (ablongman.com/mcnergney4e) and click on Technology in Practice.

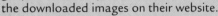

---

educational tasks can greatly affect their classroom experiences and their grades. In these same studies, researchers found that teachers can account for as much as 30 percent of students' learning. Another way to think about this point is that for some students teachers could be the difference between a grade of 70 and a grade of 100!

Stanford professor Nate Gage has argued that if a medical treatment had about one-tenth the power that teachers do, it would be declared a miracle cure (Gage, 1985). Teachers can have dramatic effects on their students, as evidenced by students' scores on tests. The key to maximizing teacher effects is understanding students' present needs and abilities. The more a teacher knows about her students' knowledge, attitudes, and how her students think, the better prepared she will be to help them succeed.

Still, students can and must help themselves. Peer feedback and self-monitoring can yield valuable information for self-guidance. When students understand how they reason and how they can collaborate with their peers, they can often improve their learning and thus their grades.

How Can Teachers Know If They Are Assessing Students Fairly?

With the increasing use of high-stakes and standardized tests comes heightened concern for fairness in testing. Most commercial producers of standardized tests review test items with great care and try to guard against built-in flaws that make tests unfair. The individual teacher who creates her own tests must also guard against a variety of threats to fairness in her own assessments. Grades and assessments count for so much in education; they are a determining factor in things like school funding and students' admission to college and training programs. Therefore, educators need to do all they can to ensure fair and accurate evaluations of all students.

Bias in Assessment

What is assessment bias, and how can a teacher avoid it? According to educational researchers, "**assessment bias** refers to qualities of an assessment instrument that offend or unfairly penalize a group of students because of students' gender, ethnicity, socioeconomic status, religion, or other such group-defining characteristics" (Popham, 2002). Assessments can offend people when they depict negative stereotypes of certain subgroups. Test items that show African Americans in stereotypical roles such as service work or sports, for example, may offend African American students. If you take a test when you are offended or angry, the result probably will not be a fair representation of what you know or can do.

Students are also unfairly penalized when their test scores are distorted because the test content puts the student at a disadvantage. The content need not be offensive, merely out of reach, for one reason or another. Young women may be penalized if test questions revolve around football or other sports with which they are unfamiliar. Students from lower socioeconomic backgrounds may be penalized by questions that require familiarity with dining out or attending high-priced entertainment events.

Sometimes students claim they have been victims of unfair tests, though, when they simply have not studied or did not pay attention in class. In these cases, the penalty for poor test performances is low grades, but it is not automatically an indication that an assessment is unfair.

Teaching to the Test

Is it wrong to teach to the test? While it is not wrong to *teach to the test*, the phrase is confusing. Teachers are supposed to create classroom opportunities for students to learn the material for which they are held accountable. Typically, this means teachers teach domains of knowledge, which are large, inclusive bodies of subject matter. Test items, if they are constructed appropriately, sample fully and fairly the knowledge contained in these domains. In short, good teaching covers the material students are supposed to learn. When this material then appears on the test, students are prepared, and teachers receive an accurate assessment of students' knowledge.

Beware, though; sometimes people use the phrase "teaching to the test" to mean teaching specific items on the test or teaching the test itself. This is wrong and doing so is poor teaching form. Remember the story that opened this chapter, the case of a Chesapeake school district teacher who left her job over charges that she taught to the test? Such charges are scary because they indicate poor teaching skills and suggest that a teacher is more interested in her students scoring well on tests than she is in what they actually learn. Although teachers are held accountable for students' standardized test scores—and the pressure to produce satisfactory scores can be intense—it is never acceptable to teach in this manner. There is much less educational value for students in learning specific test items than in learning domains of knowledge.

Multiple Measures

What is the best way to protect against unfairness in assessment? One of the best ways to ensure fairness in testing is to use different measures of success by creating multiple opportunities for students to demonstrate what they know and can do. When multiple ways for students to demonstrate their knowledge and skills are offered, definitions of success are expanded. Pressure for high scores and the best letter grades is lessened, and focus is returned to the processes of learning. For example, creating a portfolio of a student's creative writing can showcase his success in ways that standardized tests do not offer.

The state of Nebraska has a creative strategy for multiple assessment measures in its Student-based, Teacher-led Assessment and Reporting System (STARS). STARS is based on the assumption that no single assessment can meet all needs. Instead, educators need to use multiple measures to provide a full, round representation of educational success.

STARS requires school systems to develop local assessment plans that are aligned with state (or district) learning standards. These plans combine norm- and criterion-referenced assessments for students in grades four, eight, and eleven in mathematics, reading and writing, science, and social studies. The norm-referenced tests must be selected from a state-approved list. Districts can develop their own criterion-referenced assessments, including observations, portfolios, or rubrics. They can also purchase assessment tests from commercial publishers. If they develop their own, the assessments must meet certain criteria for the absence of bias (e.g., appropriate content, consistency in scoring, etc.). In addition, all students in grades four, eight, and eleven participate in a statewide writing assessment.

Every year Nebraska school districts must issue a report to local residents containing data on student performance, district demographics, and financial information. Every two years, the report must describe what is being done instructionally to help students demonstrate successful performance. And every three years, the report must contain the results of a follow-up survey of graduated students (Nebraska Department of Education, 1999).

Summary

Standards provide benchmarks against which we can judge educational success and failure. These benchmarks may come from many sources, including personal, national, and state sources. Standards are so important because they help clarify the term *accountable* when trying to determine the performances of students, teachers, school leaders, and elected and appointed governmental representatives who bear responsibility for public education.

Standards help teachers understand what is expected of their students. They also help teachers communicate expectations and support students' continuous learning. Teachers who understand the technical characteristics of classroom assessment can use them to shape teaching plans and practices. Teaching, learning, and assessment do not exist in isolation; they are processes that inform one another.

Regardless of the particular assessment used, ideas of *fairness* permeate all activities directed toward judging student performance. Efforts to develop and use *authentic* measures to assess student performance are driven by such concerns. Good teachers want to give their students every opportunity to "show what they can do" when faced with tasks that mirror the challenges they will face in real life—tasks that are real or authentic. They give students opportunities to demonstrate their abilities by using multiple measures, both standardized and nonstandardized or teacher-made. The more perspectives a teacher has on a student's performance, the more likely she is to provide a complete, fair representation of that student's achievement.

Terms and Concepts

assessment   304
assessment bias   322
authentic assessment   317
blueprint   318
content standards   304
criterion-referenced test   313
curriculum-based assessment   318
evaluation   304
high-stakes test   308
journal   317
literacy   315
measurement   304
minimum competency tests   314
norm-referenced test   313

opportunity standards   310
outcome-centered learning   314
performance standards   304
performance tests   308
portfolio   318
reliable   313
rubric   318
self-assessment   319
social promotion   314
standardized tests   312
standards   304
utility   313
valid   313

Reflective Practice

Arithmetic Test

Do this activity with a group of five to fifty peers.

Below is a problem that appeared on a sixth-grade arithmetic test taken by Freddie. How many points would you award Freddie for this problem? _____ Assume that Freddie gets the same number of points on the other nine questions. Compute Freddie's score on the test. _____ Assign a test grade (A, B, C, D, F) to Freddie. _____

Directions

Take your time and work all the problems below. Be sure to show the steps in your work:

1. If 5 bananas cost 84¢, how much would 7 bananas cost? Show your calculations.

$$5\overline{)84.0} = 16.80 \qquad 16.80 \times 7 = 117.60$$

Answer: 117.60

Issues, Problems, Dilemmas, Opportunities

Mathematics is an exact science—a closed system where there are right and wrong answers. Do you agree or disagree with your peers on the assignment of points and the giving of a grade? How might a disagreement about grading result in problems for a group of teachers?

Perceive and Value

Why might the awarding of points and grades on this simple exercise differ considerably from teacher to teacher? Can you state, in relatively few words, your own value position with regard to giving grades? Can you summarize the value positions of some of the people in your group who hold positions different from your own?

Know and Act

How might having teachers discuss their disagreement in scores and grades on Freddie's test be used to develop a common and comprehensive set of expectations for grading across a grade level or a school?

Evaluate

What does being fair mean in grading? How might you determine if you were being fair in awarding points and grades to Freddie?

INTASC Principle 8

The teacher understands and uses formal and informal assessment strategies to evaluate and ensure the continuous intellectual, social, and physical development of the learner.

Knowledge

The teacher understands the characteristics, uses, advantages, and limitations of different types of assessments (e.g., criterion-referenced and norm-referenced instruments, traditional standardized and performance-based tests, observation systems, and assessments of student work) for evaluating how students learn, what they know and are able to do, and what kinds of experiences will support their further growth and development. (Interstate New Teacher Assessment and Support Consortium, 1992)

Discussion Question

How else might you assess Freddie's understanding of this math concept?

Additional Readings

Airasian, P. (2000). *Assessment in the classroom: A concise approach* (2nd ed.). New York: McGraw-Hill.

Joint Committee on Standards for Education Evaluation (in press). *The student evaluation standards: How to judge evaluations of students.* Thousand Oaks, CA: Corwin Press.

Loveless, T. (2002). *The 2002 Brown Center report on American education: How well are American students learning?* Available online: http://www.brook.edu/dybdocroot/gs/brown/bc_report/2002/bcr_report.pdf.

Popham, W. J. (2002). *Classroom assessment: What teachers need to know* (3rd ed.). Boston: Allyn and Bacon.

Web Resources

http://www.fairtest.org

> The National Center for Fair & Open Testing works to end what they perceive as the abuses, misuses, and flaws of standardized testing.

http://nces.ed.gov/

> The National Center for Education Statistics has information that can inform both the design and conduct of educational program assessments.

http://www.ncte.org/

> This site contains Standards for the English Language Arts and is sponsored by the National Council of Teachers of English and the International Reading Association.

http://www.nctm.org/

> Find mathematics standards and teaching resources here.

http://nces.ed.gov/nationsreportcard/about/

> This is the place to learn about the National Assessment of Educational Progress (NAEP), also referred to as the Nation's Report Card.

http://www.teachervision.com/lesson-plans/lesson-4911.html

> Teachervision.com provides an overview of authentic assessment methods.

VideoWorkshop Extra!

If the VideoWorkshop package was included with your textbook, go to Chapter 11 of the Companion Website (www.ablongman.com/mcnergney4e) and click on VideoWorkshop. Follow the instructions for viewing video clips 9 and 10. Then consider this information along with what you've read in Chapter 11 while answering the following questions.

1. This chapter discusses the issue of how students' scores on standardized tests represent estimates of their abilities based on samples of their performance. Video clip 9 presents the perspective that many high-stakes tests represent only a narrow portion of the curriculum. If a school district decided to take a break from high-stakes testing for five years, what would parents, teachers, and others use to judge whether a school and its students were successful?

2. Based on this chapter's coverage of assessment and video clip 10, do you think authentic assessment or standardized testing does a better job of holding teachers accountable for students' learning? At what cost?

Benchmarks

Milestones in Curriculum, Instruction, and Assessment

1900–1920	Alfred Binet develops a systematic procedure in France for assessing learning aptitudes. Later, at Stanford University in the United States, Binet's test is revised and a formula for determining IQ is added.
1918	Franklin Bobbitt's *The Curriculum* (1918) marks the birth of curriculum as a professional field of study.
	The Commission of the Reorganization of Secondary Education issues its celebrated *Cardinal Principles of Secondary Education* (1918).
1923	W. W. Charters's *Curriculum Construction* (1923) shifts curriculum theorists' focus from content alone to the means for determining curriculum content.
1928	Harold Rugg and Ann Shumaker's *The Child-Centered School* (1928) argues for the involvement of teachers in curricular decisions.
1932	George Counts's pamphlet *Dare the Schools Build a New Social Order?* argues that curriculum and instruction should be less child-centered and more prescriptive, shaping attitudes, developing tastes, and imposing ideas.
1940–1960	Lewis Terman begins a long-term study of 1,528 gifted American children. This classic study is slated to end in 2010.
	David Wechsler develops the Adult Intelligence Scale, testing different kinds of aptitude, on which the Wechsler Intelligence Scale for Children (WISC-R) is based. This view of learners' abilities shapes teaching approaches.
1945	The Harvard Committee on the Objectives of Education in a Free Society publishes *General Education in a Free Society* (1945), a report that questions the appropriateness of curricular materials for high school students who are not college bound.
1949	Ralph Tyler's *Basic Principles of Curriculum and Instruction* (1949) stimulates the format of curriculum guides, teachers' editions of textbooks, lesson plan books, and evaluation instruments.
1960–1980	Jacob Kounin and others describe teacher behaviors that relate to teaching effectiveness and classroom management.
	Robert Mager proposes behavioral objectives stating precisely what students should know or be able to do at the end of a lesson or unit of study.
1970	Drug Abuse Education Act of 1970 (Public Law 91-427) provides for development, demonstration, and evaluation of curricula on the problems of drug abuse.
1980–2000	Global issues, such as the ecological crisis and economic interdependency, receive increasing attention in curriculum and instruction.
	National standards for curriculum are provided by various professional associations.

1994	The 1994 Ready-To-Learn Act (Public Law 102-545) establishes Ready-To-Learn Television programs to support educational programming and instructional materials for preschool and elementary school children and their parents, child-care providers, and educators.
1998	The Carl D. Perkins Vocational and Technical Education Act of 1998 (Public Law 105-32) is meant to increase the caliber of education provided by vo-tech programs by aligning them with state and local efforts to reform secondary schools.
	1998 marks the first year of funding for a five-year federally initiated family life education program. States accepting federal monies agree to teach teenagers to abstain from sex until marriage.
1999	In 1999 the Kansas Board of Education votes to delete evolution from the state's science curriculum.
	During the summer of 1999, the U.S. Department of Education sponsors a national conference on evaluating the effectiveness of technology
2002	Congress passes George W. Bush's No Child Left Behind legislation, calling for testing of children to document progress toward meeting standards.

ᗪEVELOPING A PROFESSIONAL PORTFOLIO

Assessing Students through Observation

One type of information that is potentially useful for your portfolio and likely to arise in job interviews is your opinion about student assessment. A large part of teachers' professional lives revolves around making judgments about students. Today, much of the assessment or evaluation work done to render such judgments is formal or based on standardized testing. But just as certainly, teachers gather much of the information on which they base their judgments on an informal basis—they observe the ways students behave and listen to what students say. The key to collecting good data and making sound judgments is to learn to use a variety of methods of observing a variety of activities and to use these strategies consistently and accurately. Student work samples and data on performance tasks can be used to demonstrate student academic growth over time.

Observe a teacher and her students as they interact during a lesson. Take notes on students' reactions to the lesson and list activities they work on during class. How do students demonstrate understanding of what they are supposed to learn? For example, does the teacher ask questions? Does she ask students to recite, do seatwork, and work in teams to create a product? What other activities do you see? Observe one student you think may not understand the lesson and someone else whom you believe does understand. Verify your assumptions by observing their performance in class and by talking after class with the teacher about the students. How did your perceptions fit with those of the teacher? Ask what types of assessments the teacher typically uses to inform her teaching.

Save this exercise and try it again later when you student teach. Determine how your knowledge of informal assessment has changed over time. How you judge students is a tremendously important part of your life as a teacher. Be sure to leave yourself room to grow. Changing your view of what is "fair," what is "right," and what is "wrong" are not indications of sacrificing your values. Quite the contrary. Your view of student assessment should mature over time—both you and your students will benefit in the long run if you possess a rich, robust sense of what constitutes student success.

Teaching with Census Information

When you go to the U.S. Census Bureau website (www. census.gov), click on For Teachers under Special Topics. You can download lesson plans for making sense of data from the 2000 census and from earlier years. These lessons help students recognize historical trends and contemporary issues by using real numbers about real people. Here is one exercise high school students can use to project future trends based on historical data. Complete the activity Forecasting the Future. As you do so, think about how you might incorporate this type of activity in a social studies or math lesson. What skills would a student need to be successful at this task?

Lesson 6 Activity Worksheet | **Estimating/Projecting Rates**

Forecasting the **Future**

Grades 11 and 12

● **Population Projections**

To make population projections for the United States or for individual states, demographers make assumptions about future trends in the components of population change. These assumptions, which reflect professional judgment and take into account past trends, are made in terms of rates for births and deaths, and in terms of rates or numbers for migration.

For simplicity, the population projections discussed below are based on assumptions about past trends in total population, not on assumptions about each component of population change. Table 1 shows the 1970 and 1990 census populations for four states, all with populations that increased between 1970 and 1990. Calculate numerical growth (1990 population minus 1970 population) and percent growth (population growth as a percent of 1970 population, with percent change rounded to one decimal place).

Table 1. Population of Selected States: 1970 and 1990

State	1970	1990	Population growth, 1970–1990 Numerical	Percent
2. Connecticut	3,032,217	3,287,116		
3. Minnesota	3,806,103	4,375,099		
4. South Carolina	2,590,713	3,486,703		
5. Arizona	1,775,399	3,665,228		
6. Your State				

Calculate population projections for each state for the year 2010 assuming a continuation of trends for the 1970–1990 period: first based on numerical change (an arithmetic rate of change), then based on percent change (a geometric rate of change) with the results rounded to the nearest integer.

Table 2. Population Projections for Selected States: 2010

State	Based on numerical change	Based on percent change
7. Connecticut		
8. Minnesota		
9. South Carolina		
10. Arizona		
11. Your State		

Questions about population projections

Why are the population projections for the year 2010 larger when based on percent change than when based on numerical change for the 1970–1990 period? _____

_____

_____

Source: U.S. Census Bureau (14 February 2002). Chapter 6: Forecasting the future, grades 11–12. http://www.census.gov/dmd/www/schtm03.html.

𝒜 Connected Future

𝓔very day, teachers all over the globe are shaping the future. They can't wait for policymakers and writers of textbooks to "get it right." They have places to go, things to do, and lives to change.

The newspaper *USA Today* acknowledges the importance of what teachers are doing through its annual teacher recognition program. The teachers designated as outstanding find themselves on the All-USA Teacher First Team—a team that consists of teachers deemed most worthy of professional honor:

> Long before President Bush's No Child Left Behind Act pushed for annual testing to close achievement gaps and reach every child, members of the All-USA Teacher First Team were going above and beyond to leave no child behind. The teachers . . . embody the notion of reaching out to every child, in ways that can and can't be measured by standardized tests:
>
> —An elementary school principal whose own dyslexia had kept her from reading until college, [Pam McClean] Jackson returned to the classroom in 2000 . . . [and] was so successful at reaching failing readers that the creator of the reading program she used adopted her school [in Frankfort, KY], providing professional development and reading-lab equipment for the whole school.
>
> —[Jim] Green . . . with only a pager, a beat-up car and a rented space behind a convenience store . . . combed the migrant farming pockets west of Phoenix to find . . . dropouts. Five years later, the Continuing Education Academy [CEA] team . . . was offering a full, self-paced high school curriculum in a stuccoed modular building with 32 computer stations. CEA, which serves more than 500 full- and part-time students, helped 110 seniors make it to graduation last spring. (Briggs, 2002, p. 1)

The chapters in Part 5 show that truly outstanding teaching and learning occur around the world in cultures familiar and foreign. Teachers, regardless of where they live and work, share similar goals and thus are tied to one another in many ways. They have the power to shape the future for a better tomorrow.

A Global Educational Context

CHAPTER OUTLINE

Why Learn about Educational Life outside the United States?

Why Study Education in Other Countries?

How Might We Enhance Understanding of Global Interdependence?

*C*ale Elementary School in Charlottesville, Virginia, is a school with a global outlook on education. Each year, students and teachers hold a concert to raise money for people in South America. The opening line of a recent newspaper article read, "The stuffed toucan will be flying and the cloth camel tottering along tonight as dozens of Cale Elementary students help students thousands of miles away in the school's annual Earth Day Concert" (Andrews, 2002). While this approach is unique, it is not unusual for schools around the nation to shape themselves in many ways to acknowledge the importance of making connections with their neighbors—regardless of how far away or how different those neighbors may be.

As the idea of a global community becomes reality, learning about other nations and people, as well as our place in this new community, becomes part of the educational experience. Teaching students about people around the world often happens in simple but powerful ways: "Eighty children . . . perform an indigenous tale, filled with original music and animal-puppet antics, to raise money to help build a high school in Guatemala" (Andrews, 2002).

Students are able to think big ideas when teachers make these ideas real and tangible. Bringing the world into your classroom and school makes the world's people and places tangible to students. It also prepares them to be citizens of the world. This chapter explores why it so critical to learn about educational life outside the United States, how this life unfolds in schools around the world, and where teachers and students fit in the global, interdependent community.

*W*hy Learn about Educational Life outside the United States?

People around the world live with increasing cultural, economic, political, and social diversity. Progress in transportation and communication systems is enabling people within and between nations to interact with one another in ways never before imaginable. One outcome of these technological innovations is that people are able to travel and live far from where they were born. In fact, millions of "guest workers" or migrant laborers around the world live in a country they do not call home. In 2000 slightly more than one in ten residents of the United States (28.4 million) was foreign born (Lollock, 2001).

Schools around the globe both shape and reflect this diversity, teaching multicultural education, cross-cultural education, international education, comparative education, and global studies. All these program types share two assumptions: human life is interdependent, and such mutual dependence has important implications for how we teach and learn (Cushner, 1998).

All this growth, movement, and innovation, however, can make it hard to maintain educational programs and experiences that are relevant and current for all students. Educators plan curriculum, instruction, and assessment for the "typical" student in their systems. But when the populations of these schools change by the addition of even a few students from other nations and cultures, what worked in the past may not work in the future. **What problems and opportunities might you anticipate in classrooms where students are from different cultures and countries?**

Preparing for the Future

To anticipate the future with any sense of confidence requires knowledge. We need to understand what others value, how they think, what they are likely to do and not do. Knowledge also improves our chances to perform our professional roles with sensitivity and intelligence. To learn about today's diversity of life and to imagine what it might be like tomorrow, we only have to look in schools around the world. There we can find the future leaders and followers who, in one way or another, will affect our own lives. To be fair to them and to allow them the opportunity to be part of the global community, we must give them access to as much knowledge about the world as possible. The future of politics, business, art, science, and much more depends on today's students knowing the world in which they live.

The International Baccalaureate Organization (IBO) is one unusually creative way to shape international citizens of the future. Founded in 1968, the IBO is a nonprofit educational foundation based in Geneva, Switzerland. It emerged from efforts by international schools to establish a common curriculum and university entry requirements for geographically mobile students, such as children of diplomats and military personnel. International educators also believed a shared academic experience that exposed students to a variety of viewpoints would foster tolerance and intercultural understanding among young people.

The New York Times
expect the world®
nytimes.com

Themes of the Times!

Expand your knowledge of the concepts discussed in this chapter by reading current and historical articles from the *New York Times* by visiting the **Themes of the Times** section of the Companion Website (ablongman.com/mcnergney4e).

Your Teaching Life in Practice

ARE THERE GLOBAL LIMITS TO OUR TOLERANCE?

Educators sometimes unintentionally risk offending community members when they encourage their students to study life in other nations. People in New Britain, Connecticut, discovered this simple but painful fact when a North Korean flag was displayed in the school cafeteria as part of a global studies project. Some people thought this was acceptable, but others protested.

CON A school board member who was also a Korean War veteran saw the flag hanging in the school's cafeteria and described it as "a slap in the face to everyone who served there." He wanted it taken down.

PRO The flag of the communist state of North Korea was purchased as part of a set of flags from seventy-five nations. The principal had bought the flags to accompany the global studies theme of the magnet school. "It's very decorative," said the assistant superintendent. "Many parents believe the display of flags celebrates diversity and does not honor any nation in particular."

CON When the school board member could not persuade the superintendent to take the flag down, he sought the help of a local veterans' group—many of whom thought that displaying the flag in the school honored the North Koreans.

PRO Even the school board member who first objected eventually saw some value in displaying the flag and debating it. "Korea is called the forgotten war," he said. "But at least now people are talking about it, and it is something they won't forget."

Critical Thinking Questions

What do you think should be done in this situation? Why? What might you do to limit the potential for conflict and promote understanding if you were faced with a similar situation?

To answer these questions online and e-mail your answers to your professor, go to Chapter 12 of the Companion Website (ablongman.com/mcnergney4e) and click on Your Teaching Life in Practice.

Source: Galley, M. (6 March 2002). School's display of N. Korean flag raises veterans' ire. *Education Week, 21*(25), 3. Available online: http://www.edweek.com/ew/newstory.cfm?slug=25flag.h21&keywords=global.

The IBO offers three programs: the diploma program for students in their last two years of high school, the middle years program for students eleven to sixteen years old, and the primary years program for ages three through twelve. Classes at all levels are offered in English, French, and Spanish. All the programs promote international understanding and academic excellence; see the IBO mission statement in Table 12.1.

Some eight hundred schools in over one hundred countries participate in the IBO. The IBO provides these schools with curriculum and assessment development, teacher preparation and information seminars, and electronic networking. With these materials, teachers can help students understand ideas and events around the world as they occur. Figure 12.1, for example, shows how one IBO school reacted to the events of September 11, 2001.

TABLE 12.1 The IBO Mission Statement

> **Education for Life**
>
> Through comprehensive and balanced curricula coupled with challenging assessments, the International Baccalaureate Organization aims to assist schools in their endeavors to develop the individual talents of young people and teach them to relate the experience of the classroom to the realities of the world outside.
>
> Beyond intellectual rigor and high academic standards, strong emphasis is placed on the ideals of international understanding and responsible citizenship, to the end that IB students may become critical thinkers, lifelong learners, and informed participants in local and world affairs, conscious of the shared humanity that binds all people together while respecting the variety of cultures and attitudes that makes for the richness of life.

Becoming Globally Aware

Why is global awareness important?   **Global awareness** refers to students' abilities to recognize their connections to other people and other nations around the world. Being aware of countries beyond our own is important, because the welfare of the United States depends on the welfare of other countries. We are tied to others by economics, the environment, politics, culture, and technology, not to mention by personal and familial connections. Events in distant parts of the globe—war in Israel, the discovery of fossils in Sudan, drug production in South America, and so on—create waves and ripples in the United States.

Of course, it works the other way around, too. Events in and actions by the United States affect the rest of the world in both major and minor ways. Terrorism in the

FIGURE 12.1 IBO Students React to September 11   How might schools sustain students' feelings of shared responsibility and their attention to basic human rights?

> In the weeks following the September 11 tragedy, students around the world shared their feelings with one another. Students from the Academy International Elementary School, Colorado Springs, Colorado, an IBO school, reaffirmed their connectedness to the larger world:
>
> > When school opened on Monday the students gathered for a brief flag ceremony to remember the victims of the attack and affirm their commitment as U.S. and world citizens. They then moved quickly: individuals, small groups of students and classes wanted to do things, from collecting food and clothing for families and boots for rescue workers, to raising money to send to families. The students listened to the needs of the Red Cross and decided to have an all-school fund drive, with money collected being sent to the Red Cross, with letters designating how it is to be used. For example, one class wanted the money it collected to be used to purchase flashlights and batteries for the rescue workers. Students also have been sending postcards of encouragement and condolences to the police and fire departments as well as to the victims' families. To support each other, students made red, white and blue ribbons to wear.

Source: International Baccalaureate Organization (2001). Reactions from students: 11 September events. Available online: http://www.ibo.org/ibo/index.cfm/en/ibo/services.

United States results in war in Afghanistan. A drop on the New York Stock Exchange forces the loss of jobs in Thailand. An American bicycle rider wins the Tour de France, and sports training programs around the world mimic his methods.

The daily news offers much evidence that actions in one nation—for better or worse—affect life in many far-flung parts of the world. In addition, the past twenty years have witnessed incredible advances in technology and science with far-reaching effects. For instance, more people traveling and working outside their home countries means more intercultural contact. Dramatic advances in communications technology give ordinary people around the world new opportunities for connecting with and learning from others. In some instances increased contact leads to competition and conflict. In other cases, familiarity breeds cooperation, for different people realize that they must work together if they are to survive and prosper.

To help negotiate all these effects and exchanges, people everywhere call on schools. Schools are asked to promote technical and communication skills in the hope of mutual understanding. Their curricula must continuously evolve to incorporate ever-changing politics and cultures. Schools around the globe must help tomorrow's adults learn languages, understand world history, and use a host of electronic communication systems. A global society is no longer the pipe dream of the futurist. It is an idea that people define each day as they reach around the world with their computers and fax machines.

In terms of curriculum development, programs and materials do not necessarily have to be the most cutting-edge or expensive ones available to effectively broaden students' minds. The following are some ways in which teachers can bring global ideas and perspectives into their classrooms, whether they are in Miami, Seattle, or Peoria, Illinois:

- a set of folk literature, poetry, and music from around the world for grades one and two;
- a collection of books dealing with cultural commonalities among families of the world for grades seven and eight;

Global ideas and perspectives can easily be brought into classrooms. Can you think of activities you did in school that had international influences?

- an endangered species unit for the middle grades;
- a global education section in the school library;
- and an all-school display of "Our Earth": that represents interdisciplinary work at all grade levels (Tye & Tye, 1992).

How might joining schools and classrooms from around the world on the World Wide Web affect teaching and learning? Some education professionals believe that a global perspective, aided by technology, forces people to consider problems that cut across national boundaries (Tye and Tye, 1992). Educators who think about the world also develop students' abilities to view the world from other perspectives. This process of exposing students to international perspectives has occurred for many years through associations referred to as *nongovernmental organizations,* or **NGOs.** These transnational associations—churches, scouts, farmers, chambers of commerce, physicians, athletes, educators, and so on—grew in number to more than 38,000 by 2002 (Union of International Associations, 2002). The popularity of the Web is largely responsible for the growth of NGOs and cooperative efforts that focus on problems of common interest across national borders.

Global Education Motivators (GEM) is one NGO that focuses on developing global education programs for schools and communities. Educators founded GEM in 1981 to "bring the world into the classroom." Such notables as the late Fred Rogers, of television's *Mr. Rogers' Neighborhood,* and Paul Simon, former U.S. senator from Illinois, have endorsed the work of the organization. GEM's three divisions have strong connections to the United Nations:

- GEMNET promotes video and e-mail exchanges among schools around the world.
- GEMRIM provides online instructional materials that concentrate on human rights, conflict resolution, and environmental protection.
- GEMQUEST organizes international travel to advance human rights efforts.

Clearly, the emergence of a truly global community means educators must prepare students for a world quite different from the one in which the educators themselves grew up. For teachers to enlarge their views of the world or to think globally and encourage their students to do the same, the basic curriculum and instruction in most schools must change to keep up with the times. To make these changes occur, however, a number of obstacles or competing demands must be overcome. Historically, school leaders have not considered global education to be a high priority. Teachers' limited time is already devoted to existing curricula, standardized testing, and accreditation demands. To a certain degree, the events of September 11, 2001, have changed this situation. Educators are working to bring global information and perspectives into U.S. classrooms.

Understanding and responding to crises, however, is not the only reason for globally educating students. Money and jobs also fuel interest in international and worldwide issues. Business leaders have been among the more vocal proponents of global and comparative education. They view schools as vital to the production and maintenance of a work force able to compete in a wider world.

South Carolina has been unusually successful in making a place for itself in the global marketplace. The state established special schools to train workers at no charge for any company that would create jobs in the state. The German automobile maker BMW took advantage of the opportunity and built a plant in Spartanburg in 1992. Since that time, the company has invested nearly $2 billion in the operation, paid $1.2 billion in wages, and created over 11,000 new jobs. BMW has also paid about $300 million in taxes and created another 7,000 jobs in the industries that support the auto

Voices

TEACHING IN ISRAEL

*A*s soon as they graduated from college, Esther Adams and Julie Gehm took teaching jobs in an international school in Israel. They had never been to Israel before, and they had no prior connections with a U.S. school abroad. They found their jobs through a weekend recruiting fair held in Boston. After their first teaching year in Israel, they were interviewed about their experiences.

Q: Why did you go to Israel to teach?

Esther: I knew I wanted to teach abroad. It was October 31, and I went to this information session for teaching abroad. I realized this is what I'm supposed to do!

Julie: In the international network, there are some of the most incredible individuals you will ever meet. They have traveled the world and seen so much and experienced so many different schools, and they bring something from every place they have taught. It's absolutely unreal.

Q: So you're going back this year because. . . ?

Julie: Oh, well for me I would say because of the amazing administration, and I love my kids. To be in a classroom with kids from literally all over the world is just incredible. I had children who spoke no

Esther Adams and Julie Gehm

English at all—second grade, fourth grade, and fifth grade—from all over the world. I did not speak their languages; they did not speak mine; rarely did they speak each other's. It was probably one the most amazing experiences of my life.

Esther: When I was teaching about Africa in my ESOL history class, I had kids from African countries in my class. When we were talking about civil war in Angola, Bruno added a perspective because

plant. Thinking globally can also mean realizing the importance of behaving in ways that encourage other nations to view us as partners in joint ventures.

BMW, for example, also offers internships, a cooperative education program, and training programs to move local people into career paths in the company. Interns study engineering, human resources, management, finance, and other areas of expertise. Corporate-sponsored education programs have great value to the public schools in the area. Students have opportunities to work in state-of-the-art facilities that the schools could never afford to provide. Their efforts often lead directly to good jobs after graduation.

One of the biggest challenges facing American public education is preparing students today for careers they will have tomorrow in a world that is growing smaller and faster by the day. Thomas Friedman, a columnist for the *New York Times,* puts it this way:

> Think of it: thanks to the Internet, we now have a common, global postal system, through which we can all send each other mail. We now have a common global shopping center, in which we can all buy and sell. We now have a common library, where we can all go to do research, and we now have a common global university where we can all go to take classes. (Friedman, 2000, p. 141)

Life is changing so rapidly that the future can only be imagined vaguely, if at all. **For what kind of future should schools in the United States prepare students?**

he lived there. I don't have his perspective. The classroom is so rich that you have to deal with issues of tolerance and how we listen, how we respect one another, how we understand each other.

Q: I know you do not have a lot of teaching experience in the United States, but how is teaching in Israel like teaching here, and how is it different?

Julie: Well, we seem to have boundless resources, like technology, tons of computers, just so many resources. You'd like to think that money doesn't matter, but it really does.

Esther: My colleagues treat teaching like a profession. And I also think that international schools create community because everybody is kind of out of their comfort zone, in a different culture. We're all in Israel; it's new and different for us. And especially Israel, it's incredibly intense. So, it creates this community that you can feel in the air. We're trying to create, particularly in Israel, a safe, warm, loving place for students to be.

Julie: They love to come to school.

Esther: The kids are really involved and highly motivated. And the teachers are expected to be right there with the kids.

Julie: Very high expectations.

Q: Are you frightened to be in Israel?

(laughter)

Julie: I e-mailed Esther yesterday, saying, "I don't want to bring it up, but Iraq—how do you feel about Iraq?" I don't know about Esther, but this year, we've really made peace with the idea of being in Israel, but obviously, it's constantly on our minds.

Esther: We live with it every day. You have to learn that when you move to a country, it's not your [home] country anymore. You've got to learn to mesh, to get into the culture, and Israeli culture is very intense. It's a very passionate culture; a very different culture, and you have to be willing to go and really learn. Yet, we're in an American community in another country.

Critical Thinking Question

If you were considering teaching abroad, what questions might you ask of teachers who have done so?

 To answer this question online and e-mail your answer to your professor, go to Chapter 12 of the Companion Website (ablongman.com/mcnergney4e) and click on Voices.

*W*hy Study Education in Other Countries?

International comparative education teaches that problems of educational development are common in many societies. By studying education in societies different from their own, educators learn to see these commonalities. They also develop new insights into other cultures that can lead to new and innovative ways of looking at their own societies (Thomas, 1990). For instance, the United States is not the only country that is home to a wide variety of cultural groups. Nor is the United States the only country addressing problems that arise from clashing cultures. People in other countries face these problems too, often with considerable success. Their experiences can help us learn to behave in new ways. Likewise, when we look at the education systems of other cultures, we may find they are successfully using techniques, curricula, and classroom experiences that we never considered.

With increasing globalization, multicultural understanding becomes more important for all people and all nations. The ancient Greeks were among the first to recognize the importance of learning about and from others. For Plutarch, people who studied life's lessons wherever they found them demonstrated their strength of character. Thucydides suggested that people who learn from others may be more prepared to avoid some of life's pitfalls and to capitalize on success. **What makes the transmission of culture through schooling a problem in any country?**

𝓕**IGURE 12.2 Education Around the World**   This chapter discusses education in the countries pictured here.

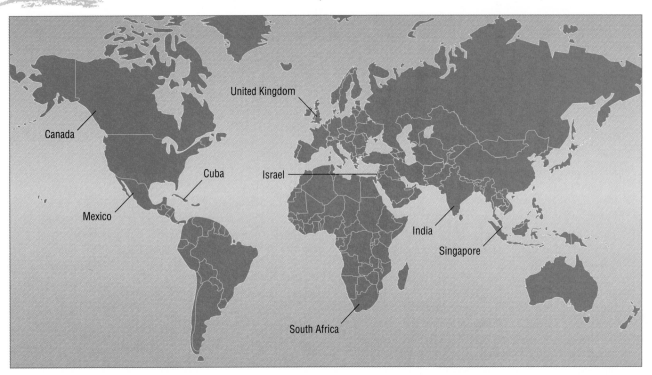

Source: http://www.educate.com/specials/specials.cfm?PC=NWGGL-GEN-0201.

Education in Canada

When the 1995 rebellion of French-speaking Canadians nearly split the country in two with a secession vote, we Americans paid little attention. Yet Canada remains our best trading partner and most trusted military ally—a friend we cannot afford to ignore. How Canada educates its citizens bears directly on how Canadians think about the United States and their relationship with us. So it is important to know how our neighbor's educational system works.

Canada's landmass makes it the second largest country in the world. Its economy is diverse and successful. Nearly two-thirds of the population live in metropolitan areas along the border with the United States. Some 60 percent of Canada's population live in two of its twelve provinces and territories, English-speaking Ontario and French-speaking Quebec. Until recently, Canada had one of the highest birthrates in the industrialized world. It has also been a home for immigrants from around the world (Fowler, 1998).

Canada is a federal state, meaning provincial governments control education, just as our individual states are responsible for U.S. education. Canada has neither a national system of education nor a central office of education. Instead, each province has its own Ministry of Education headed by an elected minister. In all provinces, schools are operated by local boards of education; the extent of their power varies across provinces. Both provincial governments and local governmental units fund schools.

Typically, children start school at age six or seven. They must attend for at least ten years, or until the age of sixteen or seventeen. The organization of school levels (elementary, middle, and high) varies by province, with some using a system of seven years in elementary, two in middle, and three in high school. Others use a 7–5, 8–4, or, as in Quebec, a 6–5–2 system. The school year runs between 180 and 200 days.

Promotion through the elementary grades is more or less automatic. At the secondary level, systems of promotion vary among the provinces, but most use the credit system. Under a credit system, students take varying levels of courses to accumulate credits for graduation. In addition, students in the provinces of British Columbia, Alberta, and Quebec must pass a graduation diploma examination. Many schools offer general and advanced levels of diplomas. On average, more than 60 percent of high school graduates go on to some form of postsecondary education (Berg, 1995).

The Canadian educational system, like many others in modern economic states, faces the challenges of the information age and an increasingly competitive global economy. Movements for teacher accountability, strengthening basic skills education, accommodating increasing cultural diversity, and addressing gender inequality characterize current Canadian education reform.

Canada, much like the United States, relies heavily on testing in schools. Increasingly, tests drive educational decision making with regard to student placement and advancement. Educators are keenly aware of the possible positive and negative consequences of testing students. For instance, they fear that testing can promote tracking—or streaming students into classes and programs designed for a particular achievement level that typecasts students and limits their opportunities for learning. The seemingly precise or scientific nature of standardized achievement tests, critics argue, encourages unfounded consumer confidence in test results. Proponents of the use of testing in Canadian schools contend that the development and use of standardized assessments have opened new opportunities for students to demonstrate what they know and can do.

Canadian schools reflect the cultural similarities among Canadians, as well as the deep division that exists between French speakers and English speakers in Quebec. There has always been a strong belief among the French Canadians of Quebec that they should split off from Canada and form their own nation. Bill 101, passed in 1977, established French as the only official language in the province and imposed many restrictions on the use of English or any other language in business and education. The bill was an attempt by the government of Quebec to preserve French culture in the face of the increasing number of immigrants entering the province, the majority of whom spoke no French. In the thirty-plus years since the bill was passed, the Supreme Court of Canada has eased these restrictions. The tension, however, remains, and every so often the move to secede reemerges.

Bill 101 has had a profound effect on education in Quebec, because immigrants to Quebec had to attend French-only schools. The Montreal Catholic School Commission, which operates more than three hundred schools in Montreal, has considered an outright ban on any language but French in its schools in recent years. (Public schools in Quebec are designated as either Protestant or Catholic and are supported financially by the government.) This ban would include all school-sponsored activities, as well as speech in the halls and on schoolyards. Offenders would be transferred to other schools, and repeat offenders would be expelled.

Many educators in the United States, particularly those in the West and Southwest, probably can identify with teachers in Quebec and the movement for single-language schools. California, for instance, has an English-only contingent that wants Spanish offerings removed completely from classrooms. **How are the positions of students with English as their primary language similar to and different from one another in the two countries? How do the positions of the language-minority students compare in both countries?**

Although they are interesting, if we relied on only the sensational events in Quebec, we would have a distorted view of life in the majority of Canadian schools. Most school jurisdictions have developed and now use multicultural curricula, particularly in social studies. The ministries of education, teachers, university professors, and publishers have cooperated to develop learning resources and instruction appropriate for the richness of ethnicity and culture that characterize all Canadian schools (Fowler, 1998).

Technology in Practice

THE JOURNEY NORTH PROJECT

Project-based learning calls for students to explore real-world problems and share what they have learned with others. Advocates argue this kind of learning beats traditional methods, hands down. They believe students develop a deeper understanding of subject matter, improve their abilities to self-learn, and sharpen their research and presentation skills.

The George Lucas Educational Foundation (GLEF) documents Web-based strategies to encourage problem-based learning. The Journey North Project is one such strategy featured on the Foundation's website, and it involves 300,000 students across three continents. As part of the Project, students trace the migra-

tion of monarch butterflies, collect data on growing tulips, plot the migration of birds and whales, and engage

edutopia®
The George Lucas Educational Foundation

[Search field] ▶▶ Search

About Us

📷 Video Gallery

Topics
Innovative Classrooms
Assessment
Emotional Intelligence
Project-Based Learning
School-to-Career
Technology Integration

Skillful Educators
Mentoring
Ongoing Professional
　Development
Teacher Preparation
Technology Professional
　Development

Involved Communities

Home > Innovative classrooms > Project-Based Learning > March of the Monarchs

March of the Monarchs　　　　E-mail this article to a friend
　　　　　　　　　　　　　　　　　　Printer-Friendly Version

by Diane Curtis

It's spring, and monarch butterflies are making their annual 2,500-mile voyage to Canada from Mexico. The beautiful, orange-brown Lepidoptera have been spotted in Virginia.

📷 play video
Running time: 4:02

"What I want you to do is mark on the paper map right now where Mexico is," teacher Frances Koontz tells her class of third graders. "We're going to follow the path of the monarchs and identify the states where they travel. If you need help with the name, look in your atlas."

Education in Mexico

What effects does the United States have on education in Mexico?　Movies, television, and the popular press portray Mexico at the extremes: culturally rich, socially warm, and humanly inviting or stunningly poor, socially archaic, and openly hostile to outsiders. These images tell only part of the story. The reality, as it usually does, lies somewhere in the middle.

The United States of Mexico is a country of thirty-one states that shares its borders with the United States of America, Guatemala, and Belize. The nation has one of the highest population growth rates in the world. Population density varies greatly among the states. The capital, Mexico City, and one of its neighboring states account for more than 22 percent of the country's total population. Mexico City is recorded as being the second largest city in the world, with twenty-five million people. Although it has not been documented, some people believe that Mexico City is actually the largest city in the world with closer to thirty million inhabitants. Overall the Mexican population is becoming more urbanized: the percentage of the population living in urban areas increased from 42 percent in 1950 to 73 percent in 2000.

The Mexican economy has been hit by a series of economic crises in the past several decades that has resulted in a continued and radical uneven distribution of wealth. High expectations surrounded the 1994 signing of the NAFTA agreement, which reduces Mexico's trade barriers with Canada and the United States of America. So far, though, the expectations for an improved Mexican economy have not been realized.

Despite our current close friendship with Mexico, there is deep anti-American sentiment in some places. The sentiment is especially strong in places of widespread and extreme poverty, such as Chiapas State.

in other tasks that span borders and time zones. They share data online.

It's spring, and monarch butterflies are making their annual 2,500-mile voyage to Canada from Mexico. The beautiful, orange-brown Lepidoptera have been spotted in Virginia. "What I want you to do is mark on the paper map right now where Mexico is," teacher Frances Koontz tells her class of third graders. "We're going to follow the path of the monarchs and identify the states where they travel. If you need help with the name, look in your atlas."

She later asks the students whether the butterflies are getting close to their hometown of Bowie, Maryland. They excitedly note that Virginia is the state next door. Daily recording of temperatures gives students an idea of optimum conditions for the arrival of the monarch butterflies.

In Koontz's class, each child maintains a folder that documents the monarchs' flight from a wildlife preserve in the mountains outside Mexico City, where the brilliantly hued insects look like a dazzling kimono as they cover the branches of the local oyamel trees. Once Journey North officials report

sightings in the southeastern United States, Koontz and her students are on high alert looking for the butterflies in their own neighborhood. They also are watchful at all times in case they see a butterfly that doesn't fit the usual pattern of travel. As soon as the students spot the monarchs, they report their observations to the Journey North databank as part of a three-continent collaboration in which 300,000 students are participating scientists.

Critical Thinking Question

If you were teaching the Journey North Project, how might you determine the success of students' efforts?

 To answer this question online and e-mail your answer to your professor, go to Chapter 12 of the Companion Website (ablongman.com/mcnergney4e) and click on Technology in Practice.

Source: Curtis, D. (2002, June 2). March of the monarchs. *Edutopia.* Online. © 2003, Reprinted with permission, The George Lucas Educational Foundation (www.glef.org). Available online: www.glef.org/journeynorth.html.

Anti-American sentiment here rises from the Mexican soil almost as effortlessly as the corn that grows nearly everywhere. It's been that way for more than 150 years, since—as every Mexican is taught in school—the United States took half of Mexico's territory, putting Texas and California on their current side of the border . . . . [T]he United States has come to represent all the world's wealth, all the heartless big business and what they see as the strangling tentacles of U.S.-led economic globalization. (Sullivan, 2001)

Spanish is the official language of Mexico, although more than ninety-three languages and dialects are present (Reyes, 1995). Nearly one million Mexican citizens do not speak Spanish, and 10 percent are illiterate.

Since 1993 the state governments have controlled the running of preschools, primary and secondary schools, and teacher-training institutes, except in the Federal District. This decentralization of power represents a major shift in education policy from a tightly controlled, centralized authority.

The Mexican education system is structured in a 6–3–3 configuration. The first six years are spent in primary school, and the next three years are for lower secondary school. For the final three years, students either pass an entrance examination to gain entry to upper secondary school (*bachillerato*), which leads to higher education, or they transfer to a three- or four-year technical school.

Mexican schools have many overage students in each grade because students repeat grades and/or drop out and then re-enroll. Overage students account for up to 30 percent of the enrollment in some grades, particularly in the fifth and sixth grades. Because overage students inflate enrollment numbers in elementary schools, pupil–teacher ratios are high, generally around thirty to one. Many Mexican students do not attend the upper secondary school level. The average educational attainment of the population over fifteen years of age is 7.7 grades (National Center for Educational Statistics, 2001).

The most serious problem at the basic level of education may be the high and persistent dropout rate, a consequence of family poverty. In 1995 only about 50 percent of entering students at any level completed their studies. In rural areas of the country, approximately 75 percent of schoolchildren did not finish the first six years of primary education (Lorey, 1995). This trend continues today.

The growing number of school-age children places a heavy burden on the Mexican educational system. Overall, national basic-education programs have emphasized access to education, rather than its relevance or quality (Lorey, 1995). Schools have had to accommodate an additional 500,000 students per year since 1950, although this trend has slowed since the mid-1980s. This expansion of the educational system, however, has not been equal in all regions of Mexico. Larger cities, as you might expect, have more residents and therefore more students, and the northern part of Mexico and Mexico City generally have the highest enrollment numbers. States in the southeast regions, which are more rural and less populated, logically have lower enrollment rates (Reyes, 1995). In fact, 23 percent of Mexican elementary schools are one-teacher schools, and 15 percent do not offer all six grades. Although some sort of accommodations are made for students with special needs, only about 10 percent of such students use them.

The immigration, both legal and not, of Mexican people into the United States along the southern border has been well publicized. By the late 1990s there were about fifteen million Mexican Americans, between two and three million of whom were illegal workers. That total number increases by 100,000 to 200,000 people each year (Huerta, 1999). What happens in Mexico, of course, can be directly linked to the United States. Latino children represent about 42 percent of the total student body in California. On average, third-grade Latino students scored 500 on the California Assessment Program, while white and non-Latino students scored 614. Eighth-grade Latino students scored 414, and whites and non-Latinos scored 567. Some 45 percent of Latino teenagers who enter ninth grade in California do not graduate. One-third of them drop out of school in the tenth grade. Across the state, the dropout rate for Latinos is double that for whites and non-Latinos.

How might teachers in the U.S. schools help Latino children succeed?   Well-intentioned people offer a variety of strategies to help Latino children: scale back or eliminate bilingual programs to reduce reliance on Spanish; create more bilingual programs and more opportunities for intercultural studies to boost Latino students' self-esteem and reduce prejudice; encourage Latino students to become more competitive, to concentrate on skill training, and to keep an eye on what matters in the world of work. These are but a few of the ideas.

Education in Japan

Critics of American education often hail Japan as an example we should be following. The Japanese, they argue, demand educational excellence and get it. On the other hand, some people believe Japan's schools foster conformity and reward obedience.

Japan is a country of more than three thousand islands in East Asia, with a population of more than 127 million. This densely populated country of city dwellers is ethnically homogeneous (with only a 1 percent minority population). Tokyo, the capital, is the largest city in the world, with more than twenty-eight million inhabitants.

From the time of its defeat in World War II until 1990, Japan enjoyed extraordinary economic success. Between 1990 and 1994, however, land values fell dramatically and industrial giants, such as Nissan, closed factories when car production fell about 22 percent. While Japanese citizens struggle with the realities of increasing unemployment and the social problems accompanying it, they continue to place a high priority on the development of a well-educated and skilled populace (Desmond, 1996).

How does Japan's educational system compare to the U.S. system? The Japanese education system closely resembles the U.S. system. Most Japanese students attend public schools in mixed-ability classrooms. Unlike the United States, there is no external examination scheme in Japan—no public or private testing service that creates, distributes, and scores a set of examinations common to students across the country. Instead only internal, school-system assessments determine students' promotion and certification of completion.

Japanese students begin school at age six, attending elementary schools (grades one to six) with an average pupil–teacher ratio of twenty to one. After completing elementary school, students attend a three-year lower-secondary school, with fifty-minute class periods and an average pupil–teacher ratio of 17.4 to 1. Nearly all lower-secondary school students study English as a foreign language. Students at all levels wear uniforms.

Upper-secondary school is not compulsory, but 96 percent of the children who complete lower-secondary school proceed to the next level. Some 70 percent of these students attend public school, while the remainder pay to attend private schools. In upper-secondary schools, 75 percent of the students pursue a general, academic course of study, and the rest enroll in specialized (streamed) tracks, such as technology, foreign languages, and computers. Students with special needs can complete secondary school by correspondence. Since 1988, some students with special needs can attend credit-system upper-secondary schools. These schools award diplomas for courses taken, instead of requiring students to pass a graduation examination. Thirty-four percent of Japanese upper-secondary school graduates continue their higher education after passing a competitive entrance examination (Kanaya, 1995).

In addition to the regular public school system, many young people in Japan attend a private after-school class. Classes may be of two types: *okeiko-goto* (enrichment classes in areas such as music, the arts, and physical education) and *juku* (supplemen-

*F*IGURE 12.3 While the Japanese have *okeiko-goto* and *juku,* Americans have such for-profit ventures as SCORE! Educational. SCORE! and other companies offer enrichment education for parents who can afford to send their children to instructional sessions above and beyond curricula offered in schools.

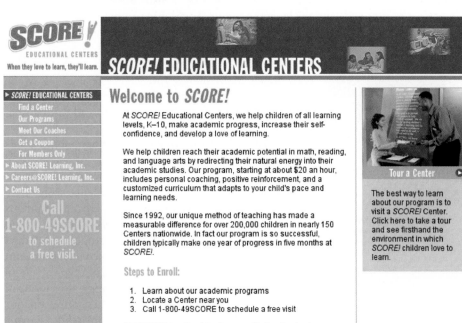

tary classes in academic subjects). Together, *juku* and *okeiko-goto* are a multimillion-dollar industry. *Okeiko-goto* often begin during children's elementary years and may continue throughout their lives. *Juku,* however, are taken exclusively during children's elementary and secondary years. *Juku* classes help young people keep up with the demanding school curriculum, provide remedial instruction in areas of weakness, and prepare students for various entrance exams.

Juku range from classes of one to three students meeting in a teacher's home to multiple schools all over the country, with dozens of classes offered at each site. Classes meet two to three times a week and may last two to three hours or more. Unlike teachers in the public schools, *juku* teachers often group their students by ability, rather than by grade level. *Juku* teachers often rotate common drill exercises with individual assistance.

Some people contend that the instruction young people receive in *juku* and *okeiko-goto* settings closes the "sensitive gap" between what is learned in public schools and what students must know to move up the educational ladder (Harnisch, 1994). Presumably, as in other cultures, this gap represents the difference between explicit curriculum (what is set forth for public consumption) and the implicit curriculum (the more subtle but quite powerful adult expectations of student performance). (See Figure 12.3 on page 343.)

Japan has a rigorous curriculum, and some reports suggest Japanese public schools demand intense rote learning and conformity from their students (Desmond, 1996). Other studies suggest that teachers in the public schools generally function more as facilitators and "knowledge guides" than as givers of information. Instead of lecturing, for example, math teachers may ask individual students to present their solutions to the class and then ask members of the class to evaluate the solutions. They use other strategies to involve students actively in instruction.

In whole-class instruction, Japanese teachers go beyond simple conceptual learning by purposely withholding the correct answer to a problem and asking the class to think of as many ways to solve the problem as possible. Presenting the material as a sort of puzzle sparks their curiosity in the subject matter and encourages them to participate (Wu, 1999).

According to some critics, the mass media frequently compare American public education to Japanese education in ways that produce a distorted view of both systems. Many news reports proclaim the Japanese system superior in producing higher achievement among its students (Berliner and Biddle, 1995). These reports often suggest that Japanese students attend school more days per year than do American students and earn higher mathematics and science test scores. Much emphasis also has been placed on Japanese schools adherence to national standards that are enforced through nationwide examinations.

But this is not the whole story. When eighth-grade American students' mathematics abilities were compared to those of their Japanese counterparts, who had been exposed to similar curricula, American students' scores were found to match or exceed those of the Japanese students (Westbury, 1992). Although Japanese students spend more days in school than do American students (240 days and 180 days, respectively), the difference in the amount of academic instruction is not profound). A typical school year in Japan includes sixty-five to seventy afternoons of either free time or nonacademic activities. Three or four days a year also are devoted to cleaning the school. Japanese students enjoy longer lunch periods and longer breaks

In Japan, some schools put up gates and issue badges to visitors to protect students. Do you think U.S. schools need to be more concerned with security?

between classes than do American students. Furthermore, although Japanese students must pass an entrance exam in order to enter upper secondary school, it is a test of elimination. For example, if 300 freshman slots are available and 304 students apply, the test is given to eliminate four students. Passing scores can be as low as 5 percent (Goya, 1994). This is not to say that one country's school system is better than another's; it is simply a caution not to make such judgments based on incomplete or misrepresented information. While we can all learn a lot by studying other nations' school systems, we must be aware of the reasons for the differences and how they influence teaching and learning.

One issue of concern to nearly all educators, including those in Japan, is violence in their schools. In recent years there has been a wave of bullying, student suicide, student-on-student abuse, and student-on-teacher violence. Some critics blame this increasing violence on pressures Japanese students face to perform and to conform. Other observers suggest the situation simply mirrors life in other countries. Whatever the reasons, Japanese educators, like educators around the world, are trying various strategies to ensure school safety.

Some schools have put up iron gates and now issue badges to visitors to protect against harm from the outside. To protect from the inside, school leaders have begun to institute programs of character education, adopting themes of unity, friendship, and helping one another.

The Ministry of Education, Science, Sports, Culture, and Technology has also been phasing out the six-day school week. As of the 2001–2002 school year, students no longer have to attend school on Saturdays. The new policy is popular among the children. "Now, I play baseball on Saturdays," boasted one student. "I sleep late," added another. Still others spend their free time swimming or taking music lessons (Manzo, 2002). But some teachers worry that they will not be able to cover all the content with seventy fewer instructional hours each year. Many parents also object to the change in policy. They work six days a week and fear that children will have too much time alone.

Education in India

India is a nation of about one billion people. In addition to being the world's largest democracy, it may be the most culturally and ethnically diverse country in the world. It is in a country known historically for its tolerance of diversity; nonetheless, regional and ethnic tensions continue. The language of commerce and of instruction in India is English, while more than a dozen regional languages (such as Hindi, Urdu, and Tamil) and local dialects are used in everyday speech in all but the major cities. In India bilingualism is the norm, and trilingualism is common.

The Indian constitution set forth in 1950 directs the government to provide free and compulsory education for all children up to age fourteen. It also provides for equal educational opportunity and the protection of religious and linguistic minority groups. The school system, which varies from state to state, is generally organized as two to three years of private kindergarten (beginning at about age three), followed by ten years of private or public basic education. This is perhaps followed by two years of private or public higher secondary education, which also may be followed by three years of tuition-free higher education. School holidays include twenty religious festivals from Hindu, Muslim, Christian, Sikh, Parsi, and Jain traditions.

In 1986 the federal parliament adopted its National Policy for Education and Policy of Action, which formed the foundation for the National Curriculum for Elementary and Secondary Education. The intent of the common core is to cut across subject areas and to encourage attention to similarities among Indians, not to exploit their differences.

The realities of schooling in India often vary considerably from the official intent and formal proclamations. The literacy rate has more than tripled since India's independence was attained in 1947, rising from 15 to 52 percent (Lloyd, 1999). Enrollment rates are greater in the cities than in the rural areas. They also are greater for boys than for girls, especially girls from disadvantaged groups (people of low castes, tribal people, and religious minorities). These numbers suggest that, similar to other countries around the globe, the desire for equality is still unfulfilled.

Despite government claims that education is open to all, caste discrimination prevents millions of children from attending school. The caste definition of "untouchable" was abolished in 1950, but the country's 200 million Dalits—now referred to as "scheduled castes" or "scheduled tribes"—routinely suffer discrimination. Dalits are at the bottom of the economic scale, often performing the most menial and degrading jobs. At least 40.5 percent of Dalit children in rural areas and 24 percent in urban areas drop out of school. At least eleven million Dalit girls between the ages of six and eleven are not enrolled in any type of school.

According to a report by the National Institute of Educational Planning and Administration, Dalit children are victims of a hidden agenda of discrimination in the classroom. They are made to sit and eat separately, and the higher-caste teachers do not touch their exercise books. In rural Karnataka, teachers refer to children from the lower castes as *kadujana* (forest people). They claim the children cannot learn unless they are beaten. Often the children are denied the right to free textbooks, uniforms, and a midday meal (Behal, 2002).

Programs run by nongovernmental organizations (NGOs) provide education programs for India's poor children. One nonprofit organization, Udbhas, promotes literacy among children living in the slums of Calcutta. Classes, which have at least forty students, are held in the open air every day from 6:30 to 10:30 A.M. There are no tuition fees, and books and pencils are distributed for free. Udbhas also provide students with free breakfasts each day and with new clothing once a year. Used clothing is provided at least three times per year. Many of the children they help live in environments where they are exposed to violence, alcohol, drugs, and abuse; to them, Udbhas is like an "oasis" (Guha, 2002, p. 207).

Four Udbhas teachers hold classes every day for a monthly salary of one hundred rupees (about $2.10), and volunteers assist with classes. The founder, Mrs. Kundu, describes the challenges of providing education services:

> It is really hard carrying on classes during the rains. We had requested . . . a raised platform with some sort of a covering over our heads, but all our efforts [to acquire this] are . . . in vain. . . . It is hard work. Many members have not been able to devote time and have left. We survive on donations and try to make the best of what we have. (Guha, 2002, p. 209)

Indian schools, like schools in the United States and elsewhere, are subject to many outside political pressures. Since the Hindu nationalist Bharatiya Janata Party (BJP) came to power in 1998, a radical Hindu-revivalist movement has promoted the "Hinduization" of education in India (Lloyd, 1999). In part the movement is an effort to counter the influence of Christian missionaries, who Hindu fundamentalists believe tricked people into conversion. Christians comprise 2.5 percent of India's nearly 1 billion people; Hindus account for 80 percent and Muslims for 12 percent.

Indian researchers estimate that about 95 percent of the rural population live in about 826,000 villages, town, and cities across the country. On average, a primary school is within a radius of one kilometer. They also indicate that 85 percent of the population has an upper-level primary school within three kilometers. In total, about 150 million children were enrolled in primary schools in 2000, while about forty million did not go to school at all (Govinda, 2002).

One of the greatest challenges facing education planners in India is simply describing the current state of schooling in the country. See Figure 12.4 for a sample

FIGURE 12.4 School Mapping in the LJ Project

The technique of "school mapping" is Lok Jumbish's special contribution to the task of mobilizing people for education.

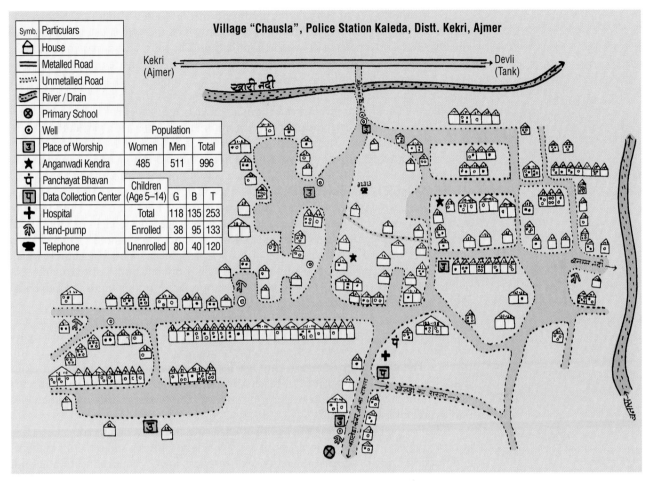

Source: Govinda, R. (2002). School mapping in the LJ Project, *India Education Report.* (p. 5). Oxford: University Press. Reprinted by permission of Oxford University Press India, New Delhi.

from the school mapping project of Lok Jumbish. The purpose of the project is to map where people are located so officials can better determine where services are needed. Project workers receive minimal training on mapping and then fan out across neighborhoods to depict households, schools, hospitals, and other buildings. The maps, or community surveys, become the basis for educational planning. Even the nonreading villagers can make proposals for improving education, thus building support for schools in the community. **How do struggles over the influence of religion on curriculum play themselves out in public schools in the United States?**

Education in the United Kingdom

More than 90 percent of children in the United Kingdom (England, Scotland, Wales, and Northern Ireland) attend publicly funded schools. These are called *state schools, government schools, maintained schools,* or *council schools* (run by local government councils). The remainder of students attend privately funded schools, called *public schools* or *independent schools*. (Note the completely opposite meaning of the term *public* from how it is used in the United States.) Attendance is compulsory for children ages five to sixteen.

Four other types of schools can be found in the United Kingdom. *Foundation schools* are publicly funded, but the properties on which they are constructed are usually owned by a religious or charitable foundation. The foundation may influence the appointment of teachers, governors, and other staff, as well as the selection of students. *Special schools* teach children with physical, educational, or behavioral disabilities. *Comprehensive schools* are state-funded secondary schools that take all local children, regardless of talent or ability. *Specialist schools* and *city technology colleges* are also state-funded schools. They teach the national curriculum but emphasize a particular subject, such as technology or the arts.

Schools are organized into two or three tiers. The two-tier system is composed of primary schools (ages five to eleven), occasionally subdivided into infant (ages five to seven) and junior (ages seven to eleven), and secondary schools (ages eleven to sixteen or eighteen), which resemble American comprehensive high schools. The three-tier system, used only in England, consists of first schools (ages five to eight or nine), middle schools (ages eight to twelve or nine to thirteen), and upper schools, which usually are nonselective (ages twelve or thirteen to sixteen or eighteen). The state church, which is the Church of England, and other churches help operate some primary and secondary schools, even though these schools are supported by public funds. **How does the existence of a state religion affect education in any country?**

Every school is run by a head teacher and a board of governors who represent parents, staff, and the Local Education Authority (LEA). LEAs are part of the local government system. They own school property and provide services to schools and parents. The central government, through its Department for Education and Skills (DfES), sets school policy and funds schools. The DfES establishes the national curriculum and the evaluation or inspection system. Schools' test results and attendance figures are published annually.

Because the United Kingdom has an official state church, religious education (RE) is a core subject in British schools. With the diversity of cultures and religions students and teachers bring to schools, the practice of emphasizing Christian education has not been without its critics. In January 1996 more than 1,500 junior school students in forty schools were withdrawn from RE courses by their Muslim parents ("Muslim parents," 1996). The boycott was prompted by parents' concern over the dominance of Christianity in RE syllabuses taught by non-Muslims. Parents worried that their children would receive inaccurate information about Islam and be confused by other faiths introduced in religious classes.

In 2001, race riots in northern England again raised questions about imposing Christian values on multifaith students. Diocesan Episcopal Vicar for Education Monsignor Kevin McGinnell justified the inclusion of religion in the curriculum. He explained that the role of school governors is to make sure school is the best it can be, while encouraging the Catholic faith, without trying to convert students (Pollock, 2002).

In addition to its inclusion of religion in the national curriculum, the British educational system had a long tradition of local control. In 1988, however, the Education Reform Act emphasized two themes in the education of all students in the British system: back to the basics and the link between education and the economy. The act was followed by pressure for a national curriculum and teacher accountability. It also promoted the idea of giving parents a greater voice in managing schools. The result was the creation of a new system of national compulsory and universal examinations.

As is the case in many other parts of the world, the United Kingdom is intent on making technology a part of teachers' lives. Education leaders had estimated that 60 percent of teachers made little or no use of computer technology. So in January 2002, the British government gave 100,000 free laptop computers to schools for teachers' use—twice the number they had planned on providing. Program originators wanted to give teachers better access to technology so they could begin to catch up with professionals in the private sector.

This program marks the first time the government has provided computers for teachers. The schools own the machines and decide which teachers receive a laptop. Government leaders claim that more computers in the classroom will allow bright pupils to move up a year and stragglers to be kept back, without changing classrooms. The success of this initiative hinges on providing teachers with advice on how to make the best use of technology in the classroom.

In addition to bringing technological advances into the classroom for teachers and students, educators are exploring other ways U.K. schools can participate in the developing global community. One of these ways can be experienced by visiting the Eden Project in Cornwall, England. It represents British aspirations for the integration of art, science, and technology in a single educational project focused on global interdependence. Described as a kind of "living sculpture and testament to our time," the Eden Project is designed to help people understand the relationship between people and plants (Devonshire, 2002). Students who are unable to travel to the large covered conservatories, or biomes, in Cornwall can visit online the living replicas of rainforests and environments in the Mediterranean, South Africa, and California to understand how plants affect people, and vice versa. (See Figure 12.5.)

No program similar to the Eden Project exists in Wales, although every head of Welsh secondary schools was given a laptop in 2000. Over one hundred other school

FIGURE 12.5 Eden's Largest Biome How do large-scale projects like Eden help stimulate curriculum development for young people?

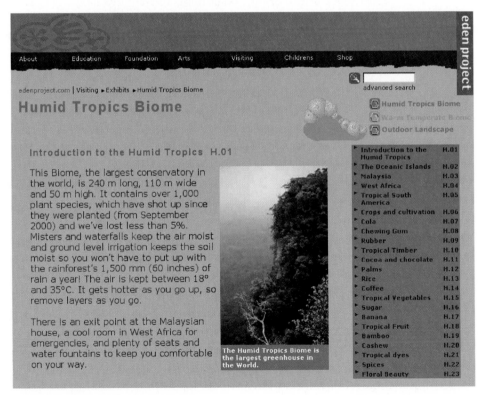

Source: http://www.edenproject.com/3464_31.htm.

leaders received them in the second stage of the program. During this same time, nine thousand Scottish teachers received small grants to help them buy home computers. Clearly then, all members of the United Kingdom recognize the benefits technology can offer teachers and students in their quest to learn about and connect with the rest of the world.

Speaking of global communities, it is too soon to know how the U.K.'s education system might be affected by its participation in the European Union (EU). One EU idea that could revolutionize education and employment is the European Personal Skills Card. "The European Personal Skills Card would accredit work skills that were not covered by paper diplomas from schools including vocational schools. In other words, the goal is to bring all workers into a credentialing system" (Spring, 1998, p. 107). The Personal Skills Cards would record people's qualifications—the skills or outcomes of learning and working. As employers across Europe recognize and use these cards, they might promote European unity. The cards might also begin to influence how educators in the United Kingdom design and deliver education.

Education in Singapore

The Republic of Singapore, a city-state on the southern tip of continental Southeast Asia, is considered the world's laboratory for experiments in social engineering. It is a multicultural society, including people of Chinese (77 percent), Malay (14 percent), Indian (8 percent), and Eurasian (1 percent) ancestries. More than three million people inhabit the 231 square miles of Singapore (Singapore Department of Statistics, 2001). The city-state, with one of the highest standards of living in Asia, bills itself as the Switzerland of Asia, the Gateway to the Future. Singapore is a city of business opportunity and a hub of high-tech development. The government tries to assure all citizens that, no matter what their ethnic or cultural background, they are first and foremost Singaporean, even though most are immigrants and their descendants.

While Singapore was a British colony, English was the required language of government and advanced schooling. The system also fostered ethnic segregation and had separate schools that taught in Chinese, Tamil, and Malay languages.

Since Singapore's establishment as a republic in 1965, however, life has changed. Today, most tourists to Singapore know that it is illegal to chew gum (actually, it is illegal to import chewing gum) and that extinguishing a cigarette on the sidewalk can draw a large fine. But few realize that the Singaporean educational system has developed innovative approaches to multicultural education. For example, even though Singapore maintains four official languages, the government has unified the English- and non-English-speaking schools (Chinese, Malay, and Tamil) into a single educational system. Leaders viewed the unification of schools, undertaken in the late 1950s, as an essential ingredient in their strategy to build a nation with its own unique identity.

The government's vigorous efforts to blend competing cultures into a unified Singaporean culture sometimes take a tough approach. For instance, the government suspended four six-year-old Muslim girls whose parents dressed them in traditional headscarves (Wood, 2002). Their suspension is an especially strong symbolic statement, because Singapore lies between Malaysia and Indonesia, both of which are Muslim countries.

Despite the government's efforts, tensions in Singapore can sometimes heighten around issues of religion, ethnicity, and race. Islam is the second largest religion among Singapore's citizens; the Buddhist Chinese community is the largest. In addition, Singapore experienced race riots in the 1950s and 1960s, the memory of which is still alive.

Overall, the government tries to balance religious freedom and social cohesion, whenever and however possible. Singaporeans celebrate their religions in private, with the blessing of the government, but the schools are supposed to be secular places. Students wear uniforms to stress the commonalities among people. Schools and apartment houses have racial quotas to ensure that racial ghettos do not emerge. Nonetheless, minorities sometimes feel left out. **Would other countries' solutions for multi-lingual education work for the United States?**

Over the past thirty or so years, Singapore has invested a lot of effort and money in education. As a result of a strong family planning program and a large investment in school facilities and teacher education, by 1968 all primary-school-age children in Singapore were enrolled in school. In 1973, educational authorities required all students to know English as either their first or second language and to know one other major language of the community. In the 1980s, authorities backed off this overly ambitious goal. Still, most students try to become bilingual, and many seek the English track as a first choice because of the access it offers to jobs and higher education.

The current education system of Singapore is comprehensive, and children begin school at age six. During their six years of primary education, they focus on English, mathematics, their mother tongue (Chinese, Malay, Tamil), music, art and crafts, and physical education. In Primary Six, all students take the Primary School Leaving Examination (PSLE) and then move on to the next stage of secondary education.

Students spend four to five years in secondary school. They take curricula based on their aptitudes and interests. In general, the subjects studied in secondary schools include English, the mother language, mathematics, science, literature, history, geography, art, technical studies, home economics, civics and moral education, music, and physical education. At the end of secondary school, students take examinations that screen them for either postsecondary education or training.

Unlike the United States, Singapore has developed close relationships among government, industry, and secondary and postsecondary education. Annual surveys estimate work force needs, and the schools and informal educational organizations respond with programs to fill those needs. These connections are especially important to a country that must depend on the talents of its people for its place in the world.

Singapore's students must leave school with strong technology skills, because people are the nation's primary resource. In 1997 the government committed 750 million

The Singaporean educational system has a cutting-edge approach to multicultural education. How do you think having four official languages would affect teaching in the United States?

pounds (about $400 million US) to build a rich technological environment by 2002—a goal that was largely achieved. Schools have about one computer for every five students, and every teacher has a laptop. The nation itself is served by one high-speed Internet system. Schools have digital cameras, data projectors, and CD burners in most classrooms. Nonetheless, teaching methods remain largely didactic, not student-centered or constructivist. Thus students have few opportunities to experiment with or explore uses of technology on their own. This has limited the power of technology in teaching and learning (Johnston, 2002).

Education in South Africa

What educational challenges does South Africa face?   South Africa is one of the most multicultural societies in the world. From 1949 to 1991, the structure of its society was shaped by an official policy of **apartheid** (pronounced "a-pár-tate" or "a-pár-tite"), or separation of the races. Under apartheid blacks lived in *homelands, black states,* and segregated *townships* outside the major cities. Whites were not allowed to enter the townships without permission, and nonwhites were not permitted to stay overnight in white urban areas without special permission. People had to carry passes at all times. Schools for white students received money, facilities, and teachers, while black schools were neglected.

Although the United States is marked by a history of slavery, it is difficult for most Westerners to imagine how apartheid could be justified in recent history anywhere in the world. The former language of apartheid in South Africa, however, must sound hauntingly familiar to Western ears. The ultimate goal of apartheid was to create "a mosaic of peoples, each with a separate national identity. They will be politically independent but economically interdependent" (King, 1988, p. 600).

The open challenge to segregated education began in 1976 to 1977 with riots in Soweto, a black township outside Johannesburg (Lemmer, 1993). This revolt was triggered by an attempt to have instruction be carried out in Afrikaans (an amalgam of Dutch, French, German, African, and Malay) instead of English. The apartheid legislation was repealed in 1991, initiating a dramatic restructuring of South African society, including a restructuring of the segregated education system that supported it. A new constitution was adopted in 1993, opening the door to free elections in which all South Africans may participate. In daily life, however, segregation continues to be reinforced by great disparities in wealth, personal attitudes, and historically separate and unequal education systems.

In general, South African schools have adopted the British view of a liberal education. Students are to be well grounded in history, languages, mathematics, the sciences, and the arts. Teaching is teacher centered, and learning is passive, with a heavy emphasis on rote and academics. Also like its Western counterparts, most all South African school systems are organized into four years of junior primary, three of senior primary, three of junior secondary, and two of senior secondary instruction.

The white, so-called coloured, and Indian schools use either English or Afrikaans as the primary language of instruction. Many black students at these schools have a mother tongue that is not English or Afrikaans. Consequently, they often do not have a sufficient command of either language (particularly in secondary schools) to cope with the academic demands made on them. The school system is made up of 82 percent blacks, 8.5 percent whites, 7.5 percent Coloureds (multiracial), and 2 percent Indians. Even though apartheid is over, these percentages, in light of most schools' use of English and Afrikaans for instruction, suggest that the current situation is still not equal.

Indeed, the battle for quality education for all of South Africa's people continues. For the blacks of South Africa the rallying cry "liberation before education" used to guide their actions. They boycotted schools and thus sacrificed their education. Now the township schools are full, but the conditions of schooling vary greatly.

Zola Senior Primary School is in one of the poorest districts in the township of Soweto. The long brick school building is on a dusty piece of shrub-covered land bordered by rubbish and rusty barbed wire. Classrooms house about fifty-five students.

> Three or four pupils often have to share a small desk and bench meant for two in classrooms that are otherwise virtually bare of furniture. . . . Three pupils have to share each textbook, but one classroom has six 10-year-old computers and the children sit in queues waiting for their five-minute slot. For some subjects there are no books, no equipment, nothing but the educator and the pupils' enthusiasm.
>
> What is lacking in terms of resources is being compensated for by everyone's determination that these pupils succeed as much as possible. Even after school there is a formidable range of activities—sporting, artistic and social—to allow the children to develop their skills.
>
> The children are proud, happy and glad to show off their talents. At one point a class of fifty-six pupils breaks into spontaneous song, moving and clapping in perfect rhythm to the amazing sound.
>
> Almost every pupil wears the school's uniform. Their parents are so proud of their child's education that, no matter what their level of poverty, they do everything possible to ensure that every day their child walks to school properly dressed. (Burns, 2002)

Hundreds of miles to the west, in a remote area on the banks of the Orange River, lies Oriana—a community of seven hundred established in 1994 by white Afrikaaners. To avoid confrontation with the government, the community calls itself a "limited company." High fencing surrounds Oriana, and there is a Strictly Private sign at its only entrance. A committee decides who can live here; there are no blacks and no coloureds, only those who believe that an all-white Afrikaaner independent state is possible.

Children in Oriana are educated in one of three ways: at home by their parents, at a traditional school, or at the community's model school. Only thirty-seven students attend the model school. To enroll, a student is required to have his or her own computer.

Oriana students, who range in age from nine to seventeen, are housed in one large classroom. The youngest children spend most of their time learning to read and write. The rest of the students sit at individual stations and work on weekly computer-based assignments in all subject areas. Computer programs allow students to assess their own learning. If they achieve 80 percent or more, students move on in the curriculum. Those completing the curriculum ahead of schedule can begin the next level of assignments or take time off from school. Slower students must stay behind at the end of each school day.

> The classroom walls are covered in shelves of reference books. The two teachers are there more as facilitators and evaluators because most of the information needed for the pupils' programmes [sic] is found on the Internet. The pupils also support each other when necessary.
>
> There is an entrepreneurial aspect to school life, with the children being encouraged to set up their own after-school businesses. These range from selling sweets to hiring out a film projector that a group of them had saved up to buy. (Burns, 2002)

Oriana's computer programs are being marketed all over South Africa. The income from sales ensures that the school is always well funded. While the curriculum encourages independent learning, critics worry that it does not promote social interaction or creativity. And at Oriana in particular, computing seems to have created another apartheid—an "educational apartheid" (Burns, 2002).

The South African government currently is in the process of reconceptualizing the school system from top to bottom. It is establishing national norms and standards for governance, finance, and the effectiveness of schooling. Change cannot be achieved overnight, however.

> A very complex system has its own momentum, and the authorities have stated that although it is important to effect changes with all speed, care must be exercised to make certain that the system does not collapse. Consequently, the changes taking place have been interpreted by some as being too rapid and by others as being too slow. (Stonier, 1998, p. 212)

How Might We Enhance Understanding of Global Interdependence?

The events of September 11, 2001, may have changed forever how Americans think about people in other nations. It shocked many of us into believing that, like it or not, we are connected to people around the globe, in ways we never imagined. In terms of economics, technology, communications, and politics, we are increasingly becoming a global community. We cannot afford to look at the world and see only ourselves and our own neighborhoods. We must work to understand others and ourselves in relation to people around the world.

The process of understanding often involves making judgments based on comparisons. Comparisons can be helpful—opening our minds and increasing our understanding—when they are reasonable and based on common conceptual ground. The International Association for the Evaluation of Educational Achievement has tried to make such comparisons of educational achievement across nations since 1959.

On one level the Trends in International Mathematics and Science Study, or TIMSS (originally named the Third International Mathematics Science Study), makes possible simple comparisons of students' test scores from different countries. By focusing narrowly on scores, these comparisons often invite simplistic arguments about who is better at educating their young. At the same time, the existence of TIMSS also encourages nations to focus on shared objectives and on methods of attaining them. As is true in most cases, test scores can provide insight, but they should not be used as the only evidence of educational achievement.

Trends in International Mathematics and Science Study

First given in 1995 and again in 1999, TIMSS is the largest, most comprehensive, and most rigorous international study of schools and students ever conducted. Researchers examined students' mathematics and science achievements by studying schools, curricula, instruction, textbooks, policy issues, and the lives of teachers and students to understand the educational contexts in which mathematics and science learning occur. The 1995 study included twenty-six countries, and the 1999 study polled thirty-eight.

The United States gave the international math and science tests to 9,000 students in 221 schools. In 1995, the fourth graders scored exceptionally well on the TIMSS tests (Martin et al., 2000; Mullis et al., 2000). By the time they reached the eighth grade in 1999, however, they had become about average. The results of the two tests suggest that U.S. students fail to sustain the achievement advantages they gain in elementary school. Some experts contend that the drop in scores occurred because our curriculum repeats itself too much and fails to challenge students.

Comparatively, in 1999, U.S. eighth graders scored above the thirty-eight-nation average both in science and mathematics, but they did not demonstrate high achievement in either subject. United States scores were well behind top scorers in Asia and Europe. The highest-scoring countries in both math and science included Singapore, Japan, South Korea, and the Netherlands.

Although scores on the eighth grade tests did not change much between 1995 and 1999, some experts believed the achievement gap between minority and white students in the United States on the tests had narrowed. On the National Assessment of Educational Progress, however, the gap between white and nonwhite students' achievements continues to increase. This is one case where test scores alone cannot determine how well and how equally students are learning.

Looking more closely at the data collected by the TIMSS tests and surveys, American students perform below the international average in geometry and measurement, but score well in fractions and algebra. In science, they score the lowest on questions dealing with physics, chemistry, and earth science, but they do well on environmental issues.

Overall, the TIMSS results raise a number of critical questions: Why do most U.S. seventh and eighth graders still review arithmetic that children in other countries have mastered by the fifth grade? Does the United States spend so much time practicing specific skills that students do not learn mathematical principles? The answers to these kinds of questions can provide much insight into the strengths and shortcomings of current curriculum standards. They also can help educators develop new programs and curricula that better prepare students for life beyond school.

Indeed, the companion TIMSS surveys of teachers and students pointed to some sharp distinctions between U.S. educational techniques and those used elsewhere in the

Issues in School Reform

WORKING LOCALLY TO STRENGTHEN OURSELVES GLOBALLY

Since September 11, 2001, patriotism has been present and accounted for in schools across the United States. You see the flag, hear the national anthem, and witness acts of national solidarity in schools large and small. As Kathleen Vail has noted, "An upsurge in patriotic feeling can be a welcome change in a society beset with cynicism and lack of trust in public institutions. But the flurry of flag-waving could be obscuring the need for deeper lessons of democracy and civic duty" (Vail, 2002).

What is needed, many educators contend, is a kind of school reform directed toward understanding the complex and difficult sides of democracy, including the importance of debate and dissent.

How can this reform happen? Vail argues that schools must implement a three-part strategy aimed at helping young people understand the rights and responsibilities of citizens in a democracy.

1. *Encourage critical thinking.* If students don't practice thinking for themselves now, how can they do so later? Critical thinking makes for informed decisions.

2. *Teach students to understand other points of view.* One excellent way to shed our egocentric ways is to learn about other cultures. Americans need to think about America's role in the world, and teachers can encourage this kind of thinking better than anyone.

3. *Link service learning to political action.* When students do volunteer work in their communities, they tend to be more politically involved than students who do not volunteer. Being involved politically at the local level—working for a candidate, circulating petitions, writing legislators—keeps democracy alive and healthy.

Critical Thinking Question

One view of U.S. history suggests that democracy does not seem to come naturally; that is, people have to learn how to function in a democracy. Leaders at all levels of the system play important roles in teaching about people living and working together harmoniously. How might you encourage students to examine the concept of leadership in a democracy?

To answer this question online and e-mail your answer to your professor, go to Chapter 12 of the Companion Website (ablongman.com/mcnergney4e) and click on Issues in School Reform.

Source: Vail, K. (2002, January). Lessons in democracy. American School Board Journal, 189 (1), 14–18.

world. Researchers found that U.S. math teachers focus on drill and practice, whereas other countries also focus on application. Ninety-four percent of students said their teachers "almost always" or "pretty often" showed them how to solve math problems when they were having difficulty. Only 86 percent of the total students polled in the thirty-eight-nation survey said this happened. Nearly 80 percent of the U.S. students said they "almost always" or "pretty often" were given time to do homework in class. Only 55 percent of students in the overall survey made the same claim. Students in the United States also indicated that they did worksheets and textbook exercises, while students abroad said they engaged in projects where they discovered mathematical or scientific concepts by applying them in real-life simulations. **How do your education experiences in math and science compare to those of student respondents?**

International Comparisons: Smoke and Mirrors?

Some critics believe that, although international comparisons of schooling are commonly used to rank educational systems, they are just as routinely abused. Gerald Bracey, for example, contends that students from the United States are often found wanting when there are no real differences between them and students in other nations. Other critics charge that international comparisons distract schools from the real issue: how to prepare our students for the future.

On the topic of the legitimacy of international comparison tests, Bracey (2002) argues that TIMSS and other such tests obscure the fact that the United States does not really have *a public school system*. Instead, he says, we have two systems: "One is for poor and minority students; the other is for the rest of us" (2002, p. 2). To support his contention, Bracey cites the rankings of American ethnic groups in reading, mathematics, and science from an international study of students in thirty-two nations. The study is called the Program for International Student Assessment (PISA) and was conducted shortly after TIMSS.

Indeed, the PISA results seem to support Bracey's claims. White students in the United States ranked second in reading, seventh in math, and fourth in science, while black and Hispanic students in the United States ranked twenty-sixth in reading, twenty-seventh in math, and twenty-seventh in science. Bracey contends that politicians' attention to international comparisons too often distracts us from the real work of dismantling what he calls the "Poor People's Education System." **Do you agree or disagree with Bracey that the real threat to public education in the United States comes from within and not from outside the system?**

Whatever the results of international comparisons of achievement are used for, they must account for students' opportunities to learn the material on which they are tested. If students in different countries do not have opportunities to learn the same things at the same time or by the same age, the value of comparing these students in terms of academic achievement is questionable. Although money is often cited as the best way to improve education, one could make the argument that smartly spending money is a more important factor in improving educational systems. When spent wisely, money can create many opportunities for students to learn. Figure 12.6 contains comparative information on national spending on education. **How closely do you think a nation's spending on education is linked to its students' performance on international comparison tests?**

Comparisons that Foster a Global View

Concepts of global and comparative education can stretch to address commonalities among people, regardless of where they live. People are naturally curious about what it is we share as a result of our humanness. **Are there activities in which we all engage that make us more alike than different from one another? How and what can we**

FIGURE 12.6 Public Direct Expenditures for Education as a Percentage of the Gross Domestic Product: Selected Countries, 1998

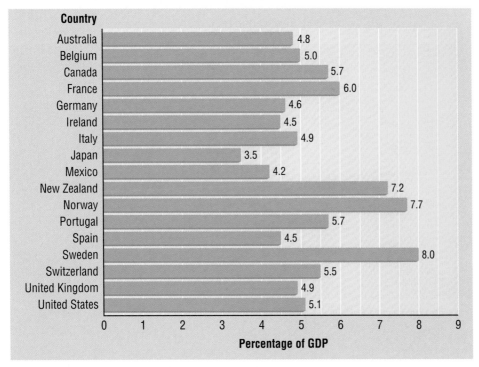

Note: Includes all government expenditures for education institutions.

Source: Organization for Economic Cooperation and Development, *Education at a glance, 2001.* Available online: http://nces.ed.gov/pubs2002/digest2001/ch6.asp#5.

learn about ourselves by learning about others who live in markedly different cultures?

Studies of teaching and learning across cultures suggest how much educators share, regardless of where they live and work. For example, the educational construct of *wait-time* has been investigated in many settings in many international contexts and with different kinds of students. Mary Budd Rowe (1986) originated the concept of wait-time as a way to describe the pauses in a classroom teacher's verbal activity. One type of wait-time occurs when a teacher asks a question and then waits for a student to respond. The other type occurs after the student responds. If a teacher can learn to wait for at least three seconds before filling the void with her talk, then the quantity and quality of students' responses increase dramatically, regardless of where in the world these events take place.

Classroom interaction studies point out common concerns among educators around the globe and highlight culture-based differences in their responses to those concerns. Research on Asian teachers, for example, suggests that they, like their U.S. counterparts, learn much by watching their students. Their learning differs in important ways, however, particularly when interpreting students' mistakes.

> For Americans, errors tend to be interpreted as an indication of failure in learning the lesson. For Chinese and Japanese, they are an index of what still needs to be learned. These divergent interpretations result in very different reactions to the display of errors—embarrassment on the part of American children, calm acceptance by Asian children. They also result in differences in the manner in which teachers utilize errors as effective means of instruction. (Stevenson & Stigler, 1992, p. 27)

$\mathcal{F}$**IGURE 12.7   Some Forces That Shape the Lives of All Teachers and Students**
What other factors operate either inside or outside people to make
them like one another? What, for instance, might all teachers believe
about teaching and learning?

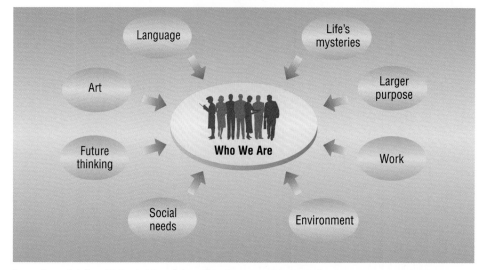

Source: http://glef.org/FMPro?-DB=articles1.fp5&-format=article.html&-lay=layout%20%231&learnl.

Regardless of where teachers and students are scattered around the globe, we are
united with one another by some common characteristics or forces that influence our
lives (Boyer, 1992). These make us more like one another than different. Figure 12.7
suggests that human dignity is shaped by some of the same kinds of forces in all cultures. Imagine how teachers might use these ideas to stimulate learners to search for
common ground.

The following are some of the things that we as humans share, no matter where we
live. They are important ideas to keep in mind as you continue to explore the occupa-
tion of teaching, and they are ideas you should share with your students.

1. As human beings we share the mysteries of the life cycle—birth, growth, and
   death. What milestone events do you celebrate in your culture? How do these
   events and celebrations resemble such events in another culture that is distant
   geographically (or philosophically) from your culture?

2. We all use languages to express feelings and ideas. Do you speak, write, or read
   a language other than English? How many of your friends and family are bilingual or multilingual? What encourages or discourages you from learning other
   languages?

3. We connect with others through music, dance, painting, sculpture, and the
   many visual arts. Is there a particular form of artistic expression that is especially
   important to you? How do artists from other nations and various cultures affect
   you?

4. We believe we are unique among living creatures in our abilities to recall the
   past and to anticipate the future. What do you imagine your future might hold?
   Personally or professionally, how is your future likely to be similar to and different from an aspiring teacher in another nation?

5. Every person belongs to groups. Some memberships are brief; others last a lifetime. To what groups do you belong? To what groups have you been assigned?

Do you share membership in any of these groups with people from different nations or cultures?

6. We are all connected to planet Earth. We all depend on the natural world for our survival. What environmental issues are important to you in your own locale? What environmental events in your immediate locale affect people who are distant from you? How might environmental events in other places be felt in your own neighborhood?

7. Work occupies our lives. Taking is key to our survival, but we all must give back if people are not only to survive but to prosper. What do you take and give back?

8. In every corner of the globe, we can find people searching for a larger purpose in life. Sometimes educators describe their desire to make a difference or to be part of something bigger than themselves. Do you have these thoughts?

Summary

The United States of America has always been a part of the world community. Recent events and increased interaction with more people from different nations make the need to learn about the rest of the world more important than ever. The revolution in communications technology only makes our connections to others faster, stronger, and more numerous. Therefore, this land of immigrants has many reasons for taking a global educational perspective that outweigh any inclinations to narrow our sights.

As we learn about education in other countries, we shape and verify our perceptions of the physical, intellectual, emotional, and social life in schools around the world. In many instances our knowledge helps us work more effectively with our close neighbors. We also learn how to support those who emigrate from distant nations to the United States. Almost

without fail, when we study educational life in other places we learn more about ourselves—why we teach and learn as we do.

Learning about education often means making comparisons between ourselves and others in the global community. Some sources of information upon which we base these comparisons, such as international performance tests, provide useful information. Comparison test results, however, should not be the extent of our interest in other countries' educational systems. When we look beyond the competition to be the best, we allow ourselves to learn new skills, ideas, and techniques that can improve education for all students. The forces that define teachers and students as citizens of the world impel us to minimize our differences and look for what we have in common.

Terms and Concepts

apartheid   352
global awareness   333
international comparative education   337

juku   343
NGO   335
okeiko-goto   343

Reflective Practice

Project Cuba

To most outsiders, Cuba is an enigma. North Americans often know the nation only as a well-developed set of images crafted during the past forty years by governments, the movie industry, and the popular press. The romantic image of this mysterious island in the Caribbean, located only ninety miles from Florida, has had remarkable staying power—so strong

that tourists' appetite for Cuban music, beaches, rum, and cigars is an emerging force in the dollar economy.

But the vivid image of life under communism also looms large over Cuba. North Americans have been taught to imagine communism as a police state that leaves its citizens powerless. In so many ways, Cubans and non-Cubans alike seem trapped by the history represented in these stereotypical images that rarely reveal much about life in Cuba.

Young Cubans do as well as most other children in the world on educational tests. Virtually all children who do not have serious disabilities advance to secondary schools, which start at grade seven. The overwhelming majority of students, about 95 percent, graduate from ninth grade.

Issues, Problems, Dilemmas, and Opportunities

What do young people everywhere, regardless of nationality, care about? What do they need in order to grow up with a sense of hope? How do they think about themselves, and how do they want others to view them? How might the goals and expectations of education in Cuba differ from those in the United States? How might they be the same?

Perceive and Value

How do you think teachers are regarded in Cuba? What might a Cuban perceive as the benefits and shortcomings of public schools in the United States?

Know and Act

What would you like to know about educational standards in Cuba? How do test scores of Cuban students compare to those of U.S. students? What percentage of Cuban students do you think attend college? How might adults help young people, regardless of where they live, stake out common ground or find common interests?

Evaluate

In Cuba, both undergraduate and graduate education are free. How might you judge the advantages and disadvantages of providing students with a free education, from start to finish?

INTASC Principle 3

The teacher understands how students differ in their approaches to learning and creates instructional opportunities that are adapted to diverse learners.

Knowledge

The teacher understands how students' learning is influenced by individual experiences, talents, and prior learning, as well as language, culture, family, and community values. (Interstate New Teacher Assessment and Support Consortium, 1992)

Discussion Question

Find someone who has moved from another country to the United States. What were the biggest language, cultural, or family, and community challenges he or she faced while adjusting to life and learning in the United States?

*A*dditional Readings

Brown, S. C., & Kysilka, M. L. (2002). *Applying multicultural and global concepts in the classroom and beyond.* Boston: Allyn and Bacon.

Davidman, L. (2001). *Teaching with a multicultural perspective: A practical guide* (3rd ed.). New York: Longman.

Martorella, P. H. (2002). *Social studies for elementary school classrooms: Preparing children to be global citizens.* Upper Saddle River, NJ: Prentice Hall.

National Research Council (1999). *Global perspectives for local action: Using TIMSS to improve U.S. mathematics and science education / A joint project of the Committee on Science Education K–12 and the Mathematical Sciences Education Board.* Washington, DC: National Academy Press.

Spring, J. H. (1998). *Education and the rise of the global economy.* Mahwah, NJ: Erlbaum Associates.

*W*eb Resources

http://www.gsn.org/

The Global SchoolNet site creates opportunities for teachers worldwide to collaborate online.

http://plasma.nationalgeographic.com/mapmachine/

National Geographic MapMachine is one of many sites offering maps of the world.

http://www.ibo.org/

Learn more about the International Baccalaureate Organization's educational programs.

http://www.ngo.org/

Explore nongovernmental organizations associated with the United Nations.

http://www.aaie.org/

The Association for the Advancement of International Schools promotes connections among educators in American schools abroad (e.g., military, diplomatic, etc).

http://www.tes.co.uk/

The *Times Education Supplement* is the place to go for information about education in the United Kingdom.

Video**Workshop** Extra!

If the VideoWorkshop package was included with your textbook, go to Chapter 12 of the Companion Website (ablongman.com/mcnergney4e) and click on VideoWorkshop. Follow the instructions for viewing video clip 12. Then consider this information along with what you've read in Chapter 12 while answering the following questions.

1. This chapter addresses the topic of global awareness. How does the influence of educational technology bring the world of education onto a global scale? How can you rec-oncile the *digital divide* discussed in the video clip with the concept of global awareness?

2. Based on what you saw in the video clip, select a topic of global importance related to education, such as equity in the classroom. Imagine you have funds from a sizable grant to spend on technology, and plan a campaign to bring together educational resources and strategies relating to your topic.

*W*hat Lies Ahead

CHAPTER CONTENTS

**How Are Teachers'
Professional Roles
Changing?**

**How Are Links to
Technology Changing
the Foundations of
Education?**

**How Are Collaborative
Networks
Transforming
Teaching and
Learning?**

**How Can Professional
Educators Prepare for
the Future?**

After setting up a table to one side of our lobby and readying his tools,
Lama Tenzin worked with quiet concentration, gradually arranging small
grains of colored sand into a design of increasing complexity. Our students stood around his table between classes, fascinated by this strange
process and the beautiful patterns swiftly emerging from the experienced
hands of its small, orange-robed creator.

By Friday, the weeklong work of creation was finally finished. But
the manner of its completion was a shock to some. Aided by a small
group of students and teachers, Lama Tenzin carried the mandala the five
blocks to New York's East River and, with ceremony and reverence,
brushed the mandala into the waters of the river. An unusual end for any
work of art.

Why destroy something on which so much labor and time have been
lavished? Part of the answer comes from the Buddha himself, who taught
that all things are characterized by impermanence and that it is our clinging to them which is the root cause of our suffering as human beings. The
destruction at the end of a mandala's creation is a powerful symbol of
this truth. (Bonnell, 2002)

As the actions of Lama Tenzin, and those of teachers everywhere, suggest, teaching
and learning give life meaning. They are hopeful acts that shape the future. This chapter discusses the unusual opportunities that now exist for teachers to make a difference

in people's lives, including trends in standards development, curriculum formation, student assessment, diversity, and character development. The chapter also examines how technology is changing the landscape of teaching and what you can expect from participation in collaborative networks of people devoted to common educational goals. The chapter concludes with suggestions on how teachers develop productive, satisfying careers in education.

*H*ow Are Teachers' Professional Roles Changing*?*

Why is now a good time to be a teacher?   There has never been a better time to be a teacher. Technological advances, innovative curricula, access to more information, highly diverse students, and the developing global community are only a few of the reasons why being a teacher today is so exciting. Many people outside the system have much to say about how teaching and learning should be improved. But teachers are there at the center of activity every day, working to inspire, inform, and support young people. They know that, in spite of negative opinions in the public and in the press, an abundance of good work is being done in classrooms. Teachers will be there, advancing civilization, when everybody else has gone home.

As the rest of this book has shown, the history and ideology of education in the United States are marked by change and evolution. From how schools are funded to what students are taught and how they are assessed, the rules and standards are constantly changing. Changes in teaching, learning, and public education can be described in terms of trends—trends toward the use of common goals and standards, toward comprehensive curriculum development and performance assessment, and toward the development of human talent in inclusive settings. As we prepare ourselves and future generations for life in a faster, smaller, and more high-tech world, it is more important than ever that teachers help shape these educational trends.

Trends toward Common Educational Expectations

Many people are worried about the public education system in the United States. Critics are worried that students are not learning the information and skills they need, that teachers are not fully trained before entering the classroom, and that a huge rift is forming between rich and poor schools. Implementing common educational expectations for all schools, teachers, and students is one way to address these issues. Advocates believe common expectations will provide educators with guidelines, while also providing ways to evaluate how well schools are doing in comparison to one another.

One of the most important moves toward common education expectations is the No Child Left Behind Act passed in 2001. A revision of the Elementary and Secondary Education Act of 1965, the No Child Left Behind Act is the most comprehensive federal legislation covering K–12 education. It affects every public school in the United States in the following ways:

- **Annual testing.** By the 2005–2006 academic year, all states must begin testing pupils in grades three to eight every year in reading and mathematics. The tests must be aligned with state standards, and fourth and eighth graders in every state also have to take the **National Assessment of Educational Progress (NAEP).**
- **Academic progress.** States must demonstrate that all students reach at least a level of proficiency on their exams by the 2013–2014 academic year. In the

---

meantime, all schools must make "adequate yearly progress." If they fall short two years in a row, they must offer students the option of attending other public schools at no cost. If the schools fall short three years in a row, they must offer supplemental services to pupils, including tutoring. The clock started ticking on failing schools in 2002.

■ **Report cards.** In 2002–2003, states must document student achievement by subgroup and by district. Districts must produce similar report cards for each school.

■ **Teacher qualifications.** By 2002–2003, all newly hired teachers must be "highly qualified," which means licensed (or certified) and teaching in content areas for which they are endorsed. By 2005–2006, all teachers must meet this require-

Cultural Awareness

JAPANESE SCHOOL REFORM

The performance of Japanese students in mathematics and science has long been the envy of other nations, particularly the United States. Although schools in Japan have an international reputation for efficiency and success, Japanese policymakers are not pleased with the high-pressure, fact-oriented nature of their schools. They are also concerned by the high incidence of teenage suicide and violence, as well as the dramatic increase in dropout rates. In an attempt to modify curriculum and instruction, policymakers have made historic changes that are somewhat controversial in a society used to having children engaged in schoolwork six or seven days a week.

When Japan began the new school year in April 2002, the national course of study—a document outlining what every public and private school should teach at each grade level—had been trimmed by about 30 percent. School on Saturday, which made for a 240-day school-year calendar, had also been eliminated. Officials also added a study period called *sogo gakusku,* designed to provide students with opportunities for project-oriented lessons on nontraditional topics, such as coexisting in a diverse society and protecting the environment. In addition, teachers, school administrators, and local boards were given more control over the curriculum.

Japan's recent curriculum changes seem to reflect the principles of progressive education that have long characterized education in the United States. It is interesting that Japan is moving more toward student-centered instruction while the United States is the midst of a "back to basics" movement. According to Thomas Rohlen, a prominent researcher in comparative education, Japan and the United States have a long history of exchanging educational policies, which often coincide with changes in the economy and the release of international comparisons of student achievement.

Why might Japan look to the United States for ideas about educational improvement? According to Japanese leaders, the U.S. educational system excels in areas such as essential life skills that Japan has neglected:

> Students seem helpless in the face of challenges that require them to think for themselves, one college instructor reports. Another college instructor at a private university frets that students are not resourceful, that they tend to seek the one "right" answer, and that they look for guidance in solving relatively simple, everyday problems. (Manzo, 2002b)

The first wave of changes in Japanese education took place in primary and junior high schools. Modifications to the more pressure-driven high schools will occur during the 2003–2004 academic year. In the midst of these changes, Japanese teachers must figure out how to deal with new requirements and address the competing demands of parents and upper-school admissions policies. A teacher of thirty years lamented, "I used to have to say to students, 'Do this, and do this.' Now, we have to take care of each child. I spend one and a half times as much time preparing lessons. . . . It takes continuous effort."

Critical Thinking Question

What characteristics of teaching and learning in the United States support a Western way of thinking?

To answer this question online and e-mail your answer to your professor, go to Chapter 13 of the Companion Website (ablongman.com/mcnergney4e) and click on Cultural Awareness.

Source: Manzo, K. K. (2002, September 25). North wind bows to the rising sun. *Education Week.* Available online: http://www.edweek.org/ew/ewstory.cfm?slug=04japan.h22&keywords=Japan.

ment. Also, all newly hired paraprofessionals or aides must have at least two years of college preparation, possess an associate's degree, or meet standards of quality. By 2005–2006, this will hold true for all paraprofessionals.

■ **Reading first.** The federal government will invest $900 million in reading programs beginning in 2002.

■ **Funding changes.** More money will flow to poorer school districts, and they will have greater flexibility on how to spend it.

How do you think these new expectations influence life in schools? Some people worry that the mandates of the act will never be implemented and enforced effectively. Others see the discrepancies in funding between rich and poor schools and argue that the proposed changes in funding are not enough to help those who need it most. Still others believe this act is merely the first step in a desirable direction.

Trends toward Comprehensive Curriculum and Assessment

Educators and other citizens of the United States are engaged in a struggle to control curriculum in the public schools. Policymakers at all levels of government, parents, philosophers, educational practitioners, citizens, and would-be citizens want to influence what is taught and learned in schools.

The public's evolving expectations for educational standards are stimulating reform in curriculum, methods of teaching and learning, and processes of assessment. These reforms will occur slowly in some places and rapidly in others. When viewed together, these reforms constitute noticeable changes in the way teachers perform their jobs.

Curricular reform requires more than continually adding and removing information to and from courses of study. Curriculum integration must blend old and new material, form links between concepts within and across content areas, structure content so students can make connections in their minds, organize people and ideas by themes,

Many groups are fighting for control over the public school curriculum. What are some areas that you think are likely to be reformed?

and team students with teachers. Reformed curricula will look different from one another, but the integration of knowledge, people, and thinking is likely to be a common characteristic among them.

As the curriculum reforms are put into effect, teachers will become increasingly responsible for creating opportunities for students to demonstrate what they know and can do in real-life settings. For instance, teachers will charge their students to study concepts of time, rate, and distance by packing them off to football fields and amusement parks with maps and stopwatches in hand. Students will be running races, timing roller coasters, and calculating the values of missing variables. In all likelihood, however, they will be doing so in virtual space, using the technological tools of the twenty-first century to solve timeless problems. And their teachers will be at their sides, helping them learn from their mistakes.

To determine how well reforms in curriculum and teaching methods are working, assessment will continue to be a major part of teachers' lives in the foreseeable future—but not only in the form of tests created by others. Educators are rethinking the practice of defining success in terms of scores on standardized achievement tests. In the future, tests that yield information on students' abilities to pick "right" and "wrong" answers will diminish in importance. In their place, educators will develop a **comprehensive assessment** of student progress. These assessments will tap students' capacities to reason, think divergently, solve problems creatively, and express themselves clearly. Comprehensive assessments need to reflect the kinds of challenges students will face in real life, and they must provide estimates of students' abilities to live and work successfully.

Such changes in curriculum development and usage, as well as changes in assessment styles, will have great impact on what teachers need to know and what they do. One could say that teachers need well-honed *clinical* skills to help students grow into independent, successful adults. That is, teachers need to base their judgments and actions on the best information they can obtain from the situations they encounter. Getting and using such information effectively is what skilled clinicians do. Teachers of the future, like physicians, will take their instructional cues from the people they serve. They will work with students to identify outcomes that are logical and attainable, and they will help students work toward these outcomes. How will teachers know when they succeed? They will judge their success by studying their own teaching and by examining the learning of their own students.

The responsibility for preparing students for the future, however, does not fall entirely on teachers. School districts are also undergoing reform to help prepare both teachers and students for the demands of the future. In a study of six school districts in five states (California, Colorado, Iowa, Maryland, and Texas), researchers found how successful school districts put data to work to improve student achievement (Armstrong & Anthes, 2001). These districts were characterized by the following attributes:

■ *Strong leadership.* The superintendent, central office staff, and school board members are committed to collecting and using data for decision making.

■ *Supportive culture for using data for continual improvement.* Data are readily available to teachers, students, and parents to guide school improvement. Teachers who did not agree with this view were encouraged to look elsewhere for a job.

■ *Strong service orientation toward principals and teachers.* The district made curriculum specialists available to schools and offered help in getting and using data to inform practice.

■ *Partnerships with other organizations.* These districts joined with universities, businesses, and nonprofit organizations to obtain expertise and technology to support school activities.

- *Mechanisms to support and train personnel to use data.* Most districts assigned a person to be in charge of data collection, analysis, and reporting. In addition, the time of others in the central office and resources from outside groups were made available.

- *Monitoring every student's performance on academic standards.* The system gave tests often and set performance targets for students to meet in between the tests.

- *Flexible time use.* Grouping and instructional patterns were changed to address students' needs and to allow teachers to plan together. Vertical integration— teachers meeting from all the grade levels—to coordinate curricula and instruction occurred in some districts.

- *Defined improvement process.* Data helped these schools identify needs. The school personnel, in turn, behaved systematically to address them.

Trends toward Education for Diversity

Standards are uniform, but children are different. If they are to achieve the same or similar outcomes, children need different levels and kinds of support. Increasingly, in the years ahead, teachers will make informed decisions about students' needs and abilities in order to deliver appropriate support. This means, among other things, that educators will develop curricula and instruction for students from different cultures and subcultures and for students with special learning needs.

GENDER SENSITIVITY TRAINING

Gender-fair education provides **gender sensitivity training** to all students. Curricula are designed to avoid sex-role stereotyping and to promote equal educational opportunities for girls and women. Some ways in which gender-fair education is implemented include using standard textbooks that draw attention to women's relevant contributions and routinely encouraging girls to take and master mathematics and science courses throughout their educational careers. In addition, education texts and classroom activities should avoid the generic use of male terms and examples.

A number of educators have created curricula that avoid sex-role stereotyping and identify opportunities for girls and women to take advantage of all their possibilities for education. The *Civitas* curriculum examines gender from three frames of references—conceptual, historical, and contemporary—and suggests directions for sharply defined study (Quigley & Bahmuller, 1991). The conceptual frame draws attention to such factors as the basis for past exclusion of women from politics, the role of feminism, arguments for and against changing women's roles in society, and women's relatively small role in the exercise of formal political power. The historical perspective emphasizes the place of women in politics at the founding of the nation, the beginning of women's political activism, the campaign for women's suffrage, and the various phases of the feminist movement. The contemporary perspective looks at gender issues as they have been articulated in the 1990s and at the start of the twenty-first century, including wage inequality and job segregation. It also considers women in politics in present-day America.

Equity between males and females might be realized as people adopt a more caring attitude toward others. Nel Noddings (1984, 1992), Madeline Grumet (1987), and other feminist educational reformers have argued that society's prevailing conceptions of gender will be changed only by transforming what and how children are taught about caring and ethics.

How can gender-fair education be provided in all classrooms? What role can gender-sensitivity training play in addressing problems of gender bias?

I have argued for a curriculum aimed at producing people who will not intentionally harm others; a transformed structure of schooling that will encourage the development of caring relations; a moral education that emphasizes maternal interests in preserving life, enhancing growth, and shaping acceptable children; and the development of a morality of evil that should help all of us understand and control our own tendencies toward evil. (Noddings, 1992, p. 678)

How far should schools go in attempting to ensure gender equity?

TEACHING ALL STUDENTS IN INCLUSIVE CLASSROOMS

The inclusion movement in special education has encouraged the teaching of children with disabilities in general education classrooms, instead of teaching them in self-contained classrooms or separate facilities. Inclusion carries the force of the law and considerable public support. At the same time, disagreement exists about which settings are most appropriate for which students and how to provide instruction for students with disabilities in inclusive classrooms.

As a classroom teacher, you will be expected to understand the needs and abilities of all students as fully as possible so you can set tasks or objectives that students with disabilities can accomplish. As you fit instruction to individuals' goals, needs, and strengths, you may need to structure teaching and assignments for students in different ways. You also will have to assess students in ways that allow them to demonstrate what they know and can do. This will mean focusing less on standard measures of learning and more on alternative assessments of what they have learned.

Trends toward Defining Diversity in Economic Terms

According to a report by the Century Foundation (2002), U.S. public schools are showing signs of economic segregation. While two-thirds of the nation's student population is middle class (not eligible for federal subsidized lunches), one-quarter of all schools have a majority of students from low-income households. To avoid becoming two United States—one rich, the other poor—the report encourages policymakers to integrate students of different socioeconomic levels. It also says that race should be a factor in integration only if economic criteria do not work. Because children perform best in middle class schools, the idea is to bring children of different races and economic classes together. Doing so should provide all students with opportunities for educational success.

To accomplish this goal, the Century Foundation recommends a policy of public school choice, accompanied by fairness guidelines:

> Within given geographic regions, parents can rank preferences among a variety of schools, each of which has a distinctive curricular theme or teaching approach. School officials then honor those choices with an eye to promoting integrated schools, a system now successfully employed in Cambridge, Massachusetts, Montclair, New Jersey, and elsewhere. Alternatively, communities might promote integration using a system of public school choice that provides substantially greater funding to low-income children, with dollars traveling with students, thereby making low-income students more attractive to middle-class communities. (2002)

Why might using incentives to accomplish economic integration be more effective than using coercion?

Trends toward Character Education

Teaching or clarifying values, sometimes referred to as **character education,** is one way educators attempt to shape young people's lives. In the past ten years or so, schools have been under increased pressure to provide students with character education in addition to the normal skill- and information-building curriculum. Karen Bohlin, Deborah Farmer, and Kevin Ryan (2001) describe three approaches to character education that currently dominate school activities: views, virtues, and values. Each approach, while somewhat different, is meant to stimulate moral and intellectual development.

The *views approach* is meant to help students develop and explicitly state their intellectual positions on controversial issues related to laws, politics, wealth, poverty, religion, and the like. Classroom discussion is the typical method used by teachers when attempting to help students strengthen their views. How well does the strategy work?

> This approach to moral issues is something like what you might see if you watch Oprah Winfrey or Jerry Springer. It might make for stimulating television, but it has little to do with character development. In general this approach generates more heat than light, and students are left with the impression that some issues are "just too complicated" or "ultimately just a matter of opinion." (p. 11)

The *virtues approach* attempts to develop good habits and dispositions (virtues) that help students develop into responsible adults. Virtues such as diligence, sincerity, personal accountability, courage, and perseverance are the things that help us develop better relationships and do our work better, thereby attaining human excellence. For instance, a virtue lesson might teach that it is not enough to value the Bible; one must also act out the Bible's rules for living with one's neighbors. Thus, "education in virtues—those good dispositions of the heart and mind that are regularly put into action—is the foundation of solid character development" (p. 12).

The *values approach* is the most popular one used in schools. This approach teaches students that values are what people want, desire, or assign worth to; the things valued can be morally good, bad, or neutral. It also teaches that, besides being a matter of personal choice, values are a personal right. Thus, teachers using the value-driven approach to character education are not supposed to indoctrinate or impose their views on students. Instead, teachers are supposed to provide students with opportunities to sort out their own values, so they can make wise choices in their lives. **How far should schools go in teaching moral values?**

A variety of character education programs have made their way into the schools. One widespread program is CHARACTER COUNTS!, a nonprofit, nonpartisan, nonsectarian coalition of schools, communities, and nonprofit organizations that holds training sessions for teachers and students, produces curricular materials, and assists local groups that promote ethics and character in sports programs. Coalition members work to advance character education by teaching the Six Pillars of Character: *trustworthiness, respect, responsibility, fairness, caring,* and *citizenship.* The six core values have been endorsed by some forty states and five hundred municipalities, school districts, business groups, and political leaders (including the president and both houses of Congress).

Another way that schools provide students with character education, in addition to a sense of belonging, is to encourage them to participate in the responsibilities of community, state, and nation. Specifically, a number of schools encourage volunteerism, or **service learning.** Some service learning programs encourage students to adopt a moral stance of caring, a political view of the value of reconstructing society, and an intellectual stance on the importance of engaging in experiences that transform the way people think. Other charity programs are organized around the moral principle of giving, the political ideal of performing one's civic duty, and the intellectual value of gaining experience by participating in service activities.

Volunteer projects can take a variety of forms and provide a variety of services for the school and the community. In many instances, volunteer groups perform their services outside school hours and receive no credit, awards, or certificates of appreciation from their school. Individual service projects, such as tutoring peers or younger children or

Voices

HOW DO TEACHERS DEVELOP STUDENTS' CHARACTER?

*L*aura and Malcolm Gauld, both experienced educators, have worked with hundreds of teenagers and their families. Much of the Gaulds's teaching has occurred in Hyde Schools, a group of public and private schools in Bath, Maine; Washington, D.C.; and New Haven, Connecticut, that focuses on character development and family growth. Often referred to as *turnaround schools,* Hyde programs have received national attention for their dramatic success with off-track, misbehaving teenage underachievers. The Gaulds explain what they have learned about character development through their work with students:

> Character is inspired. We won't teach much character if we simply post a list of ideals (e.g., respect, tolerance, honesty) and beg the kids to pay heed. In his book, *Dumbing Us Down,* John Gatto presents a comparison of the painter and the sculpture as a metaphor for great teaching. Gatto observes that a painter begins with a blank canvas and transforms it by *adding* patterns of color to create a new design. A sculptor begins with a shape that was always there, waiting to be exposed to the world. Gatto maintains that the great teachers are sculptors rather than painters. We agree. We don't pour character into our students; we summon it forth with value-forming challenges and experiences. With this view, character is a miracle that must be developed. Once developed, it must be maintained: "Use it or lose it!"
>
> We don't *give* our students anything. We help them *uncover* something that was always there. It may be buried under a lack of confidence or under a heap of family dysfunction, but great teachers remove the barriers and ignite a dormant confidence that can help a kid "take off." Parents play a similar role.
>
> The second point—site versus context—further clarifies the power of inspiration. . . . [O]ur use at

Hyde of a high ropes course [is] an effective and powerful character-development site. The high ropes course fosters courage, risk-taking, and trust. Let's take the case of sixteen-year-old Debbie, who has climbed the rope ladder to accept the challenges offered by the course. It demands that she place her trust in the person who stands on the ground thirty feet below holding her safety belt line. . . .

> Now what happens after Debbie descends from the ropes course, unfastens her harness, unstraps her helmet, and talks about the experience with her family? Let's assume her parents do not value courage, risk-taking, and trust. Perhaps her family is highly dysfunctional. Debbie cannot possibly reap the maximum benefit of the ropes course if she spends most of her time living in a context that does not reinforce its lessons. If Debbie's parents are not striving to develop their character, it is doubtful that she will continue to seek out the kind of challenges necessary for her own character development. . . .
>
> Both of these points—the power of inspiration and the idea of site versus context—add up to the same conclusion: Parents need to be critical players in the development of their children's character. (2002, pp. 21–22)

Critical Thinking Questions

Was character education a part of the curriculum in schools you attended? If so, did teachers attempt to *inspire* or *impart* character? What role, if any, did parents play in the character development program?

To answer these questions online and e-mail your answers to your professor, go to Chapter 13 of the Companion Website (ablongman.com/mcnergney4e) and click on Voices.

Source: Gauld, L., & Gauld, M. (2002). *The biggest job we'll ever have.* New York: Scribner.

working with residents in nursing homes, foster communication and intergenerational understanding. Group service projects, such as repairing bleachers or cleaning up the local park, help students learn to plan and cooperate with others to get a job done. Students who volunteer also become more responsible and develop more favorable attitudes toward the people they work with than do students who do not volunteer.

Service learning projects often provide opportunities for students to participate in the world, taking part in projects and causes that affect us all. To this end, many projects involve some form of environmental education and work. For example, science and social studies teachers work to sensitize young people to the importance of preserving the delicate balance of forces in their environment. Through lesson plans focused on issues important to students' local environments—from conserving water in the West, to controlling soil erosion in the Midwest, to raising awareness about acid rain in the East—students learn what they can do to help preserve their environments. Schools also regularly encourage student participation in such activities as Arbor Day, recycling programs, and wildlife preservation projects. In so doing, schools play an important but indirect role in educating parents about environmental issues. Perhaps, more important, these programs instill in students the belief that as part of the community it is their duty to give something back, whether it be through environmental, social, or political work.   **Should schools make service learning mandatory?**

How Are Links to Technology Changing the Foundations of Education?

Now, more than ever, it is impossible to discuss the subject of education, even at the elementary level, without referring to the power of computers. As schools develop capacities to deliver video, audio, data, and text to classrooms through electronic media, teachers will have opportunities to use technology in two ways. First, they can use it as a means of direct instruction that focuses on basic skills; second, they can use it to help students construct their own knowledge and develop a deep understanding of subject matter. Educators will also teach students to use technology for themselves. Computers will no longer be used only for drill and practice work or as rewards for students who finish their "real work" early.

The challenge educators face is determining how to use computers in ways that actually help students to think and learn. For one example of a computer-integrated classroom that works, step into Lowell School, an independent preprimary and primary school in Washington, D.C. There you might see Stephanie Heyndericks's fourth-graders manipulating eMate laptops with ease as they prepare their assigned book reviews:

> They will navigate the word-processing program by touching on-screen menus with a plastic stylus. They will type in corrections to the drafts that Heyndericks hands back. They will use infrared technology to "beam" their reviews to one another's machines—no messy writing required—and then huddle together for peer editing. Every now and then, someone will dart over to the printer, which will whir and hum and spit out a fresh draft. . . . Near the end of the afternoon, as students pack up [their computers], so they [can] continue working at home, an especially computer-literate fourth-grader name Grenville puts [the scene] in perspective. An eMate is just an "oversized PalmPilot," he says. At Lowell [School], you don't get your *real* computer until fifth grade. (Thompson, 2001, p. 18)

Most experts agree that some basic conditions must exist if computers are going to be used effectively to link students with information and people in the larger world. Computers must be available in sufficient number so that workstations can be provided for every two to three students. Teachers need training and opportunities to use computers for themselves if they are going to help students use them. Teachers also need time to restructure their curricula around computers if the machines are going to be used for anything other than drill and practice work. Finally, computers must be made available in individual classrooms, because teachers will have difficulty integrating technology with classroom instruction if students have to go to a lab to access a computer.

Educational technologists have been studying the topic of computers in classrooms to help define ways technology is being used effectively. From their studies, Mark and

Cindy Grabe (2000) have identified five themes that describe the different uses of technology in classrooms. The first theme is found when students use technology to study a particular content area; at this point, the technology has been *integrated into content-area instruction*. As teachers encourage students to learn to use general-purpose software, such as word-processing programs, they are employing a *tools approach* to technology instruction, the second theme. The Grabes identify the third theme as using technology to promote *an active role for students*. By active, they mean the mental behavior of students as they use technology to construct meaning for themselves or to solve complex problems. When students become more active, teachers may use technology to step back from their role of dispenser of information to play a *facilitative role*, or one of assisting students. The fourth theme occurs when technology is used to facilitate *an integrated or multidisciplinary approach* to teaching and learning involving a broad range of skills. Finally, technology can enhance interactions among students, providing the benefits of *cooperative learning*.

The Internet and the World Wide Web

In the coming years, if not already, teachers will use the Internet to promote any or all of the Grabes's themes. The **Internet** is a global telecommunications network that began in the 1970s as a military effort to ensure communications in case of a nuclear attack. The Internet is an international technological network that connects millions of supercomputers, workstations, laptops, hand-helds, and other devices for the purpose of exchanging data, information, news, and so on. Sometimes referred to as the information superhighway, the Internet is decentralized and unowned. It allows people

TABLE 13.1 Percent of Public Schools with Internet Access, by School Characteristics: 1994–2001

School Characteristics	Public Schools with Internet Access							
	1994	1995	1996	1997	1998	1999	2000	2001
All public schools	35	50	65	78	89	95	98	99
Instructional level[a]								
Elementary	30	46	61	75	88	94	97	99
Secondary	49	65	77	89	94	98	100[b]	100[b]
School size								
Less than 300	30	39	57	75	87	96	96	99
300 to 999	35	52	66	78	89	94	98	99
1,000 to more	58	69	80	89	95	96	99	100
Locale								
City	40	47	64	74	92	93	96	97
Urban fringe	38	59	75	78	85	96	98	99
Town	29	47	61	84	90	94	98	100
Rural	35	48	60	79	92	96	99	100[b]

[a]Data for combined schools are included in the totals and in analyses by other school characteristics, but are not shown separately.

[b]The estimate fell between 99.5 and 100 percent and therefore was rounded to 100 percent.

NOTE: All the estimates in this report were recalculated from raw data files using the same computational algorithms. Consequently, some estimates presented here may differ trivially (i.e., 1 percent) from results published prior to 2001.

Source: U.S. Department of Education, National Center for Education Statistics, Fast Response Survey System, "Survey on advanced telecommunications in U.S. public schools, K–12," FRSS 51 (1994); "Survey on advanced telecommunications in U.S. public schools, K–12," FRSS 57 (1995); "Advanced telecommunications in U.S. public schools, Fall 1996," FRSS 61; "Internet access in U.S. public schools, Fall 1997," FRSS 64; "Internet access in U.S. public schools, Fall 1998," FRSS 69; "Internet access in U.S. public schools, Fall 1999," FRSS 75; "Internet access in U.S. public schools, Fall 2000," FRSS 79; and "Internet access in U.S. public schools, Fall 2001," FRSS 82.

around the world to communicate with one another and access great resources of information on every topic imaginable. As illustrated in Table 13.1, a growing number of schools and school districts are members of the Internet community.

Teachers and students use the Internet in a variety of ways and for a variety of tasks. The ways in which people are able to access information and services are defined by *protocols,* or programs, that specify how information moves online. These are described next.

Chat is a form of real-time or **synchronous communication** on the Internet, meaning the parties involved must be online simultaneously for communication to occur. The chat program allows people to send and receive typed messages almost instantaneously.

Electronic mail (e-mail) is the most popular application of the Internet, in which messages are sent, received, stored, and forwarded to others. Teachers often establish a mailing list, or **listserv,** that allows them to send messages to all their students in a class at the same time with a single keystroke. Mailing lists are a good way to continue a class discussion outside the classroom, offering an immediacy that benefits the exchange of ideas.

A **file transfer protocol (FTP)** lets people move, or download, files from computers anywhere on the Internet to their own computers or workstations. A teacher might locate files of pictures, documents, or raw data at NASA and wish to use them with her students in a science class studying outer space. She might use an FTP to capture the files and put them on her computer and then use them whenever she or the students need them.

The **World Wide Web** (also called the Web or WWW) is a system of Internet servers that supports tens of thousands of specially formatted documents that often have text and still images, as well as audio and video. These documents are called **hypermedia.**

Websites are individual locations on the Web owned and managed by a person, group, company, or organization. They may contain a single Web page or many files, graphics, and other information, usually on the same or related topics.

A **Web browser** is a computer application that allows a user to access and view Web materials. Examples of Web browsers include Internet Explorer, Netscape, and Mosaic.

A **home page** is the first page of a website or document, and it is usually organized much like the table of contents in a textbook. Besides indicating who or what organization has posted the document, the page suggests what might be found within the site. It may also list the most recent articles or news related to the website's topic.

News groups are electronic message services that post to local, regional, national, and international Web servers. People subscribe to a news group to gain access to these messages and to post their own messages. News groups are widely used in education. They, like e-mail, are a form of **asynchronous communication,** meaning the parties involved in the communication do not have to be present online at the same time. Instead, e-mail can be sent and messages posted to news groups and viewed at a later time.

Videoconferencing is a form of synchronous communication that allows people to see and hear one another over computers. This is a useful technology for online instruction courses and meetings, as it helps people communicate across the miles.

With appropriate software and an Internet connection, one can access virtually any of the Web's documents. The range of information accessible on the Web is vast. One can travel to points all around the world, as well as find a rich repository of educational resources.

A growing number of schools give students access to the Internet through computer labs, laptops, and hand-held devices.

Your Teaching Life in Practice

ARE STUDENT LAPTOPS A LUXURY?

Across the United States, school districts are expanding teaching beyond its traditional parameters by supplying teachers and students with wireless laptops—technology that enables learning anywhere, anytime. In September 2002, the state of Maine supplied every seventh-grader with a wireless laptop computer. Editorial staff of *USA Today* criticized the move, while Angus King, governor of Maine, praised the decision:

USA Today: Maine has a mixed record of educating its children. The state has test scores that rival those in wealthier states, yet teacher salaries are low, and a high percentage of its teachers are assigned to subjects that they've never studied.

Given those problems, the state has made a puzzling decision to spend $37 million handing out laptops. . . . Surely, Maine can find better educational uses for the money than giving students individual computers that they can take home. . . . [R]esearch supporting the educational value of laptop giveaways doesn't exist. Some schools introduce laptops smoothly while others get stung. In Henrico County outside of Richmond, Va., school officials had to recall thousands of laptops for fixes last year after they discovered that students used them mostly for instant messaging and swapping game and movie files.

Given the cost, laptops are a luxury most school systems can't afford. In Maine, the $37 million budgeted for the computers could be put to better use hiring teachers who studied the subjects they're assigned to instruct. Currently, 33% of the state's math teachers in grades nine to twelve lack either a major or minor in the subject.

Computer companies are pushing hard to sell laptops as the key to preparing students for the job market. But before buying that line, educators need to pinpoint their biggest educational challenge and decide whether it's apt to be solved with the laptop.

The state of Maine is trying to transform K–12 education through the use of technology. Every seventh-grader in Maine—rich or poor, urban or rural—has a laptop computer and wireless access to the Internet.

This initiative, which extended to eighth-graders in 2003, represents collaboration between state government, local school officials, national educational leaders, and classroom teachers. The project is intended to make Maine's people the best educated—and most digitally literate—in the world, a goal Governor Angus King considered urgent as our nation makes the difficult transition to an economy relying primarily on the acquisition and use of information. . . .

Angus King: Maine studied the results of previous technology deployments to learn from their successes as well as their failures, and the state has created a system of effective professional development for teachers that focuses on integrating the technology on a daily basis. No technology can supplant the teacher, the most important educational source ever invented. But this project will give our teachers the resources necessary to meet the challenge of the knowledge explosion taking place every day. . . .

None of us can predict the future with certainty, but we can be sure that it will involve the collection and use of information, an ever-increasing role for education and a growing reliance on technology. That future will be full of both opportunity and challenge; here in Maine, our kids will be ready.

Critical Thinking Question

The jury is still out as to whether laptops will revolutionize the outcomes and the processes of education. Do you think students and teachers should be provided with wireless laptops? Why or why not?

 To answer these questions online and e-mail your answers to your professor, go to Chapter 13 of the Companion Website (ablongman.com/mcnergney4e) and click on Your Teaching Life in Practice.

Sources: USA Today (2002, September 13). Student laptops are a luxury. Our view: School funds can be better spent on, say, helping kids learn to read. *USA Today,* p. 16A; King, A. (2002, September 13). Computers key to future. Opposing view: Maine's investment in technology will better educate students. *USA Today,* p. 16A. Copyright 2002, USA Today. Reprinted with permission.

Getting information from the Web requires no permission (although some of the information may be copyrighted to restrict its redistribution), and users can share what they have with the rest of the world.

Distance Learning

Televised instruction has been a fact of life for several decades, but new technology designed to promote **distance learning** is transforming how and what students learn—and where they learn it. In its most advanced form, which usually involves Internet connections, video equipment, and special computer software, distance learning allows people to interact with one another as if they were in the same room. Students can see and hear teachers, and teachers can answer students' questions and react to students' comments instantaneously. These features are especially useful when students are located in geographically remote areas.

The Star Schools Program, established by the Department of Education in 1988 and reauthorized under Title III of the Improving America's Schools Act, has been instrumental in promoting distance education. The purpose of the Star Schools Program is to encourage improved instruction in mathematics, science, and foreign languages, as well as improved **literacy** skills and vocational education. The program uses telecommunications equipment to teach underserved populations, including low-income and nonliterate students, students with limited English proficiency, and students with disabilities. By 2000 about 2 million students in all states, the District of Columbia, and the U.S. territories had enrolled in courses in math, science, foreign language, and other subjects funded in part by Star School grants. In addition, thousands of teachers had taken courses and participated in staff development programs offered through the Star Schools Program. You can connect to any of the Star Schools websites through the U.S. Department of Education website.

Many states are already taking advantage of the Internet to establish new, far-reaching distance learning programs. By 2002, twelve states had established online high school programs, and five others were developing them; twenty-five states allowed for the creation of cyber charter schools; and thirty-two states had e-learning initiatives underway. At the same time, ten states were preparing for online testing of students. Two states—Oregon and South Dakota—were already using Web-based assessments.

According to a 2001 report by the National Association of State Boards of Education (NASBE), the virtual school movement is the wave of the future. As opposed to the traditional model of offering instruction in particular buildings according to standard calendars and schedules, e-learning allows for "any time, any pace, any place" learning. NASBE representative Michael David Warren, Jr., from the Michigan State Board of Education, described an information age education system that would be enabled by a technology-rich learning environment. The system would include:

- a focus on learning, not schools;
- learning organizations defined by mission, not by geography and facilities;
- student-focused, customized learning, not mass-produced, one-size-fits-all instruction;
- self-directed and holistic learning, not regimented recitation;
- learning on a 24/7 basis and throughout the year, not artificial schedules and calendars;
- empowerment of families and educators, not bureaucracies; and
- a number of options and educational providers for each student, not a standard model for all (p. 13).

Distance learning projects are especially important for many small, isolated school districts that have had to exclude all but basic-level courses from their curriculum due

Technology in Practice

eSCHOOLS

The Plano eSchool, in Plano, Texas, offers high school courses that are accredited through the Plano Independent School District (ISD). Students already enrolled in a school and students in homeschools can use these online courses, with approval from their school counselor, to obtain credits toward graduation.

Plano eSchool offers credit-bearing courses in typical core subjects, such as English and American government. Enhancement, or noncredit, courses are also offered in areas such as study skills and oceanography. What students take depends on what they need.

Students enrolled in the Plano ISD can take two eSchool courses at a time, earning a total of two credits by doing so. The eSchool encourages students to balance regular courses with electronic courses, with the assistance of their counselors.

It can take from six to eighteen weeks to complete a course, depending on the offering. Students access online courses on their own time, wherever they have access to a computer and the Internet. They are not allowed to use the school district's equipment while working on course assignments. Communication with the online instructor is via e-mail. Tuition for eSchool courses is between $220 and $295. In addition, students sometimes need to purchase additional materials not covered by the tuition.

Critical Thinking Questions

Have you ever taken an electronic course, either for high school or college credit? If not, would you consider doing so? What might be the greatest drawback and the greatest advantage of taking courses online?

 To answer these questions online and e-mail your answers to your professor, go to Chapter 13 of the Companion Website (ablongman.com/mcnergney4e) and click on Technology in Practice.

Source: Plano ISD eSchool (2002). Available online: http://www.planoisdeschool.net/home.html.

to budget constraints. As financial support goes down and state education standards go up, distance learning offers attractive possibilities for making connections with people and ideas. An effort must be made, however, to make sure financial constraints do not also limit computer resources and access to distance learning options for the schools that need them the most.

Telecommunications Capabilities in the Schools

To understand how technology is changing the foundations of education, we need to know how and where technology is being used. **Do educators and their students enter the "information age" when they enter schools? Or do they step back in time, technologically speaking?** As illustrated in Figure 13.1, students use computers at school in a variety of ways. But is the technology revolution touching everyone or only those in wealthy areas and in certain geographic regions of the country? How is technology affecting the formation, acquisition, and, most important, the use of knowledge?

It is always difficult to know, relatively speaking, what constitutes appropriate and sufficient use of technology. Interest in the topic can be found in a variety of places, from private enterprise to the federal government. The business sector, for instance, showed their interest at the CEO Forum on Education and Technology (2000). The Forum created a STaR Chart to help people gauge School Technology and Readiness

FIGURE 13.1 Digital Content   Digital content makes a vast reservoir of information, ideas, and experts available at any time, from anywhere. This provides powerful resources and tools to teachers and students.

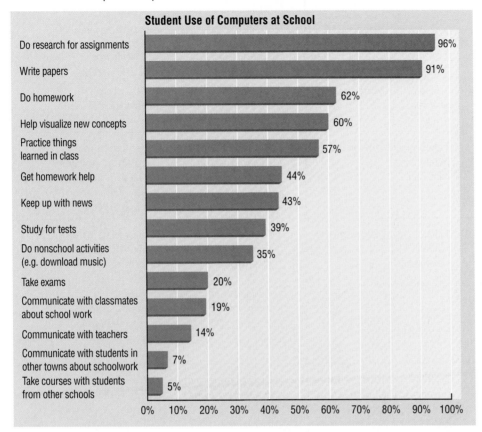

Source: CEO Forum on Education and Technology (2001, June). *Key building blocks for student achievement in the 21st century,* p. 26. Washington, DC: Author.

(hence the acronym STaR) to use technology. The chart can serve as both an evaluation and a planning device for technology use in schools. Six areas are described in the chart: hardware and connectivity, content, professional development, student achievement and assessment, integration and use, and educational benefits. It is possible to classify a school as low-tech, mid-tech, or high-tech in each of the six categories and to set targets for improvement. Figure 13.2 contains the STaR Chart standards for hardware and connectivity.

The federal government has also done much to stimulate the use of technology in schools, particularly those schools with financial needs. The Universal Service program for schools and libraries, better known as the **E-rate,** is a federal program that provides discounts on telecommunications and Internet technologies to elementary and secondary schools and public libraries. Congress authorized the E-rate discount program as part of the Telecommunications Act of 1996. The idea was to provide schoolchildren and library users with affordable access to the Internet, distance learning, and other telecommunications-based learning technologies. The program provides discounts ranging between 20 and 90 percent, with the poorest schools and libraries receiving the highest discounts. The discounts apply to Internet, telecommunications, and internal connections services. Thousands of libraries and schools, from every state in the nation, have participated in this program.

***F*IGURE 13.2   School Technology and Readiness (STaR)**

STaR Indicators	Students per Computer Connected to the Internet	Technical Support	Percent of Instructional Rooms and Administrative Offices Connected to the Internet	Quality of School's Connection to the Internet	Use and Availability of Other Forms of Hardware and Technology
EARLY Tech	More than 10	Takes several days	More than 25%	Dial-up access on some computers	VCRs, cable TV, projection devices, calculators
DEVELOPING Tech	10 or less	Takes place next day	50% or more	Direct connectivity of campus and in some classrooms	VCRs, cable TV, telephones, voicemail, projection devices, digital cameras, calculators
ADVANCED Tech	5 or less	Takes place same day	75% or more	Direct connectivity in most classrooms

Adequate bandwidth | Wide variety of VCRs, cable TV, telephones, voicemail, random-access video, projection devices, digital cameras, scanners, portals, personal digital assistants, two-way video conferencing, calculators |
| TARGET Tech | 1 student per instructional computer connected to the Internet | Tech support available 24/7 | 100% or more of all instructional rooms and administrative offices are connected | Direct connectivity in all classrooms with adequate bandwidth to prevent delays | There is broad use of a wide variety of other technologies, such as VCRs, cable TV, telephones, voicemail, random-access video, personal digital assistants, two-way video conferencing, projection devices, digital cameras, scanners, portals, calculators, thin clients, and servers. |

Source: CEO Forum on Educational Technology (June 2001). *StaR Chart: A tool for assessing school technology and readiness,* p. 18. Key building blocks for student achievement in the 21st century: Assessment, alignment, accountability, access, analysis. Washington, DC: Author.

Much of schooling is controlled and funded by state education authorities, and they are making many of the decisions regarding the availability and use of technology in classrooms. So it is important to know what state policymakers are thinking with regard to the use of technology. States may have specific criteria for evaluating computer software, audiovisual materials, CD-ROM-based reference databases, websites, and print materials. States and school districts may also help teachers with the challenging task of selecting appropriate online resources by providing one-stop access to a variety of resources, such as a statewide *digital library*. Having access to such gateway sites can save teachers much time and energy. Massachusetts, for example, sponsors a *virtual learning space* that gives each educator in the state an individualized virtual laptop that provides access to the following resources:

- state curriculum frameworks and district learning objectives;
- a personal calendar that interacts with the school and organizational calendars;
- an instructional planner or teacher plan book;
- tools to make student assessment more comprehensive and easier to administer;
- a searchable database of lesson plans, units, and courses used successfully by other teachers that meet state curriculum frameworks and their district learning objectives;
- tools to communicate with other teachers (discussion groups, bulletin boards, e-mail);
- a guide that accesses high-quality instructional Web-based content resources; and
- a "virtual hard-drive" accessible anyplace, anytime (National Association of State Boards of Education, 2001, p. 46).

The combined efforts of government and business to improve U.S. students' access to technology seem to be working. Since first measured, the ratio of students to instructional computers with access to the Internet (connectivity) has improved (12.1 to 1 in 1998 as opposed to 5.4 to 1 in 2001). By 2001, the ratio of students to connected computers was also higher in schools with the greatest numbers of low-income students: 6.8 to 1 compared with 4.9 or 5.6 to 1 in other schools (U.S. Department of Education, 2002).

From the looks of the current trends in technology availability and use, we can say that technology in the hands of ordinary people is democratizing the foundations of education. Technology brings opportunities for a person anywhere with a computer and a telephone line to make, acquire, interpret, and apply knowledge. (If you visit the AskERIC Virtual Library on the Web, you can see just how quickly and easily knowledge is available to those who seek it online.)

But is there a price to be paid for this new freedom—besides the economical one? With increasing opportunities for people to make themselves public electronically comes the necessity of sorting the good information from the poor. The kind of quality control exercised in traditional publishing does not exist in electronic communication and publication, except in a few instances. Issues of censorship that have been settled legally and practically in traditional publishing also must be reexamined with regard to the new communication technologies. **Should the creators and managers of the Internet censor materials? Should school leaders control what is appropriate and inappropriate for young people to read, see, and hear online? Who will decide? Could the Internet have a negative effect on education?**

Clearly, technology will be a key aspect of the educational system in years to come, one that is of interest to various groups and governmental levels. By its very nature, technology forces people to look forward, to anticipate not only what is important at the moment but also what is likely to be important later. When teachers consider how technology might be used to collaborate on their own professional development, they can get a sense of what their students will need to know and be able to do if they are to live successfully in the future.

How Are Collaborative Networks Transforming Teaching and Learning?

Collaborative networks are groups of people gathered voluntarily to explore and advance particular educational issues. Such groups often try to improve the education of targeted student groups through school reform. One innovative approach is to form *learning communities* that provide children with rich experiences. Learning communities are a helpful way to connect students' school lives with the children's experiences, culture, and community. This approach is part of Stanford professor Henry Levin's **Accelerated Schools** program, which he instituted in two elementary schools in San Francisco in 1986. The program now serves more than 1,000 schools across the United States and in four other nations.

The Accelerated Schools program encourages educators to build on students' strengths, giving at-risk students the kind of rich and challenging instruction typically reserved for gifted students. According to Sue Reese, kindergarten teacher at the Sheppard Accelerated Elementary School in Santa Rosa, California, "The Accelerated program has made a huge difference in our school." Some 97 percent of Sheppard's students come from economically disadvantaged homes. Reese says, "Although we can't always tell by standardized test scores, our kids are doing better. They're learning how to learn and how to make meaning out of what they learn; they are disciplined, and the attendance and transiency rates have improved." The school has been selected for the National Blue Ribbon Award for excellence in education from the U.S. Department of Education (Palmer, 2000). **Are people willing to judge the values of a teaching model by criteria other than student learning?**

For Levin, collaboration is important in the process of transforming a school into an Accelerated School: 90 percent of the staff must agree on the concept before he will work with them. Always, the adults who run schools must ask themselves a simple question: Is this what we would want for our own children? The answer to the question can spur people to behave in new and creative ways.

Levin believes people must begin changing schools by developing a deep vision of the future. Sometimes this process can take weeks or months. This vision often is not found in the typical mission statement of a school—a document that, according to Levin, frequently lacks vision. Instead, he wants people to work together to develop a set of beliefs that drive their daily behavior.

The Accelerated Schools Project, which began at Stanford University, has since moved its headquarters to Storrs, Connecticut. It is now in partnership with the Neag Center for Gifted Education and Talent Development. "Both our organizations are dedicated to raising the ceiling for kids and providing them with interesting, challenging, and enjoyable learning experiences rather than the traditional remedial approaches that have not proven to be very effective in boosting achievement or genuine engagement in learning," says Joe Renzulli, director of the Gifted Center (Palmer, 2000).

The Accelerated Schools model is only one possible model of collaborative reform. Many others have emerged in recent years. Some rely heavily on collaborations of adults and young people for their strength. Others emphasize particular approaches to teaching and learning. Most of the collaborations are intent on changing the way schools do business.

Targeting Students at Risk

Collaborative networks have been especially helpful for at-risk students. Many programs operate across the country and sometimes around the world; they offer specially designed curricula, innovative teaching methods, and specific ways to get parents and the community involved in schools and students' lives.

Since the 1970s, James B. Comer, professor of child psychiatry at Yale University, and his colleagues have been working with teachers, principals, parents, and community members to help children at risk beat the odds and succeed. Comer uses a collaborative process to create programs that foster child development. He calls the process the School Development Program. His approach is a form of site-based management, in which teams of professionals engage in "no-fault problem solving" and "consensual or collaborative decision making." In other words, people do not blame one another for problems; they work together to solve them.

*C*ollaborative networks such as the School Development Program are effective in some of the country's toughest inner-city schools.

Comer's strategy has been tried and found successful in some of the toughest schools in Washington, D.C.; Camden, New Jersey; Brooklyn; Dade County, Florida; Chicago; Dallas; Detroit; New Orleans, and many other communities. In the following passage, Comer himself describes how the School Development Program transformed one Detroit elementary school.

> I recently visited the Samuel Gompers Elementary School in one of the poorest neighborhoods in Detroit, a school with 97 percent student poverty. The Yale program has been used in this school for the past six years. The neighborhood was a disaster; the school was a pearl. The students were lively, spontaneous, and engaged in their work at appropriate times, yet quiet and attentive when they were supposed to be. They got along well with one another and were eager to demonstrate their skills to their parents and teachers. Eighty percent of the students passed the 1999 fourth-grade Michigan Educational Assessment Program (MEAP) test in reading and science, and 100 percent passed in mathematics. In 2000 they achieved the highest MEAP test scores among elementary schools in their size category in the state. (Comer, 2001, p. 3)

Collaborative networks also are transforming teaching and learning for at-risk students in U.S. high schools. In 1984, Theodore Sizer of Brown University organized the **Coalition of Essential Schools,** with nine member schools. Sizer's intent was to build and maintain viable networks of parents, students, and educators who could transform high schools into better places to teach and learn. Each school defines for itself what constitutes a good school, but participating schools abide by the nine common principles shown in Figure 13.3. Since its inception many more schools have joined the coalition, and today some nineteen regional centers coordinate member schools.

One challenge for Essential Schools is to link or integrate everything from curricula to people, and cross-discipline curriculum is a strong theme of the program. Their motto is "less is more." Therefore, high school teachers in the Essential Schools program are encouraged to think about reducing lessons from their own discipline

FIGURE 13.3   Principles of Essential Schools   If you were asked to rank by importance the attributes of an Essential School listed here, what would be your top two or three?

The Essential School should

✔ focus on helping adolescents learn to use their minds;

✔ have a single mission requiring students to master essential skills and knowledge;

✔ help all students strive for the same goals, but vary means according to students' needs;

✔ personalize teaching and learning;

✔ be guided by the metaphor of student as worker, not teacher as deliverer of instruction;

✔ prepare students to exhibit their language and mathematical skills;

✔ set a tone that communicates expectations, trust, and decency; use incentives; and encourage parents to collaborate;

✔ help staff think of themselves first as generalists and next as specialists; and

✔ provide planning time, competitive salaries, and per pupil costs of no more than 10 percent above traditional schools.

Source: Horace's school: Redesigning the American high school (1992) by T. R. Sizer. Boston: Houghton Mifflin.

specialties to the essentials and linking instruction between the disciplines. Coalition members try to adopt common themes or align similar classes and then combine the content of two or more classes into a single course of study. For instance, a theme such as "The Growth of Capitalism in nineteenth Century America" would be explored by studying history, literature, government, and the arts from the time period in a single class.

Being a collaborative network, the involvement of parents and community members is a key factor in the success of Essential Schools. Strategies for encouraging their involvement include sponsoring evening study groups in which adults explore the same educational issues that the students explore, holding public exhibitions of student work, paying parents to be classroom aides, organizing parent advisory groups, holding small-group sessions with the principal, publishing a newsletter, encouraging the local newspaper to cover educational issues, and so forth.

Success for All is another type of collaborative network for schools that can help at-risk students. Developed by Robert Slavin and Nancy Madden at Johns Hopkins University, Success for All operates in more than 1,500 schools in forty-eight states and five other countries. The main goal of Success for All is to ensure student success in reading. The program also strives to reduce referrals to special education, reduce the number of students who are retained, increase daily attendance, and address family needs. Its companion program, Roots and Wings, deals with content and experiences for children in reading and language arts, mathematics, science, and social studies.

The Success for All program supports nine specific components for helping at-risk students to succeed: (1) a reading curriculum that provides at least ninety minutes of daily instruction in classes; (2) assessment of student progress at least once every eight weeks; (3) one-to-one reading tutors; (4) a program for prekindergarten and kindergarten children that emphasizes language development and reading; (5) cooperative learning as a key teaching strategy; (6) a family support team to encourage parental support and involvement and to address problems at home; (7) a local facilitator to provide mentoring, counseling, and support to the school as needed; (8) staff support teams that assist teachers during the implementation; and (9) training and technical assistance on reading assessment, classroom management, and cooperative learning. **Should all students, regardless of achievement level, be exposed to the same basic curriculum?**

Increasing Parental Involvement

Because children's futures are linked to their parents, it is essential that teachers look for opportunities to involve parents in schooling. When parents take an interest in their children's progress—holding high but reasonable expectations for their children's performance and meeting their basic needs—good things happen: Students' school attendance, self-esteem, achievement, and prospects for living successful, productive lives all increase. It would be hard to overestimate the significance of the role parents play in their children's chances for success in school and in life.

Many ways are available for parents to take an active role in their children's educational lives. Indeed, connections between educators and families can be seen in the thousands of parent–teacher organizations that exist across the country. The most famous, the National Parent Teacher Association (National PTA), is more than one hundred years old. In 1896, when Alice McLellan Birney founded the organization as the National Congress of Mothers in Washington, D.C., she did so with clarity of purpose: "Let us have no more croaking as to what cannot be done; let us see what can be done" (National PTA, 1995–1996). The challenges she laid out were to establish and maintain lines of communication between home and school. The PTA and other such organizations made it appropriate and possible for adults in and out of the educational system to work together for children.

Too often, however, it is difficult to meet and work with the parents and guardians of the children most in need of a strong home–school support network—single parents, those working at more than one job, those pulled in so many directions by so many problems that they are struggling merely to survive. In reality, many single and overly stressed parents are children themselves. Despite the small number of glowing exceptions, far too many of these young parents fail in school, relegating themselves and their children to a bleak future. The majority of teens who start families before they reach the age of eighteen do not complete high school. Children of teenage parents often perform more poorly in school than other students and are half again as likely to repeat a grade. Figure 13.4 illustrates some of the ways teachers might overcome barriers that can inhibit parent involvement.

Enhancing Relationships among Educators

One of the most important benefits of collaborative networks is they bring educators into contact with one another for purposes of professional development and exchange of ideas. Working in cooperative settings is beneficial not only for students, but for the educators themselves. In these settings, educators are able to ask questions, receive answers, discuss current issues, exchange personal experiences, and otherwise support one another. The benefits of these networks are then taken back to the classroom.

One visible attempt to encourage education professionals to work together on relevant tasks has been the concept of the **professional development school,** or PDS. A PDS is a college–school partnership that stimulates cooperation among professors, teachers, student teachers, and pupils. A professional development school is a place where theory, research, and practice mix at the precollege and inservice levels. Thus, reform is cultivated in colleges as well as schools.

Collaborative networks for teachers also focus on content areas and mutual professional development through collegial activities. Many teachers enter the profession and stay because of their intellectual interest in the subject matter. For instance, the allure of the stage and the power of theater have attracted and sustained more than a few

FIGURE 13.4 Overcoming Barriers to Parent Involvement

- If parents do not speak English, arrange for an interpreter at meetings and conferences. Have printed materials sent home to parents translated—English on one side, the parents' language on the back.

- For parents who lack the ability to read, communicate information by way of phone calls or home visits. One-on-one meetings and other personal contacts are important. Check to see if your school system has a home–school coordinator who can assist you in efforts to connect with parents who are hard to reach.

- Learn about the backgrounds of students and find out about ways to communicate with diverse people.

- To build parents' trust in schools, encourage them to get involved in special activities like PTA and school outings. Also encourage them to visit the school, observe classes, and provide feedback. Make them feel welcome in your classroom.

- Plan one or more social events that allow teachers, administrators, and parents to interact on a social basis.

- Conduct conferences focusing on student performance at least twice a year, with follow-up as needed. Make meeting times flexible, perhaps scheduling conferences in the evenings or early mornings before school.

- Hold parent–teacher conferences at community centers or other off-campus locations that are near parents' homes.

- Make your first communication with parents a positive one. Let them know what their child is doing well or how much you are enjoying working with their child before calling to talk about misbehavior or poor performance.

- Seek out opportunities for professional development and training in parent involvement.

Sources: National PTA (1998). National standards for parent/family involvement programs—Standard 1: Communication. Available online: http://www.pta.org/programs/pfistand.htm#Standard1; National Center for Health Education (undated). Enhancing parent involvement. Available online: http://www.nche.org/.

English teachers through the years. The National Council of Teachers of English (NCTE) serves as a professional touchstone for many of them. The NCTE's programs and publications help unite English teachers by providing opportunities for professional involvement and outlets for the expression of creative energies. Science and social studies teachers, math and physical education teachers, technologists and school counselors, and teachers in other fields connect to one another through their professional associations.

Educational reformer John Goodlad has led an effort to institutionalize some new opportunities for teachers to interrelate as colleagues with common interests and to function cooperatively. He and his colleagues established the **National Network for Educational Renewal,** consisting of colleges, universities, and school districts in eighteen states. The intent of this network is to renew schools and teacher education. Members of the National Network for Educational Renewal agree to address a set of nineteen ideas, the first of which sets the tone for the organization: "Programs for the education of the nation's educators must be viewed by institutions offering them as a major responsibility to society and be adequately supported and promoted and vigorously advanced by the institutions top leadership" (National Network for Educational Renewal, 1999).

Without support, of course, even the best ideas never take hold. The give and take of colleagues who share a commitment to deal openly with difficult issues contributes to a climate that is hospitable to educational growth and development. As concern for education increases around the world, more and more collaborative networks for purposes of education that involve educators, parents, and students are forming all the time. Fortunately, through the power of the Internet and other new and evolving technologies, these networks can reach, involve, and help more people than ever imagined.

For example, CaseNEX (www.casenex.com) offers opportunities for teachers to work collaboratively on common problems of teaching and learning. Like lawyers, business people, and physicians, teachers analyze cases that describe real-life situations in classrooms. The cases they examine are multimedia representations of classrooms in schools around the world. Using both synchronous (real time) and asynchronous (any time) tools, teachers work collaboratively to identify problems and opportunities for intervention. They also examine research on teaching, forecast actions they might take if they were in a similar situation, and speculate on the possible consequences of actions by explaining how they and others might judge the effectiveness of their proposed actions.

*H*ow Can Professional Educators Prepare for the Future?

It is natural for educators to feel overwhelmed by the complexity and pace of our rapidly changing world, knowing that they have to make sense of it for themselves as well as prepare future generations. There is so much to know and so much to do. Faced with the diversity of interests that contend for attention in public education, it would be easy to either leap headfirst or be paralyzed with indecision. As professionals, educators distinguish themselves from nonprofessionals in two important ways: by what they know and by what they know how to do. To help prepare for the future, teachers use technology and participate in collaborative networks. By doing so, they build their store of knowledge and refine their repertoire of skills (see Figure 13.5). **Can collaborative networks contribute to the professionalization of teaching?**

Using Professional Knowledge

Both informal and formal sources of knowledge inform the practice of teaching. The formal knowledge base of a profession exists in books, periodicals, and other writings. This type of knowledge serves as a foundation for teacher education programs, as a basis for licensure and certification examinations, and as a benchmark by which teachers assess their own practices. The informal knowledge base exists in the minds and hearts of those who practice the profession and is derived from their experiences on the job, as well as their beliefs, values, and personal standards. For many teachers this personal source of knowledge is rich and immediately applicable to classroom life (Clandinin & Connelly, 1996).

The formal knowledge base for teaching consists of theories about what constitutes effective teaching and the results of empirical research. Educational theories attempt to explain how teaching and learning occur, while research provides the results of observations or experiments that help to explain relationships between teaching and learning. These two kinds of knowledge often complement each other, and the most useful theories and research for educators explain what teachers should do and why. Teachers who understand and can articulate the relationship between knowledge and practice demonstrate that they are ready to do their best now and to do better as their knowledge improves.

Why is formal research so important to educators? Researcher Harold Mitzel (1960) gave educators a way to think and talk about the knowledge underlying our field so we could apply it and participate in its development. Mitzel depicted a set of four

FIGURE 13.5 Uses of Collaborative Networks   People are more likely to collaborate when they have reasons to do so and opportunities for working together. What barriers, other than time and opportunity, might restrict collaboration among teachers? What other factors might enhance the likelihood of collaboration?

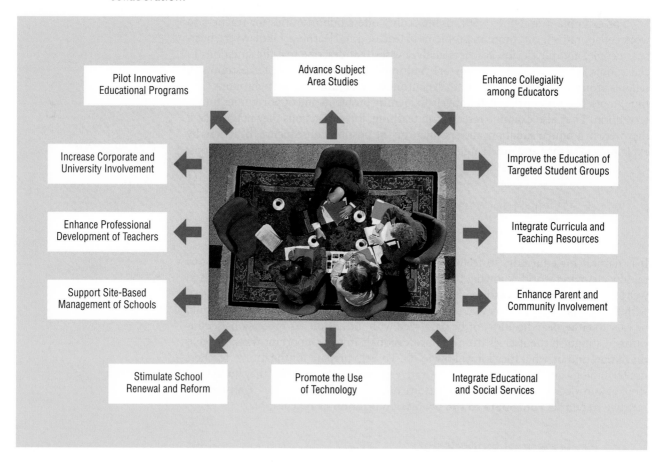

instructional variables we can use to discuss teaching and learning as interrelated activities. Those variables are teacher characteristics, teaching processes, student products, and instructional contexts. By breaking down the idea of education into these four variables, we are able to see how they interact and affect one another to produce an educational experience.

As Mitzel outlined the four variables, teachers' characteristics precede their teaching acts; for example, teachers' personalities and background knowledge influence how they approach the learning environment. Teaching process variables are demonstrated by teachers during a lesson—the questions they ask, the feedback they provide, and the like. Student product variables are student outcomes measured by tests, demonstrations, applications of knowledge, and other indications of learning. Instructional context variables are factors both inside and outside the classroom that influence teaching and learning, such as students' characteristics, school leadership, money spent on education, and children's home environments. The relationships among these variables are shown in Figure 13.6.

Another educational researcher, Herbert Walberg (1991), provided an overview of more and less effective educational practices, summarized from some eight thousand studies of teaching and learning in elementary and secondary schools. Using a statistical process of calculating *effect sizes,* he revealed the relative power of different

FIGURE 13.6 Model for Describing Research on Teaching Research on teaching cannot be conducted without the help and cooperation of lots of people—teachers, students, parents, administrators. What factors might influence your willingness to participate in research studies either as an investigator or as the subject of investigation?

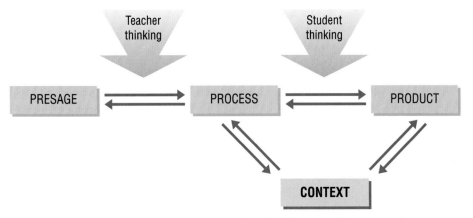

Source: Adapted from "Teacher effectiveness: Criteria of teacher effectiveness" by H. E. Mitzel, 1960. In *Encyclopedia of educational research* (3rd ed.) (pp. 1481–1486) by C. S. Harris (Ed.). Copyright 1960 and renewed 1988, by American Research Association. Used by permission of Macmillan Publishing Company.

instructional behaviors to boost student achievement. For instance, Table 13.2 shows the greater effectiveness of using manipulative materials in the teaching of mathematics over problem-solving approaches and the new math of the 1960s and 1970s.

Other researchers have noted that current research supports earlier indications of how important teachers are when it comes to stimulating student learning (Good & Brophy, 2003). This new research also focuses on the role of the student in the education process and recognizes that students do not passively receive or copy input from teachers. Instead, they make sense of it and relate it to what they already know (or think they know) about the topic.

The teachers best prepared to face the future, though, possess practical knowledge of teaching, as well as empirical and theoretical knowledge. Practical knowledge is constructed from teachers' own experiences. Teachers have always constructed their own knowledge by learning and experiencing what it takes to work with others to help them learn. In many ways, teachers' practical knowledge is far ahead of theory and research, because it comes from the classroom application of the theory and research we learn. It is through classroom application of theory and research that we learn for ourselves what really works and what does not—practical knowledge. For instance, we might

TABLE 13.2 Effects of Mathematics Methods

Method	Number of Studies	Effect Size	Graphic Representation of Effect Size
Manipulative materials	64	1.04	.xxxxxxxxxx
Problem solving	33	0.34	.xxxx
New mathematics	134	0.24	.xx

Source: Effective teaching: Current research (p. 58) by Hersholt C. Waxman and Herbert J. Wahlberg (Eds.), 1991. Berkeley, CA: McCutchan. Copyright 1991 by McCutchan Publishing Corporation, Berkeley, CA 94702. Permission granted by the publisher.

learn from theory and research that a specific style of classroom management is effective. We might learn from classroom application, however, that the management style works well for seventh grade students, but not at all for ninth graders.

Although some people believe being a teacher is something one can learn wholly on the job, practical knowledge and formal knowledge go hand in hand—one without the other is not enough. The importance of formal knowledge of teaching and learning cannot be overestimated. Empirical investigation helps separate fact from fiction and, in doing so, opens people's eyes and minds. Turning that formal knowledge into practical knowledge through classroom application is a necessary way of testing theories and staying in touch with current situations in education. Putting ideas to work in the classroom can help fine-tune theories and suggest new paths for investigation.

Knowledge, whether practical or formal, changes, evolves, and advances. As in medical research, theories and research in education can be proved wrong or incomplete. In addition, regularly comparing and contrasting how teachers and students think is beneficial to both parties, because it keeps both sides of the equations informed.

Keeping track of all these ideas and perspectives, especially when they are under constant change, can be a difficult process. Concept maps can be useful for this endeavor; they are ways of organizing relationships among ideas. To track ideas and developments, researchers who study teachers' and students' thinking sometimes use concept maps to describe what they learn. For example, when Caroline created her own concept maps of "teacher planning" at the beginning and again at the end of a two-semester course, they turned out to be very different, because her thinking had changed over time. Her second concept map of teacher planning appears in Figure 13.7. Caroline said this about her maps and her thinking:

> My initial reflections did not touch on teacher–parent interactions or on
> teacher–colleague interactions. In my end-of-year map, however, I devoted an
> entire section to communication with others. I believe the curriculum this past

FIGURE 13.7 Caroline's Concept Map of Teacher Planning   What thoughts about planning seemed most important to this teacher?

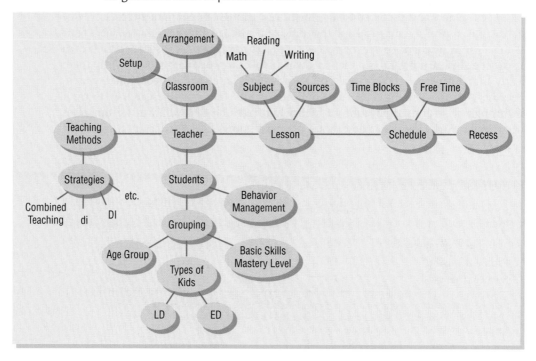

year, along with teacher training courses and student teaching, made me realize how vital these relationships are. I believe effective teachers work at reaching out to colleagues, gaining support from administrators, creating support systems, and communicating with parents from the start, not just after a problem has arisen.

Social skills are also new items on my final map. The extent to which they should be addressed depends on the students, the school, and the community. Over the course of the year, it has become increasingly clear how necessary it is for teachers to explicitly teach what is appropriate behavior, for example, how to show respect or how to respond to aggression.

With time and experience, good teachers learn how to apply their professional knowledge differently with different students. Jere Brophy and Mary McCaslin (1992) underscore the importance of teaching to individual students' needs in a series of studies they did on teachers with problem students (students exhibiting unsatisfactory achievement, personal adjustment, or classroom behavior). Teachers who had been identified by their principals as less successful in dealing with problem students described those students as underachievers, low achievers, aggressive, defiant, distractible, immature, shy, or rejected by peers. Typically, successful teachers demonstrated more willingness to become personally involved with students, showed more confidence in their own abilities to help the students improve their behaviors, and were better able to describe how to help students change their behavior and increase their learning.

Teachers' need for professional knowledge is also closely connected to their disciplines. It is not enough to possess general teaching knowledge at the expense of content knowledge, any more than it is to know the content and be ignorant of teaching practice. To teach mathematics successfully, for example, a teacher must master the subject matter, but he must also possess the teaching knowledge necessary for creating environments where students can learn mathematics. This blending of content knowledge and teaching knowledge has been called **pedagogical content knowledge** (Shulman, 1986).

Clearly, the influences of teachers and teaching in children's lives are a matter of national importance. And the knowledge teachers acquire, both formal and practical, is key to determining whether these influences will help or hinder students. In 2002, the Carnegie Corporation, the Rockefeller Foundation, and the Annenberg Foundation jointly funded a five-year initiative called Teachers for a New Era. This complex project is meant to explore not only the influence of teachers' pedagogical content knowledge on pupil learning, but also the value collegiate teacher preparation adds to their students' learning. Being prepared is one of the best assets a teacher can possess.

Reflecting on Professional Practice

Great teachers become great by continuing to learn while on the job. Those who can reflect intelligently on their own practices can learn from what they do, and they have the greatest chance of continuing to progress as teachers. In addition, these teachers are the ones best prepared to help other teachers, especially new ones, become great teachers as well. Collaboration among colleagues is important to teacher success. The five steps of professional practice noted in the following text promote such behavior.

1. In any field, professionals *perceive* problems and opportunities—they are mentally alert to what is going on around them.

2. Professionals also can articulate their *values* in relation to the values of others they work with and serve. Peoples' values help determine whether professionals' actions will be accepted or rejected.

3. Professionals possess some specialized knowledge that nonprofessionals do not. Professional educators *know* their content, and they know how to communicate

in ways that students will understand and accept. Exceptionally talented teachers, both experienced and novice, also know when they need to know more.

4. Professionals *act* on the basis of their perceptions, values, and knowledge. They continually apply their knowledge and demonstrate their skills in ways that nonprofessionals cannot.

5. Professionals *evaluate* their actions to determine their effectiveness and to plan for the future. People who can reflect intelligently on their practice—and who enjoy doing important work as best they can—turn jobs into careers.

Most teachers are not born knowing these concepts and professional standards, nor do they obtain them all at once. Teachers are students, too, and the learning never stops. Even the best among us do not always know how or why we are successful. With experience, we grow accustomed to not having all the answers all the time. We learn to rely on the best information available, as well as information acquired from successful and unsuccessful practice. No matter how professionally capable or personally adept teachers become, we will never single-handedly teach our students all that they need to know and need to do. Nor can we anticipate all the problems students will face. We must learn to work together with others (educators, parents, community members, students) to maximize our effects. The most important people with whom we must collaborate are students. By working together we model for students what we hope they in turn will model for others. We also transmit a set of democratic values that form the foundation of our society.

The best teachers stretch themselves time and again to be creative and technically proficient; they know they can call on their abilities when the need arises. They are not afraid to fail, because they have done that too and have lived to teach and learn another day. A good teacher, like a good student, gains power from doing the work.

Summary

Teachers of the twenty-first century will witness the evolution of their professional roles. They will lead their nation's efforts to set common expectations for academic success and to protect and advance the collective character of our increasingly diverse society.

Technology will figure prominently in teaching and learning in the years ahead. Teachers will use technology in many forms to plan, teach, and evaluate their student's work and, by implication, their own work. Technology will reinforce the ideas that more and better things happen when people work together to accomplish a common goal. Collaborative networks—sometimes technologically driven, sometimes not—will be the rule, not the exception.

The best teachers will be those who have the foundational preparation to continue learning on the job. These same teachers will get out of bed every morning with the anticipation of doing important work and doing it better than it has ever been done before. The great ones will relish the challenge of professional practice and savor the sweet success of a job well done.

Terms and Concepts

Accelerated Schools   380

asynchronous communication   373

character education   368

chat   373

Coalition of Essential Schools   381

collaborative network   379

comprehensive assessment   366

distance learning   375

E-rate   377

electronic mail (e-mail)   373

file transfer protocol (FTP)   373

gender sensitivity training   367

home page   373

hypermedia   373

Internet   372

listserv   373

literacy   375
National Assessment of Educational Progress (NAEP)   363
National Network for Educational Renewal   384
news groups   373
pedagogical content knowledge   389
professional development school (PDS)   383
service learning   369

Success for All   382
Synchronous communication   373
videoconferencing   373
Web browser   373
Website   373
World Wide Web   373

Reflective Practice

Turning Classrooms over to Interns

In 2002, the Kansas City, Missouri, public schools offered nine student teachers two-year full-time teaching contracts in an attempt to address the state's worsening teacher shortage. The interns were slated to graduate from state universities in December 2002.

The arrangement had the backing of the Missouri education department, and interns were offered plenty of support inside and outside the classroom. Interns received full-time pay for the two years, and they all lived rent-free the first year in the same apartment building—some even shared apartments.

Experienced teachers worked with pairs of interns, providing advice on such topics as lesson design and delivery, discipline, classroom management, and communication with parents. Faculty members from the interns' universities observed the interns' classrooms at least once a week and provided regular group and individual feedback (Manzo, 2002a).

Issues, Problems, Dilemmas, Opportunities

Visit the website for the federal No Child Left Behind Act (http://www.nochildleftbehind.gov/). How does Kansas City's arrangement square with federal guidelines for teacher preparation?

Perceive and Value

What might the student teachers in this program find advantageous and disadvantageous about the intern program?

How might parents view the program? How about Missouri's Education Association (state affiliate of the NEA)?

Know and Act

What are some of the strategies other school districts have employed to attract and retain beginning teachers? How do these efforts compare to the intern program in Kansas City? In which of these programs might you like to enroll? Why?

Evaluate

What factors should the school system consider when determining whether to expand their intern program?

INTASC Principle 9

The teacher is a reflective practitioner who continually evaluates the effects of his/her choices and actions on others (students, parents, and other professionals in the learning community) and who actively seeks out opportunities to grow professionally.

Performance

The teacher seeks out professional literature, colleagues, and other resources to support his/her own development as a learner and a teacher. (Interstate New Teacher Assessment and Support Consortium, 1992)

Discussion Question

How might this program benefit the experienced teachers who act as mentors to the interns?

Additional Readings

Dede, C. (Ed.) (1998). *Learning with technology.* Alexandria, VA: Association for Supervision and Curriculum Development.

Noddings, N. (2002). *Educating moral people: A caring alternative to character education.* New York: Teachers College Press.

Rose, L. C., & Gallup, A. M. (2002 September). The 34th annual Phi Delta Kappa/Gallup poll of the public's attitudes toward the public schools. *Phi Delta Kappan, 84*(1), 41–56.

U.S. Department of Education, National Center for Education Statistics (2001). *Technology @ your fingertips, version 2.0.* Washington, DC: The Department. Available online: http://nces.ed.gov/pubs98/tech/.

*W*eb Resources

http://www.ed.gov/Technology/guide/international/
resources.html

   The Teacher's Guide to International Collaboration on
the Internet provides resources for cross-cultural interaction and project work.

http://npin.org/

   The National Parent Information Network (NPIN) provides access to research-based information about the
process of parenting and about family involvement in education.

http://depts.washington.edu/cedren/NNER.htm/

   The National Network for Educational Renewal is an
independent, nonprofit corporation that conducts professional development programs on a wide range of edu-

cational issues. They bring together K–12, college of education, and arts and sciences faculty to advance teaching
and learning.

http://www.pta.org/index.asp/

   The National PTA is the largest volunteer child advocacy
organization in the United States. Parents, teachers, and
administrators who visit the PTA's website can find information about productive ways they can work together to
promote the welfare of children.

http://www.nsta.org/

   The website for the National Science Teachers Association (NSTA) provides information about ways science
teaching and learning, curriculum and instruction, and
assessment can be enhanced in classrooms.

Video**Workshop** Extra!

If the VideoWorkshop package was included with your textbook, go to Chapter 13 of the Companion Website (www.
ablongman.com/mcnergney4e) and click on VideoWorkshop. Follow the instructions for viewing video clips 11 and
12. Then consider this information along with what you've
read in Chapter 13 while answering the following questions.

1. Do you believe technology will ever replace human teachers in the classroom? Using what you know from the

chapter about trends affecting teachers' roles, what aspects of technology discussed in video clip 11 render
teachers irreplaceable or disposable?

2. Who do you think should be held responsible for setting
and/or maintaining standards for using technology?
Describe how collaborative networks, discussed in the
chapter, could work toward this end (see video clip 12).

BENCHMARKS

From the Past Comes the Future

1940s	United Nations Educational, Scientific, and Cultural Organization (UNESCO) is founded to broaden the base of education throughout the world and to encourage cultural interchange.
	The International Telecommunication Union (ITU) becomes part of the United Nations to promote international cooperation in telecommunications.
1960s	National Academy of Education (NAE) is founded to stimulate research in education and includes a division in comparative education.
	International Baccalaureate Organization (IBO) and the Institute of International Education are founded in the United States for international teacher education and the study of comparative education.
1970s	Telecommunications satellites, cable television, information processing, and fiber-optic technologies are developed for commercial use.
1980s	European Center for Higher Education (ECHE) implements new programs to increase student mobility across national education systems and to develop databases to facilitate transnational exchange of information.
	The Internet becomes a loosely organized, research-based network of computer users at major universities in Europe and the United States. The world's first distance learning collaborations are set up based on telecommunications and computer technologies.
1990s	National Security Education Act triples federal spending on undergraduate study abroad, overseas graduate research, and grants to support programs in international studies.
	UNESCO begins efforts to standardize educational credential reporting, licensing, and certification.
	The Internet expands to colleges, businesses, governments, individual users, and elementary and secondary schools in more than sixty-five countries.
2000	Schools in developed countries are wired for direct access to the Internet. Wireless communications and satellite technology use text, audio, and video to link people around the globe from schools to mountaintops, from offices to rainforests.
2001	The Third International Mathematics and Science Study (TIMSS) reports indicate that U.S. eighth grades do not fare well in international comparisons in either mathematics or science. Results of those studies lead researchers to ask, Are there states or local districts where this is not the case; where, in fact, their performance is world class?

DEVELOPING A PROFESSIONAL PORTFOLIO

Preparing Your Résumé

The most important element of your portfolio is your résumé. When writing letters of inquiry or application, it is common practice to include a copy of your résumé, which is a synopsis of your professional life. As such, your résumé reflects your work and educational history. Your résumé is also a plan for your future. You build it through experience with attention to what will make you a more complete professional.

While you can construct a résumé in a variety of ways in terms of content and design, there are some common expectations. As you can see in the following example, a résumé opens with personal contact information.

Nakisha Barnes
7715 Laredo Avenue
Benzinger, AZ 90220
(508) 475-0912
nbarnes@acme.com

Your contact information is often followed by your educational history.

Education	Major area	Degree
Colorado State Univ.	Elementary Education	Bachelor of Arts, 2005

Next, you can include your past work experience, which is relevant to your future employment.

Work Experience:

2004–2005:   Cashier, Colorado State University Bookstore; responsible for sales and bookkeeping.
2002–2004:   (summers): Lifeguard, Henley Swimming Pool, Greeley, CO; responsible for pool supervision and teaching beginning swimming class.
1999–2001:   Wait staff, Donuts and More, Shelby, AZ; responsible for customer orders and shop cleanliness.

You can also include your volunteer work; it shows interest in and compassion for others.

Volunteer Experience:

2002–2003:   Leader of Student Guides, Colorado Children's Museum
2004–2005:   Reader, Center for the Visually Impaired

Your basic certification and add-on endorsements demonstrate your qualifications.

Certification (or License): Elementary teaching (K–6) with endorsements in music and physical education.

List your interests to communicate balance and richness beyond your professional capabilities.

Special Interests: Piano, skiing, swimming, reading, and travel.

Finally, you will need to ask people to serve as references. You need people who can comment on your professional capabilities and your character.

References:

Mrs. Leona Tatum (The supervising teacher with whom I worked in student teaching)
Contact information, using her title, school address, telephone number, and e-mail address.

Dr. Irving Shapiro (Director of Colorado Children's Museum)
Contact information, including his business address, telephone number, and e-mail address.

Rev. Donald Spooner (minister of my local church)
Contact information, including his business address, telephone number, and e-mail address.

You can also include information in the categories of leadership positions, memberships in clubs and honor societies, and supervised field experiences.

Assume for a moment that you are reading Nakisha's résumé to hire her for a teaching position. What patterns do you see in her record? What items do you think are most important and least important? Why?

If your college or university has a career counselor or career services (placement) office, they often give workshops on writing résumés. You should attend these workshops and ask for advice. Be sure to save a digital copy of your résumé. It is an active document that will change with each new experience.

ONLINE ACTIVITY

Teaching Overseas

Have you ever considered teaching overseas? The Association for the Advancement of International Education (AAIE) exists for the purpose of encouraging such thinking and supporting those who undertake the challenge. The organization has members teaching all over the world.

Visit the AAIE website (www.aaie.org) to learn about the kinds of services the organization provides. Where is AAIE's next conference? What school-to-school projects does the organization promote that link schools around the world? Who is in the AAIE Hall of Fame, and why are they there? When and where is the next recruitment fair?

Pick a country in which you might like to teach. Why do you want to teach there? Do you have any idea of what it would be like to teach in this country? Check the Regional Associations linked to the AAIE home page. Contact the people listed for more information on your countries of interest.

A

Accelerated schools: schools designed to improve the learning of economically disadvantaged students; based on the work of Henry Levin.

accreditation: review and approval of education programs by outside experts.

Adoption and Safe Families Act of 1997: act of Congress designed to enhance the services and extend the scope of child welfare agencies.

aesthetics: branch of philosophy concerned with beauty.

alternative licensure: granting of approval to teach to individuals who have not participated in a traditional, state-approved teacher education program.

alternative school: any school operating within the public school system that has programs addressing the specific needs or interests of targeted student groups.

American Federation of Teachers (AFT): political organization of 800,000 members devoted to the advancement of educational issues and affiliated with the American Federation of Labor/Congress of Industrial Organizations (AFL/CIO). The organization has sponsored such projects as Dial-a-Teacher and Learning Line. It has also supported teacher internship programs, adopt-a-school programs, and national conferences for paraprofessionals and other school personnel.

apartheid: separation of the races.

apprenticeship: practical work experience under the supervision of skilled workers in the trades and the arts.

assessment: formal attempt to determine students' knowledge, skills, and attitudes.

assessment bias: qualities of an assessment instrument that offend or unfairly penalize students because of their gender, ethnicity, socioeconomic status, religion, or some other characteristic.

assimilation: process of educating and socializing a group to make it similar to the dominant culture.

assumption of risk: implicit responsibility assumed by people who are aware of the possible risks involved in an activity in which they voluntarily participate, thus agreeing to take their chances.

asynchronous communication: communication on the Internet that occurs at times convenient for any of the parties involved (e.g., newsgroups, e-mail).

at-risk students: children who are unlikely to complete high school; have failed one or more grades; are enrolled in special education classes; speak a language other than English; and/or are affected adversely by life- and health-threatening factors, such as poverty, disease, abuse and neglect, substance abuse, teenage pregnancy, and physical violence.

authentic assessment: assessment concerned less with students' recognition and recall of facts and more with students' abilities to analyze, apply, evaluate, and synthesize what they know in ways that address real-world concerns.

axiology: a branch of philosophy that seeks to determine what is of value.

B

behavioral objectives: objectives that describe conditions for teaching and learning, what is to be learned, and criteria for success.

behaviorism: philosophical orientation based on the belief that human behavior is determined by forces in the environment that are beyond human control rather than by the exercise of free will.

Bilingual Act of 1974: law requiring parental involvement in the planning of appropriate educational programs for children with limited English-speaking ability.

bilingual education: instruction in both English and a student's native language.

black codes: conduct codes established by southerners that allowed African Americans to hold property, to sue and be sued, and to marry, but forbade them to carry firearms, to testify in court in cases involving European Americans, or to leave their jobs.

block grant: money provided in a lump sum for several education programs in a locality.

block scheduling: organizing class schedules typically to provide longer instructional periods during the school day.

Blue-Backed Speller: Webster's *American Spelling Book,* first published in 1783.

blueprint: test specifications for the content and objectives to be assessed.

Brown v. *Board of Education of Topeka, Kansas:* Supreme Court case that determined that segregation of students by race is unconstitutional and that education is a right that must be available to all Americans on equal terms.

Buckley Amendment: part of the Family Educational Rights and Privacy Act that prohibits schools from releasing information about a student to third parties without parental or student permission.

Bureau of Indian Affairs (BIA): governmental agency established to, among other activities, oversee education programs for Native Americans.

C

career ladder: incentive program designed to acknowledge differences in the skills of teachers.

categorical grant: funding for an education program designed for a particular group and a specific purpose (e.g., bilingual education).

central office staff: superintendents and their associates and assistants.

certification: recognition by the state that a teacher has met minimum standards for competent practice.

character education: curricular approach driven by personal relevance that focuses on clarifying or unifying teaching values.

charter school: independent public school supported by state funds but freed from many regulations and run by individuals who generally have the power to hire and to fire colleagues and to budget money as they see fit.

chat: form of real-time or synchronous communication on the Internet.

Chautauqua movement: adult education movement that began in the late 1800s and led to the establishment of civic music associations, correspondence courses, lecture-study groups, youth groups, and reading circles.

chief state school officer: chief administrator of the state department of education and the head of the state board of education, sometimes referred to as the state superintendent or the commissioner of education.

Child Abuse Prevention and Treatment Act: passed by Congress in 1974 to provide financial support to states that implement programs for identification, prevention, and treatment of instances of child abuse or neglect.

Chinese Exclusion Act: legislation passed in 1882 aimed at stopping immigration.

Civil Rights Act of 1964 (Title VI): law that specifies that no one, regardless of race, color, or origin, can be discriminated against or denied participation in programs receiving federal assistance.

classroom management: collective ability of teachers and students to agree on and implement a common framework for social and academic interactions.

Coalition of Essential Schools: alternative high schools serving targeted students through school-based educational reform initiatives; based on Theodore Sizer's work.

cognitivism: philosophical orientation based on the belief that people actively construct their knowledge of the world through experience and interaction rather than through behavioral conditioning.

collaborative network: group of people who have come together voluntarily to help each other explore and advance specific educational issues.

collective bargaining: negotiation of the professional rights and responsibilities of workers (e.g., teachers) as a group.

collegiality: relationships based on the sharing of power.

Committee of Fifteen: committee that addressed the curriculum of elementary schools in 1895. Its curriculum focused on "the five windows of the soul"—grammar, literature and art, mathematics, geography, and history. It believed the role of school to be an efficient transmitter of cultural heritage through a curriculum that was graded, structured, and cumulative.

Committee of Ten on Secondary School Studies: committee established by the NEA in 1892 to standardize high school curricula.

common school: tax-supported school established in colonial times to allow all boys and girls to receive three free years of education focused on reading, writing, arithmetic, and history; predecessor of public schools.

comparative negligence: situation in which teacher and student are both held liable for an injury.

compensatory education program: program that provides children from low-income families with education opportunities beyond those offered in a school's standard program to compensate for factors (e.g., teachers, curricula, time, and materials) missing in young people's lives.

comprehensive assessment: assessment that measures students' capacities for reasoning, thinking divergently, and solving problems creatively.

concept formation: method of instruction used by teachers when they want students to analyze and synthesize data to construct knowledge about a specific concept or idea.

conflict mediation: formal efforts to help students solve their differences peaceably.

constructivism: view of knowledge as constructed by individuals acting within a social context that molds knowledge but does not determine absolutely what constitutes knowledge.

content standards: description of content to be mastered.

contributory negligence: failure of a person who is injured to exercise the required standard of care for his or her own safety.

cooperative learning: teaching model that encourages heterogeneous groups of students to work together to achieve such goals as mastery of subject matter and understanding and acceptance of one another.

cosmology: study of nature and origin of the cosmos, or universe.

Council of Chief State School Officers: nonpolicy-making organization composed of leaders of state departments of elementary and secondary education in the fifty states, the District of Columbia, the Department of Defense Dependents Schools, and five U.S. extrastate jurisdictions—Virgin Islands, Puerto Rico, Northern Mariana Islands, Guam, and American Samoa.

criterion-referenced test: test by which a student's performance is judged by comparing it to some clearly defined criterion for mastering a learning task or skill. The quality of a student's performance is measured against an absolute standard.

cultural literacy: shared information or common knowledge of a culture supposedly needed to function fully in that culture.

cultural pluralism: state in which people of diverse ethnic, racial, religious, and social groups maintain autonomous participation within a common civilization.

culture: sum of the learned characteristics of a people (e.g., language, religion, social mores, artistic expression, sexual behavior), which may be tied to geographical region. *Culture* also can be used in a "micro" sense to describe more conceptually discrete groups of people—cultures within cultures, subcultures, or micro-cultures.

curriculum: what is taught inside and sometimes outside school.

curriculum-based assessment: benchmarks for the knowledge, skills, and attitudes students must attain to master subject matter.

curriculum map: timeline indicating approximate dates when concepts and skills will be introduced.

D

dame school: educational program for boys and girls run by local women in a colonial community that typically focused on rudimentary reading skills.

direct instruction: highly structured, teacher-centered strategy that capitalizes on such behavioral techniques as modeling, feedback, and reinforcement to promote basic skill acquisition, primarily in reading and mathematics.

discrimination: differential treatment associated with labels.

dismissal: removal of a probationary or tenured teacher before the completion of his or her contract.

distance learning: capacity for teachers to communicate interactively with students or with one another over long distances.

district power equalization: relationship between state and local government in which localities establish the tax rate for educational spending and the state guarantees a set amount of money proportional to local revenue.

due process of law: mandated legal procedures designed to protect the rights of individuals.

E

early intervention: providing care and support from the prenatal period through the first years of life to enable children to enter school ready to learn.

Education Consolidation and Improvement Act (ECIA): 1981 act of Congress that consolidated many education programs into two major programs.

Education for All Handicapped Children Act (Public Law 94-142): federal law that requires all states to provide a free and appropriate public education to children between the ages of five and eighteen with disabilities. Education is to be planned through an individualized education program (IEP) and carried out in the least restrictive environment.

electronic mail (e-mail): messages sent and received via computers.

Elementary and Secondary Education Act (ESEA) of 1965: single most comprehensive extension of federal involvement in education, which resulted in policy-making power shifting to the federal level. The act provided funds to alleviate the effects of poverty through a variety of programs. It supported school libraries, the purchase of textbooks and other instructional materials, guidance, counseling, health services, and remedial instruction. It also established research centers and laboratories to advance educational practice.

emergency licensure: licensure granted temporarily until requirements and standards required for becoming a practicing teacher are met.

English academy: school established in Philadelphia in 1749 by Benjamin Franklin that emphasized the acquisition and application of knowledge thought to be most useful to the modern man.

English as a Second Language (ESL): instructional program designed to teach English to speakers of other languages.

epistemology: branch of philosophy concerned with the nature of knowledge or how we come to know things.

e pluribus unum: Latin term meaning "one out of many."

Equal Access Act: 1984 law passed by Congress that recognizes that secondary-school students are mature enough to understand that a school does not condone religion by merely allowing prayer clubs on public property.

equal educational opportunity: access to the resources, choices, and encouragement each student needs to achieve his or her fullest potential through education, regardless of race, color, national origin, gender, disability, or socioeconomic status.

equal protection clause: Section 1 of the Fourteenth Amendment, which prevents states from making or enforcing laws that abridge the privileges or immunities of citizens of the United States; deprive people of life, liberty, or property without due process of law; or deny equal protection of the laws.

E-rate: federal program that provides discounts on telecommunications and Internet technologies to elementary and secondary school and public libraries.

essentialism: philosophical orientation that acknowledges the existence of a body of knowledge that all people must learn if they are to function effectively in society.

establishment clause: clause in the First Amendment prohibiting Congress from making laws respecting the establishment of religion or prohibiting the free exercise of religion.

ethics: branch of philosophy concerned with issues of morality and conduct.

ethnicity: term describing a group of people with a common tradition and a sense of identity that functions as a subgroup within the larger society; membership is largely a matter of self-identification.

Eurocentric: curriculum and/or teaching depicting Europe as the cradle of Western culture.

evaluation: interpreting and attaching value to data relevant to people, programs, teaching, and learning.

exceptional learner: a child who has a special ability or disability that sets him or her apart from other children.

existentialism: a philosophy that emphasizes the subjectivity of human experience and the importance of individual creativity and choice in a nonrational world.

explicit curriculum: curriculum contained in policy statements, manuals of procedure, instructional materials, books, and other printed matter that explicate what and how students are to learn.

extracurriculum: noncredit-bearing activities, such as debate club and cheerleading, that are over and above the required curriculum.

F

file transfer protocol (FTP): means for moving, or downloading, files from computers anywhere on a network to a specific computer.

fiscal year: 12-month period covered by the annual budget, often corresponding to the state's fiscal year (e.g., July 1 to June 30).

flat grant: uniform or variable grant provided by the state to the school districts.

formative assessment: evaluation conducted for the purpose of shaping, forming, and improving knowledge and performance.

for-profit school: school that does not have tax-exempt status because it is run by a company to make money.

foundation program: program by which the state guarantees school districts a certain amount of money for educational expenditures and determines what proportion of that cost should be shouldered by localities.

free exercise clause: clause in the First Amendment prohibiting Congress from making laws abridging the freedom of speech or of press or the right to peaceably assemble or to petition the government for a redress of grievances.

Freedman's Bureau: government-sponsored organization established one month before the end of the Civil War to provide food, medicine, and seed to destitute southerners.

full-service school: school that attempts to meet basic needs of students by providing such things as food, clothing, showers, medical care, and family counseling.

full state funding: payment by the state of all educational expenses of school districts through a statewide tax.

G

gender bias: discriminatory treatment, often subtle or unconscious, that unfairly favors or disfavors individuals because they are females or because they are males.

gender sensitivity training: use of curricula that avoid sex-role stereotyping and the creation of educational opportunities for females to take advantage of all their opportunities for education.

giftedness: potential for high performance due to strengths in one or more of the following areas: general intellectual ability, specific academic aptitude, creative or productive thinking, leadership skill, ability in the visual or performing arts, and psychomotor development.

global awareness: recognition of people's connections to other countries and peoples of the world

H

Head Start: first major early childhood program subsidized by the federal government; provides comprehensive services to low-income three- and four-year-olds and their families.

hidden passage: educational activities that provided slaves with the intellectual power to escape bondage and to make lives for themselves after the Civil War.

high-stakes test: test used to evaluate school performance that determines students' grade promotion, graduation, and/or access to specific fields of study.

holding power: ability to keep students in school until they receive a high school diploma or an equivalency certificate.

home page: first page of a Web document.

hornbook: an instructional material used during colonial days. Letters, numerals, and other information were affixed to a piece of wood and covered with transparent material made from the horns of cattle that served as a protective layer.

humanism: philosophy that, in terms of education, calls for respect and kindness toward students and developmentally appropriate instruction in liberal arts, social conduct, and moral principles.

hypermedia: documents that consist of text and still images, as well as audio and video.

I

idealism: philosophy that suggests that ultimate reality lies in consciousness or reason.

implicit curriculum: unvoiced and often unintended lessons influenced by teachers' value orientations.

incentive program: program that offers outside incentives for good attendance and good grades.

inclusive education: education designed and offered to all people regardless of their physical, social, emotional, or intellectual characteristics; most often used to refer to education provided in mainstream or general education classrooms to students with disabilities.

Indian Self-determination and Educational Assistance Act: decision by Congress in 1975 to do away with federal reservations for Native Americans.

individualized education program (IEP): plan approved by parents or guardians that spells out what teachers will do to meet a student's individual needs.

Individuals with Disabilities Education Act (IDEA): 1990 act of Congress that amended the Education for All Handicapped Children Act by changing the term *handicapped* to *with disabilities* and by extending a free and appropriate public education to every individual between three and twenty-one years of age, regardless of the nature or severity of his or her disability.

induction program: program that provides special assistance, monitoring from experienced colleagues, and feedback on teaching performance to beginning teachers in the first one to three years on the job.

in loco parentis: term meaning "in place of the parent" that suggests that educators possess a portion of a parent's rights, duties, and responsibilities.

inquiry learning: answering and solving problems by analyzing data and creating and testing theories and hypotheses to expand the conceptual system with which one processes information.

instructional models: deliberate, explicit, complete plans for teaching that can be fitted to students and objectives.

integrated curriculum: curriculum that combines concepts and skills from different subject areas so that they are mutually reinforcing.

intermediate educational unit (IEU): collaborative organization maintained by separate districts to provide educational services (e.g., joining together to construct and maintain a technical training center for students).

international comparative education: study of education in different societies to develop new insights into these societies and to derive innovative understanding of one's own society.

Internet: electronic network with the capacity to span the globe.

Interstate New Teacher Assessment and Support Consortium Standards (INTASC): standards describing the necessary knowledge, dispositions, and performances for all teachers, regardless of their specialty areas.

J

journal: written collections of students' reflections on learning.

juku: after-school classes offered to elementary and secondary students in Japan to help them keep up with the demanding school curriculum.

K

kindergarten: educational program for young children; first established by Friedrich Froebel in 1837.

L

land grant school: public school established through federal assistance, the first of which was provided by the Northwest Ordinance of 1785.

latchkey child: child who is without adult supervision for several hours each day.

Latin grammar school: first formal type of secondary school in the colonies, established in Boston in 1635 for boys from nine to ten years of age who could read and write English.

Lemon test: tripartite test used to decide whether specific practices or policies are an establishment of religion.

licensure: process of meeting basic requirements and standards for becoming a practicing teacher.

limited English proficient (LEP): categorization of students who are qualified for instruction in English as a Second Language.

listserv: mailing list that allows a person to send a message to a group of individuals with a single keystroke.

literacy: one's ability to read, write, and calculate.

local property taxes: taxes on land and improvements firmly attached to the land (e.g., fences, barns) and on personal property, such as automobiles.

local school board: primary policy-making body for public schools, composed of elected or appointed public servants.

looping: grouping strategy that keeps students together with the same teacher for more than one year.

lyceum: out-of-school program, such as a reading circle or debating club, designed to improve the education of children and adults.

M

magnet school: alternative school within a public school system that draws students from its whole district instead of drawing only from its own neighborhood and that offers a curriculum based on a special theme or instructional method.

Marxism: philosophy based on Karl Marx's belief that the human condition is determined by forces in history that prevent people from achieving economic freedom and social and political equality.

mastery learning: one of several behavioral models that suggests that, given enough time, the inclination to learn, and instruction fitted to a student's needs, students are capable of mastering a range of subject matter.

McGuffey Reader: book first produced in 1836 by William Holmes McGuffey to teach literacy skills and to advance the Protestant ethic through stories and essays.

measurement: collection of data from individual students from a variety of sources (e.g., tests and quizzes, interviews, questionnaires, observations of in-class behaviors).

mentoring program: support system aimed at enhancing academic success and self-esteem of at-risk students; also, a program to help new teachers.

merit pay: incentive program designed to encourage teachers to strive for outstanding performance by rewarding such practice.

metaphysics: branch of philosophy that focuses on the study of reality.

minimum competency tests: tests designed to assess the lowest acceptable level of student performance.

mission school: school established by priests to convert Native Americans to Catholicism.

monitorial method: method devised by Lancaster for teaching large groups of students, by which a master teacher instructed monitors, and they, in turn, instructed younger children.

multicultural education: reform movement designed to bring about educational equity for all students, including those from different races, ethnic groups, social classes, abilities, and genders.

N

National Assessment of Educational Progress (NAEP): congressionally mandated battery of achievement tests operated by the Educational Testing Service to assess the effects of schooling.

National Association for the Advancement of Colored People (NAACP): established in 1934, the first nationwide special-interest group for African Americans.

National Association for the Education of Young Children (NAEYC): one of the largest professional associations for early childhood educators.

National Board for Professional Teaching Standards (NBPTS): nonprofit organization charged with the task of creating a national system of certification to be used to designate truly outstanding teachers.

National Center for Education Statistics (NCES): arm of the executive branch responsible for collecting and analyzing education statistics for the nation.

national certification: recognition for individual teachers, based on a national sample.

National Defense Education Act (NDEA): federal law passed in 1958 to provide funds for upgrading the teaching of mathematics, science, and foreign languages and for establishing guidance services.

National Education Association (NEA): organization with 2 million members guided by the vision of enabling students to develop themselves as people, to practice human relations skills, to learn how to be economically productive citizens, and to be responsible for their community and nation. It was instrumental in creating the National Council for Accreditation of Teacher Education (NCATE), a national organization that monitors the quality of collegiate teacher education programs.

National Education Goals: national goals established by President George Bush and the fifty governors in 1989 to ensure readiness for school; high school completion; student achievement and citizenship; excellence in science and mathematics; adult literacy and lifelong learning; and safe, disciplined, and drug-free schools. Extended by President William Clinton in 1994 to include teacher education and parental involvement.

National Governors' Association: coalition of state chief executives.

National Network for Educational Renewal: network consisting of universities and partner schools designed to simultaneously renew schools and teacher education.

National Parents–Teacher Association (PTA): largest volunteer education organization in the United States; it has long supported legislation at the state and national levels designed to benefit children.

negligence: failure to exercise reasonable care to protect students from injury.

news groups: electronic message services that post to servers locally, regionally, nationally, and/or internationally.

NGO: international nongovernmental organization that advances agendas focused on problems and issues of common interest, regardless of national interest.

nondirective model: teaching strategy in which teachers act as facilitators and reflectors to encourage students to define problems and feelings, to take responsibility for solving problems, and to determine how personal goals might be reached.

nongraded classroom: classroom in which children are grouped heterogeneously by ability, sometimes with students of various ages.

normal school: educational program established in the 1800s dedicated solely to training teachers so that they could perform according to high standards, or "norms."

norm-referenced test: test used to compare the quality of a student's performance to that of other students.

null curriculum: curriculum that is not taught in schools.

O

okeiko-goto: enrichment classes in areas such as music, the arts, and physical education that people in Japan may continue throughout their lives.

ontology: study of nature, existence, or being.

opportunity standards: standards meant to hold schools accountable for giving students a fair chance to succeed by providing them with appropriate support: books, materials, machines, teachers, time to learn, and other tools.

outcome-centered learning: focuses on results in terms of student achievement.

P

paraprofessional: unlicensed teacher aide.

parochial school: school established by one of various religious groups to inculcate their beliefs and ideas in children.

pedagogical content knowledge: particular teaching knowledge necessary to impart content knowledge.

people's profession: designation for the teaching profession that recognizes that teachers generally come from the middle-class and seek approval of and support for their practice from the people themselves.

perennialism: philosophy that exalts the great thoughts and accomplishments of the past for their own sake and for what they can offer to future generations.

performance standard: the level at which students should be able to use the knowledge they possess to solve problems.

performance tests: assessment that measure how well students can apply what they have learned.

per pupil expenditure: money allocated for educational services divided by the number of pupils to be served.

personal property: property that is movable, either tangibles (e.g., machinery, livestock, crops, automobiles) or intangibles (e.g., money, stocks, bonds).

philosophy: set of ideas about the nature of reality and about the meaning of life.

Plessy v. Ferguson: 1896 Supreme Court case that legalized separate but equal public facilities for African Americans and served to legalize school segregation.

pluralism: state of society in which members of a diverse society maintain their unique characteristics.

portfolio: purposeful collection of student work that tells the story of the student's efforts, progress, or achievement in a given area(s).

pragmatism: philosophical method that defines the truth and meaning of ideas according to their physical consequences and practical value.

Praxis Series: examination battery that purports to assess skills and knowledge at each stage of a beginning teacher's career from entry into teacher education to actual classroom performance.

primer: textbook for children designed to impart rudimentary reading skills that also reflected the religious values of the colonies.

principal: person responsible for managing a school at the building level.

private school: a nonprofit, tax-exempt institution governed by a board of trustees and financed through private funds, such as tuitions, endowments, and grants; sometimes called a *for-profit school.*

professional development school: school in which university and public school people work together to explore problems of teaching and learning.

progressive taxation: taxes, such as income taxes, that require people who earn more to pay more.

progressivism: movement aimed at using human and material resources to improve the American's quality of life as an individual; in schools this meant focusing on the needs and interests of students rather than on those of teachers. The movement was characterized by a willingness to experiment with methods of teaching and learning.

project-based learning: the involvement of students in relatively long-term, problem-based units of instruction that allow students to pursue solutions to problems posed by students, teachers, or curriculum developers.

pull-out program: program in which individual students are removed from regular classes for a period of time each day for special instruction.

R

race: classification that is not typically chosen but is instead assigned by others; defined most often by physical characteristics.

realism: philosophy that suggests that objects of sense or perception exist independently of the mind.

real property: property that is not readily movable (e.g., land, buildings, improvements).

reciprocity agreement: pact by which professional licensure for educational practice in one state makes one eligible for licensure in another state.

reduction in force (RIF): layoff of teachers.

regressive taxation: a method of taxing citizens that requires those with limited incomes to spend a greater percentage of their income on taxes than wealthy people spend.

reliable: consistent.

retention: nonpromotion from one grade to the next at the expected time because of school failure.

rubric: scoring key.

S

scaffolding: method of teaching in which a teacher provides assistance, guidance, and structure to enhance student learning and self-regulation.

school-based budgeting: allocating resources at the building level rather than at the level of central administration; sometimes referred to as *site-based budgeting.*

school board: legislative policy-making body overseeing the work of educators in schools.

school choice: idea that people should be free to choose schools for their children.

school district: state-defined geographical area assigned responsibility for public instruction within its borders.

school governance: establishment and overseeing of the structure and functions of public education.

self-assessment: evaluating one's own work.

seminary: academy for girls that was the primary means for advancing the educational skills of future teachers.

service learning: learning that results from volunteer work performed outside school hours.

site-based management: involvement of people at the school level in decisions about teaching and learning, budgeting, and hiring personnel.

social promotion: passing of children to successive grades to keep them with others of their age, regardless of their past performance or academic abilities.

social reconstructionism: philosophy based on the belief that people are responsible for social conditions and can improve the quality of human life by changing the social order.

Socratic method: teaching through inquiry and dialogues in which students discover and clarify knowledge.

special-interest group: group of people who coalesce around particular interests and try to exert pressure for the advancement of their causes.

standardized tests: tests, often multiple-choice paper-and-pencil tests, administered and scored under conditions uniform to all students.

standards: benchmarks against which progress can be judged.

state board of education: regulatory agency that controls standards for educational practice in most states and advises governors and legislators about the conduct of educational business.

state education department (SED): bureaucracy that acts as an advisor to the executive and legislative branches of a state government. An SED is organized to carry out a state's education business, including regulating or overseeing elementary and secondary schools' and colleges' and universities' conduct of teacher and administrator preparation.

state standards board: commission established to regulate professional practice in education that either has final authority or serves only in advisory capacity to policymakers.

student–teacher ratio: estimate of average class size, calculated by dividing the total number of students in a school by the total number of staff (often including noninstructional staff).

student teaching: field experience in which preservice teachers plan, organize, and provide instruction to students full time over a period of weeks.

Success for All: school reform model whose main goal is to ensure success in reading, especially for urban students at risk for academic failure.

summative assessment: assessment designed to inform a summary decision, for example, an assessment of a teacher's strengths and weaknesses to be used to make decisions about such matters as tenure and termination of contract.

superintendent of schools: executive officer of the local school board, appointed by the board.

synchronous communication: interactions that take place simultaneously.

synectics: teaching model that seeks to increase students' problem-solving abilities, creative expression, empathy, and insight into social situations.

T

teacher planning: consideration of such things as curriculum, state and local goals and objectives for student learning, instructional strategies for meeting those goals, and methods for assessing students' understanding.

teacher portfolio: compilation of products displaying a teacher's knowledge and skills, such as teacher-created tests and videotapes of one's own teaching.

teacher union: confederation of educators joined politically to advance their cause.

tenure: continuing contract that guarantees a teacher's employment unless just cause for termination can be demonstrated.

Title I: one of the largest federally funded education programs for at-risk elementary and secondary students; begun in 1965 as the first bill of President Lyndon Johnson's War on Poverty.

Title IX: provision of the 1972 Education Amendments Act that guarantees that individuals may not be excluded on the basis of sex from any education program or activity receiving federal financial assistance.

tracking: process of segregating students by ability.

tuition tax credit: provision that allows a taxpayer to subtract educational costs from taxes owed.

tuition tax deduction: provision that allows a taxpayer to subtract educational costs from taxable income before computing taxes.

U

universal schooling: educating all citizens for the common good.

Upward Bound: federally funded program to improve academic performance and motivational levels of low-income high school students.

utility: capable of being understood and used easily.

V

valid: true; measuring what it is supposed to measure.

videoconferencing: form of synchronous communication that involves seeing and hearing one another via computer.

voucher: scrip used to purchase education for a child.

W

Web browser: software that enables a person to retrieve and see what is on the World Wide Web.

website: individual location on the Web owned and managed by a person, group, company, or organization.

Women's Educational Equity Act (WEEA): 1974 law that expanded programs for females in mathematics, science, technology, and athletics; mandated nonsexist curriculum materials; implemented programs for increasing the number of female administrators in education and raising the career aspirations of female students; and extended educational and career opportunities to minority-group, disabled, and rural women.

World Wide Web: subset of the Internet consisting of tens of thousands of multimedia documents.

Z

zero-base budgeting: process of budgeting that requires all expenditures to be justified each fiscal year.

References

Chapter 1

Barber, L. W. (1990). Self-assessment. In J. Millman & L. Darling-Hammond (Eds.), *The new handbook of teacher evaluation: Assessing elementary and secondary school teachers* (pp. 216–228). Newbury Park, CA: Sage.

Darling-Hammond, L., & Berry, B. (1998). Investing in teaching. *Education Week, 17*(37), 34, 48.

Feistritzer, E. (2002). Alternative routes for certifying teachers escalate to meet multiple demands. Available online (http://www.ncei.com/).

Glickman, J., & Babyak, S. (2002, June 11). Paige releases report to Congress that calls for overhaul of state teacher certification systems. Available online (http://www.ed.gov/PressReleases/06-2002/06112002.html).

Henke, R. R., & Zahn, L. (2001). Attrition of new teachers among recent college graduates: Comparing occupational stability among 1992–93 graduates who taught and those who worked in other occupations. National Center for Education Statistics. Available online (http://nces.ed.gov/das/epubs/2001189/results_1.asp).

Hess, F. M. (2002). Tear down this wall: The case for a radical overhaul of teacher certification. Paper delivered at the White House Conference on Preparing Tomorrow's Teachers. Available online (http://www.ed.gov/inits/preparingteachersconference/hess.html).

Interstate New Teacher Assessment and Support Consortium. (1992). *Model standards for beginning teacher licensing and development: A resource for state dialogue.* Available online: http://www.ccsso.org/intascst.html#draft.

Intrator, S. M. (2002). *Stories of the courage to teach: Honoring the teacher's heart.* San Francisco, CA: Jossey-Bass.

Jacobson, L. (2002, June 19). Public wants data on teacher quality. Available online (http://www.edweek.org/ew/ewstory.cfm?slug=41penpoll.h21&keywords=Public%20Wants%20Data).

Liebbrand, J. (2002, June 20). Personal communication.

Little, J. W. (1990). The mentor phenomenon and the social organization of teaching. In C. Cazden (Ed.), *Review of research in education*, Vol. 16 (pp. 297–351). Washington, DC: American Educational Research Association.

Mehlman, N. (2002, June 24). "My brief teaching career." *New York Times.* Available online (www.nytimes.com).

National Center for Education Statistics (2001). Past and projected elementary and secondary school enrollment. Condition of education, 2001. Available online (http://nces.ed.gov/fastfacts/display.asp?id=22).

National Education Association (1999). *Beginning teacher coaching program.* Available online: (http://www.nea.org/newunion/mtdiablo.html).

New Jersey Department of Education (1999, May 20). *Professional licensure and standards.* Available online: (http://www.state.nj.us/njded/adopted/license/license.htm).

O'Han, N. (2002, Oct. 2). Inventing the future, post 9/11. *Education Week.* Available online (http://www.edweek.com/ew/ewstory.cfm?slug=05o"han.h22&keywords=cultures).

Peske, H. G., Liu, E., Johnson, S. M., Kauffman, D., & Kardos, S. M. (2001, December). The next generation of teachers: Changing conceptions of a career in teaching. *Phil Delta Kappan, 83*(4), 304–311.

U.S. Department of Education (2001). Projections of education statistics to 2011. Available online (http://nces.ed.gov/pubs2001/proj01/foreword.asp).

U.S. Department of Education (2002). Digest of education statistics. Available online (http://nces.ed.gov/).

Wadsworth, D., & Coleman, D. (2001, Oct.). From training to transformation: How liberal arts colleges can bring the best students into teaching. *American School Board Journal, 188*(10), pp. 32–34.

Chapter 2

American Academy of Pediatrics (2002). Some things you should know about preventing teen suicide. Available online (http://www.aap.og/advocacy/childhealthmonth/prevteensuicide.htm).

American Psychological Association & Music Television (undated). *Warning signs. Fight for your rights: Take a stand against violence.* Washington, DC: American Psychological Association.

Anderson, V., & Blackwood, J. (2000, October). M&M: A sweet deal for students & faculty. *Principal Leadership, 1*(2), 46–48.

Balli, S. J. (1996, Winter). Family diversity and the nature of parental involvement. *Educational Forum, 60,* pp. 149–155.

Blair, L. (2002, February). The missing link: Teacher education programs. *Southwest Educational Development Laboratory News, 14*(1), 9–11.

Borja, R. R. (2002, April 3). E-mentors offer online support, information for novice instructors. *Education Week.* Available online (http://www.edweek.org/ew/newstory. cfm?slug=29mentor.h21&keywords=tenure).

Center for Disease Control and Prevention (2000a, April 24). Table 3. Birth rates for teenagers 15–19 years, by age and race and Hispanic origin: United States and each state, 1998. *National Vital Statistics Reports, 48*(6).

Center for Disease Control and Prevention (2000b). Youth risk behavior surveillance—United States, 1999, *49*(SS-5), 1–2.

Children's Defense Fund (2002). Every day in America. Available online (http://www.childrensdefense.org/ everyday.htm).

Coles, A. D. (1999, January 20). Discontented, some districts shifting gears on anti-drug programs. *Education Week, 18*(19), 5.

Finn, C. E., Jr. (1991). *We must take charge: Our schools and our future.* New York: Free Press.

Georgia Student Finance Commission (2002). HOPE scholarship program. Available online (http://www.gsfc.org/ hope/).

Gladding, S. T. (2000). *Counseling: A comprehensive profession* (4th ed.) (p. 389). Upper Saddle River, NJ: Prentice Hall.

Grossman, K. N. (2002, May 6). Full-service schooling pays dividends. *Chicago Sun Times.* Available online (http:// suntimes.com.).

Hoff, T., & Greene L. (2000). *Sex education in America. A series of national surveys of parents, teachers, and principals.* Menlo Park, CA: Henry J. Kaiser Family Foundation, p. 31.

Interstate New Teacher Assessment and Support Consortium. (1992). *Model standards for beginning teacher licensing and development: A resource for state dialogue.* Available online: http://www.ccsso.org/intascst.html# draft.

Kominski, R., Jamieson, A., & Martinez, G. (2001). At-risk conditions of U.S. school-age children. U.S. Census Bureau, Population Division, Education & Social Stratification Branch. Available online (http://www.census. gov/population/www/documentation/twps0052. html#data).

Kozol, J. (1995). *Amazing grace.* New York: Random House.

Landau, S., Pryor, J. B., & Haefli, K. (1995). Pediatric HIV: School-based sequelae and curricular interventions for infection prevention and social acceptance. *School Psychology Review, 24*(2), 213–229.

National Association of Elementary School Principals (2002). Never say never: Violence and tragedy can strike anywhere. *School violence: An NAESP/NSPRA*

special resource. Available online (http://www.naesp. org/misc/violence.htm).

National Center for Education Statistics (2002). Science: The nation's report card. Available online (http://nces. ed.gov/nationsreportcard/science/results/television-g4.asp).

National Safety Council (2001). National report finds most states mired in mediocrity on critical public health measure: Seat belt use—thousands die as a result. Available online (http://www.nsc.org/news/nr052101.htm).

Ohio Welfare Information Network (2002). Ohio's learning, earning and parenting program. Available online (http://www.welfareinfo.org/ohioslearning.htm/).

Peterson, R. L., & Skiba, R. (2001). Creating school climates that prevent school violence. *Clearing House, 74*(3), 155–163.

The Rural School and Community Trust (2002). Results of four-state study: Smaller schools reduce harmful impact of poverty on student achievement. Available online (http://www.ruralchallengepolicy.org/nat_sum. html).

Shea, G. F. (1997). *Mentoring: How to develop successful mentor behaviors.* Menlo Park, CA: Crisp Publications.

Sheras, P., & Tippins, S. (2002). *Your child: Bully or victim. Understanding and ending school yard tyranny.* New York: Skylight Press.

Stein, M. R. S., & Thorkildsen, R. J. (1999). *Parent involvement in education: Insights and applications from the research.* Bloomington, IN: Phi Delta Kappa International.

U.S. Census Bureau (1999). Population profiles of the United States, American at the close of the 20th century, 1999. Available online (http://www.census.gov/ population/pop-profile/1999/chap06.pdf).

U.S. Census Bureau (2001). Record share of new mothers in labor force, Census Bureau reports. Available online (http://www.census.gov/Press-Release/www/2000/ cb00-175.html).

U.S. Department of Education (2000, June). The need for after-school programs. Available online (www.ed.gov/ pubs/afterschool/intro.html).

U.S. Department of Education (2001). Digest of education statistics, 2001. Available online (http://nces.ed.gov/).

U.S. Department of Health and Human Services (2001a). Child maltreatment 1999. Available online (http:// www.acf.dhhs.gov/programs/cb/publications/cm99/ cpt2.htm).

U.S. Department of Health and Human Services (2001b). *A national strategy to prevent teen pregnancy, annual report, 1999–2000.* Available online (http://aspe.hhs.gov/ hsp/teenp/ann-rpt00/index.htm).

U.S. Department of Health and Human Services (2001c). *A renewed commitment in the fight against HIV/AIDS.*

Available online (http://www.hhs.gov/news/press/2001 pres/01fshivaids.htm).

Wilson, B. L., & Corbett, H. D. (2001). *Listening to urban kids: School reform and the teachers they want.* Albany, NY: State University of New York Press.

Wood, M., & Salvetti, E. P. (2001). Project story boost: Read-alouds for students at risk. *The Reading Teacher, 55*(1), 76–83.

Chapter 3

AAUW Educational Foundation (1998). *Gender gaps: Where schools still fail our children.* Washington, DC: American Association of University Women Educational Foundation.

AAUW Educational Foundation and the National Education Association (1992). *The AAUW report: How schools shortchange girls: A study of major findings on girls and education.* Washington, DC: Authors.

Banks, J. A. (2002). *An introduction to multicultural education* (3rd ed). Boston: Allyn and Bacon.

Banks, J. A. & Banks, C. A. (2001) *Multicultural education: Issues and perspectives* (4th ed). New York: Wiley.

Brown, A. (1994). The advancement of learning. *Educational Researcher, 23*(8), 4–12.

Caplan, N., Choy, M. H., & Whitmore, J. K. (1991). *Children of the boat people: A study of educational success.* Ann Arbor: University of Michigan Press.

Carlson, D. (1998). Who am I? Gay identity and a democratic politics of the self. In W. F. Pinar (Ed.), *Queer theory in education* (pp. 107–120). Mahwah, NJ: Erlbaum.

Clemetson, L. (1998, December 14). Caught in the crossfire. A young teacher finds herself in a losing racial battle with parents. *Newsweek*, pp. 38–39.

Davis, M. (2002, May 15). Department aims to promote single-sex schools. *Education Week.* Available online (http://www.edweek.org/ew/newstory.cfm?slug= 36gender.h21&keywords=Department%20Aims%20).

Hallahan, D. P., & Kauffman, J. M. (2003). *Exceptional children: Introduction to special education* (9th ed.). Boston: Allyn and Bacon.

Hill, D. (1990, June/July). A theory of success and failure. *Teacher Magazine*, pp. 40–45.

Interstate New Teacher Assessment and Support Consortium. (1992). *Model standards for beginning teacher licensing and development: A resource for state dialogue.* Available online: http://www.ccsso.org/intascst.html# draft.

Johnson, D. W., Johnson, R., Dudley, B., Ward, M., & Magnuson, D. (1995). The impact of peer mediation training on the management of school and home conflicts. *American Educational Research Journal, 32*(4), 824–844.

Kilbane, C. R. & Milman, M. B. (2003). *The digital teaching portfolio handbook: A how-to guide for educators.* Boston: Allyn and Bacon.

Ladson-Billings, G. (1994). *The dreamkeepers: Successful teachers of African American students.* San Francisco: Jossey-Bass.

Lehrer, R., & Schauble, L. (1998). Reasoning about structure and function: Children's conceptions of gears. *Journal of Research in Science Teaching, 35,* 3–25.

Lewin, T. (1998, December 13). How boys lost out to girl power. *New York Times, 148* (51,370), section 4, p. 3.

Louis Harris and Associates, Inc. (1996). *The Metropolitan Life survey of the American teacher, 1996: Students voice their opinions on violence, social tension and equality among teens, part I.* New York: Author.

Manzo, K. K. (2002, April 24). Student–teacher says Islam lessons cost him internship. *Education Week.* Available online (http://www.edweek.org/ew/newstory.cfm?slug= 32islam.h21&keywords=cooperation).

Marlowe, B. (2001, April 18). The special education conundrum. *Education Week, 20*(31), p. 43.

McNergney, R., & Keller, C. (1999). Appendix. Some effective teachers' actions. In R. McNergney & C. Keller (Eds.), *Images of mainstreaming: Educating students with disabilities* (pp. 211–212). New York: Garland Publishing.

Metz, K. E. (1995). Reassessment of developmental constraints on children's science instruction. *Review of Educational Research, 65,* 93–127.

Mithaug, D. E. (1998). The alternative to ideological inclusion. In S. J. Vitello & D. E. Mithaug (Eds.), *Inclusive schooling: National and international perspectives* (pp. 1–23). Mahwah, NJ: Erlbaum.

Morgan, J. H. (2001, Fall). The rhetoric of hate: An AP English class unmasks racist propaganda on the Internet. *Teaching Tolerance, 20,* 22–27.

National Research Council (1996). *National science education standards.* Washington, DC: National Academy Press.

Oakes, J., & Lipton, M. (1999). *Teaching to change the world.* Boston: McGraw Hill.

Ogbu, J. U., & Simons, H. D. (1998). Voluntary and involuntary minorities: A cultural–ecological theory of school performance with some implications for education. *Anthropology & Education Quarterly, 29*(2), 155–188.

Pollina, A. (1995). Gender balance: Lessons from girls in science and mathematics. *Educational Leadership, 53*(1), 30–33.

Ponessa, J. (1995). NEA backing for gay month sparks firestorm. *Education Week, 15*(8), 3.

Rosebery, A. S., & Warren, B. (Eds.) (1998). *Boats, balloons, and classroom video.* Westport, CT: Heinemann.

Sadker, M., & Sadker, D. (1993, March). Fair and square? *Instructor*, pp. 45, 46, 67, 68.

Seymour, L. (2001, October 1). Driven by the ignored child within: Fairfax school chief intent on helping all pupils succeed. *Washington Post*, p. A1.

Sleeter, C. E., & Grant, C. A. (2002). *Making choices for multicultural education: Five approaches to race, class, and gender* (4th ed.). New York: Wiley.

Suro, R. (1998, July 19). The next wave: How immigration blurs the race discussion. *Washington Post*, p. C1.

U.S. Department of Education (2001). The condition of education: Quality of elementary and secondary school environments. Available online (http://ncdes.ed.gov/programs/coe/2001/section4/indicator 40.html).

U.S. Department of Education, Office of Educational Research and Improvement (1993). *National excellence: A case for developing America's talent*. Washington, DC: U.S. Government Printing Office.

Valdes, G. (1999). Incipient bilingualism and the development of English language writing abilities in the secondary school. In C. J. Faltis & P. Wolfe (Eds.), *So much to say: Adolescents, bilingualism, and ESL in the secondary school* (pp. 138–176). New York: Teachers College Press.

White, J. E. (2000, August 7). Are blacks biased against braininess? *Time*, p. 81.

Chapter 4

Ambrose, S. E. (1996). *Undaunted courage: Meriwether Lewis, Thomas Jefferson, and the opening of the American West*. New York: Simon & Schuster.

Barman, J., Hebert, Y., & McCaskill, D. (1986). *Indian education in Canada* (Vol. I). Vancouver: University of British Columbia.

Barnard, H. (1857, March). The public high school. *American Journal of Education*, pp. 185–189.

Berlin, I. (1974). *Slaves without masters: The free negro in the antebellum South*. New York: Vintage.

Blum, J. M., McFeely, W. S., Morgan, E. S., Schlesinger, A. M., Jr., Stampp, K. M., & Woodward, C. V. (1997). *The national experience: A history of the United States* (8th ed.). San Diego, CA: Harcourt Brace Jovanovich.

Boyd, W. (Ed.) (1962). *The Emile of Jean Jacques Rousseau*. New York: Bureau of Publications, Teachers College, Columbia University.

Boyer, P. S., Clark, C. E., Kett, J. F., Salisbury, N., Sitkoff, H., & Woloch, N. (2000). *The enduring vision: A history of the American people* (4th ed.). Boston: Houghton Mifflin.

Bullock, H. A. (1967). *A history of Negro education in the South: From 1619 to the present*. Cambridge, MA: Harvard University Press.

Coleman, M. C. (1993). *American Indian children at school, 1850–1930*. Jackson: University Press of Mississippi.

Cremin, L. A. (1970). *American education: The colonial experience, 1607–1783*. New York: Harper & Row.

Cremin, L. A. (1980). *American education: The national experience, 1783–1876*. New York: Harper & Row.

Cross, B. M. (1965). *The educated woman in America: Selected writings of Catharine Beecher, Margaret Fuller, and M. Carey Thomas*. New York: Teachers College Press, Columbia University.

Deighton, L. C. (Ed.) (1971). *The encyclopedia of education* (Vol. 9). New York: Macmillan Company and The Free Press.

Dolan, J. P. (1985). *The American Catholic experience: A history from colonial times to the present*. Garden City, NY: Doubleday.

Downs, R. B. (1978). *Friedrich Froebel*. Boston: Twayne.

Edwards, P. (Ed.) (1972). *Encyclopedia of philosophy* (Vol. 7). New York: Macmillan Company and The Free Press.

Elsbree, W. S. (1939). *The American teacher: Evolution of a profession in a democracy*. New York: American Book.

Emerson, R. W. (1884). *Lectures and biographical sketches*. Cambridge, MA: Riverside.

Flynn, G. (1971). *Sor Juana Ines de la Cruz*. New York: Twayne.

Fogel, D. (1988). *Junipero Serra, the Vatican, and enslavement theology*. San Francisco, CA: Ism.

Ford, P. L. (Ed.) (1899). *The New England primer*. New York: Dodd, Mead.

Franklin, J. H. (1980). *From slavery to freedom: A history of negro Americans* (5th ed.). New York: Knopf.

Gay, P. (Ed.) (1964). *John Locke on education*. New York: Bureau of Publications, Teachers College, Columbia University.

Gutek, G. L. (1968). *Pestalozzi and education*. New York: Random House.

Hahner, J. (1976). *Women in Latin American history*. Los Angeles: University of California.

Hallahan, D. P., & Kauffman, J. M. (2003). *Exceptional children: Introduction to special education* (9th ed.). Boston: Allyn and Bacon.

Interstate New Teacher Assessment and Support Consortium. (1992). *Model standards for beginning teacher licensing and development: A resource for state dialogue*. Available online: http://www.ccsso.org/intascst.html#draft.

Jefferson, T. (1931). Report of the commissioners appointed to fix the site of the University of Virginia. In R. J. Honeywell (Ed.), *The educational work of Thomas Jefferson* (pp. 248–260). Cambridge, MA: Harvard University Press.

Kaestle, C. F. (1983). *Pillars of the republic: Common schools and American society, 1780–1860*. New York: Hill and Wang.

Krug, E. A. (1964). *The shaping of the American high school, 1880–1920*. New York: Harper & Row.

Lannie, V. P. (1968). *Public money and parochial education: Bishop Hughes, Governor Seward and the New York school controversy.* Cleveland, OH: Press of Case Western Reserve.

Manuel, H. T. (1965). *Spanish-speaking children of the Southwest: Their education and the public welfare.* Austin: University of Texas Press.

Pestalozzi, J. H. (1898). *How Gertrude teaches her children* (2nd ed.). Syracuse, NY: C. W. Bardeen.

Richardson, R. D., Jr. (1995). *Emerson: The mind on fire.* Berkeley, CA: University of California Press.

Ronda, B. A (1999) *Elizabeth Palmer Peabody: A reformer on her own terms.* Cambridge, MA: Harvard University Press.

Rury, J. L. (1989). Who became teachers?: The characteristics of teachers in American history. In D. Warren (Ed.), *American teachers: Histories of a profession at work* (pp. 9–48). New York: Macmillan.

Steinhardt, M. A. (1992). Physical education. In P. W. Jackson (Ed.), *Handbook of research on curriculum* (pp. 964–1001). New York: Macmillan.

The Sun. (1833a, December 19), p. 2.

Tocqueville, A. (1840). *Democracy in America: Part the second, the social influence of democracy* (H. Reeve, Trans.). New York: J. & H. G. Langley.

Tyack, D. (1967). *Turning points in American educational history.* Lexington, MA: Xerox College.

Ulich, R. (1968). *History of educational thought.* New York: D. Van Nostrand.

Zitkala-Sa. (1921). *American Indian stories.* Washington, DC: Hayworth.

Chapter 5

Agee, J., & Evans, W. (1960). *Let us now praise famous men* (2nd ed.). New York: Ballantine.

Alba, R. D. (1991). *Ethnic identity: The transformation of white America.* New Haven, CT: Yale University Press.

Ayres, L. P. (1909). *Laggards in our schools.* New York: Charities Publication Committee.

Bennett, C. (1999). *Comprehensive multicultural education: Theory and practice* (4th ed.). Boston: Allyn and Bacon.

Bestor, A. E. (1953). *Educational wastelands: The retreat from learning in our public schools.* Urbana: University of Illinois Press.

Blum, J. M., McFeely, W. S., Morgan, E. S., Schlesinger, A. M., Jr., Stampp, K. M., & Woodward, C. V. (1997). *The national experience: A history of the United States* (8th ed.), San Diego, CA: Harcourt Brace Jovanovich.

Bond, H. M. (1934). *The education of the Negro in the American social order.* Upper Saddle River, NJ: Prentice Hall.

Bossert, S. T. (1985). Effective elementary schools. In R. J. Kyle (Ed.), *Reaching for excellence* (pp. 39–53). Washington, DC: U.S. Government Printing Office.

Brown, C. L., & Pannell, C. W. (1985). The Chinese in America. In J. O. McKee (Ed.), *Ethnicity in contemporary America: A geographical appraisal* (pp. 195–216). Dubuque, IA: Kendall/Hunt.

Callahan, R. E. (1962). *Education and the cult of efficiency.* Chicago: University of Chicago Press.

Carlson, R. A. (1975). *The quest for conformity: Americanization through education.* New York: Wiley.

Carnegie, D. (1936). *How to win friends & influence people.* New York: Simon and Schuster.

Carr, C. K. (2000, Winter). On writing biography. *Profile: Smithsonian National Portrait Gallery News, 1* (4), 12–13.

Catholic Campaign for Human Development, United States Conference of Catholic Bishops (2002). Poverty facts. Available online (http://www.nccbuscc.org/cchd/povertyusa/).

Cole, J. Y. (1979). *For Congress and the nation: A chronological history of the Library of Congress.* Washington, DC: Library of Congress.

Commission on the Reorganization of Secondary Education. (1918). *Cardinal principles of secondary education* (Bulletin No. 35). Washington, DC: U.S. Government Printing Office.

Cremin, L. A. (1988). *American education: The metropolitan experience.* New York: Harper & Row.

Csikszentmihalyi, M. (2000). Education for the 21st Century. *Education Week.* Available online (http://www.edweek.com/ew/ewstory.cfm?slug=32csikszentmihalyi.h19&keywords=televi).

Dabney, C. W. (1969). *Universal education in the South: Vol. II.* New York: Arno Press & *The New York Times.*

Degler, C. N. (1959). *Out of our past: The forces that shaped modern America.* New York: Harper & Row.

Du Bois, W. E. B. (1903). *The souls of black folk: Essays and sketches.* Chicago: A. C. McClurg. Available online (http://etext.lib.virginia.edu/modeng/modeng0.browse.html.).

Du Bois, W. E. B. (1904). *The souls of black folk.* Chicago: A. C. McClurg.

Edwards, J. (1991). To teach responsibility, bring back the Dalton Plan. *Phi Delta Kappan, 72* (5), 398–401.

Efron, S. (1990, April 29). Few Viet exiles find U.S. riches. *Los Angeles Times,* p. 1.

Franklin, J. H. (1967). *From slavery to freedom* (3rd ed.). New York: Knopf.

Fuchs, L. H. (1990). *The American kaleidoscope: Race, ethnicity, and the civic culture.* Middletown, CT: Wesleyan University Press.

Goodman, J. M. (1985). The Native American. In J. O. McKee (Ed.), *Ethnicity in contemporary America: A geographical appraisal* (pp. 195–216). Dubuque, IA: Kendall/Hunt.

Hallahan, D. P., & Kauffman, J. M. (2003). *Exceptional*

learners: Introduction to special education (9th ed.). Boston: Allyn and Bacon.

Harris, K. A. (1984). *Profiles of Detroit's high schools: 1975 to 1984.* Detroit: Detroit School District, U.S. District Court Monitoring Commission.

Hoff, D. J. (2002, March 20). Debate of teaching of evolution theory shifts to Ohio. *Education Week, 21*(27), 14, 16.

Interstate New Teacher Assessment and Support Consortium. (1992). *Model standards for beginning teacher licensing and development: A resource for state dialogue.* Available online: http://www.ccsso.org/intascst.html#draft.

Jennings, J. F. (1998). *Why national standards and tests? Politics and the quest for better schools.* Thousand Oaks, CA: Sage Publications.

Kliebard, H. M. (1986). *The struggle for the American curriculum, 1893–1958.* Boston: Routledge & Kegan Paul.

Kunen, J. S. (1996, April 29). The end of integration. *Time, 147*(118) pp. 39–45.

Lemann, N. (2000). *The big test: The secret history of the American meritocracy.* New York: Farrar, Straus and Giroux.

Link, A. S., & Catton, W. B. (1963). *American epoch: A history of the United States since the 1890s.* New York: Knopf.

Lippmann, W. (1922, November 1). The mystery of the "A" men. *New Republic, 32,* p. 247.

Minzey, J. D., & LeTarte, C. (1979). *Community education, from program to process to practice: The schools' role in a new educational society.* Midland, MI: Pendell.

National Commission on Excellence in Education. (1983). *A nation at risk: The imperative for education reform.* Washington, DC: U.S. Department of Education.

Painter, N. I. (1977). *Exodusters: Black migration to Kansas after Reconstruction.* New York: Knopf.

Parkhurst, H. (1922). *Education on the Dalton Plan.* New York: Dutton.

Peabody, E. P. (1886). *Sara Winnemucca's practical solution of the Indian problems: A letter to Dr. Lyman Abbot of the "Christian Union."* Cambridge, MA: John Wilson and Son.

Powell, A. G., Farrar, E., & Cohen, D. K. (1985). *The shopping mall high school: Winners and losers in the educational marketplace.* Boston: Houghton Mifflin.

Rice, J. M. (1969). *The public-school system of the United States.* New York: Arno Press.

Romo, H. D., & Falbo, T. (1996). *Latino high school graduation: Defying the odds.* Austin: University of Texas Press.

Schnaiberg, L. (1999). Calif.'s year on the bilingual battleground. *Education Week, 18*(38), 1, 9–10.

Terman, L. (1922, December 27). The great conspiracy or the impulse imperious of intelligence testers, psychoanalyzed and exposed by Mr. Lippman. *New Republic, 33,* p. 116.

Travers, R. M. (1983). *How research has changed American schools: A history from 1840 to the present.* Kalamazoo, MI: Mythes.

Tyack, D., & Hansot, E. (1982). *Managers of virtue.* New York: Basic Books.

U.S. Bureau of Indian Affairs (1974). Government schools for Indians (1881). In S. Cohen (Ed.), *Education in the United States: A documentary history* (Vol. 3, pp. 1754–1756). New York: Random House.

U.S. Census Bureau (1975). *Historical statistics of the United States: Colonial times to 1970 (Part 1).* Washington, DC: U.S. Government Printing Office.

U.S. Census Bureau (1990). *Statistical abstract of the United States* (110th ed.). Washington, DC: U.S. Government Printing Office.

U.S. Census Bureau (1995, August). *American Indian and Alaska Native populations: Selected social and economic characteristics for the 25 largest American Indian tribes, 1990.* Washington, DC: U.S. Government Printing Office. Available online (http://www.census.gov/population/socdemo/race/indian/ailang2.txt).

U.S. Census Bureau (2001). Poverty in the United States. Available online (http://www.census.gov/prod/2001pubs/p60-214.pdf).

U.S. Census Bureau (2002, May 8). *American community survey.* Available online (http://www.censuys.gov/acs/www/).

U.S. Department of Education (1998). *The condition of education 1998.* NCES 98-013, by John Wirt, Tom Snyder, Jennifer Sable, Susan P. Choy, Yupin Bae, Janis Stennett, Allison Gruner, and Marianne Perie. Washington, DC: Office of Educational Research and Improvement.

U.S. Department of Education (1999). *Digest of education statistics, 1998.* NCES 1999-036, by Thomas D. Snyder, Charlene Hoffman, Claire M. Geddes. Washington, DC: U.S. Government Printing Office.

U.S. Department of Education (2001). New report shows dropout rates remain stable over the last decade. Available online (http://www.ed.gov/PressReleases/11-2001/11152001.html).

U.S. Department of Education, National Center for Education Statistics (2002). Enrollment in grades 9–12 in public schools. Projections of Education Statistics to 2012. Available online (http://nces.ed.gov/pubs2002/proj2012/table_08_2.asp).

Vedontom, S. (2002, Friday March 29). *Washington Post,* p. A01.

Washington, B. T. (1907). *The future of the American Negro.* Boston: Small, Maynard.

Weinberg, D. H. (1997). *Press briefing on 1997 income and poverty estimates.* Washington, DC: U.S. Census Bureau. Available online (http://www.census.gov/hhes/income/income97/prs98asc.html).

Weiner, S. (2002, March). Picture imperfect. *Teacher Magazine.* (http://www.edweek.org/tm/tmstory.cfm?slug=06imperfect.h13).

Chapter 6

Adler, M. (1982). *The Paideia proposal: An educational manifesto.* New York: Macmillan.

Apple, M. (1995). *Education and power.* New York: Routledge.

Asante, M. K. (1987). *The Afrocentric idea.* Philadelphia: Temple University Press.

Asante, M. K. (1992). Learning about Africa. *Executive Educator, 14*(9), 21–23.

Banks, J. A. (1994). *Multiethnic education: Theory and practice* (3rd ed.). Boston: Allyn and Bacon.

Banville, J. (1998, August 13). The last days of Nietzsche. *New York Review of Books,* vol. 45, No. 13, pp. 22–25.

Bloom, A. (1987). *The closing of the American mind.* New York: Simon and Schuster.

Buber, M. (1970). *I and thou* (W. Kaufman, Trans.). New York: Charles Scribner's Sons. (Original work published 1937.)

Cohen, S., & Hearn, D. (1988). Reinforcement. In R. F. McNergney (Ed.), *Guide to classroom teaching* (pp. 43–66). Boston: Allyn and Bacon.

Corbin, H. (1993). *History of Islamic philosophy.* London: Kegan Paul International.

Counts, G. S. (1928). *School and society in Chicago.* New York: Harcourt, Brace.

Dewey, J. (1916). *Democracy and education: An introduction to the philosophy of education.* New York: Macmillan.

Durant, W. (1961). *The story of philosophy: The lives and opinions of the great philosophers.* New York: Simon and Schuster.

Fakhry, J. (1983). *A history of Islamic philosophy* (2nd ed.). New York: Columbia University Press.

Fine, M. (1987). Silencing in public schools. *Language Arts, 64*(2), 157–174.

Freire, P., (1998). *Pedagogy of freedom: Ethics, democracy, and civic courage.* Boulder, CO: Rowman & Littlefield, pp. 29–30.

Giroux, H. A. (1984). Public philosophy and the crisis in education. *Harvard Educational Review, 54*(2), 186–194.

Goodnough, A. (2001, March 11). For first-year teacher, 20 minds to shape, 20 mysteries to plumb. *New York Times.* Available online (http://www.nytimes.com/2001/03/11/nyregion/11TEAC.html?pagewanted=print).

Haberman, M. (1995). *Star teachers of children in poverty.* West Lafayette, IN: Kappa Delta Pi.

Hirsch, E. D., Jr. (1987). *Cultural literacy: What every American needs to know.* Boston: Houghton Mifflin.

Hirsch, E. D., Jr. (1996). *The schools we need and why we don't have them.* Garden City, NY: Doubleday.

Hirsch, E. D., Jr., Rowland, W. G., Jr., & Stanford, M. (Eds.) (1989). *A first dictionary of cultural literacy: What our children need to know.* Boston: Houghton Mifflin.

Holtom, D. C. (1984). *The political philosophy of modern Shinto: A study of the state religion of Japan.* Chicago: University of Chicago Libraries.

Hutchins, R. M. (1936). *The higher learning in America.* New Haven: Yale University Press.

Interstate New Teacher Assessment and Support Consortium. (1992). *Model standards for beginning teacher licensing and development: A resource for state dialogue.* Available online: http://www.ccsso.org/intascst.html#draft.

James, W. (1907). *Pragmatism and four essays from The Meaning of Truth.* New York: Longmans, Green and Co.

King, M. L., Jr. (1964). *Stride toward freedom: The Montgomery story.* New York: Harper and Row.

Nietzsche, F. (1924). *On the future of our educational institutions.* New York: Macmillan.

Nietzsche, F. (1961). *Thus spake Zarathustra: A book for everyone and no one* (R. J. Hollingdale, Trans.). New York: Penguin. (Original work published 1883.)

Noddings, N. (1984). *Caring: A feminine approach to ethics & moral education.* Berkeley: University of California Press.

Parziale, J., & Fischer, K. W. (1998). The practical use of skill theory in classrooms. In R. F. Sternberg & W. M. Williams (Eds.), *Intelligence, instruction, and assessment: Theory into practice* (pp. 95–110). Boston: Allyn and Bacon.

Perkins, D. (1998). What is understanding? In M. S. Wiske (Ed.), *Teaching for understanding* (pp. 39–57). San Francisco: Jossey-Bass.

Rorty, R. (1991). *Objectivity, relativism, and truth: Philosophical papers: Vol. 1.* Cambridge, MA: Cambridge University Press.

Sartre, J.-P. (1947). *Existentialism.* New York: Philosophical Library.

Schön, D. A. (1987). *Educating the reflective practitioner: Toward a new design for teaching and learning in the professions.* San Francisco: Jossey-Bass.

Shishu Bharati (2002). Shishu Bharati: School of Languages and Cultures of India. Available online (http://www.shishubharati.org/).

Skinner, B. F. (1971). *Beyond freedom and dignity.* New York: Knopf.

Westbrook, R. B. (1991). *John Dewey and American democracy.* Ithaca, NY: Cornell University Press.

X, Malcolm. (1965). *The autobiography of Malcolm X*. New York: Grove Press.

Zehr, M. (2001). Fearing potential for backlash, Islamic schools step up security. *Education Week*. Available online (http://www.edweek.org/ew/newstory.cfm?slug=03dc.h21).

Chapter 7

Achilles, C. M. (1996). Students achieve more in smaller classes. *Educational Leadership, 53*, 76–79.

Alexander, K. L., & Entwisle, D. R. (1996) Schools and children at risk. In A. Booth & J. F. Dunn (Eds.), *Family–school links: How do they affect educational outcomes?* (pp. 67–88). Mahwah, NJ: Erlbaum.

Archer, J. (1998). Breaking the tradition. *Education Week*. Available online (http://www.edweek.org/ew/1998/27jewish.h17).

Barnes, H. (1991, October). Learning that grows with the learner. An introduction to Waldorf education. *Educational Leadership*, pp. 52–54.

Boyer, E. L. (1995). *The basic school: A community for learning*. Princeton, NJ: Carnegie Foundation for the Advancement of Teaching.

Bracey, G. (2002, May 5). Why do we scapegoat the schools? *Washington Post* (Outlook Section).

Decker, L. E., Gregg, G. A., & Decker, V. A. (1995). *Teacher's manual for parent and community involvement*. Fairfax, VA: National Community Education Association.

Dickenson, T. S., & Butler, D. A. (2001, September). Reinventing the middle school. *Middle School Journal, 33*(1), 7–13.

Dornbusch, S. M., & Glasgow, K. L. (1996). The structural context of family–school relations. In A. Booth & J. F. Dunn (Eds.), *Family–school links: How do they affect educational outcomes?* (pp. 35–44) Mahwah, NJ: Erlbaum.

First Day Foundation (2002). One new First Day firsthand story. Newsletter 24. Available online (http://www.firstday.org/).

Furger, R. (2002, fall). *Rebuilding a school, revitalizing a community*. San Francisco, CA: The George Lucas Educational Foundation, 10–12

Good, T. L., & Brophy, J. E. (2003). *Looking in classrooms* (9th ed.). New York: Longman.

Interstate New Teacher Assessment and Support Consortium. (1992). *Model standards for beginning teacher licensing and development: A resource for state dialogue*. Available online: http://www.ccsso.org/intascst.html#draft.

Keen, M. (1999). Three semesters for learning. *School Administrator, 3*(56), 27–30.

Keough, R. (1999). What's up, Doc? *Education Week, 18*(33), 26–31.

Lareau, A. (1996). Assessing parent involvement in school-ing: A critical analysis. In A. Booth & J. F. Dunn (Eds.) *Family–school links: How do they affect educational outcomes?* (pp. 57–66). Mahwah, NJ: Erlbaum.

McCown, C., & Sherman, S. (2002, March). Looping for better performance in the middle grades. *Middle School Journal*, pp. 17–21.

The Met (2002). Frequently asked questions. Available online (http://www.metcenter.org/FAQ.htm#Anchor-Is_35882).

National Association of Elementary School Principals (2001). *Leading learning communities: Standards for what principals should know and be able to do* (p. 2). Washington, DC: NAESP.

National Association of Secondary School Principals (2001). *Priorities and barriers in high school leadership: A survey of principals*. Available online (http://www.principals.org/pdf/HSSurvey.pdf).

National Center for Education Statistics (2001a). Postsecondary persistence and progress: High school academic preparation and postsecondary progress. Condition of education. Available online (http://comp.cl.uh.edu/oie/Reports/Condition_of_Education_2001.pdf).

National Center for Education Statistics (2001b). Private school universe study: 1999–2000. Available online (http://nces.ed.gov/pubs2001/2001330.pdf).

National Center for Education Statistics (2001c). *Homeschooling in the United States: 1999*. Available online (http://nces.ed.gov/pubsearch/pubsinfo.asp?pubid=2001033).

National Center for the Childcare Work Force (2002). Current data on child care salaries and benefits in the United States. Available online (http://www.ccw.org/pubs/2002Compendium.pdf).

Oakes, J. (1995). More than meets the eye: Links between tracking and the culture of schools. In H. Pool & J. A. Page (Eds.), *Beyond tracking: Finding success in inclusive schools*. Bloomington, IN: Phi Delta Kappa Educational Foundation.

Oakes, J., & Lipton, M. (1999). *Teaching to change the world*. Boston: McGraw-Hill.

Olson, L. (2002). Starting early. *Education Week*. Available online (http://www.edweek.org/sreports/qc02/templates/article.cfm?slug=17intro.h21).

Phelan, P., Davidson, A. L, & Cao, H. T. (1992). Speaking up: Students' perspectives on school. *Phi Delta Kappan, 73*(9), 695–704.

Pool, H., & Page, J. A. (Eds.) (1995). Introduction. *Beyond tracking: Finding success in inclusive schools*. Bloomington, IN: Phi Delta Kappa Educational Foundation.

Rettig, M., & Canady, R. L. (1999). The effects of block scheduling. *School Administrator, 3*(56), 14–20.

Sack, J. (2002, April 24). Charter pioneers force public school officials to modify operations. *Education Week*. Available online (http://www.edweek.org/ew/newstory.

cfm?slug=32chartreact.h21&keywords=charter%20 schools).

Schwisow, A. (2002, July 21). School's future in doubt: Hearing on tap for Criglersville. *Daily Progress.*

Stricherz, M. (2001). School leaders feel overworked, survey finds. *Education Week.* Available online (http://www. edweek.org/ew/newstory.cfm?slug=12agenda.h21& keywords=principals).

Trotter, A. (2002). Boston will use new cellphones to call truants' bluff. *Education Week.* Available online (http:/ /www.edweek.org/ew/newstory.cfm?slug=31truant. h21&keywords=cellphones).

U.S. Bureau of Labor Statistics (2001). College enrollment and work activity of year 2000 high school graduates. Available online (http://www.bls.gov/news.release/hsgec. nr0.htm.).

U.S. Department of Education (1998). *1998 Regional Conferences on Improving America's Schools.* Available online (http://www.ncbe.gwu.edu/iasconferences/1998/ casestudies/denver.htm#Chicago).

U.S. Department of Education (1999). *Reducing class size: What do we know?* By Ivor Pritchard, National Institute on Student Achievement, Curriculum and Assessment. Washington, DC: Office of Educational Research and Improvement.

U.S. Department of Education (2001). Characteristics of the 100 largest public elementary and secondary school districts in the United States: 1999–2000. Available online (http://nces.ed.gov/pubs2001/100_largest/index.asp).

U.S. Department of Education (2002). Elementary and secondary education. Digest of Education Statistics, 2001. Available online (http://nces.ed.gov//pubs2002/ digest2001/ch2.asp).

Viadero, D. (2002, April 17). Study: Full-day kindergarten boosts academic performance. *Education Week.* Available online (http://www.edweek.org/ew/newstory.cfm? slug=31kinder.h21).

Wagner, M. B. (1990). *God's schools: Choice and compromise in American society.* New Brunswick, NJ: Rutgers University Press.

Walsh, M. (2002, May 22). Businesses flock to charter frontier. *Education Week.* Available online (http://www. edweek.org/ew/newstory.cfm?slug=37chartbiz.h21).

Wasley, P. A., Hampel, R. L., & Clark, R. W. (1997). *Kids and school reform.* San Francisco: Jossey-Bass.

Wasley, P., Fine, M., Gladden, M., Holland, N., King, S., Mosak, E., & Powell, L. C. (2000). *Small schools: Great strides: A study of new small schools in Chicago.* New York: Bank Street College of Education.

Zehr, M. A. (2002, May 22). Charters in some cities attract students from Catholic Schools. *Education Week.* Available online (http://www.edweek.org/ew/newstory.cfm? slug=37catholic.h21&keywords=charter%20schools).

Zill, N. (1996). Family change and student achievement: What we have learned, what it means for schools. In A. Booth & J. F. Dunn (Eds.), *Family–student links: How do they affect educational outcomes?* (pp. 139–176). Mahwah, NJ: Erlbaum.

Chapter 8

Becker, G. S. (1964). *Human capital: A theoretical and empirical analysis, with special reference to education.* New York: Columbia University Press.

Berliner, D. C., & Biddle, B. J. (1995). *The manufactured crisis: Myths, fraud, and the attack on America's public schools.* Reading, MA: Addison-Wesley.

Blair, J. (2002, June 5). Long passage. *Education Week, 21*(39), 22–28.

Borea, R. R. (2002, Feb. 6) Study: Urban school chiefs' tenure is 4.5 years. *Education Week.* Available online (http://www.edweek.org/ew/ewstory.cfm?slug= 21supes.h21&keywords=urban%20superintendent).

Bracey, G. W. (1991). Why can't they be like we were? *Phi Delta Kappan, 73*(2), 105–117.

Burrup, P. E., Brimley, V., & Garfield, R. R. (1999). *Financing education in a climate of change.* Boston: Allyn and Bacon.

Carson, C. C., Huelskamp, R. M., & Woodall, T. D. (1991). *Perspective on education in America* (3rd draft). Albuquerque, NM: Sandia National Laboratories.

Darling-Hammond, L., & McLaughlin, M. W. (1995). Policies that support professional development in an era of reform. *Phi Delta Kappan, 76*(8), 597–604.

Education Week (2002, July 10). School-based management. Available online (http://www.edseek.com/context/topics/ issuspage.cfm?id=18).

Friedman, M. (1955). The role of government in education. In R. A. Solo (Ed.), *Economics and the public interest* (pp. 123–144). New Brunswick, NJ: Rutgers University Press.

Friedman, M. (1995, June 23). *Public schools: Make them private.* Washington, DC: CATO Institute.

Guthrie, J. W., Garms, W. I., & Pierce, L. C. (1988). *School finance and education policy: Enhancing educational efficiency, equality, and choice.* Upper Saddle River, NJ: Prentice Hall.

Hanushek, E. (1989). Expenditures, efficiency, and equity in education: The federal government's role. *American Economic Review, 79,* 46–51.

Hedges, L. V., Laine, R. D., & Greenvals, R. (1994) Does money matter? A meta-analysis of studies of the effects of differential school inputs on student outcomes. *Educational Researcher, 23*(3), 5–14.

Hendrie, C. (1999, May 17). Survey finds gap between public, board members on urban schools. *Education Week, 18*(27), 9.

Interstate New Teacher Assessment and Support Consortium.

(1992). *Model standards for beginning teacher licensing and development: A resource for state dialogue.* Available online: http://www.ccsso.org/intascst.html#draft.

Kozol, J. (1991). *Savage inequalities: Children in America's schools.* New York: Crown.

National Association of State Boards of Education (1996, January). *State education governance at-a-glance.* Alexandria, VA: National Association of State Boards of Education.

Odden, A. (1984). Financing educational excellence. *Phi Delta Kappan, 65*(5), 311–318.

Pyhrr, P. A. (1973). *Zero-base budgeting: A practical management tool for evaluating expenses.* New York: Wiley.

Rose, L. C., & Gallup, A. M. (2001). The 33rd annual Phi Delta Kappa/Gallup poll of the public's attitudes toward public schools. Available online (http://www.pdkintl.org/kappan/k0109gal.htm#3a).

Sadowski, M. (1995, March/April). The numbers game yields simplistic answers on the link between spending and outcomes. *Harvard Education Letter, 11*(2), 1–4.

Schultz, T. W. (1981). *Investing in people: The economics of population quality.* Berkeley: University of California Press.

Stearns, T. M., Hoffman, A. N., & Heide, J. B. (1987). Performance of commercial television stations as an outcome of interorganizational linkages and environmental conditions. *Academy of Management Journal, 30,* 71–90.

Thro, W. E. (1990). The third wave: The impact of the Montana, Kentucky and Texas decisions on the future of public school finance reform litigation. *Journal of Law & Education, 19*(2), 219–250.

U.S. Department of Education. (2001). *Making sense of school budgets.* Washington, DC: Office of Educational Research and Improvement.

U.S. Department of Education (2001). *Digest of education statistics, 2000.* Washington, DC: U.S. Government Printing Office.

U.S. Department of Education (2002). *Digest of education statistics.* Washington, DC: U.S. Government Printing Office.

Verstegen, D., & McGuire, C. K. (1991). The dialectic of reform. *Educational Policy, 5*(4), 386–411.

Walsh, M. (2002, June 27). Supreme Court upholds Cleveland voucher program. *Education Week.* Available online (http://www.edweek.com/ew/newstory.cfm?slug=42voucher_web.h21).

Ward, J. G. (1992). Schools and the struggle for democracy: Themes for school finance policy. In J. G. Ward & P. Anthony (Eds.), *Who pays for student diversity?* (pp. 241–250). Newbury Park, CA: Corwin Press.

Williams, J. (1992). The politics of education news. In R. F. McNergney (Ed.), *Education research, policy, and the*

press: Research as news (pp. 177–200). Boston: Allyn and Bacon.

Chapter 9

Abood v. *Detroit Board of Education,* 431 U.S. 209, 97 S.Ct. 1782 (1977).

Alexander, K., & Alexander, M. D. (2001). *American public school law* (5th ed.). Belmont, CA: Wadsworth Publishing Co.

Baker v. *Owen,* 395 F. Supp. 294 M.D.N.C. (1975).

B.M. by Berger v. *State of Montana,* 649 P.2d 425 (Mont. 1982).

Board of Education of the Westside Community Schools v. *Mergens,* 496 U.S. 226 (1990).

Board of Regents of State Colleges v. *Roth,* 408 U.S. 564 (1972).

Brown v. *Board of Education of Topeka, Kansas,* 347 U.S. 483 (1954).

Bureau of National Affairs. (1993). *Lamb's Chapel and John Seigerwald, petitioners* v. *Center Moriches Union Free School District et al. United States Law Week, 61*(46), 4549–4554.

Chicago Teachers Union, Local No. 1 AFL-CIO v. *Hudson,* 475 U.S. 292, 106 S.Ct. 1066 (1986).

Conkling, W. (1991, November/December). The big chill. *Teacher Magazine,* pp. 46–53.

Data Research, Inc. (2002). *1999 deskbook encyclopedia of American school law.* Rosemount, MN: Author.

Davis v. *Grover,* 480 N. W. 2d 460, (Wis. 1992).

Davis v. *Monroe County Board of Education* (1999). 97-843, 526 U.S. 629; 119 S.Ct. 1661.

Denn, R. (2002). Seattle schools consider Native American mascot ban. *Seattle Post Intelligencer.* Available online (http://seattlepi.nwsource.com/local/75354_mascot20.shtml).

Ellis v. *Brotherhood of Railway, Airline, and S.S. Clerks,* 466 U.S. 435, 104 S.Ct. 1885 (1984).

Encyclopedia Britannica Educational Corporation v. *Crooks,* 542 F. Supp. 1156 (W.D. N.Y. 1982).

Essex, N. L. (2002). *School law and the public schools: A practical guide for educational leaders.* Boston: Allyn and Bacon.

Fischer, L., Schimmel, D., & Kelly, C. (1999). *Teachers and the law* (5th ed.). White Plains, NY: Longman.

Franklin v. *Gwinnett County Public Schools,* 112 S.Ct. 1028 (1992).

Gaylord v. *Tacoma School District No. 10,* 88 Wa.2d 286, 559 P.2d 1340 (1977).

Gewertz, C. (10 July 2002). A great day, or a dark one, for schools? *Education Week.* Available online (http://www.edweek.com/ew/newstory.dfm?slug=42voucheract.h21).

Goetz v. *Ansell,* 477 F.2d 636 (2nd Cir. 1973).

Gonzalez v. *Mackler*, 241 N.Y.S.2d 254 (N.Y. App. Div. 1963).

Goss v. *Lopez*, 419 U.S. 565, 95 Ct. 729, 42 L.Ed.2d 725 (1975).

Hazelwood School District v. *Kuhlmeier*, 484 U.S. 260 (1988).

Home School Legal Defense Association (1999). Across the states. Available online (http://www.hslda.org/).

Home School Legal Defense Association (2002). State laws: North Dakota. Available online (http://www.hslda.org/laws/default.asp?State=ND).

Honig v. *Doe*, 484 U.S. 305, 108 S.Ct. 592 (1988).

Hunter v. *Board of Education of Montgomery County*, 425 A.2d 681 (Md.App.1981), *aff'd in part and rev'd in part on other grounds*, 439 A.2d 582 (Md.App.1982).

Imber, M., & van Geel, T. (1993). *Education law*. New York: McGraw-Hill.

Ingraham v. *Wright*, 430 U.S. 651, 97 S.Ct 1401, 51 L.Ed.2d 711 (1977).

Interstate New Teacher Assessment and Support Consortium. (1992). *Model standards for beginning teacher licensing and development: A resource for state dialogue.* Available online: http://www.ccsso.org/intascst.html#draft.

In re William G., 221 Cal. Rptr. 118 (1985).

Jamieson, Jr., R. L. (2002, July 13). The mascot victory is a triumph to build on. *Seattle Post Intelligencer.* Available online (http://seattlepi.newsource.com/jamieson/78459_robert13.shtml).

Klicka, C. (1999, July 20). Personal communication.

La Morte, M. W. (2002). *School law: Cases and concepts* (7th ed.). Boston: Allyn and Bacon.

Landau, B. (2002). Educating for citizenship. *Education Week, 21* (24), 40, 44.

Lau v. *Nichols*, 414 U.S. 563 (1974).

Lee v. *Weisman*, 69 U.S.L.W. 4723 (1992).

Lemon v. *Kurtzman*, 403 U.S. 602, 91 S.Ct. 2105, 29 L.Ed.2d 745 (1971).

LRP Publications. (1996, May). Five ways to prevent peer sexual harassment. *Your School and the Law, 26*(5), 10.

Mancha v. *Field Museum of Natural History*, 283 N.E.2d 899 (Ill. App. 1972).

Martin Luther King, Jr., Elementary School Children v. *Michigan Board of Education*, 473 Federal Supplement, 1371 (1979).

McCarthy, M. M., Cambron-McCabe, N. H., & Thomas, S. B. (1998). *Public school law: Teachers and students' rights* (4th ed.). Boston: Allyn and Bacon.

Morrison v. *State Board of Education*, 1 Cal.3d 214, 82 Cal. Rptr. 175, 191, 461 P. 2d.375, 391 (1969).

National Gay Task Force v. *Board of Education of Oklahoma City*, 729 F.2d 1270 (10th Cir. 1984), *aff'd by divided court*, 470 U.S. 903 (1985).

National Organization on Legal Problems of Education (1988). *Education Law Update 1987–1988.* USA: Author.

New Jersey v. *T.L.O.*, 221 Cal. Rptr. 118 (1985).

Owasso Independent School District v. *Falvo*, 534 U.S. 426 (2002).

Peter W. v. *San Francisco Unified School District*, 131 Cal.Rptr. 854 (1976).

Portner, J. (1999, April 7). Drug testing latest tactic in prevention. *Education Week, 18*(30), 1, 16–17.

Rothschild v. *Grottenthaler*, 907 F. 2nd, 286, (1990, June 27).

Rowland v. *Mad River Local School District, Montgomery County, Ohio*, 730 F.2d 444 (6th Cir. 1984).

School District of Abington Township v. *Schempp*, 374 U.S. 203, 300,83 S.Ct 1560, 1620 (1963).

Sony Corporation of America v. *Universal City Studios, Inc.*, 464 U.S. 417 (1984) *reh'g denied*, 465 U.S. 1112 (1984).

Station v. *Travelers Insurance Co.*, 292 So.2d 289 (La. Ct. App. 1974).

Tinker v. *Des Moines Independent Community School District*, 393 U.S. 503, 89 S.Ct. 733, 21 L.Ed.2d 731 (1969).

U.S. Department of Education (1999, April 14). IDEA Regulations Published. Available online (http://www.ed.gov/pubs/EDInitiatives/99/99-03-18.html#4).

U.S. Department of Health and Human Services (1999). Child Abuse Prevention and Treatment Act. Available online (http://www.acf.dhhs.gov/programs/cb/policy/capta.htm).

Veronia School Dist. 47J v. *Acton*, 515 U.S. 646 (1995).

Virgil v. *School Board of Columbia County Florida*, 862 F.2d 1517 (1989).

Wallace v. *Jaffree*, 427 U.S., 38 (1985).

Walsh, M. (1998, June 17). Court allows vouchers in Milwaukee. *Education Week, 17*(40), 1, 16.

Ward v. *Newfield Central School District No. 1*, 412 N.Y.S.2d 57 (N.Y. App. Div. 1978).

West Virginia State Board of Education v. *Barnette*, 319 U.S. 624; 642 (1943).

Whiting, B. (1997). *The status of the American public school teacher, 1995–1996.* Washington, DC: Research Division, National Education Association.

Widmar v. *Vincent*, 454 U.S. 263 (1981).

Williams, V. L. (1999). A new harassment ruling: Implications for colleges. *Chronicle of Higher Education, 65*(41), A56.

Wisconsin v. *Yoder*, 406 U.S. 205 (1972).

Zelman v. *Simmons-Harris*, 536 U.S. No. 00-1751 (2002).

Zirkel, P. A., Richardson, S. N., & Goldberg, S. S. (1995). *A digest of Supreme Court decisions affecting education* (3rd ed.). Bloomington, IN: Phi Delta Kappa Educational Foundation.

Chapter 10

Airasian, P. W. (2000). *Assessment in the classroom* (2nd ed.). New York: McGraw-Hill.

Apple, M. W. (1998). The culture and commerce of the textbook. In *The curriculum: Problems, politics, and possibilities* (2nd ed.), pp. 157–166. Albany, NY: State University of New York Press.

Applebee, A. N. (1991). Environments for language teaching and learning. In J. Flood, J. Jensen, & J. R. Squire (Eds.), *Handbook of research on teaching the English language arts* (pp. 549–558). New York: Macmillan.

Association for Supervision and Curriculum Development. (1992, January). What the NCTM standards say. *Curriculum Update,* p. 3.

Association of American Publishers (1999). Industry statistics: 1998 preliminary estimated industry net sales. Available online (http://www.publishers.org/home/stats/index.htm).

Banks, J., & McGee Banks, C. A. (1997). *Multicultural education: Issues and perspectives* (3rd ed.). Boston: Allyn and Bacon.

Bloom, B. (1971). Mastery learning. In J. H. Block (Ed.), *Mastery learning: Theory and practice* (pp. 13–28). New York: Holt, Rinehart and Winston.

Blumenfeld, P., Soloway, E., Marx, R., Krajcik, J., Guzdial, M., & Palcinsar, A. (1991). Motivating project-based learning: Sustaining the doing, supporting the learning. *Educational Psychologist, 26*(3 & 4), 369–398.

Brophy, J. (1988). Educating teachers about managing classrooms and students. *Teaching and Teacher Education, 4*(1), 1–18.

Brophy, J. (1996, April). Classroom management as socializing students into clearly articulated roles. Paper presented at the Annual Meeting of the American Educational Research Association, New York.

Brophy, J., & Good, T. (1971). Teacher's communication of differential expectations for children's classroom performance: Some behavior data. *Journal of Educational Psychology, 61,* 365–374.

Brophy, J., & Good, T. (1974). *Teacher–student relationships: Causes and consequences.* New York: Holt, Rinehart and Winston.

Burns, M. (1995). The 8 most important lessons I've learned about organizing my teaching year. *Instructor, 105*(2), 86–88.

Carroll, J. B. (1971). Problems of measurement related to the concept of learning for mastery. In J. H. Block (Ed.), *Mastery learning: Theory and practice* (pp. 29–46). New York: Holt, Rinehart and Winston.

Cuban, L. (1992). Curriculum stability and change. In P. W. Jackson (Ed.), *Handbook of research on curriculum* (pp. 216–217). New York: Macmillan.

DeBoer, G. E. (1991). *A history of ideas in science education: Implications for practice.* New York: Teachers College Press.

Doyle, W. (1986). Classroom organization and management. In M. C. Wittrock (Ed.), *Handbook of research on teaching* (3rd ed.) (pp. 392–431) New York: Macmillan.

Eggen, P. D., & Kauchak, D. P. (2001). *Strategies for teachers: Teaching content and thinking skills* (4th ed.). Boston: Allyn and Bacon.

Eisner, E. W. (1985). *The educational imagination: On the design and evaluation of school programs* (2nd ed.). New York: Macmillan.

Eisner, E. W. (1992). The misunderstood role of the arts in human development. *Phi Delta Kappan, 73*(8), 591–595.

Eisner, E. (1994). *Cognition and curriculum reconsidered* (2nd ed.). New York: Teachers College Press.

Emerson, R. W. (undated). In R. I. Fitzhenry (Ed.) (1993). *The Harper Book of Quotations* (3rd. ed.). New York: HarperCollins Publishers, p. 136.

Emmer, E., Evertson, C. & Anderson, L. (1980). Effective management at the beginning of the school year. *Elementary School Journal, 80,* 221–231.

Frieberg, H. L., & Driscoll, A. (1996). *Universal teaching strategies* (2nd ed.). Boston: Allyn and Bacon.

Frieberg, H. L., Stein, T. A., & Huang, S. (1995). Effects of a classroom management intervention on student achievement in inner-city elementary schools. *Educational Research and Evaluation, 1*(1), 36–66.

Gage, N. L. (1978). *The scientific basis of the art of teaching.* New York: Teachers College Press.

Galley, M. (2002, May 15). Classroom microphones make voice louder, clearer. *Education Week* Available online (http://www.edweek.org/ew/newstory.cfm?slug=36headset.h21&keywords=technology).

Gehring, J. (21 June 2000). Career-prep schools let students get their feet wet. *Education Week, 41*(19), 8. Available online (http://www.edweek.com/ew/ewstory.cfm?slug=41new.h19&keywords=erosion).

Good, T. L., & Brophy, J. E. (2003). *Looking in classrooms* (9th ed.). New York: Addison Wesley Longman.

Grobman, H. (1970). *Developmental curriculum projects: Decision points and processes.* Itasca, IL: Peacock.

Gudmundsdottir, S. (1991). Values in pedagogical content knowledge. *Journal of Teacher Education, 41*(3), 44–52.

Gunter, M. A., Estes, T. H., & Schwab, J. (1999). *Instruction: A models approach* (3rd ed.). Boston: Allyn and Bacon.

Guzdial, M. (1998). Technological support for project-based learning. In C. Dede (Ed.), *ASCD year book 1998: Learning with technology.* Alexandria, VA: Association for Supervision and Curriculum Development.

Henderson, P., & Gysbers, N. C. (1998). *Leading and managing your school guidance program staff.* Alexandria, VA: American Counseling Association.

Herbert, J. M. (1999). An online learning community: Technology brings teachers together for professional development. *American School Board Journal, 186*(3), 39–41.

Hoff, D. J. (10 October 2001). Math educators tell publishers what's needed. *Education Week, 21* (6), p. 5. Available online (http://www.edweek.com/ew/newstory.cfm?slug=06math.h21&keywords=textbooks).

Hunt, D. E., & Sullivan, E. V. (1974). *Between psychology and education.* Hinsdale, IL: Dryden Press.

Interstate New Teacher Assessment and Support Consortium. (1992). *Model standards for beginning teacher licensing and development: A resource for state dialogue.* Available online: http://www.ccsso.org/intascst.html#draft.

Jackson, P. W. (1990). *Life in classrooms.* New York: Teachers College Press.

Joyce, B., Weil, M., & Calhoun, E. (2000). *Models of teaching* (6th ed.). Boston: Allyn and Bacon.

Kliebard, H. M. (1998). The effort to reconstruct the modern American curriculum. In L. E. Beyer & M. W. Apple (Eds.) (pp. 21–33). *The curriculum: Problems, politics, and possibilities* (2nd ed.). Albany, NY: State University of New York Press.

Kounin, J. S. (1970). *Discipline and group management in classrooms.* New York: Holt, Rinehart and Winston.

Langer, J. A., & Applebee, A. N. (1986). Reading and writing instruction: Toward a theory of teaching and learning. In E. Z. Rothkopf (Ed.), *Review of research in education: Vol. 13* (pp. 171–194). Washington, DC: American Educational Research Association.

Mager, R. F. (1962). *Preparing instructional objectives.* Palo Alto, CA: Fearon.

Manzo, K. K. (2002). History repeats itself in Texas for textbook-review process. *Education Week.* Available online (http://www.edweek.com/ew/newstory.cfm?slug=43textbook.h21&keywords=textbooks).

McAuliffe, J., & Stoskin, L. (1993). *What color is Saturday? Using analogies to enhance creative thinking in the classroom.* Tucson, AZ: Zephyr Press.

National Council of Teachers of Mathematics (1989). *Curriculum and evaluation standards for school mathematics.* Reston, VA: Author.

National Council of Teachers of Mathematics (1991). *Professional standards for teaching mathematics.* Available online (http://standards.nctm.org/Previous/ProfStds/TeachMath6.htm).

Rogers, C. (1971). *Client centered therapy.* Boston: Houghton Mifflin.

Rosenthal, R., & Jacobson, L. (1968). *Pygmalion in the classroom: Teacher expectation and pupils' intellectual development.* New York: Holt, Rinehart and Winston.

Slavin, R. E. (1995). *Cooperative learning* (2nd ed.). Boston: Allyn and Bacon.

Slavin, R. E., & Fashola, O. S. (1998). *Show me the evidence! Proven and promising programs for America's schools.* Thousand Oaks, CA: Corwin Press.

Sowell, E. J. (1996). *Curriculum: An integrative introduction.* Upper Saddle River, NJ: Prentice Hall.

Tyler, R. W. (1950). *Basic principles of curriculum and instruction.* Chicago: University of Chicago Press.

Walsh, M. (1999). Conservatives join effort to pull the plug on Channel One. *Education Week, 18*(30), 5.

Weinstein, C. S., & Mignano, Jr., A. J. (2003). *Elementary classroom management: Lessons from research and practice* (3rd ed.). New York: McGraw-Hill.

Wiggins, G., & McTighe, J. (1998). Understanding by design. Alexandria, VA: Association of Supervisors and Curriculum Developers. Available online (http://www.ascd.org/framebooks.html).

Wolf, D. P. (1994). *An assessment of "Creating Original Opera."* Cambridge, MA: Performance Assessment Collaboratives for Education.

Wolfgang, C. H., Bennett, B. J., & Irvin, J. L. (1999). *Strategies for teaching self-discipline in the middle grades.* Boston: Allyn and Bacon.

Chapter 11

Airasian, P. W. (2000). *Assessment in the classroom: A concise approach* (2nd ed.). Boston: McGraw-Hill.

Bloom, B. (1982). *Human characteristics and school learning.* New York: McGraw-Hill.

Bowers, M. (2001, December 11). Chesapeake teacher resigns over SOLs. *Virginian-Pilot,* B6.

Briggs, T. W. (2002, October). Gold stars for the teachers. *USA Today.* Available online (http://www.usatoday.com/news/education/2002-10-16-all-star-cover-usat_x.htm).

Carey, L. M. (1994). *Measuring and evaluating school learning* (2nd ed.). Boston: Allyn and Bacon.

Furger, R. (2002, Feb.11). Urban Academy: Where testing is anything but standard. *Edutopia.* Available online (http://glef.org).

Gage, N. L. (1985). *Hard gains in the soft sciences: The case of pedagogy.* Bloomington, IN: Phi Delta Kappa's Center on Evaluation, Development and Research.

Hoff, D. (1999). California approves math, English textbooks tied to standards. *Education Week, 18*(41), 10.

Interstate New Teacher Assessment and Support Consortium. (1992). *Model standards for beginning teacher licensing and development: A resource for state dialogue.* Available online: http://www.ccsso.org/intascst.html#draft.

Jones, E. D., Southern, W. T., & Brigham, F. J. (1998, March). Curriculum-based assessment: Testing what is taught and teaching what is tested. *Intervention in School and Clinic, 33*(4), 239–249.

Mackey, J., & Appleman, D. (1988). Questioning skill. In R. McNergney (Ed.) *Guide to classroom teaching.* Boston Allyn and Bacon, 145–146.

Maryland State Department of Education (1995). MSPAP through the eyes of a 3rd grade student. Available online (http://www.mdk12.org/mspp/mspap/2-eyes.html).

Maryland State Department of Education (2000). The Maryland School Performance Assessment Program (MSPAP). Available online (http://www.mdk12.org/mspp/mspap/how-scored/mspap_info/index.html).

National Council of Teachers of Mathematics (2000). About principles and standards and E-standards. Available online (http://standards.nctm.org/info/about.htm).

National Education Goals Panel (1998). *National education goals: Building a nation of learners.* Available online (http://negp.gov/webpg10.htm).

National Research Council (2001). *Knowing what students know: The science and design of educational assessment.* Committee on the Foundations of Assessment. J. Pelligrino, N. Chudowsky, & R. Glaser (Eds.). Board of Testing and Assessment, Center for Education. Division of Behavioral and Social Sciences and Education. Washington, DC: National Academy Press.

Nebraska Department of Education (1999). *A planning guide for Nebraska schools.* Available online (http://www.nde.state.ne.us/stars/pdf/AsmentGuide.pdf).

Olson, L. (2002, February 20). Testing. *Education Week, 21*(23), 11.

Popham, W. J. (2002). *Classroom assessment: What teachers need to know* (3rd ed.). Boston: Allyn and Bacon.

Chapter 12

Andrews, K. (2002, April 26). Cale children think globally. *Daily Progress,* p. B1.

Behal, S. (2002, April 26). Caste cruelty makes school a nightmare. *Times Educational Supplement,* no. 4478, p.18.

Berg, D. L. (1995). Canada. In T. N. Postlethwaite (Ed.), *The encyclopedia of comparative education and national systems of education* (2nd ed.) (pp. 180–189). Oxford: Pergamon Press.

Berliner, D. C. & Biddle, B. J. (1995). *The manufactured crisis: Myths, fraud, and the attack on America's public schools.* Reading, Mass.: Addison-Wesley.

Boyer, E. (1992). Educating in a multicultural world. In D. Bragaw & W. S. Thomson (Eds.), *Multicultural education: A global approach* (pp. 48–53). New York: The American Forum for Global Education.

Bracey, G. W. (23 January 2002). International comparisons: An excuse to avoid meaningful educational reform. *Education Week, 21*(19), 30, 32. Available online (http://www.edweek.com/ew/newstory.cfm?slug=19bracey.h21&keywords=timss).

Burns, J. (2002, July 26). Liberation through education. *TES.* Available online (http://www.tes.co.uk/search/search_display.asp?section=Archive&sub_section=Scotland&id=366885&Type=0).

Curtis, D. (undated). March of the monarchs. *Edutopia.* San Francisco: The George Lucas Educational Foundation.

Available online (http://www.glef.org/FMPro?-DB=articles1.fp5&-format=article.html&-lay=layout%20%231&learnlivekeywords::jargonfree=Project-Based%20Learning&-max=200&-token.1=Art965&-token.2=Project-Based%20Learning&-token.3=Innovative%20Classrooms&-find).

Cushner, K. (1998). Intercultural education from an international perspective: An introduction. In K. Cushner (Ed.), *International perspectives on intercultural education* (pp. 1–4). Mahwah, NJ: Erlbaum.

Desmond, E. W. (1996). The failed miracle. *Time, 147*(17), 60–64.

Devonshire, E. (4 January 2002). Are we nearly there yet? *Times Education Supplement.* Available online (http://www.tes.co.uk/search/search_display.asp?section=Archive&sub_section=Online+Education&id=357688&Type=0).

Fowler, R. (1998). Intercultural education in Canada: Glimpses from the past, hopes for the future. In K. Cushner (Ed.), *International perspectives on intercultural education* (pp. 302–318). Mahwah, NJ: Erlbaum.

Friedman, T. L. (2000). *The lexus and the olive tree.* New York: Anchor Books.

Galley, M. (6 March 2002). School's display of N. Korean flag raises veterans' ire. *Education Week, 21*(25), 3. Available online (http://www.edweek.com/ew/newstory.cfm?slug=25flag.h21&keywords=global).

Govinda, R. (Ed.) (2002). *India education report: A profile of basic education.* New Delhi: Oxford University Press.

Goya, S. (1994). Japanese education: Hardly known facts. *Education Digest, 59*(8), 8–12.

Guha, S. (2002). In pursuit of learning: Educational programs for at-risk children in India. *Childhood Education, 78*(4), 206–209.

Huerta, A. E. (1999). *Las Trampas de la identidad en un mundo de mujeres.* Mexico: Editorial Itaca.

International Baccalaureate Organisation (2001). Reactions from students: 11 September events. Available online (http://www.ibo.org/ibo/index.cfm/en/ibo/services/doc_library?objectid=37072050-0E28-48B0-A9AC125A468AA1F9&method=getdocument&contentid=0006105E-6240-1C7A-8EFE80C12645FE64).

Interstate New Teacher Assessment and Support Consortium. (1992). *Model standards for beginning teacher licensing and development: A resource for state dialogue.* Available online: http://www.ccsso.org/intascst.html#draft.

Johnston, C. (4 January 2002). Learning valuable lessons from the city state. *Times Education Supplement.* Available online (http://www.tes.co.uk/.../search_display.asp?section=Archive&sub_section=Online+Education&id=357692&Type=).

Kanaya, T. (1995). Japan. In T. N. Postlethwaite (Ed.), *In-*

ternational encyclopedia of national systems of education* (pp. 482–488). New York: Elsevier Science.

King, E. J. (1988). South Africa. In T. N. Postlethwaite (Ed.), *The encyclopedia of comparative education and national systems of education* (2nd ed.) (pp. 600–605). Oxford: Pergamon Press.

Lemmer, E. M. (1993). Educational renewal in South Africa: Problems and prospects. *Compare, 23*(1), 53–62.

Lloyd, M. (1999, February 19). Hindu nationalists campaign to remake education in India: Ruling party and its allies enlist academics to revise the canon. *Chronicle of Higher Education,* p. A56.

Lollock, L. (2001, January). The foreign-born population in the United States: Population characteristics. Washington, DC: U.S. Department of Commerce, Economics and Statistics Administration, U.S. Census Bureau. Available online (http://www.census.gov/prod/2000pubs/p20-534.pdf).

Lorey, D. E. (1995, March–April). Education and the challenges of Mexican development. *Challenge, 38*:51–55.

Manzo, K. K. (4 July 2002). A reporter abroad: Safety concerns up, classtime down in Japan. *Education Week, 21*(42), 21. Available online (http://www.edweek.com/ew/newstory.cfm?slug=42japan_web.h21&keywords=japan).

Martin, M. O., Mullis, I. V. S., Gonzalez, E. J., Gregory, K. D., Smith, T. A., Chrostowski, S. J., Garden, R. A., & O'Connor, K. M. (2000, December). *TIMSS 1999 International Science Report Findings from IEA's Repeat of the Third International Science and Science Study at the Eighth Grade.* Boston: Boston College, International Study Center. Available online (http://isc.bc.edu/timss1999i/science_achievement_report.html).

Mullis, I. V. S., Martin, M. O., Gonzalez, E. J., Gregory, K. D., Garden, R. A., O'Connor, K. M., Chrostowski, S. J., & Smith, T. A. (2000, December). *TIMSS 1999 International Mathematics Report Findings from IEA's Repeat of the Third International Mathematics and Science Study.* Available online (http://isc.bc.edu/timss1999benchmark.html).

Muslim parents boycott religious classes. (1996, January). *Times Educational Supplement,* p. 3.

National Center for Education Statistics (2001). Toward assessing ICT literacy: Focus on Mexico. Available online (http://nces.ed.gov/surveys/international/ines/pdf/Newsletter_Issue14.pdf).

Pollock, L. (2002, April 26). Troubling times for defenders of the faith. *TES.* Available online (http://www.tes.co.uk/search/search_display.asp?section=Archive&sub_section=GOVERNORS&id=362800&Type=0).

Reyes, M. E. (1995). Mexico. In T. N. Postlethwaite (Ed.), *International encyclopedia of national systems of education* (2nd ed.) (pp. 643–652). New York: Elsevier.

Rowe, M. B. (1986). Wait time: Slowing down may be a way of speeding up. *Journal of Teacher Education, 37*(1), 43–50.

Science study at the eighth grade. Boston: Boston College, International Study Center. Available online (http://isc.bc.edu/timss1999i/math_achievement_report.html).

Singapore Department of Statistics (2001). Census of population 2000. Available online (http://www.singstat.gov.sg/keystats/c2000/topline2.pdf).

Spring, J. (1998). *Education and the rise of the global economy.* Mahwah, NJ: Erlbaum.

Stevenson, H. W., & Stigler, J. W. (1992). *The learning gap: Why our schools are failing and what we can learn from Japanese and Chinese education.* New York: Summit.

Stonier, J. (1998). Breaking out of a separatist paradigm: Intercultural education in South Africa. In K. Cushner (Ed.), *International perspectives on intercultural education* (pp. 210–236). Mahwah, NJ: Erlbaum.

Sullivan, K. (11 November 2001). Seething south of the border. Our neighbors have some hard words for us. Are we listening? *Washington Post,* F1, F8. Available online (http://nl9.newsbank.com/nl search/we/Archives?p_action=doc&p_docid=0EFBC90E643CB66D&p_docnum=1&s).

Thomas, R. M. (Ed.) (1990). *International comparative education: Practices, issues, & practices.* Oxford: Pergamon Press.

Tye, B. B., & Tye, K. A. (1992). *Global education: A study of school change.* Albany, NY: State University of New York Press.

Union of International Associations (2002). International organizations and NGOS Project. Available online (http://www.uia.org/organizations/).

Vail, K. (2002). Lessons in democracy. *American School Board Journal, 189*(1), 14–18.

Westbury, I. (1992). Comparing American and Japanese achievement: Is the United States really a low achiever? *Educational Researcher, 21*(5), 18–24.

Wood, A. (15 February 2002). Suspended aged six for wearing headscarves. *Times Education Supplement.* Available online (http://www.tes.co.u.../search_display.asp?section=Archive&sub_section=News+%26+opinion&id=359809&Type=).

Wu, A. (1999). The Japanese education system: A case study and analysis. National Institute on Student Achievement, Curriculum, and Assessment, Office of Educational Research and Improvement, U.S. Department of Education. Available online (http://www.ed.gov/pubs/ResearchToday/98-3038.html).

Chapter 13

Armstrong, J., & Anthes, K. (2001). How data can help. Putting information to work to raise student achievement. *American School Board Journal, 188*(11), 38–41.

Bohlin, K. E., Farmer, D., & Ryan, K. (2001). *Building character in schools resource guide.* San Francisco: Jossey-Bass.

Bonnell, T. (7 August 2002). A monk, a mandala, and the meaning of school. *Education Week, 21*(43), 49. Available online (http://www.edweek.com/ew/newstory.cfm?slug=43bonnell.h21&keywords=future).

Brophy, J., & McCaslin, M. (1992). Teachers' reports of how they perceive and cope with problem students. *Elementary School Journal, 93*(1), 3–68.

Century Foundation Task Force on the Common School (2002). Divided we fail: Coming together through public school choice. New York: Century Foundation Press. Available online (http://www.tcf.org/Publications/Education/dividedwefail.pdf).

CEO Forum on Education and Technology (2000). *Teacher preparation StaR Chart: A self-assessment tool for colleges of education.* Washington, DC: Author.

CEO Forum on Educational Technology (2001, June). *Key building blocks for student achievement in the 21st century: Assessment, alignment, accountability, access, analysis.* Washington, DC: Author.

Clandinin, D. J., & Connelly, F. M. (1996). Teachers' professional knowledge landscapes: Teacher stories—stories of teachers—school stories—stories of schools. *Educational Researcher, 25*(3), 24–30.

Comer, J. (23 April 2001). Schools that develop children. *American Prospect, 12*(7), 3–5.

Gauld, L., & Gauld, M. (2002). *The biggest job we'll ever have.* New York: Scribner.

Good, T. L., & Brophy, J. E. (2003). *Looking in classrooms.* New York: Addison Wesley Longman.

Grabe, M., & Grabe, C. (2000). *Integrating the Internet for meaningful learning.* Boston: Houghton Mifflin.

Grumet, M. (1987). Women and teaching: Homeless at home. *Teacher Education Quarterly, 14*(2), 39–46.

Interstate New Teacher Assessment and Support Consortium. (1992). *Model standards for beginning teacher licensing and development: A resource for state dialogue.* Available online: http://www.ccsso.org/intascst.html#draft.

King, A. (2002, September 13). Computers key to future. Opposing view: Maine's investment in technology will better educate students. *USA Today,* p.16A.

Manzo, K. K. (2002a). Kansas City turns classrooms over to interns. *Education Week, 22*(5), 5.

Manzo, K. K. (2002b). North wind bows to rising sun. *Education Week.* Available online (http://www.edweek.org/ew/ewstory.cfm?slug=04japan.h22&keywords=Japan).

Mitzel, H. E. (1960). Teacher effectiveness. In C. W. Harris (Ed.), *Encyclopedia of educational research* (3rd ed.) (pp. 1481–1486). New York: Macmillan.

National Association of State Boards of Education (2001).

Any time, any place, any path, any pace: Taking the lead on e-learning policy. Alexandria, VA: Author.

National Center for Health Education (undated). *Enhancing parent involvement.* Available online (http://www.nche.org).

National Network for Educational Renewal (1999). *19 Postulates necessary for the simultaneous renewal of schools and the education of educators.* Retrieved from the World Wide Web, August 26, 1999. Available online (http://depts.washington.edu/cedren/NationalNetworkForEducationalRenewal.html).

National PTA. (1995–1996). *National PTA 100 Years.* Available online (http://www.pta.org).

National PTA (1998). *National standards for parent family involvement programs—Standard 1: Communication.* Available online (http://www.pta.org/programs/pfistand.htm#Standard1).

Noddings, N. (1984). *Caring: A feminine approach to ethics and moral education.* Berkeley: University of California Press.

Noddings, N. (1992). Gender and the curriculum. In P. W. Jackson (Ed.), *Handbook of research on curriculum* (pp. 659–686). New York: Macmillan.

Palmer, J. (15 February 2000). Nationally acclaimed school reform program moving headquarters to Uconn. Available online (http://www.sp.uconn.edu/~www.asp/press.htm).

Quigley, C. N., & Bahmueller, C. F. (Eds.) (1991). *Civitas: A framework for civic education.* Calabasas, CA: Center for Civic Education.

Shulman, L. S. (1986). Paradigms and research programs in the study of teaching. In M. C. Wittrock (Ed.), *Handbook of research on teaching* (3rd ed.) (pp. 3–36). New York: Macmillan.

Sizer, T. R. (1992). *Horace's school: Redesigning the American high school.* Boston: Houghton Mifflin.

Thompson, B. (2001, September 16). Learning to be wired. *Washington Post Magazine,* pp. 18–23, 45–49.

USA Today (2002, September 13). Student laptops are a luxury. Our view: School funds can be better spent on, say, helping kids learn to read. Author, p.14.

U.S. Department of Education (2002). Internet access in U.S. public schools up for seventh straight year. Available online (http://www.ed.gov/PressReleases/09-2002/09242002b.html).

Walberg, H. J. (1991). Productive teaching and instruction: Assessing the knowledge base. In H. C. Waxman & H. J. Walberg (Eds.), *Effective teaching: Current research* (pp. 33–62). Berkeley, CA: McCutchan.

Waxman, H. C. & Wahlberg, J. H. (Eds.). *Effective teaching: current research.* Berkeley, CA: McCutchan Publishing Corporation.

Name Index

A

Abu-Bakr, 160
Addams, Jane, 121
Adler, Alfred, 150
Adler, Mortimer, 156–157
Agee, James, 121
Airasian, P. W., 296, 313
Alcott, Bronson, 96
Alexander, K., 251, 256, 258
Alexander, M. D., 251, 256, 258
Al-Fārā bi, 160
Al-Kindi, 160
Ambrose, S. E., 89, 90
Anderson, V., 297
Andrews, K., 330
Anthony, Susan B., 131
Apple, M., 153, 280
Applebee, A. N., 280
Archer, J., 186
Aristotle, 148–149
Asante, M. K., 161, 162
Atkinson, Richard, 140
Ayres, Leonard, 116

B

Babyak, S., 11
Bagley, William, 157
Bahmueller, C. F., 367
Baldwin, William, 118
Balli, S. J., 33, 41
Banks, C. A., 58, 273
Banks, J. A., 58, 68, 162, 273
Banville, J., 150
Barber, L. W., 16

Barlett, Brooke, 20
Barman, J., 99
Barnard, Henry, 109–110
Barnes, H., 182
Bathurst, Charles, 101
Becker, G. S., 204
Beecher, Catherine, 101, 111
Beecher, Mary, 111
Behal, S., 346
Bennett, B. J., 296
Bennett, C., 128
Berg, D. L., 338
Berlin, I., 98
Berliner, D. C., 208, 224, 344
Bestor, Arthur, 139
Bethune, Mary McLeod, 125
Biddle, B. J., 208, 224, 344
Binet, Alfred, 118
Birney, Alice McLellan, 383
Blair, J., 201
Bloom, Allan, 157
Bloom, B., 286
Blum, J. M., 92, 94, 96, 97, 98, 118, 119, 122, 131
Blumenfeld, P., 289
Bohlin, K. E., 369
Bonnell, T., 362
Borea, R. R., 203
Borja, R. R., 35
Bossert, S. T., 134
Bowers, M., 303
Boyd, W., 88
Boyer, E. L., 192, 358
Boyer, P. S., 104, 109
Bracey, Gerald, 171, 224, 356
Brameld, Theodore, 158
Bridgmen, Laura, 102

Briggs, T. W., 329
Brigham, F. J., 27, 319
Brimley, V., 214, 219, 222
Brophy, J., 176, 285, 296, 297, 387, 389
Broughton, Charneice M., 233
Brown, C. L., 129
Brown-Smith, Linda, 127
Bryan, Hugh, 98
Bryan, William Jennings, 138, 207
Bryant, William, 126
Buber, Martin, 150, 152
Bullock, Henry, 92, 98–99
Burns, J., 353
Burns, Marilyn, 293
Burrup, P. E., 214, 219, 222
Bush, George W., 63, 133, 134, 139, 276, 305, 329
Bush, Laura, 12
Bushman, Brad, 119
Butler, D. A., 177

C

Calhoun, E., 285, 290, 291
Callahan, R. E., 118
Calvin, John, 92
Cambron-McCabe, N. H., 236, 240, 245, 253
Camus, Albert, 150
Canady, R. L., 190
Cao, H. T., 194
Caplan, N., 61
Carey, L. M., 312
Carlson, D., 65
Carlson, R. A., 121, 128, 138
Carnegie, Andrew, 118

Carr, C. K., 125
Carroll, J. B., 286
Carson, C. C., 224
Carter, James G., 111
Carter, Jimmy, 133
Cattell, James. 118
Catton, W. B., 119, 137, 138
Choy, M. H., 61
Chrostowski, S. J., 354
Clandinin, D. J., 385
Clark, C. E., 104, 109
Clark, R. W., 194
Clemetson, L., 78
Clinton, William J., 134, 189, 305
Cohen, David, 135
Cohen, S., 154
Cole, J. Y., 118
Coleman, D., 26
Coleman, M. C., 99
Coles, A. D., 52
Collier, John, 122–123
Comenius, John Amos, 87
Comer, J., 380, 381
Comer, James B., 380
Conant, James B., 178
Conkling, W., 246
Connelly, F. M., 385
Corbett, H. D., 30
Corbin, H., 160
Counts, George, 158
Cremin, L. A., 93, 99, 107, 108, 110,
    111, 123, 135
Cross, B. M., 111
Csikszentmihalyi, M., 119
Cuban, L., 279
Cushner, K., 331

D

Dabney, C. W., 121
Dalai Lama, 299
Darling-Hammond, L., 11, 229
Darrow, Clarence, 207
Darwin, Charles, 138
Davidson, A. L., 194
Davis, M., 63
de Baumont, Gustave, 96
de la Cruz, Sor Juana, 100

de Tocqueville, Alexis, 96
DeBoer, G. E.
Decker, L. E., 195
Decker, V. A., 195
Defoe, Daniel, 88
Degler, C. N., 116, 124
Deighton, L. C., 101
Desmond, E. W., 342, 344
Devonshire, E., 349
Dewey, John, 133, 138, 144, 155, 156,
    162
Dickenson, T. S., 177
Dolan, J. P., 110
Domenech, Daniel, 79
Dornbusch, S. M., 194
Downs, R. B., 89
Doyle, W., 296
Driscoll, A., 284, 296
DuBois, W. E. B., 125
Dudley, B., 67
Durant, W., 148

##

Edwards, Jonathan, 96, 133
Edwards, P., 87
Efron, S., 130
Eggen, P. D., 289
Eisner, E. W., 273
Eliot, Charles, 137
Elsbree, W. S., 101, 102, 103, 104, 111
Emerson, George B., 101
Emerson, Ralph Waldo, 86, 96, 97, 106,
    281
Emmer, E., 297
Entwisle, D. R., 195
Erasmus, 149
Essex, N. L., 244, 250, 252
Everitt, Charles, 89
Evertson, C., 297

##

Fakhry, J., 160
Falbo, T., 128
Farmer, D., 369
Farrar, Eleanor, 135

Fashola, O. S., 288
Feistitzer, E., 11
Fine, Michelle, 157, 178
Finn, C. E.. Jr., 30
Fischer, K. W., 154
Fischer, L., 250, 259
Flynn, G., 100
Fogel, D., 100
Ford, P. L., 104
Ford, R. E. , 25
Forman, Michelle, 22
Fowler, R., 338, 339
Franklin, Benjamin, 104–105, 107
Franklin, J. H., 116
Frieberg, H. L., 284, 296.
Friedman, Milton, 228
Friedman, T. L., 337
Friere, Paolo, 143, 150
Froebel, Friedrich, 89, 102, 110
Fuchs, L. H., 120
Fuller, Margaret, 131
Furger, R., 170

##

Gage, N. L., 293, 321
Gallaudet, Thomas, 102
Gallupo, A. M.
Garden, R. A., 354
Garfield, R. R., 219, 222
Garms, W. I., 202, 208
Gates, William H., III, 118
Gautama, Siddhartha, 160
Gay, P., 87
Gehring, J., 277
Gewertz, C., 233, 263
Ghandi, Mohanda, 159
Gilmer, Peachy, 89
Giroux, H. A., 157
Gladden, M., 178
Gladding, S. T., 34
Gladson–Billings, Gloria, 78
Glasgow, K. L., 194
Glickman, J., 11
Goldberg, S. S., 238
Gonzalez, E. J., 354
Good, T., 176, 285, 297, 387
Goodlad, John, 384

Goodman, J. M., 123
Goodman, Paul, 150
Gordon, William, 289
Govinda, R., 346
Goya, S., 344
Grabe, C., 372
Grant, C. A., 66
Grant, Zilpah, 101
Greenvals, R., 223
Gregg, G. A., 195
Gregory, K. D., 354
Grobman, H., 279
Grossman, K. N., 42
Grumet, M., 367
Gudmundsdottir, S., 272
Guha, S., 346
Gunter, M. A.
Gutek, G. L., 88
Guthrie, J. W., 202, 208
Guzdial, M., 289
Gysbers, N. C., 297

Haberman, M., 145
Haefli, K., 48
Hahner, J., 100
Hall, G. Stanley, 138
Hallahan, D. P., 74, 102, 131
Hampel, R. L., 194
Hansot, E., 118, 132, 134, 138
Harnisch, D. L., 343
Harris, Charles Torrey, 137–138
Harris, Louis, 77
Hastert, Dennis, 23
Hawthorne, Nathaniel, 101
Haysbert, J. W., 24
Haysbert, JoAnn W., 24
Hearn, D., 154
Hebert, Y., 99
Hedges, L. V., 223
Hegel, George Wilhelm Friedrich, 152
Heide, J. B., 218
Heidegger, Martin, 150
Henderson, P., 297
Hendrie, C., 220
Henke, R. R., 12
Herbart, Johann Friedrich, 88–89

Herbert, J. M., 274
Herbert, J. W. , 25
Hess, Rick, 11
Heyndericks, Stephanie, 371
Hildebrand, N., 26
Hill, D., 60
Hill, Oliver, 126
Hirsch, E. D., Jr., 157
Hoff, D. J., 139, 281, 305
Hoffman, A. N., 218
Holbrook, Josiah, 106
Holland, N., 178
Holtom, D. C., 160
Houston, Charles Hamilton, 126
Howe, Samuel Gridley, 102
Huang, S., 296
Huelskamp, R. M., 224
Huerta, A. E., 342
Hughes, John, 110
Hunt, D. E., 280
Hutchins, Robert Maynard, 156, 157

ibn-Sina, 160
Imber, M., 249, 255
Intrator, S. M., 3
Irvin, J. L., 296
Itard, Jean-Marc, 102

Jackson, Helen Hunt, 121
Jackson, P. W., 272
Jacobson, L., 16
James, William, 155, 156
Jamieson, A., 30, 31
Jamieson, R. L., Jr.
Jefferson, Thomas, 94, 99, 107
Jennings, J. F., 120
Johnson, D. W., 67
Johnson, Lyndon, 38, 135
Johnson, R., 26
Johnson, S. M., 67
Johnston, C., 352
Jones, E. D., 319

Joyce, B., 285, 290, 291
Judd, Charles, 118

Kaestle, C. F., 104, 106, 108, 110, 111
Kanaya, T., 343
Kannapel, Karen, 271
Kardos, S. M.
Kauchak, D. P., 289
Kauffman, J. M., 74, 102, 131
Keen, M., 191
Keller, C., 74
Keller, Helen, 102
Kelly, C., 250, 259
Keough, R., 181
Kett, J. F., 104, 109
Kilbane, C R., 20, 83
King, Angus, 374
King, E. J., 352
King, Martin Luther, Jr., 127, 159
King, S., 178
Klicka, C., 238
Kliebard, H. M., 133, 139, 271
Koch, Ed, 292
Kominski, R., 30, 31
Kopp, Wendy S., 11
Kounin, J. S., 297
Kozol, Jonathan, 33, 230
Krajcik, J., 289
Krug, E. A., 108

Laine, R. D., 223
LaMorte, M. W., 241, 245, 251, 258, 260
Lancaster, Joseph, 106
Landau, S., 48
Langer, J. A., 280
Lannie, V. P., 110
Lareau, A., 195
Lehrer, R., 79
Leibbrand, Janem 11
Lemann, Nicholas, 140
Lemmer, E. M., 352
LeTarte, C., 136

Levin, Henry, 380
Lewin, Kurt, 143
Lewin, T., 63
Lewis, Ann, 78
Lewis, Meriwether, 89
Liebbrand, J., 11
Link, A. S., 119, 137, 138
Lippman, Walter, 118
Lipton, M., 78
Little, J. W., 21
Liu, E.
Lloyd, M., 345, 346
Locke, John, 87
Lollock, L., 331
Lorey, D. E.
Luther, Martin, 149
Lynch, Deborah, 200
Lyons, Mary, 101

Madden, Nancy, 382
Mager, R. F., 286
Magnuson, D., 67
Malcom X, 161
Mann, Horace, 101, 108–109
Manuel, H. T., 100
Manzo, K. K., 280, 345
Marshall, Thurgood, 126, 127
Martin, M. O., 354
Martinez, G., 30, 31
Marx, Karl, 152–153
Marx, R., 289
Maslow, Abraham, 150
Mather, Cotton, 96
McAuliffe, J., 289, 290
McCarthy, M. M., 236, 240, 245, 253
McCaskill, D., 99
McCaslin, M., 389
McCown, C., 177
McFeely, W. S., 92, 94, 96, 97, 98, 118, 119, 122, 131
McGee Banks, C. A., 273
McGinnell, Kevin, 348
McGuffey, William Holmes, 105
McGuire, C. K., 224
McLaughlin, M. W., 229
McNergney, R., 25, 74

McPherson, Christopher, 98
McTighe, J., 284
Mehlman, Natalia, 6, 7
Mellon, Andrew, 118
Metz, K. E., 79
Mignano, A. J., Jr., 296
Millard, B., 71
Milman, M. B., 83
Minzey, J. D., 136
Mithaug, D. E., 73
Mitzel, H. E., 385
Moffett, Donna, 163
Montessori, Maria, 102, 182
Morgan, E. S., 92, 94, 96, 97, 98, 118, 119, 122, 131
Morris, Vivian, 43
Morse, Jedidiah, 105
Mosak, E., 178
Moses, Robert, 68
Mullis, I. V. S., 354
Multanowski, Edmond, 110
Murray, Linda, 203

Neef, James, 111
Nietsche, Friedrich Wilhelm, 150
Noddings, N., 367, 368

O'Connor, K. M., 354
O'Han, N., 1
Oakes, J., 192
Odden, A., 78, 225
Ogbu, J. U., 60
Ogden, Robert, 118
Olson, L., 175, 310
Owen, Robert, 97

Pacheco, Mary Ann, 195
Page, J. A., 192
Paige, Rod, 11, 53
Paine, Thomas, 93

Palcinsar, A., 289
Palmer, J., 380
Pannell, C. W., 129
Parkhurst, Helen, 133
Parziale, J., 154
Peabody, Elizabeth Palmer, 89, 101, 122
Perkins, D., 154
Pestalozzi, Johann Heinrich, 88, 102, 104, 110, 111
Peterson, R. L., 50
Phelan, P., 194
Piaget, Jean, 154
Pierce, Charles Sanders, 154–155
Pierce, L. C., 202, 208
Pinckney, Elizabeth Lucas, 112
Plato, 147
Plutarch, 338
Pollina, A., 64
Pollock, L., 348
Ponessa, J., 65
Pool, H., 192
Popham, James, 316, 322
Portner, J., 245
Powell, A. G., 135, 178
Pryor, J. B., 48
Pyhrr, P. A., 222

Quigley, C. N., 367

Reese, Sue, 380
Rettig, M., 190
Reynolds, Gerald A., 63
Rice, J. M., 116
Rice, Joseph Mayer, 116
Richardson, R. D.. Jr., 86
Richardson, S. N., 238
Rockefeller, John D., 118
Rogers, C., 290
Rogers, Carl, 150
Romo, H. D., 128
Ronda, B. A., 101
Roosevelt, Franklin, 125

Rorty, Richard, 155, 156
Rosebery, A. S., 79
Rousseau, Jean-Jacques, 87, 88, 102, 149, 150
Rowe, M. B., 357
Rowland, W. G., Jr., 157
Rury, J. L., 103
Rush, Benjamin, 94, 102
Ryan, K., 369

S

Sack, J., 185
Sadker, D., 62, 63
Sadker, M., 62, 63
Sadowski, M., 224
Salisbury, N., 104, 109
Salvetti, E. P., 36
Sartre, Jean-Paul, 150
Scalia, Antonin, 242
Schauble, L., 79
Schimmel, D., 250, 259
Schlesinger, A. M., Jr., 92, 94, 96, 97, 98, 118, 119, 122, 131
Schön, Donald, 162
Schultz, T. W., 204
Schurtz, Margaretta, 89
Scopes, John T., 207
Seguin, Edouard, 102
Sequoyah, 99
Serra, Junipera, 100
Seymour, L., 79
Shea, G. F., 46
Sheras, Peter, 50, 51
Sherman, Ruth, 78
Sherman, S., 177
Shishu, Bharati, 160
Shulman, L. S., 389
Simons, H. D., 60
Sitkoff, H., 104, 109
Sizer, Thodore, 381
Skiba, R., 50
Skinner, B. F., 153
Slavin, R. E., 288
Slavin, Robert, 382
Sleter, C.E., 66
Smith, T. A., 354
Socrates, 147

Soloway, E., 289
Southern, W. T., 319
Sowell, E. J., 273
Spencer, Herbert, 91
Spring, J., 350
Stampp, K. M., 92, 94, 96, 97, 98, 118, 119, 122, 131
Stanford, M., 157
Stanton, Elizabeth Cady, 131
Stearns, T. M., 218
Stein, M. R. S.
Stein, T. A., 296
Steiner, Rudolf, 182
Steinhardt, M. A., 101
Stevenson, H. W., 357
Stigler, J. W., 357
Stonier, J., 354
Stoskin, L., 289, 290
Stowe, Harriet Beecher, 111
Sullivan, Anne, 102
Sullivan, E. V., 280
Sullivan, K., 280

T

Tenzin, Lama, 362
Terman, Lewis, 118
Thomas, R. M., 337
Thomas, S. B., 236, 240, 245, 253
Thompson, B., 371
Thompson, Tommy, 263
Thoreau, Henry David, 96
Thorndike, Edward L., 118, 153
Thro, W. E., 225
Thucydides, 338
Tillich, Paul, 150
Tippins, Sherrill, 50, 51
Travers, R. M., 118
Truman, Harry S., 125, 127
Tyack, D., 103, 118, 132, 134, 138
Tyler, R. W., 284

U

Ulich, R., 87, 88, 89

Valdes, G., 79
van Geel, T., 249, 255
Vedontom, S., 119
Verstegen, D., 224
Viadero, D., 175

W

Wadsworth, D., 26
Wagner, Melinda B., 186
Walberg, H., 386
Walker, David, 98
Walsh, M., 183, 263, 281
Walsley, P., 178
Warczak, Christine, 249
Ward, J. G., 225
Ward, Lester Frank, 138
Ward, M., 67
Warren, B., 79
Warren, Michael David, Jr., 375
Washington, Booker T., 124–125
Wasley, P. A., 194
Watson, John, 153
Webster, Noah, 94, 105
Weikart, D. P., 35
Weil, M., 285, 290, 291
Weiner, S., 114
Weinstein, C. S., 296
Westbrook, R. B., 156
Westbury, I., 344
White, Deborah, 19
Whitefield, George, 96
Whiting, B., 249
Whitmore, J. K., 61
Whitney, Eli, 97
Wiggins, G., 284
Wigglesworth, Michael, 96
Willard, Emma, 101
Williams, Evelyn, 298
Williams, Juan, 208
Williams, V. L., 261
Wilson, B. L., 30
Winnemucca, Sara, 122
Wolf, D. P., 288
Wolfgang, C. H., 296

Woloch, N., 104, 109
Wood, A., 350
Wood, M., 36
Woodall, T. D., 224
Woodward, C. V., 92, 94, 96, 97, 98,
     118, 119, 122, 131
Wu, A., 344

Young, Ella Flag, 132

Zahn, L., 12

Zehr, M. A., 186
Zill, N., 195
Zirkel, P. A., 238
Zitkala-Sa, 99

Subject Index

A

Abolitionists, 97
Abood v. *Detroit Board of Education*, 249
Absolute Idea, 152
Academic freedom, 258–259
Academic negligence, malpractice, 254–256
Accelerated Schools program, 380
Accreditation, 11, 69
Adoption and Safe Families Act of 1997, 44
Adult education, 136, 178
Aesthetics, 146
AFL-CIO (American Federation of Labor-Congress of
    Industrial Organizations), 24
African Americans
  African philosophy, 161–162
  at-risk students among, 31, 63
  bias and, 61
  bias in assessment and, 322
  and the Civil Rights Movement, 125
  equal treatment and, 259
  higher education and, 178
  labeling issues and, 58
  and one view of teaching, 24
  preschools and, 174
  school violence and, 49–50
  as a special interest group, 206–207
  teenage birthrate among, 46
  and universal education, 124
After-school programs, for at-risk students, 38
Age of Enlightenment, 87
AIDS, 47–48
Alcohol abuse issues, 49
Almanacs, 104–105
Alternative licensure, 6, 11
Alternative schools, 179–186
American Association of Colleges for Teacher Education, 206
American Civil Liberties Union (ACLU), 207

American Federation of Teachers (AFT), 4, 23, 249
American Indian Movement, 123
American Lyceum, 106
Americans with Disabilities Association, Inc., 207
AmeriCorps, 136
Anger management, 50
Animism, 162
Annenberg Foundation, 389
Anti-Defamation League (ADL), 207
Apartheid, 352
Articles of Confederation, 94
Asian Americans
  at-risk students among, 31
  immigration of, 128–130
AskERIC Virtual Library, 379
Assessment
  academic progress, 363
  annual testing, 363
  authentic, 317
  bias, 322
  blueprints, 318
  classroom assessment triad, 311
  classroom testing, 312–313
  cognition and learning, 311
  competency testing, 16–17
  comprehensive, 366
  curriculum-based, 318–319
  definition, 304
  evaluating student learning, 295–296
  formative, 295–296
  grading and recommendations, 320
  journals, 317–318
  minimum competency testing, 314–315
  multiple measures, 323
  national examinations, 18–19
  portfolios, 318
  questions, 315–316
  report cards, 363

rubrics, 318
self-, 319
student's role, 320–321
student teaching, 18
summative, 295–296
teacher qualifications, 363
teaching to the test, 322–323
twentieth century milestones, 326–327
Assimilation, 59, 99
Assistant principals, 188–189
Association of American Universities, 137
Assumption of risk, 256
Asynchronous communication, 373
At-risk students
among African Americans, 31
among Asian Americans, 31
health and safety issues concerning, 43–49
interventions for, 33–40
poverty and, 32–33
Attendance, 191
Audiolingual language laboratories, 139
Authentic assessment, 18, 317
Axiology, 146

Baker v. Queen, 239
Before-school programs, for at-risk students, 38
Beginning Teacher Coaching Program, 21
Behavioral objectives, 286–287
Behavioral systems strategies for instruction, 285–287
Behaviorism, 153–154
Bias
and African Americans, 61
in assessment, 322
Big Brothers and Sisters of America (BBSA), 39
Bilingual Act of 1974, 259
Bilingual education, 61–62, 138
Bill for the More General Diffusion of Knowledge, 107
Biological Science Curriculum Study (BSCS), 139
Black codes, 116
Black Muslims, 161
Block grants, 210
Block scheduling, 190
Bloom's taxonomy of behavioral objectives, 287
Blue-Backed Speller, 105
Blueprints, assessment and, 318
Blues in the Schools (BITS), 71

B.M. by Berger v. State of Montana, 260
BMW, 335, 336
Board of Education of the Westside Community Schools v. Mergens, 241
Board of Regents of State Colleges v. Roth, 250
Braille, 103
Brainerd Mission, 99
Brown v. Board of Education, 73, 126, 127, 259
Buckley Amendment, 248
Buddhism, 160
Bullying, 50–51
Bureaucratization, 134
Bureau for the Handicapped. See Office of Special Education and Rehabilitative Services
Bureau of Indian Affairs (BIA), 121

California Achievement Test, 140
Canada, education in, 338–339
Career issues. See Teaching
Carlisle Indian School, 122
Carl Perkins Vocational Act of 1984, 210
Carnegie Corporation, 389
Carnegie Forum on Education and the Economy, 134
CaseNEX, 385
Categorical grants, 210
Catholic schools, 185–186. See also Parochial schools
Censorship, in curricula, 138–139
Census Bureau, 58
Center for Civic Education, 305
Central office staff, 187
Certification, 9, 22–23
Channel One Network, 281, 282
Character Counts!, 369
Character education, 50, 368–369, 370
Charter schools, 183–185
Chat, 373
Chautauqua movement, 136
Chemical Education Materials Study (CHEM Study), 139
Chicago Teachers Federation (CTF), 132
Chicago Teachers Union, Local No. 1 AFL-CIO v. Hudson, 250
Chief state school officer, 217
Child abuse and neglect, 44–45, 253–254
Child Abuse Prevention and Treatment Act, 44, 254
Child-care centers, 135
Children's Defense Fund (CDF), 43
Children with disabilities, 240. See also Exceptional learners

Chinese Exclusion Act, 129
Choice
    and at-risk students, 32
    in economic terms, 368
    existentialism and, 152
    parents and, 203
    and special education students, 261, 263
    and support for public schools, 226–228
Church-sponsored preschools, 174
Citizenship Act of 1924, 122
Civil Rights Act of 1964, 259
Civitas curriculum, 367
Classroom assessment triad, 311
Classroom management, 285, 296–297
Classroom testing, 312–313
Class schedule, 190–192
Class size, 190–192
Cluster suicides, 48–49
Coalition of Essential Schools, 381–382
Cocurricular, 273
Codes of conduct, 251
Cognition, 154
Cognition and learning, 311
Cognitivism, 153–154
Collaborative networks
    and at-risk students, 380–383
    definition, 379–380
    for enhancing relationships among educators, 383–385
    and increasing parental involvement, 383
    uses of, 386
Collective bargaining, 23
College degrees, 23
Commission on Reorganization of Secondary Education, 138
Committee of Fifteen, 137
Committee of Ten on Secondary School Studies, 137
Common schools, 108
Communication, 292–293. *See also* Telecommunication
Community schools. *See* Full-service schools
Comparative negligence, 256
Compensatory education, for at-risk students, 37–38
Competition *vs.* cooperation, 91
Comprehensive assessment, 366
Comprehensive high schools, 135–136, 178
Computers, 371. *See also* Technology
Concept formation, 289
Concept maps, 388–389
Concerned Women for America (CWA), 65
Conflict mediation, 67

Conflict resolution, 50
Confucianism, 160
Consolidation, 134, 179
Contributory negligence, 256
Cooperative learning, 288
Copyright laws, 252–253
Core Knowledge Foundation, 157
Corporal punishment, 239
Cosmology, 146
Council for Basic Education, 206
Council of Chief State School Officers, 218
Counseling, for at-risk students, 34
Creationism, 138–139
Creativity, 289
Criterion-referenced tests, 313
Cultural Awareness
    An African American View of the Profession, 24
    Charles Hamilton Houston, 126
    Éxito para Todos, 294
    Islamic Schools Step Up Security, 161
    School Mascots, 248
    Success for All Program, 294
Culture
    cultural literacy, 157
    diversity and, 57–58
    mismatches between teachers and students, 77–78
    and responsive instruction, 78–79
Curriculum
    backward design of, 284
    benchmarks in, 326–327
    in colonial schools, 104
    content of, 274–275
    explicit and implicit, 271–272
    extracurriculum, 273
    influence of professional groups and, 277–278
    integrated, 273–274
    mass media and, 280–281
    for multicultural education, 69–72
    in the national interest, 275–276
    null, 272–273
    organization of, 281–285
    post-Civil War, 137–139
    reform of, 365–366
    social issues and public opinion, 277–278
    standardizing of, 275
    state and local priorities, 276–277
    textbooks and, 280–281
Curriculum-based assessment, 318–319
Curriculum maps, 285

D

Dalton Laboratory Plan, 133
Dame schools, 95
Davis v. *Grover*, 263
Davis v. *Monroe County Board of Education*, 261
Dawes Act of 1887, 122
Day nurseries, 174
Degree creep, 137
Department of Education, 116, 133
Desegregation, 58
Detroit Federation of Teachers (DFT), 249
Dharma, 160
Dialectic, 152
Dictionaries, 105
Digital library, 378
Direct instruction, 286
Disabilities, 64, 101–102, 240. *See also* Exceptional learners
Discipline. *See* Classroom management
Discrimination, 246–247
Dismissal, 250
Distance learning, 375–376
District power equalization plan, 215–216
Diversity
    cultural, 57–58, 77–79
    exceptionality, 64, 72–77
    gender, 62–64, 367
    immigrants and, 59–61
    language and, 61–62
    and multicultural education, 65–72
    race and ethnicity, 58–59
    in sexual orientation, 65
Driver safety issues, 49
Dropouts, 30–32. *See also* At-risk students
Drug Abuse Resistance Education (DARE), 52
Drugs. *See* Substance abuse
Due process, 242–244, 243

E

Early Head Start, 35–36
Early intervention programs, for at-risk students, 35–36
Echo effect, 13
Economic Opportunity Act of 1964, 276
Edison Schools, 183
Education, aims of, 283
Educational philosophies. *See* Philosophy
Educational publishing. *See* Textbooks

Educational Testing Service (ETS), 18
Education and Consolidation and Improvement Act (ECIA), 210–211
Education for All Handicapped Children Act of 1975, 72, 210, 247, 276
Elementary and Secondary Education Act (ESEA), 119–120, 363
Elementary schools, 176
Ellis v. *Brotherhood of Railway, Airline, and S.S. Clerks*, 250
Email, 373
Emergency licensure, 11
Encyclopedia Britannica Educational Corporation v. *Crooks*, 253
English academy, 107
English as a Second Language (ESL), 61–62
Enrollment trends, and school budgets, 13
Environmental Education Act (Public Law 91-516), 275–276
Epics, 159
Epistemology, 146
E pluribus unum, 69, 120
Equal Access Act (EAA), 241
Equal educational opportunity, 58, 69, 202–203
Equal protection clause, 237
Equal treatment, 259–260
E-rate, 377
eSchools, 376
Essentialism, 156–158
Establishment clause, 235
Ethics, 4
Ethnicity, 58–59
Eurocentric, 157
European Americans
    at-risk students among, 31
    higher education and, 178
    immigration and, 123
    preschools and, 174
    teenage birthrate among, 46
Evaluation. *See* Assessment
Evolution, 138
Exceptional learners, 64, 131
    adapting instruction for, 294–295
    delivering services to gifted students, 76–77
    delivering services to students with disabilities, 72–73
    laws that support inclusion, 73
    providing for special education, 74–76
Existentialism, 150, 152
Expectations, for schools, 30–33
Explicit curriculum, 271
Extracurriculum, 273

F

Facilitators, teachers as, 79
Family Educational Rights and Privacy Act (Buckley Amendment), 248
Family life education. *See* Sex education
Federal government
    education priorities, 276–277
    influence on education, 208–211
    standards and goals, 305–307
Fields of Wings mentoring program, 46
File transfer protocol (FTP), 373
Finance. *See* School governance and funding
First Amendment, 235, 246
First Day of School America, 196
Fiscal year, 220
Flat grants, 214
Flunking, 189
Formative assessment, 16, 295–296
For-profit schools, 183
Foundation programs, 214–215
Fourteenth Amendment, 236–237
Fourth Amendment, 235, 245
Frankfurt School, 153
Franklin v. *Gwinnett County Public Schools*, 261
Freedman's Bureau, 116
Free exercise clause, 235
Full-service schools, 41–42
Full state funding, 216
Fundamentalist Christian schools, 186

G

Gallaudet College for the Deaf, 102
Gaylord v. *Tacoma School District No. 10*, 252
Gender issues
    bias, 62–64
    history of education for women, 101, 107, 131–132
    seminaries for women, 111
    sensitivity training, 367
    status of women in teaching, 132
    Title IX, 131–132
    women's rights movement, 132
Geographies, 105
G.I. Bill of Rights, 137
Giftedness, 64, 76–77
Global awareness, 331–354
Global Education Motivators (GEM), 335

Global interdependence, 354–358
Goetz v. *Ansell*, 242
Golden Mean, 148
Gonzalez v. *Mackler*, 256
Goss v. *Lopez*, 243
Grading and recommendations, 320
Grants, 214, 219
Great Books Program, 157

H

Hartford Female Seminary, 111
Harvard Project Physics, 139
Hate speech, online, 73
Hazelwood School District v. *Kuhlmeier*, 246, 258
Head Start, 35, 135, 174
Health and safety issues, 43–49
Hidden passage, 99
Higher education, 110–111, 136–137, 178–179
High school, 178
High-stakes tests, 308
Hinduism, 159–160
Hispanic Americans
    at-risk students among, 31, 48
    education for Mexican Americans, 100–101
    growth in population of, 128
    higher education and, 178
    labeling issues and, 58
    preschools and, 174
History of education
    aims of American education, 94–95
    benchmarks in American education, 82–83, 167–168, 266–267, 326–327, 393
    development of formal education in America, 102–107
    development of parochial schools, 110
    early ideas of public education, 107–108
    European thinkers' influence on American education, 87–89
    for Native Americans in America, 99
    for people with disabilities in America, 101–102
    for slaves in America, 97–99
    for women in America, 101
    federal influence on education, 119–120
    growth of higher education, 110–111
    in Spain's American colonies, 100
    in the Middle Atlantic colonies, 92
    in the New England colonies, 92
    in the southern colonies, 90–92

History of education *(Cont.)*
  leaders in the movement for universal education, 108–110
  mass media, 118–119
  national view of American education, 92–94
  post-Civil war, 115–121
  pre-Civil War, 89–90
  reconstruction era, 115–116
  reform movement, 116–117
  role of industry in, 97
  role of religion in, 95–97
  and science and philanthropy in the 20th century, 118
HIV, 47–48
Holding power, 37
Home page, 373
Home schooling, 136, 186, 238
Homosexuality. *See* Sexual orientation
Honig v. *Doe,* 247
HOPE Scholarship Program, 39
Hornbook, 104
Hull House, 121
Humanism, 148–149, 149–150
Hunter v. *Board of Education of Montgomery County,* 260
Hypermedia, 373

Idealism, 147–148
Immigrants, 59–61, 342
Immunizations, 48
Implicit curriculum, 271–272
Improved Learning and Discipline Act of 1999, 276
Incentive programs, for at-risk students, 39
Inclusive education, 66, 73, 368. *See also* Multicultural
      education
Income taxes, 214
India, education in, 345–347
Indian Reorganization Act of 1934, 123
Indian Self-determination and Educational Assistance Act, 123
Indian War, 122
Individualized Education Program (IEP), 75–76, 247
Individuals with Disabilities Education Act (IDEA), 72–73,
      210, 247, 276
Induction programs, 20
Industrialization, 97, 121, 136
Infant intervention and enrichment programs, 174
Information-processing instructional strategies, 289
Ingraham v. *Wright,* 239
In loco parentis, 245

Inquiry learning, 290
In re William G., 245
Instruction
  behavioral systems strategies, 285–287
  classroom management and, 296–299
  effective, 292–296
  information-processing strategies, 289–290
  milestones in twentieth century, 326–327
  models of instruction and, 285–291
  personal sources strategies, 290–291
  planning and organizing, 281–285
  social strategies, 287–289
Integrated curriculum, 273–274
Intellectual property, 321
Intermediate educational units (IEUs), 218
International Association for the Evaluation of Educational
      Achievement, 354
International Baccalaureate Organization (IBO), 331–333
International comparative education, 337–338
Internet, 372–373, 375
Internships, 11–12
Interstate New Teacher Assessment and Support Consortium
      Standards (INTASC), 7–8
IQ tests, 312
Iron Triangle, 208
Islam, 160–161
Israel, teaching in, 336

Japan, education in, 342–343, 363
Journals, as assessment, 317–318
Juku, 343
Junior high schools, 176–177

Kansas Fever Exodus, 127
Karma, 160
Kindergarten, 89, 175–176
Knowledge transmitters, teachers as, 79
Koran, 160

Laboratory schools, 174
Lancasterian teaching method, 106

Land grant schools, 94

Language, diversity and, 61–62

Latin Grammar School, 107

Latinos. *See* Hispanic Americans

Lau v. *Nichols*, 259, 260

Law School Aptitude Test (LSAT), 312

Learning communities. *See* Collaborative networks

Learning, Earning, and Parenting (LEAP) program, 39

Learning environments, 293

Lee v. *Wiseman*, 242

Legal Defense Fund (LDEF), 207

Legal issues

    benchmarks in educational law, 266–267

    parents' rights and responsibilities

        children with disabilities, 240

        religion, 238–239

    principles affecting public education, 235–236

    school districts' rights and responsibilities

        balancing academic freedom, 258–259

        choice, 261, 263

        educational malpractice, 260

        equal treatment, 259–260

        sexual harassment, 260–261

    students' rights and responsibilities

        discrimination, 246–247

        due process, 242–244

        privacy, 247–249

        religion, 240–242

        search and seizure, 244–246

        student expression, 246

    teachers' rights and responsibilities

        child abuse and neglect, 253–254

        copyright laws, 252–253

        negligence, 254–256

        personal codes of conduct, 251–252

        tenure, 250–251

        unions, 249–250

Lemon test, 242

Lemon v. *Kurtzman*, 242

Licensure, 3, 6, 10–12

Limited English proficient (LEP), 61, 77

Literacy, 315, 375

Literacy Volunteers of America, 136

Local property taxes, 219

Logs. *See* Journals

Looping, 177

Lotteries, 214

Lyceum, 106

M

Magazines, 118–119

Magnet schools, 179–180

Mainstreaming, 66–67

Malpractice, 260

Man A Course of Study (MACOS), 139

Mancha v. *Field Museum of Natural History*, 254, 256

Marland definition of giftedness, 64

Martin Luther King, Jr., Elementary School Children v. *Michigan Board of Education*, 259

Marxism, 152–153

Maryland Learner Outcomes, 308

Maryland State Performance Assessment Program (MSPAP), 308–309

Massachusetts Act of 1642, 92

Mass media

    curriculum and, 280–281

    learning from, 118–119

Mastery learning, 285–286

McGuffey Readers, 105

Measurement. *See* Assessment

Media, 207–208

Mentoring, 20, 39

Mentor/Mentee (M&M) program, 39

Meriam Report, 122

Merit pay, 21–22

Metaphysics, 146

Metropolitan Achievement Test, 140

Metropolitan Opera Guild, 288

Metropolitan Regional Career and Technical Center (Met), 181

Mexican Americans. *See* Hispanic Americans

Mexico, education in, 339, 341–342

Microcultures, 58

Middle schools, 135, 176–177

Migrant children, 33

Minimum competency testing, 314–315

Mission schools, 99

Monitorial teaching method, 106

Montessori schools, 181–182

Morrill Act, 111, 136

Morrison v. *Board of Education*, 251–252

Motion pictures, 119

Multicultural education. *See also* Diversity

    curricula, 69–72

    definition, 65–67

    human relations approaches, 67

    multicultural and social reconstructionist approaches, 68

Multicultural education *(Cont.)*
  multicultural approaches, 68
  single-group studies, 68
Muslims, 160

NAACP (National Association for the Advancement of
    Colored People), 116, 126, 207
National Academy of Sciences, 305
National Assessment of Educational Progress (NAEP), 140,
    306, 363
National Association for the Education of Young Children
    (NAEYC), 174
National Association of Elementary School Principals, 177
National Association of State Boards of Education (NASBE),
    206, 375
National Board for Professional Teaching Standards
    (NBPTS), 8–9
National Center for Education Statistics, 209
National certification, 22–23
National Commission on Excellence in Education, 139
National Council for the Accreditation of Teacher Education
    (NCATE), 69
National Council of Teachers of English (NCTE), 305, 384
National Council of Teachers of Mathematics (NCTM),
    278–279, 305
National Defense Education Act (NDEA), 34
National Education Association (NEA)
  Code of Ethics, 4–5
  legal issues, 249
  professional leadership, 23
  state standards boards, 217
  status of women in teaching, 23, 132
National Education Goals, 305
National Education School Improvement Council (NESIC),
    134
National Gay Taskforce v. *Board of Education of Oklahoma
    City*, 252
National Governors' Association, 218
National Heritage Academies, 183
National Middle School Association (NMSA), 177
National Network for Educational Renewal, 384
National Organization for Women (NOW), 207
National Parent-Teacher Association (PTA), 206, 383
National School Boards Association, 206
National Teachers Association (NTA), 116
Nation's Report Card, 306–307
Native Americans

  education for, 99
  parochial schools and, 92
  philosophy of, 162
  post-Civil War, 121–123
  school mascots and, 248
  as a special interest group, 206–207
Neag Center for Gifted Education and Talent Development,
    380
Negligence, 254–256
New Federalism, 120
New Harmony Community School, 111
New Jersey v. *T.L.O.*, 245
News groups, 373
Newspapers, 118–119
New York Times learning network, 281
Nirvana, 160
No Child Left Behind Act of 2001, 39, 63, 134, 139, 276, 329,
    363
Nondirective model, 290–291
Nongovernmental organizations (NGOs), 335
Nongraded classrooms, 176
Normal schools, 111
Norm-referenced tests, 313
Northwest Ordinance of 1785, 94, 111
Null curriculum, 272–273
Nursery schools, 174

Okeiko-goto, 343
Old Deluder Satan Act, 92
Online hate rhetoric, 73
Ontology, 146
Opportunity costs, 14
Opportunity standards, 310
Oriental Exclusion Act, 129
Orthodox Jewish schools, 186
Outcome-centered learning, 314
Owasso Independent School District v. *Falvo*, 249
Oyez Project, 262

𝒫

Paideia Proposal, 157
Paraprofessionals, and serving children with special needs, 74
Parent-cooperatives, 174
Parents
  family services and, 41–43

involvement of, 383
parenting programs, 44–45
parent-teacher associations, 41
poverty and, 40
rights and responsibilities of, 237–240
and school effectiveness, 194–195, 197
sex education and, 47
single, 32–33
teenage, 45–46
television and, 40
as volunteers, 42
Parochial schools, 92, 110, 185–186
Pedagogical content knowledge, 389
Peer feedback, 321
Peer-mediated instruction, 289
Peer tutoring, 39–40
Perennialism, 156–158
Performance tests, 308
Per pupil expenditures, 215
Perry Preschool program, 35
Personal conduct, 251–252
Personal property, 219
Personal sources instructional strategies, 290–291
Peter W. v. *San Francisco Unified School District*, 260
Philosophy
    African, 161–162
    benchmarks in education, 82–83
    educational, 144–147, 162–163
    Greek
        aesthetics, 146
        axiology, 146
        cosmology, 146
        epistemology, 146
        metaphysics, 146
        ontology, 146
    influence on education, 143–146
    modern
        behaviorism, 153–154
        cognitivism, 153–154
        essentialism, 156–158
        existentialism, 150, 152
        Marxism, 152–153
        perennialism, 156–158
        pragmatism, 154–156
        social reconstructionism, 158
    Native American, 162
    nonwestern, 158–159
        Buddhism, 160
        Hinduism, 159–160
        Islam, 160–161

of public schools, 145
    roots of American educational
        humanism, 148–149, 149–150
        idealism, 147–148
        realism, 148–149
        western, 146–158
Physical Science Study Committee (PSSC), 139
Plano ISD, 376, 376
Plessy v. *Ferguson*, 126, 127
Pluralism, 59–60, 138
Policy issues, 189–192
Political correctness, 71–72
Political issues, and school governance, 205–20
Portfolios
    assessment and, 318
    digital, 20
    teacher, 18
Poverty, 121
    and effect on schools, 32–33
Pragmatism, 154–156
Praxis Series™, 18
Prekindergarten, 174
Preparatory schools, 182
Preschools, 135, 174–175
Primers, 104
Principals, 188–189
Privacy, 247–249
Private (independent) schools, 182–183
Private schools, and public support for, 227
Privatization, 183, 228
Professional development school (PDS), 383–384
Professionalism
    professional organizations, 23–24, 277–278
    teaching as a profession, 3–5
    teaching as a semiprofession, 5–6
    using professional knowledge, 385–390
Program for International Student Assessment (PISA), 356
Programmed instruction, 154
Progressive Education Association, 139
Progressive taxation, 214
Progressivism, 133, 156
Project ALERT, 52
Project-based learning, 289
Project English, 139
Project Story Boost, 36
Protestant Reformation, 149
Public education, 107–108
Public opinion, and curriculum, 277–278
Public schools, philosophy of, 145
Pull-out programs, for at-risk students, 38

Q

Quakers, 97, 101
Questions, as a form of assessment, 315–316

R

Race, 58–59
Radio, 119
Reading is Fundamental, 136
Realism, 148–149
Real property, 219
Reciprocity agreements, 11
Redistricting, 32
Reflective teaching process, 25
Reform
    global awareness, 355
    inclusion of students with special needs, 74
    mentoring for adolescent girls, 46
    school consolidation, 203
    Urban Academy, 308
    urban superintendents, 203
Reform movement, 116–117, 121
Regressive taxation, 214
Rehabilitation Act of 1973, 240
Reliability, of test scores, 313
Religion, 95–97, 238–239, 240–242
Research, 385–389
Resource officers, 50
Retention, 189–190
Rockefeller Foundation, 389
Roots and Wings, 382
Rothschild v. *Grottenthaler*, 240
Rowland v. *Mad River School District*, 252
Rubrics, in assessment, 318

S

Safety, 243
Salaries. *See* Teaching
Sales taxes, 213–214
San Antonio Independent School District v. *Rodriguez*, 225
Scaffolding, 154
Scholastic Aptitude Test (SAT), 71, 140, 312
School-based budgeting, 222
School board, 187

School budgets
    and enrollment trends, 13
    and student-teacher ratios, 13–14
School choice, 32. *See* Choice
School Development Program, 380–381
School District of Abington Township v. *Schempp*, 242
School governance and funding, 201–204, 365
    benchmarks 266-267, 206–207
    educational success, 223–230
    influence of federal government, 208–210
    lobbies and special interest groups, 206–207
    local, 218–223
    National Goals, 211, 212
    political influences, 205–206
    public media, 207–208
    state funding, 211, 213–216
    state oversight, 216–218
School Math Study Group (SMSG), 139
School reform. *See* Reform
Schools
    administration of, 186–189
    alternative
        charter, 183–185
        for-profit, 183
        home, 186
        magnet, 179–180
        Montessori, 181–182
        parochial, 185–186
        private (independent), 182–183
        vocational-technical, 180–181
        Waldorf, 181–182
    consolidation of, 179
    districts, 172, 218, 366
    effectiveness of, 192–195, 196
    elementary, 176
    higher education, 178–179
    high school, 178
    junior high, 176–177
    kindergarten, 175–176
    middle, 176–177
    organizational and policy issues of, 189–192
    preschool, 174–175
    as a social institution, 172
    types of, 172–174
Scopes Trial, 138, 207
Search and seizure, 244–246
Security, 161
Self-assessment, 319
Self-fulfilling prophecies, 297
Self-monitoring, 321

Seminaries, 111

Seneca Falls Women's Rights Convention, 131

Sensitivity training, 70–71, 367

Separation of church and state, 95

September 11

    constitutional rights and, 257

    and global awareness, 333, 335

    the opening of school after, 1

    school security and, 161

Serrano v. *Priest*, 225

Service learning, 369–371

Serviceman's Readjustment Act of 1944 (G.I. Bill of Rights), 137

Sex education

    controversy over, 277–278

    parents and, 47

    and teenage parents, 46

Sexual harassment, 260–261

Sexually transmitted diseases, 47–48

Sexual orientation, 65

Shinto, 160

Shishu Bharati School of Languages and Cultures of India, 159

Singapore, education in, 350–352

Single-group studies. *See* Multicultural education

Site-based budgeting, 222

Site-based management, 229–230

Slavery

    education for slaves, 90, 93, 97–99

    ending, 116

    parochial schools for slaves, 92

Smith-Hughes Act of 1917, 276

Social Darwinism, 91

Social issues

    and curriculum, 277–278

    and effect on schools, 30–33

Social promotion, 189–190, 314–315

Social reconstructionism, 158. *See* Multicultural education

Social strategies for instruction, 287–289

Socratic method, 147–148

South Africa, education in, 352–354

Special education, 261–262

Special interest groups, 206–207

Spellers, 105

Sputnik, 133, 139

Standard English, 60–61

Standardized curriculum, 275

Standardized tests, 69, 312, 314

Standards, 4, 8

    content, 304

national, 305–307

opportunity, 310

performance, 304

personal, 304–305

standards boards, 217

state, 307–310

Stanford Achievement Test, 140

STaR, 376–377

Star Schools Program, 375

State Education Department (SED), 217

State government

    boards of education, 216–217

    chief state school officer, 217

    Council of Chief State School Officers, 218

    and education priorities, 276–277

    full state funding, 216

    funding, 211, 213–216

    National Governors' Association, 218

    oversight, 216–218

    standards and goals, 307–310

    standards boards, 217

    State Education Department (SED), 217

    and technology in classrooms, 378–379

Station v. *Travelers Insurance Co.*, 256

Student-based, Teacher-led Assessment and Reporting System (STARS), 323

Student Coalition on Human Rights, 22

Student expression, 246

Students

    acceptable use policies and, 321

    assessment and, 320–321

    laptops for, 374

    motivating, 285

    rights and responsibilities, 240–249

    self-control, 299

    sexual harassment and, 261

Student-teacher ratio, 13

Student teaching, 18

Student Teams-Achievement Divisions (STAD), 288

Subgroups, ethnic, 58

Substance abuse, 48, 52

Success for All program, 294, 382–383

Suchman Inquiry Model, 290

Suicide, 48

Summative assessment, 16, 295–296

Summerhill School, 152

Sunday schools, 124

Superintendent of schools, 186–188, 203

Synchronous communication, 373

Synectics, 289–290

T

Tabula rasa, 87
Taxes, 213–214
Teachers for a New Era, 389
Teach for America (TFA), 11–12
Teaching. *See also* Instruction
    advanced college degrees, 23
    basic professional competence, 7–8
    career ladders and merit pay, 21
    changing views of, 6–9
    child abuse and neglect and, 253–254
    codes of conduct, 251–252
    copyright laws and, 252–253
    and culturally relevant classrooms, 77–79
    education for, 11
    effective instruction, 292–296
    evaluation, 16–19
    as expert behavior, 8–9
    instructional models, 285–291
    job availability, 12–14
    licensure of teachers, 10–12
    mentoring programs, 35
    planning for instruction, 284–285
    as a profession, 3–5
    professional organizations, 23–24
    qualifications, 363
    relationships with students, 297, 299
    rights and responsibilities of teachers, 249–250
    salaries, 14–16
    as a semiprofession, 5–6
    support of teachers, 19–23
    teacher expectations, 297, 299
    teacher shortages, 13
    technology training, 371
    tenure and, 250–251
Teaching to Be Peacemakers, 67
Technology
    amplifying teachers' voices, 298
    Children's Online Privacy Protection Act (COPPA), 45
    distance learning, 375–376
    and global awareness, 335
    Holocaust Museum online, 124
    Internet, 372–373, 375
    Journey North Project, 340
    online hate, 73
    Oyez Project, 262
    professional development online, 109
    school budgeting, 221
    telecommunications in schools, 376–379
    ThinkQuest, 155
    tracking attendance, 191
    World Wide Web, 372–373, 375
Teen pregnancy, 45–47
Telecommunications, 376–379
Telecommunications Act of 1996, 377
Television
    influence on education, 119
    parents and, 40
    violence and, 51
Tenure, 16, 250–251
Test scores, and funding levels, 223–226
Textbooks, 217, 280–281
Tinker v. *Des Moines Independent Community School District*, 240, 246
Title 20, 259
Title I, 38
Title IX, 63
Tolerance, 332
Tracking, 192
Transcendental Movement, 101
Transgendered individuals. *See* Diversity, sexual orientation
Trends in International Mathematics and Science Study (TIMSS), 354–356
Troops to Teachers, 12
Truancy, 191
Tuition tax credit, 229
Tuition tax deduction, 229
Tuskegee Institute, 125

U

Unions, 23–24, 249–250. *See also* individual organizations
United Kingdom, education in, 347–350
Universal education, 108, 116, 124
Universal Service program, 377
Upanishads, 159
Upward Bound, 38
U.S. Constitution, 235–236, 266
Utility, of test scores, 313

V

Validity, of test scores, 313
Vedas, 159
Veronia School District 47J v. *Acton*, 245
Videoconferencing, 373, 375
Violence, 49

Virgil v. *School Board of Columbia County, Florida*, 258–259
Virtual learning space, 378
Vocational Act of 1963, 210
Vocational-technical schools, 180–181
Volunteerism. *See* Service learning
Vouchers, 228

W

Waldorf schools, 181–182
Wallace v. *Jaffree*, 242
Ward v. *Newfield Central School District No. 1*, 256
War on Poverty, 135
Web browser, 373
Websites, 373
Western philosophy, 146–158
West Virginia State Board of Education v. *Barnette*, 241

Widmar v. *Vincent*, 241
Wisconsin v. *Yoder*, 238
Women's Educational Equity Act (WEEA), 132
Women's issues. *See* Gender issues
Works Progress Administration, 135
World Wide Web
    future of, 372–373, 375
    and global awareness, 335
    privacy and, 45
Wounded Knee, 122

Z

Zelman v. *Simmons-Harris*, 262, 263
Zen, 160
Zero-based budgeting, 222
Zero tolerance, 243

*P*hoto Credits

PRAXIS
T. Lindfors, Lindfors Photography

CHAPTER 1
p. 2: Library of Congress;
p. 7: David Young-Wolff/PhotoEdit;
p. 10: Stewart Cohen/Getty Images Inc. — Stone Allstock;
p. 12: Elizabeth Crews/The Image Works;
p. 19: Tom Lindfors/Lindfors Photography;
p. 21: Tom Stewart/CORBIS
p. 24: Reuben Burrell

CHAPTER 2
p. 29: Getty Images Inc. — Stone Allstock;
p. 34: Myrleen Ferguson Cate/PhotoEdit;
p. 35: Tom Stewart/CORBIS;
p. 36: Syracuse Newspapers/Gary Walts/The Image Works;
p. 37: Getty Images Inc. — Image Bank;
p. 41: Laura Dwight/PhotoEdit

CHAPTER 3
p. 56: Bob Daemmrich/Stock Boston;
p. 61: Mel Yates/Getty Images, Inc. — Taxi;
p. 62: Brian Smith/Brian Smith, Photographer;
p. 63: Will Hart;
p. 66: Tom Lindfors/Lindfors Photography

CHAPTER 4
p. 86: Joesph Sohm/The Image Works;
p. 87: National Library of Medicine;
p. 88: CORBIS;
p. 89: North Wind Picture Archives;
p. 90: North Wind Picture Archives;
p. 91: Tom Stewart/CORBIS;
p. 95: North Wind Picture Archives;
p. 96: North Wind Picture Archives;
p. 98: University of North Carolina Library Photo Services;
p. 99: North Wind Picture Archives;

p. 100: North Wind Picture Archives;
p. 101, top: The Granger Collection;
p. 101, center: Lyrl Ahern;
p. 101, bottom: CORBIS;
p. 102: North Wind Picture Archives;
p. 105: Dennis MacDonald/PhotoEdit;
p. 107: Susan Van Etten/PhotoEdit

CHAPTER 5
p. 114: Jacob A. Riis/Museum of the City of New York;
p. 115: Will Hart;
p. 120: Library of Congress;
p. 122: CORBIS;
p. 125, top: North Wind Picture Archives;
p. 125, center: Library of Congress;
p. 125, bottom: Library of Congress;
p. 126: CORBIS;
p. 129: Mel Yates/Getty Images, Inc. — Taxi;
p. 133, top: The Dalton Public Library;
p. 133, bottom: Lyrl Ahern;
p. 139: NASA Headquarters

CHAPTER 6
p. 143: CORBIS;
p. 144: Will Hart/PhotoEdit;
p. 145: Tom Lindfors/Lindfors Photography;
p. 147: North Wind Picture Archives;
p. 148: North Wind Picture Archives;
p. 149: North Wind Picture Archives;
p. 153: CORBIS;
p. 156: National Library of Medicine;
p. 157: Lyrl Ahern;
p. 158: Special Collections/Morris Library Southwestern
Illinois University at Carbondale

CHAPTER 7
p. 171: Mike Brinson/Getty Images Inc. — Image Bank;
p. 175: Mel Yates/Getty Images, Inc. — Taxi;

p. 177: Tom Lindfors/Lindfors Photography;

p. 180: Monika Graff/The Image Works;

p. 181: James A. Sugar/CORBIS;

p. 184: Zigy Kaluzny/Getty Images Inc. — Stone Allstock;

p. 185: Getty Images Inc. — Image Bank;

p. 190: Mary Kate Denny/PhotoEdit;

p. 191: CORBIS;

p. 195: Michael Newman/PhotoEdit

CHAPTER 8

p. 200: Bob Daemmrich/The Image Works;

p. 203, left: Tannen Maury/The Image Works;

p. 203, right: Jacksonville Journal Courier/The Image Works;

p. 206: CORBIS;

p. 216: Bob Daemmrich/The Image Works;

p. 224: Robert Harbison;

p. 228: Tom Stewart/CORBIS

CHAPTER 9

p. 233: Syracuse Newspapers/The Image Works;

p. 234: Tony Freeman/PhotoEdit;

p. 238: Robert Harbison;

p. 243: Mel Yates/Getty Images, Inc. — Taxi;

p. 244: Hussein Akhtar/CORBIS;

p. 247: Richard Hutchings/PhotoEdit;

p. 253: Cindy Charles/PhotoEdit;

p. 256: Will Hart;

p. 257: AP/Wide World Photos

CHAPTER 10

p. 270: David Butow/CORBIS;

p. 272: Ian Shaw/Getty Images Inc. — Stone Allstock;

p. 275: Tom Lindfors/Lindfors Photography;

p. 277: Will Faller;

p. 279: Joanne McNergney;

p. 291: Victor R. Caivano/AP/Wide World Photos;

p. 293: Brian Smith/Brian Smith, Photographer;

p. 294: Mug Shots/CORBIS;

p. 296: Mary Kate Denny/PhotoEdit;

p. 298: Laima Druskis/Pearson Education

CHAPTER 11

p. 303: Will & Deni McIntyre/CORBIS;

p. 312: Charles Gupton/CORBIS;

p. 314: Zigy Kaluzny/Getty Images Inc. — Stone Allstock;

p. 315: Jim Cummins/CORBIS;

p. 316: Frank Siteman/PhotoEdit;

p. 317: Jeff Greenberg/PhotoEdit;

p. 321: Zigy Kaluzny/Getty Images Inc. — Stone Allstock

CHAPTER 12

p. 330: Lindsay Hebberd/CORBIS;

p. 332, left: Mel Yates/Getty Images, Inc. — Taxi;

p. 332, right: Lester Lefkowitz/CORBIS;

p. 334: Michael J. Doolittle/The Image Works;

p. 336: Joanne McNergney;

p. 344: John Nordell/The Image Works;

p. 351: Joe Lynch/Getty Images, Inc — Liaison

CHAPTER 13

p. 362: David Young-Wolff/PhotoEdit;

p. 365: Syracuse Newspapers/Steve Ruark/The Image Works;

p. 367: Bob Daemmrich/Stock Boston;

p. 373: Getty Images Inc. — Stone Allstock;

p. 374: Tom Stewart/CORBIS;

p. 376: CORBIS;

p. 381: Tom Lindfors/Lindfors Photography;

p. 386: John Colletti